CO-BFC-064

DISCARD

AUGUST STRIND-BERG

Benjamin Blom, Inc. Publishers, New York, 1971

AUGUST STRIND-BERG

Translated and Edited by Harry G. Carlson

MARTIN LAMM

LIBRARY

PT
9816
L 27213
C. 2

First published in Swedish by Albert Bonniers Förlag,
Stockholm, 1940/41 ; revised edition, 1948.

Translated into English from the 1948 edition
by arrangement with the copyright holder, Albert Bonniers Förlag.

©1971 by Benjamin Blom, Inc., New York, N.Y. 10025

All rights reserved
Library of Congress Catalog Card Number 69-16323

Book designed by Peretz Kaminsky

Printed in the United States of America
by Noble Offset Printers, Inc., New York, N.Y.

72-5514

MAY 1 9 1980

To Greta Wavrinsky Lamm (1888-1968)
and my parents,
Bertha A. Carlson and Harry C. Carlson

CONTENTS

CONTENTS

Part Two:
After the Conversion

PREFACE AND TRANSLATOR'S NOTE

Martin Lamm (1880-1950) was for many years professor of literary history at the University of Stockholm and a member of the Swedish Academy. It was at the special request of the Academy that he wrote *August Strindberg* (first published in 1940-42), one of the cornerstones of Strindberg criticism and research.

Professor Lamm's early research interests were in eighteenth century Swedish literature and philosophy, but in the early 1920's he gave a series of lectures which started him on his long career as a Strindberg scholar. Between 1924 and 1926 he published the two-volume *Strindbergs dramer,* a pioneering work that established the precedent of analyzing Strindberg's plays according to the two major phases of his career—before and after the traumatic psychological period referred to as the Inferno Crisis (1894-96). *Strindbergs dramer* had a great influence on Swedish productions of Strindberg's plays during the late 1920's and 1930's, particularly on the work of the distinguished director Olof Molander. In 1936, Lamm published an account of Strindberg's Inferno Crisis and religious conversion in *Strindberg och makterna.* Strindberg's significance as a dramatist has been well documented for English-speaking readers, but up to now the only broad survey in English of all his writings has been Mortensen and Down's useful but brief study *Strindberg: An Introduction to His Life and Work.* By any standards, Strindberg's literary output was prodigious: almost sixty plays, close to a dozen novels, more than 150 short stories, three volumes of poetry, scores of critical and polemical essays, and approximately 5,600 letters. The plays, of course, are his most important and influential contribution to the literature of his time, but they are like strips from a gigantic mural, and certain aspects of his talent

rarely emerge in them—his irony and warmth, for example, and his zest
for storytelling. Lamm's study deals with the entire range of Strindberg's
work and attempts to put all aspects into proper perspective. It is an
inventory of the impressions and insights of a lifetime of scholarship, a
portrait of a genius in his greatness as well as his pettiness.

The present translation is based on the second revised edition of
1948. A number of minor alterations and additions have been made in the
text to make the book more meaningful to readers not acquainted with
Swedish literary and cultural traditions, but no attempt has been made to
revise Lamm's basic viewpoints in the light of subsequent research or to
change his point of departure, which is largely biographical, a search in
Strindberg's life for the roots of his art. Today, the focus of Strindberg
research is changing, and scholars, such as Alrik Gustafson and Walter
Johnson, seek to evaluate the works more in terms of their merit as literature than as mirrors reflecting the turbulent events in the author's life and
the anguish in his heart. It is doubtful, though, that the facts of Strindberg's life can ever be completely separated from the elements of his art;
even he had trouble doing so. In this sense Professor Lamm's approach is
admirably suited to the subject. Just as it is often difficult to distinguish
between real life and fiction in Strindberg's works, so it is sometimes difficult to separate biography and criticism in *August Strindberg.*

A number of individuals and institutions assisted in the prepara-
tion of this translation, and I wish to express my gratitude: Dr. Anthony
E. Santaniello, Professor Evert Sprinchorn, The John Simon Guggenheim
Foundation, Docent Carl Reinhold Smedmark, The Swedish Institute for
Cultural Relations, Assistant Vice President Robert A. McRorie of the
University of Georgia, Professor Walter Johnson, and my wife Carolyn.

HARRY G. CARLSON

Queens College
The City University of New York
1970

AUGUST STRINDBERG

A Biographical Sketch
by Harry G. Carlson

It was August Strindberg's destiny and agony to be burdened with the conscience of a conservative bourgeois intellectual and the instincts of a romantic and sometimes radical artist. Contrary to criticisms such as the one made by R. J. Kaufmann that Strindberg was unable "to see one thing or one event simultaneously from more than one point of view," he often identified with both sides of an issue—pulled in one direction intellectually and in the other emotionally. As Professor Lamm points out, Strindberg eloquently portrayed his own dilemma in the Renaissance clergyman and artist in the short story "Evolution":

> [Botvid's] soul was split in two ever-feuding parts; he was the son of two epochs, and this gave him two viewpoints over things; the monk's and the satyr's. Although he could be moved to rapture by something great, beautiful, or good, the rapture quickly evaporated when the skeptic in him realized how ridiculous everything was. His eyes . . . no longer focused together: while one saw the front of an object, the other saw its backside.

Strindberg's dual perspective fragmented many of his basic attitudes, especially toward sex, religion, and politics. The physical act of love was simultaneously a fulfilling necessity and an abomination from which he had to seek purification; almost all his life he sought a religious belief that would give meaning to the misfortunes he suffered, yet his innate skepticism tended to undermine his faith; and although one of his most cherished ideals was the democratization of Swedish society, he shared many upper-class viewpoints and wished that he had been born an aristocrat. Strindberg paid for these ambivalent feelings with a perpetual sense of guilt. Often literally ashamed to be alive, he felt like an outcast; he was Ishmael, Ahasuerus, and the Flying Dutchman, and was continually in pursuit, either consciously or unconsciously, of atonement and reconciliation.

In *Miss Julie,* Strindberg's sympathetic understanding both of Jean's contempt for the frivolous behavior of the decadent upper classes and Julie's loathing of lower-class vulgarity and opportunism is a reflection of the conflicting feelings he had about where his allegiance lay: to his mother's humble background or to his father's higher social station and his own aristocratic aspirations and sensitivities. In writing his autobiography, *The Son of a Servant,* he felt a need, at least at the start, to dramatize the shabbiness of his origin, and so he pictured the circumstances of his birth as more plebeian than they actually were: "Three children had been born before [his parents'] marriage and Johan [i.e., August] soon after. He was probably an unwanted child, since his father had gone bankrupt just before his birth." His mother did come to his father's house as a servant—a housekeeper—and she did bear Carl Oscar Strindberg three children out of wedlock, but Strindberg's parents were married sixteen months before he was born on January 22, 1849, and his father went bankrupt four years later. Strindberg distorted or confused the facts of the bankruptcy because of his own constant worries about debts and the threat of poverty. Images of creditors appear frequently in his early works, and in the later works there are vampire-like people who sap the strength and creative energies of others.

The Strindberg family had its share of problems (only seven of eleven children survived childhood) but, despite the emphasis in *The Son of a Servant* on the deprivations the author endured, eventually there was enough money available to send him to a *gymnasium* and to the University of Uppsala, even if not in the style he would have preferred. This was no small achievement in a country where poverty forced hundreds of thousands of people to emigrate to the United States.

During his years at the university (1867-68, 1870-72) Strindberg discovered that writing fiction and drama satisfied a deep craving for self-expression, but he was uncertain about the quality of his literary talents and how far they would take him. He briefly considered a career in medicine, then in acting, but not until he worked as a journalist (1872-74) did he gain the confidence to try to make his mark as a writer.

An appointment as assistant at the Royal Library in December, 1874, solved several problems: it gave him a measure of social status and the opportunity to write. He held the appointment for eight years, and when he resigned in August, 1882, to devote all his time to writing, he had achieved prominence in Swedish literary and intellectual circles. A collection of short stories about his university days, *Town and Gown,* attracted favorable attention when it was published in 1877, and two years later a novel based on his experiences as a journalist, *The Red Room,* established him as a major Scandinavian literary figure. In December, 1881, he received his first recognition as an important playwright at the triumphant première of the prose version of *Master Olof.*

In 1882, his private life was also satisfactory. His marriage to Siri von Essen in December, 1887, had proved moderately happy and the couple had two handsome daughters: Karin, born in 1880, and Greta, in 1881 (a son, Hans, was born in 1884). But all these outward signs of material and emotional well-being belied the disturbing ambivalences that Strindberg was forced to keep in equilibrium. His union with Siri, for example, was stained with guilt. When he first fell in love with her in the summer of 1875, she was the wife of an aristocrat, Baron Carl Gustaf Wrangel. A year later he was overjoyed when the Wrangels' marriage was dissolved, but the idea of divorce troubled his middle-class conscience, and when Siri's first child by him, Kerstin, was born only a short time after their marriage and died within a few days, the experience haunted him with a shame that he never forgot.

Another kind of guilt was associated with his tenure at the Royal Library. The radical in him had felt a mission to expose the hypocrisy of the Swedish ruling classes, but in accepting the position he compromised his ideals—he was joining the Establishment instead of attacking it. In September, 1882, shortly after he left the library, his deep resentment against the class structure and vested interests, only partly expressed in *The Red Room,* exploded fully in a work of vitriolic social satire, the short-story collection *The New Kingdom.* Among his targets were the aristocracy, big business, the Swedish Academy, and the press.

Overnight, the promising novelist and playwright became a controversial figure. To many young writers and intellectuals, the candidly realistic prose style of *The Red Room* and *The New Kingdom* was a gust of fresh air in a stagnant society. But to people in high places, many of whom were ridiculed in these two books, Strindberg was a dangerous radical. *The New Kingdom* became a best seller, but the hostility it provoked did nothing to advance its author's career; he was no longer welcome in influential circles, and publishers turned cool toward his work. By September, 1883, he decided that there was only one course of action open: to go into exile.

The decision to leave Sweden came at an unfortunate time for Siri; she felt she was beginning to achieve success as an actress in plays her husband had written for her. Over the next six years, as Strindberg conducted his family from place to place in France, Switzerland, and Denmark, great strain was placed on the marriage and it began to fall apart.

A major factor in its disintegration was a series of events that became the first turning point in Strindberg's life. In late September, 1884, he published a collection of short stories, *Married,* in which he continued his attacks on the upper classes and opened a Pandora's box by exploring the subject areas where his emotions were most charged: women, sex, and marriage.

If Strindberg had been more opportunistic and tried to cater to the views and prejudices of a special audience, he would have proceeded differently. Even though *The New Kingdom* had antagonized Establishment interests, it had won him the support of those who were pioneering the liberal causes of the 1880's. One of the most popular of these causes was the feminist movement, and in *Married,* Strindberg criticized it severely, urging reaffirmation of traditional values. He glorified motherhood and the sanctity of family life and attacked the de-feminizing influences that were producing an odd generation of women with bobbed hair and mannish habits. This defense of conventional attitudes did not regain him friends among Victorian conservatives, however, for they were shocked by his frank and realistic approach to sex, especially the way he dealt with taboo subjects such as the superstitions and fears surrounding masturbation.

Strindberg expected strong reactions to *Married,* but neither he nor his publisher anticipated that the government would confiscate copies of the book and charge its author, because of a casual reference to Christ as an agitator, with blasphemy. On October 21, 1884, Strindberg appeared in court to answer the indictment in a situation that was rife with ironies. Because of the extremity of the government's action, liberals and radicals rallied to his side despite their disapproval of his anti-feminist position. On the previous day he had been given a hero's welcome at the Stockholm railroad station and a standing ovation at a special performance of his play *Lucky Per's Travels.*

But the festivities gave him little comfort. He had agreed to return to Sweden only after much pressure from friends and business associates. He was profoundly uneasy and grew more so, sensing perhaps that
he had rocked the boat once too often and that regardless of the outcome
of the trial its effect on his life would be devastating. For all his radical
ideas, he had no appetite for martyrdom. He might talk, as he did in his
poem "The Boulevard System," about the necessity for razing the corrupt
social structure, but he had no desire to become personally involved. In
short, he was caught in a vise of contradiction between his bourgeois
ambitions and his romantic instincts.

The trial ended in acquittal on November 17th, but it was a
Pyrrhic victory; Strindberg was so shaken by the experience that nothing
in his life was ever quite the same again. The following day he left Sweden
to return to his family in Switzerland, having incurred an opposition that
had ominous implications. Many Swedes regarded the verdict as a provocative travesty of justice; clergymen denounced Strindberg from their
pulpits and even newspapers that had supported him in the past warned
their readers not to allow their children to be exposed further to his dangerous influence. Before the year was out, pressure was exerted to inhibit
publication of his works, and Strindberg wrote to a friend that he feared
his "battle against the upper classes" would lead to his destruction.

His financial situation, always somewhat precarious after he took
his family abroad, began to worsen significantly in the spring and summer
of 1885, and he was no longer able to keep in balance the ambivalent feelings he had controlled in the years when his fortunes were climbing. By the
time the second volume of *Married* was published in October, 1886, his
anti-feminism had hardened into a strident misogynism that was manifested
through paranoiac suspicions and vicious accusations. *The New Kingdom*
had made him an anathema to conservatives, and now his increasingly
irrational stand on "the woman question" alienated him from liberals and
radicals. Among the disenchanted was an old friend Hjalmar Branting,
the founder of the Swedish Social Democratic Party. But, significantly,
he found a new friend in the aristocrat Verner von Heidenstam, a gifted
young writer who encouraged Strindberg's latent anti-democratic sentiments.

Strindberg's misogynism, a disruptive element in all three of his
marriages, was not simply a stubborn and intemperate reaction to those

who opposed his views on the woman question. It was a sign of the profound disillusionment that attended his quest for an impossible ideal—a woman who could satisfy his needs for intellectual stimulation, sexual gratification, and material compassion, who would be simultaneously comrade, lover, and mother. It is indicative that despite his continual insistence that women should be educated as mothers, ready to sacrifice themselves for their children, he married women who were at least as interested in furthering their careers as they were in building families.

When life began to sour for him after the *Married* trial, he blamed his troubles on an international conspiracy of irate females. It did not take long for him to suspect that Siri was one of the conspirators. Family quarrels became increasingly acrimonious, and he began taking long trips by himself. In the summer of 1887 the Strindbergs made inquiries about a divorce, and in March, 1891, they were legally separated.

The worse his personal problems became, the more vehement became his pro-aristocratic and anti-feminist sentiments—a tendency reflected clearly in the works he wrote in the late 1880's and early 1890's. The four parts of his autobiography were written in a single year—1886— yet they reveal an astonishing range of attitudes. The first volume begins with a description of Swedish society in the mid-nineteenth century that seems to have been drawn by someone with a pronounced democratic bias, but the last volume ends with a reconstruction of one of the dialogues in which Verner von Heidenstam undermined Strindberg's faith in social democracy. Strindberg's artistic focus shifted from social satire to psychological analysis, and the boundaries of his fictional worlds narrowed to an examination of the battle between the sexes in which his own problems played the dominant role.

Early in 1887 he wrote to his brother that he had doubts about whether his children were really his; he had just finished writing *The Father* in which a husband goes insane when he is unable to determine with certainty if his wife had been unfaithful to him early in their marriage. Strindberg had always feared that Baron Wrangel might seek revenge for the loss of Siri; in *Creditors,* written in the summer of 1888, a man suffers a fatal epileptic fit when visited by his wife's first husband. Much of the power in these harrowing works seems generated by a man totally possessed by jealousy and frustration, but at the same time Strindberg was capable of writing with warmth, nostalgia, and wry humor, as in the novel *The*

People of Hemsö, which he wrote between *The Father* and *A Madman's Defense,* a brutal and indiscreet autobiographical novel in which he tried to determine if Siri had been unfaithful to him from the first moment they met.

Strindberg's literary output during the last years of his first marriage was impressive, but although dramas such as *The Father* and *Miss Julie* made him famous, they brought little income. In Sweden, publishers were reluctant to accept his manuscripts and his plays went unperformed. When he returned home with his family in April, 1889, he was still *persona non grata.* Even his application for a fishing license was denied because he was remembered as the notorious author of the two volumes of *Married.* That fall he began a novel, *In the Outer Skerries,* about a high-strung intellectual who tries to find a life among the unsophisticated and insensitive inhabitants of the rugged islands of Stockholm's archipelago, but is unsuccessful and commits suicide.

When the Strindbergs were granted an interlocutory decree of divorce in the spring of 1891 and Siri was given custody of the children, Strindberg was plunged into despair. He regarded his children as his surest contacts with reality; they were his comforts in the present and his hopes for the future. In the spring of 1892 he wrote the one-act play *The Bond,* set during a divorce trial, in which a man and wife become distraught when the court takes their child from them. Several months later, Strindberg decided the time had come again to seek a new life abroad. Encouraged by his friend and countryman Ola Hansson, an expatriate who had been promoting his reputation in Germany, he left for Berlin in September.

During Strindberg's second extended exile, as during the first, there occurred a major turning point. Between 1894 and 1896 he experienced the five psychotic episodes that he called his Inferno. As was true of the tragic aftermath of the *Married* trial, the Inferno Crisis, at least at the outset, had its roots in his marital problems. After arriving in Berlin, he had several casual affairs before falling in love with Frida Uhl, an Austrian journalist more than twenty years younger than he. They were married in May, 1893, and shortly afterward went to London to stimulate interest in the production of his plays. Meeting with little success, he grew restless and left Frida in mid-June to return to the continent; she rejoined him in Berlin. In May, 1894, a daughter, Kerstin, was born, but the marriage was

doomed. Financial necessity compelled the couple to live with Frida's
grandparents in Austria, and it stung Strindberg's pride to have to accept
their charity. Once again he became involved in a round of bitter domestic
squabbles. By late summer his patience was exhausted and he went to
Paris. Frida followed him in September but left him for good in late
October; although they were not divorced until 1897, they never saw each
other again.

In addition to his very real financial problems now complicated
by alimony payments (by January, 1895, he was seventeen months in
arrears), he realized that he was bankrupt creatively. During the last years
with Siri, despite his unhappiness, he had written some of his finest work;
now it seemed that his literary resources and energies had dried up.
Between the spring of 1892 and the spring of 1897 he did no creative
writing; instead, he returned to an old love and described his decision in a
letter to Frida in July, 1893: *"Adieu les belles-lettres et bonjour la science!"*

At first he conducted rather orthodox research in botany, astronomy, and chemistry, but then, as the traumatic force of his Inferno bore
down heavily upon him, he turned to alchemy and occultism, and his experiments took on more religious than scientific significance. Undoubtedly,
his search for a way to produce gold was at least partly motivated by
economic need, but he pursued his research with a mystical fervor that
stimulated him to study the origins of alchemy in the Middle Ages, a period
he admired because it was a time when men had faith and could find paths
to redemption, a goal he desperately sought. He had always been interested
in religion, even though he flirted briefly with atheism, but during the
Inferno Crisis religion became the central experience in his lfe. In addition
to the human enemies he felt were conspiring against him, he now sensed
that there were supernatural forces — Powers — bent on chastizing and
humbling him.

The most authoritative research on the Inferno Crisis has been
done by the Swedish scholar Gunnar Brandell, who points out that the
structure of each of Strindberg's psychotic episodes was similar: "a preliminary period of general anxiety, feelings of illness, suicide fantasies,
and persecution fears. This was followed by a sudden flight from his
immediate surroundings to a new environment, where the crisis would
gradually subside."

The first episode occurred in the summer of 1894 when Strindberg's difficulties with Frida's family caused him to leave Austria for Paris. The second began in December of the same year after he hurt his hands so badly during his chemical experiments that he had to spend three weeks recuperating at the Hôpital de Saint-Louis. The third episode took place around the end of the year 1895 when he tried to forget his wife and child by having an affair with an English sculptress, but this filled him with a tormenting sense of remorse. Only after moving into the Hôtel Orfila in February, 1896, did he begin to regain his composure. According to Brandell, it was during this episode that Strindberg began to try to come to grips with his feelings of guilt and to find some moral-religious purpose behind his suffering. In the fourth episode, which began in May, 1896, his paranoid suspicions turned into terrifying hallucinations: ordinary sounds, objects, and events became omens of danger; he believed electrical currents were moving through him and he was being poisoned by gas. He fled Paris in July to stay with a friend in Dieppe but began hallucinating again and went back to Sweden to seek help from a friend who was a doctor.

For the first time, says Brandell, he began to locate "the blame within himself instead of presupposing the existence of enemies who were persecuting him." In August he was pleased to receive an invitation from Frida's family to come to Austria to see his child, but the visit was marred when two-year-old Kerstin at first treated him as a stranger. The hallucinations returned, and in November he experienced his fifth and final episode.

The Inferno Crisis did not resolve all the plaguing contradictions and ambivalences in Strindberg's personality, but it enabled him to find the equilibrium he had lost. Confronted with the full range of his shortcomings, he learned to recognize and accept them. After he returned to Sweden in December, 1896, his life entered a new and amazing phase. The following spring and summer he wrote a hauntingly beautiful account of the Inferno Crisis which was published in two parts: *Inferno* and *Legends*. In March and August of 1898 he wrote Parts I and II of *To Damascus*, the first plays he had written in six years and totally different from their predecessors. At the age of forty-eight, he started to experiment with innovations that were to influence the entire development of modern drama.

In December, 1898, he wrote an alchemist friend that he had abandoned chemistry and alchemy to devote his major energies to drama. His experiments had failed to produce gold, but he succeeded in another kind of alchemy — to take the agonizing memories of the Inferno years and turn them into brilliant dramatic images. Influenced by his readings in Emanuel Swedenborg, the eighteenth-century theologian, Strindberg came to feel that earthly life was a hell men were forced to suffer, and that their experience of reality was only an illusion, a dream that could assume nightmarish proportions. To express these visions in drama he invented a special world in which it is difficult to distingush between the real and the unreal. In *To Damascus, A Dream Play* (1901), and the Chamber Plays (1907), grotesque, phantom-like characters act on the basis of a logic that is at once improbable, ludicrous, and frighteningly believable. These strange people are stripped of every defense, every false face and disguise, until the raw truth of human weakness and corruption lies naked and exposed.

Experiences like the Inferno Crisis have destroyed many men of talent and genius, but for Strindberg it was a crucible that toughened him without crushing his sensitivity. It gave him a resiliency he had not known for a long time. Although he would repeat some of his past errors—committing himself again to courses of action that were damaging to him personally and professionally—his final years were relatively happy. There were emotional crises, of course, but he weathered them often with surprising good grace. One reason he was able to do so was that he finally achieved the financial security he had desired so long.

Between 1908 and 1910 inexpensive "family editions" of individual earlier works sold 127,000 copies, and in 1911 the publishing firm of Bonniers agreed to pay 200,000 crowns (approximately 40,000 American dollars at the 1969 rate of exchange) for rights to issue the standard edition of his collected works. Another factor was the long overdue recognition of his genius as a playwright, to which he responded with an incredible output of plays. During the periods of January, 1899, to the summer of 1902 and the spring of 1907 to the fall of 1909, he began or finished work on thirty dramas. They included, in addition to the pioneering works already mentioned, the brilliant history plays *Gustav Vasa* and *Erik XIV*, the lyrical fairy-tale-like fantasies *A Crown Bride* and *Swanwhite*, and *The Dance of Death*, which harks back to the brutal naturalism of *The Father*.

Many of his earlier works were staged successfully, some for the first time in Sweden. Between 1908 and 1912 there were 1,550 performances of his plays presented in Stockholm alone. A production of *Miss*

Julie in December, 1906, by August Falck, an enterprising young actor-manager, revived one of Strindberg's oldest hopes: to establish a theatre whose primary function was to perform his works. In 1888 and 1889, stimulated by André Antoine's example at the Théâtre Libre in Paris, Strindberg had founded the Scandinavian Experimental Theatre in Copenhagen, but it closed after one performance. Four years later, he had expectations of starting a theatre at Djursholm near Stockholm, but nothing came of them. August Falck's energy and interest prompted Strindberg to collaborate on new plans. In June, 1907, they rented a building in Stockholm, and Strindberg invested a considerable amount of his own money to finance the venture. On November 26, 1907, the Intimate Theatre opened with the première of the Chamber Play *The Pelican*. When the theatre closed three years later, it had produced twenty-four of Strindberg's plays and had added immeasurably to his stature as a playwright.

In the fall of 1910, while searching for someone to play the leading female role in the première production of *To Damascus,* Strindberg met and fell in love with a beautiful Norwegian actress, Harriet Bosse. Defying warnings from friends that it was ridiculous for a man over fifty to court a woman in her early twenties, he and Harriet were engaged in March, 1901, and married in May. Life brightened considerably for him once again, but only briefly. In June, Harriet went off to Denmark by herself, having tired of delaying her honeymoon while her husband waited to find omens and portents indicating that it would be safe for him to go abroad. He joined her after a short time, but their marriage held little promise of happiness. She was a vivacious young woman who loved meeting people, and he was an aging, touchy recluse who feared and distrusted strangers. Over the next three years their relationship followed a pattern of long separations and brief reconciliations. Their only child, Anne-Marie, born in March, 1902, was a source of great joy for Strindberg, and he continued to see her regularly after he and Harriet were divorced in 1904.

In contrast to his dealing with his other wives, Strindberg maintained an intimate correspondence with Harriet for a long time after their divorce. Not until she remarried in May, 1908, did he stop hoping that they would be reunited. Several months later he sold many of their belongings, left the apartment they had shared, and moved to his final home, which he called The Blue Tower. Unlike his other divorces, this last one did not shatter him psychologically or cause his creative resources to wither, partly because he had learned resignation and partly because a short time before Harriet's remarriage he had taken a personal interest in another young actress, Fanny Falkner. The difference of more than forty years in their ages did not discourage him from proposing to her in the fall of 1909 and again in the spring of 1910. On each occasion she accepted him and then backed down. He swallowed his disappointment and plunged back into his work.

In some ways, the post-1900 Strindberg resembled the acerbic young social critic whose future seemed so bright before it was clouded by the *Married* trial. His opposition to the upper classes, big business, and hypocrisy of all kinds was rekindled, and he renewed his friendship with Hjalmar Branting, who now headed a Social Democratic Party that had grown considerably in power and influence. In 1903 Strindberg resumed his campaign against the Establishment with *The Gothic Rooms,* a novel he regarded as a sequel to *The Red Room,* but it lacked the sting of the earlier work because he was out of touch with Swedish social, political, and economic realities. Nevertheless, it was clear that the Inferno Crisis had not subdued his curiosity, vitality, and appetite for conflict.

In the spring of 1910, Strindberg initiated what came to be called "The Strindberg Controversy" by beginning a series of approximately one hundred provocative and contentious articles on art, religion, and politics. One of the institutions attacked and ridiculed was an old enemy: the Swedish Academy. In a mock interview Strindberg asked himself:

> Is it a Learned Society?
> Moderately. But if it is to be the high tribunal of literature, it should contain people competent to judge literature.

In *The New Kingdom* he had attacked the reactionary permanent secretary of the Academy, Carl David af Wirsén, and this cost him the Nobel Prize for Literature. He was in good company, however; Ibsen, Tolstoy, Zola, Hardy, Chekhov, and Mark Twain were only a few of his contemporaries bypassed in favor of people such as R. F. A. Sully-Prudhomme, Theodor Mommsen, R. C. Eucken, and Henryk Sienkiewicz. The injustice did not go unnoticed in Sweden. In 1911 a sum of money was raised by national subscription and given to Strindberg as an "Anti-Nobel Prize."

And on his birthday in 1912 a giant torchlight procession of workers and students marched past The Blue Tower to honor him. From a balcony where he stood with his daughter Anne-Marie, he tossed rose petals down on the passers-by.

Strindberg's dual perspective on life was both a curse and a blessing. For all the searing agony it brought to him personally, it strongly influenced the choice of dramatic dialogue as his primary form of literary expression. When he used his own experiences as the chief source for this dialogue, it was not a vindictive or exhibitionist act, but a courageous self-sacrifice, fulfilling what Conrad Aiken has called "one of the responsibilities of a writer—that he should take off the mask." Like his persona Arvid Falk in *The Red Room* and *The Gothic Rooms,* Strindberg "was a vivisector who experimented with his own soul, and his open wounds always showed." He was well aware that he had caused pain and embarrassment to intimates and enemies alike, but if he was ruthless and indiscreet in exposing the frailties of others, he was no less hard on himself. Another of his personae, the writer Falkenström in the novel *Black Banners,* delivers a confession that could be Strindberg's own:

> My friends, . . . during my writing career there has always been a misunderstanding between my readers and myself. They believed I was punishing them when in fact I was reacting against the evil in myself. In order to be able to write my works, I have offered up my life and my person.

During his battle with stomach cancer, which ended with his death on May 14, 1912, Strindberg said to his daughter Karin: "Everything is atoned for."

Queens College
The City University of New York
1970

PART ONE

Before The Inferno Crisis

Chapter One

THE EARLY YEARS

Childhood Home

Johan August Strindberg's career as a writer began in 1869 when he was twenty years old. From that time on, life and art were inseparable to him. His experiences constituted the raw material for his work, and his works became the significant events in his biography. This relationship was so evident to him that during various periods in his life he complained that he was unable to distinguish between what he experienced and what he wrote. Childhood and adolescence, therefore, are the only periods of Strindberg's life that one can discuss without simultaneously analyzing his work.

It is important to remember, however, that the principal source of information about Strindberg's early years, his autobiography, *The Son of a Servant (Tjänstekvinnans son)*, is also a work of fiction. The images of childhood anguish in the early part of this four-volume work were created by an adult whose perspective was affected by modern psychological theories and social concepts. It is difficult to conceive of that much sorrow, that much self-reflection and hypersensitivity in a child, or even in a precocious adolescent. The actual letters, essays, and compositions he wrote as a young man and later inserted into his autobiography seem conspicuously tame in comparison with the adjoining text. On the other hand, there is no documentary support for the picture that certain scholars have attempted to construct of a young Strindberg who, before he was buffeted by the storms of life, was a mild, neatly combed Sunday school student. Even the earliest of Strindberg's personal letters show evidence of his rebellious temperament. That this temperament is not as strongly manifested in his earliest writings is partly because he did not possess the artistic means to express it. Also he was determined to appear calm and reasonable. But even there he explodes with elemental violence.

3

Can the origin of so unique a personality as August Strindberg be explained? While writing his autobiography in 1886 he was firmly convinced that it could, but during the final period of his life, he was only too ready to regard himself as an exceptional individual and his childhood as an unprecedented and inexplicable martyrdom. In 1890, the Swedish writer Ola Hansson called Strindberg a brilliant refutation of Taine's precept that a writer is a product of his time and milieu. The wisest course in trying to understand Strindberg's childhood is to discount a portion of his portrait of youthful melancholy, but to remember that the feelings he described in his autobiography were valid for him for the greater part of his life, even for the years in which he was growing up.

Strindberg always considered himself to be suffering from what may be called an inferiority complex,[1] and his father was influential in its development. Witnesses other than Strindberg have testified that Carl Oscar Strindberg, because of business reverses and because he married beneath his station, felt that he had lost social status and prestige. He withdrew within himself and became a domestic tyrant, demanding that everything in the home be run according to his arbitrary rules. Above all, disobedience and lying had to be punished. One need not take too literally Strindberg's accounts of trials conducted under torture during which he was compelled to confess to minor offenses that he had not committed, but the final impression his accounts give is that the father was governed by the same demons of suspicion and dogmatism that would later hound the son.

Even as a small child, Strindberg kept close track of his brothers' offenses. "If they were not punished, he felt deeply wronged; if they were rewarded undeservedly, his sense of justice suffered."[2] This remained his attitude toward his fellow men throughout his life, and it was sharpened by his sense of always being treated wrongly, always being the stepchild. Referring to himself by his first name throughout his autobiography, Strindberg notes that "Johan was no one's favorite. He felt it and it grieved him."[3] Because he had inherited his father's uncommunicativeness and his mother's touchiness and temper, he could not have been a manageable child.

Even in later years, Carl Oscar never took notice of his son's talent. According to Strindberg's sisters, their father once said, "August is so strange; he'll never amount to anything." Even when his son's one-act play *In Rome (I Rom)* was accepted by the Royal Dramatic Theatre in 1870, the old man greeted the news with the word "fiasco." Although he lived until 1883, he paid no attention whatsoever to his son's literary successes. Strindberg's stepmother,[4] with whom August lived at loggerheads while he was growing up, seems to have shown a greater interest.

"Bringing up a child was something no one had time for. The school took charge where the servant-girls left off," Strindberg said in *The Son of a Servant.*[5] His father interested himself only in maintaining strict discipline, and his mother felt much too inferior socially and intellectually to be able to contribute anything. Strindberg regarded his first period of schooling as "a preparation for hell and not for life."[6] As a result, he became, and for the rest of his life remained, a capricious and willful child. He was capable of being affable, but sooner or later the volcanic part of his nature would erupt. At an early age he became aware of the blend of hypersensitivity and brutality that marked him, impulses that are sharply revealed in one of his earliest self-portraits, the story fragment "The Beginning of Å Bogsveig's Saga" ("Början av Ån Bogsveigs saga"), and are underscored in many of his youthful letters. As he became more confident of his position as a writer, he gave vent more uninhibitedly to these impulses.

Whenever Strindberg tried to explain his behavior, he referred to his insatiable need for maternal tenderness. Describing the first time he was separated from his mother to go on a summer journey, he wrote: "This loneliness and longing for his mother followed him throughout his life. Had he arrived in the world abortively? Was he incomplete? Why was he so bound to his mother?"[7] This passage has provoked a variety of psychological interpretations, including those based on the Oedipus complex. But what haunted him was an abstraction, an ideal, not his feelings for his real mother; in another place in his autobiography he says that after her death he missed her for hardly more than several months. She had favored the other children, betrayed him to his father, and, as he grew older, seemed to him to be uneducated.

With the passage of time, however, he came to create what he called a purified and glorified image of her. Throughout his life he felt a sense of loss and longed for an ideal maternal figure, an ideal maternal embrace, in which his stormy emotions could be cradled to rest. He worshipped the mother in all the women with whom he fell in love during his lifetime. To him, sexual desire, once it had been satisfied, was a profanation. His program for sexual reform as stated in the preface to the story collection *Married (Giftas)* culminates in a glorification of woman as mother.[8]

The feeling of being a stranger in his own home, of being different from the others and therefore out of favor, became the foundation for Strindberg's later relationship with the outside world. He felt unwelcome everywhere, as if people made a place for him reluctantly, only for as long as they could use him. And when setbacks were finally too numerous to be explained away as instances of human animosity, he created a world of "Powers" and spirits and accused them of the same faults he found in his fellow men: jealousy, pettiness, and iniquity.

During the time that Strindberg was engaged in writing *The Son of a Servant,* he was in a mental state not unlike his later (1894-1896) "Inferno Crisis," as he called the period of his greatest psychological disturbance. The lawsuit brought against him for blasphemy in the first volume of *Married,*[9] although decided in his favor, made him suspect that he was being persecuted by a world-wide league of women. Gradually the fear that he was suffering from persecution mania obsessed him and he felt that he was in danger of being confined. In a curious statement[10] written the year before he began his autobiography, he gave instructions "in the event I should be attacked by insanity. . . . My brain has been on fire since I was a child," the document continued, and he described how he was frustrated and humiliated in his own home and then for a long time prevented from enjoying literary success because of the machinations of his enemies.

Strindberg believed that his most effective answer to those who might suspect that he suffered from persecution mania was the argument that he really was persecuted. This is one of the reasons his childhood memories acquired so dark a coloring that he himself was sometimes astonished. When he was writing about himself as a fourteen-year-old, he acknowledged that his life "was not so damned eternally melancholy during those years as it later seemed in retrospect." His choice of facts was conditioned by the need to demonstrate that from the beginning he was oppressed by his parents, tormented by his teachers, and hated by his comrades.

There is quite another view of Strindberg's childhood home in the

introductory poem in his verse cycle "Exile" ("Landsflykt"), written in 1883 at a time when he had not yet felt the need to protect himself against suspicions of delusions of persecution. Here is a picture of a comfortable and congenial environment with well-rubbed mahogany furniture, walls covered with faded lithographs, and Swedish classics in the bookcase. Strindberg's frightening father contentedly keeps time to a Haydn quartet with the nodding of his pipe, his mother flits about the house like a good fairy, and his grandmother is absorbed in her book of homilies:

> The warmth of Sunday nights at home,
> gay sisters, happy brothers.

If one looks closely, one can find similar details in his autobiography. But the childhood home stressed there is the tenement near Klara Church with the pitch-black backyard, the garbage bin, and the big rats; the furniture consists mostly of cradles and beds, and children lie on ironing boards and chairs: it is "a prison workshop for breadwinners and a hell for children." This is the dismal childhood home that Strindberg painted in ever darker colors the older he became, driven by the desire to justify the picture of his childhood as a period of undeserved suffering. Transformed poetically, the same home became the macabre setting for the Chamber Play *The Burned House (Brända tomten*— 1907).

Strindberg's happy childhood memories appear less frequently in his writings than the somber ones, but traces can be found in such works as the short stories "Pål and Per" ("Pål och Per") in *Swedish Destinies and Adventures (Svenska öden och äventyr),* "The Romantic Organist on Rånö ("Den romantiske klockaren på Rånö"), the drama *Midsummer (Midsommar),* and the poem "Journey to Town" ("Stadsresan"). The strongest traces are in the essay collection *Old Stockholm (Gamla Stockholm);* Strindberg declared that during its writing he "imagined himself sitting and telling his child about the good old days."

The phrase "the good old days" is an indication of the nature of some of these memories. There were musicales in the home, at which even Strindberg's severe father became sociable, and holidays were celebrated every year with the same ritual. Strindberg was never more easily moved than when he thought about Christmas, Easter, and Midsummer, and these holidays provided the setting for a number of his works. Above all, there were picnics and summer excursions to the Lake Mälar skerries when, before the steamboat departures, his father would reveal another side of his nature: a happy, youthful man "who joked with the berry-brown steamboat captains and wore a handsome, benevolent smile." When Strindberg first thought of recording his reminiscences, he considered limiting himself to the summer sojourns and reposing "in the happy memories of my life." If these intentions had been carried out, we would have had a completely different picture of his childhood. But, as he said in a letter, "this terrain was deliberately bypassed" to be spared for other works. The gloominess and heartsickness of his childhood were thus exaggerated and the reader is not given an accurate picture of how the author thrived in the only setting in which he ever really felt at home—Stockholm and its environs.

Adolescence

As a child, Strindberg was so self-assertive that one might overlook an important aspect of his personality: his inclination toward self-torment.[11] He himself did not ignore it, and in several places in *The Son of a Servant* he describes how he reveled in self-torment and vaunted his martyrdom before his brothers. It would be unwise to underestimate the influence of this characteristic upon his later religious development. The urge toward self-sacrifice was and remained the first article of his faith. It was fitting that Kierkegaard was his prophet throughout his life.

Strindberg's mother and stepmother were adherents of Pietism, and this was the source of his religious awakening. Emphasizing simple puritanical virtues, Pietism appealed to the poverty-striken and downtrodden and was opposed by the more conventional, orthodox State Lutheran Church. Strindberg read the German theologian Friedrich Wilhelm Krummacher (1796-1868) and Thomas à Kempis, who was to become his favorite again after his interest in religion was renewed following the Inferno Crisis; he visited Pietistic meetings or conventicles and had heated disputes with his family, whose religious practices he found inconsistent. He once refused to accompany the family on a Sunday excursion so as not to be guilty of a breach of the Sabbath, and instead went to Bethlehem Church to hear the renowned Pietistic evangelist Carl Olof Rosenius (1816-68). Afterward, as he strolled in Haga Park, he shuddered at the thought that the humble tradespeople picnicking there with their children were just as surely damned as the fine gentlemen and ladies who drove by in barouches.

According to his own statement, he tormented himself with an almost fanatical passion when, at the age of fifteen, he fell in love with the landlord's thirty-year-old daughter. He wrote for her in French the religious essays that appear in translation in his autobiography. Their unctuous tone foreshadows the meditations of *A Blue Book (En blå bok)*, the huge *omnium gatherum* of ideas on literature, philosophy, science, and religion published in four volumes from 1907 to 1912. During the final years of his life, Strindberg resumed his visits to Bethlehem Church and wrote of hoping to be able to attain "that religious outlook the world calls Pietism." He also found this religion to be in accord with his temperament at the time he was writing his autobiography: "Melancholy by nature, although full of spirit, he loved the melancholy."[12]

There was nothing melancholy, however, about the cheerful and optimistic Unitarianism of the American Theodore Parker (1810-60), which followed Pietism as Strindberg's next profession of faith when he was fifteen years old, but then he was always balanced between extremes. And yet even Parker's optimism became material out of which to make a martyr. Strindberg now called himself a freethinker, and his relationship with his parents, which had already been tense, became unendurable. He agitated in the classroom, instigated a strike against the matins among his classmates, quarreled with the theology teacher, and was rebuked by the principal. The young *gymnasium* student had developed a taste for life's pleasures and went to balls, sang in a quartet, drank Swedish punch, went drinking at the Andalusiskan restaurant, and carried on "mild flirtations with waitresses." But although he became hostile to Pietism after accepting Unitarianism, he could not emancipate himself from the conscientious scruples it had engendered. The flagellant and ascetic still lived within him and was reawakened by Ibsen's *Brand*, which he read in 1869, and by Kierkegaard, whose work he first came to know while he was at the University of Uppsala in 1870. "His new self opposed the old, but they continued to live together in discord throughout his life, like an unhappy married couple unable to separate."[13]

"Had I been born several hundred years ago, I would have donned a clerical frock and gone out to preach," Strindberg wrote to Bjørnstjerne Bjørnson in 1884.[14] During his school years he dreamed of a clerical calling, and once, while working at a summer job, he had an opportunity to preach—presenting a cautious form of his Parkerian faith. After passing his university qualifying examination, however, he felt that he was not sufficiently orthodox a Unitarian to be able to take the ordination oath. But the sacrificial tendency and the desire to preach remained with him, and the careers that beckoned to him during his student years were more "callings" than professions.

After his first, desultory semester at the University of Uppsala, he took a position (in 1868) as an elementary school teacher in Stockholm. It was regarded as a disgrace for a university student to become an elementary school teacher, but Strindberg's craving to sacrifice himself, to "step down" and debase himself, was strong, even though he had hoped to be able to satisfy this craving less conspicuously in some rural area. He was terribly uncomfortable with the catechism lessons and the ragged and foul-smelling lower-class schoolboys. He had dreams about carrying out teaching reforms, but they turned out to be illusory. In his disgust for his work he made wild plans about enlisting in the Foreign Legion. Instead, he was attracted by the idea of becoming a doctor.

His decision to choose the medical profession was motivated by the desire "to learn and to preach," for he believed that "these new prophets" were the successors of "the priests and the confessors."[15] He was satisfied with his new life as a science student as long as he was able to conduct his own studies in Stockholm, but when he failed the first part of his preliminary examination in chemistry for the University of Uppsala in the spring of 1869, he abandoned the medical calling. Nevertheless, he retained his passion for natural science and medicine even after he turned to the study of the humanities at Uppsala in 1870. In his short-story collection *Town and Gown (Från Fjärdingen och Svartbäcken—1877)* and in the third part of his autobiography, *In the Red Room (I röda rummet—1887)*, chemists and doctors are pictured as sound, sober, and prosaic people, whereas humanists are idealistic and fatuous. Time and again during the 1880's, Strindberg was on the verge of becoming a chemist or doctor. In the beginning of the 1890's, the laboratory experimentation he had never completely abandoned took precedence over his writings, and he began dreaming of the grandiose chemical and alchemical projects that were to occupy him until his death.

On the day he failed his chemistry examination at Uppsala, Strindberg came upon Levasseur's French actors talking and laughing in Karolina Park, and a new way of life beckoned to him. But the sudden impulse to be an actor led to an even worse fiasco than his decision to become a doctor. He dreamed of making his debut as Karl Moor in Schiller's *The Robbers;* instead, after putting in time as a supernumerary and auditing classes at the Royal Dramatic Theatre School in Stockholm, he was assigned the bit part of Härved Boson in Frans Hedberg's *Wedding at Ulvåsa (Bröllopet på Ulvåsa).* He finished out the fall term as prompter for the student show, then returned to the university in 1870, where he remained except for a brief interval until the spring of 1872. That fall he made another attempt to become an actor at the theatre in Gothenburg but was equally unsuccessful.

It might not appear that these desires to be an actor—whose importance to his later work is obvious—had much in common with his desire to preach. But for Strindberg they were part of the same impulse: "In these theatrical ecstasies something reemerged that he had felt when he preached and when he opposed the prayers in school—the proclaimer, the prophet, the speaker of truth."[16]

And "proclaimer, prophet, speaker of truth" was what Strindberg wanted to be when he found his real "role in life"—writing. He would never cease to maintain that literature in itself was a useless game. Time and again he wanted to renounce its lies in order to be able to write "the pure, unadulterated truth." That he constantly returned, after longer or shorter digressions, to "the beautiful groves of art" was due not only to an ineradicable creative drive, but also to his discovery after each effort as preacher or social reformer that his words did not become resonant until they were clad in artistic form.

His passion for truth was fervent and his faith in his mission unshakable. It annoyed him to be called "poet" because he regarded himself as engaged in a more serious pursuit. But his art was destined to be remembered longer than his ideology, and our primary concern must be with Strindberg the artist, not Strindberg the religious reformer or advocate of social betterment.

Notes to Chapter One

1. Alfred Adler, the originator of the term, was influenced in the development of his concept by *The Son of a Servant*. This trait in Strindberg has been analyzed in an ingenious way by Torsten Eklund in *Tjänstekvinnans son, En psykologisk Strindbergsstudie* (Stockholm, 1948). The first chapter, "Barndomsintrycken och karaktären," treats in detail the period that is touched upon here only briefly.

2. *SS*:XVIII, p. 15. [Except where otherwise noted, Professor Lamm has referred throughout to the standard edition of Strindberg's works: *Samlade skrifter* (55 volumes, 1912-19), edited and annotated by John Landquist.—Translator]

3. *Ibid.*, pp. 15-16. Eklund strongly emphasizes how much Strindberg suffered because his next older brother Oscar was the family favorite *(Strindbergsstudie,* pp. 10 ff.).

4. Strindberg's mother died in 1862, when he was thirteen years old. His father remarried in 1863.—Translator

5. *SS*:XVIII, p. 14.

6. *Ibid.*, p. 39.

7. *Ibid.*, p. 46.

8. Cf. Eklund, *Strindbergsstudie,* pp. 134 ff., who disputes the existence of an "incestuous tendency" in Strindberg.

9. The specific charge concerned a passage in the story "Virtue's Rewards" that referred to "the shameless fraud practiced with Högstedt's Piccardon at 65 öre per bottle and Lettström's corn wafers at 1 krona per pound, which the clergy gives out to be the flesh and blood of the demagogue Jesus of Nazareth, who was executed over 1800 years ago."—Translator

10. *See* Birger Möorner, *Den Strindberg jag känt* (1924), pp. 167-68.

11. This was not neglected by Eklund, however, who strongly emphasizes it in *Strindbergsstudie,* pp. 29 *et passim.*

12. *SS*:XVIII, p. 129.

13. *Ibid.*, p. 163.

14. *Strindbergs brev* [*Letters*], IV, p. 145.

15. *SS*:XVIII, p. 287.

16. *Ibid.*, p. 313.

Chapter Two

WORKS OF A NEOPHYTE

The Early Plays

Strindberg completed his first significant play, the prose version of *Master Olof,* in 1872, but prior to this, between 1869 and 1871, he was engaged in a number of experiments in dramatic form worthy of attention. Interestingly enough from a biographical viewpoint, all of them, except the very first one about which we know next to nothing, glorify idealistic heroes who battle and sacrifice everything for their beliefs, just as Strindberg believed he was sacrificing everything for his Parkerism.

His first play, a two-act comedy entitled *A Name-Day Present (En namnsdagsgåva),* is not extant. It was begun in the fall of 1869, the day after he failed his test as an actor, and was completed in four days. *The Son of a Servant* states¹ that he recast an idea from Zachris Topelius's *Stories of an Army Surgeon (Fältskärns berättelser)* to describe how after being alienated from his father, he became reconciled with him through his stepmother.

His second play, *The Freethinker (Fritänkaren),* written in November of the same year and published in 1870 under the pseudonym Härved Ulf, was also based on conflicts in the Strindberg family, but does not end in a reconciliation. The hero, Karl, is an ardent apostle of Theodore Parker, who is compared to Christ, Socrates, and Luther. Karl sacrifices everything for his faith—his fiancée, his parents, and his friends. Threatened with the loss of his teaching position in an elementary school, where he has struggled in vain to teach his beliefs, he steadfastly endures all vicissitudes. As the curtain falls, he is prepared to go to the United States to preach his faith in Parkerian Unitarianism.

The play is similar to other Scandinavian works connected with

13

the tradition-shattering breakthrough of realism in the 1870's and 1880's, in which we find the same boundlessly self-sacrificing heroes, cast in the mold of Ibsen's Brand. Throughout Northern Europe at this time, religious questions delineated the boundaries between generations.

Strindberg began by drawing a picture of a gentle preacher "of the religion of truth and love." Karl is impressionable and lyrical like the earliest characterization of Master Olof. But the original intention was not realized; like Olof, Karl flares up and slashes out at the slightest challenge, even though his original purpose was to be a peacemaker. He breaks off with his Pietistic childhood friend Gustav because the latter will not accept Parker's gospel. According to Karl, Gustav is a false swearer who is stirred not by the idea for which he is fighting but by the fanaticism his "imaginary belief" produces. Karl is just as intolerant toward his parents and his fiancée. The motto printed on the title page of the play is: "I came not to send peace, but a sword,"[2] and it is almost a prophecy.

Despite its one-dimensional characterization and awkward dialogue, *The Freethinker* is arresting because of its brisk, breathless tempo. One feels Strindberg's agitated spirit pulsating through it. The next few plays have less spontaneity; they are stylistic experiments in verse and prose that attempt to satisfy conventional tastes. This is particularly true of the three-act play *Greece in Decline (Det sjunkande Hellas)* which was finished in December, 1869, a month after *The Freethinker*. In early 1870 it was submitted to the Royal Dramatic Theatre, but not accepted. Revised, it was sent under the title *Hermione* to the Swedish Academy, where it received honors. By this time the play had been expanded from three acts to five.[3] Strindberg states in *The Son of a Servant*[4] that this tragedy "was his first true 'work of art,' as the phrase goes, since it did not deal with anything that actually happened to him." It exemplifies the petrified forms from which Strindberg had to liberate himself.

Hermione plans to murder Philip of Macedon, but at the crucial moment, like Schiller's Maid of Orleans, she falls in love with the enemy general. Strindberg decked out this dramatic nucleus in conventional style and borrowed heavily from his predecessors. There is a misunderstood oracular response, as in Goethe and Schiller, and the model for the portrait of the born leader Philip is Shakespeare's Julius Caesar. Furthermore, Strindberg borrowed unabashedly from the scene between Brutus and Mark Antony for the debate between Demosthenes and Aeschines;

the similarities are particularly evident in each playwright's treatment of the ignorant and unruly mobs.

Presumably the Royal Dramatic Theatre found that the play did not contain enough historical color, for in the revised version Strindberg devoted a great deal of space to a depiction of the immorality of moribund ancient Greece, with touches borrowed from Viktor Rydberg's popular novel *The Last Athenian (Den siste athenaren*—1859). In the statement of praise from the Swedish Academy, drafted by Carl Wilhelm Böttiger, Strindberg's "assiduous attention" to local color was commended, although it was emphasized that he did not succeed "completely in utilizing the Greek tone and costume." Although the play was treated kindly and considered a "beautiful promise for the future," it was sharply criticized for its weak verse and its occasional colloquial language.[5]

The twenty-year-old poet diligently imitated the various trends in contemporary Swedish historical drama. For example, there are many learned, classical turns of phrase that have a flavor of Johan Runeberg's play *The Kings on Salamis (Kungarne på Salamis*—1863), which according to Strindberg was a favorite for reading aloud in the 1860's. There is also evidence of the influence of Carl August Hagberg's mid-nineteenth century translations of Shakespeare, and these were the primary sources that inspired Strindberg to take the rather awkward, colloquial liberties that offended the Academy judges. However, Strindberg did not yet have a true understanding of Shakespeare's use of realism. Only after reading Georg Brandes would this become clear to him.

After *Hermione,* Strindberg made two other attempts at conventional tragedy. The first, *Jesus of Nazareth,* was supposed to "shatter once and for all the divine image and eradicate Christianity"[6]—presumably to prepare the way for Theodore Parker's Unitarianism. After having written several scenes, Strindberg found the subject too demanding, and no manuscript remains. Of the first version of *Erik XIV* (King of Sweden, 1560-68), which was begun and burned in the fall of 1870, we know only that Erik's controversial associate and advisor Göran Persson (*ca.* 1530-68) was portrayed as "a hater of nobility and a man of the people."[7] In a review two years later of Georg von Rosen's famous painting of Erik, his mistress Karin Månsdotter, and Göran Persson, Strindberg, in an obviously personal interpretation, described how Persson grew up under continual persecution because he was the son of a priest who had turned

Lutheran and married, and how he became bitter watching his mother "constantly subjected to unjust contempt."[8] Since Strindberg associated his review with the burned play, one can assume that this autobiographical reference to the relationship between Persson and his mother was also included in the play.

One of Strindberg's friends at Uppsala, Gustaf Eisen, suggested that he write a one-act play in order to gain acceptance at the Royal Dramatic Theatre as a playwright. Strindberg followed this advice and completed a verse comedy that he had begun before returning to Uppsala for the second time in 1870. This unpretentious play about the Danish sculptor Bertel Thorvaldsen (1770-1844), *In Rome (I Rom)*, became his earliest performed work when it was produced at the Royal Dramatic Theatre in September, 1870.

In Rome, a dramatic parable, mirrored Strindberg's own situation at the time. After a row with his father, he received the small inheritance left to him by his mother and departed for Uppsala, promising solemnly not to waste time writing. But he did write, and then quelled his pangs of conscience by justifying himself through the character of Thorvaldsen. The play shows how the young sculptor, while studying in Italy in 1803, is spared from having to return to Denmark as his father requested when the great English art collector Sir Thomas Hope (1770-1831) orders a finished version in marble of Thorvaldsen's statue of Jason. Most of the dialogue consists of discussions between Thorvaldsen and his friend Pedersen about whether one should listen to "God's calling" or to the wishes of one's father. Strindberg's Thorvaldsen, contrary to history, cannot bring himself to smash his model of Jason but is fundamentally uncertain about his career as an artist. The play contains an unspoken wish on the part of Strindberg to find a patron like Sir Thomas Hope, and this was realized after Strindberg's next play when King Charles XV (1826-72) took an interest in the young author. Contemporary taste found the short play appealing, with its Roman artistic milieu and elegant dilettantism; one newspaper suspected that the play was actually written by the Norwegian Lorentz Dietrichson (1834-1917) who was a popular lecturer in Stockholm from 1867 to 1875 and very familiar with the milieu the play depicted.

Although *In Rome* contains an attack on the flowery poetry of a romantic, backward-looking Uppsala literary coterie called "The Signatures" *(Signaturerna)*, its verse differs little from the stylistic tendencies of that group. As a matter of fact, during the time the play was written, Strindberg and five poetically oriented Uppsala comrades founded a coterie of their own, the Runa Society *(Runaförbundet)*, which also looked to the past for poetic ideals, as is evident both in Strindberg's accounts and in the preserved records of the Society.[9] The Runa Society dreamed about a purified Swedish language with style and vocabulary linked to Icelandic; the members tried to eliminate the Latin names for the months, admired Norwegian and Danish literature, and in general cultivated idealism and patriotism. But Strindberg later satirized his fellow society members as "echoes" and pointed out their alienation from contemporary problems: "Life, general interests, daily politics, the present did not exist; they lived in dreams."[10]

Strindberg had a taste for demanding subjects, and in the fall of 1870 tackled the story of the eleventh-century figure, Blotsven, "perhaps the biggest subject in all of Swedish history," he wrote to Frans Hedberg. The play, which dealt with the struggle between paganism and Christianity, was annihilated by the criticism of a newly admitted society member, Josef Linck, before it was finished. In early 1871, Strindberg revised it into the one-act *The Outlaw (Den fredlöse)*.

Strindberg later acknowledged[11] that he had used Bjørnstjerne Bjørnson's *Between the Battles (Mellem slagene*—1855) as the model for the revision. Like Bjørnson's play, *The Outlaw* depicts a modern family conflict in an ancient Scandinavian context and culminates in reconciliation. A pagan Swedish viking, Earl Thorfinn, modeled after Strindberg's father, becomes reconciled with his wife, allows his daughter (who had been a secret Christian) to marry her lover, and with his final breath addresses an invocation to the higher power he had earlier denied. In a letter to his actor friend August Dorum, Strindberg wrote that he tried with this figure to portray "a self-sufficient human being who is forced to acknowledge a higher being; a Titan, a Prometheus who battles against the gods, or a King Fjalar who defies fate." But he was aware that he had failed to realize his intentions; when he sent the final script to the director of the Royal Dramatic Theatre, Frans Hedberg, he complained that during the revisions "all the old fogies [in the play became] . . . so wretchedly sentimental—the icy coldness . . . disappeared—Nordic stoicism is soft."[12]

Thorfinn, too, is soft, although his daughter reproaches him for his inhuman harshness. This softness is particularly evident in a scene inspired by the Danish writer Adam Oehlenschläger's *Earl Haakon (Hakon Jarl*—1805), in which Thorfinn, deserted by everyone, seeks help from a thrall who turns out to be a secret Christian. When Thorfinn describes, in a verse monologue, how he sailed in a broken boat one stormy fall day and landed on a rocky islet, he expresses Strindberg's own sense of loneliness:

> Then it became still.—Oh! such long days!
> Only cloudless heavens above me
> and endless, deep-blue sea around me!
> No sound of living creature!
> No gull to wake me with its screech!
> not even a breeze sufficient to splash
> a tiny wave against a stone.
>
> It seemed that I was dead;
> I talked and shouted loudly,
> but the sound of my voice frightened me
> and the dryness bound my tongue.
> Only the even beat of my heart
> made me aware I existed.

A seal watches him with moist eyes:

> Now I was no longer alone.
> I stretched out my hand to caress
> its rough body; but it fled
> and I was doubly alone.[13]

This is the first bit of true poetry Strindberg wrote. It is characteristic that it was inspired by the simultaneously liberating and frightening sense of loneliness Strindberg felt whenever he visited the outermost fringe of the Stockholm archipelago. Interestingly enough, he uses here the same free verse he later chose for *A Dream Play (Ett drömspel)* and *The Great Highway (Stora landsvägen),* although here, of course, the verse has not yet reached its full power.

Most of the play reveals Strindberg's debt to his great Scandinavian colleagues. Oehlenschläger, whom he had studied carefully, was a general influence. From Ibsen he took the driving hammer-blow dialogue, and from Bjørnson the dramatic pause: "the silence that kills more than words." At times, Strindberg's heroes forget themselves, drop their lapidary speech, and toss off surly colloquial phrases. Sometimes, they deliver feverish rhetorical tirades that typify the way Strindberg's anguish expressed itself at this time. The ardent revolutionary faith that would be shown by Gert Bookprinter in *Master Olof* is anticipated in the passage in which the poet Orm, the author's spokesman, becomes the herald of a new era:

> Feel how the earth is shaking under you—that means an earthquake! The whole world is quaking these days, because it's in labor—it's about to give birth, with grievous pain, to a magnificent hero. . . . He's about to be born, this young, strong, handsome ruler, whose reign will be universal. His sceptre is made of love and his crown of light—and his name is The New Era![14]

When Strindberg left Uppsala and the Runa Society for several months in early 1871, he began to develop a hostility toward the Society's sentimental old Scandinavian idealism. In his senior thesis on *Earl Haakon* written in the spring of 1871, he disclaimed his former idol Oehlenschläger and showed that he was influenced by the Shakespearean realism that Georg Brandes advocated in *Reviews and Portraits (Kritiker og Portraiter*—1870). But Strindberg warned, referring to Kierkegaard for support, against allowing this realism to result in materialism. He called Hauch,[15] Bjørnson, and Ibsen "genuine embryonic Shakespeares," but did not think that they had given Scandinavian the drama it needed: "No, the time itself in its fullness shall breed a drama. For the present, there is no other study to recommend to our dramatists than the time itself."[16]

The Messiah of Swedish drama was a role Strindberg sought to fill himself when in December, 1871, he drew up the first outline for *Master Olof.*

Prose Narratives

Two prose narratives, written in the spring of 1872 when Strindberg left Uppsala to become a journalist in Stockholm, describe his attitude toward the literary calling during the period when he was occupied with what he called his "journeyman piece"[17]—*Master Olof.*

The question of "poetic predestination" was discussed heatedly in the Runa Society, as Strindberg relates in *The Son of a Servant:*

> He and one of the most poetic of the members had developed strong doubts about their calling. Often, when they had drunk a great deal, they asked each other if they believed. By this they meant did the one believe that the other was "called" to be a poet? It was the same doubt Johan experienced when he wondered if he were a child of God.[18]

This doubt, which appeared earlier in the Thorvaldsen drama, asserted itself with renewed strength.

In the short story "Martyrs For Art" ("Konstens Martyrer"),[19] two incurably fanatic amateur musicians, Lampa and Nyberg, one an inspector of weights and measures and the other a teacher, try to maintain faith in their calling through mutual admiration. But when a violinist tells Lampa one evening that he has neither an ear nor the slightest sense of tempo, Lampa burns his flute:

> I know people laughed at me, I know that. But still I was able to live because I believed in my calling. Now I no longer believe. So, it's finished.—But who gave me this faith? Our Lord, perhaps. Then didn't He intend anything with it?[20]

He finds himself in the same bottomless despair that Strindberg did when he burned his play *Blotsven* late in 1870. And when Nyberg is compelled to sell his violin after Lampa dies, he too discovers that he has nothing to live for.

The story is written in the narrative style of the popular novelist and playwright August Blanche (1811-68)[21] who usually depicted two eccentrics in a Stockholm milieu. The misadventure that occurs when Lampa will not stop playing his flute long enough to sell a pound of potted cheese has close parallels in Blanche.

When Strindberg told Gustaf Eisen about the story, he begged Eisen not to disclose that he was the author, "because I do not recognize these hasty sketches as successors to *The Outlaw*—it is only to be able to write drama that I dash off such trash; they bring in bread."[22] The short story was published under a pseudonym in the women's magazine *Svalan*.

A completely different mood—the certainty of success—characterizes the fragment "The Beginning of Ån Bogsveig's Saga." This reworking of an Icelandic saga was intended for a literary almanac in Uppsala to which the Runa Society members contributed. When the story was submitted, its realism aroused the displeasure of one of the editors, Fredrik A. Fehr. Strindberg scornfully demanded the return of his manuscript: "How could such a ragamuffin and such scum as Ån be introduced among refined people [whose literary garb consists of] . . . alcaic heels and iambic fancy dress?"[23] Strindberg said that after the story was finally printed people referred to it as coarse and tasteless, because "the word naturalism was not yet in vogue."[24] During the time he was writing the tale, Strindberg explained in a series of articles, "Perspectives" ("Perspektiver"), that "realism is what our time requires":

Complete reality in art, poetry, in all of life's situations—this is what we need after having escaped the preceding decade's whining, sickly, false idealism, which reached its epitome in that infallible barometer: the poetry of the day.[25]

Strindberg pointed out that in the character of the "coal-chewer" in the saga he portrayed himself as the acknowledged black sheep of the family.[26] This was the first time he described himself as the stepchild despised by all. It was also the first time he gave fictional form to his "berserker"[27] spirit.

Ån's father brutally provokes his son in a scene reflecting the author's own family difficulties:

"Are you a man, you—lying there like a lump of dung?"
Ån remained silent.
Björn took a skewer and struck him across the neck.
Ån turned around.
Björn struck.
Ån raised himself on his elbows and looked his father in the eye.
Björn stopped.
"Get up!"
Ån did not move.
Björn threw aside the skewer.
"This is the end, Father!" said Ån. And when he shoved his father onto a wooden frame bed, one of the boards fell out.[28]

But this young Viking is also nervously hypersensitive. When his father discovers lumber missing from his workshop and accuses Ån of having stolen it to make a chair for his mother—a fictional version of an incident involving missing screws in *The Son of a Servant*—it grieves the young man so sorely that he bursts into tears and buries his head in his mother's lap: "Then his entire body was wracked with moans and groans."

Ån is tied to a pine tree to prevent him from going along in his brother's Viking ship, but as the anchor is raised, he jumps on board with the uprooted pine tree still on his back. When his brother declares that Ån is the biggest and the strongest, Ån asks, "Why didn't you say that before?" The fragment ends as the ship sails off into the roaring wind, while behind them the shoreline turns into a light blue band as it disappears.

Pulsating warmly beneath the coarse and sometimes grotesque realism of the saga is Strindberg's happiness over finally being sure of his way, conscious of his own power. It is a poetic declaration of his coming of age, written when he decided to stake his very existence on the completion of the play *Master Olof*.

Notes to Chapter Two

1. *SS*:XVIII, p. 340.
2. Matthew 10:34.—Translator
3. An introductory scene appears for the first time in this second version. It contains, newly dressed in classical costume, the same student dormitory discussion in the first act of *The Freethinker*. In the original version the heroine was poisoned by her father while she sang a song of homage to Philip. In *Hermione*, Strindberg, in a more heroic fashion, has her stabbed by her father—in other words, the Virginia legend. The original three-act play exists in manuscript form in the Birger Mörner collection at the Örebro Municipal Library, along with a manuscript of the revised version. [The original version edited by Erik Gamby was printed in 1960 by Bokgillet in Uppsala.—Translator]
4. *SS*:XVIII, p. 344.
5. *See* Henrik Schück, *Svenska Akademiens historia*, VII (1939), pp. 208 ff.
6. *SS*:XVIII, p. 346.
7. *SS*:XIX, p. 14.
8. *SS*:LIV, p. 181.
9. Published in *Samlaren* (1925).
10. *SS*:XVIII, p. 364
11. *SS*:L, p. 10.
12. *Brev*, I, pp. 80, 84.
13. *SS*:I, p. 238.
14. *Ibid.*, p. 234.
15. Johannes Carsten Hauch (1790-1872) was a poet and professor of aesthetics at the University of Copenhagen. Although his poetry and drama were once highly regarded, he is best remembered today for his novels.—Translator
16. *SS*:XVIII, p. 427.
17. *Brev*, I, p. 97.
18. *SS*:XVIII, p. 392.
19. The title of the story in the 1912 edition of *I vårbrytningen (SS*:III) is "For Art" ("För konsten").—Translator

20. *SS*:III, pp. 192-93.
21. Strindberg alludes directly to his teacher when he mentions in the story that Lampa, even before he died, had been an object of ridicule as a character in one of Blanche's novels. This occurs in *Flickan i Stadsgården*.
22. *Brev*, I, p. 98.
23. *Ibid.*, p. 105.
24. *SS*:XIX, p. 59.
25. *SS*:LIV, p. 187.
26. Göran Lindblad has followed up more intensively the parallels with childhood events in *The Son of a Servant* in *August Strindberg som berättare* (1924), pp. 11 ff.
27. In Norse folklore "berserkers" were a class of warriors who went wild in battle, foamed at the mouth, howled, and bit their shields. They were believed invulnerable.—Translator
28. *SS*:III, p. 202.

Chapter Three

MASTER OLOF

Early Sketches, Drafts, and the Prose Version

The first sketches for *Master Olof* were executed during Strindberg's final stay at Uppsala in late 1871,[1] and are dominated entirely by the title character, Olaus Petri (1493-1552) or "Master Olof," the writer and clergyman who converted from Catholicism and became Sweden's foremost Lutheran leader during the Reformation. In the sketches Master Olof is a religious zealot who, like Kierkegaard, wants to "arouse God's kingdom." "It is not Catholicism he wishes to combat—it is the spiritually dead." In the opening scene of the first sketch, Olof has not yet left the Catholic church and is secretary to Bishop Mathias; as he translates the Bible in a room at the bishop's monastery, he declares himself to be "tired of this dead academic work." His situation is Strindberg's own. In a letter to Frans Hedberg, his old teacher at the Royal Dramatic Theatre School, Strindberg called Uppsala "this city of dead academicism and examination preparation—where, remarkably enough, no trace of spiritual life can be found."

In the sketches, Olof's tragedy, like Brand's in Ibsen's play, is that he goes too far in his idealism. He runs into conflict with his devoutly Catholic mother and his bishop, just as Strindberg, because of his Parkerian faith, battled with his parents and teachers. Olof is eager to extend the Reformation beyond the religious break with Rome; he comes to desire political as well as spiritual freedom for his country. But King Gustav Vasa, the monarch responsible for forging the political unit that is modern Sweden, is wary of the influence of the Reformation. At first it is useful to him as a tool to obliterate Rome's influence in Sweden, then he wants it arrested, viewing it as a threat to the political stability of the state. As a result, Olof works against Vasa and makes common cause with his father-in-law Gert Bookprinter who, when he first appears in the later sketches (the character was invented entirely by Strindberg), is a Catholic opposed to the king. The historical Olof was subsequently condemned to death for treason and then pardoned upon the payment of a huge fine, but in one of Strindberg's sketches, Olof—abandoned by everyone except a prostitute —goes to meet death, his spirit unbroken.

It was largely his deference to historical truth that later compelled Strindberg to have Master Olof acknowledge his guilt, plead for mercy, and be spared. But there were also other influences. Before revising the early drafts in the summer of 1872 on the island of Kymmendö, Strindberg had become familiar with two works that changed his viewpoint toward Olaus Petri and the Reformation: Georg Brandes's *The Emigrant Literature (Emigrantlitteraturen)* and Thomas Buckle's *History of Civilization in England.*

Brandes's work, the first part of *Main Currents in Nineteenth-Century European Literature (Hovedstrømminger i det 19:de Aar-hundredes Litteratur)*, had already been debated in the press for several months[2] when Strindberg got hold of a copy through his Uppsala comrade Eugéne Fahlstedt. It was an absolute revelation to him. In a letter to his friend in May, 1872, he wrote that Brandes must have "ascended Mount Everest, if that is indeed the highest mountain on earth, because only from there would one be able to see as far as he does."[3]

Brandes believed that the spirit of revolution once again prevailed in most of Europe. But in Scandinavia reactionism survived and preserved a conservative, abstract religious idealism that was manifested in an ascetic prophet like Kierkegaard and a fictional figure like Ibsen's Brand, "whose moral law, if realized, would compel half of mankind to starve to death for love of the ideal." Strindberg was quick to accept Brandes's view and told Fahlstedt that Kierkegaard and *Brand* belonged to the literature of reaction. Kierkegaard was "the last gasp of Christianity before it drowns."[4] Although this by no means signified that Kierkegaard and *Brand* ceased to influence Strindberg, his reading of Brandes resulted in a distrust of abstract idealism which lasted through the 1880's.

For the religious idealism he rejected, Strindberg substituted a Brandes-inspired revolutionary idealism. Brandes called revolution the legitimate offspring of the Reformation, which in turn had descended from the Italian Renaissance, although the Reformation preferred not to acknowledge the kinship. In the series of articles "Latin or Swedish?"

("Latin eller Svenska?"), written under the immediate influence of *The Emigrant Literature,* Strindberg explained that "the bracing, liberal, daring ideas" from the Renaissance had been salvaged from the catacombs "after Christianity degenerated into a wretched papism and bullied its way to tyranny over free thought." He glorified "revolution, the great mine sprung in 1789."[5]

Whereas the early drafts show a hero who failed in his purpose because he went to extremes and became embroiled in political intrigues, the completed prose play portrays Master Olof as a reformer who stops half-way and capitulates to his king. The real hero of the play becomes Gert Bookprinter, the revolutionary who remains adamant when his son-in-law bows before royal power. There are echoes of Brandes's revolutionary enthusiasm in Gert's subversive ideas and demands for spiritual life and spiritual freedom. During the time the play was revised, the increasing emphasis on revolution began to overshadow the theme of religious reformation, and Master Olof became a half-reluctant tool for Gert. Buckle's influence further complicated the play's thematic statement.

Buckle's *History of Civilization in England* with which Strindberg became familiar the same spring, is written from the point of view of positivism, declaring that all ideas, especially religious ideas, are relative and temporally conditioned. Buckle states that "what in one period is attacked as a paradox or heresy, is in another period welcomed as a sober truth; which, however, in its turn is replaced by some subsequent novelty."[6] This is the same line of thought that Master Olof expresses in a conversation with his mother in the completed prose version, when he tells her that the truths by which she has lived have become lies. "When you were young, Mother, you were right. When I get old, perhaps I'll be wrong. We don't change with the times."[7] The logical consequence of this argument should be that all truth is relative, but Olof is reluctant to accept this conclusion. "Am I supposed to have lived and fought for a lie?" he wonders in the final scene with the Lord Constable. "Shall I be compelled to declare my whole youth and the best years of my manhood lost, useless, wasted? I'd rather die with my delusions!"[8]

Intellectually, Strindberg accepts Buckle's relativism, but emotionally he defends himself just as zealously as Olof does against this kind of conclusion to his premises. Gert is, at least in part, speaking for Strindberg in the final act when he tells Master Olof: "Never believe that a lie

ignited a human soul. . . . The day you deny yourself, you're dead."⁹ Gert
never yields, and at the end, when he is being taken away to be executed,
Olof hears his accusing voice crying out from offstage: "Renegade!"
Crushed by the charge Olof sinks down on the pillory.

Buckle's influence on the prose version of *Master Olof* is a temptation against which Strindberg fights with all his strength. This version is
a drama about the greatness and permanent value of ideological enthusiasm, about the duty to preach and die for one's conviction. Gert goes to
the block in the certainty that the name of each new martyr becomes a
battle cry for a new following, and this underlying meaning gives the play
a warmth and a power that the subsequent versions lack.

Another merit of the prose over the later poetic version is the
fresh realism. A passage in *The Son of a Servant* indicates that the author
was "audacious after reading Goethe's *Goetz,* with its sixty-odd tableaux,
. . . [and] decided to break with the prevailing drama as it was patterned
after the work of Fryxell and Afzelius."¹⁰ He describes later how he forswore verse, declamation, and the unity of place, and permitted the tragic
and comic, the great and small "to alternate with each other as in life."¹¹

Brandes in *Reviews and Portraits* praised Shakespeare's naturalism
in opposition to the practices in conventional Danish tragedy. He pointed
out that Shakespeare ventured to depict scenes that were not directly
connected with the action but which made it more vivid, and that he
brought fully rounded people on stage instead of the specific character
types necessary to the dramatic action. In Brandes's brilliant essay "The
Infinitely Small and the Infinitely Great in Poetry" (Det uendeligt smaa
og det uendeligt store i Poesien"), he applied this observation to *Henry
IV, Part I,* with special praise for the inn yard scene in the second act in
which the carriers go down to the stable at dawn to saddle horses, and the
audience is permitted to overhear their quite aimless conversation. Strindberg inserted a big tavern scene in a corresponding position in *Master
Olof;* it too falls outside the story line, but its rigorous realism adds another
dimension to the action. Brandes also focuses attention on the scene in
which Hotspur angrily describes how an affected nobleman recommended
to him "parmaceti for an inward bruise." In Strindberg's first sketches
and drafts, a recipe for spiced Rochelle plays a conspicuous role and crops
up in the completed play during the monks' vigil at Olof's mother's deathbed where the Dominican, Brother Nils, rattles off the ingredients to his

colleague, Brother Mårten. One can understand Strindberg's desire to include the recipe when one reads Brandes's admiring commentary on the phrase in Hotspur's speech:

> Why this [parmaceti]? To what purpose the fullness of detail and the citing of so insignificant and ridiculous a trifle? Because this little trifle is a touch of reality, and evokes illusion. The very fact that one does not understand why such a trivial and moreover carefully defined detail is described makes it seem impossible that it was contrived. But linked to this little word are all the other images, the entire chain of illusion.

Thereafter, the creation of the illusion of reality through small, sure details became Strindberg's aesthetic creed, both as dramatist and novelist. In 1889, he praised Zola because "in the capacity of naturalist [he] cannot disdain the infinitely tiny as *ingredient*."[12] Strindberg continued to recognize the necessity of including the vividness of everyday life in the treatment of historical material long after he forswore naturalism. Many years later, discussing the historical dramas he wrote after the Inferno Crisis, he said that he reverted to his "style of dramaturgy from the first *Master Olof*" and, "following his teacher Shakespeare," sought to sketch "people in their greatness and their triviality" and "not to avoid the right word."[13]

Brandes's analysis of Shakespeare made Strindberg realize that his own candid approach to the depiction of reality was a great, unexploited resource. It was this approach that enabled him to rejuvenate Swedish literature. He became a naturalist before the word acquired the meaning it has now, and before he established contact with any foreign naturalists.

For *Master Olof*, Strindberg studied more primary historical sources than he ever would again. Of course he by no means submerged himself as deeply in historical source material as Scandinavia's other great naturalist, the Danish writer, Jens Peter Jacobsen, who spent several years in exhaustive preparation for his novel *Marie Grubbe* (1876). Jacobsen examined seventeenth-century letters, memoirs, and maps in the Danish Royal Archives; he visited museums and castles to obtain intimate knowledge of furniture and interiors, made costume sketches, and finally produced a novel in which virtually every detail is historically accurate. Strindberg said that during his own library studies he filled large sheets "with what he called local color, and that from them he borrowed a touch here and there so that the intention of the play would not be too transpar-

ent."[14] A few of these "large sheets" still survive and some of the amusing
and bizarre items Strindberg recorded actually grew into short episodes,
but generally they were simply inserted at random, often in a casual conversation. He also included vague allusions to events of his own day,
which fortunately were explained later in his autobiography; otherwise
we would not be able to recognize them. The character of Master Olof is
modeled on himself, and the other leading figures speak out frankly on
controversial questions of the day. The sequence of events is also grotesquely unhistorical—Strindberg was already beginning to avail himself
of his method of "condensing historical time in accordance with the
demands of the contemporary theatre."[15]

Nevertheless, the play's atmosphere has a scent of genuineness
about it, like a breath of air from the Reformation. The opening scene in
the flowering monastery garden is wonderful. Olof, with his students, is
reading aloud from the play often attributed to the historical Olof—*The
Comedy of Tobias* (*Tobie Comedia*—ca. 1550)—and a little later the stiff-
necked Catholic Bishop Brask and the violently resolute young King Gustav Vasa make their entrances. Act One is crowded with history-making
events: Olof holds a Mass, although forbidden to do so by the Church
authorities; Gert proclaims his republicanism; and the growing conflict
between papal and royal power is expressed in the brief clash between
Bishop Brask and the King.

The second act, with its tavern scene modeled on Shakespeare, is
a marvel of historical milieu depiction. Here, too, is an exuberant profusion of events; the prostitute chased by the mob and protected by Olof; the
anarchistic anti-Catholicism of Knipperdolink and his Anabaptists. An
amusing interlude between the tipsy sexton and his wife is followed by a
scene in the sacristy during Olof's first sermon, a collision between him
and his religiously conservative mother, and a declaration of love between
Olof and his future wife, Kristina. The various scenes are not logically
joined and often succeed each other in arbitrary fashion. But a brilliant
picture is evoked of a time when spirits were awakening, when new ideas
were seething everywhere. One is not at all put off by the ideas from
Buckle and Brandes mouthed by the leading characters, by the echoes of
Ibsen in the lovers' conversation, or by the hollow phrase, taken verbatim
from *Camille,* with which Olof addresses the prostitute: "God has forgiven
you—people never will!"[16]

Does Jacobsen's novel *Marie Grubbe,* with its purely craftsman-like cultural-historical setting, its endlessly fastidious portrait of the time, give as strong an impression of the seventeenth century? In certain passages, perhaps, but precisely because Jacobsen took such pains in these passages to achieve historical accuracy, the modern elements evident elsewhere in the characterizations seem doubly disturbing.

The difference between the two writers appears most clearly in their handling of dialogue. Jacobsen attached primary importance to reproducing historically accurate dialogue. As Paul V. Rubow shows in an excellent study, Jacobsen was not satisfied to study linguistic sources endlessly and plow through Christian Molbech's 1833 Danish dictionary (the first substantial work of its kind)—he also tried to invent expressions that were consistent with the style of speech in the era he described. He was fairly successful in re-creating the written language of the time, using letters, sermons, and so forth, but his dialogue is stilted because of its peculiar sentence structure and too numerous gaudy metaphors and foreign words. Jacobsen had a tendency, as Rubow points out, to believe that everything contrary to modern language usage was genuine seventeenth-century speech.

Strindberg deliberately followed opposite principles. Shortly after the prose version was first submitted to the Royal Dramatic Theatre, a notice about the play appeared in the newspaper *Norrköpings tidningar* (August 19, 1872). He probably wrote it himself; it is mentioned by him in a letter to Fahlstedt in the fall of 1872. The notice stated: "This play will be original in that the language in it, in contrast with other historical plays, is completely modern and free from old-fashioned turns of phrase, idioms, and expressions." He also stressed in the autobiography that he permitted people in the play "to speak simple, everyday speech, as people use off the stage."[17] As in the historical dramas written after his Inferno period, Strindberg was not entirely consistent in his handling of dialogue. At times his characters seem to remember that they are in the sixteenth century and blurt out archaic phrases of doubtful authenticity. Now and then there are also outbursts of pathos in Schiller's style, as well as sententious, symbolic, allusive lines in Ibsen's style. But the rhythm of everyday speech manages to assert itself everywhere and gives the style power and life. This bold challenge to current theatrical conventions delayed the production of the play for nine years, but it made *Master Olof* the beginning of an epoch, not only in the writing of Swedish historical plays, but in Swedish drama in general.

The style of realistic dialogue developed in *Master Olof* and used in the later plays and even in large measure in the novels, became Strindberg's chief means of character delineation. Brandes had pointed out that Shakespeare's characters "portray themselves in every phrase they utter without ever saying one word about themselves." Strindberg became closest to this ideal in the depiction of the many subordinate characters in *Master Olof*. Reveling guests in the tavern, the sexton and his wife, the two Dominican friars, and others come to life through their speeches. This is a clear indication that Strindberg built on the dramatic prose style of Hagberg's translations of Shakespeare, although Strindberg's dialogue had a more naturally Swedish flavor than Hagberg's. He also succeeded in suggesting the different temperaments of the leading characters. For example, the depiction of the king's character through his speeches is splendid: now passionately aglow, now surly and growling. The character has some of the stature later developed in the play *Gustav Vasa* (1899). "Dispense with formulas if you want me to listen to you," Olof says at the pillory to his brother Lars, who is assiduously preaching to him. Strindberg took the phrase as his motto when fashioning his hero's speeches.

Strindberg never intended Master Olof to be a replica of the historical figure. He used himself as model, giving the character the contradictions of his own personality: "Ambitious and weak-willed; ruthless when it mattered, and meek when it did not; great self-confidence mingled with deep depression; reasonable and irrational; stern and soft."[18] The later Strindberg nearly always sided with the heroes he created in his own likeness; here he made a serious attempt at objective self-examination.

In the opening scene of the prose version we meet Master Olof as a young and preoccupied novice who only reluctantly undertakes the preaching mission being forced upon him. He has no desire to lead the way; his task is to look on while others battle, to "heal the wounded" and "whisper peace in the ears of the dying." Lars Andersson, a religious reformer who urges him to become a leader, knows him better than he does himself: "Olof! You were born to offend; you were born to strike."[19] Despite his reluctance, his contrariness and taste for battle drive him onward. "To a man like you," says Gert, "one says 'Don't do that' when one wants something done!"[20] But he is not convinced of his calling, any more than

Strindberg seemed to be. Reluctantly caught up in a whirlpool, he is compelled to become further involved by his belligerence and his desire to
assert himself. "I want to do my work—not yours,"[21] he says to Gert. Unwittingly, however, he becomes a tool, alternately in the hands of the king
and of Gert.

Olof is unhappy even before he learns the import of the fateful
1527 resolution of the *Riksdag* (Parliament) of Västerås, which legitima-
tized the confiscation of church property in the name of the state and thus
signified the triumph of the Reformation in Sweden. He despairs because
the battle is almost over and the goal is in sight: "No more struggle—this
is death! . . . It wasn't victory I wanted, it was the struggle!"[22] When Gert
later tempts him with the conspiracy against the king, he makes only a
weak attempt to resist. He repeats Gert's exhortation that the king must
die so that all may live, but adds: "Let's go before I regret it!"[23] How like
Strindberg himself in every way—better a snap decision with the risk of
regret than hesitation and deliberation. One is reminded of the Stranger's
words to the confessor at the end of Part Two of *To Damascus:* "Come,
priest, before I change my mind."

What purpose is there in Olof's struggle for the sake of struggle?
"You tear down and tear down, Olof," says his brother Lars Petri, "so
that soon there'll be nothing left. But when someone asks: 'What have you
to offer instead?' you answer, 'Not that! Not that.' You never answer—
'This!' "[24] Olof can only reply that he wants to create suspicion of the old,
"not because it's old, but because it's rotten."[25] This is an early version of
the general demolition program Strindberg would advocate in his poem
"The Boulevard System" ("Esplanadsystemet") in 1883. It is no wonder
that young men with similar feelings recognized themselves in Master
Olof when the prose version of the play was finally produced in 1881. And
when a medal was struck in honor of Strindberg after the lawsuit over
Married in 1884, the motto chosen for the inscription was one of Olof's
lines from the play: "The truth is always insolent."[26]

The prose version was much more appropriate for the young radicals than the verse version in which the influence of Eduard von Hartmann's world-weariness put a damper on the joy of the struggle. In the
prose version Gert states: "Aim for the sky and you'll at least hit the edge
of the woods."[27] But in the verse version this assurance that effort implies
some achievement has disappeared. In his final speech in the latter ver-

sion, Olof proclaims to his disciple Wilhelm that one will fail if one
follows a star: "For even the stars in heaven fall."

The Revisions and the Verse Version

Strindberg's own constancy was severely tested when he submitted
the manuscript to the Royal Dramatic Theatre. He was told that in order
for the play to be accepted he would have to expunge Gert's cry, "Renegade!" "I shall not alter this *renegade!*" he wrote to Fahlstedt in September, 1872. "For then I should be one myself. The thought of a possible
triumph has tempted me to strike out the word, thus permitting the
play to be performed! But I cannot! Now my piece will not be performed! And I shall never get to say what I wanted."[28] He was in the
same position as his hero, who could "win time to work for humanity"
only by apologizing.

Strindberg did compromise somewhat, however, when in October, 1873, he submitted a largely unaltered copy of the Kymmendö prose
version to a Swedish Academy competition.[29] The drama still bore the
original title of *A Renegade (En avfälling),* but in a newly written preface
scarcely in harmony with the work itself, Strindberg attempted to justify
the title as ironic and wondered "whether it was not necessary to be a
'renegade' to a certain extent in order to realize one's ideal." The same
thought was on his mind when he began his first attempt at a revision by
adding to the final scene.[30] Now King Gustav Vasa answers Gert's accusation: "Olof, I am a renegade, and I thank God, not on behalf of myself
but of my people, that I am one." Whereupon, more in accord with Buckle
than with history, the king describes how once, as a young enthusiast, he
wanted to tear down the decaying religion of the Swedish people and drive
out their monks but found that the people were not ready for deliverance.
Consequently, for their sake, he relented: "I am a wretched renegade, and
I confess it before God, because He willed it."

This new scene indicates the direction the revisions of the play
would take. Gradually, Gustav Vasa becomes the author's spokesman in
place of Master Olof, assuming such dimensions that he overshadows the
title character entirely. "Is life the greatest sacrifice God demands?" he
asks Olof. "Are not conscience and peace of mind greater?" Another
speech, which appears in the Kymmendö manuscript but not in the printed

play, has Vasa declaring: "To accomplish anything in this world, one must abandon morals and conscience."

The reading of Tocqueville's *Democracy in America* and Prévost-Paradol's *The New France* had turned Strindberg anti-democratic. Consequently, Gert, the martyr for freedom, was reduced in the revisions to a partially deranged fantast. Strindberg's first contact with the pessimism of Eduard von Hartmann had fed his own skepticism, and he found increasing relevance in Buckle's theory that the masses, not the individual, really determine the course of history. This led him also to forsake his former teacher, Shakespeare. "Shakespeare has only individuals, therefore lacks wider significance," he noted in the Kymmendö manuscript. The realistic features of the first *Master Olof* were rejected, and even the tavern scene was eliminated; Strindberg was trying to reshape the work into a drama of ideas.

The figure of Master Olof now became a portrait of the author at a younger, more naive time, when he still saw himself as an optimistic and enthusiastic social reformer. Between 1872 and 1874 Strindberg was active as a journalist while he worked on the verse *Master Olof*. When in December, 1874, he abandoned his free-lance writing and accepted a position with more financial security as an assistant at the Royal Library, he felt like a renegade; he had turned his back on his newspaper colleagues and on social reform and had rejoined respectable society. Therefore, Strindberg's primary interest in the revised version of the play became that of allowing Olof—the renegade—to retain his honor as he pleaded for mercy.

Strindberg's efforts to re-create his hero so confused the plot and the main themes of the play that the reworking and elimination of scenes from the earlier version was a slow process. Olof becomes unnecessarily brusque and thoughtless, and Strindberg could not refrain from having him preach Buckle's theories. "What you're saying is the truth, isn't it?" Kristina asks. Olof replies: "It isn't the truth yet—but it will be, until in turn it becomes a lie." Since Olof is conscious of the relativity of truth, it is difficult for him to be a persuasive reformer. Gustav Vasa had assumed such overwhelming dimensions at Olof's expense that Strindberg had to pare his role more and more, and finally expel him from the play. In the verse version Vasa's dramatic function is served by the Lord High Constable.

The verse version of the play, begun in the spring of 1875 and completed a year later, has a clearer design and a more consistent title character than the earlier versions. In some respects, Strindberg had returned to the first sketches. Olof is a pale and impoverished canon who lives camp-fashion and sleeps with his sword: a figure reminiscent of the ascetic Strindberg in his Kierkegaard period; but he is no longer identified with the author. "I have tried to put something over by throwing together some rather beautiful things while in the most uncertain state of mind," Strindberg wrote in October, 1875. "I think M. Olof is a simpleton who should have been sent to a business school—God in Heaven, I am going to laugh one day if I succeed even for a moment into tricking the audience into weeping.—I was eager to reread the first act to see if the irony is too obvious."[31]

Strindberg was in a profoundly pessimistic mood at the time he was completing the play, and the mood is reflected directly in Bishop Brask's last monologue and indirectly in the Lord High Constable's speeches. Master Olof himself is not handled with irony—this would happen later in the Epilogue—but we see too little of the inner struggle that resulted in his conversion from Catholicism to Lutheranism. At the end of the verse version, Olof refuses to capitulate to the king until he learns that Luther himself had to submit to political authority. Then he too surrenders, but is spared the ignominy of capitulation; he can justify his own submission by citing Luther's example. The Reformation no longer seems very important to him. Gert's and Olof's paths cross without coinciding, and the conflict between Olof and Kristina—between the demands of a man's work and the needs of a woman's love—which had occupied such a prominent place in the earlier versions, is resolved through compromise.

Strindberg's dissatisfaction with the conclusion led him to add an Epilogue when the play was published in 1878. Master Olof is now a fat and secure *pastor primarius* who at a pre-Christmas market gets homesick for his mother and her cooking. The burghers suggest scornfully that his mouth has become as empty as his stomach has filled out. In this inserted marketplace scene a dash of bitter Schopenhauer-Hartmann pessimism is served up in a thin medieval gruel.[32] Olof and his sons are in a crowd witnessing an ironic medieval mystery play in which God is presented as having created the world only to see how human beings might starve and suffer, and the Devil is a beneficent force teaching men that life is evil and that they exist only to provide "amusements" for the gods. As the mystery play ends, the spectators shout their demand for a happy ending, and when the theatre director protests that this is the play the playwright wrote, they beat him. In a sense, Strindberg himself had surrendered to such a demand in the vain hope of getting his play performed. In the Epilogue, his need to attack and criticize, curbed in the verse edition, is expressed in a way he must have found satisfying.

In Sweden, the verse version of *Master Olof* has held the stage more successfully than the prose version, and this is understandable. The former is a brilliant theatre piece—surely and firmly constructed. The completely transformed first act is itself a work of art. Its depiction of the monastery, fragrant with roasting meat and wine, is the most suggestive historical picture Strindberg created before his short stories in *Swedish Destinies and Adventures* (1882-91) and also provides a graphic representation of the corruption Master Olof was battling. But the most significant factor in making the verse version more popular in Sweden than the prose version is the use of *knittelvers,* an irregular verse pattern (rhymed couplets, four to seven feet per line) that permits great flexibility and vitality in rhyme and rhythm. In the verse *Master Olof* Strindberg ranges from the nonchalant commonplace to soaring lyrical flight. In comparison, the fine naturalistic dialogue of the prose version may not seem as impressive; although Strindberg would develop the naturalistic style to perfection in the post-Inferno historical plays.

When Strindberg first tried to versify lyrical passages in the interim version of *Master Olof,* he turned to blank verse, but could not go beyond prosaism; he found the freedom he needed in *knittelvers.* From statements in his letters it is evident that he originally planned to versify the entire play, and six of the first eight scenes are in verse. In its final form, the play became a prose drama with versified insertions; each of the final acts has three or four scenes in verse. The high points are Olof's frequent monologues, which Strindberg tried to express in prose in the interim versions.

Strindberg still lacked—and would continue to lack in the plays immediately following—the ability to integrate lyricism into his prose which was often banal. In Olof's famous monologue at his mother's deathbed[33] the lyricism did not become expressive until it was reworked in *knittelvers.* By then the monologue had also become a tribute to Strindberg's birthplace, Stockholm, and foreshadowed the opening of his novel *The Red Room (Röda rummet*—1879).

Despite its display of poetic skill, however, the verse version is inferior to the prose version, for it lacks the earlier work's seething life and spontaneity. It is a child of reflection, more free of faults, but also less interesting. In addition, it is the first of a series of less daring, more academic examples of Strindberg's historical drama. Not until after the Inferno Crisis would he resume the bold experiment begun with the prose version: to shape historical dramas on naturalistic patterns.

Notes to Chapter Three

1. The sketches and different manuscript versions of *Master Olof* are located in the Gothenberg Municipal Library. *Cf.* Per Lindberg, *Tillkomsten av Strindbergs "Mäster Olof"* (1915).
2. *See* Holger Ahlenius, *Georg Brandes i svensk litteratur* (1932), pp. 57 ff.
3. *Brev,* I, p. 103.
4. *Ibid.*
5. *SS:* IV, p. 259.
6. Thomas Buckle, *History of Civilization in England* (1882), I, p. 129.
7. *SS:*II, p. 70.
8. *Ibid.,* p. 181.
9. *Ibid.,* p. 179.
10. *SS:* XIX, p. 27. [The historical sources Strindberg referred to were Anders Fryxell's *Berättelser ur svenska historien* and A. A. Afzelius's *Svenska folkets sagohäfder.*—Translator]
11. That Strindberg read *Goetz* during preparations for *Master Olof* can be gathered from his admiring statement about "the formless *Goetz von Berlichingen*" in an art review dated March 21, 1872 (*SS:*LIV, p. 176). And the bold attempts at reform on which he prided himself, he had already proclaimed as necessary a year earlier in his senior candidacy essay on *Earl Haakon,* citing Brandes as a reference.
12. *SS:*XVII, p. 287.
13. *SS:*L, p. 240.
14. *SS:*XIX, p. 27.
15. *SS:*L, p. 240.
16. *SS:*II, p. 59.
17. *SS:*XIX, p. 27.
18. *Ibid.,* p. 32.
19. *SS:*II, p. 10.
20. *Ibid.,* p. 85.
21. *Ibid.,* p. 58.
22. *Ibid.,* p. 128.
23. *Ibid.,* p. 167.
24. *Ibid.,* p. 150.

25. *Ibid.*
26. *Ibid.*, p. 27.
27. *Ibid.*, p. 23.
28. *Brev,* I, p. 121.
29. For a discussion of the rather harsh verdict *Master Olof* received there, *see* Schück, pp. 222 ff.
30. *See Lindberg,* p. 75.
31. *Brev,* I, p. 254.
32. Eklund *(Strindbergsstudie,* p. 289) has pointed out that the Epilogue was inspired primarily by Schopenhauer. He calls it "an allegorical transformation of Schopenhauerian metaphysics."
33. The prose version of this monologue is reproduced in John Landquist's commentary in *Samlade skrifter.*

Chapter Four

THE NEOPHYTE PROSE WRITER

The Skerries Writer

The six years devoted to the writing and rewriting of *Master Olof* had not brought Strindberg the recognition he sought. Almost thirty years old, he was still comparatively unknown as an author. Although for a time (1872-74) he managed to make a living as a journalist, mostly free lance, the rigorous day-to-day work left little opportunity for extensive creative writing. After "Martyrs For Art" in 1872, he wrote no fiction about Stockholm until the novel *The Red Room* in 1879. The Viking novel that he was supposed to develop from "The Beginning of Ån Bogsveig's Saga" for the newspaper *Handelstidningen* was never written. But he did enjoy some modest success between 1872 and 1875 writing about the beautiful archipelago that lies between Stockholm and the sea—the skerries— although here, too, he did not follow through on his intentions.

Strindberg's love for the skerries went back to his school days. There is a famous passage in *The Son of a Servant*[1] in which he described his first sight of the skerries; he was a *gymnasium* student and his Volunteer Rifle Corps group practiced on Tyreso: "idyllic spots; bleak, rugged, gray-stone islets dotted with spruce, scattered about in great, stormy bays, with the endless sea as a background at a safe distance." He swore that neither "the Swiss Alps, the Mediterranean olive groves, nor the Normandy cliffs" could ever supplant his love for the skerries. While on the Italian Riviera he wrote that after a time he tired of staring out into empty nothingness: "and then my imagination planted several green islands here and there out in the blue, not islands with oranges, bayberries trees and marble palaces, but small, rough hills of gneiss with spiny spruce trees and red cottages."[2] In a letter from the coast of Normandy he tried to show with sketches how the line of the horizon was limited instead of enlarged at the open sea. He longed to have the sea once again "at a safe distance." And when he was staying near the Lake of Constance in Bavaria in 1887 —tormented by homesickness—he sat down and wrote his great novel about the skerries, *The People of Hemsö (Hemsöborna)*.

It was in the Stockholm archipelago in 1871 that the twenty-two-year-old Strindberg found what he called in a letter in 1889 "the only spot on earth I love (my island).[3] Kymmendö, this paradise in the skerries, was closed to him after the publication of *The People of Hemsö*—the landlords he described unsympathetically in the novel no longer wished to rent a summer cottage to him—but it shimmered in his imagination even as an old man:

> Oh, my verdant isle,
> flower basket on the waves of the sea!
> Fragrant with hay newly-mown
> I saw you in a dream.[4]

In his autobiography[5] Strindberg said that he began writing about the skerries when he was appointed to the telegraph office at Sandhamn in the fall of 1873; he apparently forgot that his first effort was composed a year earlier. On September 4, 1872, a letter-essay appeared in the newspaper *Dagens Nyheter* with the title "Life in the Stockholm Archipelago" ("Livet i Stockholms skägård").[6] Because it was unsigned, it only recently has attracted the attention of Strindberg scholars, but a letter from the editor of *Dagens Nyheter*, Rudolf Wall, to Strindberg mentions the latter as its author. "It seems to me," Wall wrote, "that you have exhausted the subject in one breath, but it would not be unpleasant if I were wrong." Wall was wrong if he believed that Strindberg had said all he felt about the skerries. But in this modest bit of reporting, the writer did tell—with youthful enthusiasm—everything he saw in the skerries. Included was his first impression of Kymmendö:

> Here are wild and steep rocky shores, with gulls and dead-white driftwood for accessories; here are ground depressions with undergrowth; regal oaks escorted by noble, elegant hazel bushes in a glade; here are reedy coves with an atmosphere reminiscent of Lake Mälar: ledger-tackle and ducks' nests; here are heaths with cloudberries and tussocks of bog bilberries and alder bushes harboring grouse; all this on an island that is not [one and one-half miles] ... long.

The letter is an unadorned and dispassionate account devoid of the picturesque verve that Strindberg would later display in his Sandhamn letters ("Sandhamnsbrev"). Nevertheless, it gives a clear indication of what he would always love about the skerries: the contrast between the cultivated and the wild, between the luxuriant inland and the rocky shoreline. In his introduction to the letter Strindberg says that a person traveling the outer route through the archipelago would find nature anything but engaging. It is only when one has traversed the steep, desolate shores that one discovers "smiling meadows, lush pastures, and groves of hazel bushes and oaks; perhaps also—if the island is large—a little lake edged in reeds."

The remainder of the unsigned letter contains a brief preview of the characters who would later appear in his stories about the achipelago. There is a typical skerries man: independent, proud, and conservative. He ekes out a living from fishing and farming, but is often exasperated by the fisheries inspector who tries to control his catches. The minister of the State Lutheran Church is considered by "a certain sect" (i.e., the Pietists) as "dead" (not awakened to the new life); Strindberg preferred him this way because he was thus "less diligent in spreading soul-killing teachings." Finally, there is the customs agent, about whom Strindberg would later write one of the best short stories in the collection *Men of the Skerries* (*Skärkarlsliv*—1888). The skerries had once been a haven for smugglers, but no smuggled goods had been seized since the 1860's, a dozen years earlier. As a result, the agent's job had come to be regarded as a joke; it consisted of sailing with his crew of two seamen from place to place as long as the water remained free of ice.

Strindberg's first attempt to exploit this material in fiction, an unfinished novel[7] about a group of university students in the skerries, foreshadows both the short story collection *Town and Gown* and the novels about the archipelago. A young natural scientist from the University of Uppsala is traveling by boat from Dalarö to Nämndö; on Ådholm he meets three students, the most important of whom is Örn (i.e., Eagle, Strindberg's Runa Society name), the author's persona in the story. In the same way Strindberg would begin the novels *The People of Hemsö*— and *In the Outer Skerries (I havsbandet):* a newcomer sails into the archipelago and we see it through his eyes.

It is uncertain whether Strindberg knew how he wanted the novel to develop. After sketching a self-portrait in Örn, he obviously tired of the work. The most successful passage is the picture of the easygoing summer atmosphere on Dalarö that opens the novel; the same passage, abridged and revised, was later transferred to the short story "How I Discovered Sehlstedt" ("Huruledes jag fann Sehlstedt"). Here is the beginning as it appears in the novel fragment:

> It was five o'clock on a summer morning. Dalarö was still asleep, weary from the tiring idleness of the previous day. The sun had just worked its way apart from a threadbare, van Dyck brown cloud with Neapolitan yellow edges, and was trying hard to dry out the damp seesaw on the customs dock; gulls were spearing fish in the glare of the sun on the placid channel; a flycatcher was catching flies on a bench near the steamship pier, where the day before the captain's careless servant girl had let a piece of butter stand in the sun; customs house attendants and pilots snored at an open window in the customs shack; an American flag hung like a wet snuff handkerchief up on the roof of the inn; the tar began to smell in the joints of the customs yacht that was moored at Spegel's pier; then, in the distance to the south, a faint puff of steamship smoke rose over the edge of the woods.

In a discussion of his Sandhamn letters in his autobiography, Strindberg wrote that because of the oil paintings he had done of seascapes his eyes had "become, as it were, sharpened, so that he conceived of details strongly and by accumulating and arranging them, could evoke for the reader a powerful image of what was being described."[8] The influence of painting is obvious in the use of palette colors ("van Dyck brown cloud with Neapolitan yellow edges"). In another "skerries" story, written in 1875, "Markus Larsson—Lawyer" ("Markus Larsson advokat"), he made Larsson a storyteller solely to justify the same kind of reference to painting. Whenever Larsson describes something, his hand moves as though it held a brush, and he qualifies nouns with epithets "that produced the effect of red adjacent to blue . . . it was chromatics applied to language."[9]

In the novel fragment Strindberg did not confine himself to visual impressions. Sounds and smells are described; there are aromas of tar, steamship smoke and paint, as there would be in all of Strindberg's later harbor images. Childhood years spent around a steamship office were not wasted. The sensory details have a cumulative effect, even though they are not presented in an orderly fashion; they are even haphazard in the story revised from the fragment, which is only one half as long as the original.

Vivid but abrupt images are given in short sentences that follow one another without transition and are separated by dashes; a technique we recognize from Strindberg's earlier letters. He personifies nature, as did Dickens and Hans Christian Andersen; the gulls over the channel display the same fussy eagerness as the sparrows over Moses Heights do later in the novel *The Red Room,* and even the sun has domestic chores.

Strindberg used this impressionistic approach to nature description until well into the 1880's, when he came under the influence of "scientific" description in the style of Zola, but he would return to his earlier approach whenever sketching familiar motifs. A morning scene at the same place—the Dalarö customs pier—in the short story collection *Married* (1884), is executed with the same technique of short, coordinate sentences and clusters of narrative details, although by then his style had acquired an elasticity it did not have in the youthful efforts, and the landscape comes into clearer focus.

In the novel fragment the transitions from descriptions of nature into descriptions of people are brief, and both are executed in a playfully mocking way. An accountant goes down onto the customs pier and curses all doctors as he passes the seesaw, for he has to drink Carlsbad mineral water and is forbidden to sit down: "He is unhappy because he had dreamed all winter of summer fun on the seesaw." The most vivid picture is of the customs agent, who loves to tell of the last seizure of contraband in the Stockholm archipelago in the 1860's, but who now—since the new customs decree made smuggling unprofitable and pointless—has nothing to do but poach fish, hunt seabirds out of season, and draw his pay, which is then converted into schnapps *(brännvin),* tobacco, and coffee.

The eccentric life of the young university students on Ådholm is not as effectively described. Strindberg had difficulty sustaining the young men's joviality, and his attention was drawn more to creating in the demoniacal Örn a picture of himself during that summer when he "sensed Kierkegaard on the horizon and wanted to be ethical, and fulminated against aesthetics."[10] He was disinclined, however, to describe Örn directly; we get a picture of him primarily through what his comrades say about him. Örn has rejected "the paradox that God became human" but clings to the doctrine of suffering, and his comrades think that he is obsessed with the need to make himself suffer. To a certain extent his ideal is Ibsen's Brand, and his favorite argument is that a person who can hate is greater than God, for God can only love because He is love. Hate, contempt, and pity are the only emotions he believes in. But one of his comrades claims to have seen through him and found that, despite his protestations, Örn feels an attachment for his friends: "Because attachment is just what this man needs and therefore he calls it hate." The answer to the puzzle of Örn's soul lies in his past, which Strindberg does not describe.

The fragment is keen self-analysis, and it corroborates the picture of Strindberg we have from his autobiography and the few contemporary documents. Even at this time, the tough exterior concealed a tender and vulnerable interior; he was both spiteful and hypersensitive. Unfortunately, the story ends just as Örn is about to speak for himself.

"A writer is only a reporter of what he has experienced," Strindberg wrote in June, 1875.[11] He later returned to this belief in the beginning of the 1880's when he tired of the prefabricated or "synthetic novel" of the naturalists and wanted it replaced by reporting.[12]

One of his first journalistic efforts, occasioned by two shipwrecks and the attendant official investigations, was published in *Dagens Nyheter* in December, 1873. Strindberg, at twenty-four, was then a telegraphy apprentice tapping out weather reports. The letter was well received and he was offered a position on the paper, which he accepted. His most ambitious contributions to the paper were articles about the skerries: the previously mentioned sketch "How I Discovered Sehlstedt," written in the summer of 1874, and "On Kanholm Bay" ("På Kanholmsfjärden"), a description of a regatta from the same summer. In addition to articles for *Dagens Nyheter,* he published the short story "Markus Larsson—Lawyer," based on one of the shipwreck inquiries, in the women's magazine *Svalan* in 1875.

A decade later Strindberg said of the first Sandhamn letters: "A light skepticism mixed with a bit of sentimentality gave something airy to the style, and without realizing it he had hit upon the very tone that made people take notice."[13] His description is correct, but it is doubtful that he adopted this chatty style as spontaneously as he suggested. Today it seems rather labored when it is mocking and when, as in the Sehlstedt sketch, it overflows into sentimentality.

Strindberg is not really himself in these sketches; the first Sandhamn letter begins with a jesting, topographical-ethnographical account of Sandhamn patterned after Heine's *Die Harzreise.* Strindberg belonged

—then and long into the 1880's—to the fanatical worshippers of Heine.[14] In the novel fragment Strindberg had inserted a verse parody of Heine, mentioning Örn as the author, and in the Sehlstedt sketch there is another parody "furnished as a reproof to those who have overworked themselves reading a well-known writer about the sea." To what extent Heine is imitated or parodied in the later, long verse cycle, "Exile," is difficult to say.

Heine's influence on the style of the Sandhamn letters often is expressed in a forced liveliness which is also closely reminiscent of the work of Carl Fredrik Dahlgren (1791-1844): "Kanholm Bay is like a circus. The White Mare whinnies in her wooden joints and the Harö windmill stretches its arms and turns cartwheels on the edge of the woods. —Kanholm Bay is like a newly-swept dance floor, and a southwest wind strikes up a double-reefed topsail reel."[15] This style—with paradoxical figures of speech chasing one another—becomes even more eccentric when color images are introduced and an occasional Norwegian word is inserted, calling to mind the realistic novels of Jonas Lie (1833-1908).

Strindberg was still far from an accomplished prose artist; his eagerness to be original at any cost made him at times breathless, florid, and insipid. Nevertheless, these beginner's excesses could not obscure the signs of a born writer. The glitter of the sun on the sea, the billowing foam, the smell of seaweed and fresh breezes give a saltiness to the Sandhamn sketches; the archipelago of east-central Sweden had acquired its first congenial portraitist.

Town and Gown

Having tested his powers, Strindberg longed to write about his life as a journalist—especially about the famous red room in Bern's Restaurant, the stimulating meeting place for Stockholm's younger, lesser-known artists and intellectuals. "Oh, if only I could write the story of the Red Room," he wrote longingly in July, 1875,[16] "it would be the abstract of the story of our time!" A month earlier he had despaired of pleading "the cause of the oppressed before those who possess power or who have stolen it. I feel like a deaf-mute, because I cannot speak and am unable to write. Sometimes I stand in the middle of my room and feel as if I were in a cell. I want to scream until the walls and ceiling fly apart, but I have so much to scream that I hold my tongue."[17] He did not yet dare to plunge into social satire for fear of losing his newly appointed position as assistant librarian at the Royal Library and of having *Master Olof* permanently rejected.

At this time Strindberg was attempting to write about the Red Room coterie in dramatic form. He chose to do it as a comedy and tried to disguise the people and events portrayed by shifting the time back thirty years. Of course, this anachronistic approach made the social satire in the play—*In the Year '48 (Anno 48)*—completely pointless, and it is not surprising that Strindberg put the work aside. But two years later, in 1877, he threw down the gage with *Town and Gown.*

Strindberg later wrote that he began this first volume of prose with the intention of "writing about his student memories" and not with the intention of exposing unsatisfactory conditions or caviling or seeking revenge. This was undoubtedly true. The earliest story, "A Popular Entertainment" ("Ett folknöje"), about a Latin examination at "Flunker's Hall" at the university, had already been published in 1874 in the newspaper *Svenska Medborgaren,* where he had also published reminiscences about his schooldays. Indeed, some of the stories in the beginning of the book are only anecdotes about amusing perpetual undergraduates or depictions of the boarding house where Strindberg stayed during his first period as a student. But the more he wrote, the harder it became to suppress his stifled belligerence. The last story in the book, "The Old and the New" ("Det gamla och det nya"), became a vehement settling of accounts with antiquated Uppsala and its collegiate romanticism and "Boströmianism"—a political conservatism named for a long-time (1840-63) professor of practical philosophy, Christopher Jacob Boström (1797-1866).

During his studies at Uppsala, Strindberg had been an idealist among idealists, but the subsequent years in Stockholm had cured him. In 1872, he paid a chance visit to Uppsala and noticed that the members of the poetry group he had belonged to, the Runa Society, were the most old-fashioned young people there: "The students in general—the great mass of them—were realists, skeptics, scoffers, as befitted those who were of their time, but the poets were credulous fools with the 'Signature'[18] ideal in their hearts."[19] A year later he met one of his former Runa Society comrades on Dalarö and discovered that the man "had replaced idealism with an unimaginative Philistine view of life." Strindberg wanted to "indulge in blaspheming, deriding, and cursing the wretchedness of life," but his former friend "had not been educated in the Red Room and did not respond."[20]

Strindberg felt no more at home with the new Uppsala than with the Uppsala of his student days. And so in *Town and Gown* he lashed out in all directions; naive idealism and unimaginative Philistinism were treated with the same skeptical disdain. Not even the fifteen-year-old fledgling student of the final story, the spokesman for the future, is entirely safe from the author's irreverent irony.

Most of the stories in the book have the same pattern. A student, either because of innate refinement, earnestness in study, or an idealism acquired in the *gymnasium,* detaches himself from his comrades and so becomes an object of contempt. This unique individual has exalted expectations which are usually wrecked; as a result, he eventually abandons entirely his idealism and ambitious goals and seeks a safe harbor. At times, Strindberg contrasts him with a student of an opposite type—who wins success by changing his goals to conform with conventional tastes. A long-haired idealistic "serious poet" plays the role of "broken genius" at Uppsala, but ends up as a jovial lumberyard inspector in northern Sweden, while a poetic competitor who achieved success in his college[21] with mundane, realistic subject matter—writing "about the price of firewood, about the woman who cleaned his room, about the hole he ate in"—turns to more lucrative pursuits after graduation by becoming a fashionable court poet, in attendance at all royal weddings and funerals. In the story "Primus and Ultimus," Primus has a nervous breakdown at graduation because of overwork. On the other hand, although Ultimus, who devoted himself to studying the natural sciences (esteemed by the author in *Town and Gown*), sees his dreams about a great discovery dashed, he nevertheless succeeds in making several practical improvements at a porcelain factory where he takes a modest position. The fundamental theme in all the stories is that Uppsala makes a student unfit for the demands of real life. But Strindberg's purpose had a wider scope: we must abandon our convictions, relinquish our ideals in order to continue to live—the same disillusioned theme as the verse version of *Master Olof.*

The similarity to *Master Olof* is most striking in the story "The Victim" ("Offret"), which, despite the subtitle "A Fragment of Farm Life" ("Ett stycke bondeliv"), is to some extent autobiographical. A

young farm boy, because of his father's heartlessness and stinginess, suffers the same deprivation at Uppsala that Strindberg did. Life at the university is a constant series of disappointments and humiliations. Finally,
on Walpurgis Night,[22] when he spies on a student celebration through a
keyhole and listens to speeches by the president of a student association
and the faculty advisor, he feels "as if something had gone wrong for him.
He believed that everyone lied—the students in their singing, the student
president in his speech, and the faculty advisor in his."[23] Why should he
not do as everybody else—lie—in order to make an easy living? He
acquiesces to his father's wish and becomes a curate in his home parish.
"Now he is much beloved by the people of his parish, respected as a kind
and honorable man, and so he is; but strangers from the city who heard
him speak in church say he is 'dead'."[24]

This fat curate with inaccessible eyes and lifeless ideals is fundamentally the same character as the Master Olof of the Epilogue. The story
suggests how he got that way. His cruel father, for the sake of vanity,
wanted his son to enter the ministry and tried to bribe him by promising
to pay for his studies. But the young man did not want to be a minister
since he was not "of the pure [i.e., Augsberg] confession." He resisted
stubbornly and tried to make his own way at Uppsala. After failing in this
effort and seeing everyone else compromise with his conscience, he too
capitulates. Strindberg describes somewhat clumsily but movingly how
the young man at first refuses to admit defeat and tries to compel himself
to believe:

> He wanted to become a true Christian, but could not; he wanted to test
> himself through mortification, self-inflicted suffering, but he could never
> experience ecstasy. Once he hung on his wall a printed placard proclaim-
> ing "Come to Jesus!" To be sure, this caused him to suffer a little shame,
> but it was so little in contrast with what he suffered before that he took
> down the placard.[25]

Although this state of affairs is characterized by the author as "absolute
stupidity," one observes how very reminiscent it is of the ascetic period he
himself endured under the influence of Kierkegaard.

"The Victim" anticipated the bold Scandinavian novels of the
1880's—the period of the "breakthrough," when the spirit of realism hit
Northern Europe full force, breaking ties with tradition and the past. Cultivating ground broken by Brandes and Ibsen, the novelists of the 1880's

dealt with the struggle between two generations; they emphasized problems of conscience, satirized the "official lie," and became engrossed in
social problems. In 1883, six years after "The Victim" appeared, the
Norwegian writer Arne Garborg (1851-1924) established his reputation
in Scandinavia and throughout Europe with his novel *Peasant Students*
(Bondestudentar), which demonstrated how inadequately university life
prepared peasants for the harsh reality of a class-conscious urban society.

The last story in the book, "The Old and the New," examines the
ideas of those university students, a decade younger than Strindberg, who
became part of "Young Sweden," a coterie of forward-looking authors of
diverse temperaments whose faith in evolution and progress motivated
them in the 1880's to break with the conservative traditions of the past.
Two years after *Town and Gown*, in 1879, the leaders of Young Sweden
responded warmly to Strindberg's radical realism in *The Red Room*, and
for a time he became their rallying point.

The cocky little fifteen-year-old freshman of the story, a symbol
of the new generation, is terribly matter-of-fact and sober; he cruelly
smashes the romantic illusions of a perpetual undergraduate and singer of
old ballads. The youngster despises the concept of romantic love:

> It is a detail of life and must not be anything more! . . . We have
> ceased to draw sustenance from your poetry; we study economics and
> natural science; we regard our time at the university as a transitional
> period; you took it for a vocation. . . . You were ready with opinions on
> everything; you sang freedom songs; you cheered the . . . proposal [for
> reform of Parliamentary representation]. We cheer for everything; we
> sense that something is coming and so we keep our eyes open. . . . We
> are conservative because we fear mobocracy. Young people who are
> conservative! It's unprecedented! But that's what the mob has done. You
> were royalists: we are ready to become imperialists, if that's what's
> needed![26]

He meets little vigorous opposition from his older colleague until
he attacks the ideas of Professor Boström, the great Uppsala political
conservative: "What sort of nonsense is this philosophy of yours? You
think it flowed from a classical spring, when it's only an echo of the
Enlightenment, one hundred years after its time. It should have been submitted as an article in a small-town German magazine." When the older
man protests against this abuse, his adversary retorts that Boström was not
"great, he was insignificant!"[27]

The story is so skillfully organized that the reader is never certain if the young radical is the author's spokesman. Strindberg handled the younger generation's cocksureness and dry rationalism with irony. Nevertheless, one recognizes the author's own ideas, sharpened into paradoxes. His bottled-up hatred of the old and antiquated breaks through, partly against his will, and Uppsala's philosophy and romanticism are not the only things put to the sword. Strindberg's anti-democratic sentiments, fostered by his reading of Tocqueville, are expressed so strongly that one is reminded that later he would anticipate Nietzsche. His proclamation of life as "a great joke" is a portent of the ending of *The Red Room,* in which Doctor Borg declares his nihilism and describes all existence as "bosh."

If the entire book had been written in the same spirit as the final story, we would be left with a bitter impression of Uppsala. It was fortunate that Strindberg began the collection in a good humor, attempting to create an entertaining general picture of the city and university. The opening story, "The Boarders" ("Inackorderingarna"), describes how a novice comes "directly from the nursery to Uppsala," and by the time graduation is depicted in the next-to-last story, "Primus and Ultimus," all aspects of contemporary life in Uppsala have been presented without the author having made the slightest pretense to methodical order.

Town and Gown is still unrivaled as a realistic picture of Uppsala, and Strindberg had few predecessors in this kind of story-telling. The foremost was probably Orvar Odd (pseudonym for O. P. Sturzen-Becker— 1811-69), whose work Strindberg read when he was young.[28] Strindberg's story of the fun at the Latin examination has a counterpart in Odd's description of a translation test for a government position in "The Royal Chancery Official" ("Kunglig sektern"). Odd used pointed satire in his "physiologies" to depict typical citizens of the Stockholm of his day— "The Young Man in the Factory" ("Den unga mannen i verken"), "The Man Who Had Been Abroad" ("Mannen som varit utomlands"), "A Loafer" ("En dagdrivare"), and so forth. Often, he allowed a person's title or a personal pronoun to serve as introduction, beginning offhandedly with "he." For example, "The Man Who Had Been Abroad" begins with: "He took a little trip by steamship last summer from Malmö to Copenhagen." The same technique appears in *Town and Gown,* where eight of the twelve stories begin this way.[29] Again like Orvar Odd, Strindberg often continues into the story by stringing together present-tense sentences, opening with "He."[30] Sometimes he even concludes narratives in the same way as his predecessor—with an ironic *coup de grâce* in the style of a pretentious newspaper biography. Odd had the young man in the factory end up "with a title in front of his name and a star on his chest; elected to boards of directors and committees with the public's confidence: member for three silver riksdaler per year in the Bible Society and the Society Pro Patria." In the same spirit Strindberg wrote the following about his "court poet":

> He had written poems for one queen's funeral (for which he was awarded a diamond stickpin), one coronation, two ordinations, eighteen weddings, six christenings and many, many banquets, and was reported to have received a commission for a cantata for the next jubilee, whatever it happens to be! Since his *Collected Poems* have been published as well, his name belongs to literary history. He was biographed twice (the second time in two editions) and the boxwood has already been chosen for his official portrait.[31]

These parallels between Strindberg and Orvar Odd are stressed because the same satirical journalistic style appears again in *The Red Room* and the story collection *The New Kingdom (Det nya riket)*. But even in *Town and Gown* Strindberg demonstrates a command over a wider range of expression than Orvar Odd, whose prosy, bantering style lacks subtlety.

Ever since 1920, when Anton Blanck detected that Strindberg had contributed to the 1874 Swedish translation of Hans Christian Andersen's fairy tales, scholars have pointed out Andersen's stylistic influence in *Town and Gown*. Göran Lindblad claims to have discovered evidence of Andersen's influence in both form and content, but this is surely an overstatement. Not until seven years later, in *Married*, would Strindberg consciously follow Andersen's lead and produce a sparkling, playfully colloquial dialogue style. The style in *Town and Gown* was not really influenced by Andersen. It is true that Strindberg used long periodic sentences and occasionally even the florid phraseology that was characteristic of his predecessor. But most of the time he either struck a facetiously solemn tone, as August Blanche might have done, or he appropriated student slang. On the whole, it is not the style itself that gives the book its eminent position—it is the brisk narrative tempo, the amusing situations, and the light ironic tone. *Town and Gown* does not have *The Red Room's*

charged and energetic prose or its bold figures of speech and lyrical radiance. The story collection also lacks *The Red Room's* visual clarity in the
portrayal of character, milieu, and landscape. In *Town and Gown* the outlines of characters are sketched sparingly; people emerge more as types
representing different categories of students than as living individuals, as
in the following laconic picture of the "serious" poet—the "bard"; "He
wore long hair, had a bad chest, and drank absinthe." And Strindberg
devoted very little attention to the flat countryside of Uppsala that he
detested so heartily.

But precisely because the book attempts only to present a cross
section of Uppsala, the style is extraordinarily appropriate—with its bubbling good humor and its mocking tone now and then interrupted by a
brief touch of pathos. This little book has greater artistic unity than
Strindberg's next few works.

Notes to Chapter Four

1. *SS:*XVIII, pp. 192-93.
2. *SS:*XVI, p. 258.
3. *Brev,* VII, p. 380.
4. *SS:*XXXVII, p. 243.
5. *SS:*XIX, p. 102.
6. Reprinted in Torsten Eklund's *Före Röda rummet* (1946) pp. 28-33.
7. *See* Ruben G. Berg, *Litteraturbilder* II (1919), pp. 196 ff. The novel fragment has been published under the title *A Narrative from the Stockholm Archipelago (En berättelse från Stockholms skärgård* (1948). The editor, Torsten Eklund, concurs with Berg's opinion that it was written during the winter of 1871-72. Evidently, Strindberg wrote about his first summer on Kymmendö (1871) when he was studying for his *kandidatexamen* [roughly equivalent to an American M.A. degree—Translator]. One observes, however, that the university students in the novel claim it is their second summer on the island. According to Eklund, the novel should be dated earlier than the above-cited letter from the skerries.
8. *SS:*XIX, p. 102.
9. *SS:*III, p. 139.
10. *SS:*XVIII, p. 433.
11. *Brev,* I, p. 190.
12. During his journalistic years in the early 1870's he was close to arriving at the same conclusion.
13. *SS:*XIX, pp. 102-3.
14. Among other Swedish writers who honored the master by parodying him were the popular poet Elias Sehlstedt (1808-74) and Gustaf Fröding (1860-1911), the great master of verse forms.
15. *SS:*III, p. 131.
16. *Brev,* I, p. 203.
17. *Ibid.,* p. 187.
18. *See* Chapter II, The Early Plays.—Translator
19. *SS:*XIX, p. 58.
20. *Ibid.,* p. 89.
21. The Swedish word here is *nationen,* a university association or club composed of people from the same province or town.—Translator

22. The last day of April at Uppsala is the traditional signal for university students and alumni to welcome the coming of spring with boisterous celebrations.—Translator

23. *SS:*III, p. 72.

24. *Ibid.*, p. 75.

25. *Ibid.*, p. 74.

26. *Ibid.*, pp. 105-6.

27. *Ibid.*, pp. 107-8. [Strindberg's contempt for Boström's rational idealism is reflected in the autobiography where he associates the professor with "the abominable philosophy of reaction, which derives so drearily and darkly from the eighteenth-century Enlightenment." —Translator]

28. As a portraitist of the university itself, Strindberg had no real predecessor. William Bäckman's story about students, "Pencil Sketches in the Notebook" ("Blyertsteckningar plånboken") published twenty-seven years earlier, has been referred to as a model, but it is poorly written and could hardly have inspired Strindberg. August Blanche, Strindberg's old teacher, was more influential, as contemporary critics pointed out. His good-natured tales about amusing student types and academic pranks foreshadow Strindberg's in places. The latter's "The Bard and the Poet" ("Skalden och poeten"), for example, resembles Blanche's "Kalle Utter."

29. This manner of introduction seems very curious, but Strindberg's precedent became obligatory for stories about students. Gustaf af Geijerstam (1858-1909) used it, as did Ola Hansson (1860-1925) in his collection of stories *Student Life (Studentliv)*.

30. Compare, for example, Orvar Odd's "A Loafer" ("En dagdrivare") with Strindberg's "The Field Mouse" ("Sorken").

31. *SS:*III, p. 59.

Chapter Five

THE RED ROOM

Sources and Social Satire

The Red Room, sometimes called the first modern Swedish novel, was published in November, 1879. On the title page is Voltaire's familiar quotation that nothing is as disagreeable as being hanged in secret; up to now this had been Strindberg's lot. *Master Olof* had been quietly turned down by the Royal Dramatic Theatre and the Swedish Academy. *Town and Gown* received kind but feeble praise. *The Red Room,* however, provoked an immediate storm. With one stroke Strindberg became Sweden's most debated author.

The Red Room was shocking because of the boldness with which Strindberg invaded and ruthlessly exposed the hypocrisy in every stronghold of established respectability. The novel describes how Arvid Falk, a naive and idealistic young civil servant, flees from his stultifying life as a government bureaucrat and tries to make his way as a journalist and author. In each of the social spheres he enters he discovers that the weight of tradition and the power of vested interests have created more corruption than he had dreamed possible. In scenes of often savage satirical force, Falk finds hypocrites everywhere—among politicians, newspaper publishers, religious leaders, theatre people, philanthropic matrons, and financiers. Even his older brother Carl Nicolaus, a smug merchant, turns out to be a hypocrite. For companionship, Arvid Falk turns (as did Strindberg) to a circle of bohemian friends who meet in the Red Room, a dining room in Bern's Restaurant in Stockholm. The group includes Ygberg, a clerk and would-be philosopher; Olle Montanus, a pathetic young man who is so influenced by Hartmann's pessimistic philosophy that he eventually commits suicide; and two painters—Sellén, a *bon vivant,* and Lundell, a practical businessman.

Although the social satire in *The Red Room* alludes to conditions that prevailed at the time the book was published in 1879, Arvid Falk's trying experiences as a journalist are identical with those lived through by the author a half-decade earlier (1872-74).[1] When he left Uppsala, Strindberg began as a staff writer on the radical *Stockholms Aftonpost,* but the newspaper was shut down shortly thereafter, in May, 1872. After his second unsuccessful attempt at acting the following fall in Gothenburg, he became editor of a trade publication for insurance companies, *Svensk försäkringstidning,* during the first part of 1873. But because he sharply criticized the shady practices of certain insurance companies, they withdrew financial support and the journal collapsed. The letters from Sandhamn in December, 1873, earned him a regular position on Stockholm's *Dagens Nyheter,* but he clashed with his editor and had to leave. In the spring of 1874 he turned to the Agrarian Party newspaper *Svenska Medborgaren;* in the few short months he spent there "he experienced the greatest adversity, sickness, and humiliation he had ever known."[2] Consequently, he felt literally saved from starvation and ruin when in the fall of 1874 he received a special appointment as assistant librarian at the Royal Library, a post that offered not only security but social standing as well. Now he had time to write essays and articles for a variety of newspapers and magazines.

As a journalist, Strindberg could not be himself. It is true that in his autobiography he recalled with pleasure his position on *Dagens Nyheter:* "The editorial desk fascinated him as an observatory from which one looked out over the world and watched history unfold."[3] But because he could not always check the flow of vitriol from his pen, he quarreled constantly with his superiors and fellow workers, and the job became unbearable. Whatever he was assigned on *Dagens Nyheter*—literary criticism, theatrical criticism, the Danish-Norwegian news desk, stockholders' meetings, sessions of Parliament, expositions, or banquets—his subjective writing style betrayed him. Actors threatened to beat him up for his play reviews, and he received complaints from members of Parliament because he reported not what they said, but what he thought they should say.[4] On *Svenska Medborgaren* he apparently pasted up news items, as does Arvid Falk for *The Worker's Banner (Arbetarfanan)* in *The Red Room.* On the different magazines he was compelled to work for, he had the hardly rewarding job of writing captions and short verses to accompany woodcuts.

Strindberg acknowledged his aversion to "taking the bit between

his teeth and crawling into the harness."⁵ He explained his inability to
write news reports by stating that he embraced "the larger point of view,
by which things of importance in ordinary, everyday life were treated as
bagatelles."⁶

A group of radicals with whom Strindberg was most sympathetic
broke up during 1872, and as a result, he was politically homeless. Although he felt closest to the political programs of the Agrarian Party and
finished out his journalistic career as a contributor to the party house
organ, he discovered to his dismay that it followed a narrow partisan
approach. He regarded the early years of King Oscar II's reign (1872-
1907) as signaling a reactionary turn in every area. The bureaucratism,
the proposal for military conscription, the spreading Pietism, and the
growing number of bogus financial schemes and speculations gave him the
impression that "the engine had reversed, and the train rolled down-
grade."⁷ These contemporary trends were the subjects for satire in both
The Red Room and *The New Kingdom.*

Strindberg did not choose his close friends from among newspaper colleagues, for he hated them from the first time he joined them at
La Croix Café—an incident described in detail in a passage cut from the
novel before publication. He much preferred the Red Room coterie of artists and bohemians whom he first met in the spring of 1872 at a banquet
given at the Lidingö Bridge Inn by Per Ekström, the Sellén of the novel.
The banquet is described in the chapter "Happy People" ("Lyckliga
människor").⁸ Later that fall, the group adopted as a regular meeting
place the room at Bern's furnished with red sofas—the Red Room. They
met there until the spring of 1874, when several of the members left the
country.⁹

Strindberg's earliest use of his experiences from the Red Room
days was in the extraordinarily naive comedy *In the Year '48*, written in
1876-77. Since we lack any preliminary sketches for *The Red Room*, the
play can be helpful in illuminating the genesis of the novel. *In the Year '48*
takes place during the time of the Stockholm riots of March, 1848. Brewer
Larsson, a reactionary royalist, anxious about the revolutionary spirit sweeping Europe, foolishly aggravates the tension by proposing in Parliament
that all servants be dressed in gray so that in the event of trouble the
army would know at whom to shoot. Although the periods in which the

play and the novel are set are twenty years apart, the two works really have the same milieu: family life, artistic and theatrical worlds, the press, and—in a very cautious form—politics.

The model for the play's central character, the boastful and vulgar Larsson, captain of municipal cavalry, seems to have been Strindberg's "progenitor from the brewery wagon"—his grandfather Zacharias Strindberg. Larsson's nephew Arvid is a forerunner of *The Red Room's* Arvid Falk; he submits his "great poem" to the editor of a liberal newspaper who throws it in the wastebasket and offers him a lowly position as proofreader. As in the novel, Arvid is the connecting link between the Philistine world and the bohemian life. The latter is represented by the painter Per, who experiences the same success at the end of the play as Sellén does in *The Red Room:* he sells a painting and is accepted by the Academy of Art. Per even appears in the same triumphal costume as Sellén—with a flower in his buttonhole and field glasses hanging on a strap over his shoulder.

The theatrical world is represented in part by the old actor Klinger, who corresponds to the character of Falander in the novel, and in part by the stagestruck bookkeeper Lundquist who, like Strindberg himself, wants to play the role of Karl Moor in Schiller's *The Robbers*. Lundquist also serves the same function as Olle Montanus in the novel; at a workers' meeting he gives a lecture on the dignity of labor, just as Montanus gives a lecture "About Sweden" ("Om Sverige"). In content, however, Lundquist's speech is more closely related to Montanus's bitter writings on the curse of manual labor, found on his body after his suicide.

Strindberg asserted in his autobiography that Arvid Falk's brother Carl Nicolaus was "a fabricated figure," and that his "famous party on Österlång Street, room decorations and all," was "completely invented."[10] But Sten Linder has pointed out that Carl Nicolaus's manipulation of his brother's inheritance and his indignation over Arvid's becoming a radical scandalmonger are reminiscent of Strindberg's conflicts with his father. Linder further points out that Carl Nicolaus was accustomed to thinking of himself as a father to his brother, who was fifteen years his junior.[11] Overall, however, the play is more obviously based on Strindberg's life than is the novel.

A baptismal celebration in *In the Year '48* is a preparatory study for the party on Österlång Street in *The Red Room*. At the baptism, Larsson shows the same unwillingness to lend money to his friend, the curate's assistant Gren, as Carl Nicolaus Falk shows toward his crony, Fritz Levin. The assistant also has the same responsibilities as the teacher Nyström in the novel—to make flattering speeches to his hosts on gay occasions, to sing songs, and at night to recite double-entendre verse. Even the furnishings in the room are the same in the play and the novel, and when Larsson speaks, he uses the same stolid, bullying tone as does Carl Nicolaus Falk.[12]

In the Year '48 contains no true social satire. Not until 1878, when he first read Dickens, did Strindberg really try "to launch a similar massed assault on all society, with which he had never been able to reconcile himself."[13] But other circumstances had whetted this desire. He connected the origin of The Red Room with the financial crisis of 1878, which resulted from the years of reckless speculation in Europe following the Franco-Prussian War—the grunderjahre. Strindberg describes this period in his autobiography:

> The iron industry expanded its activities, bought and built; the timber people chopped and sawed; the farm owners took out mortgages and cleared new land; the railroad companies laid track parallel to each other past every house; hitherto untouched abundances of peat and pit coal were excavated; companies were founded, often with good intentions; at times, less than good.[14]

Downturns in market conditions for the leading Swedish exports—timber and iron—also helped produce the crisis, which was particularly injurious because a great amount of capital had been committed to building railroads, capital that would take a long time to return interest. The crisis played such a prominent role in The Red Room because the thirty-year-old Strindberg was a victim of it. In January, 1879, a year after his first marriage, he was forced into bankruptcy. He had borrowed money on his wife's capital stock certificates in one of the failing firms, and it was not until July of that year that he was able to put his affairs in order.

Strindberg wrote in his autobiography: "When the matter was settled and he found some peace again, he sat down to write his novel, sine ira et studio,"[15] but, in actuality, the novel was written while the bankruptcy investigation was in progress and he feared for his very livelihood. A letter in July, 1879, written while he worked on the concluding chapter, bears witness to his mood; he was angry, vengeful, anxious to strike "until the dogs cry out—for I write not to be called poet, but to fight."[16] His resentment over what he suffered was so deep that it lasted for the rest of his life. More than thirty years later, in 1910, he complained in *Talks to the Swedish Nation (Tal till svenska nationen)*[17] that the bankruptcy had disgraced him for life, although eventually he did pay off all his debts, some even twice over. Strindberg's tendency to regard all business affairs as swindles also dates from this time. During the final decade of his life, market conditions in Sweden were favorable, but he stubbornly insisted in *The Gothic Rooms (Götiska rummen*—1904) and elsewhere, that the nation stood on the brink of ruin.

Strindberg had begun planning the novel before the crisis brought him hardship. He related that he first thought of creating "a Swedish Pickwick Club," obviously with the Red Room coterie as a counterpart to the Dickens group. Neither title nor subtitle—"Scenes of Artistic and Literary Life" ("Skildringar ur artist-och författarlivet")—is satiric or belligerent, but this peaceful mood disappeared when his financial troubles began to exert their influence. Carl Nicolaus Falk, who in the beginning of the novel is content to operate his linen-goods business, at the end establishes a dubious banking enterprise, The Deposit Guarantee Company, and Lundell, the practical artist, ends up painting only lucrative portraits of managing directors. Everything in the novel was transformed into business. A chapter each is devoted to "The Newspaper Syndicate *Gray Coat*" ("Tidningsaktiebolaget Gråkappan"), "The Triton Marine Insurance Society" ("Sjöförsäkringsaktiebolaget Triton"), and "The Phoenix Theatrical Company" ("Teateraktiebolaget Phoenix"). Furthermore, everything is corrupt, not only high finance: government bureaucracy, Parliament, charity, religion, and art. Strindberg had a natural talent for faultfinding and the exposé, and the crisis of 1878 brought it to the fore; he lashed out in every direction. In a letter to his publisher, Josef Seligmann, Strindberg called the novel "a contemptuous ridiculing of all the things people deluded the hero into believing were so-called ideals . . . until the moment arrived when he discovered that these things, whatever they were, were not ideals."[18]

What distinguishes Strindberg's social satire from Dickens's, which he indicated was his model, is the absence of a systematic political and social point of view behind his attack. This becomes apparent when one compares the description of "The Salary Commission For Civil Servants" with Dickens's Circumlocution Office in *Little Dorrit;* Strindberg's contemporaries observed the parallel. Strindberg was satisfied just to relate how the commission frittered away money and wasted time. Dickens's satire probed more deeply—with fervent indignation he used an imaginative narrative style to show how all the forms, etiquette, and bureaucracy of government life combine to strangle the individual. The Norwegian novelist Alexander Kielland (1849-1906), who somewhat later than Strindberg imitated the same scene from Dickens in his *Working People* (*Arbeidsfolk*—1881), was not as independent of his predecessor as Strindberg and came closer to Dickens's intentions. Not until the serious and comprehensive social criticism of *The New Kingdom* (1882), did Strindberg develop a consistent point of view. This is why *The New Kingdom,* although artistically inferior to *The Red Room,* had more influence on the younger generation.

As for Dickens's humor, Strindberg did not appreciate it and never commented on it. "People think that the purpose of humor is fun," said Strindberg in a review of an American humorist.[19] "No! It is very serious business. An author does not dare to state truth nakedly, it is too appalling. He must mask it; he must serve it up under the less dangerous label of humor." Torsten Eklund has pointed out[20] that this idea is in harmony with Strindberg's descriptions of the selections of American humor he edited and in part translated in two volumes in 1878-79. In his autobiography, Strindberg said of these humorists that "the public took their joking as joking," whereas he "took them seriously. . . . [Their joking] was the harbinger of the anarchy of thought that would later burst out; it was the settling of accounts with the old view of the world, the beginning of the demolition work."[21]

Strindberg overrated the American humorists he read before he rediscovered Dickens, but their influence on the social satire in *The Red Room* is indisputable. The Americans distorted Dickens's caricaturing into preposterous jesting. But whereas their "wild west" stories of inkwell battles, shootings, and fistfights in newspaper offices had scarcely any deeper implications, Strindberg used the same technique to brand easily recognizable contemporaries. In a letter to Edvard Brandes he named several of the contemporary events and institutions he used in *The Red Room;* other references can be identified from newspaper articles of the time, particularly ones written by Strindberg himself.[22]

Strindberg's method of dealing with his contemporaries in the novel is demonstrated in his treatment of newspaper critics. When the verse version of *Master Olof* was published in 1878 and harshly attacked in the conservative newspaper *Aftonbladet,* Strindberg satirized the staff of the paper, which he called *Gray Coat* in the novel. The literary critic is an unsuccessful poet who, after his own work was devastatingly criticized, swore "eternal death to all Swedish literature." The drama critic qualified for his work in a sanitation department office in "X-Town" and furthermore is deaf. The art critic has "never held a brush in his hand" and reviews paintings before they are finished. The satire is in the same vein as Mark Twain's humorous stories about newspaper conditions in southern America, where book reviews are assigned to people who never wrote a book, drama reviews handled by shoemakers and pharmacy apprentices, and agriculture discussed by unsuccessful poets. Strindberg also borrowed other stylistic devices from the American humorist, such as the use of fabricated reports and news items.

Strindberg had particular people in mind in the satirical chapters but disguised his figures "so as not to expose private individuals,"[23] and this sometimes spoiled the effect by making the characters psychologically incomplete. Pastor Skåre, for whom Gustaf Emanuel Beskow[24] was the closest model, is "a papier-mâché skeleton thrown together from all sorts of bone collections." The same could be said of Smith the publisher and other caricatures. But it was primarily the social satire, expressing what many thought but no one dared to say, that caused many younger men to rally to the author and his book.

Skepticism and Pessimism

Strindberg said that most of his friends in the Red Room group never became successful because they "misunderstood my worldly skepticism and wanted to put into practice the theories I had stated ironically."[25] But the novel gives the impression that it was the good-natured idealist Arvid Falk who was instructed in skepticism by his comrades. The truth probably lies somewhere in between. It was through his association with the Red Room circle that Strindberg was initiated into the teachings of positivism—he borrowed some of Buckle's writings from Martin Nyström. He soon assumed the philosophical leadership, however, especially after he assimilated Hartmann's pessimism. Undoubtedly, this is the "worldly skepticism" that Strindberg believed was so fateful for his friends of the Red Room. In his autobiography he said: "Johan, who did not wish to discuss problems at length, assumed a skeptical tone and cut short attempts to argue with a clever evasion, an interjection, or an expression of doubt."[26]

The first stage in the development of Strindberg's thinking during the Red Room period is illuminated by a small unpublished manuscript entitled "Observations of a Skeptic" ("En tvivlares anteckningar"), from the years 1872-73.[27] Strindberg wanted these observations included in his autobiography as "the whole program of his future writings," but only a short summary was published. In a note added to the manuscript, Strindberg pointed out that these reflections were "probably based mostly on Thomas Buckle" and were included in *The Red Room*. Several appear as aphorisms left behind by Olle Montanus after his suicide.

"Observations of a Skeptic" reveals that Buckle's relativistic approach to religion and his liberalistic distrust of the state and its measures to protect itself made a deep impression on the young Strindberg and contributed to his skepticism. It was a line of thought that would have far-reaching consequences for him. Buckle's eagerness to preserve the freedom of the individual led him to attack the concept of the division of labor, which according to him made people cogwheels in the machinery of society and threatened to transform them into spiritual cripples.[28] Strindberg made several references to this idea in "Observations of a Skeptic" and formulated it as an aphorism in *The Red Room:* "The great idea of our time—the division of labor—means success for the race and death for the individual." This idea, which Strindberg associated with Rousseauism, caused him to doubt the optimistic belief in evolution presented by Spencer and others. Perhaps evolution was retrogressive instead of progressive.

"Observations of a Skeptic" contains reservations about Hartmann, who is characterized as "a good mind, but behind the times."[29] Gradually, however, Strindberg assimilated Hartmann's pessimism, especially after he assisted several friends with the translation of Hartmann's *Philosophy of the Unconscious* during 1877-78.[30] "It was true, then—as he had dreamed so often—that everything was bosh," Strindberg wrote in his autobiography when giving an account of his principal impression of Hartmann. The same definition of existence, put in the mouth of Arvid

Falk's tough-minded friend, the medical student and objective man of science Doctor Borg, concluded the original manuscript version of *The Red Room*.

Strindberg stated in the autobiography that the validity of Hartmann's pessimism was long obscured by his own religious idealism. In Strindberg's mind, Hartmann's and Schopenhauer's disdain for the worldly became part of the disdain he found in Pietism and Kierkegaard. This is demonstrated both in "Observations of a Skeptic" and in Olle Montanus's aphorism: "Pietists and pessimists proceed from the same principle, the wretchedness of existence, and aim at the same goal, to leave this world and live with God."[31] Another character, the irreverent actor Falander, proclaims that pessimism is the truest idealism and a Christian doctrine "because Christianity teaches us about the world's wretchedness, from which we should seek release."[32] In a tirade, strangely enough placed in the mouth of the sly, conservative journalist Struve, disdain for the worldly develops into a disgust with existence itself: "If you want to avoid the self-immolation that you as a fanatic are headed for," Struve says to Arvid Falk,

> then adopt a new perspective on things as soon as possible. Train yourself to take a bird's-eye view of the world, and you'll see how small and insignificant everything seems. Start with the idea that it's all a garbage dump, that people are the refuse—the egg shells, the carrot tops, the cabbage leaves, the rags. Then you'll never again be caught off guard, never again be stripped of an illusion. On the contrary, you'll experience great pleasure—every time you see a fine action, a beautiful deed. In a word, adopt a calm and serene disdain. And don't worry—it needn't make you heartless.[33]

Up to this time, the image of life as a garbage dump—which would be used frequently during the Inferno years—was for Strindberg more a persistent anxiety than a consistent way of looking at things. This is evident in Arvid Falk's answer to Struve, in which the tone of personal conviction is unmistakable: "I don't share that opinion yet, it's true, although I am cynical to an extent. But this is my misfortune, for as soon as I see any token of generosity, I'm in love with people once more. Then, I expect too much of them and am deceived afresh."[34]

As a rule, the "nihilism" adopted by Strindberg during his Red Room period is not expressed by Arvid Falk. It is usually delivered by other figures in the book, all voicing a pessimism appropriate to their individual occupations and dispositions: Struve, in a glib, journalistic style; Falander, in the jargon of the actor. Olle Montanus jots down wildly formulated paradoxes, while Doctor Borg uses the medical terminology so cherished by the naturalists. But sometimes not even these distinctions are observed. When Strindberg wants to express an opinion, he allows the bearer of the message to blurt it out, even if it is not in character.[35] He was aware that the characterization in *The Red Room* was somewhat careless and once admitted to Jonas Lie, after reading Lie's novel *The Family of Gilje (Familjen paa Gilje*—1883), that "I have too low an opinion of people (mostly acquired through personal experience!) to be able to deal with characters this exhaustively."[36]

Amid blasphemers and skeptics, Arvid Falk is an ingenuous idealist whose illusions are betrayed at every turn. The hopes with which he enters journalism from civil service are quickly frustrated, and he learns to regard man "as a mendacious social animal." Finally, the only thing he believes in is the worker, because "his cause is the burning issue of the near future, and all your politics aren't worth two cents in comparison."[37] He leaves the liberal newspaper *Red Cap (Rödluvan*—Strindberg's fictional name for *Dagens Nyheter)* to take a position on the workers' paper *Worker's Banner.* But editing a newspaper that caters only to the uneducated worker does not satisfy him, even though he still believes in the workers' struggle for justice and has no faith "that the cause of the oppressed lies in good hands. . . . It is vital to inform people about what public opinion is—especially printed public opinion—and how it originates. And the cause—that I shall never abandon!"[38] But he is forced to betray this lofty promise as well.

At the end of the novel we see him again working in the same government office he once scorned, silencing his conscience with numismatics, just as Strindberg drowned his hopes and despair in Sinological studies at the Royal Library. But Doctor Borg suspects that Arvid could not for long stifle his political fanaticism in dry, austere studies, and neither could Strindberg. A half-year after *The Red Room* appeared, he wrote to Edvard Brandes:

> I have retired to my home (I am married) and avoid questions of the day. I bury myself in the 200,000 volumes of the Royal Library (I am an assistant there!); studying sinology, geography, archeology—for a while. But underneath something begins to rankle and ache until a boil like *The Red Room* breaks out. Then I feel relieved and happy![39]

Because Arvid Falk's experiences are Strindberg's in disguised form, there has been a tendency to interpret the character as a self-portrait, and to a certain degree this is valid. Strindberg did try to sketch himself as he thought he was at the time he joined the Red Room circle. But in his later years he was eager to ascribe to himself as a young man a greater measure of naivete and idealism than he probably had. Time and again, Johan in the autobiography allows himself to be deluded into magnanimous reconciliations that he later bitterly regrets. He expects the best of people and cherishes the brightest of hopes for the future. In this way the author was trying half-consciously to defend himself against accusations that he was suspicious, ungrateful, vengeful, and contemptuous of people.

Strindberg clearly did not want to identify himself completely with Arvid Falk. He did not give the character the same combination of toughness and vulnerability that is found in his earlier self-portraits: Master Olof, or Örn in the novel fragment. Arvid Falk has no sharp edges; he is mostly good-natured and submissive and certainly not belligerent. His love letters are absurdly romantic, and his poetry is in the most banal "Signature" style.[40]

It is therefore difficult for the reader to take Doctor Borg seriously when he predicts Arvid Falk's future in the last pages of the novel. Are we really to believe that Falk, now married and settled, is "inscrutable" and a member of "one of the secret societies that the forces of reaction and militarism have produced on the continent"? He has appeared to be an open book. Why fear that his political fanaticism—of which we have seen little sign—will ultimately explode?

But the book itself is the explosion that Doctor Borg prophesied, and its author belonged to the freemasonry of new ideas in Europe. Strip the masks off Arvid Falk and other characters in *The Red Room,* and we find August Strindberg staring open-eyed at the reader—menacing, deeply melancholy, anxiously searching.

Romantic and Naturalistic Touches

Illusionless pessimism also characterizes the attitude toward art in *The Red Room*. The actor Falander flatly denies all poetic value in Shakespeare, and in the chapter entitled "Nihilism," Olle Montanus confesses to a thoroughgoing hostility toward art that is also expressed in the notes found later on his body.[41] This hostility had its origin in Strindberg's reading of Plato's *Republic*, with which he had become acquainted earlier and to which he would return continually in his polemical essays.[42] Plato recognized, says Montanus, "the futility of art, calling it but an illusion of the illusion (i.e., of reality). This is why he eliminated the artist from his ideal state."[43] Art does not create anything new—it can only "alter, amend, arrange."

I shall return later to this condemnation of art, in which utilitarianism is combined with a contempt for esthetics that was inspired by Kierkegaard; significantly, Montanus glorifies Savonarola and the Dutch iconoclasts. At this point I wish only to emphasize that early in his career Strindberg was opposed to the naturalists' demand to copy reality. This is one reason he reacted so strongly against contemporary criticism characterizing *The Red Room* as programmatically faithful to naturalism or realism. He was especially unwilling to be regarded as a disciple of Zola— a point he emphasized in a letter to his old university professor, Carl Rupert Nyblom, in 1882. There is also every reason to trust the assertion in the autobiography[44] that only after the publication of *The Red Room* did Strindberg first read a book by Zola—*L'Assommoir,* the novel with which Zola made his name in France and elsewhere.

This is not to say, of course, that Strindberg had had no contact with French naturalism when he wrote *The Red Room.* In 1875 he had been much taken by Flaubert's *Madame Bovary* and had wished to translate it into Swedish. And novels by the Goncourt brothers were part of the library he left behind when he went abroad in 1883. In the preface to *Miss Julie* he says that the novels by the Goncourts appealed to him more than "anything else in contemporary literature." When, in 1875, he spoke for the first time of his desire to write the story of the Red Room, he added: "It would be the abstract of the story of our time." This is reminiscent of the Goncourt brothers' declaration in their famous preface to *Germinie Lacerteux* that the novel should be *"l'histoire morale contemporaine,"* and *The Red Room* was indeed an attempt to fulfill this purpose. Whereas social satire in Dickens is only one element of the plot, *The Red Room* is a procession of investigations into one social sphere after another. At times the novel threatens to disintegrate into small pieces, each devoted to a single aspect of society: civil service, literature, commerce, Parliament, theatre, and so forth. Throughout, attention is called to decadence and corruption, in the same way that the naturalists in France exposed the rottenness of

their society. It is understandable that *The Red Room* came to be regarded
as the first naturalistic social novel in Scandinavia and in this capacity
served as a model for such later writers as the Norwegians Alexander
Kielland and Arne Garborg.

If one seeks a progenitor among the French naturalists, the most
likely candidate is Daudet, whose reputation in France and Sweden was
established earlier than that of Zola. In *Fromont jeune et Risler âiné*
(1874) Daudet dealt with crooked business transactions,[45] and in *Le Nabab*
(1877), he unveiled a panorama of the corrupt financial world of Paris,
exposing prominent people and public institutions behind very transparent disguises. The sensation this novel aroused in Sweden was mentioned by Strindberg in 1878 in the magazine *Finsk tidskrift:* "They talk
about Daudet as if he were a native Stockholmer, and closer track is kept
of his latest work than of the works of Jolin and Hedberg."[46]

The same international reversal in market conditions in the late
1870's inspired the descriptions of swindling in *Le Nabab* and *The Red
Room*. Similarities in details between them could be coincidental,[47] but it
does appear probable that it was from Daudet that Strindberg got the idea
of using wide-scale social criticism and references to the scandals of the
day. *The Red Room's* bold indiscretion, its frank descriptions, and its
caustic tone had the same strong effect on Strindberg's readers as the
French naturalists had on theirs. Strindberg, however, made no attempt to
adopt the naturalists' documentary technique and scrupulous investigation of reality. Artistically, as other scholars have pointed out, he was the
product of a literary school of an earlier vintage.

A romantic strain runs through the chapters dealing with the Red
Room group; in them, Strindberg abandoned social problems and evidenced a fresh sense of humor in a way he seldom did again. Later, in his
autobiography, he was more faithful to reality when describing the coterie,
but the carefree tone had evaporated. In *The Red Room* he sketched
the members with swift, sure strokes: the gay, playful artist Sellén, the
"practical" artist Lundell, eccentric Olle Montanus, and envious Ygberg.
The scenes involving the group—at the shack in Lill-Jans Woods just
north of Stockholm, at the magnificent party at Bern's Restaurant with its
epilogue in the prostitute's apartment, and in the deserted photographer's

studio on Regerings Street where Sellén and Montanus are staying—have never been equalled as descriptions of the bohemian artistic life style in Sweden.

As soon as the book appeared, the critic Karl Warburg questioned whether Strindberg had been inspired by Henri Murger's classic novel *Scènes de la vie de Bohême* (1848). Many similarities have been pointed out by Göran Lindblad, but he does not regard them as the result of a direct influence of Murger on Strindberg. He believes that the artists gathered in *The Red Room*, "all individual differences to the contrary, have something in common with the universal breed of romantic artists" who also appear in Murger's work.[48] He points out that Strindberg characterized his artistic comrades as "post-romantics," who were true to "the bohemian type; for there is always a delay before the swell of great tides reaches the remote Scandinavian coasts."[49] But this argument does not conclusively exclude the possibility that Strindberg had Murger's bohemians in mind when he drew his friends. Several of the scenes in which Strindberg portrays the vagabond life of the coterie are so similar to Murger's in mood that, in retrospect, one is uncertain as to whether they appeared in *The Red Room* or in *Scènes*. For example, there is the Lill-Jans Woods shack scene in *The Red Room* in which Sellén, having run out of white paint, makes a bundle of his shoes and stockings, Rehnjelm's vest, and the only two sheets from the bed and sends it with Olle Montanus to the pawnshop to get money to buy paint, as well as six French rolls and two half-pints of beer for the hungry artists. Or the scene in the old photographer's studio where Sellén and Montanus, after having burned up the floorboards to keep warm, fix themselves a common bed with bits of canvas and old drawings for a covering and portfolios for pillows, and try to drive away hunger by reading aloud recipes from a book borrowed from Ygberg. Per Ekström—the real-life Sellén—has called both scenes distortions of what actually occurred,[50] and Martin Nyström (Ygberg) never mentioned the borrowing of a cookbook. It appears that Strindberg used Murger to supplement reality.

At the same time, one notices an obvious attempt by Strindberg to avoid false romanticizing, and for the most part he is successful. The Swedish bohemians have more calloused hands and a coarser view of existence than their French comrades: for them, Bacchus takes precedence over Venus. Nevertheless, some of the rosy glow of Murger's bohemian world lingers in *The Red Room*. The novel might have seemed more naturalistic without this element but also less vibrant.

People and Milieus

Charles Dickens's influence is evident in the treatment of both the Red Room coterie and the more conventional people in the novel. We are obliged to Göran Lindblad for demonstrating this through striking parallels, but some additional comments are in order. Referring to Strindberg's method of characterization, Lindblad says: "An eye for a person's outward appearance, for the picturesque or eccentric in their dress or manner —this he obtained from Dickens."[51] This is true, insofar as Strindberg adopts directly from Dickens the technique of first describing the way a character looks at his initial entrance and then keeping the image alive by emphasizing particular gestures and quirks. But Strindberg lacked Dickens's intense visual imagination in portraiture. As an example, we can take the description of Doctor Borg at his first entrance:

> a broad-shouldered thirty-year-old man with a square head, the front of which was supposed to represent a face. The skin looked like the half-rotten plank of a bridge in which worms have plowed their labyrinths; the mouth was carved wide and constantly ajar, thus permanently exposing four finely-polished eyeteeth; when a smile appeared, the face split in two parts, opening a vista as far back as the fourth back tooth. Not a strand of beard ventured forth from that barren soil; the nose was so badly fitted that from the front one could see a good distance into the head; and on top of the skull something was growing that resembled coconut matting.[52]

The portrait would be in the best Dickens tradition except that it fails to give the reader a clear impression of Borg's mien. And although Strindberg—still following Dickens's example—gives the fearful doctor the habit of sticking out his tongue, he is still no more successful in bringing the character to life than he is with the journalist Struve, whom he has blink and tug at his right whisker. Only when the people in *The Red Room* begin to speak can they be visualized clearly by the reader. This is especially true of Arvid Falk's brother Carl Nicolaus, to whose outward appearance the author devotes little attention: "He had fair hair, a fair mustache, fair eyebrows and eyelashes. He was rather stout, and so could squeak around rather well in his shoes, which screamed under the weight of his thickset body."[53] Hundreds of Stockholm wholesale merchants could answer this description. Not until he starts talking does Carl Nicolaus Falk become a unique, alive individual.

It was through directly rendered or reported dialogue that Strindberg was able to give life to his people, a talent he shared with Maupassant. In the preface to *Pierre et Jean,* Maupassant explained that his own method—as opposed to Zola's physiological approach and Bourget's technique of psychological analysis—was to allow characters to reveal themselves through their speech and gestures. Strindberg immediately concurred. In both his autobiography and his preface to *Miss Julie* he condemned the Dickens-type characters—"organ-grinder's puppets"—who derive individuality not through what they say, but through external criteria: a red nose, a wooden leg, or a mechanically repeated phrase.

But if he condemned Dickensian character description, he greatly admired Dickens's ability to create milieu and contrasts it with Sir Walter Scott's and Zola's overburdened methods: "Dickens blew life into inanimate objects and made them play a role, harmonizing the setting with the character and the situation."[54] There is no aspect of Dickens's technique that Strindberg assimilated more completely than this ability to blend setting, action, and character, and to give inanimate objects a fantastic fairy-tale lustre. During later periods in Strindberg's life, these objects acquired mystical lives, becoming portents and symbols, but in *The Red Room* he was content simply to personify them. Contemporary critics expressed admiration for the description of the provincial X-Town, in which the afternoon drowsiness of a rural town is suggested through an interior picture of the town hall restaurant.

> The main room of the town hall restaurant was still quiet and peaceful. . . . The graduated liquor bottles stood in their places, having an afternoon nap. Opposite them were the brandy bottles, with the metal pendants of their noble orders around their necks; they were on leave until evening. The grandfather clock, never permitted an afternoon nap, was like a tall peasant standing upright against the wall, retailing the time.[55]

Strindberg then described the long narrow room in terms of a stable, with the tables projecting from the wall, like tied-up horses, "and one could see that they were asleep, since flies walked undisturbed on their backs."[56] Lindblad has cited a parallel from Dickens—the description of a bedroom, where a bed, a wardrobe, chairs, and tables are asleep in the same way: "they were plainly apoplectic and disposed to snore." The passage is from Chapter III of *Martin Chuzzlewit*, which was included in Strindberg's earliest library. But one must emphasize that this desire to personify all things came naturally to Strindberg.

Strindberg was most successful in *The Red Room* when he was able to harmonize depiction of milieu with situation and dialogue, as in the party scene. Falk's office is swept and spruced up. Near the door are two crates "out of which the necks of bottles protruded, sealed with red and yellow foil and wrapped in pink tissue paper. In the middle of the floor was a table covered with a white tablecloth; upon it was enthroned an East Indian bowl and a heavy silver candelabrum."[57] Carl Nicolaus is dressed in a frock coat, and the atmosphere is a bit formal at the start. But when his guests Nyström and Levin begin eating, "a tremendously benign smile" spreads over Falk's features, and he sits "like a coachman, clicking his tongue and cracking his whip" over two famished dogs:

> Go on and eat, Nyström; you don't know when you'll get your next meal! Stow it away, clerk; you look as if you could use some meat on your bones. Are you making faces at the oysters? Maybe they're not good enough for a fellow like you—eh? Take another piece! Help yourself! Can't manage it? What kind of nonsense is that? There you are! Now for some beer, boys! Go on—drink! Have some more salmon! Dammit, you'll have another piece of salmon! Eat—dammit! It won't cost you any more![58]

These snatches from Falk's table conversation render the frenetic excitement during the meal better than any description.

Six months after publication, Strindberg recommended that Edvard Brandes examine closely the scene at Carl Nicolaus Falk's party because "so much fine detail work" had been executed there.[59] The fair copy of the manuscript shows that there had been much altering, eliminating, and adding. Here dialogue is used indirectly to show how the mood changes from wrangling to sentimentality:

> Falk talked about his wife, how good he was to her; he talked about how uninspiring his work was, how deeply he felt the lack of education, how misspent his life was. And when he had drunk his tenth liqueur, he confided to Levin that he had really wanted to devote himself to the clerical profession—even become a missionary. They became more and more spiritual. Levin talked about his dead mother, about her death and funeral, about an unhappy love affair, and finally about his religious view, "which one didn't talk about to just anyone." Now they were into religion.

The setting changes at the same time:

> The office lay in a dimness of tobacco smoke that obscured the glow of the gas-light. The seven candles in the candelabrum had burned down,

and the table had a melancholy appearance. Here and there a glass had lost its foot, cigar ashes were scattered on the soiled tablecloth, matches lay strewn about on the floor. Through the hole in the window shutter daylight now squeezed in and broke into long beams through the cloud of tobacco, creating a cabalistic figure on the tablecloth between the two champions of the faith, who were earnestly engaged in revising the Augsberg Confession.[60]

After the guests leave, Stockholm's presence is felt as Falk opens the shutters and a fresh breeze streams in from Skepps Bridge through narrow Ferkens Alley, whose solitary row of houses is illuminated by the rising sun.

When in the latter part of the novel Strindberg portrayed another party scene—the reception at Norrbacka after the funeral for Struve's child—he resorted to a cruder, harsher style not very different from the one he would cultivate in his later novels. In so doing, he achieved a formidable intensity in the description of drunkenness, but we perceive less of the mental state of the people involved than in the earlier scene, and the various images follow one another in an unmodulated and violent way. The reader's impression is not that of being admitted into a crowd of hard drinkers, but of having been thrown into a cage of wild animals.

The Stockholm Landscape

Strindberg was also Dickens's pupil in his handling of nature. In the opening description of the beautiful May evening on Moses Heights every natural phenomenon is personified: first, the garden at the inn where the snowdrops "worked their way up through last year's layer of leaves," lilacs were waiting for a south wind before blooming, and the unbroken buds of the linden trees offered a screen for the love-making of the chaffinches. The sparrows hunt for nesting materials:

They tugged around fragments of rocket shells from last autumn's fireworks display; they plucked off the straw covers from the young trees that had been transplanted the year before from the nursery at Rosendal—and they didn't miss a thing! They found pieces of barège in summer arbors, and from between the splinters on the leg of a chair were able to pull away hairs from dogs who had not fought there since the previous summer.[61] What a life and what strife![62]

Lindblad pointed out that Strindberg learned from Dickens how to group together different sense impressions and with magnificent narrative art merge them into a picture. But Strindberg was also building on a century-long Swedish tradition. Not since the great balladeer Carl Michael Bellman

(1740-95) had Stockholm a portrayer with such feeling for picturesque disorder—idyllic animal life among the rags, broken glassware and pottery, and gutter mud. And Strindberg's description of the east wind's passage through the harbor channel is similar to a description of the wind's journey into Stockholm in Carl Fredrik Dahlgren's *Mollberg's Epistles (Mollbergsepistlar—1819-20)*.[63]

The vivid descriptions of Stockholm were the one element in *The Red Room* that won unanimous approval from contemporary critics. And today, when so much of the novel's social satire has lost its immediacy, the images of the city are a central factor in the book's continuing appeal.

Partly for the sake of discretion and partly because he wanted to refer to certain features of the Stockholm landscape that had disappeared during the large-scale renovation and modernization of the city in the 1870's, Strindberg suggests that the action of the novel takes place in 1868-69, a decade before the book was published. Although he approved of the modernization, at least in theory,[64] his heart clung to the old. Nostalgia colors the scene in which Arvid Falk strolls through the orchards and fields of the Humlegården district (now the heart of the city). Cows belonging to the Commanding General of Ordnance still graze, the carousel and rotunda are still standing, and truant schoolboys sit under the old apple trees playing a game of "buttons." Arvid feels like a boy himself and begins to throw stones in the duck pond. Actually, all this idyllic charm had disappeared in 1877, two years before *The Red Room* was published, when the old buildings were torn down and Humlegården became the dull city park with broad sand walks that it is today. Arvid could walk northward "over the large tobacco field" and behold another idyllic spot already doomed: the gate to Lill-Jans Woods, with three cottages nearby nestled among blooming lilacs and apple trees.

The feeling of a bygone Stockholm also slips into the satirical sections. One of the places visited by Pastor Skåre's charitable society is a dilapidated shanty in the Vita bergen section of Stockholm, the kind of dwelling that August Blanche never tired of describing: "an old one-story wooden house that had scrambled up a hill and now looked as if it had joint disease."[65] And when the Red Room coterie pays a visit to a prostitute after Sellén's big party, Strindberg locates her residence near Ladugårds Field in a building that formerly was supposed to have been an executioner's house. Set in the wall over the door of this stone structure are two grinning sandstone heads flanking a sword and broadaxe. In *The Author* (*Författaren*), the fourth section of his autobiography, Strindberg reported that in truth he had never seen the Vita bergen district and scarcely knew where it was. The model for this strange building, whose ornamented façade seems somewhat inappropriate for its fictional tenant, was apparently an old gabled house on Skeppar Street actually called the Executioner's Residence, which was torn down in 1908.[66]

Until May, 1936, one could still identify Carl Nicolaus Falk's linen-goods business at 18 Österlång Street, just opposite Ferkins Alley. Although the business had long since closed, the sign over the store had not been repainted: "M. Nordman, Sailmaker, Flag Manufacturing, Cordage Merchandise." This was the last remnant of the shop where each morning Falk's assistant used to hang out "a tuft of flax, a fish trap, an eel basket, a bundle of fishing rods, and a fishgarth filled with unstripped quills."[67]

Strindberg said[68] that while writing *Old Stockholm* he was so absorbed with childhood memories that he depicted as antiques things that during proofreading had to be rejected as entirely too modern. In *The Red Room* this same affinity for the period in which he grew up gave much of his portrait of Stockholm an atmosphere that was a bit too old. Carl Nicolaus Falk's old-fashioned linen-goods business and his similarly old-fashioned money-lending activities are not consistent with his up-to-date stock-exchange maneuvers and bogus companies. Strindberg had never ceased to live imaginatively in the Stockholm of his youth. This is noticeable in the first chapter, as Arvid Falk stands looking down on the city's center from a hill in the south, his eyes blazing, his clenched fist raised against the city below him as if at an enemy. Although the opening lines suggest a big city, what Strindberg remembers are the sights and sounds of his childhood:

> Far below him the burgeoning town clamored: steam winches whirled down on the Stadsgård piers, the open ironwork gates rattled in the iron weighing machine, the sluice-keepers' whistles shrilled, steam boats near Skepps Bridge steamed, Kungsback omnibusses bumped clatteringly along on the uneven cobblestones; noise and yelling came from the fish market, and sails and flags flapped out in the channel; there were screams of seagulls, bugle signals from Skepps Island, shouted rifle commands from Södermalms Square, the clattering of the wooden shoes of laborers on Glasbruks Street—everything contributed to an impression of life and bustle.[69]

When the city's church bells rang at seven o'clock, Arvid's mood suddenly changed, and as he listened to the peaceful evensong of Klara Church,

> his features softened, and his face expressed the pain a child feels when he finds himself deserted and alone. And he was alone, for his father and mother were lying [across the harbor] in Klara churchyard, from whence the bell could still be heard. And he was a child, for he still believed in everything, in truth and fairy tales alike.[70]

Throughout the novel sensory images from the author's childhood in Stockholm have a strange softening effect on the harsh satire. Even during the hero's worst crisis in the office of the *Worker's Banner* on Kindstu Street, the dark shadow of pessimism cannot quite prevail over the Stockholm landscape. The sun blazes into the room, and as Arvid Falk opens the window he is assaulted "by stunning fumes from the gutter" and a terrible din: "The tinsmith below him began to hammer tinplate so that the house and windowpanes trembled; a couple of laborers went by pushing a rumbling, stinking cart, and from the bar across the street poured the smells of schnapps, beer, sawdust, and pine branches."[71] Strindberg would become famous for his masterly evocation of sombre moods, but in this scene, in spite of everything, an idyllic Stockholm emerges—open-hearted, dirty, and noisy. Toward noontime the bells of the German church begin to play "O Blessed Land" ("Här är gudagott att vara") and "My Life Is a Wave" ("Mitt liv är en våg"), and an Italian street organ near Brända Tomten Square, as if possessed by the same idea, begins to crank out "The Blue Danube" with an obbligato flute-like voice. At this point the tinsmith, exhilarated by all the music, turns to his tin plate with redoubled zeal. It is clear that Strindberg relished the vulgar clamor. In a memorable passage in his autobiography, he recounts a journey to Gothenburg where he despaired to find that city "gloomy, priggish, expensive, conceited, reserved" in contrast with "Stockholm's rich and smiling character."[72]

"Stockholm and its environs are a part of the skerries," Strindberg says in the preface to *Men of the Skerries,* and the Stockholm of *The Red Room* is inconceivable without the fresh ocean breeze blowing in from the skerries in the east. It is no coincidence that Strindberg opened the novel by describing the wind's westward journey—through Vaxholm, past Sjötullen, in back of Hästholmen, and onward to the south shore with its smell of coal, tar, and whale oil. Carl Nicolaus Falk's linen-goods business on Österlång Street is situated "so nearly opposite Ferkens Alley that the clerk, when he looked up from his novel—which he was surreptitiously reading under the counter—could see part of a steamer, perhaps the wheelhouse or a jib-boom, and a treetop on Skepps Island plus a bit of the sky above it."[73] When Arvid Falk leans out the window of the dirty office at the *Worker's Banner,* he sees "in the far distance a part of a steamer, several waves in Lake Mälar glistening in the sunlight, and a ravine in Skinnarvik Hill just beginning to turn green in crevices here and there."[74] In its published form, the action in the novel ends when Doctor Borg finds Arvid Falk in a bar where he is drinking with several writer friends and takes him to a naval supply store where Borg buys him a pair of canvas shoes. From there Arvid is led to Stadsgård Harbor where the cutter *Uria* is waiting to sail out to the skerries, and the chapter ends with Borg shouting: "Now strike out for summer fun on Nämndö. All aboard! No arguments! - - - Ready? - - - Cast off!"[75]

In manuscript form the novel had a final chapter, later eliminated, where we encounter Arvid Falk as a newly married man. He is living in the ugliest alley in Stockholm and in the alley's gloomiest and dirtiest building, "an old dowager house of poverty, sloth, neglect, and vice." Yet through the window overlooking the yard, one can see above the little garden "the sky and the mastheads of the timber barges in Nybro Harbor."[76] The closeness of the sea and the archipelago helps to brighten an otherwise gloomy scene.

Many of the elements in Strindberg's portraits of his native city can be traced to a traditional way of describing Stockholm that began with Carl Michael Bellman and continued with Fredrik Cederborgh (1784-1835), August Blanche (1811-68), and Elias Sehlstedt (1808-74). But Strindberg added something new to the tradition in *The Red Room.* The critic and poet Oscar Levertin pointed this out in "Stockholm's Scenery in Swedish Literature" ("Stockholmsnaturen i svensk dikt") when he wrote:

> One might think he learned his impressionistic brush technique from the painters who were among his friends during the early years of struggle and privation, were it not that this form of depiction and the thematic emphasis on the poverty and bohemian living conditions of big city life did not begin to appear in Swedish art until a decade later. In his genius, Strindberg anticipated an approaching trend.[77]

The qualifying note in Levertin's statement seems to have escaped the attention of later scholars who casually assumed that *The Red Room* is indebted to impressionistic plein-air painting. The water colors of Strindberg's long-time friend Carl Larsson (1853-1919), for example, have often been cited as sources, without a proper understanding of the contemporary situation in Swedish art and of Strindberg's own attitude toward it.

Strindberg made abundantly clear in articles on art written in the late 1870's[78] that he did not appreciate French impressionism and found no validity in the emphasis on plein-air technique. A painting was to be looked at indoors, and so its color values became untrue if it were painted outdoors.[79] He deplored the fact that his artist friend Per Ekström (Sellén in the novel) lost his Nordic originality and his color sense when he went to Paris: "He now painted like all the others: anemic, colorless, purplish, like the *impressionists!*"[80] He also disapproved of the first paintings Carl Larsson sent back from Paris, asking: "Is there really so much for him to learn in Paris that could not be acquired at home? Certainly not!"[81] The masterpieces of French impressionism only annoyed him; they were "like photographs in which the subject did not sit still, or photographs of trees during a storm."[82]

Strindberg always painted his seascapes at home in his room. Scholars who try to demonstrate the influence of plein-air technique in *The Red Room* usually cite the scene where Sellén stands in front of his easel in Lill-Jans Woods. But it is not at all certain that Sellén is painting the scenery before him; we know only that he has moved his easel outdoors into the spring warmth. He is probably painting the same subject he later completes inside the shack. This finished painting, the one that brings Sellén his great success at the exhibition, represents an entirely different scene from the one he had before him at Lill-Jans: "The subject was simple and grand. A stretch of shifting sand on the coast of [the Swedish province of] Halland with the sea in the background. . . . And it was painted with inspiration and talent; the mood produced the color and not vice versa."[83] According to Strindberg, the older school of painting, which he praised and copied in his own paintings, had sought "truth in color," in contrast with the "inexplicably luminous, colorless manner of the impressionists."[84]

One might describe Strindberg's literary landscapes as impres-

sionistic, but there was no connection between them and the French school
of painting. He was "impressionistic" in the same way that the earlier
Stockholm portrayers were, by reason of the freshness and immediacy
with which he rendered his impressions. He had abandoned the rather
forced suggestion of palette colors of the Sandhamn letters, but he had
retained his practice of viewing the landscape with the eyes of an artist and
then hastily sketching its contours. Göran Lindblad has sought to detect
signs of impressionistic water-color technique in the little view of Skepps
Bridge and Skepps Island seen through Ferkens Alley from Falk's linen-
goods shop.[85] The similarity to impressionism in choice of subject matter
is undeniable, although probably coincidental; moreover, Strindberg did
not indicate a single color in the image. What he used fundamentally was
Dickens's narrative technique but with a more modern tendency toward
sketchiness.

Lindblad also finds "Impressionism, literary plein-air painting"
in the author's "portrait of Lill-Jans Woods [that was] captured entirely at
the easel." Strindberg would surely have protested; he would have declared that it was composed at his desk and had nothing at all to do with
the pointless, luminous, plein-air paintings of the French. Furthermore,
the Lill-Jans Woods scene is more than a little reminiscent of Carl Michael Bellman's classic description of disorder and chaos in Mummen's
half-dilapidated inn garden[86] and deserves to be quoted:

> Here was a perfect idyll. A rooster, perched on the shafts of a whisky
> barrel, was crowing; a watchdog lay shooing flies in the heat of the sun;
> and bees hung like a cloud about the hives. The gardener was kneeling
> near the hotbeds, weeding the radishes. Willow warblers and redstarts
> were singing in the gooseberry bushes; and half-dressed children chased
> chickens who were trying to investigate the fertility of diverse newly-
> sown flower seeds. Overhead was an all-blue sky and behind, the black
> woods.[87]

Lindblad has attached special importance to the painterly description
of bees hanging "like a cloud" around the hives. One might add that it was
typical of Strindberg's sense of tonality to make the woods black, not
green. But here, as elsewhere, Strindberg combined these "impressionistic" touches with his technique of constructing pictures of nature out of
small details, of transforming description into narrative, and of personify-
ing all events. Dickens and Hans Christian Andersen used the same
approach, but it is also part of an old Swedish tradition of nature portrayal
and probably originated in animal legends and fables. Like many of his

predecessors, Strindberg, for purposes of humor, had animals and plants and sometimes inanimate objects perform complicated actions. Here, chickens investigate the fertility of newly sown seeds, and in Humlegården the old bald apple trees try to sprout buds.

Strindberg is also able to make these nature scenes, constructed from a painter's viewpoint, come alive by introducing an animate presence. When the Red Room group leaves the prostitute's room in the Executioner's House, Strindberg's painter's eye lingers over the color effect of her hair as she waves farewell from her window to the company down in the alley:

> Magdalena was leaning out of the open window. The sun shone on her white face, and her long black hair, tinted dark red by the sun, trickled down past her throat and seemed to hurtle down in several rivulets into the street. Over her head hung the sword and broadaxe and the two grinning faces. And in an apple tree on the other side of the alley perched a black and white flycatcher, singing the melancholy stanza intended to express his joy that the night was over.[88]

These last lines about the flycatcher round off beautifully a scene whose color brilliance is in sharp contrast with the wretchedness of the subject.

Strindberg described his artist comrades of the Red Room as mood painters in the style of Corot and Théodore Rousseau. He maintained that the setting for his own seascape paintings was never ordinary daylight, always sunset or moonlight. Something of the same preference for mood painting distinguishes his descriptions of Stockholm in *The Red Room*. The most beautiful example is the often-cited section of the first chapter where Arvid Falk, after having quit his government job and talked with Struve on Moses Heights, ends up alone on a bench on the quay of Skepps Island:

> He felt like a bird who had flown against a windowpane and now lay defeated, just when he thought he could lift his wings and fly straight into the open. He sat down on a bench near the shore and listened to the lapping of the waves; a light breeze whispered through the flowering maple trees, and the half moon shone faintly on the dark water. There were twenty or thirty boats moored to the quay, and they tore at their chains and popped up their heads, one after the other, for just an instant, and then dove down. Wind and wave seemed to chase them onward, and they made runs toward the bridge like a pack of excited hounds, but the chains jerked them back, whereupon they bumped and pitched as if they wanted to break loose.[89]

Levertin tried to see an expression of revolutionary pathos in this passage: "The tender notturno of the Stockholm night is transformed into a turbulent cadence suggesting the rumble of the advancing working masses." Surely this is to read something alien to Strindberg's intention. The underlying meaning is indicated in the opening words; after his first attempt to liberate himself from a bureaucratic society, Arvid feels like a bird who has broken his wings and now lies beaten. He finds something of the same futile striving for freedom in the moored boats that try vainly to tear their leashes and put to sea. Arvid Falk's ultimate capitulation is foreshadowed at the close of the scene. At midnight the wind falls asleep, the waves go to rest, and the fettered boats tire of tearing at their chains.

In the beautiful autumnal picture of Katarina churchyard, the mood of nature is even more obviously linked with the feelings of the observer:

> The September afternoon lay gray and warm and still over the capital as Falk climbed the hills in the south. At Katarina churchyard he sat down to rest. He felt a curious sense of satisfaction when he saw how the maples had frozen red during the last few nights, for he welcomed the coming of autumn with its darkness, its gray clouds, and its falling leaves. Not a breath was stirring; it was as if nature were resting, tired after the work of the short summer. Everything was at rest. The people lay under their plots of earth, more quiet and well behaved than they had ever been in life, and he wished they were all there with him.[90]

One cannot help being struck by the similarity to Carl Michael Bellman, who also loved to see Katarina churchyard in autumnal dress and, like Arvid Falk, linked autumnal decay with his own sense of mortality. But of course there is a vast distance between Bellman's tranquil elegiac tone and Strindberg's dark pessimism.

Lindblad, who attached special importance to this last passage, indicates[91] how ironically Strindberg treated his own habit of harmonizing his moods with those of nature. In the beginning of the chapter "Settlers in Lill-Jans" ("Nybyggarna på Lill-Jans"), Arvid Falk, disgusted with both his brother and himself, wanders through the streets in the brilliant May sunshine, but "he wished it were overcast and he were in base company."[92] The longing for base company may not seem as natural as the hostility toward beautiful weather and sunshine that anyone might feel when depressed or annoyed, but Strindberg had a constant and unmistakable tendency to enjoy the times he was dispirited and wanted his surroundings to be as dismal as he felt. The above description of autumn is a good example of this. In another passage at the end of the novel, a place intensifies Arvid Falk's mood of uneasiness in the same way nature

did earlier. He has been dragged away by a couple of shabby newspaper-
men to the "Star" restaurant on Österlång Street:

> He felt a strange sense of pleasure from the odor of the cooking and the
> buzzing of the flies and the smell of the half-rotten bouquet of flowers
> standing next to the filthy cruet stand. His base companions too—with
> their slovenly linen, their stained coats, and their unkempt, jailbird
> appearances—were in such harmony with his own degraded condition
> that he experienced a wild joy.[93]

Arvid Falk had found the base company he wished for during his beautiful
spring promenade to Lill-Jans Woods.

Scenes of poverty and big-city bohemianism—which Levertin
maintained anticipated the choice of similar subject matter by graphic
artists—are not many in number; on the whole, Strindberg preferred to
picture the more picturesque side of life in Stockholm. But the few scenes
that are included are powerful. Perhaps the most striking one is the
description of the house in the Vita bergen district, the first part of which
has already been cited:

> At the base of the house grew dandelions, nettles, and knotgrass, all of
> them man's faithful companions in adversity; and sparrows were bathing
> in the scorching dirt that sprayed about them. Urchins with swollen
> bellies and pale faces, who looked as though they subsisted on ninety-
> percent water, were tying dandelion necklaces and bracelets, and other-
> wise trying to embitter their miserable lives by molesting and abusing
> each other.[94]

It is particularly effective to describe first the sparrows bathing in the
scorching dirt and then to turn—without drawing a direct parallel—to
the urchins. Strindberg's most successful evocation of the proletarian milieu was through nature description. Later in the novel, when he tried to
portray the diverse, squabbling, destitute families directly, the impression
is not as forceful, and when the charity society ladies led by Mrs. Carl
Nicolaus Falk enter the scene, everything lapses into tendentiousness.

With a few masterful strokes the graveyard of the poor in Nya
Cemetery is sketched: "a gray and somber sky hung over the huge, desolate sand field, where white sticks stood like the phantoms of small children who had gone astray. The edge of the woods was outlined in black
like a background for a shadow play, and not a breath of wind moved."[95]
This association between the small, white pieces of wood and the strayed
phantoms of small children is splendidly appropriate for the shabby funeral of Struve's child, which must be conducted without a minister because

the child died unbaptized—a funeral that later, at the reception, turns into a wild drinking orgy.

The great strength of Strindberg's descriptions of Stockholm in *The Red Room* is their turning, almost imperceptibly, into images of humanity, images of life. Strindberg would later add more colors to his palette and be able to render the city not only through magnificent panoramas but through visionary, dream-like moods as well. Never in his later works, however, would Stockholm's atmosphere steal in as exquisitely as in *The Red Room*. It is the unifying element in the novel's varied action, and a continuous accompaniment to the characters' thoughts and feelings, which at this time Strindberg could more easily depict through parallels in the surrounding city landscape than through direct analysis.

Style

In a chapter numbered twenty-three that was excluded at publication, the editor of *The Gray Coat* speaks disparagingly of Arvid Falk's newly published collection of poems. He reads aloud several titles, quotes several lines of verse, and exclaims: "It is unpoetic because it is false; truth is poetry's most beautiful jewel."[96] *The Red Room* demonstrates that Strindberg himself had some difficulty with poetic imagery that rang false, especially when he tried to evoke pathos. An example is the notorious passage, written in August Blanche's worst flowery style, in which Mrs. Carl Nicolaus Falk sees an anticipated triumph, during one of the meetings of the Bethlehem Day Nursery Charity, turn into defeat:

> Alone in the large rooms, she burst into violent sobbing. But these were not the tears that fall like a May rain on an old, dust-covered heart; these were the venoms of wrath and evil that now obscured the mirrors of the soul and later dripped down like corrosive acid on the roses of health and youth.[97]

Then there is the scene in which Arvid Falk attends the stockholders' meeting of The Triton Marine Insurance Society. When he inspects the gathering with eager and defiant glances, his eye encounters another eye some distance away against the wall, "and that eye—which so resembled a pair now lifeless, but which once looked upon him with love—was green with malice and pierced him like a needle. It made him want to weep with sorrow to think that a brother could look that way at a brother."[98] The reader needs a moment of reflection to understand that Arvid Falk, seeing his brother's eyes, is reminded of his mother. Such farfetched images tumble off Strindberg's pen at unguarded moments even in the best chapter in the book. When Carl Nicolaus Falk throws open the window shutters after his party with Levin and Nyström, Strindberg makes the following sentimental disgression: "The clock chimed four—that little wonderful time of chiming, usually heard only by the poor wretch longing for morning, tossing sleeplessly because of trouble or sickness."[99]

These occasional faults are perhaps due to the fact that Strindberg no longer strove for the light elegance that was his ideal during the writing of *Town and Gown*. He was now attempting to make his style expressive and rich in imagery, and the inner bond with Dickens's exaggerated manner asserted itself quite often. Of the famished Ygberg we learn: "He was pale and cold like a corpse, cold and resigned like a corpse that had given up hope of resurrection."[100] And Struve's battered top hat is said to have "genuflected of its own weight and seemed to mourn its lost youth, for it bore mourning crepe." [101] This reflects the same desire to personify inanimate objects that appears in Strindberg's depictions of nature and interiors, and he filled the entire novel with similar metaphors and similes—they positively crowd each other. A copy of the newspaper *The Gray Coat* foams over with rage and barely catches its breath before receiving a new blow: "Now the wind struck *The Gray Coat,* and it flapped like a rag on a stake."[102]

The style is a conscious exaggeration of reality. People "hurl shells" or "pointed bullets" with their glances; they "fire off" rejoinders, and even in rather calm moods they "snort" and "grunt." Carl Nicolaus Falk's squeaky shoes "scream" under his weight. And when Arvid Falk enters the press box in Parliament, "there was not much for his eyes to *rest upon* as they *groped* about the empty walls, but they finally *perched* on the old wall clock."[103]

Throughout the book Strindberg tried to replace threadbare expressions with new and original ones; in his autobiography he emphasized that the real-life Red Room circle created an entirely new language which demanded "brutal candor in speech and thoughts" and rejected "empty phrases and borrowed expressions." Occasionally, this caused the style in *The Red Room* to become much too elliptic and strained, but these efforts are more obvious here than in Strindberg's later prose where fundamentally the same stylistic technique was practiced.

Sometimes one finds critics asserting the mistaken notion that

Strindberg's style was free of periodic sentences; perhaps because he so often ridiculed the prolix "chancery" style of language.[104] But the practice of alternating between a spontaneous colloquial style—with short, choppy, often coordinate clauses—and a fuller, periodic style remained a characteristic of his.[105] Even in dialogue, where Strindberg was more obviously colloquial, he was liable to swell out in long periodic sentences, especially when a character happened to be his spokesman. But he was also capable of recognizing when he had exceeded the probabilities of spoken language. In the expunged twenty-third chapter, Strindberg had Doctor Borg fire off a diatribe against the insipid verse written in the "Signature" period;[106] afterward, "Borg was red in the face from the strain and refreshed himself with a cognac."[107] When the same tirade was inserted into the final printed version, it had been wisely changed into a newspaper article that is read aloud from the proofs.

Strindberg's contemporaries appreciated the liveliness and ready wit of his prose, but they found it "coarse" and were irritated by the casual syntax and colloquialness. No one seemed to have noticed its lyrical quality and passionate vibrato, although these are the qualities that give the style of *The Red Room* its mark of distinction. There are many Strindberg works with a better balanced prose style but scarcely another with a style so intensely personal. The obvious shortcomings in the novel—the awkward, rambling composition, the tendency of the characters to merge with one another in the reader's mind, the ill-prepared mixture of romantically conceived bohemianism and ruthlessly photographed realism—are in some measure forgivable when we recognize that it is Strindberg's own voice we constantly hear: in the dialogue, the satirical sallies, and the cynical observations, as well as in the tender twilight dreams. The voice does not yet have the orchestral breadth and subtlety of nuance it would later possess, but it has a tremolo of wounded young idealism that it would never again recover. One can understand how Alexander Kielland could feel grateful for the "bracing twinge of pain" he experienced when reading *The Red Room*.

Notes to Chapter Five

1. The third part of his autobiography, *In the Red Room,* can be read as a running commentary on the novel.
2. *SS:*XIX, p. 117.
3. *Ibid.,* p. 107.
4. An account of Strindberg's journalistic activities by a fellow worker, Klas Ryberg, can be found in the Kalmar newspaper *Barometern,* December 13 and 18, 1897. *See also* Torsten Eklund, "Strindbergs verksamhet som publicist 1869-80," in *Samlaren* (1930).
5. *SS:*XIX, p. 114.
6. *Ibid.,* p. 108.
7. *Ibid.,* p. 116.
8. The coterie, whom Strindberg came to know through his sculptor friend Alfred Nyström, at that time ate together at the place described in the beginning of the novel as "The Sauce Pan" ("Grytan"), a little inn on Grytgjutar Street where one could dine on credit.
9. One of the members of the coterie, Martin Nyström (Ygberg in the novel), has given valuable and evidently quite accurate information about the origin and development of the group in his diary accounts. I am obliged to Fru Gerda Nyström who gave me portions of them. Also apparently reliable are Per Ekström's (Sellén) statements in an interview with Herman Seldener in the newspaper *Nya Dagligt Allehanda* (August 9, 13, and 20, 1922), insofar as they are confined to the Red Room coterie. His statements concerning the factual bases for other events in the novel cannot be verified.
10. *SS:*XIX, p. 165.
11. Sten Linder, *Ibsen, Strindberg och andra* (1936), p. 39.
12. One observes too that in both the play and the novel Strindberg created a special embodiment of his own dream of being an actor. As in the play, the character is divided. In the novel Rehnhjelm in "X-Town" is the counterpart of Arvid Falk in Stockholm: Rehnhjelm has a cynical mentor (Falander), just as Arvid Falk has his (Borg), and Rehnhjelm's unfaithful lover, the cunning actress who calls herself Agnes Rundgren, is the same person adored by Arvid Falk—the waitress, Beda Pettersson. Strindberg undoubtedly retained this unusual doubling effect, as Fredrik Böök

has pointed out, because he wanted to avoid damaging his own
and his wife's prospects at the Royal Dramatic Theatre. And so
the setting for the satire on the world of the theatre was shifted
from Stockholm to the provinces. *See* Böök, "Teatern i Röda
rummet" in *Från åttiotalet* (1926). Henry Villgrund, in an article
in the newspaper *Svenska Dagbladet,* September 8, 1934, quarrels
with Böök's interpretation, and makes valuable observations about
the similarity in details between Rehnhjelm's theatrical experiences
in X-Town and Strindberg's in Gothenburg. But he seems not to
have noticed that the satirical handling of the theatre manager
(in the manuscript, the director) was aimed at the manager of the
Royal Dramatic Theatre, Frans Hedberg, whose dramas are mercilessly caricatured.

13. *SS:*XIX, p. 160.
14. *Ibid..* pp. 68 f.
15. *Ibid.,* p. 163.
16. *Brev,* II, p. 72.
17. *SS:*LIII, p. 73.
18. *Brev,* II, p. 90.
19. *Dagens Nyheter,* January 2, 1877.
20. *Samlaren* (1930), p. 169.
21. *SS:*XIX, p. 109.
22. *See Brev.,* II, p. 166; Georg and Edvard Brandes, *Brevveksling med
    nordiske Forfattere og Videnskabsmaend* (1939-42), I, p. 6; and
    Eklund, *Samlaren* (1930).
23. *SS:*XIX, p. 165.
24. Gustav Emanuel Beskow (1834-99) was a popular Pietist preacher.
    Almost a decade later, in *The Son of a Servant,* Strindberg said,
    "Beskow made Pietism aristocratic and fashionable . . . Pietism
    was then what spiritualism is now: a five and dime philosophy."
    —Translator
25. *Brev,* I, p. 203. The same idea was suggested in an earlier letter
    (Ibid., p. 168).
26. *SS:*XIX, p. 48.
27. In a private collection. See my *Strindbergs dramer,* I (1924), p. 143.
28. In his article, "On the Freedom of Science," in *Essays,* a book which
    was in Strindberg's library.
29. The expression can probably be explained by Hartmann's zealous
    opposition to Darwinism. Subsequently, however, Strindberg con-
    curred with Hartmann.

30.   An enlightening essay about Hartmann's pessimism and its signi-
      ficance for Swedish literature can be found in Axel Herrlin, *Från
      sekelslutets Lund* (1936).

31.   *SS:*V, p. 362.

32.   *Ibid.,* p. 265.

33.   *Ibid.,* pp. 235 f.

34.   *Ibid.,* p. 236.

35.   This is why it is rather futile to speculate—as numerous scholars have
      done—about the transference of ideas among the characters. Linder,
      for example, presumes that Struve acquired the foundations for
      his nihilistic philosophy from Doctor Borg, but Strindberg never
      indicates that such an exchange took place. It is true that young
      Rehnhjelm believes that it was through associating with Falander
      that Olle Montanus acquired his new philosophy, "which tears
      everything down and turns things upside down until they are
      topsy-turvy" *(SS:*V, p. 318). But Strindberg has clearly put this
      in only to prepare the reader to accept Olle Montanus—who
      hitherto was presented as an obdurate Boströmian—as the author
      of the notebook found on his body.
            The best analyses of the characters in *The Red Room* are
      found in two newspaper articles by Algot Werin, *Svenska Dag-
      bladet,* November 2 and 16, 1924, reprinted in *Svenskt 1800-tal*
      (Lund, 1948).

36.   *Brev,* IV, p. 22.

37.   *SS:*V, p. 309.

38.   *Ibid.,* p. 323.

39.   *Brev,* II, p. 165.

40.   *See* Chapter II, The Early Plays.

41.   In "Nihilism" Montanus declares his intention (p. 245) to read
      publicly an essay "on art and its high mission." But Strindberg
      changed his mind and had Montanus give his lecture "On Sweden."
      Actually, it is an art lecture directed against Lorentz Dietrichson
      (*see* Chapter II, The Early Plays), who had made Måns Jönsson,
      the model for the character of Olle Montanus, an object of vicious
      notoriety.

42.   Plato's *Republic* provoked similar remarks in "Observations of a
      Skeptic."

43.   *SS:*V, pp. 258-59.

44.   *SS:*XIX, p. 164.

45.   *See* Arne Lidén in *Samlaren* (1938).

46. Johan Jolin (1818-84) and Frans Hedberg (1828-1908) were two of the most popular Swedish playwrights of the day.—Translator

47. The Bethlehem Day Nursery in *The Red Room* has a counterpart in a nursery of the same name in *Le Nabab,* which is run according to the same methods. Both novels treat parliamentary humbug, high finance, and upper class philanthropy with the same biting satire, and Daudet, like Strindberg, resorted to the somewhat old-fashioned technique of reporting bits of action in the novel by means of letters and diary notations.

48. Lindblad, p. 119.

49. *SS:*XIX, p. 8.

50. In actuality, according to the interview with Per Ekström cited in note 9, above, they boarded at the Lill-Jans Woods shack with an old lady who provided good food; they never experienced anything like the difficult time described by Strindberg. As for the period he lived with Måns Jönsson in the photographer's studio, Ekström said: "It's true, it was pretty cold there sometimes; still, it was never so bad that we had to wrap ourselves up in old bits of paper and brushes, as Strindberg wrote."

51. Lindblad, p. 85.

52. *SS:*V, pp. 250-51.

53. *Ibid.,* p. 24.

54. *SS:*XVIII, p. 174.

55. *SS:*V, p. 181.

56. *Ibid.*

57. *Ibid.,* pp. 52-53.

58. *Ibid.,* pp. 59-60.

59. *Brev,* II, p. 166.

60. *SS:*V, p. 69.

61. Strindberg actually wrote: "since Josefina's [Name] Day," i.e., August 21.—Translator

62. *SS:*V, pp. 5-6.

63. *See* Greta Hedin, *Manhemsförbundet* (Akad. avh. Göteb.) (1927), p. 295.

64. His approval is evident in the poem "The Boulevard System."

65. *SS:*V, p. 220.

66. An article about this by Carl Magnusson appeared in the newspaper *Svenska Dagbladet,* July 30, 1940.

67. *SS:*V, p. 21. At the time *The Red Room* was being written the shop

was owned by N. P. Tull, a sailmaker; Nordman was then an employee.

68. *SS:*XIX, p. 173.
69. *SS:*V, p. 7. [In the original Swedish the harbor sounds have a unique clatter and rhythm, and Professor Lamm wonders "if it did not amuse Strindberg to emphasize the almost toy-like effect of this symphony of sound."—Translator]
70. *SS:*V, p. 8.
71. *Ibid.,* p. 325.
72. *SS:*XIX, p. 56.
73. *SS:*V, p. 21.
74. *Ibid.,* pp. 324-25.
75. *Ibid.,* p. 336.
76. *SS:*XXII, pp. 59-60. This is a description of the house in which *The Red Room* was written, located in what was called "The Long Row" (Långa raden) on the east side of Norrmalm Street (now Bibliotek Street).
77. *Svensk konst och svensk natur,* pp. 249-50.
78. Gotthard Johansson was the first to demonstrate this in an analysis unfortunately never published.
79. *SS:*IV, p. 154.
80. *Ibid.*
81. *Ibid.,* p. 190.
82. *Ibid.,* p. 149. In a letter in June, 1884, Carl Larsson took exception to Strindberg's conservatism regarding the art of painting, and particularly his condemnation of Manet in *This and That.* He wrote to Strindberg: "You find Zola and his confreres good and necessary, but paintings which say precisely the same things just as well—yes, even better . . . have no justification?" But Strindberg was implacable: "Zola and Manet. I do not honor Zola because he depicted les Halles, but because he said that man is both an animal and a natural deity! Manet's melon has not spoken any truth to the world—more likely a lie, since a melon does not look that way in nature" (*Brev,* IV, pp. 204, 106).
83. *SS:*V, p. 84.
84. *SS:*IV, p. 156.
85. Lindblad, p. 74.
86. Bellman, *Fredmans epistlar,* p. 214. [A recently published critical biography, Paul Britten Austin's *The Life and Songs of Carl Michael Bellman,* New York: American-Scandinavian Foundation,

1967, contains translations of a number of Bellman's songs and many interesting reproductions of paintings and drawings of Stockholm in the eighteenth century.—Translator]

87. *SS:*V, p. 33.
88. *Ibid.,* p. 157.
89. *Ibid.,* p. 20.
90. *Ibid.,* pp. 246-47.
91. Lindblad, p. 90.
92. *SS:*V, p. 31.
93. *Ibid.,* pp. 328-29.
94. *Ibid.,* p. 220.
95. *Ibid.,* p. 254.
96. *Ibid.,* p. 394. The criticism suggests the aesthetic program Strindberg later described in the poem "Singers." One should not be bewildered by the fact that the words are uttered by the same editor of *The Gray Coat* who earlier in the novel was characterized as a conservative and idealistic poet. Neither should one be surprised that Doctor Borg's tirade which follows—criticizing poets who write only dirges bemoaning their own misfortunes and who never give expression to controversial ideas of the day—is spoken in the published form of the novel by the drunken editor of the scandal sheet *Copper-Snake (Espingen).* Strindberg cared very little—especially in the latter part of *The Red Room*—about which character spoke his opinions. Lindblad has pointed out that both the titles and verse quotations from Arvid Falk's collection of poetry were taken from a newly published collection of poems, *Nya Dikter,* written by one of the poets of the "Signature" group (*See* Chapter II, The Early Plays), C. L. Östergren, whose pseudonym was "Fjalar."
97. *SS:*V, p. 180.
98. *Ibid.,* p. 164.
99. *Ibid.,* p. 70.
100. *Ibid.,* p. 46.
101. *Ibid.,* p. 234.
102. *Ibid.,* p. 143.
103. *Ibid.,* p. 112. Italics mine.
104. The Swedes retain even today a formal, sober, dignified written style, primarily for use in government reports and judicial decisions. Sometimes praised for its clarity and consistency, it is also criticized for being "extraordinarily heavy and un-Swedish." (Einar

Odhner, *Svenska* [1951], p. 81.—Translator
105. *See* Nils Svanberg, "Ur Strindbergs prosautveckling" in *Nysvenska studier 1935,* and Helge Gullberg, *Berättarkonst och stil i Per Hallströms prosa* (1939), especially pp. 157 ff.
106. *See* Chapter II, The Early Plays.
107. *SS:*V, p. 395.

Chapter Six

ROMANTICISM AND NATURALISM

The Historical Dramas of the 1880's

In the third section of his autobiography[1] Strindberg describes himself as in a transitional state between romanticism and naturalism "like the blindworm, which retains rudimentary lizard feet inside its skin," and declares this double nature to be "the key to his personality and to his writing." Although he did not formulate this self-evaluation until 1886, the uncomfortable feeling of being a "half-breed romantic" and of standing in the cross fire between two battling schools plagued Strindberg from the moment he published *The Red Room* in 1879.

The novel made him the most logical standard-bearer for the radical young writers known as Young Sweden, but he had a difficult time adapting himself to the role. In January, 1882, he complained in a letter that he had been pressed into being "the bandit captain of a school they call the realistic" and had become a realist "without having prepared myself for it." To the new generation he was "idealist, deist, traditional conservative," but he wanted to "daydream" and retain his "naive belief in God." He wanted the right to admire Fritz Reuter[2] as well as Zola: "But—do you think I am allowed to? No, they have to drag you out by the horn and incite you with a red flag to get you to come into the arena! I'll go, all right, when duty calls, but I don't want to be hounded out and bound hand and foot to a program; nevertheless, this is what is happening!"[3]

This letter was written when Strindberg had already agreed to formulate Young Sweden's program of realism for publication. But his reluctance to run with the herd was genuine. It was partially out of fear of being ignored that he assumed the leadership of Young Sweden, whose disapproval of prevailing social conditions he shared. In another letter we find a foreshadowing of his social criticism in the satirical story collection *The New Kingdom:* "I find society to be more than anything a clique; I do not see the best people leading the way; I find institutions that have no purpose other than busy-work, and wherever I see an institution, I see misfortune and the absence of freedom." This structure must be razed completely "and I have no qualms about using dynamite in politics."[4]

When the dynamite was detonated with the publication of *The New Kingdom* in 1882, Strindberg wrote that what he had feared a year earlier had become a reality: "Standing between two epochs at odds with each other, I shall be crushed to death."[5] The fundamental theme of his observations at this time was that he was by inner inclination a romantic, by social conscience a realist.

The conflict within Strindberg between romanticism and realism asserted itself first in the historical dramas he wrote after *Master Olof: The Secret of the Guild (Gillets hemlighet*—1880), *Lucky Per's Travels (Lycko-Pers resa*—1882), and *Herr Bengt's Wife (Herr Bengts hustru*—1882). Indeed, upon closer examination we discover that all three plays are debates upon this polarity. They are more romantic than *Master Olof,* yet contain modern realistic elements within their historical frames.

According to Strindberg, *The Secret of the Guild*—the first work he wrote after *The Red Room*—was regarded by Young Sweden as a defection.[6] This is understandable: it is a transparent glorification of romanticism. In the play—which concerns the building of a tower to complete Uppsala Cathedral in 1402—two men, Jacques and Sten, compete to be elected master builder of the guild in charge of the project. Through intrigues, Jacques, who is selfish, boastful, and unimaginative, gets himself elected to succeed to the post once held by his father Hans and swears falsely that he knows how the tower is to be completed; he knows the "secret of the guild," which everyone presumed was lost. Jacques gains possession of the guild's chest containing a parchment with a clue to the "secret," but he cannot decipher the writing, and the tower he builds for the cathedral collapses. Consequently, his competitor, the capable and unselfish Sten, who had been demoted from master to journeyman when his construction plan was rejected by Jacques, becomes master builder and interprets the secret:

You say that the secret is lost, and you, Jurgen, think the basic plan of the cathedral has been forgotten. Take out your parchment, Jacques, and examine it: you will see a cross on it. That's the secret. If you had been present when the foundation was laid, you would have seen how the original planners laid their stone cross in the earth: this is the basic plan of the Christian church. . . . Or shall I read the lines written by the unknown master builder on your parchment:

"You who build this church
do not depend on your own strength.
Build on the cross: This is Faith!"

Strindberg later explained in *Talks to the Swedish Nation* that the collapse of the vault symbolized the destructiveness of doubt and that the missing secret was the faith that had been lost.

And so, although Jacques won the post, the final triumph goes to the pious and romantic Sten. Strindberg stated in 1884 that the play was hostile both "toward the old 'Young Sweden,' which had trampled on our sensitivities and lived according to [outworn] beliefs, and toward the young 'Young Sweden,' which had lost its faith!"[7] By the "old 'Young Sweden'" he meant the Signature school, represented by Jacques who knows only the beliefs taught to him by his father.

In his portrayal of the rivalry between the two builders, Strindberg identified himself with Sten; Sten's construction plans were rejected, just as *Master Olof* had been turned down. The real-life parallel to the rivalry between Sten and Jacques was apparently a contest with the Signature poet Edvard Bäckström over who would be first to achieve recognition as an important playwright. Bäckström had won this victory. In March, 1877, a half-year after Strindberg's *Master Olof* was refused definitely by the Royal Dramatic Theatre, Bäckström's weak, derivative play *Dagward Frey* had a successful première and was heralded as the first masterpiece in modern Swedish drama. In an early draft of *The Secret of the Guild*[8] Sten is killed when the tower collapses and so is never able to put his proud building plans into effect. This was the fate that Strindberg himself expected, because he felt caught in a vise between two literary factions. Consequently, the optimism that stamps the present conclusion of the drama is somewhat forced.

The most interesting element in this disjointed play today is the concept of retribution, inspired by the theory of Nemesis as propounded by the great botanist Linnaeus;[9] later this theory would play an important role during Strindberg's Inferno period. In an essay written in 1887,

Strindberg wrote that Linnaeus believed that God "punishes the criminal, even if not until the children of the third or fourth generation." In the play, Jacques believes that his misfortunes are punishment for his father's transgressions: "I believe that crime grows in the blood, like sickness or blight, and that it can never be cured until it bursts out: I believe that one inherits these sensations as one inherits debts." He is convinced that his father's crime was so great "that it needed two men to atone for it."[10] The possibility of one person expiating the sins of others is the same concept that Strindberg would advance in the post-Inferno play *Easter (Påsk)*. We find the following in *The Secret of the Guild:* "It seems to our dim eyes that the suffering is more important than the identity of the sufferer."[11]

Strindberg's next drama, *Lucky Per's Travels,* appears to be more romantic than *The Secret of the Guild.* On Christmas Eve a fairy visits Per—a fifteen-year-old boy who had been locked up in a church tower by his Scrooge-like father—and gives him a wishing ring. The boy uses it to escape the tower to search for love and happiness. He finds, however, that there is hypocrisy everywhere and that the world often stones the reformers who discover and reveal this truth. He also learns that love, the one thing worth having, cannot be acquired simply by searching for it. Nevertheless, although life may be a desert, it is a desert "that has its flowers." In the end, when Per has learned to love someone other than himself, he is reunited with his beloved Lisa, whom he met, then lost while on his travels, and will henceforth devote himself to hard work instead of wishing.

The play's fairy-tale form reminds one of Hans Christian Andersen and Dickens's Christmas stories.[12] The third act, however, is a piece of realistic social satire that helps to shed light on *The New Kingdom.* In the town square a statue is to be unveiled to former Mayor Schultze, whose scheme it was to have the city's streets paved with cobblestones. Although the stones are rough and hard both on feet and vehicles, they are responsible for the prosperity of the local wagonmaker, chiropodist, and shoemaker, and so Mayor Schultze is a hero. "Idealistic songs" are sung "idealistically" in his honor. When Per suggests that the rough cobblestones be replaced by smooth, flat ones and dares to express everyone's real feelings about the late mayor,[13] he is put into a pillory. "People are dissatisfied," says Per, "but when you try to eliminate the cause of the dissatisfaction, they throw stones at you!"[14]

Per's éducation in the nature of hyprocrisy follows the same course as Master Olof's and Arvid Falk's. Reality deprives him of one ideal after another, and he is driven toward a bankrupt pessimism. But when he finds the primary fault in himself, he is reconciled with existence. This solution was Strindberg's first attempt to escape from his pessimism. In the last act, a bier that for fifty years has seen nothing but corpses complains that "life is so black!" But a nearby broom will not accept this gloomy view: "What are you doing prating about life, you old bier! You, who have seen only death! Life is black on one side and white on the other!"[15] In *The Red Room,* pessimism is the result of facing up to the harsh truth of reality rather than walking with one's head in the clouds. In contrast, *Lucky Per's Travels* proclaims that pessimism is a product of exalted expectations; it is a relic of a romanticism alien to the ways of the world. Happiness lies in unremitting labor, in affirming existence and not in seeing only its dark side.

Herr Bengt's Wife examines marriage from the same realistic point of view. Strindberg called the play "a farewell song to my romantic ideals."[16]

During the early Reformation in Sweden, Margit, a young aristocrat, enters a cloister but is unhappy there. When the Lutherans gain dominance, she is romantically rescued and married by Herr Bengt, a young lord with whom she had earlier been in love, but problems soon invade their happiness. Misunderstandings accumulate and the couple decide to separate, but in the end Margit and Bengt are reconciled, promising each other to temper the romanticism of their marriage with a more candid and realistic approach to life.

The play is also a farewell to historical drama, to which Strindberg would not return until the turn of the century. Properly speaking, however, *Herr Bengt's Wife* is really a contemporary drama just adequately reupholstered in historical fabric. It was completed in September, 1882, at the same time that Strindberg was planning *Swedish Destinies and Adventures,* in which he would transfer, in an unabashed way, his own experiences and modern social problems to the late Middle Ages and early Reformation. Anachronisms are more obvious in the dramatic work than in the short stories, and Bjørnson remarked in a letter to Strindberg that contemporary ideas put an excessive strain on the credibility of the medieval setting of the play. Actually, Strindberg had portrayed his own marital relationship while simultaneously contributing to the Doll's House debate.

Ibsen's *A Doll's House* had become a bone of contention in Strindberg's marriage, as well as in countless other Scandinavian homes,[17] but it is not certain how his wife felt about it. Their daughter, Karin Smirnoff, has written that at the time the first volume of *Married* appeared in late 1884, Siri detested *A Doll's House* just as much as Strindberg did, but Mrs. Smirnoff also presents evidence that her mother had earlier held another viewpoint.[18]

Strindberg's position on the issue is obvious in his chapter on women in the historical-essay collection *The Swedish People (Svenska folket)*, written at the same time as *Herr Bengt's Wife* (1881-82). There we find[19] that it was "the despotic and debauched eighteenth century that transformed woman into—a doll." Man, through his gallantry (a relic of "obscene" medieval chivalry, made woman into an angel and then later in the era into a "beautiful soul." By estranging her from reality, he estranged her from himself and, busy with his breadwinning, could not follow her soaring flight. The situation finally deteriorated to the point where men avoided marriage "for fear of the doll tyranny that awaited them."[20] Ultimately, a reaction sets in against this worship of woman, and man's unquestionable right to be woman's master is asserted.

Interestingly enough, this declaration, inspired either directly or indirectly by Rousseau, has Strindberg actually concurring with Ibsen's thesis that it was man who treated woman as a doll—a position he would later fervently repudiate. But he did not see the solution where Ibsen saw it—in woman's intellectual and legal equality with man; he saw it in her being trained morally to fulfill her duties as wife and mother.

In *Herr Bengt's Wife*, he tried to be more impartial than in the essay collection by dividing the blame, but his effort went unrecognized because the domestic situation in the play was so similar to his own. The class distinctions between husband and wife are strongly emphasized. The first act—the best in the play—depicts Margit as an innately proud and degenerate aristocrat who despises her low-born comrade in the cloister, Metta, and calls her a bondwoman because she had not been, like herself, "born twenty times of parents who never worked." Margit has an abnormal desire to be scourged and finds pleasure in looking at a picture of Christ being nailed to the Cross by a soldier with swelling arm muscles.

There are traits reminiscent of Madame Bovary and J. P. Jacobsen's
Marie Grubbe in Strindberg's portrait of this hysterical and highly strung
young woman. Margit is hurt by Bengt's vulgarity; he enjoys eating roast
veal, for example, but he shows no appreciation for the roses that decorate
the table. The gulf between them is widened when the day after their
wedding Herr Bengt incurs financial burdens that are suspiciously like
Strindberg's own. In order not to worry his wife, Herr Bengt keeps her
ignorant of his problems, and she continues her romantic dreamings. She
even hastens his downfall: on harvest day she sends all the manor's servants to fetch water for her rosebushes. She is distressed because her husband has dragged "dust from the cattle fields" into their home; a stormy
scene develops, and it is at this point that they decide to seek a divorce.

In Act Four we see that Margit has developed a better understanding than her husband of their situation and how to cope with it. She
has sold her jewelry and taken over the management of the household,
while Bengt can only stand bewildered in the face of misfortune. The roles
are reversed; now it is Bengt who represents romanticism. When he asks
Margit what she plans to do after the divorce is granted, and she answers:
"Work!—Serve!" his rejoinder is: "Serve!—Work! Can the butterfly—
whom God created a butterfly—work?"[21]

Margit's frustration at the end of Act Four is similar to Nora's at
the end of A Doll's House. She is disturbed that she had not been apprised
earlier of the family's problems. She criticizes Bengt for having loved her
as one of his possessions, for having treated her as though she were a hunting horse he did not want to hitch to a wagon. For his part, Bengt
reproaches himself for having hesitated to "lay his heavy thoughts on the
butterfly's wings"[22] and for having treated Margit as "a beautiful cageling
who was supposed to be beautiful and nothing more."[23]

Act Five, however, brings about Margit's and Herr Bengt's reconciliation. "I love you though I don't want to!" says Margit, and Bengt
replies: "Love is stronger than your will!"[24] At the final curtain there is
the suggestion that their marriage—reconstructed on a foundation of
resignation and realism—can still be romantic. "The eagle has to live, even
with a broken wing," says Bengt, "the bluebird has to live, even if her
color has faded." And Margit adds: "Let us teach our child that heaven is
up above, but we live on the earth."[25]

When Strindberg rewrote the play a year later as a short story in

Swedish Destinies and Adventures, the moral evolved as "love is a great power, surpassing all our understanding, and against which our will cannot prevail." In the preface to the first part of *Married,* Strindberg declared *Herr Bengt's Wife* to be "an apology for love as the natural force that survives all fads and subdues free will." But this understanding of love's irrational side—which would become the central element in Strindberg's campaign against the idealism of *A Doll's House*—was only half-assimilated at the time he wrote the play. In a letter on December 10, 1882, he explained that "the piece glorifies—but, alas, not with complete honesty—the victory of reality."[26] And a month later he acknowledged that as a realist he gave the heroine her due after she had learned life's responsibilities, "but as a romantic . . . I cry over the fact that a beautiful picture has been defaced."[27]

The statements in these letters are quite indicative of Strindberg's attitude at the time. Despite his realistic tendencies he still had a lingering affection for romanticism. His attempt to administer Solomonic justice in the debate over *A Doll's House* cannot conceal the fact that his position on the emancipation of women was still ambivalent.

These three historical dramas do not signify any artistic advance over the prose version of *Master Olof.* The historical color is weaker, and Strindberg bowed more to theatrical conventions. To a certain extent they were written to provide his wife with rewarding roles and to ensure his acceptance at the Royal Dramatic Theatre. *The Secret of the Guild,* particularly, is disfigured by a number of mawkish scenes. Quite obviously, Strindberg's primary interest at this time was narrative prose, not drama.

The New Kingdom

Young Sweden was eager for Strindberg to put forward a program of realism and launch a new attack on society. In January, 1882, the journalist and author Pehr Staaff (1856-1903) tried to incite him by relating how Lorentz Dietrichson[28] had attacked him as a naturalist: "I hope this will act like a spur on a racehorse as regards your article on idealism."[29] Not until the summer, however, was the article in question, "About Realism" ("Om realism"),[30] published in *Ur dagens krönika.*

The article was actually a reply to criticism about the brutal realism and the indiscreet depiction of easily recognizable individuals in *The Red Room.* For Strindberg, the characteristic thing about realism was the use of living models—actual personages; moreover, he asserts, this technique had been used by all the world's greatest writers. He also defends himself against accusations of sordidness and without mentioning him by name praises Zola who, although he "unequivocally detested meanness and wretchedness, was able to depict the humbug and corruption of the Second Empire. . . . If the description drips with filth, it is not the author's fault." But although Strindberg accepts on behalf of himself and his adherents the name naturalist as a title of honor, he is careful to divest the term of its programmatic literary import. To be a naturalist is to love nature, hate the new social conditions, the police and military state, and detest the artificial and contrived—this is Rousseau and Buckle. Strindberg's reluctance to commit himself to any one literary school is shown by the way the article ends, with a quote from the "renowned realist" the poet Esias Tegnér (1782-1846), who was actually both a Gothic and a romantic.

"About Realism" failed to satisfy the expectations of Young Sweden, as did the social criticism in the short stories in *The New Kingdom,* which appeared three months later. It was true that Strindberg's satire was brutal and candid, but no reader could fail to notice that Strindberg's primary concern was not literary or political criticism. He wanted to settle accounts with personal enemies and answer attacks made on an earlier work, *The Swedish People.* This two-volume collection of cultural-historical essays written in 1881 and 1882 consists of episodes from the lives of ordinary Swedish people from the ninth century to 1865. The very idea of such a work—a Swedish history that focused attention on the lives of commoners—was directly contrary to the prevailing theory, as articulated by the great conservative historian Erik Gustaf Geijer (1783-1847), that the history of the Swedish people was the history of its kings. It was little wonder that the essays met with widespread hostility. But the criticism struck Strindberg more deeply than any other literary setback. He had suffered a defeat in the area of scholarship—the very sphere to which he had withdrawn after the clamor over *The Red Room,* and where he had believed he was safe. "He felt as if his person were annihilated, his ego nullified, as if he were dead," he said in his autobiography.[31]

The day after the publication of the first installment of *The Swedish People* Strindberg wrote to Kielland: "I have knocked over an old idol (Geijer) and now the people want to stone me."[32] And there is little doubt that his attack on this respected poet and historian in the pre-publication announcement about the book occasioned the unusual severity of the critics' attacks. The same day the first installment appeared, the conservative newspaper *Aftonbladet* carried a long, stinging article, and from then on the work sailed constantly against the wind. Strindberg became increasingly exasperated as he saw that not even the liberal newspapers would come to his defense. He felt he was treated unjustly, because when he attacked Geijer's history as "primarily the story of the royal family, officers of the army, and civil servants," he had only been following Buckle's exhortation to historians to occupy themselves with "those subjects that alone determine man's fate, and abandon the petty details with which we have all too long been weary, details touching on the lives of kings, the intrigues of ministers, and the gossip of courtiers."[33]

Strindberg also feared that criticism of his scholarship would cut his career as assistant at the Royal Library. In a letter to a colleague at the library, Richard Bergström, in August, 1881, he wrote that he had heard a rumor that he was "regarded as canceled out"[34] of his position. He threatened not to spare the head librarian, Gustaf Klemming, in his next book if he were not able to obtain additional leave of absence to complete *The Swedish People*. The letter is characteristic of the agitated state of mind of the thirty-two-year-old author; he continued rather desperately to publish new installments, but as soon as each appeared, it was annihilated by the critics.

His conflict with "official" historical writing provoked in Strindberg a permanent hatred of all recognized scholarly and scientific authority; a hatred that found its final monument in the four-volume essay collection *A Blue Book* (1907-12). Opposition to tradition and authority was the point of departure for *The New Kingdom*, the central theme of which is the grotesque misuse of the name of "the Swedish people." Geijer is castigated at every opportunity, as is all Swedish writing on history and archaeology. The targets of next importance were all the people who had the effrontery to criticize *The Swedish People* or could be suspected in any way of having instigated the attacks. His belligerent mood prompted him to take out after all his other old enemies: those who had opposed *Master Olof* or criticized *The Red Room*. The Royal Dramatic Theatre, which had refused the play, was accorded a chapter; and the Swedish Academy, which had not awarded it a prize, another. Strindberg used the title

"Vengeance" ("Hämnden") for the chapter in his autobiography dealing with *The New Kingdom,* and he chose the right word. He exacted a cruel and merciless retribution for all the injustices he had suffered.

Oscar Wieselgren has brought to light Strindberg's associations with the scandal publications of the time and points out that Strindberg adopted their methods of character assassination.[35] This consisted of singling out people indirectly but so unmistakably that virtually every contemporary Stockholmer knew the identity of the party in question, of tossing off censorious insinuations without expressing open accusations, and, in those cases where he administered an exemplary chastisement, of disguising incidents by placing them in a different historical setting, as he did in the virtuoso chapter "Claris Majorum Exemplis," in which he stigmatized the editor of *Figaro,* Hugo Nisbeth, one of his most malicious antagonists. Ethically, *The New Kingdom* was scarcely on a higher plane than *Figaro.* Strindberg's correspondence shows that he was not even above using the same threatening, not to mention blackmailing, tactics that according to *The New Kingdom* made the editor of *Figaro* "the most feared magnate in the kingdom."[36]

Strindberg was worried even before the book appeared, for the publisher had requested him to sign an affidavit assuming legal responsibility. He thought of fleeing to Paris and begged Pehr Staaff to find out if he could be extradited from there; on this point presumably he received reassuring information. The book provoked a far greater scandal than *The Red Room* and must be regarded as Strindberg's most ruthless polemical writing, the novel *Black Banners (Svarta fanor*—1904/07) not excepted. If it no longer seems shocking, it is because the individuals accorded the worst treatment are by now almost forgotten. But for Strindberg the feeling of having incurred enemies everywhere was so strong and unmistakable that the following year (1883) it forced him to leave Sweden for six years.

The New Kingdom is the finest polemical work in Swedish literature. The book lacks the personal warmth and technical versatility that distinguishes *The Red Room,* but it is more unified in style and purpose and is buoyed up by a fresh humor that is captivating from first page to last. It is remarkable that a book based on the scandal and gossip of its day could remain vital so long after its publication. The chapter "A National Educational Establishment" ("En nationell bildningsanstalt") is

still the classic caricature of the Royal Dramatic Theatre, despite the fact
that few readers of today are familiar with the French drawing-room
comedies that Strindberg ridicules or the style of acting he parodies. Most
Swedes would probably still find validity in the attack on the Swedish
Academy in "That's How Things Go!" ("Så går det till!"). Yet this
depiction, inspired partially by Daudet's famous academy episode in *Les
Rois en exil* (1879), contains the most preposterous ingredients. The
setting is presumably one of the academy's annual commemoration days
in the 1880's, but Strindberg, reveling in his hatred of Geijer, took an
actual speech that Geijer delivered on the famous Swedish admiral Claes
Fleming at the Academy of Literature in 1832 and made it into a prize-
winning memorial address given by a young *gymnasium* student. In the
same way, in the chapter "About the Official Lie" ("Om den offentliga
lögnen"), Geijer's tribute to his fellow poet Esias Tegnér in December,
1846, at the Swedish Academy is transformed into a funeral address for
and old printer. Strindberg attempted to point up Geijer's hypocrisy by
contrasting the address with hostile remarks Geijer had made about Tegnér
earlier in his letters. Several of the quotations are in Geijer's most sublime
prose, but Strindberg, by adding ironic parenthetical remarks, succeeds
in making them seem like drivel.

The author's skill in ridicule and indirect attack is evident throughout the book. By describing the Volunteer Rifle Corps sympathetically,
he indicated that compulsory military service—even in the unpretentious
form put into practice after 1878—was "an attack on the freedom of the
people . . . an insidious betrayer, which under the borrowed banner of
freedom sought to put a people in bondage."[37] Likewise, he suggested
that the railroads were destroying the life of the Swedish peasant. After
a parodic description of the dedication of a new railroad branch line,
Strindberg gives a picture of a nearby farmer plowing his fallow land under
the burning afternoon sun. At the unfamiliar roar of the locomotive, the
farmer's oxen "turn tail to the wind, wrenching the plow off its course,"
and a long gully is cut through the newly sown autumn rye. The cham-
berlains aboard the dedication train find it tremendously funny: "The
roars of laughter die out . . . but the farmer's curses—they do not die!"[38]

The note of pathos in this passage is not only due to Strindberg's
hatred of the railroads as an instrument for "ruining farmers and exploit-
ing the land," as he put it in an essay which came out several years later—

"About the Universal Dissatisfaction" ("Om det almänna missnöjet").[39]
He is also dealing with his favorite theme—the worthlessness of industrialized, technological society. As early as 1880 he had described himself
in a letter as "a Jean-Jacques-ist of the most serious intention."[40] And
earlier the same year he wrote to Edvard Brandes: "I am a socialist, a
nihilist, a republican—everything contrary to the reactionaries! And I am
these things instinctively, for I am Jean Jacques's *intime* when it concerns
the return to nature."[41]

This Rousseauism accounts for the hostility toward the state in
The New Kingdom. Rousseau's famous passage[42] about the first division
of property is paraphrased in Strindberg's explanation of the origin of the
contract-by-tender system:

> In small societies and debauched nations that have lost the gift of the
> spirit of enterprise, there readily comes into being an unfortunate state
> of affairs, more particularly known by the name contract-by-tender sys-
> tem. All that is necessary is for a man with a few connections to step
> forward, "appropriate" a position, and say: "This is mine." His friends
> support him immediately and say: "It is his, and will be for his life-
> time. Woe to him who even dares to glance toward that position."[43]

Rousseau's and Buckle's hatred of society coalesce; the chapter ends with
an evocation of Buckle's old specter "the protective spirit" system.[44]

Similarly, Rousseau and Darwin are coupled together in the
chapter "The Newly-Ennobled" ("De nyadlige"). Artillery Sergeant-
Major Lundquist's son, who is compelled to take the university qualifying
examination and become an officer in order to "ennoble the race of
Lundquist," ends up as a degraded bohemian in Paris. After studying
"Darwin's theory about the origin of the species and the theory of evolution," the son, by comparing himself with his bold, aggressive father, has
"come to the conclusion that he had been corrupted by his upbringing and
thus rendered incapable of continuing the struggle for existence." This
theme of the corrupting influence of the refinements of a civilized society
first appeared in *The Red Room* and would shortly appear again in the
short story "Cultivated Fruit" ("Odlad frukt") in *Swedish Destinies and
Adventures*.

Strindberg's correspondence during the writing of *The New
Kingdom* proves that he proceeded rather unsystematically in creating the
"goblin images" of the people and social phenomena that irritated him.

Consequently, it is even more remarkable that the book has a firm structure and a unified viewpoint. The introductory chapter, "The Days of Illusions" ("Illusionernas dagar"), with its bright, vivid First of May procession during the reign of Charles XV in the 1860's, expresses the fundamental principle that all subsequent reactionism has its origin in the lofty but unfulfilled promises of the Parliamentary Reform of 1865. In the following essays "the Swedish people" are presented, the honorable Swedish people who are tyrannized by civil servants, swindled by entrepreneurs, blinded by the stardust of idealists, and fed official lies and festival speeches.

In *The New Kingdom* Strindberg did not explore individual psychology because he was probably aware that character delineation in prose fiction was not his strength. He was able, however, to conceal this shortcoming cleverly by merging different portraits into types. The individual entrepreneurs and idealists are not especially well drawn, but they come alive as types. The chapter on Jews, "Moses," is unquestionably a masterpiece. From at least a score of different real-life models Strindberg created an exquisite collective figure, a playfully malicious study in race psychology. He effortlessly fused together the different individuals by calling them all Moses and showed that they are present everywhere in society, just as there are idealists crawling like earthworms under every social compost heap. Lindblad has rightfully maintained that this technique of working through accumulation has its model in Dickens—*Little Dorrit*, for example, where members of the Barnacle family are found in every government office, in every lucrative post.

Strindberg's satire was influenced not only by Dickens but by his various foreign pupils. Here and there one discovers echoes of Orvar Odd.[45] It is also possible that Strindberg was influenced by the scandal-mongering that had precedents in novels about Stockholm as far back as the eighteenth century.[46] But these models are no longer important. In *The New Kingdom* Strindberg found his own satirical tone, his own derisive manner, which would return in his polemical works, although seldom with such consummate artistry. He used exaggeration as frequently as the American humorists, but not in the same grotesque and obvious way. The book was written in a matter-of-fact journalistic style that makes the devastating irony even more effective. There is no defense against this kind of tricky swordplay which makes unexpected lunges and thrusts in every direction, all the while maintaining the appearance of a harmless game.

One of Strindberg's contemporaries, Karl Warburg, has testified that probably no work contributed more to creating the bitterness of the youth of the 1880's than *The New Kingdom*. This is understandable. In spite of the fact that a desire for revenge played a role in the writing of the book and partially distorted it, its purpose had universal application. It was directed against the social lie, against antiquated ideals, against oppressive authorities, prejudicial cliques and conventions, against the gilding and the secretiveness with which society attempts to conceal its inner corruption. For the generation that was first incited by *Brand* to put an end to all compromise and official hypocrisy, the book must have seemed more profitably revealing and straight-forward than it may seem to our time. Strindberg also brilliantly captured a number of Swedish national failings: the taste for rhetoric and stiff bureaucratic forms and the love of jubilees and chauvinistic hero worship. But it is not a profound analysis of the Swedish temperament; Strindberg was content to stigmatize sharply a few glaring traits.

The book attracted a wider audience than any of Strindberg's earlier works. It is indicative that Michel Perrin's[47] rebuttal, *The Newest Kingdom (Det nyaste riket)*, which stripped the anonymity from the persons attacked and then delivered a heavy-footed defense of them, went through two printings before the end of the year. Perrin made a few personal allusions to the book's author, among others to his bankruptcy, which infuriated Strindberg. Consequently, Strindberg's own rebuttal, *The Old Kingdom (Det gamla riket)*, was so vulgar and offensive that no publisher could be found for it,[48] and Pehr Staaff had to undertake his defense. Although Strindberg provided material and support for Staaff's pamphlet *"The New Kingdom" and Its Author (Det nya riket och dess författare)*, it must have grieved him when Staaff, too, expressed disapproval of the attack on Geijer.

The repudiation of *The New Kingdom* by Young Sweden was interpreted by Strindberg as a betrayal, because they had induced him to write the work and so put his very survival at stake. Though a final breach did not come until after the legal battle over *Married* in late 1884, feelings between him and the Young Sweden group were strained, and he expressed his disappointment both in *Swedish Destinies and Adventures* and in the volume *Poems (Dikter)* in 1883. In terms of his own development this growing conflict would be crucial.

Swedish Destinies and Adventures

"I am writing beautiful things now! Like an idealist!" Strindberg wrote to his publisher Looström in October, 1882.[49] He was beginning work on his historical narratives—set for the most part in the late Middle Ages and Renaissance—which appeared in two parts under the title *Swedish Destinies and Adventures* in the years 1882-83.

He had made plans for the work while writing *The New Kingdom* and conceived of it as a fictional counterpart of *The Swedish People.* This is apparent in a tentative title, *The Chronicle of the People. From Immemorial Times to the Present (Folkets krönika. Från hedenhös till våra dagar).* But at the same time he was firmly resolved to continue under historical camouflage the battle of ideas he had waged in *The New Kingdom.*

After *The Red Room* Strindberg had imagined that in his writing he could work alternately as an "idealist" and a realist. But realistic questions of the day asserted themselves even in his historical dramas. By the time he began *Swedish Destinies,* he was fully conscious that he could not exclude contemporary debates from any of his writing. Historical disguise became a concession to romanticism that he allowed himself almost grudgingly, and the importance of naturalism was made clear to him through acquaintance with Zola. The longest of the "destinies"— "Evolution" ("Utveckling")—reflects more clearly than any other of Strindberg's works the dissension within him between conflicting artistic viewpoints and attitudes toward life.

Strindberg continued to add to *Swedish Destinies* at long intervals, right up into the 1890's, but in the later narratives, his purpose was scarcely more than that of transporting to the past what he did not dare depict in contemporary milieu. This was the case with "The Isle of Bliss" ("De lycksaliges ö"—1884), in which he resumed the mocking satire of historical and archaeological research begun in *The New Kingdom.* The difference was that in the "destiny" Strindberg sought revenge for the harsh criticism professional historians accorded *The Swedish People* by alluding to them as believers in "Rudbeckianism," a reference to an eccentric scholar, Olaus Rudbeck (1630-1702), who claimed that ancient Sweden was in reality the lost civilization of Atlantis.[50] The historical veneer is even thinner in "A Witch" ("En häxa"), an almost verbatim copy of the first part of his contemporary novella "Short Cuts" ("Genvägar"). In both "A Witch" and the long story "Tschandala,"[51] Strindberg simply transplanted his own experiences into a seventeenth-century setting.

These later "destinies" led critics to the erroneous conclusion that Strindberg had little regard for historical accuracy, and they underestimated the artistic ambitions with which he began the series. His contemporaries were enthusiastic about the apparently authentic period flavor in the first "destinies" that appeared, and the question might well be raised whether Strindberg ever again reached such heights as an historical narrator. But even though it was not until years later that he defended himself with Goethe's famous expression, that all true literary art lives and breathes only in anachronisms,[52] the fact was that he had used anachronism ever since the prose version of *Master Olof*. Consequently, when one accuses him of offenses against historical truth, one must take into account that they were often intentional. Fredrik Böök has quite correctly pointed out[53] that a cultivated man of letters like the knight Sten Ulvfot, the hero of the opening story "Cultivated Fruit," would have been an unlikely figure in the Middle Ages when there were no differences in education between knights and peasants, but Strindberg was fully aware of this. In *The Swedish People* he cautioned his readers not to nurture romantic illusions about how well educated the average knight was, describing him as simply "a rich peasant whose training in the use of weapons had given him a certain smartness of behavior."[54] And shortly before "Cultivated Fruit" he had drawn in Herr Bengt a knight with peasant manners.[55]

Strindberg also deliberately broke away from historical truth in "Higher Purposes" ("Högre ändamål"). The central conflict in the story is based on a decree made at a church council meeting in the town of Skänninge which stipulated that married clergymen had to separate from their wives before the end of the year. He knew very well from his studies that this decree was never observed in Sweden at all.[56] To salve his historical conscience he has the archdeacon in the story offer to let the poor parson keep a "housekeeper," as long as she was not his former wife.[57]

As Böök has pointed out, Strindberg also took liberties with historical accuracy in "Pål and Per." The story deals with the relationships between Stockholm and the provinces in the seventeenth century, and Strindberg could have used the rather impressive primary source materials he had collected for *The Swedish People* and *Old Stockholm,* as well as Clas Odhner's authoritative book on the origins of Swedish cities which he had since acquired. But it did not embarrass him to deviate from history if by so doing he could make the story livelier or underscore his purpose more effectively.

Probably the main reason *Swedish Destinies* has been found so deficient in historicity is that Strindberg did not place emphasis on the traditional elements of historical fiction: the painstaking portrayal of costume and milieu. During his school years he had been bored to death by Sir Walter Scott's tedious descriptions. It is certain, too, that he found little to admire in Jacobsen's depictions of costumes and interiors based on sketches in museums. When Strindberg did attend to costume detail, it was for reasons other than to create an historical patina. In "Evolution," for example, he evoked the fever of unrest during the rule of King John III (1569-92) by noting several small changes in fashion. People had "new clothes and new faces, but they did not seem happy over their new clothes; they wore high collars as if they feared for their necks and wore their cloaks over both shoulders for safety's sake, since new winds were continually blowing."[58]

It was an integral part of Strindberg's program not only as a realist but as an historian to portray ordinary "Swedish People on Holiday and Workday" and not just important characters from the past. Consequently, the people we meet in *Swedish Destinies* are from the lower social classes: citizens, monks, scribes, craftsmen, and peasants.

There is scant attention given to chivalric bravura and battle scenes in *Swedish Destinies.*[59] When war situations do appear, the author's purpose is to express his pacificism. The best example is the description of the battered Sweden of slain King Charles XII in 1718, in the story "At the Wake in Tistedalen" ("Vid likvaken i Tistedalen") written in 1891. In just a few bold strokes the author provides a vivid picture of the ugly side of Charles XII's campaign against Norway. In the dawning of a grayish-yellow December day, army wagons and cannon roll over "broken mounds of debris that were once members of the Jönköping Regiment and the King's Own Dragoons, a mixture of human entrails and scraps of clothing, a shoe with a foot in it, a glove with several fingers, an

ear packed in a ball of hair."[60] Zola, in *La Débâcle* (1892), needed many
pages to produce an equally intense picture of the carnage of war.

Rather than war scenes, Strindberg preferred to depict gay folk
festivals and holidays, such as the wedding in the restaurant of the Stockholm City Hall, the high point of "Cultivated Fruit," or the celebration of
the traditional early service on Christmas Day in "Pål and Per," or the
comparison of busy commerce down on the Stockholm docks with life up
in the town in "Evolution."

In addition to *The Swedish People,* Strindberg drew his source
material from *Old Stockholm,* in which he had given accounts of high
holidays and popular celebrations. Despite a number of curious anachronisms in the "destinies," one senses the spirit of the early Reformation
and the dawning of the age of national states. But it is extremely difficult
to draw the line between historical and contemporary milieu, because the
historical costume Strindberg chose for Stockholm was a varied one, collected from all the sources with which he had become familiar through his
cultural-historical studies. A good example is the brilliant opening of
"Evolution." It begins with the breakup of the ice on Lake Mälar, where
the April sun and the waves liberate the great ice floes and send them east-
ward past the city to the sea: "The ice hole expands, the bay increases in
size, and then away it all goes, unrestrainedly, out, out, toward the sea."[61]
Strindberg then follows the course of the floes until they pile up against
the pillars of Norr Bridge in the center of town. The channel is filled with
foreign sailing vessels:

> Dutch schuyts with clothes, Lübeckian with beer, French with wine, and
> Spanish with spices and precious metals from the newly-discovered world
> on the other side of the ocean. . . . Up in the town there was life and
> movement; people swarmed like ants whose hill had been torn up; cavalry-
> men and soldiers thronged, and the city's journeymen worked on the
> walls.[62]

From an historical viewpoint it is noteworthy that the ships and people are
so numerous that one would think the scene was a modern seaport. But
perhaps Strindberg was inspired by the awkward old engravings from the
seventeenth century, in which countless ships are crowded together near
Skepps Bridge, and the artists avoided sketching street perspectives by
filling all empty spaces with figures.

In other stories Strindberg provided pictures of life more familiar
to modern inhabitants of the old section of Stockholm: *staden mellan*

broarna—"the city between the bridges." Böök pointed out that the depiction in "Pål and Per" of the Christmas Day early service and the journey to it is based on Strindberg's own childhood memories, which he had already used in *Old Stockholm*. But even if it is anachronistic, the bleak mood of winter is exquisitely captured: "It was as if everything was blighted by the cold, so that the wind itself did not stir and the stars flickered like tiny coals trying to keep alive. A lonely night watchman almost ran along the street so as not to freeze his toes off, and there were cracking sounds from the old wooden houses as the beams shrank together."[63]

People gathered in Stor Square for the departure: "And they were already sitting in their sleds--stout brewers and bakers—and the whole square was lit up by their smoking torches. Crack! The bells rang and the procession started moving down the bank and out through the north gate of the city."[64] Even if one keeps in mind Böök's remarks that this Christmas service and the drinking of glögg—the traditional spiced wine and brandy—afterward at the Stallmästargården inn belong to the period of Strindberg's childhood and not to the seventeenth century, the reader's imagination manages to redecorate everything in a seventeenth-century setting.

Or take the extraordinary portrait of the Franciscan monastery on Ridder Island in "For Good and Evil" ("På gott och ont"). Lindblad is surely correct that Strindberg had the Royal Library in mind in his description of the monastery library. The scene that stays longest with the reader is the one in which lazy Brother Franciscus lies in a window-opening sunning himself in the blazing July sun: "He saw how the pitch on the shingle roof was melting and dripping down into the sea. Each time a drop plopped on the water's surface a school of bleak[65] rushed to see whether it was fit to eat, but it was not—it just turned into a lot of oily rings in all colors of the rainbow."[66] The old monastery wall is still there today, and Strindberg's description is so vivid that one half-expects to see Brother Franciscus leaning out one of the windows, lazily watching the playing of the bleak on the surface of the water.

The Stockholm landscape was not the only locale Strindberg used for his blending of historical intuition and love of nature. The Lake Mälar archipelago is also rendered beautifully, as in "Evolution," the setting for which is the island of Gripsholm and the town of Mariefred. "New Weapons" ("Nya vapen") supposedly takes place on the island of Öland off the southeast coast of Sweden, but the actual locale is the Stockholm skerries, and elements in the story are similar to those in the novel *The People of Hemsö:* "Jost walked in the lead with the oxe and harrow, and his father, Thomas, sowed the spring corn; afterward came the wagtails picking up worms, and in the woods, crows were perched, waiting."[67]

It may seem absurd to maintain that *Swedish Destinies* is still the most vivid of all Swedish historical fiction, when it can be proven that so much in them is contrary to known historical data. But is absolute accuracy so vital for historical fiction? For each new generation and with every pioneering historical study the image of the past is changed. We expect something else from historical fiction, something more lasting: the ability to project the reader into a bygone age through historical intuition; a genuine feel for the period is scarcely ever made obsolete by new scholarly discoveries. Perhaps we should simply venture the paradox that *Swedish Destinies*—for all its glaring anachronisms—has given more inspiration to modern Swedish cultural-historical research than most other Swedish historical novels and short stories.

Strindberg said that in *Swedish Destinies* he dealt with "all the social concepts he had touched upon lightly in the satires,"[68] but one concept was given special attention: his Rousseauism, which now took on firmer contours and for the next few years became the unifying element in his world view.[69] Earlier, Rousseau's influence had actually led Strindberg to anarchistic conclusions. In the summer of 1881 he wrote to Edvard Brandes that he regarded all halfway measures in politics as unsatisfactory: "It is my absolute conviction that civilization is stupid and cursed and that a regeneration can only come about through a return to nature. Cities must be abolished; the state must be broken up into village communities with no sovereign over them, for a superior authority is intolerable whether he be called king or president. The Nihilists are my people!"[70] Strindberg was demanding a *Ragnarök* to enable a new culture to rise from the ashes. The same Rousseauistic nihilism was the foundation for the social criticism in *The Red Room* and *The New Kingdom*.

Hatred of civilized society is just as fervent in *Swedish Destinies* and is apparent even in the first story, "Cultivated Fruit." As a remedy for the evil, Strindberg recommends Rousseau's means—alter the way man is brought up. Just as in the opening of *Emile*, civilized man is compared to a fruit that has become sterile through overbreeding: "When nature is left alone, she makes masterpieces; when man joins in and wants to assist, the result is a mess. . . . Therefore, the practice of cultivating selected individuals must cease, particularly since it is always done at the expense of others."[71] Sten Ulvfot, the bookman, is destroyed because he is overcultivated, and in "Pål and Per" urbanized society is treated as a decadent manifestation of overrefinement. Its citizens live like parasites off peasants who are forced to feed them and receive only useless trash in exchange. This is the distinction between the "producing" and "consuming" classes that Strindberg would make a year later in his essay "About the Universal Dissatisfaction."[72] During the writing of "Pål and Per" in March, 1883, he announced to his publisher that he planned to settle down in the skerries as a peasant the following fall.

Recognizing that both the individual and society were corrupted through overrefinement, Strindberg, like Rousseau, doubted that the development of life on this planet was moving in a forward direction. This is the theme of a story that has much significance as an ideological and psychological document: "Evolution." Its fundamental thesis is that the path of progress is circular. The asceticism of the Middle Ages was succeeded by the pagan worship of beauty of the Renaissance, but this was crushed by the hostility to art of the Reformation and by the Counter-Reformation. The world moves constantly in a circular course, like the earth around the sun: "eternally new, but eternally beginning again, and everything new was only the resumption of something old."[73]

Above all, however, "Evolution" is important as a self-evaluation. In the contrast between the pious painter-monk Botvid and the pagan, life-worshipping Renaissance artist Giacomo, Strindberg depicted his own sense of being alien to naturalism and the ideals of Young Sweden. As Nils Erdmann pointed out,[74] these two characters mirror different sides of Strindberg's own nature;[75] even the Lutheran minister who preaches the perishability of the beautiful and the worthlessness of art has a covert kinship with the author. Botvid is commissioned by a Catholic Carthusian monastery outside Stockholm to paint the Virgin Mary, but he has always been shy in dealing with women and is not convinced he can paint a portrait that will be both lifelike and pious. When he becomes ill, he is replaced by the hedonistic Giacomo, who shocks Botvid but also arouses his admiration by boldly choosing as his model (and mistress),

Maria, a girl who lives close to the monastery. Botvid envies Giacomo's hunger and zest for life and beauty until he sees that it is a philosophy that comes to grips only with the surface of life. When Maria contracts plague and is disfigured, Giacomo abandons her. In her dying moments she is obliged to turn for solace to the faithful Botvid.

The story is similar to *The Red Room* in a number of ways. It contains aphorisms that originated in "Observations of a Skeptic" at the time of *Master Olof* and were repeated in *The Red Room* by Olle Montanus. Botvid, like Arvid Falk, is a docile and ingenious young idealist, standing somewhere between Giacomo and the minister, who represent respectively, as do Doctor Borg and Olle Montanus, the antithetical poles in the central character's nature: life-affirming naturalism versus cynicism, and the worship of beauty versus the condemnation of art.

An early draft of the story demonstrates—again as in *The Red Room*—how the disillusioned hero learns to compromise on matters of conscience. Although Botvid finds that the Renaissance worship of antiquity is as empty of meaning as the asceticism of his youth, he continues to paint on commission in order to stay alive. This early version ends with his going home to "work on a Leda and swan, which would hang in the duke's bedroom." But Strindberg discarded this conclusion. In the published version, Giacomo is struck down by a treacherous arrow and continues to avow his defiant atheism even as he lies dying. Botvid then leaves his native land and retreats into a German Carthusian monastery. At this time, Strindberg inserted the often-quoted passage in which Botvid feels that his soul is "split in two ever-feuding parts; he was the son of two epochs, and this gave him two viewpoints over things: the monk's and the satyr's."[76] Several lines crossed out in the manuscript mention that he had "lost faith in the old because it did not satisfy, and he had lost faith in the new."

This was Strindberg himself at the crossroads. We are reminded of his statement made immediately after the publication of *The New Kingdom:* "Standing between two epochs at odds with each other, I shall be crushed to death." He states in his autobiography that he had often prophesied, during the time of his first meetings with the men who were to constitute Young Sweden, that his role as transitional figure would be "to be ground between the old and the new eras."[77] The coterie's atheism and repudiation of immortality were difficult for him to accept as "a romanticist and individualist." (In letters to Staaff he declared he could never become an atheist.)

But he was not entirely unaffected by this new heathenism. Just as Botvid is partially drawn to Giacomo's persuasions and feels they express his own hidden thoughts, so had Strindberg been fascinated by Zola's naturalistic glorification of the rightness of sexual desires in *La Faute de l'Abbé Mouret* (1875), a book he commended in January, 1882, to his old university professor, Rupert Nyblom, as a colossal work of art, and he retained this opinion for the rest of his life.[78]

Zola's novel is directed against the celibacy of Catholicism in particular and sexual continence in general. Strindberg travels the same path in "Higher Purposes"—written before "Evolution"—when he allows Parson Dominus Peder of Rasbo, who was separated from his wife through the decision of the Council of Skänninge, to be reunited with her during the spring season's reawakening of love. The deacon wants to separate them again, but the parson refuses and declares that "the gods that our forefathers worshipped above the clouds and in the sun" are much greater "than these Roman and Semitic procurers and debt-collectors, whom you have imposed on us."[79] He leaves the church to devote the remainder of his life to "converting Christians to heathendom."

Nevertheless, Strindberg could not wholeheartedly profess this naturalistic Pan-cult that worshipped elemental forces. One can see this in "Evolution." Even Giacomo trembles at the minister's warning words, and Botvid, who for a time is captivated by Giacomo's hedonistic teachings and regrets the abstinence of his earlier years, returns to the cloistered life.

These ambivalent feelings toward romanticism and naturalism were common among serious Scandinavian writers of Strindberg's generation. In 1886, the year after "Evolution" appeared, Levertin emphasized that a great deal of modern Scandinavian literature dealt with characters who were suspended between the old and the new and who could never plant their feet on solid ground.[80] In Jacobsen's *Niels Lyhne,* which Strindberg read shortly before he began writing "Evolution," the hero regards himself as a transitional figure between two epochs and sometimes thinks he was born half a century too late, sometimes half a century too soon:

> His talent had its roots in the past and could live only there; it could not draw sustenance from his current opinions, his convictions, or his

> sympathies. [The past and the present] . . . floated away from each other
> . . . and like water and oil could be shaken together, but could not
> merge, never become one.

This is reminiscent of Botvid's complaint that he was the son of
two epochs and unable to "get a stable view of life, capable of carrying
him to a goal."[81] Yet Strindberg's position was different from that of
Jacobsen, whom he called "the old romanticist, as we well know."[82] On
certain issues, Strindberg's basic outlook on life was rooted in the past,
while his "talent"—his artistic temperament—had more affinity with naturalism. Lindblad has pointed out that *Swedish Destinies* is Strindberg's first
work in which the influence of Zola's descriptive technique can be traced,
although as of yet it was on a limited scale. Strindberg continued to adhere
to his Platonic theory that art was meaningless, because it was only "an
illusion of the illusion." Therefore, Zola's demand for an exact reproduc-
tion of reality was an abomination to him. The minister condemns Giacomo as "an ape who tries to mimic what God made and people ruined. . . .
Useless is what you are, and clown is your name."[83] In the poems in
Somnambulist Nights (Sömngångarnätter), Strindberg would preach the
futility of imitating a nature that God created and man spoiled.

Poems

On June 8, 1883, Strindberg wrote triumphantly to his publisher
Looström: "The bubo in my brain has burst and nothing but verse is
streaming out. Beautiful and savage!" Before the year was out he had
published his first volume of ballads and lyrics—*Poems,* consisting of
three groups of works: the first group (under the collective title "Youth
and Ideals"—"Ungdom och ideal") written between 1869 and 1872, the
second ("Storms"—"Stormar") from the middle of the 1870's and the
last group (in two sections, "Wound-Fever"—"Sårfeber" and "The Height
of Summer"—"Högsommar") begun in 1882 and completed in the
summer of 1883.

The letter to the publisher was written on the island of Kymmendö, also the setting for the "beautiful" verses included in the section
"The Height of Summer." They depict mushroom-gathering and sailing:

> Hold hard to the rig of the foresail
> for the wind blows against us fair,
> I watched the flow of your streaming veil
> and your wild and unruly hair![84]

The fiery satirist has fled to nature, the balm for his wounded breast, but finds that there he is a disturber of the peace: "Everything flees the feared one who fled people."[85]

The calm of a Saturday evening makes his raucous instrument yield gentle tones:

> The wind is at rest, the bay like a mirror,
> The mill is asleep, the sailors haul in sail,
> The oxen are turned out in grassy meadows,
> And all make ready for the Sabbath.
> The woodcock "roads" his way through the brush;
> Near the barn the hired hand plays his accordion,
> The porch is swept, the yard is raked,
> Garden plots are watered and lilacs treasured.[86]

One beautiful June morning the poet plays the role of a friendly brownie who takes care of his cucumber bed, rids the cabbages of worms, throws kisses to his wife and children, and picks cowslips and orchids before settling down to his writing in a bower by the water:

> Sea and sun and billows blue!
> Now he writes satires!

After his handiwork, he returns for breakfast and kisses his children:

> Since the satire did not strike at them
> They are well-behaved and quiet![87]

It is curious that this idyllic milieu inspired the "savage" poems in the section "Wound-Fever," which gives the collection its merit. Strindberg said in his autobiography[88] that he chose verse instead of prose in order to "hold himself above the level of the pamphleteers." This may have been his intention, but the results are quite different. Verse whetted his appetite for battle. With increasing animosity he tackled new opponents. Not until he had submitted the greater portion of the manuscript did he realize that it would force him to leave Sweden. He left in September, 1883, and after arriving in Paris, fired off the collection as a farewell salvo. Despite the caustic and merciless attacks on adversaries, most of whom are now forgotten, these lampooning verses have something of the sun and bubbling salt spray about them. It obviously gave Strindberg a sense of liberation to be able to burn his bridges and properly sing out what he only dared to suggest in *Swedish Destinies*. This is evident in the first poem in "Wound-Fever," "Biographical" ("Biografiskt"), whose dejected opening mood is transformed into a triumphant note at the conclusion. One notices it too in "The Boulevard System," whose thesis—that demolition creates air and light—became a battle cry of the 1880's.

At the time *Poems* was being written, the violent acts of the nihilists were spreading fear throughout Europe. Strindberg, too, sang the praises of dynamite, which would soon liberate Russia and then supposedly the whole world. He prophesied the coming of a Midgard serpent, which would prepare on the Volga, along the Seine, and in the Pyrenees, a *Ragnarök* out of which a new generation would emerge.

He had not as yet had any close contacts with revolutionary movements in Europe. When somewhat later he happened upon some Russian nihilists in Switzerland, he was impressed by their apostolic mildness and utopianism; for a moment he forgot the "great, beautiful hatred" that gave his Loki figure its legendary radiance in the poem "Loki's Blasphemies" ("Lokes smädelser").

But Strindberg did not really come into his own in "Wound-Fever" until he resumed the guerrilla warfare of *The New Kingdom*. Fortunately, events in Sweden provided him with new material for satire. The 250th anniversary jubilee of the battle of Lützen (1632)—a magnificent but tragic victory in which Sweden lost her great king Gustav Adolf—produced no poem as audacious as Strindberg's "For the Freedom of Belief" ("För tankens frihet"). Recognizable are all the pretentious, elaborate paraphernalia from the jubilee festivals parodied in *The New Kingdom*. The poem begins with the preparations:

> The trumpeter polishes his white trumpet
> And the master chef is busy,
> Cracking lobsters and stirring batter
> And larding the hazel hens to make them crisp.
> *   *   *   *
> And the Guardsmen blow a chorale
> In the morning in the tower of the church.[89]

Then comes the description of the official part of the celebration with opera singers, great ladies, lieutenants, and speeches—each stanza of the section ending in the refrain: "a festival for the freedom of belief." Throughout, Strindberg stresses the irony of the fact that Gustav Adolf fought not to extend religious freedom, but the influence of Lutheranism.

This is *The New Kingdom* in a rejuvenated and poetically embellished form. Scholarly historical research also comes in for criticism. The liberal politician and war historian Julius Mankell had been criticized by historians because he had portrayed Gustav Adolf from the somewhat unsympathetic viewpoint of the 1880's. With collegial sympathy Strindberg devoted a section of the poem to Mankell's martyrdom. In the conclusion he remembers his own unlucky fate for having dared to attack Geijer as he mentions that although Gustav Adolf had to give his life for his belief, the King still retained his honor:

> I know a man who for a different belief
> Had to yield his honor but retained his life,
> But the rabble will never give up
> Until his life is torn to shreds.
> What art does it take to die in splendor
> With a coffin topped by a crown?
> No, it's harder to bear the contemptuous sting
> Of the mob, with no honor to call your own.[90]

Strindberg was more effective with random attack and counterattack than with a systematic campaign conducted from prepared positions. It is often astonishing how the shabbiest of causes could give him the inspiration for superb polemical poems. For example: "Dissimilar Weapons" ("Olika vapen"), an attack on the reactionary Carl David af Wirsén, was provoked by a review in which Wirsén dismissed Strindberg by saying he would not cross his sword with a dagger. With setting and verse form from the Spanish *El Cid* romances and a pinch of Heine for seasoning, Strindberg created a masterpiece of literary satire.[91] Another example is the poem provoked by a parody of *Herr Bengt's Wife*—"Idealistic Criticism" ("Idealistkritik")—a magnificent squaring of accounts with the false idealism of the "Signature" school. Here, Strindberg defended his right to write about beautiful things if he chose to do so and also refuted the charges that he sought out only the ugly and burrowed in filth. In other poems, such as the one directed against Edvard Bäckström, "My Friend and I" ("Min vän och jag"), in which he pokes fun at the latter's elegant language, Strindberg says that he has fallen in love "with the naturally ugly." It is clear that romanticism and naturalism continued to battle for his soul, and he knew it. In the North Sea cycle "Exile," from the section "Storms," he grumbles about his "damned old heart," which loves churches and missals and pines away for romantic Charles XII. This is in sharp contrast to the poems in which he ridicules the religiosity and punchbowl-inspired patriotism of the "Signature" clique.

Strindberg's deep ambivalence is also evident in the poem intended to be his definitive statement on aesthetics: "Singers!" ("Sångare!")

from the section "Wound-Fever." As long as he is poking fun at the cradle songs of the older generation of poets—with their cracked serenading voices and clattering fatherland appeals clad in rusty armor—he feels on firm ground and is jaunty. But when he tries to formulate the poetic credo of the younger generation, an uncertainty appears:

> Why do you still label the illusion of beauty
>   as truth?
> Truth will be ugly as long as beauty is only
>   illusion.
> Ugliness is truth![92]

Here is the conflict between Olle Montanus's Platonic condemnation of all art that imitates reality and naturalism's demand for the right to reproduce ugliness. It is true that Strindberg inserted a reservation. Ugliness is truth "as long as beauty is only illusion." But can beauty, according to his definition, ever cease to be an "illusion"?

"Ugliness is truth." The public response to this statement misled both contemporary and later critics in their evaluation of Poems, and the foreword Strindberg wrote in October, 1883, in Paris does not clarify things. After declaring verse an antiquated form to be abandoned by the new age, Strindberg defends himself against the intimation that "with clear intention" he had broken the laws of poetry. But in the same breath he declares that he was justified in breaking them "since I regarded my ideas as more significant than a metrical foot or a rhyme."[93]

Strindberg's biographer, Erik Hedén, has called him "a lyricist against his will." This is true; on principle, he damned lyricism, as he did all belles-lettres. But one must not think, therefore, that he deliberately wrote bad verse.[94] When he handled ordinary rhymed stanza forms, only his realistic vocabulary set him apart from his contemporaries. This is true of a portion of the poems in "Wound-Fever." "Loki's Blasphemies" has no striking faults in meter or rhyme, but it does have a rather tiresome prolixity. Strindberg's originality emerged most clearly in unrhymed verse, although it is not likely that he had aspired to be original at the start. His first title for the collection—New Wine in Old Bottles (Nytt vin på gamla flaskor)—shows that he intended to restrict himself to conventional forms so as to be able to propagandize more effectively for his ideas. During the writing he was drawn unintentionally to experiments, but these were only partially carried out. In order to fill out the collection, he gathered together virtually every bit of verse he had ever written.

In the foreword he says that he "polished" his youthful poems here and there so as not to seem proud of demonstrating in print how badly he wrote at twenty years of age. Unfortunately, only occasionally is it possible to determine how he proceeded in this polishing, as in the poem written in 1870 in the town of Visby, "On the Nikolai Ruins" ("Pä Nikolai ruin"), which was radically changed before it was finally published in 1883. The poem's original religious element disappeared, and wherever possible Strindberg followed Heine's example and thrust in mood-breaking modern words.

The cycle "Exile"—unfortunately difficut to date[95]—seems to mark a turning point in Strindberg's poetic style. It is true that from the very first he had pursued what he called "Heinesque echoes," but these early copies of Heine are poetically insignificant, teetering between imitations and parodies.[96] In "Exile," Strindberg was able to assimilate in a more personal way the free-verse metrics and bizarre style of Heine's images of the North Sea, and the parodic element is perhaps even more strongly underscored than earlier. But as Fröding observed, Strindberg now ridiculed not only "Heine, but poetry in general, and for that matter the whole world, including the author himself."[97]

His technique in "Exile"—with its endlessly long adjectives, its compounds, and attempts in Heine's self-parodic way to attach comic effects to pathos—seems strained at times. His contemporaries probably appreciated the cycle because Elias Sehlstedt (1808-74) had already accustomed them to parodies of Heine written in a broad style.[98] Strindberg was well aware that he used the travel narrative form only as a disguise. In a letter in July, 1883, he called the cycle "Deviltries and pessimistic bits rendered in the form of travel impressions from my Paris journey."[99]

From this time on Strindberg strove for a more casual tone. Some of the poems begun in the older style were completed in the new or provided with additional stanzas that changed their character considerably. For example, the section "Height of Summer," devoted largely to his wife, opens with a gracious little poem, "Perseus and Andromeda," which describes how Andromeda, chained to a rocky ledge, is freed by Perseus, who is rewarded by being offered her as his wife. In other words, we have the same theme as in *Herr Bengt's Wife*, where the knight liberated Margit from the cloister. After having written the piece, however, Strindberg apparently found the diction too polished and academic and could not resist the desire to add a bantering final stanza:

> And so goes the legend by Herodotus told,
> whose interest was strictly narration,
> he had nothing to add that was new to the old
> and it needed no consideration![100]

Another example is the popular ballad "Herr Beaujolais of Beaune" ("Herr Beaujolais av Beaune"). It first appeared in the story "Cultivated Fruit," where Sten Ulvfot sings it to a lute accompaniment. Although it is alleged in the story that the song is "in the style of the old Provençal singers," it seems hardly likely that any reader would seriously believe that Strindberg was trying to imitate troubador poetry. But this is exactly what happened.

In an early draft of *The Secret of the Guild,* master builder Sten comes from Provence because Strindberg intended to have him sing a "Provençal song," but the idea was discarded after a first draft.[101] For the early version Strindberg went to great trouble to find rhymes for the names of the different Provençal towns: Barcelonnette, Durance, Mont Philine, and so forth. He found a troubador's name in Ahnfelt's literary history which he introduced into the rhyme scheme:

> Där bodde den unge Sieur Mauléon   There lived a young Sieur Mauléon
> Han älskade rosor och vin och sång.   He loved roses and wine and song.

But although he had hit upon the setting—a castle at the foot of the Alps and a threatening ice avalanche—he could not find a form for the poem until he boldly seized two names he remembered from wine labels:

> Herr Beaujolais   Herr Beaujolais
> Herr Beaujolais de Beaune,   Herr Beaujolais de Beaune,
> han byggt sin borg   he built his castle
> han byggt sin borg vid Rhône.   he built his castle by the Rhône.

With this, the poem acquired the contagious rhythm that Gustaf Fröding said rang continually in his ears during his youth.[102]

Unfortunately, contemporary literary critics were too influenced by historical tradition to be able to appreciate this new kind of "troubador poetry." Karl Otto Bonnier took a chance when he published the poetry collection and was made to see the error of his naive and inexperienced judgment. When the volume received withering newspaper criticism, he was scoffed at during family gatherings for the poor taste he had shown.[103]

In general, critics were displeased because they felt Strindberg had recklessly scribbled down stanzas and rhymes without revising them, and this undoubtedly contributed to the vehemence of their attack. But one hardly gets the impression of poetic carelessness from Strindberg's notes or the earlier versions of the poems. Rhyme and meter did not come easily to him, unless by chance he hit upon an eloquent rhythm. Although he was—in contrast with Fröding[104]—musical to his fingertips, his lyrics are seldom singable. Occasionally in *Poems* he was able with diligence to construct sturdy verses, but more often than not he made a virtue of necessity. Not until *Somnambulist Nights,* where he was able to cultivate the form he loved best—loose *knittelvers*[105]—did his lyrical qualities come into their own, and they were quickly recognized. It is indicative that Strindberg referred only to *Somnambulist Nights* when years later in *Talks to the Swedish Nation* (1910) he asserted his position as a forerunner of the lyricism of the 1890's. As far as I know, he nowhere suggested that *Poems* was as important a contribution. Twenty years were to elapse before he would again try, in *Word-Play and Minor Art (Ordalek och småkonst),* to write lyrical poetry.

Somnambulist Nights

During the summer of 1883 on Kymmendö when he produced the major part of *Poems,* Strindberg told his publisher about plans to write "several Swedish farewells." This was the impulse for *Somnambulist Nights in Broad Daylight (Sömngångarnätter på vakna dagar),*[106] and the original manuscript in Birger Mörner's collection[107] still bears the crossed-out title *Three Farewells (Tre farväl).* But not until he arrived in Paris in the fall did he manage to complete the first "night," which was included in the first edition of *Poems.* The three remaining "nights" were written the same fall and, together with the first one, published as a separate book early the following year. The title was changed because Strindberg, now on foreign soil and longing to return to his homeland, dramatized this longing in the forms of "somnambulist nights": journeys made by a restless dreamer, defying time and space, back to Sweden.

The sketches and original manuscript demonstrate, as Henry Olsson has shown,[108] that the opening stanzas set in a French milieu were written later than the main body of the poems. Never had Strindberg's homesickness found so spontaneous and moving an expression as in these introductory sections. They describe how ill at ease he was in the autumnal fog and street noises of Paris, and his happiness at being able to travel north in his dreams—through the clover meadows and buckwheat fields of the province of Skåne, the stony hills of Småland, and the plains of Öster-götland to the edge of Lake Mälar just west of Stockholm, where everything was welcome and familiar. While walking in the Bois de Boulogne, he is moved by the sight of a Scandinavian spruce among the walnut and acacia trees, conjuring up memories of blooming reeds, white birches, groves of lilies of the valley, and perch shoals, and finally of the high days and holidays of a Swedish Christmas. The fourth "night" culminates in a stately apostrophe to Sweden: "Live free and proud in your rugged nature."[109]

He hoped to be back on Kymmendö by the following summer. Everything displeased him in Paris, from the cast-iron stoves to "the Frenchmen's food fit only for dogs."[110] In an 1884 article concerning the problems of running a Swedish household in Paris,[111] he described his fruitless wanderings in grocery stores hunting for dill to serve with lamb. He had never before been away from Sweden for any length of time and was astonished at the way his longing continually pulled him homeward:

Like a child wandering to his mother's grave,
so unreasonably, so pointlessly.[112]

Homesickness induced Strindberg to review his childhood and to evaluate his past and present philosophy of life and art. In these evaluations, new ideas impressed him less than old ones. He attacked Darwinism and research into the basic nature of the living cell: How childish people were to "believe in shoes, but repudiate the shoemaker," to imagine that experimentation with protoplasm could liberate man from the torment of existence or that one could "satisfy souls with cells!"[113] To Strindberg, modern scientific specialization was an example of the decadence of the times and would cause the scientist and his whole profession to languish and die. His attitude here was the same as his distrust of "the division of labor," which, using Buckle as a point of departure, he had expressed in "Observations of a Skeptic" and had had Olle Montanus preach in *The Red Room*. In a draft for the fourth "night" we find: "The scientist crippled with learning specializes in a speck.—What does he know? Nichts! Bosh!" Strindberg did not really develop this argument until the essay written immediately after *Somnambulist Nights*, "About the Universal Dissatisfaction," and he gave it its sharpest satirical expression in the story "The Isle of Bliss." Nevertheless, it is present in *Somnambulist Nights* behind the ridiculing of the scientist engaged in such picayune activities as "counting the hairs on an unknown cockroach, / which will later bear [his] great name."[114]

Strindberg questioned whether any purpose was served by all the scientific investigation that was the focal point of seething modern society. "Would you please lend me Rousseau, the part dealing with the injurious-ness of the arts and sciences to the human species?" He asked his friend Leopold Littmansson in December, 1883.[115] He had already applauded Jean-Jacques earlier in the second "night." Man, ruined by culture, has in turn ruined nature. The Boulogne woods are only theatrical set pieces and wings, with clipped trees and rocks appearing as though they were molded of wax, and the Jardin d'Acclimation, a "business enterprise for the better-ment of nature." And what is art? "A laboratory specimen, / a makeshift, a substitute / for the nature man destroyed."[116]

The feeling that it is useless for art to try to copy or revise what God created is stronger here than in any of his earlier works. In the second "night" Strindberg admits that he had once found the ancient Olympian world of beauty refreshing after "Christ and His cruel teachings." Now, antiquity is not only foreign to him but ugly, "a cartload of old plaster."[117] Apollo's head is askew and the neck of the Venus de Milo is too long. Only the statue of "The Knife-Grinder" finds favor in his eyes, not be-cause the figure is handsome and idealistic, but because it is ugly and naturalistic. He repeats his conviction from "Singers" that the truth is ugly and claims that "The Knife-Grinder" constitutes an entire theorem, filling a gap in his poetic system: "even the ugly must have its place / in this marble palace of beauty!"[118]

Strindberg began to realize, however, that this "theorem" was untenable if art were conceived as a meaningless imitation of the originals found in nature. The more naturalistically the artist proceeded, the less value his works would have. In the second "night" he interprets the dilemma this way:

> And yet, how can an artist touch a heart
> Unless he traces nature's pattern;
> But then what is achieved is not by art,
> Though one might be led to believe it.[119]

The short essay written after this—"About the Universal Dissatisfaction" —was an attempt to solve the riddle by applying a Rousseauan, idealistic ethic. The sculpture of antiquity is "a representation of nature before it was ruined by civilization" and is therefore "a remarkable example of an idealism that was on the right track and can almost be called realism."[120] The big feet and long neck of Venus de Milo demonstrate only the relativity of the concept of beauty. She was beautiful to the ancient Greeks, but not to us. There is no mention here of "The Knife-Grinder" as representative of the ugly and true. But in a somewhat later essay, "The Overrating of Cultural Activity" ("Kulturarbetets överskattning"), Strindberg harshly condemns all imitation of nature in art. He says that "a well-painted ugly cadaver," such as the painting of Christ by Philippe de Champaigne in the Louvre, is as insignificant as a decoration.[121] And in "The Isle of Bliss" he toyed with the notion that "a cow excreting" was an unpleasant sight that became beautiful once it was drawn.

It is evident from the manuscript that the optimism apparent in *Somnambulist Nights* developed as the work progressed. This is corroborated in a letter to Bjørnson, which accompanied a copy of the volume: "It is a struggle with myself! It ends with self-reproach and a penitential sermon! The latter part was written after I became acquainted with you!"[122] (The poems are dedicated to Bjørnson and Jonas Lie.)

In the fourth "night's" prophecy of a new ice age that will bury Western culture, one catches a glimpse of Hartmann's theory about the coming destruction of the world. But since this development was still many thousands of years away, Strindberg urged mankind to make itself happy for the remaining time by living according to the principle that "what is best for the many is the highest good." Instead of following the outline of the first draft and concluding with his favorite deprecatory expression, "bosh," he shakes off the cowardly doubt that whispers "that everything is naught and nothingness" and urges himself to a new struggle in which the spirit will awaken and faith will win triumphs; a struggle that will be carried on honorably, with unsheathed swords, and will distinguish between "the trivial individual and the great idea."

In the verse epilogue written after the main body of the fourth "night," hopeful contemporary signs are cited, such as the growing power of the peasants and the indefatigable struggle for the freedom of the press. The poet Count Carl Snoilsky is praised for having stretched his hand toward "his brother, the peasant." *Somnambulist Nights* thus gave rise to an optimism that would animate Strindberg until the lawsuit over *Married* broke open old wounds. His foreign sojourn taught him not only to expose his opinions to unbiased criticism, but to debate them with himself as adversary. He was not disturbed by the attacks of opponents or by his confederates' impatience. In many ways the continuous inner dialogue that characterizes *Somnambulist Nights* gives a clearer insight into Strindberg's thought processes than his later cocksure preachings.

The style of *Somnambulist Nights*—with its deliberate nonchalance—has an irresistible charm. The improvisational, colloquial verse form, inspired primarily by Ibsen's "Balloon Letter to a Swedish Lady," (1870), was extraordinarily well suited to his temperament. The loose metrical form, *knittelvers,* which he had already tested satirically in "For the Freedom of Belief," is used in a variety of forms in *Somnambulist Nights,* from choppy, epigrammatic sentences to long, lyrical bow strokes or passionately flowing torrents of words in which we detect the pulse of spoken language almost more clearly than in his argumentative prose.

At the conclusion of the second "night" Strindberg bids a solemn farewell to the "surging rivers and green groves" of the world of beauty. He does so reluctantly and concludes by imagining a partnership between the beautiful and the practical:

> But if beauty will yield its ground
> and with function be meekly bound,
> it will have a period of grace—
> so speaks one who'd utility embrace.[123]

Similar reservations can be found in the essays in *This and That (Likt och olikt),* written immediately after *Somnambulist Nights.* Working on the essays delighted Strindberg because he could express his thoughts on questions of the day "without having to encase them in literature's candy box." He condemns all literature as useless, but acknowledges that "we who were nurtured at the flower-decked trough of romanticism" had a difficult time making the sacrifice. He predicts that it might take three generations before writers learn to speak the truth.[124] But he himself feels no compulsion to abandon literature entirely, "because someone who has worked as hard as I have is entitled to intervals of rest and play."[125]

Strindberg sees romanticism as an antiquated style, but also thinks that the representatives of naturalism suffer from a fever that drives the blood to the brain and causes "an unnatural magnification of objects." He tells of his amazement when, with the memory of Zola's *Le Ventre de Paris* (1874) in mind, he once again saw les Halles and discovered that it was not at all as big as Zola had suggested. He claims to doubt that art is the "appropriate instrument with which to investigate social questions of an intimate nature" and regards the era of French naturalism as the final era of art: it "will transport literature into the newspaper article—the literature of the future."[126]

This last idea was followed up in an article on Bjørnson in May, 1884, in which Strindberg declared his intention to give up belles-lettres for newspaper writing. The modern novelist is "a magician who practices his art with 'human documents.'" But the day after his novel comes out, newspaper writers are ready to expose his most subtle artistic device, and the public loses its illusions, asking: "Ah, is that all it was?" Why should novels be written when reports of court trials are available in the newspapers?

When Strindberg now insisted that Zola's true greatness lay in reporting, he had to some degree returned to his utilitarianism of 1875, when he asserted that a writer was only a reporter of what he experienced. It was along these same lines that he later developed his opposition to naturalism and proclaimed that autobiography is the only justified form of literature for the future, because novels are only synthetic concoctions.

Strindberg's intention of abandoning belles-letters entirely did not have very serious consequences. In a fatherly letter Bjørnson earnestly requested him to turn back to creative work. Strindberg replied, during the time he was writing the Bjørnson essay, that his distaste for art assumed a kind of fanatical religious character."[127] But he also conceded that for him to be useful to mankind he had to be read, and that in order to be read he had to write "art." He said that he had just completed a story, "Remorse" ("Samvetskval"), which demonstrated "that I still possess the full power of my art," and he had "plans for the most splendid works of art." But he felt it was his duty to continue writing *This and That* until his works were ignored. "The world is so damned spoiled by your devilish art and esthetics that it vomits up every naked word of truth." Two weeks earlier, however, Strindberg had written to his publisher that he was tired of politics and yearned for "the beautiful groves of art in prose."

When the dam burst after four months of abstaining from literature, Strindberg was alarmed over his productivity. He told Bonnier that
he was writing *Married* like a sleepwalker, allowing himself no time to
reread the manuscript: "I think it is immoral to write stories and my conscience weighs heavily upon me. That is why things are moving at express
train speed. One day I wrote the equivalent of sixteen printed pages."[128]
At the same time, he was working on stories for *Utopias in Reality*
(Utopias i verkligheten) and *Swedish Destinies,* allaying his bad conscience by continuing his social reform in fiction.

Notes to Chapter Six

1. *SS:*XIX, p. 140.
2. Fritz Reuter (1810-74) was a German novelist perhaps best remembered for *Ut mine Stromtid* (1864), one of the most popular pastoral romances of the nineteenth century.—Translator
3. *Brev,* II, pp. 356-57.
4. *Ibid.,* p. 363.
5. *Brev,* III, p. 136.
6. *Brev,* II, p. 357.
7. In the essay "Literary Reactionism in Sweden" ("Den literära reaktionen i Sverige"), *SS:*XVII, p. 325.
8. In Birger Mörner's collection.
9. It is apparent in *The Swedish People (Svenska Folket)* that Strindberg had by this time read Linnaeus's observations on Nemesis.
10. *SS:*IX, pp. 120-21.
11. *Ibid.,* p. 128. During the final part of his life Strindberg set great value on *The Secret of the Guild,* not the least because he thought it had been the inspiration for Ibsen's *Master Builder.* In the first draft, where Sten dies as the tower collapses, the similarity between the two plays is more striking.
12. Strindberg, after having just written the work, declared in a letter to Helena Nyblom on January 30, 1882, that he felt "like a truant schoolboy, like a fugitive from the prison of civilization" (*Brev,* II, p. 363).
13. This alludes to Strindberg's attack on the long-respected romantic poet and historian Erik Gustaf Geijer (1873-1847) that appeared in his pre-publication announcement about *The Swedish People* and provoked a storm against him. Olle Hultén has pointed out in a still unpublished essay that the most undisguised attack on Geijer is in a dialogue exchange in Act Four where Per declares to the Official Historiographer that the titles Official Historiographer and Court Historiographer "are six of one and half a dozen of the other."
14. *SS:*IX, p. 331.
15. *Ibid.,* p. 377.
16. *Brev,* III, p. 136.
17. One need not attach too much importance to Strindberg's claim in the autobiography (*SS:*XIX, p. 174) that not until two years later

did he first read the Ibsen play; the statement is contradicted in
several places.

18. Reprinted in Karin Smirnoff's book *(Strindbergs första hustru*, 1925,
     p. 143). It is a pro-feminist statement written by Siri before her
     marriage to Strindberg.
19. *SS:*VIII, p. 290.
20. *Ibid.,* p. 296.
21. *SS:*IX, p. 230.
22. *Ibid.,* p. 231.
23. *Ibid.,* p. 229.
24. *Ibid.,* p. 260.
25. *Ibid.,* p. 263.
26. *Brev,* III, p. 137.
27. *Ibid.,* p. 169.
28. *See* Chapter II, The Early Plays.—Translator
29. Letters from 1882, Royal Library Collection.
30. *SS:*XVII, pp. 191-200.
31. *SS:*XIX, p. 183.
32. *Brev,* II, p. 283.
33. *See* Sölve Nettbladt, "August Strindberg som svensk kulturhistoriker"
     (Svenska kulturbilder. N. F. III; 6, 1936, pp. 319 ff.).
34. *Brev,* II, p. 274.
35. In the newspaper *Svenska Dagbladet,* January 7 and 9, 1933.
36. For a publishing transaction Strindberg needed a loan of 3,000
     kroner. He urged his publisher to show the banker A. O. Wallen-
     berg the unpublished chapters "Moses" and "Claris Majorum
     Exemplis" and added in his letter that if Wallenberg granted the
     loan, the chapters mentioned would be revised, "for one must
     sacrifice something for a great purpose" *(Brev,* III, p. 70). Wallen-
     berg granted the loan, and three allusions to "the Palmstruch
     Bank's" connections with *Figaro* were altered. Strindberg had
     alluded to a popular rumor circulating to the effect that Wallenberg
     used *Figaro* for his own purposes. K. O. Bonnier, who called atten-
     tion to the episode *(Bonniers, En bokhandlarefamilj.,* IV, pp.
     33 f.), doubts—certainly with justification—that Wallenberg saw
     the original version. But it is evident that Strindberg believed he
     had obtained his loan through such a maneuver; in a letter to
     Pehr Staaff at the time he said: "The reason A. O. W. patronizes
     me cannot be entrusted to paper, and *that* he does so must remain
     a secret to the grave" *(Brev,* III, p. 92).

37. *SS:*X, p. 17.
38. *Ibid.*, p. 31.
39. *SS:*XVI, p. 81.
40. *Brev.* II, pp. 182-83.
41. *Ibid.*, p. 166.
42. In *Discours sur l'Inégalité.*
43. *SS:*X, p. 54.
44. One of Buckle's central theories was that the speed of the progress of civilization at any given moment was dependent upon whether the influence of "skepticism," which encouraged doubt, investigation, and change, was greater than that of "the protective spirit," which sought to maintain the status quo.—Translator
45. *See* Chapter IV, *Town and Gown.*
46. I doubt Lindblad's supposition (pp. 161 ff.) that Strindberg was inspired by Offenbach's operettas or by the classic Uppsala student farces. The farces date for the most part from a later period and it is more likely that they were inspired by *The New Kingdom.* Several scholars have sought to trace influences from Zola, but I feel the differences are greater than the similarities.
47. Pseudonym for Wilhelm Bergstrand.
48. An excerpt from it, "The Tale of Hercules" ("Sagan om Herkules"), was printed in 1883 in a small edition of thirteen manuscripts. It was based on the legend of the Augean stables with reference to Ibsen's *Enemy of the People.* (The phrase "enemy of the people" actually appears in the text.) There are also references to Ibsen's plays in *The New Kingdom.*
49. *Brev,* III, p. 99.
50. *See also* Chapter VIII, *The Isle of Bliss.*—Translator
51. "Tschandala" appeared in the third edition of *Swedish Destinies and Adventures* in 1904.
52. *SS:*L, p. 237.
53. In "Tre noveller ur Strindbergs *Svenska öden och äventyr*" (Publications of Modersmålslararnes förening, 1915, pp. 6-7).
54. *SS:*VII, p. 92.
55. Strindberg might have defended his creation of a Sten Ulvfot by pointing out that J. P. Jacobsen—whose novel *Marie Grubbe* he was attempting to dramatize during the time he was planning *Swedish Destinies*—had no historical support for making his heroine "flower-delicate" or sketching Sti Høg as a gentle melancholic.

56. Cf. *SS:*VII, pp. 125-26.
57. The parson's response was to refuse this "obscene offer."—Translator
58. *SS:*XI, pp. 262-63.
59. In this regard Strindberg sharply parts company with Walter Scott. Lindblad is right when he finds "a distant similarity" between the introductory part of "Cultivated Fruit" and the beginning of Scott's *Quentin Durward.* A letter to Claes Looström *(Brev,* III, p. 99) demonstrates that Strindberg requested that he be sent this very Scott novel before he began work on the story. But Strindberg was little influenced by Scott, both here and elsewhere. The stories of Gustaf H. Mellin (1803-76), which Strindberg mentions as predecessors to *Swedish Destinies* in *Talks to the Swedish Nation* in 1910, first came into his hands during the work on *Swedish Destinies,* but he apparently found them disappointing.
60. *SS:*XII, p. 390.
61. *SS:*XI, p. 195.
62. *Ibid.,* pp. 195-96.
63. *Ibid.,* p. 264.
64. *Ibid.,* p. 267.
65. A European fish of the carp family.—Translator
66. *SS:*XI, p. 149.
67. *Ibid.,* p. 295.
68. *SS:*XIX, p. 193.
69. *See* Böök, *Teatern i Röda rummet,* pp. 18-19 and *Svenska litteraturens historia,* III, pp. 109-10.
70. *Brev,* II, p. 267.
71. *SS:*XI, p. 56.
72. *SS:*XVI, p. 17.
73. Eklund has demonstrated *(Strindbergsstudie,* pp. 245 ff.) that this viewpoint is traceable to J. Moleschott's *Der Kreislauf des Lebens* (1852), with which Strindberg was probably already familiar at the time he wrote *Master Olof.*
74. *August Strindberg: En kämpande och lidande själs historia* (1920), II, p. 63.
75. In a letter to Jonas Lie on June 1, 1884, Strindberg wrote: "You have to read a *Swedish Destiny* in the second volume entitled 'Evolution.' There you have me in two parts" *(Brev,* IV, p. 194).
76. *SS:*XI, p. 258.
77. *SS:*XIX, p. 186.
78. *Brev,* II, p. 357. He praises it even in *A Blue Book.* Pehr Staaff,

during his reading of the first part of "Evolution," asked Strindberg if it did not contain "subtle loomings from *Abbé Mouret.*" Lindblad has done an extraordinary job of analyzing this novel's significance for *Swedish Destinies* in *August Strindberg som berättare.*

79. *SS:*XI, p. 113.
80. *See* Henry Olsson, *Från Wallin till Fröding,* p. 258.
81. *SS:*XI, p. 259.
82. *Brev,* III, p. 55.
83. *SS:*XI, pp. 248-49.
84. *SS:*XIII, p. 106.
85. *Ibid.,* p. 103.
86. *Ibid.,* p. 117.
87. *Ibid.,* p. 121.
88. *SS:*XIX, p. 193.
89. *SS:*XIII, p. 74.
90. *Ibid.,* p. 87.
91. "Dissimilar Weapons" later inspired Gustaf Fröding's "The Traitor" ("Förrädarn"—1894).
92. *SS:*XIII, p. 26.
93. The foreword is dated in October, 1883. However, according to a letter to Looström on July 12, 1883 (*Brev,* III, p. 260), there seems to have been a foreword included in the then still incomplete collection of poetry; unfortunately, we know nothing of its contents.
94. Three years later in the fourth part of his autobiography *(SS:*XIX, p. 196) Strindberg is still very indignant that the reviewers of *Poems* considered him ignorant of the laws of poetry, "notwithstanding that he had had a classical education and probably had written twenty thousand verses in his time and, what was more serious, had received honorable mention from the Swedish Academy for a verse drama."
95. *See* Henry Olsson, pp. 80-81.
96. *Ibid.,* pp. 69-70.
97. Fröding, *Samslade skrifter,* IX, p. 187.
98. *Cf.* Lindblad, pp. 21-22.
99. *Brev.* III, p. 260.
100. *SS:*XIII, p. 92.
101. Reproduced in facsimile in Mörner, p. 196.
102. Fröding, p. 186.

103. *Bonniers,* IV, pp. 48 f.
104. Fröding is renowned as a master of rhythm in Swedish.—Translator
105. For an explanation of *knittelvers, see* the end of The Revisions and
      the Verse Version, Chapter III.—Translator
106. Henry Olsson, "Strindbergs Sömngångarnätter," pp. 77 ff.
107. *See* note 3, Chapter II.
108. Olsson, p. 86.
109. *SS:*XIII, p. 279.
110. *Brev,* III, p. 331.
111. *SS:*XXII, pp. 77-78.
112. *SS:*XIII, p. 275.
113. *Ibid.,* pp. 269-70.
114. *Ibid.,* p. 274.
115. *Brev,* III, p. 375.
116. *SS:*XIII, pp. 228-29.
117. *Ibid.,* pp. 230-31.
118. *Ibid,* p. 235.
119. *Ibid.,* p. 228.
120. *SS:*XVI, pp. 58-59.
121. *Ibid.,* p. 131.
122. *Brev,* IV, pp. 46-47.
123. *SS:*XIII, p. 238.
124. *SS:*XVI, p. 50.
125. *SS:*XVII, p. 329.
126. *Ibid.,* pp. 328-29.
127. *Brev,* IV, pp. 144-45.
128. *Ibid.,* p. 210.

Chapter Seven

THE BATTLE OVER *MARRIED*

The Years of Exile

During the last half of the nineteenth century the expatriate's life had an appeal which seems puzzling to us today. Particularly in the Scandinavian countries, where young writers felt restrained by a stultifying cultural environment, the word "exile" took on an enticing ring. From foreign bastions they hoped to be able to conquer the conventionalism and subservience to authority of the critics back home. This is what Ibsen succeeded in doing in 1879 with *A Doll's House,* while his fellow exiles, Bjørnson and Lie, were well on the way toward becoming world famous.

The dream of exile was born early in Strindberg's imagination. On June 26, 1881, he wrote to Edvard Brandes: "When I am finished with my cultural history, which will unmask the entire Swedish nation, I shall go into exile in Geneva or Paris and become a real writer! Not the kind who works with belles-lettres, but one who writes the things he cannot speak! Ruthlessly!"[1] He attempted to realize this hope two years later in Paris, where he wanted to make his way as a socio-political writer in French.

The storm provoked by his attack on Geijer in the pre-publication announcement about *The Swedish People* strengthened his resolve. On October 3, 1881, he wrote that he felt "hellishly alone in this conflagration I prepared":

> There is no one who does not want to roast me in the fire! I think I misjudged my people—they are so thickheaded and conservative that there are none who agree with me, and those who should be with me are jealous, so they leave me in the lurch. Next fall I too shall go into exile.

The same year he began his plans for *Married;* perhaps he thought he

139

could win renown more quickly by contributing to the debate over *A Doll's House.*

During the next year or two the thought of exile was a recurrent theme in Strindberg's letters and writings. It appeared in several of the stories in *Swedish Destinies* and motivated the verse cycle "Exile" (1876), in which one might say he gave vent to his homesickness in advance. Although he was finding it unendurable to stay in Sweden after the uproar over *The New Kingdom,* another year would elapse before he finally left.

No matter how much Strindberg talked about "de-Swedenizing" himself and becoming a naturalized citizen of France or Switzerland, the separation from his homeland was costlier than he had imagined. This is evident in the first "somnambulist night," written shortly after his arrival in Paris, and in his letters, where he usually referred to his yearning for home as a "physical" thing. When after a four-year sojourn abroad he tried to explain in his autobiography why an attempt by an adult to emigrate from his native land was doomed to failure, he referred to "the spirit's dependence on matter":

> Even if you do not leave anything precious behind, do not own a stone in your ancestral home, not a clod in a field; even if you are happy to have emerged from an environment that was intolerable, and like the queen bee you carried everything along so that you have not the slightest cause to long for home, your body still feels homesick.[2]

Because Strindberg was extremely set in his ways, the change, in physical surroundings alone, caused him anguish. It is difficult to understand why years later in *Talks to the Swedish Nation* (1910) he ridiculed so severely "the five lines" in Verner von Heidenstam (1859-1940) in which the latter professed to long not for people but for the land—"the stones where I played as a child." Strindberg's own homesickness was of the same variety. Although the novelty of foreign surroundings frequently charmed him for a time, when he compared them with Stockholm and the skerries, the new impressions quickly lost their appeal. No matter how comfortable he felt in a new locale, the feeling was only temporary; the place soon became hell. And so the Strindbergs wandered constantly from place to place: Strindberg's daughter, Karin Smirnoff, enumerated twenty-two different places the family set up housekeeping during the six years of exile, and from time to time her father went off on short trips by himself.

It was during this period that his marriage—which had already undergone numerous storms—was permanently shattered. Most of the time he and his wife had no other company than each other. Siri, who had pursued her acting career while in Sweden, now had to devote herself to catering to Strindberg's unpredictable whims and satisfying his fastidious tastes. She was not only his housekeeper, but also a model in his work, even for the first volume of *Married,* despite the denials of Strindberg and others. "I hit out at my own wife," he wrote from Geneva to Jonas Lie in October, 1884, before journeying home for the blasphemy trial. "It was a personal sacrifice that I had to make." He was aware that *Married* would alienate him completely from former friends: "[I've] broken with every-thing, advanced over corpses, to triumph and defeat! Look about me! There lie the wounded! Friends, ideals, dear ones, everything!"

Strindberg had achieved the international fame to which he had aspired. When the first part of *Married* was published in French in the spring of 1885, half a year after the trial in connection with the Swedish edition, the Paris newspapers began to talk about the notorious woman-hater. But it was a dearly bought triumph.

The First Volume of *Married*

Strindberg had two contradictory explanations for the origin of the first volume of *Married.* On the one hand, according to his autobiog-raphy, he began the book "while living in happy eroticism," venerating woman almost superstitiously and even intending to help her escape her oppressed state. By the time he had written half the book, however, he found that "it was not turning out as expected." Supposedly, unpleasant experiences with women in the Swiss pension where he lived[3] had soured his attitude.

On the other hand, according to *A Madman's Defense,* he wrote the entire book in the midst of tumultuous warfare with his wife. An unmarried woman, a friend of his wife, arrived from Scandinavia "full of those crazy ideas about female emancipation" and brought with her "a bad book by a sexless man." Indignation enabled Strindberg to shake off his depression, and he began "a book which will be like a gauntlet thrown in the faces of emancipated women, these fools who want to have freedom at the cost of man's suppression."[4]

The first version is the truer one, although it was probably Strind-

berg's own marriage complications rather than his experiences at the pension that altered the character of the book during the time it was written.

In the spring of 1883, before his trip abroad, Strindberg was
occupied with plans for "a salable publication—*Portraits of Women
(Kvinnobilder),*" which he wanted to introduce between installments of his
slow-selling historical stories. When he returned to the idea a year later,
he explained to K. O. Bonnier that he had laid the foundation for the work
"several years ago under the title *Portraits of Women,* which I want now
to change to *Married People (Gift folk)."* It was true that Strindberg was
returning to an old project; in November, 1881, he had offered for publication in *Politiken,* Denmark's leading radical newspaper, a series of fifteen
stories illustrating the same social problem. As Landquist pointed out,[5]
this was the first plan for *Married.* On the same day, Strindberg also
offered the series to several other newspapers,[6] and a comparison of the
letters reveals that the subject matter of the collection must have concerned
women. The purpose was to "examine small human questions on a large
scale" and deal with "social problems in living pictures."

Unquestionably, Strindberg's intention from the start was to
state his views on the Doll's House question, the most debated subject of
the day. He had already taken a stand on it in *Herr Bengt's Wife* and *The
Swedish People,* and the argument that man's gallantry toward woman
had made him a victim of a "doll tyranny" reappears in the preface to
Married. As work proceeded on the book, his attitude toward the Ibsen
play became even more antagonistic.[7]

After about two-thirds of *Married* had been written, Strindberg
reread *A Doll's House,* which he had had sent to him from his library in
Stockholm. Shortly thereafter, on June 24, 1884, he wrote to Pehr Staaff
that Ibsen's play had the drawback of depicting only "a single exceptional
case. My present opinion is that it is a bit simple-minded. From my standpoint." When he had finished writing *Married,* he wrote that the preface
contained "the most radical program for women ever seen." By radical,
Strindberg meant that although he was suspicious of the modern emancipated woman, he was willing to make extreme proposals toward the goal
of more equality of the sexes. For example, his preface recommends
co-educational schools, an easing of divorce laws, and the right of women
to vote and to choose (to a certain extent) their own occupations. "But I
scold Ibsen," he wrote, "for his devilish idealism in *A Doll's House.*

Bjørnson's *A Gauntlet (Handske)*, as well. Idiotic flirting, old-fashioned gallantry."

The most important result of Strindberg's rereading of the Ibsen play was the short story "A Doll House" ("Ett dockhem"), in which the play was made the source of conflict in a marriage.

Strindberg had intended to write an entertaining book and promised his publisher to begin with "something especially pleasant." Although the promise of something "pleasant" was not fulfilled, the bitterness of misogyny is absent in the first few stories.[8] The earliest one, "Virtue's Rewards" ("Dygdens lön"), was a continuation of the Zola-inspired battle against asceticism and celibacy initiated in the *Swedish Destinies* stories "Higher Purposes" and "Evolution." As has often been pointed out, Strindberg presented, half-seriously, his own erotic misadventures as a youth.[9]

Even less hostile to women is the next story, "Compelled" ("Måste"), which develops into a burlesque panegyric on marital bliss. Similarly, one can find little misogynistic propaganda in the third, "Love and Bread" ("Kärlek och spannmål"), in which two newlyweds are equally unreasonable and therefore have to suffer the consequences equally.

Not until the next two stories do we begin to discern the feminine profile that was to recur in more or less unaltered form: a small, stubborn, illogical woman, inclined to quarreling and attacks of hysteria. Although in the first of these stories, "Compensation" ("Ersättning"), the dark clouds threatening a marriage are driven away by the arrival of a child, in the second, "Bad Luck" ("Otur"), dissension suggested by Strindberg's own marriage begins to appear. The husband, a mild-mannered wholesaler, is forced to sit in a riding-academy grandstand and watch his wife's nightly riding lessons. It pains him to see the riding master put his arms around her waist to help her into the saddle, and to see her male companions follow her movements with "ardent eyes." "There was lewdness in the air and mischief took place unseen."[10] One night when he is home alone, he answers the door and finds his wife helplessly drunk after one of her lessons, during which great quantities of champagne had been consumed. Later he reads "horrible things" in the newspaper about a certain society lady, but although it is obvious to him that the woman in question is his wife, he cannot prove it. (Here is a foreshadowing of the monomaniacal jealousy in *A Madman's Defense.* One need only convert the *manège* into a theatre auditorium and the riding companions into actors to recognize the real-life situation.)

The story "Natural Obstacle" ("Naturhinder") contains a variation on the same theme. The wife works in the baggage department of the railroad and her jealous forester husband spends unbearable hours waiting for her in the office. Sometimes his arrival is announced by a bookkeeper with the sneering expression: "The lady's husband is waiting for her." These are the times Strindberg waited for his wife in a narrow alley outside the stage door. Sometimes the man's wife does not return home until early morning, drunk on champagne and hanging on the arm of one of her male colleagues.

These stories marked the first appearance of the Strindbergian domestic martyr. The common theme is that feminine emancipation results in marriages in which man is the slave, because he is the one who loves. "And believe me, women are the ones who rule the world, even if they can't vote."[11] In "Natural Obstacle" the forester had entered into "a proper spiritual marriage" when he married a self-supporting woman who kept her job. But when he fails to appreciate her friendships with male co-workers in the baggage department, he is told that he has betrayed "their great faith, the faith in . . . woman's liberation."[12] Ultimately, after he is forced to assume some of his wife's domestic responsibilities in the caring of their child, he comes to the conclusion that there is no "hope that women can be emancipated from natural laws—*under present conditions,* he was wise enough to add."[13]

The radical program for women in the preface of Volume I of *Married,* of which Strindberg was so proud, was weakened when its most important proposals were qualified with the reservation—not to be put into effect "under present conditions." For example, he suggests that "woman has the right to hold any job, and practice any occupation she prefers."[14] But he adds that the competition would be devastating if the doors of the labor market were immediately thrown open to several million women. He also says that woman "can be given the right to vote as soon as possible." But in a fictitious interview that was printed with the preface, Strindberg emphasizes that if in France one were immediately to extend suffrage to all the priest-educated, boarding-school girls, as Dumas *fils* was urging, Jesuits and Capuchins would be elected and the Empress Eugenie placed on the throne. Unfortunately, the ambivalence of his position is not resolved in the later essay "Equality and Tyranny" ("Likställighet och tyranni"), which was written before the first volume of *Married* was available in the bookstores in late September, 1884. Some passages in the essay advocate giving women the vote and others reject the idea. Throughout, he retreats behind the obstacle that makes marriage unbearable—the "present conditions": "Consequently, I have not attacked woman, I have attacked—spell it out in capital letters—THE PRESENT CONDITIONS."[15]

In time the validity of Strindberg's argument in the first volume of *Married* was recognized and became influential in bringing the feminist movement back from the byroads into which it had strayed during the debates over *A Doll's House*.[16] Strindberg felt himself the pupil of Rousseau when, in contrast to Ibsen's bloodless idealism, he championed the rightfulness of natural instincts and pointed out the distortions created by the bias in favor of woman's rights. In late August, 1884, he wrote to Jonas Lie: "My Rousseauistic perspective, using nature as norm, does not permit me to go along with the modern idealistic gallantry that makes women into angels and men into devils." In the preface he was skeptical about the importance of the question of emancipation for women, because it concerned only educated or "cultured" women, a mere ten percent of the population. Moreover, if the "cultured" woman understood more clearly the "natural"—i.e., the peasant's—life, the problem would never have arisen. Certainly, "the peasant's wife cannot envy [her husband's] free position, since it is not more noble or honorable to stir the manure pile than the soup pot."

The *Married* stories, however, which stress the need to respect what is healthily animalistic in man, and which praise motherhood and fecundity, have more in common with Zola than with Rousseau. It was from a Zolaesque point of view that Strindberg perceptively criticized Ibsen's drama—especially its failure to acknowledge that the simple process of living together can unite people who are ill-matched by personality. "Have we not educated each other, and planed off the rough edges?" asks Captain Pall of his wife in the story "A Doll House." "Surely you remember," he continues, "that in the beginning everything was spikes and spurs."[17] Strindberg's reaction to the intellectualism of the Doll's House

debates on the nature of marriage is contained in the sea captain's answer
to his wife's question as to whether he has *thought* about their marriage.
" 'No,' he said, as if he had his parry planned. 'I have merely felt about it!
You see, I believe love is a matter of feeling. If you sail according to your
feeling about where the land is, you make port. But use a compass and
chart, and you'll run aground.' "[18]

To a certain extent, *Married* is a step toward Zolaesque naturalism. It consists—as Strindberg tirelessly maintained—of a collection of
"cases" drawn directly from real life, supposedly to illustrate a universal
"law." Strindberg made little effort, however, to observe the objectivity
that was proclaimed to be the highest virtue of the naturalistic writer. He
was also aware that from the naturalistic standpoint he had erred by not
including any detailed descriptions. He was to correct this deficiency in
several of the stories written shortly afterward for *Utopias in Reality*.

In the author's interview with himself in the preface to Volume I
of *Married* the "interviewer" brings up the criticism Strindberg anticipated might come from the naturalists—that the book was not "detailed":

> If you knew how right you are! It isn't detailed! That's exactly the point.
> You see, my purpose was to depict a rather large number of cases, ordinary
> cases, of the relationship between husband and wife. . . . Therefore, I
> have not detailed more than one supper at Stallmästargården, in which we
> have two kinds of salmon with dill, freshly pickled cucumbers, small
> beefsteaks with Spanish onions, chicken and strawberries. In addition, I
> have crayfish (female) at Rejners, pancakes at Djurgården; a garden on
> Nortulls Street with blooming apple trees, six kinds of flowers and a
> pair of nightjars. Furthermore, I have Adolf Frederick's Church and a
> fencing foil, and at least thirty nautical terms which I took out of a
> nautical dictionary! Now isn't that realistic?[19]

This obvious irony shows that Strindberg did not set great store
on the naturalistic approach, with its descriptions of accessories and its
documentary method. In the stories themselves critical remarks are also
made about "synthetically-concocted stories" whose plot structures are
contrived.

The story that retained most of the Zolaesque style that Strindberg had imitated earlier in *Swedish Destinies* is "Virtue's Rewards," and
most of the examples mentioned in the interview can be found there. It
contains descriptions of nature which, through a somewhat ponderous
symbolism, are supposed to herald the awakening of man's natural in-

stincts. We find the whirling pollen of apple trees in bloom, the wedding song of mosquitoes, the "purring siren strains" of nightjars, the "lustful screams of cats," the buzzing of dung beetles—all to remind Theodor, the young *gymnasium* student in the story, of "nature's command." There are also descriptions of his sexual dreams and his battle against the intoxication of the senses that nature provokes. Once again Strindberg took as his model Zola's *La Faute de l'Abbé Mouret,* but he was now considerably bolder and more candid in his descriptions than he had been in "Evolution."

The supper party at Stallmästargården mentioned by Strindberg in the preface, with its facetiously grotesque exaggerations, is a good example of the Zolaesque physiological method. The autobiographical point of departure was a breakfast Strindberg had at Tre Remmare restaurant after his confirmation. According to his account in *The Son of a Servant,* [20] he had a drink and a beefsteak, which brought warmth to his body, tears to his misty eyes, and caused him to "feel strength and vigor flow in his half-empty veins, restoring his nerves for life's battles." In "Virtue's Rewards," the adult Theodor, now an ascetic theologian, experiences even stronger sensual intoxication at a supper party when he is confronted with eighteen different side dishes in addition to the main dishes. He cannot resist tasting the schnapps:

> And it warmed him strongly. And a thin, warm veil fell over his eyes and hunger raced like a wild animal in his insides. There was fresh salmon with its half-rancid taste and dill with its torporific narcotic. Radishes clawed at the throat and cried out for beer. There were small beefsteaks and Portuguese sweet onions that smelled like a warm dancing girl, and lobster-à-la-daube with aromas from the seashore. And the freshly pickled cucumbers with the poisoned taste of verdigris, which crunched so beautifully between the teeth. And then the chicken stuffed with parsley, which brought to mind the gardener. The beer ran in his veins like warm streams of lava, and then, bang, popped the champagne over the strawberries, and the girl brought the sputtering drink, which flowed like a fountain. . . . And Theodor sat there like a newly sapped tree, and the food effervesced inside him until he felt like a volcano. [21]

Taken out of context, the passage might seem intended as a parody of Zola's technique, but this was hardly the purpose. Zola, too, could exaggerate in the same half-joking way, as in the famous goose dinner scene in *L'Assommoir* (1878), of which Brandes once observed that there could not have been a stronger effect if an elephant had been roasted. But

Zola does not use the fresh and original similes that distinguish Strindberg here.

The fault with descriptive passages of this kind is that they are ends in themselves. It is true that the section above goes on to mention that "new thoughts, new feelings, new opinions, new viewpoints fluttered like butterflies about" Theodor's head, but it is difficult to understand how they were kindled by the opulent party. Strindberg is much more successful when he employs a straightforward narrative approach, as in the famous crayfish-eating scene that opens the story "Compelled." The thirty-two-year-old bachelor comes to life for us despite the fact that description is limited to two details: he is a schoolmaster and his glasses are steamed over. For twelve years he has been coming to eat crayfish at this restaurant, and we understand the rhythm of his life and the world of his thoughts. This is Dickensian psychological realism, and it is another example—which would occur often in Strindberg's later writings—of his superiority to Zolaesque naturalism, with its orgies of taste and smell, its nervous physiological fastidiousness, and its paroxysms of drunkenness.

Most of the *Married* stories begin with a very brief description of husband and wife. Indeed, so sketchy are the descriptions that the majority of the central characters seem like the same couple in different situations. Domestic problems quickly accumulate and become intensified, and the resolution often derives from the birth of a child, which mitigates the conflicts, at least temporarily. In the later essay concerning *Married* and the blasphemy trial, "The Confiscation Journey" ("Kvarstadsresan"), there is a statement that indicates that Strindberg apparently considered having all the stories end in this way.[22] The uniformity is intentional; the sameness of modern marriage is the thing he wanted to illustrate.

To some extent, Strindberg availed himself of the same story technique he employed in *Town and Gown*.[23] We recognize the sketchy, nonchalant Orvar Odd manner[24] of beginning most of the stories with the pronouns "he," or "she," or "they" somewhere in the opening sentence, and only later revealing the identity of the person or persons mentioned: "He was a genius at college and there was no doubt he would amount to something" ("Compensation"). "He had had his eyes opened to the world's stupidity" ("Skirmishes" — "Slitningar"). "She had observed with disgust how girls were brought up to be housekeepers for their future husbands" ("A Reform Attempt" — "Reformförsök"). "They had been married for six years, but they were like an engaged couple" ("A Doll House").[25]

The influence of August Blanche's narrative technique is also still in evidence. In "Compelled" there is a short account, between asterisks—exactly as in Blanche's *Pictures From Reality (Bilder ur verkligheten)*—of the hero's curriculum vitae: "Schoolmaster Blom had at twenty years of age discontinued his studies at Uppsala and gone to the capital as an assistant teacher." Elsewhere, there are situations narrated with the same ironic gravity found in Blanche. "Compensation" contains an amusing portrayal of an acting district judge who marries a cooper's daughter:

> The cooper got drunk at the wedding and was delivering an indecent speech to the girls. But the judge found his behavior so natural and agreeable that instead of silencing the old man, he encouraged him to continue. He felt very comfortable with these simple people; one could be one's self.[26]

It is not surprising that critics believed *Married* was influenced by contemporary French prose style, in particular by Maupassant, but one must be cautious about presuming such an influence.[27] Although both writers have a brisk narrative style devoid of unnecessary description, Maupassant's conciseness is different from Strindberg's: his French is classically decorous, and although he frequently depicted lascivious or outrageous situations, his vocabulary retained the most extreme propriety. In Strindberg it is the coarse words and brutal outspokenness that are abrasive, not the subject being portrayed. Whereas Maupassant endeavored to be naturalistically objective, the *Married* stories have the subjective and improvisatory character of sketches. Strindberg is chatty, interrupting the story line to insert short, amusing reflections and making no effort to avoid the impression that each story is another verse in the same old refrain.

A more important influence on *Married* than Maupassant was *Novelettes (Noveletter*—1879) by the Norwegian writer Alexander Kielland (1849-1906). They were elegant and ironic, and Strindberg admired them very much. It has been said that Strindberg sought to imitate their nonchalant, superbly witty tone, and if he did not succeed completely, it was due to his more somber temperament and less aristocratic style. Strindberg's humor is more tendentious and morally indignant than Kielland's.[28]

In the essay "The Confiscation Journey," Strindberg posed an important question about style: "Should one write as people speak? Yes, one ought to, because writing must be veracious; depictions of life must resemble life."[29] In another passage he claimed to have introduced the novelty of "allowing each person to speak approximately as he might in real life, yet avoiding the bluntest of vulgar words which, although spoken by the upper classes, are not written (at least not presently in Sweden)."[30] In his earlier prose works colloquialisms appeared only in dialogue; in *Married* the prevailing style is colloquial since virtually everything has been transformed into dialogue. Many passages that are not actual dialogue exchanges are reports of conversations. Even the author's personal remarks—short questions and exclamations—have a conversational tone. The stylistic model was Hans Christian Andersen, as is evident in the description of the wedding in "Love and Bread":

> And then there was a wedding on a Saturday night! And then there was Sunday morning! Hey, what a commotion! Isn't it wonderful to be married! Isn't marriage a wonderful invention! You get to do whatever you please. And then, parents and brothers and sisters come to congratulate you, to boot![31]

This is Andersen's method of grabbing the reader's lapel and forcing him to share the feelings of the characters portrayed.

Typically Strindbergian—although also not without ties to Andersen—is the abrupt tempo: mere clauses, which more often than not begin with "and," as in ordinary, conversational speech. "And then the room was in order. And the bedroom was like a little temple. And the two beds stood there alongside each other like two carriages. And the sun shone on the blue bedspread and the white, white sheets."[32] Indeed, even when Strindberg uses more complex sentences, he scarcely troubles himself to work them out syntactically or logically; he is satisfied with artless suggestion: "It was during strawberry time, in the parsonage, that he saw her for the first time. He had seen many girls before, but when he saw her, he knew she was the one."[33] The intentional awkwardness of this opening to "The Phoenix Bird" ("Fågel Fenix") is not without charm. It is a genuine fragment of the emotional world of a shy *gymnasium* student.

Character descriptions, too, are rendered in a few quick and rather astonishing similes. The girl in the parsonage is characterized as follows:

> Her hair was yellow and transparent white like clear honey and always hung like water spray around her face. Her eyes blazed and her skin was

> fresh and soft like a doeskin glove. They were engaged; and in the
> garden, in the woods, under the linden, they kissed like birds. Life was
> like a sunny, unmowed meadow for them.[34]

Of course, such a passage does not give us a clear visual image, but it is
not intended to do so; instead, we are left with a feeling of spring and
lighthearted youth. Throughout the stories, Strindberg draws his figures in
this way, without the lengthy caricaturing descriptions of outward appearances found in *The Red Room*. To characterize the emancipated seminary
student Ottilia in "A Doll House," Strindberg borrowed Captain Pall's
nautical terminology: she "was tall like a stav[35] and had cut her hair short
so that from behind she looked like a swabbie." The same technique
appeared later in the novel *The People of Hemsö* (1887), in which Strindberg used words and idioms from the world of the men of the skerries.

The typically Andersenian intonations are perhaps most noticeable in the ironic lamentations that conclude many of the stories: "Oh,
how cruel, how cruel—that life[36] cannot provide grouse and strawberries
for everyone. How cruel, how cruel!"[37] ("Love and Bread"); "But she
still insists she is his slave. She is, too, and this is her only comfort in
distress, poor thing!"[38] ("Natural Obstacles"). And even when a story
ending is in a lighter key, one can recognize Andersen's coquettish appeal
to the reader: "And she became his wife and comrade as before, but, in
addition, the mother of his child, and that, he thought, was the best of
all"[39] ("A Reform Attempt").

The clearest evidence of Andersen's influence is probably in the
story "Compensation." A husband has livened his marriage by singing
"The Rose in the North Woods" ("Rosen i Nordanskog") while his wife
listened attentively and crocheted antimacassars. After a year, the house
is filled with antimacassars and "The Rose in the North Woods" has
begun to wear thin. With the arrival of a child, everything is changed as if
by magic. The wife has other things to do than to crochet antimacassars
and "The Rose in the North Woods" is brand-new to little Harald. "And
they sang 'The Rose in the North Woods' and Harald squealed along.
And they danced to 'The Rose in the North Woods' and rocked the cradle
to it, and it never wore out, no never!"[40] This is thoroughly Andersenian
in style —in the light-hearted, galloping cadence and in the little phrase
"no never," tacked on to the stately *tirade*-like rise at the final lines in
order to undermine the rhetorical effect.

Sometimes the sequence of events in the stories also takes on this restless, playful rhythm. For example, in "Love and Bread" Strindberg bridges passages of time in fairy-tale fashion with short, staccato phrases: "The months go by! The moment approaches. The time for cradles and tiny clothes!" Or: "The day has come and the night is here! He has to get dressed and run for the midwife!"[41] This fairy-tale technique is splendidly appropriate for the portrayal of two married children living in the moment, without any thought for the future.

Shortly after Volume I of *Married* was published on September 27, 1884, Karl Warburg, in the section of his review in the Gothenburg newspaper *Handelstidningen* concerning the story "Compelled," stated that "not since the days of [Carl Michael] Bellman has life in Stockholm had such a portrayer." Twenty years later Oscar Levertin was of the opposite opinion and complained that in *Married* "the Stockholm milieu emerges so unartistically and plebianly conceived that one almost thinks of Blanche." Today's reader would probably agree with Warburg. The stuffed easy chairs, dried-flower bouquets, and antimacassars of the 1880's (the despair of the highly aesthetic 1890's) have taken on time's patina, and one does not lament that the idyllic Stockholm life pulsating in the *Married* stories is reminiscent of August Blanche. As was his custom, Strindberg preferred to depict the Stockholm of his childhood or his youth rather than contemporary Stockholm. Even in the malicious second volume of *Married* he took time to describe his beloved Klara churchyard and the old rotunda in what is now the park (Humlegården) around the Royal Library.

The best of the stories dealing with Stockholm, as Warburg mentioned, is "Compelled," with its incomparable images from the old restaurant, Rejners. In the glassed-in veranda the schoolmaster celebrates the brief Swedish crayfish-eating season with the seriousness of a religious ceremony. Later, in the inner dining room, he drinks a toddy with the bookseller and the Polish violinist. The story also includes a Stockholm Midsummer celebration that surpasses the holiday descriptions of bygone Christmases and Easters in *Old Stockholm* (1880). Today, no one recalls the time when workers' families used to picnic in the middle of Berzelii Park, when people ate boiled eggs, crayfish and pancakes out of baskets, as mothers nursed their children, and a police constable faithfully watched the idyll with a glass of beer in one hand and a sandwich in the other. One suspects that even in the 1880's such things no longer took place. In "Compelled" the famous Hasselbacken restaurant still has the same motley group of customers it had in Blanche's day in the 1860's:

> High up in the back sat officers, blue in the face from food and drink. Alongside them were representatives of foreign powers, gray and exhausted from the strenuous work of defending the cause of several drunken fellow countrymen who were beaten up near the harbor, or from having to attend gala spectacles, christenings, weddings, and funerals and so forth.[42]

Out in the open spaces of the big park (Djurgården) near the restaurant are holiday visitors: the chimney sweep of Ladugårds Field and his family, the restaurant keeper at "Kungen i Helvete," and the assistant at the Sjubben pharmacy. This splendid story gives a remarkably vivid picture of Stockholm on holiday. The account begins with the sound of the chiming of church bells, then come images of flag-bedecked barges, steamboats out in Nybro Harbor, and the Volunteer Rifle Corps marching out to their drill field (Gårdet) to the resounding music of a brass band. The story ends in an evening panorama, with the steamboats returning home, and fine ladies with white-powdered hair riding through the streets in lacquered carriages.

In *Married,* as in all of Strindberg's works, the Stockholm archipelago plays a part. It is probably most noticeable in "A Doll House":

> And so reveille sounded. The drawn-out notes of the bugle rolled out between the green islands over the shining water and returned by other routes behind the pine woods. And then came the order for all hands on deck, and the Lord's Prayer and "Jesus, at the day's beginning" were read. The little church tower on Dalarö answered with a faith chiming, for it was Sunday morning. And now came the cutters in the morning breeze; flags were flying, guns cracked, and light-colored summer clothing flashed on the customs pier. The steamboat, trailing a red wake, sailed up from Utön, the fishermen hauled in their nets, and the sun shone on the billowing blue water and over the greening islands.[43]

This portrait of Dalarö is similar to one included in the novel fragment discussed earlier in connection with Strindberg's first sketches of the skerries, and it foreshadows the idylls in the later stories *Fairhaven and Foulstrand (Fagervik och Skamsund*—1902). A portrait of the skerries painted in a minor key appears in the most beautiful story in the second volume of *Married,* "Autumn" ("Höst"). The summer cottages on Vaxholm are boarded up, gardens are plundered, verandas minus their tent awnings look like skeletons, and the bays of the island are dark blue and enclosed by yellowing birches.

Interior scenes in Volume I show the small apartments of newly-weds, with embroidered pillows, pier glasses with enormous sheets of plate glass, writing tables with innumerable draws ("walnut every one"), and Captain Pall's enchanting cabin room in the Långa raden section of Skepps Island near Stockholm, which "was like nothing in the world. On the walls hung Japanese parasols and armor, East Indian miniature pago-das, Australian bows and lances, African drums and dried flying fish, sugar cane, and opium pipes."[44]

Just as Strindberg can make a character visually clear for the reader in *Married* without mentioning outward appearance, so can he bring an interior to life without going into details. In portraying the interior of the little dining room in Rejners restaurant ("Compelled") he did not need to resort to the kind of painstaking description used for X-Town's provincial restaurant in *The Red Room*.[45] The atmosphere in the dining room is evoked through the conversation of the trio of toddy drinkers and through information given about the restaurant keeper, an old sea captain who "fell in love with the forecabin" and whose wife keeps an eye on him through the kitchen opening while he tends bar; at closing time he is permitted a bowl of rum toddy for a nightcap:

> And then it was twelve o'clock. The piano one flight up, which pounded a noisy accompaniment for a mixed male and female chorus, became silent. The waiter stopped running across the floor from the kitchen opening to the veranda. The restaurant keeper recorded in the ledger the last champagne bottles sent one flight up. The gas was turned down.[46]

During the time the storm over *Married* was raging, Strindberg wrote that one day the book would be used as a reader in schools for girls, and his prophecy proved true. Today no one takes offense at the tenden-cies his contemporaries found so shocking, and its once notorious indecency is no longer considered dangerous for modern female *gymnasium* students. The book deserves to be included, with *Town and Gown* and *The Men of the Skerries,* among Strindberg's classic story collections.

The Trial and the Second Volume of *Married*

Shortly after Volume I of *Married* was published in September, 1884, the state confiscated copies and charged the author with blasphemy.[47] Strindberg, living in Switzerland, was shocked and frightened, and at first it appeared he might let his publisher take all the blame. He finally returned, however, and went to trial on October 21, 1884. On November 17, 1884, he was acquitted, but the ordeal had a crushing effect on him.

Bjørnson's accusation that Strindberg was guilty of cowardice because of his initial reluctance to return for the indictment was to some degree unjust. Strindberg was not a moral coward. Although extremely sensitive to criticism, he was capable of flouting public opinion and risking his citizenship on the turn of a card, if it mattered. But he was to some extent a physical coward; he was afraid of bulls, savage dogs, and, above all, the police. In the very first chapter of *The Son of a Servant* there is an account of the panic he felt as a child when police appeared in the kitchen of his home. He was afraid his father would be arrested, but it turned out that there was only a fine to pay because a slop pail had been emptied into the gutter by one of the servants. This fear of the police and of the island prison on Långholmen in Stockholm followed Strindberg throughout his life. Whenever he became apprehensive about indictment or prison, he completely lost his nerve, which is exactly what happened when he first heard that *Married* had been confiscated.

It took the pleading of friends and a special trip to Switzerland by the publisher to convince Strindberg to come back to Sweden. Friends and supporters crowded to greet him as a martyr at the Stockholm railway station, but after his first court appearance only the fear of being shadowed everywhere by detectives prevented him from immediately fleeing abroad again. Following the acquittal, he was a broken man, physically and psychologically, and remained so. That fears of persecution were beginning to take root in him can be detected in the account of the trial he wrote after returning to Switzerland, "The Confiscation Journey." These fears are even more evident in a letter written from Geneva to Jonas Lie, who seems to have been his closest friend at this time. Exacting from Lie an oath of "honor, faith and secrecy," Strindberg revealed to him on December 2, 1884—in other words, shortly after his return—that he had had meetings in Stockholm with "young, educated *fanatici.*" They had wanted him to join them in an assassination attempt against the Bernadotte dynasty. "A national government was chosen, basic laws rewritten, ground plans drawn of the palace, and the terrain reconnoitered; the mines and many other things were all ready. . . . I was asked to guide the reins from Geneva. I made a promise, but won't keep it." On the last page of the letter is a sketch by Strindberg of how the assault would be carried out. He alleged that the detectives who were following him were more afraid of him than he was of them.

His situation worsened as he became intermittently aware that he was suffering from persecution mania. After he left Switzerland for Paris, he wrote to Lie in April, 1885: "The solitude in Switzerland became unwholesome. I believed I was persecuted and saw betrayal everywhere, nothing but enemies who tricked me." The same year he wrote the peculiar document in which he asked to be poisoned by some skillful doctor, or else sent to a place of treatment in Belgium where the patients were not locked up "in the event I should be attacked by madness, which is not at all inconceivable, since a sane person can actually become deranged when he sees idiots and scoundrels running the world."[48]

Strindberg had also managed to have a falling out with the two most important literary camps—the Young Sweden group and the conservatives. It is true that Young Sweden supported and defended him during the trial, but they were resolutely critical of his attitude toward Ibsen and the woman question. Immediately after the first volume of *Married* appeared, Young Sweden's disapprobation was registered in a letter from Pehr Staaff. He disapproved of the story "A Doll House" and of the preface, and demanded "a story about woman's rights." In a short time the break was complete. In conservative quarters, of course, people were revolted by the book's alleged indecency.

Strindberg's indignation was vented primarily on the emancipation movement which had been gaining ground during the two years he was away from Sweden. He believed that the indictment against *Married* was prompted by the feminist leader Countess Sofie Adlersparre (1823-95), with the Swedish queen acting as intermediary. Beginning with "The Confiscation Journey," he would henceforth miss no opportunity to strike out against the Scandinavian feminist movement and its representatives. At the same time, he felt that he was being persecuted by an international league of women all over Europe who were bribing men to write books against him and had agents shadowing him everywhere.

After the publication of Volume I of *Married*, his financial situation was more desperate than ever. "I have been in adversity, for the first time in real adversity, ever since I brought this child into the world," he wrote to K. O. Bonnier on December 31, 1884. When his wife reacted against his misogyny, he began to suspect her of conspiring with his feminine adversaries and of trying to have him rendered helpless by placing him in an institution. Gradually, these suspicions developed into the accusations of infidelity that appear in *A Madman's Defense* (1887).

Strindberg's persecution complex, which in various forms continued into the Inferno Crisis, explains the vehemently militant foreword he wrote in 1886 for the second volume of *Married*, the stories for which were written in June, 1885, but not published until the following year.

The foreword, half of which was cut before publication,[49] reiterates all the reforms Strindberg demanded in the first volume of *Married*. Marriage is viewed as a form of prostitution by contract which, as a consequence of woman's indolence and ambition for power, has imprisoned the husband in a state of complete slavery. Women were responsible for all of history's monstrosities—religious persecution, war, and so forth—and they had made progress toward reintroducing matriarchy by acquiring inheritance rights (for married women) and gaining admittance into the labor market, although man was still expected to remain the breadwinner. "In other words: Watch out, men!"

To a certain extent this vehemence prejudiced both contemporary and subsequent critics against the stories in Volume II, several of which are not at all concerned with the woman question, while others are relatively moderate polemics. The long opening story, "Autumn," cannot even be called unfriendly to women. It is an exquisite mood picture, portraying a marriage that has drifted over the years into boredom and resignation. It is evident that Strindberg's own experiences provided the raw material, but they are pictured in a conciliatory light. Something of the same mood lingers over the following story, "Bread" ("Brödet"), in which marital harmony becomes impossible because of constant anxieties over having enough bread to feed the family. (These two stories were written in French and translated into Swedish by someone else.) But there are also other stories in the collection that are free from controversy over the woman question. I need only mention the touching little narrative admired by Victoria Benedictsson, "It Is Not Enough" ("Det räcker inte"), which describes how a mother wears herself out for her egotistical and ungrateful sons.[50]

Only the latter part of the second volume is written in the same spirit as the foreword. Sometimes Strindberg does not even take the trouble to cloak his ideas in story form; he simply attacks women by citing examples. Sometimes he draws upon the experiences of married couples easily recognized by the contemporary reader, and sometimes he shows us samples of his own domestic "martyrdom."

But even this latter part of Volume II has superb sections. The character of Hélène in "For a Consideration" ("Mot betalning") is the first sketch for Miss Julie—probably Strindberg's most splendidly drawn female figure. Furthermore, Hélène—the degenerate and discontented daughter of a general—foreshadows Hedda Gabler.[51] The last half of the story, showing how Hélène torments and exploits her husband in order to advance the cause of feminine emancipation, is quite unbelievable; she is transformed into a very ordinary kind of Strindbergian shrew. But the character of Hélène at the opening of the story is quite striking: a brittle, proud girl who was raised as an exceptional, privileged being, nourished by romantic literature, and accustomed to regarding sexual love as unclean and man as her natural enemy.

Other stories are as well constructed but betray the author's obsessions. "The Child" ("Barnet"), for example, begins with a beautiful picture of a boy's childhood, obviously reminiscent of Strindberg's own, but then turns into an extremely biased polemic against sibling tyranny. The same can be said about "A Duel" ("Tvekamp"), which deals with professional rivalry between man and wife—a theme Strindberg would later develop in Comrades (Komraterna—1886). In the story the husband is a lawyer and the wife is a dramatist (an obvious transformation—Siri von Essen was an actress), whose successes—as the husband candidly acknowledges—make him jealous.

Strindberg presents his own domestic misery casually throughout the second volume, but the final story, "The Breadwinner" ("Familjeför-sörjaren"), was the one that did most to arouse public indignation. It even induced the great Social-Democratic leader Hjalmar Branting, then one of Strindberg's warmest friends, to declare in a review that he could not understand how Strindberg could write a story which invited a scandal-hungry public "to defame—and then, too, largely without justification—the person closest to him." In the story a cognac-drinking, pleasure-loving, and demonic wife is a painter who endeavors persistently to have her husband confined in a mental institution. Strindberg, who in the earlier stories appeared in the roles of professor, lawyer, English shipyard manager, and so forth, makes no attempt to disguise himself; the husband is a writer living in a foreign pension, literally working himself to death to make money to support his extravagant wife and family. Aside from the autobiographical element, the story, although ruthlessly brutal and psychologically unbelievable, has undeniable power.

After the two volumes of *Married* (a third volume was contemplated but never written), Strindberg was no longer able to write about the woman question without dragging in his own marriage. *Comrades, The Father (Fadren),* and *Creditors (Fordringsägare),* which continue his crusade against women, are largely autobiographical, and *A Madman's Defense,* which was originally planned as a novel about his marriage, became a formal indictment against his wife.

Notes to Chapter Seven

1. *Brev,* II, p. 267.
2. *SS:*XIX, p. 194.
3. *Ibid.,* pp. 218-19.
4. *SS:*XXVI, pp. 321-22.
5. *SS:*XIV, p. 419.
6. The series was offered to *Handelstidningen* through Karl Warburg and a day later to *Östgöten* through Isidor Kjellberg.
7. Shortly before he began writing *Married,* he confessed in a letter to Bjørnson on May 4, 1884, that he had begun to develop "a slight hatred" of Ibsen after *Enemy of the People.* "And *A Doll's House!* Woman-hater Ibsen! There was a maneuver that possessed the great virtue of success. When Fru Hwasser wrote to ask him what he intended with the piece, and if Nora would come back, he answered that he did not know! There you have the aesthete and the knight commander!" (*Brev,* IV, p. 146). [Ibsen had recently received a decoration from the Turkish government.— Translator]
8. The order in which the stories were written and submitted is indicated in Strindberg's correspondence with the publisher. *See* Landquist's commentary on *Married.*
9. He pointed out to his publisher that ideas from the essay collection *This and That,* particularly from the essays about the upper classes, "haunted the story: I was on the point of forgetting entirely the relationships between the sexes."
10. *SS:*XIV, p. 145.
11. *Ibid.,* p. 149.
12. *Ibid.,* p. 182.
13. *Ibid.,* p. 186.
14. *Ibid.,* p. 31.
15. *Ibid.,* p. 36. Strindberg was actually poorly acquainted with the practical reforms urged by the feminist movement. Not until after the completion of *Married* did he read John Stuart Mill and Herbert Spencer on the woman question, on which he then commented in the essay "Equality and Tyranny."
16. Much of the reform of the feminist movement was due to the efforts of the pioneering writer Victoria Benedictsson (1850-88; pseud.: Ernest Ahlgren) and the feminist leader Ellen Key (1849-1926).

In a letter to Mörner on March 21, 1896, Strindberg wrote: "Yes, now, after thirteen years, Ellen Key is saying what I said thirteen years ago and had to suffer for!" (Mörner, p. 120).

17. *SS:XIV*, p. 198.
18. *Ibid.*, p. 201.
19. *Ibid.*, p. 8.
20. *SS:XVIII*, pp. 149-50.
21. *SS:XIV*, p. 70.
22. *SS:XVII*, p. 27.
23. Strindberg wrote to K. O. Bonnier before beginning *Married* (April 11, 1884) that he longed to "be able to return to *mes premières amours,* prose pictures" *(Brev,* IV, p. 112).
24. *See* Chapter IV, *Town and Gown.*—Translator
25. The same technique is used extensively in the second volume of *Married,* but it does not appear in the work written between the volumes—*Utopias in Reality*—nor in *Swedish Destinies.* It is clear that in *Married* Strindberg intended to suggest that he was presenting rough-cast sketches, not full-blown stories.
26. *SS:XIV*, p. 131.
27. To judge by a statement in *This and That (SS:XVI,* p. 112), Strindberg at this time did not appear to have a very high opinion of Maupassant.
28. It is indicative that the "novelette" by Kielland most similar to the *Married* stories is "Eroticism and Idyll" ("Erotik og Idyl"), of which the author himself disapproved because his indignation over the casual way babies were being produced had made him didactic. For a discussion of the similarity between this Kielland short story and Strindberg's "Love and Bread," *see* Torsten Svedfelt, "Alexander Kielland och det svenska åttitalet" *(Edda,* 1931, p. 295). *Cf. also,* Sten Linder, *Ernest Ahlgren,* 1930, p. 120.
29. *SS:XVII*, p. 23.
30. *Ibid.*, p. 28.
31. *SS:XIV*, p. 82.
32. *Ibid.*, p. 81.
33. *Ibid.*, p. 211.
34. *Ibid.*
35. A large rope or wire used to support a mast.—Translator
36. Here, Strindberg uses the Danish expression—"Att det livet. . . ."—Translator
37. *SS:XIV*, p. 93.

38. *Ibid.*, p. 187.
39. *Ibid.*, p. 176.
40. *Ibid.*, p 139.
41. *Ibid.*, p. 90.
42. *Ibid.*, p. 117.
43. *Ibid.*, pp. 190-91.
44. *Ibid.*, p. 192.
45. *See* Chapter V, People and Milieus.—Translator
46. *SS:*XIV, p. 108.
47. *See* note 9, Chapter I.—Translator
48. Mörner, p. 167.
49. The missing portion of the foreword was later published (1920) in *SS:*LIV, pp. 244-63.—Translator
50. *Cf.* Sten Linder, *Ernest Ahlgren,* 1930, pp. 253-54.
51. Sten Linder has assumed that Ibsen was influenced by Strindberg, and his thesis is plausible. See *Ibsen, Strindberg och andra,* 1936, pp. 88-89.

Chapter Eight

UTOPIAS IN REALITY

The short stories, set in Switzerland, which Strindberg worked on both before and during the *Married* ordeal, were given the ambiguous title *Utopias in Reality* in order to show that Utopia could be realized here on earth and had already been partially realized.[1] If one's knowledge of Strindberg came only through these stories, he would seem an optimist. In each he prophesies a future society which, although of rather ill-defined shape and form, is generally based upon the communistic ground plan laid down by the predecessors of socialism—Etienne Cabet (1788-1856) and Claude Saint-Simon (1760-1825). But Strindberg's visions were only castles in the air, and his instinct for demolition razed them. Even before he finished *Utopias* he informed Jonas Lie (on Christmas Eve, 1884) that he was "intellectually bankrupt." After having studied the problem of social organization in three languages, he had arrived "at the same nihilistic position as when I wrote *The Red Room*. . . . The skein is too snarled to comb out. It can only be cut. . . . All attempts by the socialists to better the position of the workers are nonsense."

A half-year earlier he had written for inclusion in *Swedish Destinies* "The Isle of Bliss" which, in the spirit of Rousseau and Defoe (in *Robinson Crusoe*), begins as an attempt to glorify the natural state and ends up, as does *Candide*, poking fun at man's incurable desire to comfort himself with utopian dreams.

In the *Utopias in Reality* story "Above the Clouds" ("Över molnen") Strindberg's spokesman, Aristide, declares that the idealism of his youth was a futile journey "above the clouds," devoid of any roots in reality. Soon, Strindberg came to think of his own ideas on social reform as "above the clouds," and to regard his concept of socialism as an "after-

glow" of the idealism of his youth. During the entire six years of exile
following his departure from Sweden in 1883, he restlessly changed one
viewpoint for another, swinging from pessimism to optimism and then
back to pessimism. Again and again he declared himself "intellectually
bankrupt," only to find a new point of view to cling to for a time.

After the first *Married* volume, Strindberg's interest in reform
focused primarily on the utopian refashioning of marriage and the family,
as in the *Utopias* stories "Relapse" ("Återfall") and "Reconstruction"
("Nybyggnad"), which he once considered including in the second volume
of *Married.* But "Remorse," which was written before *Married,* does not
deal with marriage and the woman question at all.

Remorse

Somnambulist Nights (1884) ends on an optimistic note, and this
mood of hope and conciliation emerges even more clearly in the essay
collection *This and That* (1884). Although Strindberg thought of calling
these essays *The Faultfinder (Felfinnaren),* and although the first essay is
titled "About the Universal Dissatisfaction," the dissatisfaction is specifically with modern industrialized society, which produced, through division
of labor and specialization, the degenerate urban man. Of all the social
classes the peasant is the most fortunate because he "avails himself least
of the division of labor."[2] If all artificial obstacles were removed and
nature were allowed to operate freely, civilized man could regain his health
and happiness.[3]

An indication that Strindberg's pessimistic mood dissipated when
he left Sweden is the change in purpose that took place between the planning and execution of an essay that was to be titled "Fira-Kanna's Journey
in Sweden" ("Fira-Kannas resa i Sverige"). At first he contemplated having a Japanese visitor expose "all the absurdity in our institutions," but in
the final version, titled "Nationality and Swedishness" ("Nationalitet och
svenskhet"), Strindberg, using ideas from *The Swedish People,* has the
educated Japanese observe that everything regarded as indigenously Swedish was actually borrowed from abroad. The implication is that a Swede
should be proud that the history of his national development is "so universally European" and should look forward with confidence to Sweden's
entry into a "general European confederation of free states."

Strindberg emphasized that one source for the idea of a coalition of European states was the celebrated Swedish utopian thinker Nils Herman Qviding's book *The Final Settlement of Swedish Law (Slutlikvid med Sveriges lag)*, a work he read with great admiration. Another important influence was his contact with the Swiss canton system, in which different nationalities lived peaceably together. When he first arrived in Switzerland in January, 1884, Strindberg was distrustful of every kind of social order. In his foreword to "About the Universal Dissatisfaction," Switzerland is described as a typical police state with edicts and prohibitions, but he soon changed his mind and saw it as an ideal society. He considered extolling it in an essay he was working on, "One Thing and Another About Switzerland" ("Ett och annat om Schweiz"), for inclusion in *This and That,* but instead wrote the short story "Remorse," depicting Switzerland as a miniature model for a united states of Europe.

There are hints in this beautiful story that after his agonizing struggles Strindberg had found peace in the national setting of the Alps. "Nature has cured me," he wrote to Lie (May 13, 1884), "and I have just written a story for [the journal] *Ude og Hjemme* that is so beautiful I feel ashamed."

From his comfortable exile Strindberg had intended "to begin bombardment of the Swedish kingdom" with a blistering attack on political and literary reactionaries in an essay called at this time "What Is the Battle About? and What Has Happened?" ("Vad gäller striden? och Vad har hänt?"), which was to be a continuation of the *New Kingdom* campaign. He changed his mind, however, and reclaimed the manuscript in order not to provoke new storms against himself; not until two years later was the essay published, although in shortened form.[4]

In a passage deleted from the published version Strindberg objected violently to the attempts made to persuade him to lay down his arms: "This reminds me of the French who, after declaring war on the Prussians, wanted to forbid them to bombard Paris. And when the French were beaten, they talked about a violation of international law at the same time they were using snipers."[5] Strindberg admitted that during a month's solitude in Switzerland he underwent a serious crisis and was at the point of wrongfully yielding to his enemies:

> I have too soft a heart to meddle in politics! I see myself as an officer
> in wartime who ordered enemies to be shot! Well—he did the right

thing! Nevertheless, he doesn't sleep well nights. He would have been a traitor, of course, if he hadn't shot his enemy, but he would have slept better.[6]

After stopping the publication of "What Is the Battle About?" Strindberg used the idea of the officer receiving orders to execute snipers in "Remorse."[7] At the beginning of the story the basic theme is suggested through expressive symbolism. The time is the Franco-Prussian War; a young German lieutenant named Bleichroden has thrown his stiff-collared tunic over the back of a chair in his room, "and there it hung limp and shrunken like a corpse, as if the empty arms were spastically clutching the chair legs to guard against a headlong fall."[8] As he sits and writes in his shirt-sleeves he is a warm-hearted human being, but the minute he puts his tunic on, he is transformed. The tunic symbolizes his official self, the soldier, and the friction between his public and private selves tortures him. When a French priest tries to put in a word for a group of captured freebooters, Bleichroden tears open his tunic and cries out: "Why can't we always be human beings? Why do we have to have alter egos?"[9] After the prisoners are executed, the lieutenant has a mental breakdown and becomes schizophrenic.

In the story the beauty of nature is contrasted with the harsh rules of war. Strindberg himself was torn by the same painful contrast. In February, 1884, he wrote to Bjørnson and Lie: "Here it is 15 degrees [59 degrees F.] in the shade and 25 [77] in the sun. Very beautiful! But such a terrible conflict exists between this beauty and the battle going on within me that I become depressed."[10]

We find the same "conflict" in the story. The lieutenant is stationed in the meeting and dining hall of the abandoned Marlotte art colony. The walls are decorated with faded red painting caps, a besmeared palette, and canvases painted in the style of the 1860's. While the execution is taking place in the yard, the young officer wanders aimlessly with his patrol through Fontainebleau woods and sees everywhere in nature "the terrible struggle for existence," a struggle as cruel as man's. He returns and is nauseated by the sight of an elegantly set supper. Everything —the meat, the red wine, the red radishes, the red caps—reminds him of the blood stains by the grape trellis that he stumbled upon just moments before.

The last half of the story, to borrow Strindberg's phrase to Bjørnson, is "ultra-optimistic"; it is also inferior to the first half. Lieutenant Bleichroden's mental balance is restored in Switzerland's "clean, lie-free air," where all controversial international problems are smoothly and effortlessly solved. By acquiring Swiss citizenship, he becomes European instead of German. His vision of the future includes the belief that armies will disappear once women get the right to vote.

Several weeks after Strindberg wrote this happy ending he was immersed in work on *Married*. He did not permit his utopianism to emerge again until the preface to the first volume of *Married*, which was written after the stories. In the preface, he declares that in the society of the future everyone would be educated and supported through a just distribution of the wealth. Consequently, the permanent economic bond of marriage would be unnecessary and could be replaced by an oral or written contract for a specified period, either long or short. This communistic solution to the marriage question is also recommended in the next two *Utopias* stories—"Relapse" and "Reconstruction."

Relapse and Reconstruction

"The Swiss stories will include 'New Marriage,' the continuation of *Married*, and people will see that I am not a reactionary on the woman question," Strindberg wrote to Albert Bonnier on October 8, 1884. Two months earlier, when discussing a suitable title for the still-unnamed *Married* collection, he wrote, "I should have preferred to call the book *Old Marriage* after having read Tchernishevski's narratives about 'new human beings.' " Of all the socialistic and communistic literature that Strindberg devoured at this time, Nicolas Tchernishevski's *What Is to Be Done?*[11] subtitled *A Book About New Human Beings*, made the strongest impression on him. He wrote to Jonas Lie in August, 1884, that it was "epochal for his writing career"; it had taught him that just to criticize was not enough, one had "to paint a picture of the future."

This Russian anarchist's novel, written in the Peter-Paul Prison, is devoid of a conventional plot. The main emphasis is focused upon a series of conversations sprinkled with scientific terminology in which humanity's problems are solved in a casual way. The heroine, Vera, has a vision in which she glimpses the paradise that will come into being when all work would be conveniently done by machines that need only be switched on. The major part of each day would be spent in a giant palace of aluminum where the choicest menus would be served on a dinner service also made of aluminum. Only during harvest time would one have to live in Russia proper. Once the fields were mowed, everyone would journey to the shore of the Black Sea where the earth will have been transformed by machines from wasteland into paradise, and people would amuse themselves by singing and dancing in a giant dance hall. Most of the ingredients of the ideal state are present and everything is painless and happy.

Strindberg tried to demonstrate in *Utopias* that Tchernishevski's dream was realizable.[12] In "Reconstruction" we have the author's interpretation of the *familistère* or community settlement at Guise in northern France, which was established by "France's noblest, if not most famous man,"[13] deputy Jean Baptiste Godin (1817-88). Although Strindberg had never seen the place, he described how at Guise an end had been put to the stultifying conventions of ordinary family life. Six hundred families lived under the same roof. Because the children were accommodated in a common nursery, in the evenings husbands and wives were free to go to restaurants, lectures, and the theatre. The formal lectures seem superfluous, however, for in the story, as in Tchernishevski's book, everyone lectures. Even farm laborers lecture to their children, explaining that from manure comes wheat, and from wheat, bread, and from bread, people—"calm, tranquil people." In the outside world the story's heroine Blanche and her beloved Emile had separated when they realized that they could not accept the enslaving responsibilities of marriage, a relationship in which happiness was defined as "two beds, a dinner table, six rattan chairs." Now they are reunited in the liberating surroundings of the *familistère*. "Wasn't it terrible traveling in the old world?" Blanche asks Emile on his return from a business trip. He replies, "It was like walking in Pompeii and Herculaneum. No, I don't want to think about it."[14]

After the publication of *Utopias*, Strindberg visited Guise to gather evidence to show that he had not, as critics claimed, just painted "beautiful mirages of the future." What he found, however, was contrary to what he had expected, and although in a letter sent from the *familistère*[15] he made an effort to conceal his disillusionment, he could not resist remarking that the only emancipated people were the women, who not only were freed from housekeeping duties and child care, but also had the right to control the property of their working husbands. Less than a year later he had altered his early opinion of the *familistère* so completely that in a section omitted from the foreword to the second part of *Married* he described the communal settlement as a devilish invention for the enslavement of men: "That is the ultimate goal of emancipation—to make a lazy and idle woman the guardian of a ten-hour-per-day slaving man! Watch out, men!"[16]

According to Strindberg, "Relapse"—which he wanted to publish in French because it contained intimate pictures of his own family life —would serve to show "the 'liberal' ladies how seriously I have thought about the new marriage." In the story an exile Russian anarchist Paul Petrowitsch, who supports himself in Switzerland by cultivating roses, has a common-law marriage with a countrywoman from a distinguished family. The couple's daughters are taught to ignore commands so that they will not grow up to be slaves. But when a son is born, the mother has a relapse to more conventional behavior and wishes to baptize him—an event also depicted in *A Madman's Defense* (1887) but in such a way as to portray the wife in a more unfavorable light. Paul yields, but his capitulation upsets their relationship and he leaves her. Away from home, he regrets his departure and realizes that by judging his wife harshly, he had demanded too much of life. He hears an inner voice: "Love is a mystery that you'll never solve, that we'll never solve. It cannot be defined as sympathy for one another, Paul, because we feel antipathy. And yet we are still in love." He consoles himself with the knowledge that "marriage was created for the future generation."[17]

In "Reconstruction" Emile explains to Blanche that love is "a mystery whose prosaic solution you can't bear to hear!" He swears that he loves her, although his common sense warns him against her, and he cannot find any good qualities in her. It is not until they are in the *familistère,* where all family ties and domestic problems disappear, that he can hope for happiness in love: "As my mate—you are free; as a human being— free, eating your own bread. That is the realization of our utopia. And those wicked people said it could never be realized."[18]

The optimism present in *Utopias* was grounded on pessimistic assumptions. In the foreword, written in July, 1885, Strindberg says that the book is an attack on overcivilization or degeneration. The process of natural evolution itself is retrogressive. Since creation lacked a personalized authoritative will, there could be no purposeful development.[19] The mastodon was more impressively endowed than the elephant, and the modern bear is a degeneration of the extinct cave bear. In the same way, civilized society has caused man's development to regress, and "all of the current destructive activity being manifested in the war against society is only a natural reversion to a condition when man was better prepared for the battle for survival."[20] Only after man acknowledges the futility of illusions and ideals and the validity of his own egotism could a new society be built upon the union of individual interests into a coalition: "This is socialism. The talk about wanting to combat socialism is as great an absurdity as wanting to combat politics."[21]

Despite the note of assurance in this last statement, Strindberg's faith in socialism at this time was shaky. Six months after he finished the foreword, he wrote that his study of social problems had warped him: "I am in a word bankrupt—and confound me I no longer know what to believe. Skepticism again—like at the time of *The Red Room*. A conglomeration of old and new." The poet and aristocrat Verner von Heidenstam (1859-1940) would cure him permanently of all socialistic obsessions.

The heroes and heroines of these stories attacking overcivilization and preaching socialism are all scientists whose brilliant minds are threatened by mental illness and whose emotional lives are tainted with degeneration. Lieutenant Bleichroden in "Remorse" is a geologist; Paul Petrowitsch in "Relapse" a doctor. And it seems that for Emile (a chemist) in "Reconstruction" and his beloved Blanche (a doctor), the universe can hold no secrets. Despite differences in certain attitudes the *Utopias* heroes foreshadow the intellectual and scholarly fishing commissioner, Borg, in the novel *In the Outer Skerries* (1890). Like Borg, they refute all arguments in advance, and they too look down over the world from the exalted standpoint of science, arranging their lives in thoroughly rational ways.

Bleichroden wants to liberate humanity from the problem of sustenance by enabling human lungs to utilize directly the nitrogen in the atmosphere. If this could be done, a golden age would be ushered in. From letters to Hjalmar Öhrvall in 1884, we know that Strindberg himself was seriously engaged in similar speculations.[22]

Blanche and Emile in "Reconstruction" are also exceptional individuals. They are superior intellectually to ordinary people and have more refined tastes, although they do not find happiness until they join the two thousand inhabitants of Godin's *familistère*. One need only read the long description of Blanche's ecstatic experience involving perfume inhalation to realize that we are close to the decadent sophistication displayed by the fishing commissioner in *In the Outer Skerries* when he intoxicates himself on laughing gas. And when Emile declares his love for Blanche, he articulates it in the same scientific vocabulary later used by Borg:

> I am almost certain that if I were killed right now, and an autopsy were performed immediately, a microscope would reveal your image on my retina, and in every lung cell, every bit of heart tissue, and in the very marrow of my bones. Every drop of blood would contain your reflection and every brain cell, like a microphone, would render your dear voice— you, beloved![23]

The heavy scientific ballast in *Utopias* reveals the influence of French naturalism to a greater degree than any of Strindberg's earlier works. Blanche's perfume ecstasy is reminiscent of the famous symphony of smells in Zola's *Le Ventre de Paris* (1874) and also foreshadows the artificial paradise that the decadent hero, des Esseintes, creates for himself in Huysman's *À Rebours*.[24] As in Zola, it is surprising how the exposure to commonplace substances can produce such strong physiological effects. For Blanche, an opened bottle of lily of the valley perfume evokes visions of "early summer landscapes with unmowed meadows and blooming fruit trees, children playing, and gently moving clouds." She hears "alpine horns and the rushing of brooks, steamboat bells and boys' choirs." When the different perfume fragrances blend together, Blanche imagines herself watching a passion play in the cathedral at Fribourg. The long passage culminates in a description of the playing of a giant organ, a vision that foreshadows the most famous sections of the story "The Romantic Organist on Rånö." As in Zola, sensual ecstasy is intensified into hallucination.

The depiction of Paul Petrowitsch cultivating roses in "Relapse" is in a somewhat calmer style. But here, too, Strindberg's horticultural descriptions surpass similar pictures in Zola, such as the rose images in *La Faute de l'Abbé Mouret*. In Strindberg each variety is singled out for special attention:

> Lofty tea and perpetual roses stood in long ranks and in full bloom, arranged according to their colors. The back rank was made up of *Maréchal Niel*, with their huge yellow bowls stained with faint orange-red shimmers like the afterglows of sunsets; then, the small, tight balls of *Gloire de Dijons*, yellow like raw silk dipped in Madeira and with a

> fragrance like a song; the sulphur-yellow of *Safrans,* which stung the
> eyes; then, a platoon of white *Boules de Neige,* as white as their name.[25]

Eight additional kinds of roses are enumerated and described, and together
they produce the kind of ecstasy of colors and fragrances one associates
with similar Zolaesque descriptions:

> It was sensually intoxicating to see and feel the fragrance of this forest
> of roses. It aroused all sensations simultaneously; as powerfully as by
> well-prepared food, as intoxicatingly as by wine, as bewitchingly as by the
> presence of a woman, as innocently as by a child's caresses or stories about
> angels; like a blend of meat newly butchered and burning Madeira, rouge
> and angel's wings, a woman's breast and children's kisses, sulphur and
> auroral blush, blood and milk, violet and linen.[26]

For Paul, however, who is a "new person," roses "are his last
concession to a sense of beauty, a tedious legacy, from which his children
would probably escape."[27] Strindberg shared Paul's attitude: he accepted
naturalism's poetic-scientific portrayal of nature as a necessary evil under
the existing social conditions, just as he accepted art in general. A similar
theme is expressed in the story "Above the Clouds," in which the author's
spokesman Aristide prophesies that someday literature would consist of
new ideas, and people would enjoy the beauty of nature without trying to
create useless imitations in words. To illustrate the meaninglessness of a
literary representation of nature, Aristide points to a cloud-enveloped
silver-white Alpine peak. He asserts that it would be impossible to describe
such a natural phenomenon so that the reader would be given a true picture: "Let's make a poem of it! I'll try to compare it to something, for a
poem is always a comparison. I could compare it, for example, to a reliquary shrine of newly molten silver borne by a legion of angels, gliding
along over the earth."[28] His friend Henri finds the comparison beautiful,
but Aristide thinks it vulgar to compare a ten-thousand-foot-high mountain with one of man's works and to turn a veil of clouds into angels,
"fictions that no one believes in." Henri then asks if "human beings of
the future" will create poetry out of the Alps by relating the information
that the secondary calcareous layer of the Dent du Midi is mixed with
dolomite and covered with three milimeters of snow.[29]

In the novel *In the Outer Skerries,* written five years later, Strindberg would utilize the same dryly scientific portrayal of nature that Henri
scornfully proposes—describing, with the aid of geological handbooks, the
rocky islets of the skerries according to their mineralogical characteristics.[30]

"The Isle of Bliss"

Strindberg's difficulty in remaining faithful to the implications of his utopian theories is best demonstrated in "The Isle of Bliss," a story published not in *Utopias* but in *Swedish Destinies*. In Paris in the fall of 1883, Strindberg wandered daily in the Jardin d'Acclimation (he lived nearby), planning a story involving American Indians, whom he admired greatly. It was to be set in the seventeenth century in the Wilmington, Delaware, settlement of New Sweden.[31] When he returned to the idea in April, 1884, his intention still was to glorify the natural state. He contemplated a Swedish *Robinson Crusoe*, which would "include Indians and all that, of course, but it will also contain the entire history of culture."[32] While working on the story in July, however, he informed his publisher: "The name of the 'destiny' is 'The Isle of Bliss' and it is dreadful. It won't do as a Robinson! Don't consider it as such."

One can see from the early drafts and outlines that Strindberg really intended to write a Rousseauistic *Robinson Crusoe*—a depiction of the origin and development of an entire culture. In "The Isle of Bliss" a group of colonists are shipwrecked on an island on their way to New Sweden and learn to enjoy living a simple, primitive life in the natural state. Then, when a volcano erupts, their island disappears and the settlers are forced to begin again on another island where the climate is more rigorous. This time they create a more complex "civilized" society, passing through all the stages whereby happy, natural human beings are transformed into quarrelsome, civilized individuals. They go through the hunting and pastoral phases, and ultimately, just as in Rousseau, agriculture is invented and the concept of private property is introduced. At this point —again following Rousseau—a social order is established to protect the rich against the nonpropertied classes.

The first drafts of the story are not entirely free from pedantry, and in places the narrative seems indeed intended for children, although no Indians appear.[33] During the course of the writing, however, Strindberg's desire to satirize became increasingly stronger. It would perhaps have been appropriate for the story to end with the colonists from the ship *The Swedish Lion (Svenska Lejonet)* restoring the social conditions they had left behind—those of the reign of King Charles XI (1655-97). But

Strindberg could not stop there, and the story continues until the island becomes the Sweden of the late nineteenth century, the Sweden of *The New Kingdom*—with its humbug, official lies, class injustices, theatre, Swedish Academy, and above all, the unjust monopoly enjoyed by certain authorities in the area of historical research.

Among the colonists are two Uppsala University students, being deported to New Sweden because they were "found guilty of having spoken slanderously in the inns of the city and in a provincial business establishment about His Majesty's Professor Serenissimus Olaus Rudbeckius[34] and his recently published *Atland eller Manhem.*"[35] By repudiating Rudbeck's theory that Sweden was the location of the lost city of Atlantis, they became targets for the same kind of calumny Strindberg did when he dared to call into question in *The Swedish People* the infallibility of the respected historian Erik Gustaf Geijer. Ironically, the students eventually become connected with the same kind of chauvinistic hypocrisy in historical research that they had once attacked. One of them, who had become king on the "civilized" island, is the subject of an official history after his death. The history, supported by evidence from the deceased king's copy of Rudbeck's *Atlantica* "proved conclusively that the present kingdom was truly the most perfect of all kingdoms, and that it was actually Atlantica or The Isle of Bliss. The isle upon which their forefathers had lived and where they had imagined they were blissful, had never existed; it was only an invention of [the opposition party] The Discontented to make people discontented."[36]

The story goes on to portray the development of historical research through the centuries. Chauvinism and imperialism become official doctrine in *The Book of Kings,* which praises all the kings "from Lasse I to Per Erik, and particular praise went to all ambushes and plunderings in foreign lands."[37] New sciences are created, and the name of one of these has become a Swedish catchword: "Buttonology" ("Knappologi"). Intended as a device to ridicule a typological system devised by the Swede Oscar Montelius, the word became part of the Swedish language, referring to any systematization of useless information. Art and literature are also attacked. Strindberg probably never gave so stinging an expression to his utilitarian's contempt for art: "The useful had become despised and the useless was honored. Consequently, it was more honorable to draw a picture of an apple, for which one became professor and was knighted, than to cultivate an apple tree, for which one only became liable to taxation."[38] At the conclusion of "The Isle of Bliss," Strindberg pokes fun at the various social-betterment projects into which people frenziedly throw themselves after they have sunk into complete cretinism. He examines the different solutions to problems advocated by anarchists and socialists, and concludes by mentioning, approvingly, that a third sect, the "Bosh-man-ites," consider the problems unsolvable and recommend "a general explosion of the whole planet Tellus. Inasmuch as the planet was created from nothing, the safest course would be to return it to its origin."[39]

For a time, Strindberg had turned for inspiration alternately to Rousseau, the great prophet of the natural state, and to Voltaire, its greatest detractor. In a letter to K. O. Bonnier on June 6, 1884, he recommended that *Discour sur l'inégálité* and *Candide* be translated; both works influenced "The Isle of Bliss."[40] But as happened so often before, Strindberg ultimately returned to Hartmann's theory of the destruction of the world. It was the universal remedy to which he resorted when all other prescriptions proved ineffectual.

Notes to Chapter Eight

1. "With the phrase 'in reality' I wanted to indicate that these plans, which are still being discussed and which appear in my book, have already been carried out in *several places*, and I wanted to reassure the reader that he had firm ground under his feet" (*SS:*XVI, p. 311).

2. *Ibid.*, p. 19.

3. When K. O. Bonnier pointed out the similarity between Strindberg's essay and Max Nordau's recently published *Die konventionellen Lügen der Kulturmenschheit* (1884), which combined positivism and Rousseauism in the same way, Strindberg admitted that he found most of his viewpoints in Nordau, but insisted that he had presented them earlier. He explained the similarity by pointing out that the ideas expressed had originated neither with him nor with Nordau but were based on those of Darwin, Spencer, Mill, and the Socialists. "And our ideas are quite simply those of the time" (*Brev,* IV, p. 71). Nevertheless, he considered the idea "about the division of labor as the cause of the wretched state of things" to be his own. As we have seen, however, this was something he adopted from Buckle.

4. It bore the title "Literary Reactionism in Sweden" ("Den litterära reaktionen i Sverige"). The passages cut from "What Is the Battle About?" are included in Landquist's edition (*SS:*XVII, pp. 313-30).

5. *Ibid.*, p. 318. A similar comparison is made in a letter to Bjørnson and Lie on February 12, 1884 (*Brev,* IV, pp. 37-39), in which he discusses whether to publish "What Is the Battle About?"

6. In an essay, "Strindbergs Samvetskval" (*Edda,* 1939), Arne Häggqvist correctly pointed out that the idea for the story was contained in this letter to Bjørnson and Lie, but he has not noticed the statement in "What Is the Battle About?"

7. "Remorse" was first published in *Ude og Hjemme* and then included in *Utopias.* In his autobiography (*SS:*XIX, p. 212) Strindberg states that in the story he had portrayed his own remorse over having cut down enemies. Characteristically enough, he adds bitterly that "hoary culprits turned up the whites of their eyes and regarded themselves as vindicated martyrs because he had begged them for forgiveness." Obviously, none of his contemporaries except Bjørnson and Lie could guess the personal motive behind

the story. It was assumed that Strindberg was arguing for pacifism, and this was indeed his intention in January, 1884, when he ordered books about the Franco-Prussian War. One of my students, Tore Andersson, has established that among these books was a publication with the title *The German Armies in France (De tyska arméerna i Frankrike*—published in Stockholm in 1871). Among other things, the volume contains a narrative about a young officer who was ordered to execute 25 snipers and because of the execution became mentally ill. For a discussion of Strindberg's position on the question of peace and Qviding's ideas about a European union of states, *see* Häggqvist, *Edda* (1939), pp. 279 *et passim.*

8. *SS:*XV, p. 176.
9. *Ibid.,* p. 184.
10. *Brev,* IV, p. 39.
11. Published in German as *Was Thun?* in 1883.
12. In "Relapse" an anarchist exiled in Switzerland celebrates the twentieth anniversary of the publication of Tchernishevski's novel.
13. *SS:*XV, p. 79.
14. *Ibid.,* p. 91.
15. *SS:*XVI, pp. 311-36. The letter was first published in 1885 in the newspaper *Politiken.*
16. *SS:*LIV, p. 260.
17. *SS:*XV, p. 139.
18. *Ibid.,* p. 92.
19. Several years later this train of thought would lead Strindberg to a repudiation of all natural laws. *See* Eklund, *Strindbergsstudie,* pp. 249 ff. In his "Vivisections" (*SS:*XXVII, p. 183) Strindberg maintains that his Darwinism was dependent on his belief in an organizer and lawgiver. This belief collapsed when he became an atheist.
20. *SS:*XV, pp. 7-8.
21. *Ibid.,* p. 9.
22. Strindberg's insistence in the cited correspondence (*see* Mörner, pp. 183-90) that cows derive nourishment from nitrogen in the atmosphere returned in "Antibarbus" in 1893. Here, Strindberg says that ten years earlier he experimented with the idea at the home of a peasant in Switzerland (*SS:*XXVII, p. 178).
23. *SS:*XV, p. 61.
24. It seems hardly likely that Strindberg would yet be familiar with this novel published in 1884.

25. *SS:*XV, pp. 99-100.
26. *Ibid.,* p. 100.
27. *Ibid.,* p. 101.
28. *Ibid.,* p. 169.
29. *Ibid.,* p. 170.
30. This radical skepticism about the validity of belles-lettres also induced Strindberg to make plans for a gigantic work on "the European peasant." Later, he was able to liberate himself from "synthetic literature" by writing his autobiography.
31. Nova Svecia was established by Swedish settlers in 1638.—Translator
32. *Brev,* IV, p. 92.
33. One year later (March 26, 1885), Strindberg informed Heidenstam of his plan to deal with the question of the upper and lower classes by writing an allegorical narrative about an English botanist's adventures among Indians (*Brev,* V, pp. 58-59).
34. *See* Chapter VI, *Swedish Destinies and Adventures.*—Translator
35. *SS:*XII, p. 51.
36. *Ibid.,* p. 101.
37. *Ibid.,* p. 106.
38. *Ibid.,* p. 109.
39. *Ibid.,* p. 115.
40. The *Candide* influence is especially noticeable in the beginning of the story, where the two Uppsala students become counterparts of Candide and Pangloss: "Lasse, because of his nature and his education, had arrived at the conviction that everything that happens is for the best. Peter, on the other hand, believed that everything was hopeless" (*SS:*XII, p. 52).

Chapter Nine

THE AUTOBIOGRAPHICAL WORKS

The Son of a Servant

Virtually all of Strindberg's works are autobiographical, inasmuch as the author continually depicts himself in different attitudes and disguises and transforms poetically fragments of his own experiences. But he also had a persistent desire, long before he achieved literary renown, to write a straightforward autobiographical account of his childhood and youth.

If we accept his statement in a letter to Edvard Brandes on December 5, 1885, he wrote an autobiography in French as early as 1864.[1] It was probably a language exercise similar to the French compositions he wrote as a schoolboy and then later translated into Swedish for inclusion in *The Son of a Servant*. In any case, this memoir of a fifteen-year-old is lost. In 1874, Strindberg wrote a long description of his life as a *gymnasium* student at Stockholm's Lyceum. It was published in two installments in the newspaper *Svenska Medborgaren* under the title "A Place of Refuge During the Reign of Terror" ("En fristat under skräckregeringen").

But the immediate inducement for Strindberg to reveal himself directly to the public was the *Married* trial. In the periodical *Tiden* on October 25, 1884, he published an autobiographical article, "Souls Had Awakened" ("Andarne hade vaknat"), with the subtitle "August Strindberg on His Youth" ("August Strindberg om sin ungdomstid").[2] The article describes his debates about religion at the gymnasium (later inserted in abbreviated form in *The Son of a Servant*) and further clashes on the same subject occurring after he took the university-qualifying examination; it concludes with an appeal to public opinion for support against his indictment for impiety. One month later he offered *Tiden* a series of autobiographical sketches with the title *In the Country. Memories of Middle Sweden From the Forest and Lakes. (På landet, uppsvenska minnen från skog och sjö).* The proposal was accompanied by a table of contents indicating that the sketches were to be descriptions of all Strindberg's summer vacation journeys, from the very first summer on Drottningholm to the Kymmendö and Sandhamn sojourns. A half-year later (August 2, 1885) he proposed a similar project to Albert Bonnier, explaining that in *Utopias* he had "said everything" and now regarded himself as old. "Like all old people I am becoming more tranquil. . . . I am sick and want to linger over the happy memories of my life." The book was still to be called *In the Country* and was intended for the Christmas book season.

The writing went more slowly, however, than Strindberg "in several optimistic moments" had hoped, and a letter on September 3, 1885, has him taking back his commitment to a Christmas deadline. The work had developed other dimensions. It was becoming a multi-volume study, each volume "with an independent title, [and] together summing up my entire life in small pictures, but chronologically arranged thus: In the Country—In the Capital—At the University—Abroad."[3] A week later he wrote that he was uncertain "whether interrelated individual stories would be best or an objectively touched-up memoir." He was torn between the desire to speak his mind in an autobiography and the hope of winning back his lost popularity by relating his summer sojourns (which is what he did later in *The People of Hemsö*—1887 and *The Men on the Skerries*—1888). The autobiography came first, partly because Strindberg found a French prototype to serve as a model—the autobiography of the Communard Jules Vallès (1832-85), published as a serial, beginning in 1878, under the title *Jacques Vingtras.* He asked Albert Bonnier in February, 1886: "What would your reaction be if—since I am already dead physically, morally and financially—I wrote about my own life? I should be interested in writing it subjectively-objectively like Jules Vallès in *Jacques Vingtras.*"

By April 25, 1886, Strindberg was not only able to submit the first part of the autobiography to his publisher, but was able to indicate the titles of the five parts with which he intended to bring the story up to the present. He first planned to issue the succeeding parts as separately titled volumes, but then gave them all the common title *The Son of a Servant.*

Jules Vallès's book, much discussed at the time because of the author's recent death (the third part was published posthumously in 1886),

was an autobiography in the form of a novel. Strindberg surmised that
publisher and public alike would wonder when confronted with *The Son
of a Servant* whether it was a novel, a biography, or a memoir. He pointed
out to Albert Bonnier in April, 1886, that he wanted to write his autobiography "as truthfully as a biography can be written," with primary emphasis
on psychology, but also to present "a history of Sweden from 1849 to
1867." The novel-like characteristics of the autobiography are limited to
Strindberg's speaking about himself in the third person (using his second
baptismal name, Johan), giving fictitious names to people (when he names
them at all), and discreetly changing place names here and there. Actually,
the autobiography is intended to be as factual as possible.

As far as we know, Strindberg had no early notebooks to use as
sources and asked his brother Axel to send every scrap of writing he could
find relating to their childhood. Since Axel had difficulty satisfying the
request, Strindberg included as documents in the first two parts of the
autobiography only some school compositions, his senior thesis essay, a
youthful love letter that was never mailed, and several letters he had received. He also ordered copies through Bonnier of a number of the works
he had read in his youth, as well as several political and cultural-historical
texts to be used as reference materials. These sources were not extensive,
and generally Strindberg relied on his extraordinary memory, which seldom
misled him[4] as long as he was not attempting to reinterpret events for
polemic reasons.

In a letter to Gustaf af Geijerstam in March, 1886, he explained
what he meant when he said he presumed people would regard the book
as a novel:

> I am now beginning to write myself to death on a big novel in four, five
> parts: "My novel."[5] Type: *Jacques Vingtras* by Jules Vallès. An "ad-
> vanced" form of naturalistic novel that includes historical, psychic, and
> social milieus together with the author's opinions, which are the most
> important things, for he has to stand above his subject and, like God . . .
> teach his readers to understand what they are reading.

Strindberg had already suggested a year earlier that naturalistic
novels should be autobiographical: "Literary writing will gradually cease.
Future societies should establish bureaus in which every person at a specified age would anonymously deposit a truthful biography. This could
serve as source material for a true science of man, if such a thing were
needed."[6] Further justification for the idea is contained in a preface-inter-

view to *The Son of a Servant* that was excluded on the advice of his publisher.[7] Here, Strindberg calls his work an "attempt at the literature of the
future." The novel is moribund: "Zola has made the last compromise with
the form and now seems to have recognized its weaknesses."[8] It is doomed
because it is arranged, contrived: "How can one know what is going on in
other people's minds? How can one know the complicated motives behind
another person's actions? How can one know what so-and-so said in an
intimate moment? Well, one fabricates. . . . One cannot really be familiar
with more than one life—one's own."[9] He reiterates his proposal that as
a substitution for "synthetic" literature every citizen should be enjoined
to deposit his autobiography in a communal archive. "Now, *that* would be
documentation!"

Strindberg's old aversion to belles-lettres led him to try to outdo
the naturalistic novel in documentation, something he would also attempt
to do by other means in *In the Outer Skerries*. In referring to the subtitle
of *The Son of a Servant—The Story of the Evolution of a Human Being
1849-1867 (En själs utvecklingshistoria 1849-1867)*—in the preface-
interview, he added:

> I admit [the subtitle] should have continued: in Middle Sweden and
> under the specific conditions indicated in the book—the son's inheritances
> from his mother, father, and wet nurse; circumstances during his fetal
> period; his family's economic situation; his parents' philosophy of life;
> the nature of his companions; his schools and teachers, friends, siblings,
> servants, and so forth.[10]

Strindberg made a sincere effort to delineate all these factors,
particularly in the first part of the autobiography. We find that he had
inherited his father's aristocratic instincts and his mother's—the servant's
—"slavish blood," and that he had contracted "twitching nerves" from
his wet nurse. The importance of his upbringing and family environment
in the development of his character is carefully stressed, just as he tries to
show how the political and social milieu influenced him. He disagrees,
however, with Zola's insistence on the importance of physiological aspects
and certain purely incidental elements, citing as an example a scene from
La Curée (1874):

> If a woman is seduced in a hothouse, it isn't necessary to relate the
> seduction to all the potted plants found there and list them all by name.
> But on the other hand, the furniture in a child's home is another matter
> since it indicates the family's general economic status; likewise, the books

in the family library play a significant role in the development of a literary person.[11]

Strindberg's psychological approach was similar to a trend in France begun by Paul Bourget and Edouard Rod as a reaction to Zola's "physiological" method. At this time, though, Strindberg could scarcely have known Bourget and Rod except through hearsay. The primary influence on Strindberg, as on Bourget, was Théodule Armand Ribot,[12] whose association psychology left traces everywhere in *The Son of a Servant,* perhaps most obviously in the often-quoted concluding passages of the first part, in which the author attempts to present his state of mind at the age of eighteen. Using Ribot as a point of departure, Strindberg denies the integrity of the ego; it is only "a conglomeration of reflexes, a complex of instincts, desires."[13] His own ego, "because of much crossbreeding of blood lines, conflicts in the home, rich experiences from books, and many ups and downs in life," had become "a rich but disorganized source of material." Up to this point he had not found his "role" and was actually "characterless."

> Had he been able to look at himself objectively at this time, he would have found that most of the words he used came from books or from companions, his gestures from teachers and friends, his facial expressions from relatives, his temperament from his mother and wet nurse, and his inclinations from his father, perhaps his grandfather. . . . What then did he posses that was of and in himself? Nothing.[14]

Strindberg stressed the importance of these psychological speculations. He told Albert Bonnier in May, 1886, that he wanted to use the autobiography to "investigate the concept of character—upon which all literature rests," and he resumed the investigation two years later in the introduction to *Miss Julie.* Scholars can be grateful that he was so generous in citing the many influences and impulses he believed explained his character and behavior. Whereas most autobiographers show a sensitive reluctance to acknowledge dependence on others, Strindberg never hesitated to show how his life had developed because of his inheritance, his milieu, his reading, his encounters with important contemporaries, and even by trifling, casual occurrences. Because he was so firmly convinced of his own uniqueness and originality, he did not feel the need to conceal the identity of the sources that had influenced him.

Strindberg's description of himself as "characterless" is partially a commendation. A "character," according to his definition, is an individual whose basic attitudes are petrified:

> He sees the most complicated situations in life from only one point of view; he has resolved to have a single definite opinion on anything for the rest of his life. And in order not to be guilty of characterlessness, he never changes his opinion, however foolish or unreasonable it may be. Consequently, a character must be a very ordinary person and, one might say, a little stupid. . . . Moreover, a character is supposed to know what he wants. But what does one really know about what one wants? One wants or does not want, that is all.[15]

Strindberg thus makes no effort to hide or excuse the fact that he changed his mind many times. On the contrary, he often exaggerates the importance of the changes out of conviction that this intellectual agility was a mark of distinction. He maintained that one of the basic elements of his intellectual makeup was a skepticism that made it impossible for him to accept ideas uncritically—he was compelled to develop and combine them. "This is why he could not become an automaton and be considered an ordinary member of organized society."[16] At the same time, he was conscious that in spite of these changes he was always the same within, even when he held diametrically opposed opinions. The first part of the autobiography ends with his going out into the world "to evolve, to develop, and yet to remain forever the same."[17]

In order to understand the importance of *The Son of a Servant* as a document, it is necessary to examine the profound changes in opinion that Strindberg went through during the short time—barely a year—it took to write all four parts. When he wrote the final part, *The Author,* he described it as closing the book on his past and requested the publisher to look over the last three chapters so "that you may see the position I now find myself taking and how important immediate publication is."[18]

When Strindberg began writing *The Son of a Servant,* his mind was dominated by misogyny and socialism, and this caused him to view his childhood from a warped perspective. Although his opinions on the woman question were the same throughout the period the autobiography was in progress, his misogyny is most obvious in the first part, written immediately after the *Married* ordeal.

Part One begins with a survey of the years following the ascension to the throne of King Oscar I, during whose reign (1844-59), Strindberg complains, daughters were granted equal inheritance rights with their brothers "without a simultaneous lightening of the sons' burdens as future breadwinners." The same hostility toward women appears in the discussion of the relationship between his parents. Although a careful reading of the autobiography gives one the impression that Strindberg felt his father's uncommunicativeness and sullenness had cast a gloom over the author's childhood home, one can also detect an intention to throw some blame on the mother. From her the children receive food; from the father, punishment: "In this way, the children became accustomed, unfairly, to regard her as the provider of all good and the father of all evil."[19] Strindberg saw his father suffering the same breadwinner's martyrdom that he thought he himself was undergoing:

> This is the thankless position of the father in the family. Provider for all, enemy of all. If he came home tired, hungry and depressed, and found the floor still wet from scouring and the food badly prepared, and then dared to make a comment, he would receive a curt reply. It was as if he lived on sufferance in his own home, and the children hid themselves from him.[20]

In this context, his mother, a woman burdened with the responsibilities of a large family, seems almost as indolent as the ladies in pensions he had so brilliantly depicted in *Married:* "She drank her coffee in bed in the mornings; to assist her she had wet nurses, two servants, and her mother. Very likely she did not strain herself."[21]

It is true that Strindberg's hostility toward the family as an institution was deep rooted. But when in his autobiography he calls the family a washing and ironing establishment and an uneconomical way to feed people—pointing out that a restaurant manager with several hundred people to serve used scarcely more help than was needed in his home—what emerges is his old enthusiasm for the *familistère*. And the often-cited fiery tirade against the family ("Glorious, moral institution! . . . The Family! Home of all social evil. . . .") more accurately reflects the biased attitude prevailing throughout the volume than it does the thinking of the boyish Johan.[22]

For Strindberg at the time he was writing *The Son of a Servant,* the problem of social organization was exemplified in the conflict between the upper and lower classes. Before he began work on his autobiography, he was uncertain about which class he identified with. In January, 1885, immediately after the *Married* trial, he wrote Albert Bonnier that he would soon abandon his position as " 'great man' and 'martyr' " and "strip down to my shirtsleeves in earnest. I was born a democrat, though fate (in the form of an aristocratic bourgeois father) leaned me toward the upper classes as well." In a letter to Heidenstam six months later, however, he attacked "the lowly ones" who tried to hinder him; parenthetically, he added: "Of course I was upper class and never needed to fear for my position." In another letter to Heidenstam in September he said that an acquaintance had openly suggested that the roots of the discord between Siri (first married to a baron) and himself "lay in U. C. [Upper Class] and L. C. [Lower Class]. Perhaps."

And so, on the one hand, Strindberg regarded himself in terms of origin and sympathies as lower class, despite his father's higher social standing and his own marriage into the aristocratic class. When he began writing *The Son of a Servant,* he decided to identify himself with the lower classes and to write for them. Indolent upper-class women and their enslaved men were the people who had persecuted him during the *Married* ordeal. But on the other hand, the title *The Son of a Servant* represented only one side of the author's makeup, and throughout the volume the conflict between his mother's and his father's lineage asserts itself. When as a little boy he paid his first summer visit to Drottningholm outside Stockholm and met the Crown Prince (later Charles XV) near the summer castle there, he says that he glimpsed—

> the splendor of the upper classes from a distance. He longed to be with
> them as if he longed to go home, but the slave blood he inherited from
> his mother rebeled against it. He instinctively revered the upper classes,
> but revered them too much to dare to hope to join them. Furthermore,
> he felt he did not belong there, but he did not belong with the slaves
> either. This feeling of being torn between two worlds would become one
> of the torments of his life.[23]

When he was eight years old he was transferred from Klara School to Jacob's School where the students were poorer. He admitted, in the chapter "Contact with the Lower Classes" ("Beröring med under-klassen"), that he had "come down," but alleged that he had wanted to. "He did not wish to climb higher and push anyone down, but he suffered because of pressure from above. He did not want to be higher than anyone else, but neither did he want anyone else higher than he. Still, it annoyed him that his old classmates thought he had come down."[24]

In spite of his ambivalent feelings about the lower classes, he seems to miss no opportunity to defend them.

> In all cases in which the lower classes are not pressed by necessity, they are more conscientious than the upper classes. They are also more charitable toward their peers, more forbearing to children, and above all more patient. How long have they not endured being exploited by the upper classes before they finally became impatient![25]

It was a mistaken impression, the author asserts, that the lower classes want to be above the upper classes; they want only equality: "this explains their expressed desire to want to raise themselves."[26] But although observations such as these abound in Part One of the autobiography, they are presented rather half-heartedly, without the burning conviction that marked the essays about class distinctions in *This and That*. The truth was that even while he was representing himself to the public as the son of a servant, his democratic beliefs were beginning to totter. In June, 1886, in a letter to Albert Bonnier concerning the newly completed second volume, Strindberg made a surprising statement. He said that Part Two was:

> written for cultured people and so the lower or middle classes won't be able to read it. It is addressed to the academically cultured, for whom I really should be writing. I get no pleasure when Tom, Dick, and Harry fail to understand me, and I am unable to convert them.

The cause of this shift in the author's intention can be found in another letter to his publisher sent a month earlier (May 14, 1886) from Brunegg in Switzerland. Strindberg had visited Verner von Heidenstam in a mountain castle, where they "matched coins in the castle hall and fenced with armor from the fifteenth century, . . . drank beer, played backgammon and talked socialism." Strindberg later saw fit to reproduce the entire discussion on socialism as a conclusion to the fourth part of his autobiography, evidence that this particular visit at Brunegg with the young Swedish aristocrat and writer had far-reaching consequences.

During earlier meetings, the two men had had "endless conversations about socialism," but Strindberg had not been won over to Heidenstam's anti-socialistic position. This time Heidenstam's arguments had a more potent effect because (according to a passage cut from the fourth part of the autobiography) Strindberg "had stamped out his last belief in idealism by studying the latest advances in psychology." (A year earlier Strindberg had repudiated deism and adopted atheism, under the influence of several stories in Oscar Levertin's *Conflicts—Konflikter.)* In the published dialogue between the two men[27] Heidenstam says that Strindberg's socialism is "only Christianity with the addition of a theory of privation, from which you cannot liberate yourself. . . . It is remarkable . . . that you, who are unable to believe in anything—either in God, woman or art—believe in poverty and the worker."[28] He urges Strindberg to "unmask poverty as you unmasked art. Try to see the other side of that, too! Perhaps it too is humbug, taken all in all."[29] In response, Strindberg admits that he wondered if his democratic obsession did not conflict with his nature; his conscience troubled him when he re-read *The Son of a Servant* (the first part had just been published).

Anti-democratic sentiments begin to appear in the second part of the autobiography, *The Time of Ferment (Jäsningstiden)*. In the second chapter, when describing his work as a primary school teacher in 1867-68 —a period when he strongly favored democratic ideals—he disputes Ibsen's assertion that the workers were the nobility. It tormented him to see the deformed bodies and smell the bad odor of the lower classes because through his upbringing he had become an aristocrat. "Life had given him much, in spite of everything, and these daily reminders of misery plagued him like an awareness of evil."[30] This is a reiteration of a Heidenstam observation that Strindberg's upbringing and natural aptitude had elevated him to the upper classes and only because of a bad conscience did he believe in the cause of the poverty-stricken.

Strindberg also declares in *The Time of Ferment* that when he was a school teacher he never tried to give the impression that he was a "friend of the people":

> One has no control over one's sympathies and antipathies, and for the lower classes to demand love and self-sacrifice from the upper classes is idealistic. The lower classes are sacrificed for the upper classes, but, by God, they have offered up themselves willingly. They have the right to recover their rights, but they will have to do it themselves. No one gives up his position voluntarily, therefore the lower classes should not wait for kings or upper classes to disappear. Pull us down—but all at once![31]

In the Brunegg discussion Heidenstam says that it amused him to think of the lowly, stooped peasants in the forest of his family estate back in Sweden who were toiling in order for him to be able to visit foreign lands and live in a castle. "Stupid wretches. If I were in their place, I would do just what they are planning to do." But the upper classes, Heidenstam continues, have the right to resist by using "our power—the military! Notice that I don't talk about justice, for that's only a word; justice doesn't exist. To want to rise up in the world, to be uppermost and to tear down what's on top—this is a natural law that cannot be changed."[32]

Strindberg was already close to agreement with Heidenstam on this Darwinian power philosophy[33] in Part Two of the autobiography, particularly in the chapter "How He Becomes an Aristocrat" ("Huruledes han blir aristokrat"). Inspired by the Brunegg debate, Strindberg re-evaluated some unpleasant contacts he had had with lower-class vulgarity on a canal trip to Copenhagen when he was twenty years old. The lower classes, "the upper classes [i.e., tyrants] of the future, . . . had become his enemies. The bridge between them and him was now drawn up. But the ties of blood remained and he shared their hostility toward society and toward those who were unjustly elevated."[34] In the Brunegg debate Strindberg quotes Heidenstam as saying: "At bottom we are all anarchists: Let's have no one above us—that's anarchism."[35] And at the end of the debate, after apparently turning his back unequivocally on all his earlier utopian ideas, Strindberg outlines to Heidenstam a generally anarchistic program for the future. The old concept of the state would be shattered, and all untilled land parceled out to peasants' sons, crofters, cotters, and unemployed urban workers. The family would be replaced by the family association, wives would "be forced to go out and work instead of petitioning as they now do with lamentations and threats," and all children would be given a common upbringing. Consumers' cooperatives would make middlemen unnecessary, large cities would be broken up into village communities, and "private socialism" would replace "state socialism." The current varieties of socialism and idealism are "diseases generated by the indolence that is the result of working with machines, which tire neither the brain nor the body."[36]

Johan (Strindberg) "talked until his lips were blue," but the result is only a hodgepodge of earlier Strindbergian utopian ideas. In a letter to Heidenstam he declared that he had renounced socialism and become a revolutionary. Meanwhile, as he repudiated his former support for social reform, he was becoming reconciled with belles-lettres. In June, 1886, after completing *The Time of Ferment,* he wrote to his publisher: "This is perhaps the kind of work that interests me most, and I feel myself straightening out in the process. It was a necessary step in enabling me to return to writing." In subsequent letters, he repeats time and again that "ephemeral political or social so-called problems or questions" no longer appealed to him and that he hoped to be able "to bring into being an artistically valid psychological literature." But it was not only his dislike for "so-called problems" that turned Strindberg back to the "beautiful lies" he had censured so persistently in the preceding years. Although the autobiography was intended solely as factual narrative, it gave Strindberg more opportunity to exercise his poetic imagination than had his recent fiction. Irrespective of its merit as history, the autobiography is a work of art and one of Strindberg's finest achievements.

Like Rousseau, Strindberg used his childhood as an object lesson to illustrate the failings of society, the shortcomings of current child-rearing methods, the egotism of parents, and the tyranny of family life. Every sequence of events is analyzed psychologically: little Johan is explained and diagnosed as a clinical case; scarcely any of his actions, thoughts, feelings, and reactions escape comment. This approach has its dangers but also its advantages. Absent from the book is any suggestion of a child's naive lightheartedness. The boy already has a faultfinder's eye and the corners of his mouth are turned down with disillusionment. His pain is redoubled when he recalls every injustice, setback, and humiliation.

As Strindberg describes his childhood martyrdom in this vehement, accusatory tone, he also sketches sharply and clearly the Strindberg of the 1880's. We may be skeptical about the authenticity of sections of his story, especially the rendering of childhood impressions and experiences, but the author's reactions to his past bring the adult Strindberg to life for us. "Afraid and Hungry" ("Rädd och hungrig") is the revealing title of the first chapter of the autobiography; in the third, "Away from Home" ("Borta ifrån hemmet"), he says: "He came into the world afraid and lived in constant fear of life and people."[37] This fear of existence is probably the most memorable impression the book creates; the same gloomy vision of childhood is reflected in Strindberg's writing both prior to and following *The Son of a Servant.*

But the story is not painted in only sombre colors; there is warmth and humor, and a number of fine character portraits. His father is splendidly drawn: "basically an aristocrat, to the very last habit": his manservant has to wear gloves when brushing his boots. Marriage and economic misfortunes have wounded him in ways he tries to conceal.

Reserved, serious, pedantically self-righteous, he stays at home constantly and never accepts an invitation to visit anyone because he cannot return it. His only pleasures are playing the piano and cultivating pelargoniums in the window. These same flowers play a role in Strindberg's little cameo description of his mother:

> In later years, when Johan had grown older and his mother was dead, every time he tried to picture her the image of a pelargonium followed, or both came together. His mother was pale; she had had twelve confinements, and was consumptive. Her face was like the pelargonium's transparent white leaves with its blood-red veins, which grow darker toward the bottom where they form an almost black pupil, black as his mother's.[38]

Particularly beautiful are the short descriptions of excursions in the country—the brightest memories of the years he was growing up. The first is the boat trip to Drottningholm summer castle, during which the youngster looks out a cabin window and sees gliding past, as if in a panorama or theatre, small red and white houses, green trees, and great green expanses with red cows on them, "just like Christmas toys."[39] Another scene depicts the wonderful discovery of the Stockholm archipelago during the excursion with the Volunteer Rifle Corps that was discussed earlier.[40]

There is often touching humor in the sketches of Johan's infatuations: the twelve-year-old's crush on an inspector's daughter is like "a quiet sorrow . . . a madonna worship, which desired nothing more than to make some great sacrifice, preferably like drowning himself in the bay, but, of course, only if she were watching."[41] At fifteen he experiences a platonic love for a spinster of fully thirty years.

The finest of these scenes of early love is probably the one in *The Time of Ferment*, which describes his shy courtship of a waitress at Stallmästargården restaurant, an affair which comes to a sad end when as a name-day gift Johan gives her a risqué poem written by an older friend, a teacher, and tries to pass it off as his own. The girl recognizes it as a poem given two years before by the teacher to " 'old Majken, who was a bad girl. Oh, Johan!' "[42] Whereupon the young student, desperate with shame, grabs his hat and dashes out into nearby Bellevue Park. The episode had already been used in the *Married* story "Virtue's Rewards," but there it was told without the psychological subtlety it has in the autobiography.

The last two parts of the autobiography are artistically inferior to the first parts. The author is much too concerned with books and ideas, too defensive, and too anxious to repudiate views he once thought valid; he has no time to develop psychologically interesting situations. But even these final parts have brilliant passages. It was important for Strindberg to have his entire life pass in review in this way, to confront his own temperament. Not until he made this inventory of his treaure of memories did he discover how wealthy he really was, and what little cause he had to feel he had exhausted his writing potential. While working on the third part, he promised in a letter to his publisher (July 4, 1886) that afterward he would pack away all his books and return to "belles-lettres, which entice me again."

A Madman's Defense

During his work on *The Son of a Servant,* Strindberg had thought of several ways to fit the story of his marriage to Siri von Essen "into the evolution story." At first he collected their correspondence under the title *He and She (Han och Hon)*[43] and intended to add to it a presentation of his wife's theatrical career in the form of a novel—*The Fate of an Actress (En skådespelarskas öden).* But when his publisher refused to publish the correspondence, Strindberg decided (at the end of 1886) to reshape the entire story of his marriage into a novel, retaining the name Johan for the hero so that the volume might be considered the fifth part of the autobiography. *Le Plaidoyer d'un Fou,* written in French between September, 1887, and March, 1888, was the realization of this goal, as Landquist shows in his note to *He and She.* Landquist also points out that Strindberg had originally intended the work to be lighter in tone than it subsequently became. This is probably true, for at the time Strindberg declared in a letter that he had escaped the woman question and "was living idyllically"; but the idyll was only a brief respite.

The purpose of *A Madman's Defense* was to expose Siri as a means of protecting Strindberg from the danger of confinement in a mental hospital. By a curious irony of fate, it has served as evidence of his derangement. As early as 1894 the same year the book came out in German under the title *Die Beichte eines Toren,* the German psychologist Wilhelm Hirsch, in *Genie und Entartung,* said that Strindberg was a typical paranoiac, suffering from pathological jealousy. But as Eklund has emphasized,[44] the jealousy mania was not confined to that period alone, despite the insistence of later psychiatrists such as Karl Jaspers. Strindberg suffered from abnormal jealousy in all of his marriages. The reason it is expressed so violently in *A Madman's Defense* is that it was reinforced by the fear that he was being persecuted and threatened with confinement.

During and after the *Married* trial Strindberg was plagued with the idea that there were people persecuting him, and it was not long before he included his wife among them. In a letter to Isidor Kjellberg on January 14, 1885, he said that his wife had received a letter from the feminist leader Countess Adlersparre, and he concluded that Siri was being persuaded to join the international league of women, which he suspected of being behind the *Married* indictment. Supposedly, the object of the league was to prevent him, at all costs, from continuing his anti-feminist campaign. He felt he was being persecuted in Switzerland, so he went to Paris and then to Grez, all the while sensing plots. That these fears were not invented later is indicated in his letters to Jonas Lie and other friends that constantly mention feminine intrigues against him. Suspicions about his wife's infidelity and perversion appear for the first time in a letter to Kjellberg from Grez (October, 1885). The wording of the letter makes it appear that both he and Siri were anxious to find out all they could about the "dastardly insinuations" in order to refute them.

At the end of 1886, a manuscript for an essay, "The Final Word on the Woman Question" ("Sista ordet i kvinnofrågan"), was mislaid, and its disappearance further inflamed Strindberg's persecution fears.[45] When the manuscript was found, he did a turnabout and wrote to Heidenstam that "the termagants" had tried to break up his marriage by "arousing my suspicions that Siri took a manuscript."

It appears from evidence in her daughter Karin's book[46] that at this time Siri, anxious over Strindberg's mental condition, told a Swiss doctor who knew him that she thought her husband was deranged. Strindberg became aware of his wife's suspicions, and when he found out about her conversation with the doctor was convinced that she intended to have him confined. The situation reached a crisis that was reflected in his work. Early in 1887, Strindberg wrote *The Father,* a play whose basic theme is a wife's attempt to get her husband to compromise himself so that she can have him put away.

A Madman's Defense is a strange mixture of real events and wild imaginings. The wife Maria (Siri) thinks her husband mad right from the beginning of their marriage and tries to provoke him to actions that will justify having him confined. Siri kept a King Charles spaniel from her first marriage, and the dog was a constant source of friction during the Strindbergs' honeymoon. In the novel the narrator says that "if it is established that I am crazy—as my wife alleges," it is his own fault, because he had lacked the courage to poison the disgusting animal.[47] When Maria joins the critics in attacking her husband's book (i.e., *The New Kingdom,* which the narrator asserts attacked sexless women), she is accused of having gone over to the side of the enemy, and as a result, says the narrator, a newspaper circulated "a 'rumor' that I was crazy."[48] A trip by Strindberg to Paris in 1883 is described in the novel as being motivated by a wish to see old friends who understood his eccentricities and paradoxes, and who "could judge the present state of his mind." Furthermore, the narrator states, he wanted to place himself under the protection of certain Scandinavian writers then living in Paris "in order to counteract more effectively Maria's criminal intentions, which aimed at nothing less than having me confined in a nursing home."[49] "A prominent Norwegian author" (Bjørnson) urged him to remain in Paris for several years, but his wife wanted him isolated from his friends and forced the family to return to the French-speaking part of Switzerland. When they arrived there, "from the first moment she posed publicly as the keeper for a harmless lunatic. She got to know the doctor, warned the proprietor and his wife, and even alerted the servants and the other pension guests."[50] When the narrator corresponded with friends in Sweden, he could see "what they thought of my mental condition"[51] by their guarded language and fatherly advice. His worst fears were confirmed: "She had triumphed." He sensed that he was close to becoming mentally ill and noticed the first signs of persecution mania. But he checks himself: "Mania? Why call it mania? I was being persecuted, and there was nothing irrational about believing it!"[52]

Why had his wife spread the rumor that he was deranged? Because she was an adultress. "So, you have betrayed me," accuses the narrator, "and in order to deceive the world you spread the fable about my madness. To conceal your crime more effectively you try to torment me to death."[53] First, she was after his life insurance, which she tried to get by driving him to madness and suicide; then, she wanted the rights to his writings so that she could enjoy them undisturbed with her lover.

During the writing of *A Madman's Defense,* Strindberg re-evaluated how he had felt about Siri right from the beginning of their acquaintance. Although he had their correspondence in front of him as he wrote, his imagination restructured their entire relationship. His tendency to be jealous may not have been restricted to this period, but it can be assumed, as Jaspers has established, that it was by means of this systematic review of the past that his suspicions grew into accusations. He asserted that during his first reading of *The Wild Duck* he found nothing to remind him of his own situation. Now he saw clearly that Ibsen had portrayed him as Hjalmar Ekdal and Siri as Gina. It also appears that Strindberg did not at first find anything suspicious in a caricature of him in an artists' album in the hotel in Grez; it was drawn, after all, by one of his best friends. Now, the narrator finds that the artist had obviously decorated the sketch with "a horn, cleverly constructed with a lock of my hair"; from this he concludes "that my wife's infidelity was known; everyone in the world was aware of it except me."[54]

Strindberg's suspicions about the identity of Siri's alleged lover were not restricted to a single person. In letters to his brother Axel and to Pehr Staaff, one name after another is mentioned as the culprit, but by the time Axel or Staaff had refuted an accusation, Strindberg's thoughts were elsewhere. Suspicions that his wife had been untrue and that his children were not his became deeply rooted within him. The more impossible it was to find proof for his fears, the more his fever rose: "Why would people have offended me, taunted me as a betrayed husband, pictured me with a horn, and so forth, unless they knew something?"[55]

The narrator speaks of opening his wife's letters, setting traps for her, subjecting her to cross-examinations, and constantly noting her behavior. If she is happy and lighthearted, it is a sign of her guilt; if she is distressed, that too is a sign. If she takes pains with her clothes, it is to please others. If she is careless about her appearance, it is a sign that she does not love him. Sometimes he suspects her of amusing herself by making him jealous, sometimes, of intentionally driving him to distraction and madness by letting him believe that she has had love affairs with others. But above all he is tortured by the uncertainty of never knowing what actually happened, because he finds neither his wife's denials nor the confessions he believes he extorted from her to be convincing.

The entire complex of past and present feelings became even more chaotic when during his work on the novel he and Siri experienced happy if brief reconciliations. In *A Madman's Defense* the narrator describes returning from a visit to Vienna in the spring of 1887: "It was a month of enchanted springtime for us, to the chirping of starlings. Our love was boundless; we hugged and kissed as if we could never stop. We played duets on the piano and rounds of backgammon. The best times we had had in the last five years seemed pale by comparison."[56] A similar picture of how Strindberg and Siri quarreled violently and then spent deliciously fond hours together "as if nothing happened" is contained in a letter to Strindberg's brother Axel in February, 1887: "You probably know that as a writer I blend fiction and reality, but all of my misogyny is only theoretical; I could never live without the company of a woman."

One must have a clear impression of these changeable states of mind in order to understand the work Strindberg did during the remaining years of his first marriage. The grim aspects of the marriage emerge in the plays *Marauders (Marodörer)* later revised and called *Comrades, The Father, Miss Julie,* and *Creditors,* and these works contrast with those produced in happier times: the novel *The People of Hemsö* and the story collection *The Men of the Skerries.* Even his divorce proceedings provided an inspiration for his work, resulting in the powerful one-act drama *The Bond (Bandet).* But when the divorce was final and he was separated from his children, his productivity quickly dried up and was not renewed until after his religious conversion.

Notes to Chapter Nine

1. *Brev,* V, p. 218.
2. *SS:*LIV, pp. 223-27.
3. A draft in Birger Mörner's collection shows that the last part was to include all of Strindberg's travels abroad, beginning with the trip to Copenhagen up to the second sojourn in Paris and Grez.
4. This is not true about dates, which Strindberg treated rather nonchalantly. Hence the origin of a number of unintentional misconceptions that later reappear in möst of the biographies of Strindberg.
5. The words "my novel" are in English in the original text.—Translator
6. Mörner, p. 168.
7. It was first published in Landquist's edition, *SS:*XVIII, pp. 453 ff.
8. *Ibid.,* p. 457.
9. *Ibid.,* p. 456.
10. *Ibid.,* p. 452.
11. *Ibid,* p. 456.
12. In a section cut from the foreword to Volume II of *Married,* Strindberg mentions Ribot's *Les Maladies de la personnalité* (1885).
13. *SS:*XVIII, p. 218.
14. *Ibid.,* p. 219.
15. *Ibid.,* pp. 212-13.
16. *Ibid.,* p. 219.
17. *Ibid.*
18. Strangely enough, destiny decreed that this part was not to be published until twenty years after it was written; Strindberg then wrote a new foreword, in which he declared that the writer portrayed in the book was now just as much a stranger to him as he was to the reader and just as unsympathetic.
19. *SS:*XVIII, p. 13.
20. *Ibid.,* p. 14.
21. *Ibid.,* p. 13.
22. Strindberg asserts that in *Master Olof* for safety's sake he allowed Kristina instead of Olof to voice his opposition to parental authority. Hostility to this same authority reappears in *The Red Room* where Olle Montanus protests against "the most horrible of all forms of authoritative rule: family tyranny."
23. *SS:*XVIII, p. 34.
24. *Ibid.,* pp. 59-60.
25. *Ibid.,* p. 62.
26. *Ibid.,* p. 66.

27. In this dialogue Strindberg also quoted as part of the discussion bits out of Heidenstam's earlier letters to him. This is not to say, of course, that these arguments were not reiterated orally.

28. *SS:*XIX, p. 283.

29. *Ibid.*

30. *SS:*XVIII, p. 260.

31. *Ibid.*, pp. 260-61.

32. *SS:*XIX, p. 284.

33. Heidenstam goes on to say that he believes that his class will be beaten in "the free struggle for existence": "We are too cultured or too weak to employ barbarism, like them; consequently, we shall go down, and with us, culture" (*SS:*XIX, p. 284). Strindberg assimilated this conception completely in his theory about the superiority of "the lowly ones" over "the great." Later, he would reinforce it with arguments borrowed from Nietzsche.

34. *SS:*XVIII, p. 324.

35. *SS:*XIX, p. 285.

36. *Ibid.*, p. 293.

37. *SS:*XVIII, p. 47.

38. *Ibid.*, pp. 12-13.

39. *Ibid.*, p. 30.

40. *See* Chapter IV, The Skerries Writer.—Translator

41. *SS:*XVIII, p. 78.

42. *Ibid.*, p. 268.

43. This correspondence, which includes only the transitional period 1875-76, was first published by Landquist in the collected works (*SS:*LV). Strindberg's letters to Siri are reproduced in *Brev*, I.

44. Eklund, *Strindbergsstudie*, pp. 172 ff.

45. This time, his suspicions were directed against a "feminine cabal" led by Fru Anna Branting; he suspected her of intercepting the manuscript before it reached her husband and "confiscating" it. —Translator

46. Smirnoff, p. 243.

47. *SS:*XXVI, p. 263.

48. *Ibid.*, p. 299.

49. *Ibid.*, p. 313.

50. *Ibid*, p. 316.

51. *Ibid.*, p. 317.

52. *Ibid.*, p. 318.

53. *Ibid.*, p. 368.

54. *Ibid.*, p. 330.

55. Letter to Axel Strindberg, October 22, 1887; *Brev*, VI, pp. 285-86.

56. *SS:*XXVI, p. 360.

Chapter Ten

THE NATURALISTIC CONTEMPORARY DRAMAS

Marauders-Comrades

Strindberg had approached naturalism in his novels and short stories and created a substitute for *le roman expérimental* in his autobiography, but had as yet made no effort to utilize Zola's suggestions for reforming drama, although he had been familiar with them for several years. In a letter on May 10, 1883, he described a current Swedish play as "a hopeful step toward *le naturalisme au théâtre*," and several weeks later tried to persuade Daniel Fallström, the editor of the newspaper *Puck*, to publish excerpts from Zola's manifesto.[1] But it was not until he came in contact with psychological experiments with the power of suggestion that he was able to see new possibilities in naturalistic drama; it was then that he set in motion plans that undoubtedly had long been brewing in his mind.

His first contemporary drama, *Marauders-Comrades*, cannot in any way be considered naturalistic. It is an attempt to confront the partisans of the woman question in the arena where they preferred conducting the struggle—the theatre. While the first volume of *Married* was at the printer, Strindberg planned a drama against "the tigresses," and after the blasphemy trial he considered attacking, among others, Countess Sofie Adlersparre in a play entitled *Duel (Tvekamp)*.[2] In August, 1886, these plans were realized in the writing of the play *Marauders;* only a few copies were reproduced in manuscript, however, and the play did not reach the public until 1888, when it was revised and issued under the new title *Comrades.*

The title *Marauders* is explained by the hero, Axel, a painter, when he remarks to his wife Bertha, also a painter: "It's strange, but I feel as if you're trespassing, marauding where we [men] were struggling while you [women] sat home by the stove."[3] Feminine encroachment upon the masculine labor market was one of Strindberg's favorite themes in the recent *Married* campaign. The play attempts to ridicule the entire feminist movement, including its drama, and is primarily an answer to *A Doll's House*. A man is tyrannized to such an extent that his wife is nearly able to force him to dress as a female Spanish dancer for a costume ball. Ultimately, he throws off his oppression and slams the door in her face. Another similarity to *A Doll's House* is the repetition of the phrase "the miracle." Ibsen's Nora implies that "the greatest miracle" would be if her husband were able to treat her as a true partner in marriage instead of a plaything subordinated to his will. Strindberg's answer is Abel, a mannish emancipated woman, who says that it would be a "miracle" to find a man who could dominate a woman.

Except for the first act, the action of *Marauders* is set in Paris, and a number of the characters were modeled on members of the Scandinavian colony there. In a letter on May 27, 1887, Strindberg described the artist couple whom he represented in Axel and Bertha: "They compete for the salon and he is turned down; she is accepted. The marriage falls to pieces." In the first four acts of the play Strindberg appears to follow the same course of events. But in the last act it is discovered that the accepted painting was actually Axel's, not Bertha's. Because he knew he was the better artist, he wanted to help his wife, and he exchanged the numbers on the paintings they submitted to the salon. His triumph is complete when his wife, in order to humiliate him, invites his friends to a celebration in their home and arranges for the rejected painting to be carried in and displayed.[4] Bertha discovers that the work is hers, and she is the one who is humiliated. *Marauders* concludes with Axel generously surrendering the house and all his possessions to Bertha.

When Strindberg and his wife were temporarily reconciled in the fall of 1887, he allowed his Danish translator and collaborator Axel Lundegård to revise the piece into a comedy with a happy ending, ridiculing both husband and wife: the two "dull fogeys" whose idealistic demands had made life dark and gloomy. But after finishing *A Madman's Defense* in March, 1888, Strindberg found the conclusion too tame. When he revised the play as *Comrades,* he had Axel drive his wife out of the house and threaten to have her locked up if she bothered him again. Before

Bertha has had time to leave, the maid announces that Axel's mistress has arrived.

Marauders-Comrades bears the marks of having come into being during varying stages of the crisis in Strindberg's marriage. The first act of *Marauders* (discarded in *Comrades*), written almost three months before the rest of the play, is a fresh and gay opening to the comedy, with satire directed primarily against women appropriating masculine fashions and forcing men to adopt feminine modes. In the second act too, in which the playwright arbitrarily moves the entire cast of characters to Paris, broad farce is still in evidence. But thereafter, the mood changes. The conceited Bertha, "like a cannibal," devours Axel's soul to nourish her own, and the mild and dreamy Axel develops into a combination of domestic martyr and keen exposer of human frailty. For the first time we meet the two protagonists of the Strindbergian marital drama. Despite the playwright's fierce bias in these scenes, their intensity makes them engrossing. The harsh duel between husband and wife completely arrests the spectator's attention. In his next drama, *The Father,* Strindberg would rise to true greatness.[5]

Vivisections

Between the writing of *Marauders-Comrades* and *The Father,* Strindberg became intrigued by psychiatric studies and was introduced to the phenomenon of the power of suggestion, which he first dealt with in works that were part story, part essay, published in the Vienna newspaper *Neue Freie Presse.* His intention was to collect these pieces in a book under the title *Vivisections (Vivisektioner).* However, the most important influence of the concept of suggestion on Strindberg's work was not on the *Vivisections* essays but on his naturalistic dramas.[6] He saw suggestion as a means of delving into hitherto unexplored areas of spiritual life. As he was writing the first of his "vivisections," "The Battle of the Brains" ("Hjärnornas kamp"), in January, 1887, he informed Heidenstam: "I have discovered a new genre and will present it in *Neue Freie* in several months, I hope."

Landquist has noted that Strindberg's primary source on suggestion, Hippolyte Bernheim's *De la Suggestion* (1884)—cited in the opening of "The Battle of the Brains"—had indicated that suggestion could be defined as the ordinary influence our fellow human beings have on us. Landquist emphasized that Strindberg "added the struggle for power to the suggestion theory and as a result made it fruitful for drama and the short story." As Torsten Eklund maintained,[7] however, the idea of suggestion as a struggle for power was also expressed in popular form by Max Nordau in a book much admired by Strindberg—*Paradoxes psychologiques* (1885). According to Nordau, suggestion is "the transfer of the molecular movements of one brain into another brain." In the process, the more complete person practices "suggestion on the less complete, but not reversely." Strindberg was using this theory in "The Battle of the Brains" when he claimed to have discovered through an experiment "that suggestion is only the stronger brain's struggle with and triumph over the weaker, and that this procedure is applied unconsciously in everyday life."[8]

Strindberg performed his experiment in the fall of 1886 on a traveling companion, Gustaf Steffen, an engineer. He suspected Steffen of wanting to use him and resolved therefore to exploit the "exploiter."[9] In "The Battle of the Brains;" written in early 1887, he describes how by means of suggestion he used his superior brain and stronger nerve power to "pulverize" his adversary's brain. For many years afterward as Eklund has shown,[10] the "battle of the brains" became the formula for Strindberg's attitude toward human relationships and was the inspiration for his belief in the ability of one brain to prey like a parasite on another, like a vampire sucking its victim empty.

A similar theme is handled in the novella "Short Cuts:"[11] in which Karl Billgren exposes two spiritualists, a hypnotist and a medium. At this time, Strindberg's preoccupation with suggestion made him skeptical about the validity of hypnotic sleep: "The hypnotist says sleep and the person sleeps, or at least behaves like someone asleep. The hypnotist puts a broom in his hand and the broom sways about. But this is no more remarkable than when a recruit presents arms at a corporal's order!"[12] Similar expressions of doubt about hypnotism are found in *The Father* and *Miss Julie,* all demonstrating that whenever people talked about hypnotism, they were actually referring to a transfer of psychic power through conscious suggestion from a stronger individual to a weaker one.

It was characteristic that during his first contact with these psychic phenomena Strindberg saw himself as a dispassionate scientist, who eschewed spiritism and superstition. This attitude is also evident in

Vivisections, although he arrives at conclusions that are almost occultist. In the essay "Nemesis Divina,"[13] Strindberg says that "with a different outlook on life" he might easily have imagined that he was living under the direct protection of a deity. As he reviewed the events of the preceding four years of his life, he noted that he had remained unscathed while people who persecuted, criticized, or ridiculed him had fallen into misfortune ("seven dead, one in a madhouse, six ruined"). Nevertheless, although he acknowledged that Linnaeus in his Nemesis theory believed in "a god's direct intervention in man's faith,"[14] Strindberg said he thought such coincidences could be explained in a natural way.

The length to which Strindberg was prepared to stretch the definition of the term "scientific" is evident in several other essays. In "Mysticism—For the Present" ("Mystik—tills vidare"), a doctor tells how he managed to save his seven-year-old daughter from a potentially fatal attack of cramps when, in his desperation, he momentarily forgot his atheism and at the urging of his wife began to say his childhood prayers. This too was a case of suggestion: "I have irrefutable scientific proof that my nerve currents regulated those of the child through contact and conduction."[15] To explain how these nerve currents could be made operative through prayer, the narrator declares that prayer is a manifestation of either actual or imagined faith, and that faith is "a concentration of wish and desire, intensified to the point of conscious will."[16] It was this conscious will that brought about the child's recovery. In this example of the force of suggestion, Strindberg's atheism had come close to a faith in the miracle-working power of prayer.

Of greatest significance regarding Strindberg's naturalistic drama, however, is the essay "Phychic Murder" ("Om själamord"), published in the spring of 1887. Using Ibsen's *Rosmersholm* as a point of departure, Strindberg describes a series of real and fictional psychic murders and concludes that the struggle for power, formerly purely physical, had "become more psychic, but not therefore less cruel."[17] He believes that "because of hypnotism and suggestion," even the most fantastic stories no longer seemed mysterious.[18] The world had been transformed into a torture chamber where strong minds used psychic means to destroy the weaker ones.

Hypnotic-psychiatric writings had an important effect on belles-lettres in the 1880's, both in Sweden and in Europe generally. In France, where the writings had their origin in naturalism's scientific orientation, they eventually created a reaction against naturalism. The same course of events occurred in Sweden, influencing writers like Strindberg and Ola Hansson (1860-1925). Strindberg apparently discovered the writings on suggestion independently, and not until later did he become acquainted— mostly through Hansson—with the writers who exploited these new ideas for literary purposes. On December 26, 1888, he borrowed some works by Edgar Allan Poe from Hansson and stated that he believed Poe "was a stimulus for Bourget, Maupassant (in *Pierre et Jean*), *Rosmersholm,* and *The Father,* not to mention all the mind readers and hypnotists!"[19] In a reference to the same writers and works in a letter to K. O. Bonnier several days earlier, Strindberg declared his intention to abandon "Zolaism." Up to this time, Strindberg believed he was following good naturalistic procedures by experimenting with the new psychological discoveries, although he was aware that his emphasis on psychology differed from Zola's physiological documentation approach.

In *Paradoxes psychologiques,* Nordau revealed his belief in the aristocracy of the intellect through his comments on suggestion. According to him, a crowd of people, a city, indeed an entire nation, could be completely remolded by a brilliant individual's power of suggestion, and the masses were capable only of "repeating what the genius accomplished earlier."[20] Strindberg was following the same line of thought in "The Battle of the Brains" when he asserted that "the politician's, the thinker's, the writer's brain compels the brains of others to function automatically."[21]

This division of people into geniuses and mindless followers led Strindberg to his theory of "the great" and "the lowly," which is exemplified in several of the "vivisections." Strindberg thought he anticipated Nietzsche in these essays, but perhaps it would be more accurate to say that he anticipated his own brand of Neitzscheanism.[22] Strindberg may have used Nietzsche's terminology, but his supermen—for all their superior brain power—fail. It was self-evident to Strindberg that because their intelligence was over-refined, they were doomed to go down before "the lowly," who were not only superior to "the great" in numbers, but also better equipped for the struggle for survival. Earlier, in "Cultivated Fruit," he had declared that the earls would die out and the thralls survive, and Heidenstam further convinced him that the aristocratic upper classes would eventually succumb to the barbarian plebians.

The Father

Shortly after he began the *Vivisections* series in February, 1887, Strindberg wrote *The Father*. It had been debated whether or not this drama should be called naturalistic. But although Strindberg did not preface the play with a programmatic statement alluding to Zola as he did with *Miss Julie,* a remark he made in a magazine article that same spring suggests that he had his French contemporary in mind. He wrote that the Swedish neo-classical poet-dramatist Carl Gustaf af Leopold (1756-1829) had followed French classical drama "which, scorning melodramatic effects, sought to concentrate interest on psychological development; it neglected stage machinery and properties in order to analyze states of mind—in other words, our own Zola's newest dramatic program—something Ibsen had already had in mind for a long time."[23]

The Father occupies an intermediate position between Ibsen and Zola. It is constructed like *Ghosts* (a work for which Strindberg never lost his admiration): in three acts with the unities of time and place observed. As in *Ghosts,* the fateful presence of the past broods over the play. Strindberg's choice of theme and his emphasis on the psychopathological elements in emotional life, push *The Father* a step closer to naturalism than Ibsen's play. In "Psychic Murder," the afore-mentioned *Vivisections* essay about *Rosmersholm* (written after the completion of *The Father,* but before its publication), Strindberg showed how Ibsen should have proceeded in order to explain Rebecca West's "psychic murder" of Mrs. Rosmer. Rebecca is called "an unwitting cannibal who devoured the soul of the late wife" by making her suspicious, precisely the way Iago murdered Othello without having to resort to rapier and dagger:

> We never learn in *Rosmersholm* how Rebecca committed her murder; this in itself might have constituted the entire action in the play, which presently develops in a different direction. She presumably used the old familiar method of persuading the weaker brain that it was sick and then "proving" to her or making her believe that death was a blessing.[24]

Strindberg assumes that Rebecca began by persuading Mrs. Rosmer to believe that she had an overly suspicious nature. "Naturally, she became more suspicious when her senses were sharpened in this way and it was impossible for her to obtain any proof. And so it is quite probable that the wife really became overly suspicious. It was then an easy matter for Rebecca to drive her crazy."[25]

Strindberg had reconstructed *Rosmersholm* in the image of his own drama, and what he describes are Laura's tactics with the captain. Equipped with greater strength of will and stronger nerves than her husband, she suggested to him so strongly that he was mentally ill that he finally became ill. "You were able to hypnotize me while I was awake, so that I neither saw nor heard anything, but just obeyed," says the Captain. "You could give me a raw potato and make me believe it was a peach."[26] And when Laura has completed her "psychic murder," her brother, the Pastor, says to her: "Let me see your hand! Not one spot of blood to give you away, not a trace of that treacherous poison! A little innocent murder that the law can't touch—an unconscious crime—unconscious? What a beautiful invention!"[27]

What makes this dramatic "vivisection" so absorbing is that Strindberg turned the dissecting knife on himself, describing the nightmare in which he found himself during the writing of the play. To Lundegård, he confessed: "I do not know whether *The Father* is a fiction or whether my life has been. But it seems to me as if soon, in a decisive moment, they will merge, and then I shall either collapse into remorseful madness or take my life."[28]

Siri's consultation with the Swiss doctor about Strindberg's state of mind opened terrifying prospects for him—the brink of madness. In 1882, the year before he left Sweden, he had written to his family doctor that he feared for his reason and asked him to prescribe a trip abroad.[29] He quaked at the thought that this letter might have fallen into his wife's hand. In *The Father* a letter becomes Laura's most dangerous weapon: to convince the doctor of her husband's derangement, she tells him that six years earlier the Captain had admitted in a letter to his doctor that he feared for his reason. Later, when the Captain asks Laura how she plans to have him declared incapacitated, she produces the letter and informs him that a copy is in the hands of the authorities. This diabolical move causes the Captain to lose his senses, and picking up a burning lamp from the table, he flings it at his wife.

The play's similarity to *A Madman's Defense* is so obvious that it almost seems to be a preparatory study for the autobiographical work. Almost all the situations in *The Father* can be found in the novel, and at times the dialogue is strikingly similar. Like *The Father, A Madman's Defense* is a mixture of fiction and autobiography, written under the conditions Strindberg described in a letter to Lundegård in November, 1887:

> It seems as if I'm walking in my sleep, as if fiction and life were jumbled. . . . Because I've written so much, my life has become a shadowy existence. I imagine myself no longer on earth, but floating weightlessly in an atmosphere, not of air, but of darkness. Whenever light falls on this darkness, I crumple, shattered.[30]

Purely literary influences could never have played the decisive role in the creation of so intensely felt a work as *The Father*,[31] but several of the references made by the author deserve attention. In an unpublished essay about the play, written in French,[32] Strindberg mentioned as a source of inspiration a magazine article, "Le Matriarcat," by the French sociologist Paul Lafargue in *La Nouvelle Revue* of March 15, 1886. Lafargue argued that matriarchy was humanity's original form of social organization and that only by means of violent battles between the sexes was patriarchy established. If an attempt should be made to restore matriarchy, similar violent sexual battles would be risked. The thesis made a deep impression on Strindberg because of its implications regarding the woman question, a theme he returned to in essays and letters in 1886-87. At the same time he was writing *The Father*, he said in an essay that another sexual war would bring the downfall of men. Women's struggle against men was the struggle of the lowly against the great. Women try to coax Hercules' club away from him, and if matriarchy triumphed, a new era of barbarism for humanity would be at hand "because women belong to the community of beasts."[33]

The idea that conflict in marriage was an integral part of a larger, historic struggle gave *The Father* its wild frenzy as well as its greatness. "Sexual love is conflict," says Laura, and the Captain confirms it. "This is like race-hatred." The Hercules symbol appears again: "Omphale! Omphale! You cunning woman, who championed peace and invented disarmament. Wake up, Hercules, before they take your club away. . . . Brute strength has fallen before insidious weakness."[34]

The article "Le Matriarcat" was also important because it directed Strindberg's attention to Greek tragedy, which, according to Lafargue, mirrored the terrible battles that preceded the establishment of patriarchy. Strindberg pointed out in his essay "The Final Word on the Woman

Question" (1887), that whereas Clytemnestra has no qualms about killing Agamemnon, "Orestes dreads killing his mother," in other words, Aeschylus regarded the murder of a mother as a crime of greater magnitude than the killing of a father. Strindberg believed he had created a kind of counterpart to the *Oresteia* in his drama. The instant the Captain uses violence against his wife he is lost, although in reality, Laura is the killer —she cunningly provokes him to an irrational act and then has him bound in a strait jacket. Lundegård, who was with Strindberg constantly during the world premiere of *The Father* in Copenhagen in November, 1887, characterized the play as "a story of the fate of a contemporary person presented with a suggestion of the implacable gravity of ancient tragedy."[35] The comparison was undoubtedly inspired by Strindberg himself.[36]

Due to the influence of classical drama, *The Father* has elements absent in Strindberg's earlier drama: a compact and simple structure, a small cast of characters, an action limited almost entirely to the moment of catastrophe, intensified pathos, and the universal sense of the tragic. The Captain and his wife are doomed to engage in a battle taking place between forces they cannot control; forces that for centuries have incited man and woman against each other.

Shakespeare, too, was in Strindberg's mind at this time, as is evident in his reference to *Othello* in the *Rosmersholm* essay as well as in the Captain's paraphrase of Shylock's great soliloquy ("If you prick us. . ."). The Captain has some of the greatness of such Shakespearean heroes as Othello, Macbeth, and Lear: the somber temperament and the violent passions which, once set in motion, inevitably destroy the men possessing them. These heroes move us in the same way the Captain does—through their greatness and their clumsy helplessness. They too are in conflict with a world of shortsighted pygmies and they are physically broken before death finally catches up with them. At the very moment of death, there is a faded splendor about them and they display a heroism and a magnanimity, albeit blunted, that they had not earlier demonstrated.

Shakespeare's influence in *The Father* is especially evident in the last act. Seldom before the Inferno Crisis did Strindberg show so forcefully his ability to compress within the frame of a few short scenes the most varied moods—blending the tragic and the grotesque, the brutal and the tender. The Captain has lost all inner balance and is only a ruin of his former self. His humor is macabre and cutting; and he almost literally frightens his daughter to death. He takes a revolver from his weapon collection, but when he discovers the cartridges removed, he collapses in a torpor. His old nurse uses the opportunity to trick him into the strait jacket, distracting him by prattling about his childhood. When he discovers that he is bound, he can only utter desperately: "Captured, shorn, caught off guard, and unable to die!"[37] As Laura spreads a shawl over him, he thinks about the bittersweet memories of the early days of their marriage:

> I feel your soft shawl against my mouth. It's warm and gentle like your arm, and it smells of vanilla, like your hair when you were young! Laura, when you were young, and we walked in the birch woods—the primroses and thrushes, lovely, lovely! Think how beautiful life was then—and what it's become![38]

But the nostalgic mood lasts only a short time. The Captain fancies that the shawl is a cat and it annoys him: he wants to be covered with his military tunic instead. New curses against woman rush from his lips. He raises himself to spit at his wife, but falls back again on the sofa, mumbling a childhood prayer. He rises one more time, then falls with a scream. The apoplectic fit has come.

When *The Father* was to be performed in Copenhagen, Strindberg gave suggestions to Lundegård about the qualifications of the actor who would play the leading role. Preferably, he was to be:

> an actor with an ordinarily cheerful temperament. [The Captain], possessing the superior, self-ironic, lightly skeptical tone of a man of the world, conscious of his superiority, goes to meet his fate with rather jaunty courage, becoming mortally enveloped in the spider's webs that natural law prevents him from tearing apart. [The role should be played] subtly, calmly, resignedly, like an otherwise healthy modern man accepting his fate as though it were an erotic passion. . . . In particular, he represents to me a manliness which people have tried to degrade, trick out of us, and transfer to the third sex! It is only in front of woman that he is unmanly, because she wants him that way, and the law of adaptation obliges us to play the role our mistress demands.[39]

The statement is characteristic of the way Strindberg identified the hero with the manly ideal toward which he himself aspired. The letter was sent from the Bavarian town of Lindau, where he felt very much at home; he was delighted to be in a virile, patriarchal society. His friends included officers who, like the Captain, knew Latin and Greek, and his militaristic zeal drove him to the point of asking his publisher to give him

money for a horse ("my Kingdom for a horse") so that he might participate as a correspondent in the war he anticipated between France and
Germany. For all his zeal, however, he was only able to give his character
the trappings of a military hero; behind the Captain's blustering and cocksureness lurks fear. He admits that he was born without will, that his big,
powerful body is deficient in nerves, that he is unmanly, and that despite
his superior talent he listened to his wife like a "foolish child." The
suggestion Strindberg made later—that in the figure of the Captain he had
portrayed the superman—must be taken with reservation. As in many other
cases, he was more candid and honest when writing the text than when
interpreting it. The Captain belongs to the category of humanity that
Strindberg referred to as "the great"—defenseless, gigantic children,
whose lot it is to be broken by the cunning machinations of "the lowly."

What actually destroys the Captain is not jealousy but suspiciousness. When Laura consults the doctor, she learns that her husband could
go mad if his suspicions were aroused. She exploits this information with
subtle skill in a conversation with the Captain by remarking nonchalantly:
"You can't be sure you're Bertha's father!" At first, he takes this as a
joke, but Laura continues the attack: "Suppose I were ready to endure
anything—being driven out, despised, anything—in order to keep and
control my child. And suppose I was sincere just now when I said: Bertha
is my child, but not yours! Suppose. . . ."[40]

With this, the Captain's suspicions are provoked, and Laura has
made sure that he will never again be certain if she had actually been
unfaithful to him or only lied in order to obtain control over her daughter.
Even when she offers to take an oath that he is truly Bertha's father, the
Captain cannot be convinced: "What's the use, when you said before that
a mother can and should commit any crime for her child?"[41] He makes
every effort to extract a confession of guilt from her. Finally, he is compelled to admit to her that he would prefer to be told she was guilty,
because it would give him a certainty he could not otherwise obtain. After
the Captain is imprisoned in the strait jacket and Laura declares openly
that his suspicions about his daughter's parentage were unfounded, his
agony is intensified:

> That's what's so horrible! If they were real, there would at least be some-
> thing to hold onto, to cling to. Now there are only shadows, lurking in
> the undergrowth, poking their heads out to laugh. Now it's like fighting

with air, like battling in maneuvers with blank cartridges. Reality, no matter how terrible, would have aroused opposition, braced body and soul for action, but now . . . thoughts dissolve into mist, and my brain grinds emptiness.[42]

The situation may appear improbable, but Strindberg lived through a similar one during the time he wrote *The Father*. Using every means at his disposal, he tried to compel his wife to confess her infidelity. He beseiged his friends to learn the name of her lover. When he was met by denials, his agony over feeling morbidly suspicious increased, and he accused Siri of attempting to drive him insane by giving the appearance of having been unfaithful to him.

The Captain battles desperately to escape the strait jacket, but all the time he feels the net tightening around him, strand by strand. Are these suspicions that are entangling him the work of spiteful enemies or the promptings of his own mind? The second possibility is the one he fears most of all. We are reminded of what The Stranger says in *To Damascus, Part I*, when he discovers that the phantoms haunting him in the kitchen are only scouring rags flapping in the moonlight: "Everything is so simple and natural, but that's exactly what disturbs me." It is more reassuring to believe that one is battling against treacherous powers than against one's own delusions.

The Father is in certain respects a psychological case history, and it is also the first play in which Strindberg demonstrated his mastery of the style that would become characteristic of all his naturalistic dramas, including those that were written after the Inferno Crisis. His works are the culmination of the nineteenth-century trend toward transforming dramatic dialogue into a judicial procedure in which interlocutors cross-examine and refute each other with the skill of trained lawyers. Strindberg's dialogue, however, is not as contrived as Dumas *fils'*, nor as calculated as Ibsen's; the tempo is quicker, and transitions, which earlier playwrights would have regarded as indispensable, are omitted. Phases of action and points of view that Strindberg's predecessors would have developed over several acts are confined by him to one point: the moment when the characters feel their fate is being decided, and they brace themselves for the worst. Strindberg would eventually omit act divisions and finally reduce a play to a single scene—the crisis.

Strindberg's dialogue is more illogical and ungrammatical than that of Ibsen or his French predecessors: there are no sententious phrases or clever repartee, no enlightening asides. At the conclusion of the play, the spectator is as much in the dark as the characters are; he is no more certain than the Captain that Laura committed an infidelity, and he is no more certain than Laura that the Captain seriously believes her guilty. The play is less clear than its predecessors, perhaps also less plausible; nevertheless, it renders a more harrowing impression of reality.

Zola wrote a now-famous letter to be included in the French translation of *The Father*, and the play was accepted for production under his aegis at the Théâtre Libre (although it was not actually produced in France until 1894). Strindberg wrote his next two plays—*Miss Julie* and *Creditors*—for the same theatre and adhered more closely to the naturalistic approach.

Miss Julie

Strindberg offered *Miss Julie* to the publisher K. O. Bonnier in a letter on August 10, 1888, describing the play as "the first Naturalistic Tragedy in Swedish Drama."[43] He continued: " '*Ceci datera!*'—this play will be recorded in the annals." It was an accurate prophecy. *Miss Julie* is a masterpiece of naturalistic drama. Whereas other attempts made in the 1870's and 1880's to bring naturalism into the theatre are today often of interest only to literary historians, *Miss Julie* is still performed regularly. It is bolder and more original in design than its contemporaries, and it is executed with greater artistic integrity.

The preface to *Miss Julie* shows that Strindberg observed the demands for technical reforms advocated by Zola and the Théâtre Libre. He wanted to remove the footlights, replace kitchen utensils painted on the scenery with real ones, allow actors to speak their lines in profile or with their backs to the audience, introduce dumb show, and so forth. All this was in conformity with naturalism's striving to transform the stage into a room whose fourth wall has been replaced by the proscenium opening.

Strindberg also took pains to emphasize that he had depicted a "case," that he had chosen, as he states in the preface, a "theme from a true story I heard a number of years ago, which made a strong impression on me."[44] (A letter written to Heidenstam in October, 1888, indicates that

the model was a certain titled young lady who seduced a stableman.[45])
Strindberg's sensational story, partly drawn from life, supposedly proved
(again in accordance with Zola) a natural law: the stronger survive in the
struggle for existence.

Miss Julie is the last representative of a noble house whose blood
line has run thin. She is doomed to be destroyed; whereas the valet Jean is
a "species originator" with a fresh appetite for life and without any cumbersome feelings about honor. Strindberg, using the terminology of "Cultivated Fruit," says in the preface that "the thrall has this advantage over
the nobleman: he lacks a fatal preoccupation with honor. And in all of us
Aryans there is something of the nobleman or of Don Quixote."[46] The
word "Aryans" suggests that Strindberg had discovered Nietzsche,[47] but
these ideas had been in his mind earlier, and they were intensified by his
association with Heidenstam. Heidenstam represented himself as belonging to "the vanishing inheritance nobility"—too refined, too unbarbaric to
be able to stay on its feet in the struggle for existence; whereas he regarded
Strindberg as a representative of "the new intellectual nobility, which will
have its own House of Lords."[48] Strindberg obviously recalled this remark
when he wrote in the preface that Miss Julie is "a relic of the old warrior
nobility now giving way to the new intellectual nobility or aristocracy of
great minds." Strindberg tries to persuade himself that he will welcome
this inevitable development:

> When we grow as strong as the earliest French revolutionaries, we shall
> feel unconditionally happy and relieved to see the national parks cleared
> of rotting, overage trees which have stood too long in the way of others
> equally entitled to a period of growth—as relieved as when we see an
> incurable invalid die![49]

The spectator is not similarly relieved, because Strindberg, in
spite of his approval of her fate, portrayed Miss Julie's downfall as tragedy.
She is an aristocrat with high-strung emotions who has lost her way
among the lower classes who do not understand her; they trample her
ideals, are amused by her humiliation, and hound her to death. It is possible that when Strindberg first approached the subject he identified more
with the socially ambitious "species originator," Jean, but during the
writing he was drawn to Miss Julie, with whose hypersensitive nervousness
he felt an affinity. Strindberg felt that the superman was a vanishing race
and that the earth would be dominated by "the lowly." Another example

of his interpretation of the superman cult is in the novel *In the Outer Skerries*. Like Miss Julie, the well-educated fishing commissioner Borg is defeated in his struggle with representatives of the lower classes—the crude fishermen and their families.

Strindberg was not content to discuss the "problem of social climbing and falling" in the preface and then have it confirmed in the play's outcome. In his eagerness to underscore the importance of the problem he has the two protagonists, Miss Julie and Jean, make specific reference to it in the dialogue. They talk extensively to each other about their origins, obsessions, and inherited tendencies. Miss Julie had had a recurrent dream in which she climbs to the top of a column and longs to fall down; Jean often dreams that he is lying under a tall tree and longs to climb to the top. In a long, impassioned speech Miss Julie forecasts the extinction of her line and the ritual smashing of her family's coat of arms against her coffin; Jean tells of his ambitious plans to rise above his lower-class status.

Strindberg undoubtedly realized how improbable it was for such reflections to be made in the same fateful hour when Miss Julie becomes a victim of Jean's opportunism and is driven to suicide. In a passage omitted from the preface he justifies the reflections by maintaining that it was permissible in modern drama for characters to discuss Darwinism,[50] and he points out that the gravedigger in *Hamlet* spoke "Giordano Bruno's philosophy."

Apart from Miss Julie's and Jean's discussion of the problem of degeneration and their tendency to analyze each other's feelings, the play is a strict application of Zolaesque principles. Zola had acknowledged the legitimacy of the classical unities because they were in keeping with his demand for an illusion of reality, but in his own plays he was only able to observe the unity of place, since he was fettered by the cumbersome plots he was dramatizing. Strindberg criticized him in the essay "On Modern Drama and Modern Theatre" ("Om modern drama och modern teater") especially his overemphasis on the importance of realistic décor and his failure to recognize the necessity for unity of time. In *Thérèse Raquin*, for example, Zola made "the mistake of having a year elapse between the first and second acts." For Strindberg, classical French drama was the model to follow: "With Molière, French drama had entered a phase in which all scenic effect was abandoned, and the nuances of emotional life became the most important element. Observe how the delicious vivisection of Tartuffe takes place in one room furnished with two taborets."[51] In *Miss Julie*, the action occurs in one setting so that the characters can "develop in their milieu." And although it is evident in the early drafts that Strindberg originally planned an act division, "as an experiment," he dispensed with having the curtain fall during the play and made the action continuous.

The one-act form necessitates drastic simplification in terms of number of characters and plot. *Miss Julie* contains three speaking roles and only a few rudiments of an Ibsen-like intrigue. For example, the opening scene is a symbolic foreshadowing of the future action: Kristin, the cook, is preparing food for Miss Julie's bitch Diana who has displeased her mistress by sneaking out with the gatekeeper's pug-dog. When Kristin later learns of Miss Julie's indiscretion, she recalls that Miss Julie's pride was such that she wanted Diana shot. Ibsen's method of illuminating future action through parallel scenes is used in the later episode with the greenfinch: Miss Julie insists on taking her pet bird with her on her flight abroad to prevent its falling into the hands of strangers. When Jean kills it, she becomes hysterical: "Kill me too! Kill me! You, who can butcher an innocent creature without blinking an eye!"[52]

In his next play Strindberg would simplify even further. He felt that *Miss Julie* was a "compromise with romanticism and stage decoration" but that *Creditors* was "thoroughly modern" and a better play: "three characters, a table and two chairs—and no sunrise!" Obviously, it now displeased him that in the final scene in *Miss Julie* he had—as Ibsen hand done in *Ghosts*—allowed the sunrise to establish a jarring contrast to the mood of desperation within the room.

Strindberg's rules for dramatic characterization set forth in the preface are actually only an application of Théodule Ribot's concept of the ego as a complex of multiple, often mutually hostile, impulses. In his autobiography, Strindberg had already criticized the tendency on the parts of novelists and dramatists to conceive of character as "a very simple, mechanical contrivance. . . . A 'character' and an automaton seem almost identical. Dickens's famous characters are organ-grinders' puppets, and 'characters' in the theatre are required to be automatons."[53] The same criticism appears in the preface to *Miss Julie,* where Strindberg is opposed to "simple stage characters" whose psychological identity can be expressed in a single word and whose uniqueness is evidenced through a physical defect, a habitual gesture, or a constantly repeated expression. Instead, he claims to have made his fingers "characterless" in order to show "how rich soul-complex is." Therefore, he has depicted them:

> vacillating, disintegrated, a mixture of old and new . . . My souls (characters) are conglomerations of past and present phases of civilization, bits from books and newspapers, fragments of humanity, torn pieces of once-fine clothing that has become rags, patched together as the human soul itself.[54]

Strindberg's intention was to go beyond simple explanations for actions and to present the multiplicity of conscious and unconscious motivations upon which actions are based. In his preface he lists the circumstances that led inevitably to Miss Julie's seduction: "the mother's basic instincts, the father's wrong methods in rearing the girl, her own nature, and her fiancé's influence on a weak, degenerate mind; also, and more immediate—the festive mood of Midsummer Eve."[55] When Georg Brandes found the heroine's suicide psychologically unbelievable, Strindberg enumerated a large number of motivations contributing to her decision in his letter of reply: "Notice that Miss [Julie] left to herself would have lacked the power, but now she is driven and tormented by the multiple motives."

Even as Strindberg worked to simplify the play's structure, he tried to complicate its internal mechanism, although to a certain degree these attempts remained drawing-board fantasies. The preface was written after the play, and Edvard Brandes was probably correct in his suspicion that *Miss Julie* was not the result of the application of conscious theory. Strindberg best realized his intentions in the portrayal of the heroine. Miss Julie wavers under the influence of many different impressions and is torn between the most contradictory feelings: tenderness and contempt, ecstasy and irony, vanity and the wish to degrade herself, erotic desire and chaste modesty. She is capricious, unrestrained, tactless, sometimes cruel and heartless. We are, nevertheless, touched by sympathy for her. She matures as a person under her misfortune, whereas Jean becomes more despicable in his mood of triumph. Her inherited pride, which earlier found expression in a rigid and insecure haughtiness, takes on a tragic dimension when she goes to her doom with the razor in her hand.

The personalities of the other two characters in the play are more simplified and do not present the psychological enigma Miss Julie does. Jean is an exuberant figure drawn with grotesque humor: innately vulgar and yet possessing fastidious habits and manners. "Polished, but coarse underneath," is the way Strindberg describes him in the preface. Particularly in the beginning of the play, when Jean poses as a fussy connoisseur of food, wine and feminine beauty, his cockiness is irresistible. Unfortunately, Jean displays a sophistication that is not consistent with his character at the beginning of the play. Without intentionally caricaturing him, Strindberg provides Jean with witty repartee that one does not expect to hear from a valet with lower-class origins.[56]

Kristin—with her sullenness, her uncharitable religiosity, and her inveterate respect for class distinctions—is a typical representative of one aspect of the Swedish national temperament. Her class consciousness is so great that she is unable to be jealous of Miss Julie. "No, not of her," she says to Jean. "If it had been Clara or Sofi, I would have scratched your eyes out! Yes, that's the way it is. Why—I don't know. - - - Oh, it's disgusting!"[57]

As in his subsequent naturalistic dramas, Strindberg begins *Miss Julie* at a brisk pace by avoiding obvious exposition. The opening line by Jean—"Miss Julie is crazy again tonight, completely crazy!"—thrusts the spectator immediately into a situation that is quickly made clear through the servants quarreling. The description of the mistress of the house is corroborated by her first entrance: She is at once aristocratically condescending, coquettish, and provocative; and we are reminded of Jean's story about her mother who wore blouses with dirty cuffs, but insisted that all her buttons have the Count's coronets on them. Not until after the seduction are we motivated to shift our sympathy from Jean to Miss Julie. Strindberg depicts effectively the shifts in Julie's emotions from numbed shock to the terrifying discovery that this man to whom she has given herself is more despicable than she could have dreamed possible.

The final scene is perhaps the best in the play, containing that blend of naturalism and fantasy that is so typical of the later Strindberg.

The final effect, however, was produced only after repeated revisions. An early draft shows that Strindberg originally thought of having Miss Julie grab the razor away from Jean after all possibilities of escape were blocked and the Count's bell had sounded to summon his valet. She slashes her wrists in full view of the audience, crying triumphantly: "You see, lackey, you weren't capable of dying." Fortunately, Strindberg's interest in the phenomenon of suggestion provided the impulses for a different resolution. In the published version Miss Julie wants to commit suicide, but cannot do it of her own free will. She must be compelled to it by an external command. She asks Jean if he has ever seen a hypnotist in a theatre: "He says to his subject: 'Take the broom,' and it's taken. He says: 'Sweep,' and the person sweeps." When Jean protests that the subject has to be asleep, Miss Julie answers ecstatically: "I'm asleep already . . . the whole room is like a cloud of smoke . . . and you look like a stove . . . shaped like a man in black with a tall hat . . . and your eyes glow like coals when the flames die down . . . and your face is a white patch like ashes."[58] The sunshine streams into the desolate room, and Miss Julie rubs her hands as if warming them before a fire: "It's so nice and warm . . . and so bright . . . and so peaceful!" Jean puts the razor in her hand and whispers in her ear that she must take it with her to the barn. But once again her courage deserts her, and Jean feels himself growing powerless as he thinks of the Count's bell and the police. Not until the bell rings sharply twice again can he straighten himself up: "It's horrible. But there's no other way out . . . Go!"[59] Miss Julie now has the determination necessary to go to her death.[60]

In the preface Strindberg maintains that he had not made his people into catechists who sit and ask stupid questions in order to elicit clever replies:

> I have avoided the symmetrical, mathematical and contrived construction of the dialogue in French drama, and have let people's minds operate as irregularly as they do in real life where, in conversation, no subject is completely exhausted, and one mind finds a cog in another mind with which to engage. Consequently, the dialogue, too, wanders, gathering in the opening scenes material which is later picked up, reworked and repeated, developed and embellished, like the theme in a musical composition.[61]

Strindberg is not, however, as free from contrivance as he believed; the rambling purposelessness of *Miss Julie* is more apparent than real. The play contains some old-fashioned theatrical repartee, and Strindberg did not attempt to write dialogue that sounded like the ordinary everyday speech that Zola recommended and later naturalistic dramatists like Granville Barker and Chekhov pushed to extremes. But in comparison with Strindberg's earlier dialogue, the language in *Miss Julie* is denser and richer in texture, probing beneath surface reality into the unconscious: the characters become intoxicated by their own words, and while they speak about one thing, their minds are elsewhere.

The scenes after the seduction offer clear examples of how Strindberg attempted to put into practice his principles of naturalistic dialogue. Jean, who alternates between a feeling of triumph and a fear of the consequences of his action, talks rhapsodically of the future, of traveling with Julie to Switzerland and founding a hotel with the daughter of a count as cashier. Julie, her feelings torn between shame and erotic longing for the man who conquered her, is only half listening and she responds anxiously: "That's all very well! But Jean. . . . Say that you love me!" When talking has finally restored Jean's composure, he says to her: "Sit down there! I'll sit here and we'll talk as if nothing has happened." She bursts out desperately: "Oh, my God! Have you no feelings?" To which Jean replies: "Me! No one has more feelings than I do, but I know how to control myself."[62] Strindberg constantly reminds us of the disparity between what people say they want and what they really want. Jean talks about his ambitious plans for the future while his thoughts are constantly occupied with how to get rid of Julie and retain his position on the estate. Julie pleads for assurances of affection in order to preserve at least the illusion that she committed her indiscretion for love. Deep down she feels a burning shame at having given herself on a whim to a man for whom she has no feelings. Not surprisingly, their mutual pledges of love and devotion turn into exchanges of bitter invective in a matter of minutes.

When Kristin prevents them from fleeing at the decisive instant, Julie hits upon the kind of bizarre idea common in moments of desperation: all three of them will go to Switzerland. She now tries to sell to Kristin the same travel plans, the same proposal for starting a hotel on the shores of Lake Como with which Jean had regaled her earlier. Her speech becomes more and more agitated as her courage sinks. Then, when Kristin asks her if she really believes what she is saying, she collapses: "I don't know. I don't believe anything any more."[63]

Contained in these passages are all the innovations in revelation of character that Strindberg wanted to express through dialogue: the irregular operation of the mind, the contrast between thought and speech, the reiteration of the same theme with new psychological implications. Perhaps the author's intentions are too obvious, but they are brilliantly executed.

During the writing of *Miss Julie,* Strindberg was eager to create a prototype for naturalistic drama, a counterpart to what the Goncourt brothers produced for the novel. In the preface he declares that he chose their "documentary novels" for models since they "appealed to me more than any other contemporary literature." "Modern people" are not satisfied to see something happen; they want to know how it happens. "We want to see the wires, watch the machinery, examine the box with the false bottom, pick up the magic ring to find the join, look at the cards to see how they are marked."[64] It is the presence of this "machinery" that makes *Miss Julie* less spontaneously moving than *The Father.* In the dramas immediately following this artificiality shows up even more strongly.

Creditors

Strindberg claimed to have carried "the new form" even further in *Creditors,* which was written right after *Miss Julie.* The central themes in the play are the power of suggestion and the battle of the brains. There are three speaking parts, and the setting for all three scenes in the play is a seaside resort drawing room occupied by Adolph, an artist, and his wife Tekla. The third character is Tekla's first husband, whom Adolph has never met, and who has come seeking revenge, a creditor trying to collect old debts.

Creditors was intended for Antoine's Théâtre Libre and Strindberg at first did not want to publish it in Swedish, "because my enemies always write commentaries on my dramas designed to hurt me." Finally, he submitted a manuscript to Joseph Seligmann, who had published *Miss Julie,* but Seligmann had misgivings about accepting it, presumably because the characters resembled too closely Strindberg, Siri, and her first husband. Strindberg tried to disabuse the publisher by persuading him

that the model for the female character was the feminist writer Victoria
Benedictsson and not Siri.[65] Fortunately, *A Madman's Defense* had not
yet been published, otherwise Seligmann might have noticed greater resemblances, as dialogue and situations in the play were borrowed directly
from the novel. Even the title of the play is from the novel, where the
narrator accuses Maria of wanting to get rid of "the troublesome creditor"
after she has drained him and lived on his ideas.[66] Adolph is the first to use
the word in the play, and it has the same implication as in the novel. After
having seen his wife try to appear brilliant by using his ideas, he says:
"And so I became the disagreeable creditor, whom one only wants to get
rid of. You wanted to cancel your debt to me."[67] Tekla is exposed, however, by the other "creditor," her first husband, who boasts triumphantly
in the final scene: "Now I've canceled your debt to me." Wherever the
expression occurs in Strindberg's works it has a bloodthirsty ring.

Tekla's first husband is named Gustav, as is the baron in *A
Madman's Defense* and, of course, Siri's first husband. These are not
coincidences. Strindberg did indeed fear that his predecessor would seek
revenge, not only during his marriage, but as late as the 1900's. Gustav
of *Creditors,* with his superman's mental powers, foreshadows the domina-
ting intellectuals in later works—in the play *Pariah (Paria),* the story
"Tschandala," and the novel *In the Outer Skerries.*

By the time Gustav appears (incognito), Adolph is already half-
murdered by Tekla who, like Bertha in *Comrades,* is a female cannibal
who has devoured her husband's soul to nourish her own. "But this is pure
cannibalism," exclaims Gustav upon hearing about Adolph's martyrdom.
"Do you know what cannibalism is? Well, savages eat their enemies in
order to acquire their outstanding characteristics! - - - She has eaten
your soul, this woman; your courage, your judgment."[68] Gustav delivers
the *coup de grâce* when he uses the power of suggestion to induce a fatal
epileptic fit in Adolph.

It is characteristic in this play, as it is in a number of Strindberg's
later works, that all the characters burn with the same savage desire to
torment one another. During their marriage, Adolph and Tekla have tried
to blot out the memory of her first husband. At the same time, Tekla, like
a vampire, has drained poor Adolph's lifeblood. When Gustav appears, he
becomes the evil messenger of death, relentlessly avenging himself on
them both. First, he tries to persuade Adolph to take courage and revolt

against Tekla, then he takes cruel pleasure in destroying him. Adolph complains:

> You pull me out of the icy water only to hit me on the head and push me under again! As long as I kept my secrets to myself, I still had something within me, but now I'm empty. There's a painting by some Italian master, showing a torture scene. The intestines of a saint are being wound out on a winch. The martyr lies watching himself become thinner and thinner, as the roll on the winch becomes thicker and thicker.[69]

The three characters are full of a hate so intense that it threatens to explode at the slightest disturbance. "What terrible power you must have!" Adolph says to Gustav. "It's like coming in contact with an electric generator."[70] They torture each other with words, thoughts, suggestions. The entire atmosphere around them is charged with suspicion; even inanimate objects reveal terrible secrets. When Adolph takes out a photograph of Tekla, Gustav examines it and remarks that her cynical eyes are searching for someone other than her husband. Adolph notices this, too, and bitterly rips the picture to pieces. Later, when Tekla sits on the sofa and discovers that the seat is still warm and that there is a hollow as if made by an elbow, she knows immediately that someone has been there trying to separate her and Adolph. Signs of affection are construed as evidence of a guilty conscience. Tekla gives Adolph a kiss when she returns from her trip, and his reaction is: "What have you been up to?"[71] At the same time, the characters never cease talking about their gentle natures. "Have I ever raised a hand against you in all these years?" Gustav asks Tekla: "No!" he continues, "but the minute I get here and look at you, you go to pieces!"[72]

Despite their savage conflicts, Strindberg evidently felt this trio to be congenial company. In a letter to Seligmann he calls *Creditors* "human, agreeable, with all three characters sympathetic."

Creditors was the work which established Strindberg's name abroad, and the play has remained in the repertoires of European theatres for an astonishingly long time. Strindberg confessed his fondness for it on a number of occasions, and it is often called his best naturalistic drama, but it is difficult to share this view. The explosive power of *Creditors* is in its expert handling of dialogue and its tight composition. The play begins in the middle of one of Adolph's lines, without any introductory exposition, and then rises in an unbroken crescendo. But although *Creditors* also has many of the criteria Strindberg demanded of a naturalistic drama, as the play unfolds the action and motivation become completely absurd.

A ghost story by Alexandre Erckmann-Chatrian gave Strindberg the idea of having Gustav turn Adolph into an epileptic through the power of suggestion. Gustav acts like an epileptic and when Adolph is compelled to imitate him, he is fatally afflicted.[73] In the story, an old woman in a provincial French town induces a number of people to hang themselves from the same spot—the sign in front of an inn—by disguising herself as her intended victim the night before, drawing the victim's attention to herself as she stands in a window opposite the inn, then persuading him to copy her movements.

There are indications in *Creditors* that the new psychological discoveries were pulling Strindberg away from naturalism: the play has an atmosphere of horror that foreshadows the Inferno dramas.

The Scandinavian Experimental Theatre

Strindberg's following short one-act plays, *Pariah, The Stronger (Den starkare)*, and *Simoom (Samum)* were written for The Scandinavian Experimental Theatre, which he established during the period when he lived in Denmark (1887-89). Founded in Copenhagen after the moderately successful production of *The Father*, the theatre gave only one public performance in the city, on March 9, 1889, and one in Malmö a short distance away in southern Sweden.[74] Its *directrice* was to be Siri von Essen, but the Strindbergs separated even before the premiere; he suspected her of having an affair with Viggo Schiwe, a member of the company who had played Jean to her Miss Julie.

The theatre's small and untrained group of performers naturally required an undemanding repertoire, and the three plays were written with this in mind. *The Stronger* has only one speaking role; *Pariah*, two; and *Simoom*, three; and all of the plays are short. Strindberg made a virtue of necessity: in his essay "On Modern Drama and Modern Theatre," he declares that the short, single-scene, one-act play is "the model theatre play for modern people." The idea for the repertoire came from the Théâtre Libre, founded two years earlier; Antoine (who also used amateur actors) produced short, one-act pieces called *quarts-d'heure*, often based on a violent and sensational theme. The form was not entirely inappropriate for Strindberg's fiery temperament. He had an extraordinary ability to evoke dramatic tension with a few snatches of dialogue. In November, 1888, he gave an account of his new art form in another characteristic way —a culinary metaphor: "In France I always ate five lamb chops, to the great astonishment of the natives. You see, each chop consisted of a half-pound of bone and two inches of lard, which I left on the plate. Within was a back muscle—*la noix*. This I ate. 'Give me the nut!'—is what I want to say to the dramatist."[75]

. *Pariah* was freely adapted from an Ola Hansson story[76] dealing with unconscious impulses, irresponsibility, and compulsion in human behavior. It concerns a man who had to flee to America when he became a forger against his will. When he was young, as a whim he had copied a signature on a check without intending to use it for his own ends. Then, as if in his sleep, he had gone to a bank and cashed it. He was unable to explain his action: "I wonder if it wasn't related to the strange temptation that comes over certain people to touch an object for no reason or purpose at all, just for the sake of touching it."[77] The forger's confession is reported by the narrator, who meets him at Ringsjön, a lake in southern Sweden. The narrator concludes his presentation with the following words: "It is possible that he was lying [about what motivated him], but it is not entirely impossible that he was telling the truth."[78] Hansson obviously preferred the latter alternative.

Strindberg, however, who always showed a greater inclination to convict than acquit, held a contrary opinion right from the start, and as he dramatized the story, his antipathy toward Mr. Y, the poor forger, grew. Mr. Y's inquisitor, the keen-sighted Mr. X, exposes him as a born criminal who not only forged the check for sordid gain, but also committed a petty theft for which he has yet to be punished. Mr. X shows that Mr. Y got the idea for his story about unconsciously forging the check from Mr. X's copy of Bernheim's book on suggestion, which Mr. Y had read surreptitiously. The play ends with Mr. Y being driven out the door as an exposed felon.

Ola Hansson had difficulty recognizing his story in this form: "My 'Pariah' concerns an individual who commits a single crime and then suffers the consequences. In Strindberg's version, on the other hand, there is a duel between two men, both almost equally 'driven,' over who can bring the other down."[79]

Strindberg admired the story because of its theme—the influence of the unconscious—and it is easy to see what induced him to alter the plot; he saw it as a "battle of brains." For Ola Hansson, the title "A Pariah" did not contain any Nietzschean import; his forger is only a pariah in the sense of being cast out, "marked." For Strindberg, the word had a different meaning. In the play, Mr. X, apparently to entice Mr. Y into confessing, risks exposure and arrest by admitting to an act of manslaughter committed in his youth and never discovered. But the admission has more than one role to play in the drama. Strindberg, who originally thought of calling his version *Aryan and Pariah (Arier och paria)*,[80] wanted to show the contrast between someone like Mr. X, who committed a crime only because of circumstances, and someone like Mr. Y, who was a born criminal—the contrast between a superman and a petty thief.

At the same time, the play was a veiled polemic against Nietzsche, with whom Strindberg was in correspondence. He took exception to Nietzsche's *Götzen-Dämmerung,* in which the criminal is portrayed as a strong person, a barbarian who was alienated from society and whose instincts, therefore, were wrongly directed. In *Pariah,* the unfortunate forger pleads that it was his "uncivilized self, the barbarian who doesn't acknowledge conventions," who committed the crime. But Mr. X ruthlessly demonstrates that Mr. Y is a born criminal and, furthermore, stupid. Strindberg, influenced by the physical descriptions of "instinctive" or "born criminal types" in the French translation of the *L'uomo delinquente* (1876) by the noted Italian criminologist and psychologist Cesare Lombroso, has Mr. X say to Mr. Y: "You are so terribly narrow between the ears that I sometimes wonder what race you belong to."[81] In a letter to Nietzsche, Strindberg referred to Lombroso's indices and protested that Nietzsche had flattered stupid and degenerate lawbreakers.

Strindberg's *Pariah* lacks completely the merits that distinguish Ola Hansson's story. The gentle summer atmosphere of southern Sweden has been replaced with an air of terror and suspicion. The subtly constructed psychology has been coarsened. Instead of a blue-eyed, ingenuous forger, who acted under compelling impulses and committed a crime without any true motive, Strindberg created a habitual thief who trembles in fear of the police and, for an instant, tries blackmail. Mr. Y presents his confession—which is the rationale for the forgery in the story—"with empty enthusiasm, theatrical gestures, and false accents." But although by this time the spectator is thoroughly convinced of Mr. Y's villainy, it is not possible for him to feel sympathy for the exposer, the brutal Mr. X.

In spite of these objections, it cannot be denied that Strindberg brought dramatic intensity to a theme that does not seem at all suitable for a play. As a drama of crime, the play's tension and concentration put it in a class by itself. It is no accident that it has remained on the stage so long, although it is not among Strindberg's more important works. It shows his proficiency in a genre he did not otherwise cultivate.

The Stronger is also a battle of brains. Here, the two combatants are women and the one with the stronger brain, the actress Mrs. X, has such a decisive advantage right from the start that her colleague Miss Y never gets to speak; she can only register her feelings through facial expressions and bodily movements. Although Strindberg has sucessfully reduced the number of characters in the play, the spectator may get the unfortunate impression that Miss Y is suffering from some form of asphasia.

In a passage intended for the preface to *Miss Julie,* Strindberg had spoken about "thought transference" *(Gedankenübertragung).* In *The Stronger,* he obviously tried to produce a kind of inner communication between Mrs. X and her adversary. Mrs. X reads Miss Y's thoughts, but at the same time she feels Miss Y is inducing her to express everything she is thinking. "You've sat there staring at me and winding all these thoughts out of me like raw silk from a cocoon—thoughts, perhaps suspicions."[82] She discovers that Miss Y is the woman with whom her husband has been having an affair and that she is a vampire: "Your soul bored its way into mine like a worm into an apple, eating and eating, boring and boring, till there was nothing left but the skin and a little black mold."[83] But suddenly Mrs. X becomes aware that she herself is "the stronger" and that Miss Y's silence is not an evidence of strength—it only means that she has nothing to say. In a letter to Siri, who was to perform the role for the Experimental Theatre, Strindberg explained that Mrs. X is the stronger because she is more supple. "What is rigidly inflexible breaks, but what is pliable bends and returns to its shape."[84] Nevertheless, even with this commentary, it is difficult to be convinced of this talkative woman's superiority in this battle of brains.

Strindberg apparently wrote *Simoom* shortly before the opening of the Experimental Theatre, but it was not produced there. Its exotic setting—an Arab burial vault in Algeria—gives it a unique position in

Strindberg's work. In a letter to Ola Hansson in March, 1889, Strindberg called the play "a brilliant Edgar Poe piece." He also said that reading Poe had confirmed his belief that one could use psychic influence to produce sickness in another person. It is by means of this kind of "psychic murder" that the Arab girl Biskra, in order to get revenge against the French for having killed her lover Ali, destroys the feverishly ill Zouave lieutenant with the help of the Simoom, the desert wind.

The drama is based upon the hypnotic experiments conducted by the Nancy school of psychology. First, the hapless lieutenant has to sip sand from a bowl in the belief that it is water. Biskra then deludes him into believing that he has been bitten by a rabid dog, prompting in him what Strindberg's authority Bernheim called a retroactive hallucination. After this, the Frenchman is entirely in her power. Through ventriloquism and other means, Biskra makes him see terrible visions—his wife's infidelity, his best friend's treachery, and the death of his only son. Finally, she brings out a skull and persuades him that it is his own and that he has been executed for desertion. When she shows him the spot where the executioner's axe supposedly fell, the officer drops dead of terror.

This summary might suggest that the play is a world of ghosts and phantoms, but Strindberg is anxious at every moment to give a rational, scientific explanation of the actual psychic course of events. The spectator can see too many of the strings to become really involved in the story, and the total effect is that of a magic demonstration by a clever hypnotist. Strindberg would be able to manage scenes like this much more successfully after the Inferno Crisis, when he himself unreservedly believed in such phenomena as if they were miracles.

Notes to Chapter Ten

1. In a letter to Looström (June 8, 1883) *(Brev,* III, p. 252) Strindberg requested a copy of Zola's Théâtre.
2. The information is contained in a note in Birger Mörner's collection. [Countess Adlersparre was a feminist leader. In the preface to *Married* she is one of those referred to in the statement: "The four Swedish authoresses now writing live in childless wedlock." *SS:*XIV, p. 23.—Translator]
3. *SS:*XXIII, p. 285.
4. That this plot complication was not conceived until after a large portion of the play had been written appears evident in that Axel takes it very badly when his wife is accepted and he rejected. In his dejection he even turns to retouching photographic plates.
5. Strindberg announced in a letter to Bonnier on December 20, 1886, that *Marauders-Comrades* would constitute the intermediate piece in a trilogy and told Edvard Brandes in a letter on January 3, 1887, that the first part would be "about the father and Bertha's childhood" and the third part "about Bertha's later fate as mother and wife of a lard merchant." *(Brev,* I, p. 98). The connection between *Marauders* and *The Father* consists only of Bertha's mother wanting her to be trained as a painter and of the appearance of a minor character, Dr. Österman. It does not seem as if the third piece was ever executed.
6. Landquist pointed this out in his interesting study "Litteraturen och psykologien," *Dikten, diktaren och samhället* (Stockholm, 1935), pp. 71-121.
7. Eklund, *Strindbergsstudie,* pp. 361 ff.
8. *SS:*XXII, p. 123.
9. *Brev,* VI, p. 60.
10. *Edda,* 1929, pp. 132-33.
11. This was published under the German title "Schleichwege" in the fall of 1887 in *Neue Freie Presse.* It was first presented to the Swedish public in historical dress in the story "A Witch" in *Swedish Destinies and Adventures.* The original German version has been translated into Swedish by Landquist and published under the title "Short Cuts" in *Efterslåtter (SS:*LIV, pp. 7-114). According to Strindberg, the factual basis was a seance at the Hôtel Rydberg during the *Married* trial, during which he exposed a medium.
12. *SS:*LIV, p. 92.

13. *See* Chapter VI, The Historical Dramas of the 1880's.—Translator
14. *SS:*XXII, p. 163.
15. *Ibid.,* p. 180. [Strindberg believed he had saved his own daughter's life under similar circumstances, according to Erik Hedén, *Strindberg, En ledtråd vid studiet av hans verk,* Stockholm, 1926, p. 216. —Translator]
16. *SS:*XXII, p. 186.
17. *Ibid.,* p. 192.
18. *Ibid.,* p. 195.
19. *Brev,* VII, p. 218.
20. Nordau, p. 180.
21. *SS:*XXII, p. 123.
22. As Eklund demonstrated, this was due primarily to the influence of Nordau.
23. *SS:*XVII, pp. 257-58.
24. *SS:*XXII, p. 196.
25. *Ibid.,* p. 195.
26. *SS:*XXIII, p. 67.
27. *Ibid.,* p. 77.
28. *Brev,* VI, p. 298.
29. *SS:*XXVI, p. 304.
30. *Brev,* VI, p. 298.
31. Echegaray's play *O locura ó santidad* (1877), which a number of scholars has associated with *The Father,* can scarcely have had much significance, even though it is plausible that Strindberg was familiar with it. Neither do I find completely convincing A. Jolivet's parallels (*Le Théâtre de Strindberg,* Paris, 1931, pp. 157 ff.) between *The Father* and Dumas *fils' L'Affaire Clemenceau* (1866) and Maupassant's masterly story "Monsieur Parent" (1886). However, Strindberg certainly knew and appreciated both of these works. When he received a friendly letter from Maupassant involving the French translation of *The Father,* he requested Edvard Brandes to publish it in *Politiken* with an introductory remark about Maupassant having treated the problem of paternity in "Monsieur Parent" and *Pierre et Jean (Brev,* VII, p. 591.)
32. Included in another series of *Vivisections* that Strindberg wrote in 1894, according to a letter to Mörner (Mörner, p. 105). The manuscript is in the Royal Library in Stockholm.
33. *SS:*LIV, p. 303.
34. *SS:*XXIII, p. 94.

35. Axel Lundergård, *Några Strindbergsminnen knutna till en handfull brev,* Stockholm, 1920, p. 69.

36. Johan Mortensen, who conversed a great deal with Strindberg about his literary sources, has underscored, as have later scholars, the classical element. *See* Mortensen's *Från Röda rummet till sekelskiftet,* I, pp. 147-48. Jolivet considers such an influence inconceivable, since Aeschylean drama is moralistic and religious (*op. cit.,* p. 157). But the criterion that a work must be religious or moralistic in order to be considered as inspired by antiquity is not valid—O'Neill's *Mourning Becomes Electra* is an example. Moreover, Strindberg proceeded from Lafargue's sociological interpretation of the *Oresteia.*

37. *SS:*XXIII, p. 89.

38. *Ibid.,* p. 93.

39. *Brev,* VI, p. 282.

40. *SS:*XXIII, p. 42.

41. *Ibid.,* p. 65.

42. *Ibid.,* pp. 92-93.

43. *Brev,* VII, p. 104. The play was refused by Bonnier, but accepted by Joseph Seligmann on the condition that the publisher had the right to cut and edit. On September 14, 1888, Strindberg wrote to Seligmann that "after accepting the ultimatum" he agreed to the publisher's proposals for changes *(Brev,* VII, p. 116). But it seems that Strindberg did not closely examine the changes until after publication, for he then became very disturbed over Seligmann's "idiotic and presumptuous collaborations." On January 3, 1889, Strindberg ordered his Danish translator, Nathalia Larsen, to place the following on the title of her version: "Translation from the restored original, excluding the Swedish bookseller's literary efforts within the author's text." *(Ibid.,* p. 219). Although this statement appears on the title page, Landquist has assumed that it was unwarranted since the Danish text follows the Swedish with relatively few changes.

   The original manuscript of *Miss Julie,* bequeathed to the Nordic Museum in Stockholm in 1936, shows that Seligmann not only carried out the changes recommended by Strindberg and removed objectionable sections with Strindberg's permission, but also made a number of exclusions, corrections and changes on his own initiative, some of a linguistic nature. Since they impaired the text, Strindberg's indignation was fully justified.

Strindberg had only the published version in his possession when
the Danish translation was to be made, and consequently was able
to make few alterations in the text. When the play was reprinted
in his collected dramatic works *(Samlade dramatiska arbeten)*,
he had completely forgotten the affair.

[Discussions about the textual problems in *Miss Julie* can be
found in Harry Bergholz, "Toward an Authentic Text of Strindberg's *Fröken Julie*," *Orbis Litterarum, IX* (Fasc. 3, 1954), pp.
167-92, and *August Strindberg's dramer*, ed. Carl Reinhold Smedmark, Vol. III, Stockholm, 1964, pp. 494-506.—Translator]

44. *SS:*XXIII, p. 100.
45. *Brev*, VII, p. 142. Strindberg informed Edvard Brandes in an earlier
    letter that the woman did not commit suicide—she took a position
    as a "barmaid at Hasselbacken" restaurant *(Brev,* VII, p. 126).
46. *SS:*XXIII, p. 106.
47. Strindberg recommended Nietzsche to Heidenstam on May 17, 1888
    (Brev, VII, p. 91).
48. *SS:*XIX, pp. 283-84.
49. *SS:*XXIII, p. 101. As Eklund *(Strindbergsstudie,* pp. 385-86)
    showed, this ruthless concept was not inspired by Nietzsche as has
    been earlier believed, but by the psychiatrist Henry Maudsley.
50. Strindberg believed, of course, that he had transferred Darwin's
    theory of the struggle for existence and the survival of the fittest
    into the socio-political sphere. But we know that Darwin himself
    received the impulse for his ideas from political economics, in
    particular from Malthus. It was later, through Darwin, that the
    belief that certain individuals, families and races are fated to give
    way to newer, more vital ones became inbued with the biological
    hallmark and authority that made it a universal dogma. Since the
    belief had already gained acceptance by Strindberg's time, it is
    impossible to indicate the specific source that inspired him.
51. *SS:*XVIII, pp. 288, 285.
52. *SS:*XXIII, p. 174.
53. *SS:*XVIII, p. 212.
54. *SS:*XXIII, p. 104.
55. *Ibid.,* p. 102.
56. Interestingly enough, Strindberg became indignant when he first read
    the Danish translation of Jean's bold answer to Julie's violent
    outburst against him and the entire masculine sex: "Now the
    aristocrat is talking! Good, Miss Julie! Just don't let the cat out

of the bag!" He wrote to his translator that the speech was to be "cut completely, since it was written by bookseller Seligmann." The request was carried out. The original manuscript shows, however, that Strindberg himself inserted the speech in the margin.

57.   *SS:XXIII*, p. 169.

58.   *Ibid.*, p. 186.

59.   *Ibid.*, p. 187.

60.   In a passage cut from the preface Strindberg states that Miss Julie does not accept Jean's command in hypnotic sleep, but is subjected to "open suggestion, a variation of sleeping." The power of suggestion operates through the people involved (each influencing the other), the milieu (the greenfinch's blood), and the attribute (the razor). He also "had 'Gedankenübertragung' [thought transference] carried through an inanimate medium (the Count's boots)." In the published text, on the other hand, Strindberg declares that he "makes the weaker [person] steal and repeat words from the stronger, making characters derive ideas, or 'suggestions' as they are called, from each other." It is clear that Strindberg's fundamental conception of the relationship between Julie and Jean was as a "battle of brains" in which the lackey—the stronger—emerges the victor.

61.   *SS:XXIII*, p. 108.

62.   *Ibid.*, p. 147.

63.   *Ibid.*, p. 179.

64.   *Ibid.*, p. 109.

65.   As late as November, 1889, he asked Geijerstam to refute "all the whispering and lying" about his having written his wife into *Creditors*.

66.   *SS:XXVI*, p. 235.

67.   *SS:XXIII*, p. 241.

68.   *Ibid.*, p. 210.

69.   *Ibid.*, p. 216.

70.   *Ibid.*, p. 218.

71.   *Ibid.*, p. 224. In *A Madman's Defense,* the same question is directed to the wife in a similar situation.

72.   *Ibid.*, pp. 265-66.

73.   Strindberg refers to the story in the essay "Psychic Murder," and believed that the phenomenon described could be used to explain how the power of suggestion operated. A half year later Strindberg read Poe for the first time and believed he had "anticipated" him

when he had Gustav "produce the falling sickness" in Adolph
(*Brev*, VII, p. 218).

74. In addition a private performance of *Miss Julie* was given by the
Student Society. *See* Harry Jacobsen, *Strindberg i Firsenes Koben-
havn,* 1948, pp. 79-164.

75. *Brev,* VII, p. 184.

76. In November, 1888, Strindberg came across Hansson's story "A
Pariah" ("En paria") in the journal *Ny jord.* He wrote immediately
to the author that he had found in him "the makings of a dramatist who does not construct with conscious intrigues" (*Brev,* VII,
p. 164) and suggested that Hansson dramatize his story for the
Scandinavian Experimental Theatre. When it developed that Hansson was unable to do so, Strindberg did it himself in January,
1889, following his own recommendations to Hansson: "have
everything take place within the room in twenty minutes' time in
the form of statements and revelations, then a parting, a dissolu-
tion of the friendship, and so forth" *(Ibid.)*

77. Ola Hansson, *Samlade skrifter,* III, p. 98.

78. *Ibid.,* p. 99.

79. *G. H. T.* 1920; cited by Erik Ekelund, *Ola Hanssons ungdomsdikt-
ning* (1930), p. 156.

80. *Aryan* is from the Sanskrit *ärya,* meaning noble, member of the
upper castes; a *pariah* in southern India and Burma is a member
of a low caste.—Translator

81. *SS:*XXIII, p. 383. During a summer visit to Skovlyst castle near
Copenhagen, Strindberg believed he had actually used his detective
instincts to spot a criminal. Gotthard Johannsson, in *Forum* (1915),
pp. 381 ff., points out the similarities between *Pariah* and the
story "Tschandala." *Cf.* Harry Jacobsen, *Digteren og Fantasten*
(1945).

82. *SS:*XXV, p. 221.

83. *Ibid.,* p. 222.

84. Smirnoff, p. 276.

Chapter Eleven

THE SKERRIES TALES

The People of Hemsö

It is ironic that Strindberg's two masterpieces about the Stockholm archipelago, works that contain much warm humor and nostalgia, were written during one of the stormiest periods of his life. He said he was "distressed and tired, harrowed, hunted like a wild animal"[1] when in August, 1887, he began the novel *The People of Hemsö*, which was published between *The Father* and *A Madman's Defense.* And the best story in the collection *Men of the Skerries*, "The Romantic Organist on Rånö," was written in May and June of 1888 in Skovlyst, the ghostly castle at Holte near Copenhagen, a place described in the story "Tschandala." There is some validity to Strindberg's statement in a letter to Pehr Staaff that his surroundings exerted no influence on his work.

The bracing sea atmosphere in both books can be explained largely by the fact that after long uncertainty Strindberg had finally found the literary forms suitable for describing "his summer memories from the unforgettable days in Stockholm's archipelago."[2] As early as 1883, during his last summer on Kymmendö(Hemsö), he had planned a poem, a realistic idyll in hexameters, "The Christening" ("Barndopet"), which was to have been illustrated by Carl Larsson, "who was familiar with all the old guys out here." Although no trace of the work remains, it long engaged Strindberg's imagination. He characterized the idyll in a letter in 1886 as "grotesque as nature (in the skerries), with a drunken minister and lots of boozing."[3]

Strindberg had also long considered depicting his Kymmendö sojourn in prose. It has already been noted that his original plan for the autobiography was a chronological account of his summer vacation trips, beginning with his childhood. As we saw, however, *The Son of a Servant* took on an entirely different tone. He also thought of adapting the material

235

into a novel with the proposed title *In the Country (På landet)*, or into "Auerbachean peasant stories."[4]

But it was not until he arrived in German-speaking Switzerland that he was inspired to write a realistic picture of peasant life. He became acquainted with the peasant novels of Jeremias Gotthelf (1797-1854)— who at this time was praised as a forerunner of naturalism—when he settled in Gotthelf's home canton, Aargau. On December 10, 1886, he promised Albert Bonnier "a Swedish provincial novel into which I am investing my great Kymmendö assets, which I saved as long as I had hope of returning there again. . . . Toward this end, I am studying Jeremias Gotthelf, a divine Swiss who was much ahead of his time in many ways." A half-year later the novel bore the title *The People of Bunsö* when Strindberg offered it as a serial to the newspaper *Stockholms Dagblad*.[5] He described the work, then only half-finished, as the first authentic novel he had produced and said that it overflowed with "Swedish landscapes, peasants, inspectors, ministers, organists, and the like." The list of items indicates that he intended to include some material that would not actually be used until later in *Men of the Skerries*.

The main action of the novel—the story of a farmhand who through his cleverness and capability becomes master of the manor—is similar in certain ways to Gotthelf's masterpiece, *Uli, der Knecht*.[6] The similarity is most noticeable in the first few chapters, where the hero, Carlsson, like Uli, comes to a neglected farm, tidies up the manure piles and the cowshed, and in general makes the farming operations more efficient. He also has to struggle against the distrustful owner, old widow Flod, as well as the envy of his fellow workers; through his persistence he succeeds, bit by bit, in taking over the management of the farm. But whereas Gotthelf's Uli has certain moral failings to begin with and develops into an exceedingly fine farmer, Carlsson goes in the opposite direction. After marrying widow Flod and assuming complete responsibility for the manor, he adopts the habits of a gentleman, begins to mismanage the farming, has an affair with one of the servant girls, and spends all his time trying to persuade his wife to disinherit her son, Gusten, by making a will in his favor. All of his efforts go for nothing when the old lady discovers his infidelity and orders Gusten to burn the document. When, after her death, Carlsson is reduced to living on the dole, the whole parish is pleased.

But Strindberg was not entirely unsympathetic toward this shrewd man who comes as an outsider to the skerries from the west-central province of Värmland. In October, 1887, the same month Strindberg completed *The People of Hemsö*, he wrote to Lundegård that he tried to show in his novel "how an easygoing farmhand with sound nerves and no rancor can make his way through life, taking whatever is offered, and relinquishing without tears whatever he could not hold onto."[7]

The form of the first part of *The People of Hemsö* shows the influence of Strindberg's earlier narrative poetry and the classicism of Gotthelf's description of folk life: the changing seasons are suggested through descriptions of the different farming activities and celebrations. Böök, without knowledge of the book's pre-history, pointed out the Homeric atmosphere lingering over the hay-mowing scene in the third chapter: "The enumeration of the men mowing and the girls raking is reminiscent of [Homer's] catalogue of Greek ships, and in the description of the work there is a truly great rhythm."[8] Strindberg compares the activity of mowing to that of a pitched battle, and the description has counterparts in his earlier narrative poetry, as well as in Swedish landscape depiction of the eighteenth century:

> And so the battle moved forward. Two dozen white shirtsleeves advanced in a wedge like swans migrating in the fall, with scythes heel to heel. Behind them, scattered like a flock of sea swallows, came the girls with their rakes, playfully flinging and tossing the hay, yet keeping it together, each girl following her own mower.

Midsummer flowers fall before the scythes, and the animals of the field, frightened by the din of battle, crouch down for protection; "but high above the battlefield swung a pair of titlars whose nest had been trampled by an iron heel."[9]

Strindberg told Pehr Staaff in August, 1887, he was "returning to belles-lettres after a series of experiments, and was using modern psychology as an auxiliary science." It was clear that he did not intend to produce a faithfully naturalistic novel. His mentioning of "modern psychology as an auxiliary science" indicates his intense interest in the psychological experiments he was writing about in *Vivisections*. In the first chapter of *The People of Hemsö* there is evidence that Strindberg considered staging a "battle of brains" between Carlsson and Gusten Flod.

When Carlsson enters the Flod cottage, the first thing to attract his attention is an old mahogany chiffonier, its finish smudged and dirty:

"That's an awfully pretty chiffonier, that is." When Widow Flod replies
that there is not much in it, Carlsson pokes his little finger in the keyhole
and says ingratiatingly: "Oh, I bet there's plenty of stuff in there."[10] After
meeting the widow's suspicious son, he crawls into his bed in the kitchen
and imagines as he lies half-asleep that he has a bunch of keys in his hand.
But just as he is about to put a key in the chiffonier, the keyhole becomes
round and large, like a gun muzzle. Over the end of the barrel he sees
Gusten's red ruddfish eye take aim sharply and treacherously, as if trying to
protect his gold. The conflict between Carlsson and Gusten is thus anticipated, and in the final chapter, the vision materializes as "Carlsson's
Dreams Come True" ("Carlssons sanndrömmar"). Gusten has put a seal
over the chiffonier's keyhole and when Carlsson tries to break it, Gusten
aims his gun at him.

    Strindberg believed he had anticipated Nietzsche's theme of the
will to power and in 1894 stated that in the "vivisections" "The Lowly"
("De små"), "The Great" ("De stora"), and "The Battle of the Brains,"
and in *The Father* and *The People of Hemsö,* he had "adopted the point of
view now regarded as Nietzsche's."[11] Böök maintains that there is a
struggle for power in *The People of Hemsö* and concludes from Strindberg's statement that the clever Carlsson is a kind of superman "on the
sly." To support his conclusion he refers to Carlsson's farming reforms and
to Strindberg's notation on the galley proofs that Carlsson is the superior
man in comparison with the "peasants" and their "vacantly smiling bovine
philosophy." Böök also compares Carlsson with the fishing commissioner,
Borg, in *In the Outer Skerries.* But although Carlsson is described in
the beginning of the book as having "a capability above the level of those
around him" and as being able to read people's thoughts and guess their
secret desires,[12] it was hardly Strindberg's intention to make him a superman like Borg. From the beginning, the character is developed with humor
and irony; he is a jack-of-all-trades with "a pronounced aversion to physical
labor" and "an unbelievable talent for inventing ways of avoiding this
unfortunate consequence of Adam's fall."[13] As a native of the agricultural province of Värmland, he does have a better understanding of farming than the men of the skerries, but when he introduces crop rotation, he
can give only a foggy explanation of its advantages.[14] Furthermore, Carlsson's complete ignorance of "sea subjects" is in contrast to Borg who,
though lacking in practical sailing experience, understands the principles

of navigation immediately, thanks to his scientifically trained mind. Carlsson is also hopelessly inferior to the townspeople with whom he associates. He abases himself before the music professor, makes 'a fool of himself over the professor's servant girl, and is completely duped by the director of a feldspar company who comes to buy mineral rights. Ultimately, even his peasant shrewdness fails and he becomes more naive and gullible than he appeared in the beginning. The sullen and stolid Gusten is his superior, and the battle of the brains ends with Carlsson's downfall; one would have expected the reverse outcome.

One ought to keep in mind that Strindberg did not intend to write a novel of ideas, but to "create a Swedish and amusing and coarsely droll book,"[5] and this purpose was true to the tradition of storytelling about the Stockholm archipelago. His closest predecessor, Frans Hedberg, had been writing skerries stories since the 1870's and published the collection *Stockholm Life and Skerries Atmosphere (Stockholmsliv och skärgårdsluft)* the year before *The People of Hemsö*. In Hedberg's work, the inhabitants of the skerries ("skralpiggarna") are interpreted for the most part as ridiculous figures. During the summer they rent out their cottages to important Stockholm merchants with refined manners and well-bred daughters; in the fall they parade around in their tenants' cast-off clothes and straw hats. Just as in *The People of Hemsö*, Hedberg's characters realize windfalls through the sale of feldspar deposits. There is even a story about harvesting in his collection "At Mowing-Time" ("Vid höstlåttern"), but it lacks the artistic brilliance of the parallel scene in *The People of Hemsö*.

Strindberg felt that he had proprietary rights in this world of sea and rocky islands: he had been intimate with it from the days of his youth. Whenever he glorified the peasant as a reminder of how happy man could be in the natural state, it was primarily the man of the skerries he had in mind, and when he toyed with the idea of becoming a farmer, the place in which he wanted to settle was the Stockholm archipelago. Although he had no illusions about "the aborigines" there, their faults did not arouse his indignation—he regarded them as amusing eccentrics. Despite his resolutions, Strindberg did not apply "modern psychology" to his treatment of the people of Hemsö-Kymmendö as he did later—with mixed success—in several of the *Men of the Skerries* stories. In the novel, the skerries inhabitants appear exactly as he saw them. Here and there—particularly in the end—a current of sympathy for his characters emerges, which was unusual for Strindberg at this time.

The fundamental tone in the novel is richly, genially humorous. Strindberg's contemporaries had little awareness of his greatness as a humorist, in spite of *The Red Room* and the first volume of *Married,* and even today, many people probably think of *The People of Hemsö* as a brilliant exception, perhaps because his humor in the other works is almost always intertwined with satire and is too stridently tendentious to afford uninterrupted pleasure.

In *The People of Hemsö* he produced "pure descriptions of nature and folk life—*L'art pour l'art.*"[16] In the introduction to *Men of the Skerries,* Strindberg tried to write a detailed, analytic study of the temperament of the skerries man, but it is labored. He was far more successful when he approached the task simply and spontaneously in *The People of Hemsö;* all he had to do was speak plainly about his hosts, their neighbors, and their servant girls and farmhands.

Böök is correct in observing that *The People of Hemsö* is "written in part from the point of view of the summer visitor"; Strindberg was following still another tradition in skerries storytelling. Sometimes he even stooped to rustic farce. Carlsson's love letter to the professor's housemaid, Ida, is an absurd document. To heighten the humorous effect, Strindberg larded it with several old folk ballad phrases and even an illusion to the farewell address of King Gustav Vasa. To justify their inclusion, he notes that Carlsson had read *Swedish Folk Songs* and Afzelius's *Saga Annals of the Swedish People* at the home of a farm overseer in Värmland. The desire to amuse also led Strindberg to allow a character as skillfully drawn as Carlsson to make some rather obvious, clichéd remarks. For example, after the Widow Flod (now Mrs. Carlsson) makes Carlsson the beneficiary of her will, he treats everyone to schnapps, " 'For,' he said, 'every minute is precious; let's eat and drink, for tomorrow we'll be dead! Ho!' "[17] Some of the coarseness that the publisher asked to have deleted was also in this same vein of rustic humor; and the dramatization made of *The People of Hemsö* two years later is entirely dominated by it.

That Strindberg constantly struggled against temptations of this kind is most evident in the revisions he made in the opening lines of the book. In the earliest version,[18] the opening scene is in a bar on Dalarö, where an intoxicated Carlsson, awaiting his boat trip to Hemsö, gets into a fight with a boat pilot who has flirted with some Hemsö servant girls. A second version, on the other hand, begins with the trip itself. Carlsson is still rather drunk and becomes increasingly so with gulps out of his eathernware bottle. He scratches the mast in the belief it will produce wind and thinks that broom-head buoys are real brooms. For the published version, Strindberg found an eloquent opening line: "He arrived like a squall one evening in April, with an earthenware bottle slung on a strap around his neck." The newcomer is now a completely sober individual with no landlubber eccentricities. He is an artful diplomat and alert observer who plans to make a good, dignified first impression.

Strindberg resisted another opportunity to write rustic comedy at the end of the novel. The published version has a trace of tragedy: while helping Gusten to transport his mother's body from Hemsö for burial, Carlsson is unable to make it safely across an ice field before the sea, "on its nocturnal plundering expedition," breaks the field up. Late the following afternoon, after searching in vain for the missing bodies of Carlsson and his wife, the island's inhabitants gather on the shore in the red evening glow reflected from the rocks. Pastor Nordström reads the funeral service out in a skiff, and the hymn "Toward death I go" is sung:

> The last notes died out and echoed against the skerries through the cold air. There was a pause, during which one heard the sighing of the north wind through the pine needles, the splashing of waves on the rocks, the screaming of gulls, and the bumping of the boats as they touched bottom. The Pastor turned his wrinkled old face out towards the bay, and the sun shone on his bald head, around which gray wisps of hair fluttered in the wind like lichens on an ancient spruce.[19]

This description, in which even the otherwise burlesque and alcoholic Pastor Nordström becomes an imposing figure before the majesty of death, ends on a defiant note as Gusten, the new master of Hemsö, has his farmhands row him home afterward, "and he pilots his own craft across the windy bays and green straits of a capricious world."[20]

After sending the manuscript to the publisher, Strindberg had second thoughts about killing off Carlsson and devised a new ending which was never used.[21] The skerries people, after returning from the funeral, begin to tell each other ghost stories. Suddenly, a rooster crows and a light flashes on the snow near an opening in a fence. It is Carlsson lighting his pipe. "Yes, God have mercy on us!—if I don't think it's him!"[22] It was fortunate that this postscript was never added, but it would not have completely violated the novel's style. The work entwines pathos and humor in a way that is difficult to separate, but because of it, the novel has a salty, fresh quality. It even contains the warmth of conciliation. After the funeral ceremony is concluded, Gusten, in spite of the fact that he and his late stepfather were enemies to the last, asks the Pastor if an additional word ought not to be said for Carlsson. The Pastor, "more moved than he wished to be," replies: "The service was for both, my boy!"

The natural setting of the skerries gives a poetic touch and holiday mood to ordinary workaday experiences. In the mowing scene, Strindberg takes us through an entire brilliant July day, from dewy morning to the half-darkness of a Scandinavian summer evening, when the men who mowed and the girls who raked pair off, climb over the stile, and disappear into the hazel brush. A boy from Kvarnö appears with a girl from Fjällång who is flushed from dancing: "Her teeth flashed in a broad smile of abandon," and with her arms crossed behind her head, she threw herself headlong into his arms. Another magnificent passage is the description of the outermost skerries where the Pastor and Gusten camp out on Norskär, drink schnapps, play cards, and discuss the wrongness of Carlsson's marriage to Mrs. Flod:

> Beyond lay the gleaming open sea, where the skua gull conducted his plundering hunt in competition with terns and sea gulls, and where the sea eagle could be seen piloting his somber, muffled flight, seizing, whenever possible, a sitting eider duck.... Only several bald rowan trees stood among the rocks, but in the crevices grew the gorgeous spindle tree with its fiery red berries. The glen was covered with a thick carpet of heather, crowberry sprays, and cloudberries that were just beginning to turn yellow. Scattered juniper bushes lay as though trampled flat on the slabs of rock, and it seemed as if they were hanging on by their nails so as not to be blown away.[23]

The skerries landscape also plays a role in the wedding of Carlsson and Mrs. Flod. This chapter was probably foremost in Strindberg's mind when he told Lundegård that he chose "Dutch genre painting as a model, because it always seemed to me to resemble the life of the common people in the Swedish provinces."[24] The scene does resemble a wild kermis in the Low Countries, what with its orgiastic abundances of food and drink; the publisher blue-penciled quite a lot to make it fit to print. Any reader familiar with the book will remember how Pastor Nordström becomes dead drunk during the dinner and is later found in the Carlssons' wedding bed. But perhaps less memorable in the wedding sequence is the picture Strindberg inserted as a bridge between two boisterous scenes: the view of the skerries in the bewitching perpetual twilight of a Scandinavian summer night:

> The dancing went around like a mill and the fiddler sat by the fireplace, scraping away. Sweaty backs hung out of open windows to cool off in the freshness of the night air. The old people sat on the ground outside, enjoying [the noise of occasional gun play fired off by boisterous celebrants], smoking, drinking, and cracking jokes in the half-darkness and by the faint glow coming through the ,window panes from the kitchen fireplace and from the candles around the dance floor.
> Out on the meadows and slopes couple after couple wandered in the dewy grass under the faint shimmer of the stars in order to quench—amid the scent of new-mown hay and the sound of the cricket's song—the fires ignited within them by the heat inside the cottage, the strong glow of the barley spirits, and the rhythmic tramping of the music.
> The midnight hours danced by and the heavens began to brighten in the east, the stars retreated into the sky, and the handle of the Big Dipper pointed straight up, as if it had tipped out its contents. Ducks began quacking among the reeds, and the gleaming bay already mirrored the lemon colors of dawn between the dark havens of alder trees, which seemed to stand on their heads in the water and reach down to the bottom of the sea. But the dawning lasted for just a moment; clouds loomed up from along the coast and it was night again.[25]

Swedish critics often refer to the naturalism in *The People of Hemsö,* and Strindberg's contemporaries believed the wedding sequence was inspired by the famous goose dinner in *L'Assommoir.* It is possible that Strindberg was influenced; in any case, like Zola, he had a taste for candid descriptions and later greatly admired the peasant novel *La Terre.*[26] But Strindberg's descriptions differ from those of Zola: he used personification for humorous ends, as he did in *The Red Room,* but he was careful not to allow it to constitute an end in itself. In the first draft, Carlsson's initial journey out to Hemsö is framed in a richly detailed, magnificently beautiful picture of a frosty evening in early spring. In the published version, the section is pared down to a few lines that render just the boat trip as seen through the eyes of the newcomer:

> The skiff splashed ahead between holms and skerries, while the long-tailed duck derided behind the rocks and the black grouse tuned up in the fir woods. It sailed across bays and over ocean currents until darkness fell and the stars began their procession. Then it rode out on open water where the Huvudskär lighthouse was blinking.

The journey ends as the skiff glides in through a canal in the reeds, "which rustled against the sides of the boat, and startled a spawning pike that was speculating around a ledger tackle."[27]

Here, as elsewhere in the novel, we observe the prominent role played by animal life—the mocking cries of the birds and the maneuvers of the fish in the reeds. Even inanimate objects and changes in the wind and water are vividly characterized by Strindberg through images derived from the vocabulary of the skerries men. The sky in the outer skerries is "blue-white like skimmed milk," and snowflakes fall "big as hen's feathers." A grass snake scoots along the ground "like the end of a rope on a sail," and Carlsson's new cabin is "red as a cow." The whole style of the novel—not just its dialogue—is colored by the language of the people it depicts.[28]

In later years, in letters to Heidenstam and others, Strindberg would refer to *The People of Hemsö* as "publisher's literature" that he was forced to turn out to subsidize the writing of his naturalistic tragedies. But although he called the work "an *intermezzo scherzando* between battles," his extensive revisions show that he approached his task more seriously than he would later admit. Indeed, one wonders if he ever produced another work that is as harmonious and well balanced. The atmosphere of rustic idyll gives *The People of Hemsö* its epic repose and its graphic clarity. Naturalism keeps the descriptions from becoming too idealized, but is not permitted, as later occurred in *In the Outer Skerries,* to damage them by excessive "scientific" details. "I have put aside the woman question, banished socialism, politics, all nonsense," Strindberg wrote to Lundegård in October, 1887. This helps to explain why *The People of Hemsö* has its contagious good spirits and was to become Strindberg's most popular work in Sweden. In *Men of the Skerries,* contemporary problems are brought up, and as a result, the lighthearted mood disappears.

Men of the Skerries

Even before *The People of Hemsö* was printed Strindberg contemplated a sequel. "Tell the publisher that another volume of *The People of Hemsö* is possible, if such a thing seems desirable," he wrote to his brother Axel in October, 1887, "for Carlsson can remarry and have new adventures, even if he is buried." It was presumably at this time that he drafted the scene in which Carlsson, to the dismay of the people of Hemsö, reappears at the gap in the fence, smoking his pipe. The idea continued to appeal to Strindberg even after the novel was published. The continuation of *The People of Hemsö* was to deal with "Flod's [i.e., Gusten's] *ménage* and Carlsson's remarriage; along with infidelity, child murder, tenantcy, duck-hunting, the problems of child support, education, and arguments about the same, university students, . . . an ambulating elementary school, etc., but interlarded with the small pictures that are my strong point."[29] He said that he would prefer to write "small pieces": "pieces— not Spencerian psychology or social-democracy—but in the genre of *Town and Gown*. A novel would nauseate me and be too bluestocking and Ohnetian."[30]

A month earlier, influenced by his friends in Denmark, Strindberg had begun to believe that his novel was a failure, and he felt his old distrust of "the synthetic novel." He wanted to utilize the remainder of his Kymmendö memories in a work to be called *From Skerries and Lighthouses (Från skär och fyrar)* "with modern, that is to say hitherto less rehashed subject matter, and new points of view." In April, 1888, he submitted to K. O. Bonnier all of the *Men of the Skerries* stories except two: "The Sea Distress Promise" ("Sjönödslöftet"), written to replace "The Girls' Love" ("Flickornas kärlek"), a story rejected by the publisher, and "The Romantic Organist on Rånö," which Strindberg originally thought of setting on the mainland and publishing as a separate book.

The "new points of view" mentioned were in part identical with the ones presented in *Vivisections;* indeed, some of the skerries stories were planned for the latter collection. "My Summer Minister" ("Min sommarpräst"), for example, is a variation on the theme of the power of suggestion. But, of course, some new ideas were also evident. In the story "Höjer Takes Charge of the Farm" ("Höjer tar gården själv"), he illustrated the Nietzschean theory that "he who is not born to be master, never becomes master," and in "A Criminal" ("En brottsling"), dealing with an inquest into a woman's murder, he experiments with Lombroso's criminal psychology. Andreas Ek, a customs house attendant who has drowned his wife and stuffed the body down a privy, will not give any reason for his action. He declares simply that he had longed for years to do away with her and finally felt as if this craving were "an order from my superior. . . . Year after year it got stronger until I felt that if I didn't do it, I'd be neglecting something that had to be done."[31] He is sentenced to life imprisonment and stubbornly refuses to seek an appeal. The judge feels sympathy for the dead wife because he "had had his ears filled with fairy tales about downtrodden female slaves," and he regards Ek as a hardened criminal. But a doctor who is summoned declares that it was the wife who demonstrated criminal tendencies: "She was the criminal." A juror who knew the victim is also convinced of this. But Ek abides by a superstition prevalent among the people of the skerries that "a husband never criticizes his wife," and so he refuses to explain in court how he came to hate her.

The best stories in *Men of the Skerries* deal with shattered illusions. In "The Pastor's Moose" ("Pastorns älg") the theme is handled humorously. A pastor has expectations of being generously reimbursed when the Crown Prince hunts moose on his land, but his hopes go up in smoke, and at Christmas time he has to subsist on herring: "For that's what can happen when you play games with important people." The story "The Tailor Had to Give a Dance" ("Skräddarns skulle ha dans") is more complex. A little hunchbacked tailor lavishes much time and attention on a beautiful garden around his home, but when he gives a dance, his guests get drunk and his little paradise is devastated. Furthermore, he has to sit and sew for eight days to compensate for the amount of alcohol his guests consumed. He got so drunk himself that he passed out at the beginning of the party and missed all the excitement, but when his sister later assures him that his guests had a good time, he considers that he received full value for his money: "Well, it was fun, anyway!" An interesting implication becomes apparent: imagination has to compensate for what life has denied us.

The same implication is spelled out with a strong autobiographical strain in the stories "The Customs Agent" ("Uppsyningsman") and "The Romantic Organist on Rånö." ("The Customs Agent" first bore the title "Flying Dutchman." The published version begins with the typically Strindbergian introduction: "He traveled in his sloop like the 'Flying Dutchman,' never coming to rest." This is the first appearance of the theme in Strindberg's work; henceforth, always haunted by a feeling of rootlessness, he would readily apply the image to himself.) The character of the customs agent was based on an actual person who is first mentioned in Strindberg's skerries letters and who later appears in the unfinished skerries novel.[32] Strindberg's first plan was to introduce him in *The People of Hemsö,* and in the dramatization of the novel he appears exclusively as a comic figure. He is also comic in the beginning of the short story, but something suggests that he is a martyr to his imagination as well, like the Rånö organist.

The customs agent inherited his occupation from his father, who once was awarded ten thousand crowns[33] for seizing contraband. This almost fairy-tale adventure lured the son into the profession, but now the customs duties are so low that people rarely smuggle. Nevertheless, his imagination causes him to see each approaching vessel as a potential treasure ship laden with precious cargo, whereas it is likely to be just a Norwegian brig carrying English pit coal. When his wife dies, all his property is sold at auction and he no longer has a home on land. All year round he lives on his sloop—an old bawley boat with a patchy, posset-colored mainsail and a dirty yellow cabin. He sails back and forth without purpose. If he stays in one place too long, the customs controller forces him to move: " 'Just sail!' 'Where?' 'Any damn place at all, as long as you sail!' "[34] As the phantom ship with its black rigging glides past the red summer cottages, people refer to it as the Flying Dutchman.

But the agent does not look "at all remarkable or romantic. More like a wizened little store clerk from the country. With his legs bowed from standing at the helm, his whiskers thin and scrawny, his face pale and lean, he was not at all the type of sailing man the girls picture as a 'sloop commander'!"[35] But something happens during the November storms when the old sloop seems "like a decaying oak tree bursting into leaf"; the cordage is clothed in ice crystals; snow, looking like the wadding used to pad windows, lies on gaffs and booms; and the black hull is over-laid with bluish ice. The little man at the helm takes on "a touch of great-ness and power as he stands there in his sheepskin coat and sealskin cap. . . . [For] several hours his energies are tested in a struggle. For what purpose? Just for the sake of the struggle!" When he goes into the light-house and the keeper greets him with coffee and schnapps, his only remark is: " 'The weather's not fit for a dog to be out in!' "; "he has ceased to reflect on the purposelessness of the long journey that will be done only when he is done." After he has warmed himself in the pilot house and slept, he goes out to test the wind: " 'I think we'll sail again!' he said to his seamen. And so away they sailed again!"[36]

This excellent story gives the impression that only during the actual writing of it did Strindberg become conscious of the customs agent's life as a counterpart to his own—with its aimless wandering from place to place and its never-satisfied dreams of happiness; a life without a home, without firm footing. One can almost see the figure develop as Strindberg thinks about his own hard and purposeless struggle for life. As he wrote *Men of the Skerries* in Denmark ("in order to cure my homesickness"), his personal life had become more insecure than ever. Not only had his marriage completely fallen apart, but he was faced with the terrifying thought that he might have to abandon his career as a writer and be forced to seek a position as bookstore clerk, commercial correspondent, or head waiter: anything to be able to support himself and his family. "If this [*Men of the Skerries*] misfires with Bonnier," he wrote from Klampenborg, Denmark, in April, 1888, "then all I can do is go to Copenhagen, find a position, and rent a room and kitchen for the family, for I will not give in!"

When the publisher congratulated him on "The Customs Agent," Strindberg said that he had some anxiety about not having followed the prevailing fashion, "which only wants a perfect imitation, and has no desire to use the writer's mind as a stereoscope through which to view the object."[37] He was obviously turning to a more subjective artistic approach than that of naturalism. For the first time in many years he gave free rein to his imagination, and the result was "The Romantic Organist on Rånö."[38]

"The Romantic Organist on Rånö"

None of Strindberg's earlier works heralds his later symbolic writing as clearly as "The Romantic Organist on Rånö." He would often point out that he wrote the story "before the Pepita assault and the Byronic snob-school's return." *Pepita's Wedding (Pepitas bröllop)*, a pamphlet published a year later in 1890 by Verner von Heidenstam and Oscar Levertin, attacked "little naturalism" and "shoemaker realism" and predicted a non-naturalistic renaissance in Swedish literature.

During the actual writing of the story, however, Strindberg had no great expectations. In a letter to Heidenstam in mid-May, 1888, he complained about being compelled out of deference to public taste to throw together an idyll about an organist-sexton; "more idiotic than *The People of Hemsö*." But when he had finished it, he was aware of its merit.

"I believe that it is fine; not too idiotic, I hope, for the public," he wrote on July 2, when he submitted it to the publisher. And when he reread it at the end of the month, he wrote: "It was intended to be a trivial sketch about an uninteresting organist, but it has become far more than that."

The story underwent a significant transformation from the time it was planned to when it was completed. On May 10, 1888, Strindberg first mentioned a long-cherished plan to write a story to be called "The Organist in Vidala." On the manuscript he noted a reference to the third chapter of *The Son of a Servant* in which he described the summers when he and his brothers were boarded with the kindly organist-sexton of "Vidala," Strindberg's fictitious name for Ardala, a town on the mainland southwest of Stockholm. One month later he wrote that "the organist story, for reasons over which I have no control, has sneaked out into the skerries and feels more at home there; consequently it will be included in *The People of Hemsö,* Part Two, or what we are referring to as *Men of the Skerries.*" In the first draft of the story, the opening section takes place in the coastal city of Nyköping. Later, Strindberg changed Nyköping to Trosa, a coastal city closer to the skerries, and altered a lake to the sea, a land wind to a sea wind, and so forth.[39]

The early section of the story takes place in the 1850's. A young store clerk, Alrik Lundstedt, travels to Stockholm's Academy of Music to be educated as an organist and schoolteacher. Although he has talent and high expectations, he eventually has to settle for the modest position of organist-sexton on Rånö—near Utö—where he has right to preferment because it is his native parish.

In the seventh section or "chapter" of this long story, there is an account of the organist's childhood that seems to contradict what we have learned about him earlier. We discover that his idiosyncrasies—such as his tendency to live silently in his own imagination—are due in part to his isolation in the skerries and in part to his feeling of guilt because he never revealed that he was present when his father murdered his mother with an ice pick "during a severe winter when the fish were not running." After this, he lived alone with his father, "who now no longer spoke." In his loneliness and guilt, the boy developed the habit "of muddling the real and the unreal," and found expression for his feelings in music "in which he could tell his story without anyone else understanding what he said or suspecting that he had a secret to keep."[40] These new facts are hard to reconcile with the first part of the story, where Alrik is portrayed as a placid and childish fantast and his father as a simple, sociable, and alcoholic fisherman. The additional details were undoubtedly added to connect "The Romantic Organist" more closely with the prevailing theme of criminality in *Men of the Skerries,* but it is also evident that while working on the story, Strindberg started to identify with the organist.[41] He regarded the early death of his own mother and his relationship with his uncommunicative father as factors contributing to his habit of "toying with his imagination." Just as the organist used music, so Strindberg could use literature "to tell his own story without anyone else understanding him."[42]

The intimate connection between Alrik's imaginings and Strindberg's later dream visions can be demonstrated with a single example. For a time Lundstedt played the great organ in Jakob's Church in Stockholm. Then one day he saw a picture in *Meyer's Universum* of the basalt grotto on the island of Staffa in the Inner Hebrides. "From that day on, the [Jakob's Church] organ was a great basalt grotto and the organ bellows was Aeolus, King of the Winds."[43] During the graduation ceremony in *A Dream Play* the great organ is transformed into the same grotto—Fingal's Cave on Staffa Island.

But perhaps most characteristic of the similarity between Alrik Lundstedt's and Strindberg's powers of fantasy is the description of how Lundstedt's chance discovery of a cork on the shore of Rånö sets his imagination in motion:

> If he found a cork on the strands of seaweed, . . . it became a cork from Russia and occasioned a half-hour of reflections: Did it once sit in the neck of the Czar's breakfast wine? Or did one of the descendants of the heroes in *Fänrik Stål*[44] have his corkscrew in it? If he found a broken oarlock, he conjured up a picture of a terrible shipwreck. And an empty bottle was always examined to see whether it contained a note from someone who had deposited his last wish as his ship was sinking.[45]

This is the same way Strindberg speculated during the Inferno period about objects he found on the sidewalks of Paris or, after returning to Stockholm, about debris that washed ashore in one of Stockholm's bays *(Djurgårdsbrunnsviken),* always convinced that they had some mysterious significance. The things, however, that Strindberg would interpret as visions and miracles after the Inferno Crisis were at this time regarded more realistically.

The organist is too much of a daydreamer to realize his grandiose hopes of achieving musical greatness. But although he has to be content with teaching the island's children and playing the miserable little organ in the Rånö chapel, his ability to "conjure" allows him to experience imaginatively what reality has denied him. When he plays on the little Rånö organ the same fugue he performed the day after his examination at the Academy of Music, he is carried away by the same reverence for his own greatness as he experienced then. The little organ is transformed into the great Jakob's Church instrument; his feet work nonexistent pedals, and his hands play octaves that are not there and pull out imaginary stops. "The Romantic Organist on Rånö" shows how imagination makes man unfit for reality; the compensation is that imagination gives him an inner reality of greater value. Strindberg knew he was asserting one of romanticism's favorite themes; and before sending the manuscript away, he altered the original title, "The Organist on Rånö," to include the word "Romantic."

As several scholars have pointed out, Ernst Hoffmann's "Der Goldene Topf" is similar to "The Romantic Organist," and we know that Strindberg admired Hoffmann in his youth.[46] Hoffmann's real-life model, a poor student who always fell victim to bad luck just when he believed he was making the big move of his life, becomes a symbol for the poet in the story. Anselmus is on the verge of being won back to prosaic reality, of becoming a Philistine like everyone else and of marrying Konrektor Paulmann's daughter Veronica, but at the crucial moment he flees and continues his fantastic adventures, becoming the happy husband of the snakegreen Serpentina in poetry's Atlantis.

Strindberg's organist, too, has a choice to make between the worlds of imagination and reality. From the organ loft in Jakob's Church he falls in love with a young girl he sees in a distant pew, but never even tries to talk to her. In his imagination he names her Angelika[47] and becomes engaged to her. Later, on Rånö, he has another chance for love. The housekeeper at a nearby farm is interested in him, and for a moment he feels the temptation to enter respectable society at her side. But then he changes his mind:

> No—sooner go free and play, bend and mold the whole universe with his imagination, satisfy all his whims and desires, feel no compulsion, not be discontented with his position, never envy anyone, and never own anything that one fears losing. Sooner have Angelika for eternity than a wife on a manor for a lifetime.[48]

If the story had ended here, it would have been similar to "Der Goldene Topf." Instead, Strindberg permitted a reconciliation between poetry and prose. Lundstedt's experience with the housekeeper together with a frightening return to the memories of his childhood deprive him of "the gift of playing." He can only recover his "gift" through new contacts with reality. "Something new had to come along, something real, something tangible, to cover over the other things, and then he would once again have the gift of playing, and if he could only play, he would soon be happy again."[49] Finally, he marries the lighthouse keeper's daughter and they have children: "And now he plays the dearest games with real toys."[50]

One may wonder whether this compromise was advantageous to the story, but it was a genuine expression of Strindberg's own needs. He was aware that in order for his imagination to bloom, it required a constant supply of raw material from reality. He was much less romantic than Hoffmann, although he once revealed that Edvard Brandes thought him too romantic and laughed at his "utopias." In an essay in *Talks to the Swedish Nation* there is an account of a meeting with George Brandes in Kongens Nytorv, a square in Copenhagen. Strindberg pointed up to the statue of Adam Oehlenschläger in front of the Royal Theatre and said: "There is the literary idol of my youth—Oehlenschläger." When Brandes answered that Oehlenschläger was a child, Strindberg retorted: "Yes, but that's the way I have dreamed of poetry—as naive—although I have come a long way from childhood. But I hope to return." The essayist adds parenthetically: "I was then writing 'The Organist on Rånö' and had published *The People of Hemsö;* my break with pure realism, which *preceded* the alleged Swedish renaissance of the 1890's."[51]

Even though this conversation was reported years after the event and perhaps did not accurately represent what took place in 1888, there can be no doubt that he felt he was returning to romanticism at the time he wrote the story. But he did not go all the way; the organist marries respectably and retains his romantic dreams as a charming eccentricity. Strindberg never really identified with his hero; at the end of the story he was uncertain whether to call him the "bewitched" or the "idiotic" organist. "The Romantic Organist" did not initiate a new phase in Strindberg's work. It was but a foreshadowing of a distant revolution, for it was followed by a relapse into naturalism.

The first part of the story is the most satisfying. The reader is

gradually led into young Lundstedt's fantasy world as he lies by an open
window and marvels at the way the moonlight and the warm sea breeze
lend a magic life to the silhouettes of chimney tops:

> First, the great metal cap took on the form of a witch wearing a black
> hood; then the snake-head of the weather vane poked out of the cowl,
> exposing its teeth and its outstretched stinger; then the balance beam
> swung its round disk forward and in profile became a safety valve on a
> steam engine; and then witches danced with dragons around the four-
> cornered pipe, from which smoke belched as if from an Easter-Eve
> bonfire.[52]

When he turns back into his room, he sees on one of the beds "a carpet-
bag, packed, but still open, like a great toad that had choked on the
dozen wool stockings and the roll of music sheets visible through its
iron-sheathed jaws."[53]

Although Lundstedt is referred to as "the dreamy young clerk,"
his tendency to "play" and pretend is not really developed until the car-
riage journey to Södertälje when he imagines that he is Napoleon returning from Moscow in a sled and pretends that the shocks of rye along the
way are troops watching him pass. When he is accepted as a student at the
Academy of Music in Stockholm, he wanders through the streets and
alleys of Old Town "as proudly as a lord high constable." At noon the city
guards parade by with their weapons, the church bells ring, and the cannon thunder on Skepps Island—all in his honor. On Präst Street he pretends that he is a knight in Venice, beset by a swarm of beautiful chate-
laines, until he is shocked into reality when a washbasin is emptied above
and spills down in front of him.

His daydreaming ecstasies culminate in the organ loft at Jakob's
Church. Even Carl af Wirsén, generally unsympathetic to Strindberg,[54]
admired the description of the organ; he pointed out that Strindberg, following the example of Victor Hugo's treatment of the cathedral in *Notre-
Dame de Paris*, had given the organ a spectacular life of its own. The similarity in approach is undeniable and perhaps intentional on Strindberg's
part.[55] But here, as with the organ image in *Utopias*, we can also detect
the influences of Zola's manner of portraying inanimate objects as living
beings and of encumbering description with technical terms and historical
comments. Strindberg says that "a more educated bent of mind than that
of the young store clerk" could have related the entire history of the organ
through references to the apparent confusion of different elements in the

instrument's apparatus, whereupon the author briefly recapitulates this history.

At the end of the story there is a beautiful passage describing the depression Lundstedt experiences when he temporarily loses the Aladdin's lamp of his imagination. "Everything became melancholy [and] gray. . . . Dreams turned into sharp, piercing thoughts that cut to pieces all the veils he wanted to suspend to obscure the past, into reflections that corroded and disintegrated things."[56] The little Rånö organ that he had transformed into the Jakob's Church organ dwindles to life-size, and its pipes cough and wheeze. The schoolroom that he had peopled with heroes from novels about American Indians turns out to contain only the scurvy sniveling children of fishermen. The seashore—his kingdom of adventure—becomes a garbage heap; the clouds lose their human form and consist only "of aqueous vapors, as described in Berlin's natural science textbook." Apparently, Strindberg also suffered a shattering of illusions as he returned to naturalism. Two years later, he created in the fishing commissioner of *In the Outer Skerries* another person for whom clouds are only aqueous vapors.

Another indication of Strindberg's retreat from romanticism is the preface to *Men of the Skerries,* written in September, 1888. In the interim between the completion of the stories and the writing of the preface, he wrote *Miss Julie* and *Creditors* and proclaimed to his publisher that naturalism would be obsolete only when it could be said that "Darwinism —of which [naturalism] is the consequence—was [outdated]; *hoc est:* never." The naturalism in the preface is reflected in the abundance of geological and biological terminology. There is talk of morainal gravel, glacial flora, gneiss and pegmatite; we find animals and birds enumerated, and even advice on how to cook duck. Its didactic tone is a foreshadowing of *In the Outer Skerries.* The Rånö organist is mentioned as an example of the tendency on the part of lonely and isolated skerries inhabitants to degenerate into fantasts and fall "prey to their subjective impressions." For the author, the organist had become strange and irrelevant, and he no longer regarded "the art of playing" as a propitious baptismal gift.

Notes to Chapter Eleven

1. *Brev,* VI, p. 293.
2. *Cf.* my essay "Förhistorien till Strindbergs *Hemsöborna"* in *Svensk litteraturtidskrift* (1938), pp. 41 ff. and Knut Landmark in *Edda,* XLI (1941).
3. It is evident from this that the alcoholic Pastor Nordström in *The People of Hemsö* was to have figured in this poem, which presumably was to have been a verse version of the wedding scene in the novel. An earlier letter to Geijerstam (May 10, 1883—*Brev,* III, p. 231) called the Ornö minister who served as the model for Pastor Nordström "the one I portrayed in the christening scenes." Thus, it is possible that "The Christening" was at least partially executed.
4. The German author Berthold Auerbach (1812-82) depicted the life of the south German peasant in a number of novels in the 1850's and 1860's.—Translator
5. *Brev,* VI, p. 255.
6. *Cf.* A. Jolivet in *Études Germaniques* (1948), pp. 305-8. Presumably, this was the book Strindberg had in mind when in a September, 1889, letter to Albert Bonnier (*Brev,* VII, p. 369) he mentioned Gotthelf's "glorious *veduta* paintings and undeniably classic folk descriptions which influenced me in *The People of Hemsö."*
7. *Brev,* VI, p. 293.
8. Böök, "Tre noveller," p. 118.
9. *SS:*XXI, pp. 61-62.
10. *Ibid.,* pp. 11-12.
11. *SS:*LIV, p. 323.
12. *SS:*XXI, p. 41.
13. *Ibid.,* p. 40. In the first draft the point is added that Carlsson was quite right in that "mental work is more useful, more honorable, more comfortable and more financially rewarding." But this statement is hardly evidence of an overwhelming respect for Carlsson's "intellectual powers."
14. Strindberg's emphasis on Carlsson's farming reforms was due to his utilization of insights developed while doing research on French peasants for *Bland franska bönder* (1886, 1889).
15. *Brev,* VI, p. 293.
16. *SS:*XIX, p. 148.
17. *SS:*XXI, p. 145.

18. Reproduced by Knut Landmark, pp. 109 ff.
19. *SS:*XXI, p. 178.
20. *Ibid.,* p. 179.
21. Landquist found this ending on the reverse sides of several manuscript pages of *Men of the Skerries.*
22. *SS:*XXI, p. 408.
23. *Ibid.,* pp. 111-12.
24. *Brev,* VI, p. 293.
25. *SS:*XXI, pp. 131-32.
26. Rather than Zola, however, the Swedish reader is likely to think of the chiaroscuro in Anders Zorn's (1860-1920) painting *Midsummer Dance (Midsommardans),* and Strindberg's passage about "the strong glow of the barley spirits and the rhythmic tramping of the music" probably calls to mind the swinging reel rhythms of the poet Erik Karlfeldt (1864-1931).
27. *SS:*XXI, pp. 8-9.
28. On the other hand, the unique speech patterns of the skerries inhabitants are no more than suggested, and Strindberg has Carlsson resort to his Värmland dialect only when the character wants to appear "impressionable and ingenious." In the introduction to *Men of the Skerries* Strindberg explained that there was no true provincial dialect for the Stockholm archipelago but "a mixture of many." I cannot say whether this is so; in any case, the archipelago is not identified as a unique region poetically. It is often emphasized that the southern (Skåne province) peasant fiction of Ola Hansson and Ernst Ahlgren foreshadowed the regional romanticism of the 1890's in Swedish literature. Unfortunately, it is easily overlooked that this was accomplished to an even greater extent in *The People of Hemsö.* Strindberg was correct in pointing out (in the preface to the fourth part of the autobiography in 1909) that in *The People of Hemsö* he had rendered "descriptions of nature and folk life pure and simple" before people had begun shouting about a renaissance of nationalism.
29. *Brev,* VII, pp. 20-21. About this same time Strindberg thought about dramatizing *The People of Hemsö,* but he did not do it until the beginning of 1889. The drama has the quality of clumsy peasant farce and is a vandalization of the novel; it can be bypassed.
30. The French writer Georges Ohnet (1848-1918) was the author of a series of novels centered on the same simple, idealistic character. —Translator

31. *SS:*XXI, p. 294.
32. *See* Chapter IV, The Skerries Writer.—Translator
33. Worth, at 1969 exchange rates, approximately two thousand U. S. dollars.—Translator
34. *SS:*XXI, p. 339.
35. *Ibid.,* p. 341.
36. *Ibid.,* p. 342.
37. *Brev,* VII, p. 83.
38. The Swedish term for this position—"Klockare"—is difficult to translate. In Strindberg's day, the position included such duties as playing the church organ, and serving as parish clerk or sexton and schoolteacher.—Translator
39. The changes are not consistently carried out. For example, in the definitive text the hero Lundstedt passes by the Svärdsbro Hostelry on his way to Södertälje, which is geographically impossible if he is coming from Trosa.
40. *SS:*XXI, p. 246.
41. To the publisher's criticism of this portion of the story Strindberg replied that he did not dare to change it: "And I think that under the influence of fever the author received the right impulse, even though afterwards in his sober senses he thinks some things might have been done differently" (*Brev,* VII, p. 103). Three weeks earlier he had declared his intention of writing an addendum in order to explain the sexton's "second sightedness." [Strindberg uses the Danish word *fremsynthed* here.—Translator.] Instead, he mentioned it in the preface to *Men of the Skerries.*
42. Evidence of Strindberg's ability to transform impressions of reality into fantasy can be found early in the depiction of childhood and adolescent memories in *The Son of a Servant.* After the Inferno Crisis he kept a diary about these "occult" experiences: he discovered pillows taking on the forms of artistic reliefs, the perianths of pansies resolving themselves into human faces, telephone poles and wires playing wonderful melodies, and cloud patterns evoking illusions of Alpine landscapes.
43. *SS:*XXI, p. 232.
44. *The Tales of Ensign Stål (Fänrik Ståls sägner),* written in Swedish by the great national poet of Finland, Johan Ludvig Runeberg (1804-77), is a cycle of thirty-five patriotic poems dealing with the heroism of Swedo-Finnish forces against Russia in the War of 1808-9.—Translator

45. *SS:XXI*, pp. 236-37.
46. Apparently Strindberg did not reread "Der Goldene Topf" before
    writing "The Romantic Organist," for he asked Ola Hansson a
    half-year after completing the story: "Don't you think we could
    still read Hoffmann's tales with profit?" (*Brev*, VII, p. 218). But
    of course he could have been recalling things from his youth.
    Hoffmann is mentioned among Strindberg's early reading matter
    and is believed to have influenced his first story—"Martyrs for
    Art." When Strindberg first mentioned "The Organist in Vidala,"
    he said that he had "mulled it over for a long time" and thought
    it would evolve as "a classic story set in the '50's and '60's, prob-
    ably like a *Precentor in Fichtenhagen* who lives a long life."
    (*Ibid.*, p. 89). What he is alluding to, as Gunnar Ollén pointed
    out (*Strindbergs 1900-talslyrik,* 1941, pp. 162-63), is Gustav
    Nicolai's very popular *Die Geweihten, oder der Kantor aus Fich-
    tenhagen* (first published in a Swedish translation in 1833 and
    republished in 1871 with a preface by Strindberg's friend Richard
    Bergström). This novel, which seems most strongly inspired by
    Goldsmith's *The Vicar of Wakefield,* has only a general thematic
    similarity to Strindberg's story. Precentor Graupner of Fichten-
    hagen travels to Berlin with the ambitious plan of winning re-
    nown as the composer of an oratorio and while there is persuaded
    to write music for an opera as well. His greatest thrill is when an
    acquaintance, the organist of the Berlin cathedral, arranges for him
    to play his fugues on the great cathedral organ, an experience
    similar to Alrik Lundstedt's treasured moments in the organ loft
    of Jakob's Church.
47. "Angelika" is the name of a famous poem by Bernhard Malmström;
    it was honored with a grand prize by the Swedish Academy in 1840.
48. *SS:XXI*, p. 243.
49. *Ibid.*, p. 254.
50. *Ibid.*, p. 257.
51. *SS:LIII*, p. 557.
52. *SS:XXI*, p. 193.
53. *Ibid.*, p. 194.
54. *See* Chapter VI, *Poems.*—Translator
55. The organ is said to be "a human creation that has no inventor, as
    the cathedral is" (*SS:XXI*, p. 217).
56. *Ibid.*, pp. 247-48.

Chapter Twelve

THE SUPERMAN AND NATURE

Nietzsche and "Tschandala"

On May 17, 1888, Strindberg wrote to Heidenstam: "Buy yourself a modern German philosopher by the name of *Nietzsche,* about whom G[eorge] B[randes] has given lectures. There you can read *everything.* Do not deny yourself this pleasure! N. is also a poet."[1] His next letter to Heidenstam on May 25, 1888, speaks of a "boundless hatred of Christ," which he felt was a spontaneous result of his Nietzscheanism. Christ is called "the little, degenerate, asexual sophist, . . . the democrat—that is, the little tyrant I now find so disgusting, since I see that the ideal of freedom means the freedom to tyrannize." He declared that he hated both the lowly "who sit on high" and "the stupid tyrants down here." In a letter the following October, he wrote of goals that he would like to see accomplished: "The strongest and wisest on top! The lowly as manure and underlying warmth! below! Read Friedrich Nietzsche *(Jenseits von Gut und Böse).* I waver between suicide and immortal life!" Strindberg was completely captivated by the new prophet.

The May, 1888, letters were sent from Skovlyst, the ramshackle, former royal hunting lodge of King Frederik VII (1808-63) near Holte outside Copenhagen, where Strindberg rented living quarters from May to September and where, in a conflict with the lodge's gypsy manager, he fought his first "superman" battle. The facts of the incident are bizarre.[2] Strindberg charged Ludvig Hansen, the manager of the lodge—which boasted a pack of wild dogs and a countess who played a hurdy-gurdy—with theft; he in turn had an affair with Hansen's sister and was accused of rape by several conservative Danish newspapers. The upshot was that he fled in fear to Berlin for several days before returning to take up residence in a hotel near Holte.

Strindberg reproduced these events, disguised as historical fiction, in "Tschandala," published in the series *Swedish Destinies and Ad-*

ventures. The action of the novella is laid in southern Sweden during the latter part of the reign of Charles XI (1660-97). A university professor, Andreas Törner, comes into conflict with the gypsy manager of a decaying manor house owned by a baroness. With his superior mind, Törner is able to exercise the power of suggestion over the hapless gypsy and manages, through the artful use of a magic lantern, to have his enemy torn to pieces by his own dogs. Strindberg, quoting Nietzsche's *Götzen-Dämmerung* (1888), cites the terrible Hindu laws against the Tschandala caste instituted by the wise Manu, whose purpose was "to create, through these degrading laws, a brutalized race that would lie beneath the noble Aryan stock as a warming and nourishing manure; in this way, the Aryan stock could shoot up and flower every hundred years, like the century plant."[3]

Although Strindberg and Nietzsche apparently shared certain anti-democratic sentiments, their views of what constituted a "superman" were radically different. Nietzsche, an overworked university professor, envisioned a man with primitive jungle instincts and the characteristics of a predatory animal, whereas Strindberg's ideal was always intellectual. Törner in "Tschandala"—like the fishing commissioner in *In the Outer Skerries*—is a cultured, learned man who is reluctant to join battle with his barbarian adversary. "He felt like a Hellenist fighting the barbarian in a struggle the barbarian was certain to win because he was the most savage."[4] Only by transforming himself into a barbarian, by resorting to "primitive self-defense against a primitive human being,"[5] is Törner able to triumph.

When Strindberg wrote "Tschandala" shortly before Christmas, 1888, he had already protested to Nietzsche about his glorification of the criminal as a brilliant person. In Törner, Strindberg tried to sketch an intellectually superior and distinguished scientist who meekly suffers endless insults and mistreatment before he finally feels compelled to administer justice. But the story lacks psychological credibility. It is difficult to understand why Törner would ever want to associate with such a subnormal individual as the gypsy and have an affair with his sister. Furthermore, since Törner could have left the place any time he pleased, one cannot understand either his fear of the gypsy or the necessity for putting him to death.

It is obvious that Strindberg was describing his own persecution mania. In the disagreeable Skovlyst environment, he experienced his first

Inferno. Reality itself was a nightmare he could not escape, just as later in Paris he could not escape from the various "filthy hells" in which he landed. His persecution mania became more and more aggravated and developed into a desire to persecute. In November, 1889, a year after he had written about Törner killing the gypsy, Strindberg, then staying in the skerries, was still anxiously preoccupied with the whereabouts and activities of the Skovlyst manager. He exulted over a rumor that the gypsy was sentenced to six months in prison, but became frightened on hearing that he had been freed. Ola Hansson, who was living in Holte at this time, received detailed instructions to inquire about the manager after his release because Strindberg felt that he was an ever-present threat: "I carry a revolver and will shoot him down if he shows himself.—He'll never leave me alone."[6] This sense of being hounded by an enemy foreshadowed Strindberg's agony in Paris when he believed that a Polish friend, Pryzbyszewski, had turned vindictive and was persecuting him by telepathy from Berlin.

"Tschandala" is interesting as a psychological document, but artistically it is one of Strindberg's weaker works. He did not allow himself enough time to digest the actual events. Furthermore, the original manuscript, which was first published in a Danish translation in 1889, was lost when it was sent to a translator in Germany. As a result, the Swedish version published in 1897 is a rather indifferent retranslation from the Danish.

Strindberg's mastery is evident only in the depiction of milieu. Törner's journey to the lodge is through a devastated Inferno landscape with ruins of castles and half-burned windmills. In the entrance hall of Bögely (i.e., Skovlyst) castle, where Törner and his wife have rented rooms, they are greeted with "a stench caused by either rotten meat or wet dogs." The dilapidated main hall is furnished mostly with broken musical instruments. Two half-empty glasses have stained a table top with rings, and next to them lie bread crusts and a bacon rind—"remains of a meal eaten on the dirty corner of the table." In the black, soot-besmirched kitchen, the floor is covered with scraps of food; someone is lying in the kitchen bench-bed, but only a matted head is visible close by where a rooster has flown up to perch. In a bedroom, two dogs are standing on the bed, a bird cage with half-dead greenfinches and turtledoves is in the window, and from the ceiling hangs a stuffed stork with a withered viper in its beak. Their landlady, the baroness, has a round, sunburned cat-face with fish eyes and ugly teeth, and looks like a grocery peddler. The gypsy manager has what appears to be a horsehair wig, a large flashy stone on one of his dirty hands, tattered and ill-fitting clothing, and eyes that never look at the person to whom he speaks.

In this bewitched environment, Törner feels he is "in a struggle with invisible powers."[7] Three months of isolation from educated, refined people saps his strength. He believes that he is threatened in the same way civilized peoples in antiquity were threatened by barbarians; he is "the civilized man, the human being developed to live in a higher form of society."[8] As a civilized man, he resorts to modern weapons in his "battle of brains": the sophisticated crime-detection techniques of code decipherment, trail analysis, and so forth.

Shortly after writing "Tschandala," Strindberg read Edgar Allan Poe for the first time, and it is not surprising that he felt he had been mystically influenced by the American. He notified K. O. Bonnier in late December, 1888, that with "Tschandala" he intended to abandon Zolaism and enter into a new phase in his writing, but the following fall, in the novel *In the Outer Skerries,* he was once again in harmony with Zola. The Skovlyst experiences appear once again, but this time in a more naturalistic way.

In the Outer Skerries

In the Outer Skerries was at first the name for a contemplated collection of short stories, "a third part of *Men of the Skerries,*" and was to deal with "pilots, lighthouse keepers, customs spies, harvesters, divers, Utö mines, shipwrecks, and the like," as Strindberg said in a letter to K. O. Bonnier in January, 1889. But the first story, which was tentatively titled "The Master" ("Mästaren") and was to deal with a fishing commissioner,[9] grew during the spring into an independent novel that required over a year to write. The first seven chapters were completed during the summer and fall of 1889, but the latter half of the novel was not begun until the spring of 1890 and was finished that June.

Although Strindberg was probably certain at first about the main direction of the action of the novel, it is evident that he changed his intention during the writing. The seven chapters written in 1889 portray an intellectual conqueror of the same species as the heroes of "The Battle of the Brains," "Short Cuts," and "Tschandala." Commissioner Borg is sent out to an island in the skerries to find the cause of and possible solution for a diminution in the supply of herring. A fastidiously dressed man, interested in scientific investigation and experimentation, he is an outsider among the coarse, ignorant inhabitants of the skerries, somewhat as Carlsson was in *The People of Hemsö*—an alien among "the lowly." Borg, however, is superior to Carlsson in intelligence and training. He not only possesses the detective ability to expose and destroy enemies that Strindberg's other intellectual conquerors had, he is "a titan who storms the universe." In the seventh chapter he even succeeds in doing what Strindberg felt was more difficult: he so conquers Maria, the scornful woman he loves, that she humbly begs for his love. The next day, in honor of her birthday, he uses some scientific trickery to produce a mirage, thus compelling the superstitious skerries people to worship him as a higher power.

Up to this point, the novel develops in the same direction as "Tschandala." Even after its completion, Strindberg maintained in a letter to Ola Hansson in June, 1890, that it asserted "the stronger's (the wiser's) undeniable right to oppress and treat the lowly, in their own best interest, as manure,"[10] just as Manu, in "Tschandala," had decreed.

When Strindberg began the novel in May, 1889, he was back in the archipelago—alone in a fishing cottage on Runmarö, "enraptured, in love with nature in the skerries," as he wrote to Heidenstam and as is evident in the opening chapter, where the description of nature is still fresh and immediate without the scientific ballast with which it was later weighed down. He had requested from his publisher, however, a large number of books on biology, geology, and geography, together with works on the herring and the salmon, and informed Ola Hansson on July 6, 1889, that he was "doing an enormous amount of scientific reading." Indeed, even while writing his "modern novel in the footsteps of Nietzsche and Poe," he was collecting material for a book on chemical investigations and theories, *Antibarbus* (1894). His enthusiasm for his work grew and so did his ambitions; he dreamed of defending his theses in Copenhagen and of winning a professorship, as had the author Viktor Rydberg, who was appointed professor of cultural history at the University of Stockholm in 1884. "And now I swear," he declared in a letter to his brother Axel (July 27, 1889), "that if I live ten more years, I shall be a professor and a knight in at least six foreign orders." The majority of Borg's remarkable scientific experiments in the archipelago are clearly Strindberg's own, and the triumphant moment when the commissioner—with six miniature decorations on his dress coat—conquers Maria, mirrors Strindberg's grandiose dreams.

The last seven chapters of the novel were written under different circumstances from those of the first seven. Months had passed, and in the interim, economic troubles had compelled Strindberg to look for a position at a bookstore or a publisher. For a time he even thought of becoming a traveling salesman. Separated from his wife and children, he was tormented by his sense of isolation in the skerries. In a letter sent from Runmarö in May, 1891, a year after the publication of the novel, he told Ola Hansson that people conspired to refuse him food: "I could very easily perish here—both from sorrow and want! And I do not yet have persecution mania—and I do not need it, either, for all the men of the skerries are my enemies—but I might develop it."[11] The ambitious and power-hungry fishing commissioner in the novel also walks in isolation among the fisher folk, unable to determine whether he is actually being persecuted by them or whether he is suffering from persecution mania.

His hero has another pathological trait from which Strindberg feared he might be suffering—megalomania. When Borg opens his manuscript case and surveys the boxes filled with slips of paper upon which he is trying to classify natural phenomena, he feels that he is "actually the Power who brought order out of chaos, who separated light from darkness. . . . He intoxicated himself with his thought, felt his ego expand."[12] The last section of the book depicts the gradual disintegration of Borg's world as he becomes progressively unbalanced: his relationship with Maria is shattered, and he finally commits suicide. Toward the end, the symptoms of megalomania actually increase: the more his nervous system approaches the breaking point, the more grandiose his projects become.

When Strindberg corresponded with Nietzsche at the end of 1888, the latter's mental illness took the form of delusions of grandeur. At first, Strindberg was impressed by Nietzsche's "strong self-esteem," but then he noticed that it exceeded normal bounds and that he himself had similar symptoms. Shortly after receiving Nietzsche's last, completely irrational letter, he wrote to Ola Hansson on January 28, 1889: "I think Nietzsche is making me blind, because my brain is injured from overwork! But he is also making me crazy, because the extraordinary self-assurance in his books has produced a similar tendency in me! But this won't prevent the gray matter of my brain from bursting, which it probably is!"[13] Before he began writing *In the Outer Skerries*, he heard the rumor that Nietzsche had been confined, and perhaps this influenced him to have Borg end in a state of distraction, although memories from Skovlyst undoubtedly also played a role. In any case, Borg is doomed to succumb to "the lowly." After completing the novel, Strindberg wrote Ola Hansson that it dealt with "the persecution of the strong individual by the lowly, who instinctively hate the strong. Alone, persecuted from above and below, his soul goes to pieces bit by bit."[14]

Behind this conflict, however, between the superman and the pariahs, we glimpse another conflict—between man and nature. Borg, who treated nature as an inferior servant, is ultimately defeated by its superior power.

In his excellent essay on *In the Outer Skerries*,[15] Torsten Eklund has shown that whereas Nietzsche in his chief works is anti-intellectual, Fishing Commissioner Borg is distinguished by his intellectual superiority. It was Zola who induced Strindberg to make his hero an experimenter in the natural sciences. For Borg, all of existence is only a series of scientific problems, and he appraises every phenomenon from a scientific point of view. He sacrifices even himself to the dissecting knife: he "used himself as a psychological specimen, vivisected himself, experimented with himself, planted fistulas and fontanelles."[16]

When the book's weighty erudition was criticized, Strindberg turned for precedents to Zola[17] who, with the help of technical dictionaries, price notations, and seed catalogues, described mines, factories, department stores, and gardens. Strindberg went one step further by dealing with nature in the wild, a subject Zola generally left untouched, but from a scientific standpoint he does not seem to have succeeded any better than Zola. Sten Selander established that in the nature descriptions in *In the Outer Skerries*, Strindberg made only superficial use of his sources.[18] Although contemporary critics were impressed by the vivid images of the sea fauna Borg studies through his telescope, Strindberg was actually relying on the imprecise descriptions and woodcuts in Brehm's *Djurens liv* and hence made a number of mistakes. (For example, he inadvertently confused the picture of one fish with the description of another.)

Strindberg's knowledge of geology also left much to be desired: nevertheless, he attempted to produce an "exact" description of nature in place of the "poet's version," which he had ridiculed in earlier works. Borg, geological map in hand, informs Maria that the untrained eye and the undeveloped ear perceive everything too simply:

> You look around here and see only gray rocks, and the painter and the poet do the same. That's why they paint and portray everything so monotonously: that's why they find the skerries so monotonous. And yet, look at this geological map of the area and then glance out over the landscape. We are sitting on a region of red gneiss. . . .
>   Listen to "the roaring of the waves," as the poets summarily describe this symphony of sound. . . . First, you hear a roaring that sounds like what you hear in a machine shop or in a big city. That's the great mounds of water smashing against each other. Then you hear a hissing—that is the lighter, smaller water particles.

After listening to this long lecture, the young woman exclaims: "Yes, but nature is spoiled for us this way!" To which Borg replies: "This is the way to become intimate with nature! It is reassuring to learn these things, and thereby escape the poet's half-hidden fear of the unknown, which is nothing more than a reminder of the barbarian stage of literature."[19] Borg will not admit that landscapes can be portrayed according to fleeting sense impressions and moods. He wants to isolate the components involved, to analyze the constituent parts. Instead of painting the landscape as he sees it, he gives its geological structure, its flora and fauna. In this way, nature becomes a living textbook for him, instructing him not only in the true essence of things, but also in their origin and development. Borg finds the archipelago landscape captivating because it reproduces "creation in the form of a story with exclusions and abridgements."

Strindberg was obviously trying to surpass Zola in scientific scholarliness, but the book is not naturalistic in the accepted sense. It is true we learn that the commissioner regards nature "not with the poet's dreamy imagination," but "with the calm eye of the researcher, the alert thinker." But even his approach to fish involves some poetic imagination: a pike hovering near the water's surface dreams "about the flowery meadows and birch groves above him, where he can never go."[20] The description of the "harmony of sound" made by different varieties of sea birds is supposed to give the reader an aural portrait of the progress of evolution "from the reptile's first feeble effort to express wrath by hissing, right up to the music of man's harmonious vocal instrument." But instead of being ominously erudite, the passage is vividly poetic:

> There was a hissing, like that of an asp, from the eider duck, when the drake wanted to bite her in the neck and push her under the water; there was the quacking of the merganser, the shrieking of the terns, the croaking of the mews, the child-like cries of the gulls, the growling of the eider ducks like tomcats at rut time. But above all, highest and therefore most beautiful, was the wonderful music of the long-tailed ducks, almost but not quite song. It was an impure major triad, sonorous like a herdsman's horn, and no matter how or when it joined in, it harmonized with other triads into an untuned chord; a canon for hunting without beginning or end, reminders of humanity's childhood from the earliest times of the herdsman and the hunter.[21]

It is true that in the landscape portraits Strindberg inundates the reader with long lists of trees and flowers, and the geological accounts include mention of white quartz and black mica and rosy feldspar, of hornblende schist, of sparkling black diorite and the elegant, lightly colored hälleflinta. But when Borg goes out in a boat to make observations, he passes through an arctic landscape in an ultramarine blue sea where the ice has thrown up arches, constructed caves and built towers so wonderful,

> that they seemed fashioned by an enormous human hand. . . . Here, the blocks had piled up like Cyclopean walls, arranging themselves in terraces like an Assyrian-Greek temple. There, the waves through repeated assaults had excavated a Roman barrel, and fretted a round arch that sank into an Arabian horseshoe arch.[22]

Once again Strindberg's eagerness to render "the recapitulated story of creation" induced him, against all his intentions, to give rein to his imagination, and the result is a foretaste of the dream-like skerries pictures he would paint after the Inferno Crisis. In interior scenes, Strindberg has objects telling the stories of their origins. The motley selection of colors in the rag rugs in Öman's fishing cottage form:

> an album of memories from grandfather's jacket, grandmother's jumper, mother's cotton dress, and father's uniform from the time he was a pilot. There were the girls' red garters, the boys' yellow military service stripes, the summer guests' blue bathing suits, duffel and corduroy, cotton and baize, wool and jute, from all styles and wardrobes—the poor man's and the rich man's.[23]

Despite his resolve to be sober and prosaic, Strindberg occasionally returns to forms of expression he had used in earlier stories, but repudiated as too poetic. His spokesman Aristide in the story "Above the Clouds" in *Utopias* has disapproved of likening a white, cloud-enveloped

Alpine peak to "a reliquary shrine of newly molten silver," for he found it vulgar to compare a ten-thousand-foot-high mountain with an object made by man. But in *In the Outer Skerries* the morning mist is compared to "newly molten silver" through which "the sunlight was sifted."[24] And two pages later there is mention of the fog-silvered sunlight lying "like a long silver ingot" on the crests of the waves. The apparent motivation for this kind of imagery is that Strindberg's learned commissioner illustrates natural phenomena by using similes drawn from science and technology. The water at the shore, for example, is transparent "like compressed liquid air," and the colors of the seaweed on the ocean floor shine "as if fused in a mass of glass."

In order to understand this desire to transform nature into a collection of artifacts, one must take into account influences other than Zola's. Mortensen has already pointed out that Strindberg was influenced in his depiction of Borg by Huysmans's decadent hero des Esseintes in *À Rebours* (1884). Strindberg's letters to Ola Hansson at this time establish that he was much taken with Huysmans, although he was uncertain whether to regard him as a representative of a new trend or as a naturalist who was trying "to overtake and pass Zola." It was in *À Rebours* that Huysmans, earlier one of Zola's most faithful adherents, was first influenced by symbolist writers, although retaining Zola's descriptive technique. Huysmans's influence is evident in Strindberg's description of Borg's outward appearance. Although Borg's personality traits are Strindberg's own, including overexcitedness, petulance and suspiciousness, his appearance scarcely corresponds to Strindberg's manly ideal; with his spindly physique, his monocle, his *glacé* gloves, his crocodile shagreen boots, and his gold bracelet, he suggests the effeminate men Strindberg could not endure.

Des Esseintes is an aesthete filled with disgust for the modern age. Since he is enormously rich, he is able to free himself from the monotony of everyday life by creating an artificial paradise on his estate outside Paris. Although the resources on the little skerry Österskär will not permit such an expensive arrangement, Borg manages to transform his room in the little fishing cottage into an enchanted apartment by using the gaudily colored covers of magazines. In place of the perfume intoxication that transports des Esseintes, Strindberg's hero turns to ordinary drugs. Borg intoxicates himself with a laughing gas composed of ammonium nitrate and suppresses his desires with potassium iodide. By giving Maria a series of medicines, beginning with asafoetida, Borg makes her believe she is wandering through Stony Arabia, along the shores of Brittany, and so forth. In place of the exquisite, sumptuous feasts in *À Rebours,* Strindberg stages a picnic on an island, during which sardelles, chestnuts, and Russian caviar are served on Borg's remnants of a china collection, which include pieces from every period since the Renaissance. Borg's motive for starting the collection is exactly the same as in Huysmans: "Fear of the general descent into banality taking place in art, industry, and daily life had compelled the owner to participate in a new search for the unusual; the dreadful triviality of the present day and its hatred of originality had forced him like so many others into overrefinement."[25]

Des Esseintes has tired of nature's tedious landscapes and lighting effects. There is no moonlight that cannot be produced more effectively with electric light, no waterfall that cannot be surpassed by hydraulic power, and no rock that cannot be reproduced in papier-mâché. Borg appears to be taking des Esseintes's suggestion when he creates a mirage by using dynamite, an ax, wire, and a paintpot to change a desolate skerry into an Italian landscape.

But these similarities only show Strindberg's eagerness to follow the most modern trends in French belles-lettres. Actually, he was not temperamentally akin to Huysmans. As an outdoor person and nature lover, with preferences for swimming, physical exercise, and simple, plain cooking, Strindberg shared few of his hero's exotic tastes. In one passage, even Borg admits that "although both light and air could be produced by machine, he preferred the sun's unexcellable ether vibrations and the atmosphere's inexhaustible source of oxygen."[26]

Huysmans's aestheticism was totally foreign to Strindberg's purposes. Although when Borg transforms the little island into an Italian landscape he is said to have "corrected the Maker's bad penmanship," his real goal is to "attack and engage in a struggle with nature" and "frighten the rabble," that is, the fisher population on Österskär. For Borg, everything is a power struggle, a "souls' melée." Even in his relationship with Maria, his primary concern is to assert his masculine authority, and from the moment he meets the men of the skerries he regards them as his natural enemies. He finds it ridiculous to live "in sickly anxiety over the welfare of the lower classes" and is indifferent to whether or not "these desolate skerries can sustain a half-starving, useless stock of people." His sole interest in them is how they can be manipulated. "It would give him the greatest pleasure to sit inconspicuously, regarded as an idiot, and guide these people's fates."[27]

Why does he fail? Certainly he feels that he "stands high in the terrestrial chain of creation"; his intelligence is unlimited, and he knows it. Nature is "an inferior who could serve him; and it amused him to be able to trick this mighty adversary into placing its powers at his disposal."[28] One might say that the primary cause of his defeat lies in his intellectual refinement. When he reviews his life, he acknowledges that in common with his generation he had suffered from nervousness, because he was born "in the era of steam and electricity, when the process of life was accelerated." Drawing on his own life for examples, Strindberg describes how Borg would become "depressed for many hours when his morning coffee was not strong enough; and a crudely painted billiard ball and dirty cue could induce him to pick up and be off."[29] Behind these feelings one can discern the theory Strindberg had held since his youth—that culture makes man unfit for life's struggle by overrefining him.

Significantly, it is the isolation and not the hostility of the fisher folk on Österskär that undermines Borg's peace of mind. Long before the skerries men begin to plot against him, "the delicate wheels of his thinking processes" begin "to run unevenly." When he encounters a strange boat in the fog while on a sailing trip, he feels that it is pursuing him. It turns out, however, after Borg lands on an islet, that his supposed persecutor is only the local minister out for a sail. Now begins a familiar Strindbergian vicious circle. Borg isolates himself more and more and in the process becomes more and more convinced that the minister's appearance on the islet was "deliberate spying, paid for by certain people who wanted to persecute him. In calmer moments he rejected the idea, for he knew very well that fear of persecution was the first sign of the illness that can result from isolation." But he will not concede that he is actually suffering from persecution mania, because ever since his school days he really had been persecuted "from below by inferiors and from above by the mediocre."[30]

Why then does he not leave this isolation on Österskär which he feels is upsetting his mental balance? Because he fears being confined. Earlier, when he paid a visit aboard a navy corvette, he noticed that the doctor shook his head when hearing about Borg's experimental projects and recommended that Borg go for a vacation at a resort. But this would be impossible. "Sooner stay in absolute solitude and pass for an idiot among the 'redskins' than be condemned to a civil death by peers from whose authority and jurisdiction there is no appeal."[31]

Everything seems to conspire against him. Even the sea, which he loved, seems confining, its waters surrounding him in a turpentine-green gray circle as if within a prison. The skerries men despise him; the servant girls pity him. Ultimately, this proud aristocrat of the intellect becomes a poor idiot called "nincompoop" by children who throw stones.

As Borg's mental machinery deteriorates and his brilliant plans dissolve into wild fantasies, he retains his hatred of Christ, "the declared God of the lowly," "the Idol of all criminals and worthless people." When on Christmas Eve he exerts the last remnants of his energy and sets sail in his little boat for the open sea and certain death, the great star in the east toward which he steers is not the star of Bethlehem, but the star Beta in Hercules: "Hercules, the moral ideal of Hellas, the god of strength and good sense. . . . Out toward the new Christmas star the journey proceeded, out over the sea, the mother of all, from whose womb life's first spark was kindled, the inexhaustible spring of fruitfulness and love, life's origin and life's enemy."[32]

Strindberg's blasphemy probably never assumed a more defiant form. We notice, nevertheless, that a new divinity, nature, is about to take the place of the deposed one. Earlier represented as man's obedient slave, nature has become an all-powerful force, completely determining his fate. It is not a rational force, guided by a purposeful will, but a force at war with itself: at once man's creator and destroyer, his benefactor and enemy. It is this nature the fishing commissioner tries to understand in his investigations into "the great disorder and the great coherence"; it is this force he feels he is battling, and vengeance is finally wreaked upon him because he "toyed with nature's spirits."

In the Outer Skerries is one of Strindberg's most ambivalent works. First, it not only marks the high point of his worship of the superman, it also demonstrates that he could not use such a concept to harden his heart against the outside world. Second, although the novel does not contain the slightest indication of religious faith, or even respect for the religious conviction of others, it suggests an approaching change. The commissioner's atheism forbids him to believe in any purposefulness or

adherence to law in nature; to do this would be tantamount to acknowledging a providence or cosmic organizer. Everything is accidental and
chaotic, but on the other hand, natural settings appear as if "a supposed
creator" arranged them, and the formations seem fashioned by "an enormous human hand." What for Borg is only speculation would become
complete reality for Strindberg during the Inferno Crisis when he convinced himself while wandering in the Jardin des Plantes that animals
were "created by hand."

The aesthetic program presented in the novel is just as ambivalent.
Strindberg not only wanted to oppose Heidenstam's proposition that naturalism had played itself out, he also wanted to indicate a truly viable new
direction. As he tried to push Zola's scientific scholarliness to its ultimate,
he glided over into fantasy and sometimes came close to symbolism. This
is especially evident in his treatment of the landscape; what a difference
there is between the bright water-color picture of the skerries at the opening—with the herring boat rocking in the breeze of a warm May evening
—and the brooding storm images at the conclusion. In the beginning of
the book, a whistling buoy lying offshore brightens the monotonous
surface of the sea with a splash of red like the seal on a letter; later, it
becomes a giant organ playing a solo for Titan to the accompaniment of a
storm. Finally, when Borg is about to strike out on his last journey, it
screams in one, never-ending clang, as if crying for help. And Borg has
a dream in which he is a whistling buoy, torn loose, drifting to find a
beach to be thrown up upon. (In a similar way, Strindberg would use a
whistling buoy in *A Dream Play* as a symbol for life's anguish.)

In the Outer Skerries is a powerful but uneven book that lacks the
sunny humor and tender nuances of the earlier skerries tales. The style is
somber and the contempt for mankind bitter, as in Strindberg's novels
written after the turn of the century. The shadow cast by the forthcoming
Inferno, which is evident in the image of nature as a demonic force,
broods even more darkly over the last work of fiction he worked on before
his departure for Germany in September, 1892—the story "The Silver
Marsh" ("Silverträsket".)

"The Silver Marsh"

The published version of "The Silver Marsh" was completed in
Lund in 1898, but when Strindberg submitted the story to the journal

Vintergatan, he said that "the principal elements" were drawn from life and that the first draft had been written eight years before. This is corroborated by earlier letters. A month after the completion of *In the Outer Skerries,* on July 13, 1890, Strindberg notified K. O. Bonnier that he intended to write a Christmas book "for the altar of the home" with the title "The Silver Marsh." Two years later (April 1, 1892) the contours of the work came into sharper focus: "a long, subjective story about the *Silver Marsh* with no natural science, but much psychology and many nature descriptions."[33]

The story is based on experiences that date from Strindberg's last two years on Runmarö, where the Silver Marsh is located. In the summer of 1890, he lived on the island with his wife and children, but in a separate cottage, just as the curator does in the story. He returned alone the following spring after he and Siri were divorced. A letter to Ola Hansson in May, 1891, describes his mood:

> Since you and I last saw each other I have lived through horrible days, horrible! And when I came back out to Runmarö yesterday evening— alone!—Once again seeing the red cottages and green meadows where I played with my children last summer!!! Oh!
> I am living in a cottage where two years ago a childhood acquaintance lived at the time he drowned himself in a marsh nearby because—his wife left him and took the children with her. Slept in the same room where he slept on his last night and was the horrible victim of "suggestion" from—the marsh! Dreamed so vividly that the house was invaded by barbaric people who abused me physically—that I lit a lamp and placed a loaded gun near the bed, waiting for daylight, which fortunately came an hour later. I have never had so vivid a dream![34]

The letter, which describes the same power of suggestion that the Silver Marsh exerts on the hero, shows that the story's main action and its mood date from the early 1890's. A curator, who spent a summer on the island with his family, returns alone the following year and stays in the cottage of a childhood friend who had drowned himself because of marital discord. Against the stern warnings of the islanders, the curator fishes in the marsh and thus incurs their enmity. The outline is reminiscent of *In the Outer Skerries,* but the central theme here is the struggle with the invisible forces of nature.

The marsh has an air of mystery about it that intrigues the curator. Legend has it that the islanders once deposited a store of silver there when it appeared a Russian invasion was imminent, and that the silver was never recovered. On his way back from his first visit to the marsh the curator loses his way, in spite of the fact that he is carrying a compass and knows how to use it. Everything seems to be conspiring against him. A wasp stings him; he picks up a clump of moss under which lies a snake. When he sits down, ants crawl on him and he interprets it as a personal attack:

> The hunter felt he was at war with something. He could not accept that it was with himself, for surely he was not against himself. Was it then with something else? With whom? They were certainly not blind powers, for they had eyes in front and behind, and behaved as if they were as calculating, deliberate, and cunning as he was, and even more so.[35]

Nor could it be blamed on chance, for chance could just as well have taken him the right route instead of astray.

Even though this particular section first took shape in 1898, it probably reproduces rather faithfully Strindberg's earlier experiences on Runmarö. His persecution mania was no longer directed solely against people. Nature itself is transformed into a conspiracy of treacherous and invidious Powers: every tuft of grass in the wanderer's path was placed there intentionally, every trifling event was prearranged.

Later in the story, the curator starts trying to explain the curious things he encounters through numerology—a technique also used in *Inferno* (1897). He sees repetitions of the number 107 everywhere, and it leads him to the conclusion that the Silver Marsh is actually the site of an abandoned silver mine, the treasure of which "now seems guarded by jealous powers."[36] In Strindberg's later writings, strange repetitions and coincidences would prove the existence of occult patterns in the world, but in "The Silver Marsh" the curator discovers that he made some mathematical errors and that the entire preoccupation with the number 107 was little more than a ridiculous guessing game. This does not, however, entirely relieve the curator's anxiety. He is no longer a proud superman, but a perplexed, compulsive searcher for truth, with whom the powers of nature play a game of hide-and-seek.

Notes to Chapter Twelve

1. *Brev*, VII, p. 91. For accounts of Brandes's significance in Strind-berg's acquaintanceship with Nietzsche *see* Ahlenius, pp. 136-37; Landquist's introduction to *Georg og Edvard Brandes Brevveksling,* Copenhagen, 1939-42 (I, pp. xxv f.) ; and Eklund, *Strindbergs-studie,* p. 394.

2. *See* Karin Smirnoff, pp. 253-65, and Harry Jacobsen's excellent ex-amination of the factual background in *Digteren og Fantasten,* 1945.

3. *SS:*XII, p. 375. The same idea can be found, illustrated appropriately by a similar botanical image, in Nietzsche's *Jenseits von Gut und Böse* (p. 258).

4. *SS:*XII, p. 330.

5. *Ibid.,* p. 352.

6. *Brev,* VII, p. 394.

7. *SS:*XII, p. 298.

8. *Ibid.,* p. 362.

9. The fishing commissioner, who provokes the enmity of the skerries men because he wants to check their catches, is mentioned in Strindberg's first skerries letter in 1872. As previous scholars have pointed out, he is also mentioned later in *This and That (SS:*XVII, pp. 98 ff.), where he makes himself ridiculous by trying to inves-tigate the salting of herrings. There, Strindberg makes him—in the spirit of Buckle—a warning example of a case of "too much authority."

10. *Brev,* VIII, p. 58.

11. *Ibid.,* p. 267.

12. *SS:*XXIV, p. 134.

13. *Brev,* VII, p. 236.

14. *Ibid.,* p. 58.

15. *Edda* (1929), pp. 119-20.

16. *SS:*XXIV, p. 65. The closest counterpart to *In the Outer Skerries* is Zola's *Le Docteur Pascal* (1893), in which the hero conducts research in the laws of heredity. Glimpses of the same character are evident earlier in the Rougon-MacQuart cycle.

17. *Brev,* VIII, p. 128.

18. In an investigation unfortunately published as yet only in part in *Stockholms Dagblad,* April 8, 1928.

19. *SS:*XXIV, pp. 124 ff.

20. *Ibid.*, p. 39.
21. *Ibid.*, pp. 41-42.
22. *Ibid.*, p. 40.
23. *Ibid.*, p. 88.
24. *Ibid.*, p. 161.
25. *Ibid.*, p. 115.
26. *Ibid.*, p. 30.
27. *Ibid.*, p. 97.
28. *Ibid.*, p. 29.
29. *Ibid.*, pp. 56-57.
30. *Ibid.*, pp. 223-24.
31. *Ibid.*, p. 220.
32. *Ibid.*, p. 243. Torsten Eklund has shown (*Edda,* 1929, p. 139) that Nietzsche honored the star Hercules as the symbol of the superman in *Jenseits von Gut und Böse,* and that these final words of the novel were inspired by a statement of Ola Hansson in his Nietzsche essay in *Ur dagens krönika* (1890).
33. We learn from other letters (to Albert Bonnier on November 21, 1893, and to Frida Uhl from Paris in December, 1894) that Strindberg worked on the story in the years during which he had otherwise abandoned all belles-lettres activity.
34. *Brev,* VIII, p. 267.
35. *SS:*XXVII, p. 501.
36. *Ibid.*, p. 518.

Chapter Thirteen

STRINDBERG AND SWEDISH
ANTI-NATURALISM IN THE 1890's

Strindberg and Heidenstam

It was always a matter of pride to Strindberg that he was not bound to any literary school. He had not aligned himself with the Young Sweden movement, and he had been a *frondeur* within the ranks of the naturalists. On the other hand, he was always eager to experiment with new ideas. He was the first in Sweden to make literary use of the new discoveries in psychology and the power of suggestion and the first to respond to Nietzsche's gospel. It was therefore a hard blow for him when Verner von Heidenstam was recognized as a more important literary reformer than he.

Shortly after Strindberg wrote his first naturalistic dramas, *Miss Julie* and *Creditors* in 1888, his acquaintance with Ola Hansson brought him into closer contact with the new currents in French literature. When he submitted "Tschandala" to K. O. Bonnier in December, 1888, he announced that he was on the point of abandoning Zola: "Zolaism . . . seems to be on the way out. Therefore, don't be surprised that I don't want to trail behind, since I'm used to being in the vanguard." He named Bourget, Maupassant, and Ola Hansson as representatives of the new trend he intended to follow. Shortly thereafter, Ola Hansson persuaded him to read Poe, and he discovered that he had been Poe's disciple before having read him.

He gave a public indication of his break with naturalism in the essay "On Modern Drama and Modern Theatre," published in March, 1889, in the Danish journal *Ny jord*.¹ In it, he condemns "the objectivity that is so beloved by those who have nothing to say, by those devoid of temperament—the soulless ones, as they ought to be called." Strindberg is criticizing "photographic" realism which reproduces "everything, even

277

the speck of dust on the lens of the camera." It is nothing more than "a technique elevated into an art form." In contrast to this, he extols the "great naturalism" that takes delight in the war between natural forces: "This is the grandiose art we found in *Germinal* and *La Terre.*"[2] He says that as a naturalist, Zola did not disdain "the infinitely tiny as *ingredient,* but never worshipped the tiny as great, according to the Christian conception; instead, he has asserted, with full consciousness of the justness of his power, the prerogatives of the strong."[3]

Strindberg had carried his familiar theme of the contrast between "the lowly" and "the great" into the area of literary criticism. He wrote to Ola Hansson on November 9, 1889, that in his essay he denounced "realism as the trivial style of the lowly, in order to proclaim the greatness of naturalism, the style in which I wrote *Miss Julie* and *Creditors.*"[4] Later, he believed that he had thus anticipated by several months the distinction Heidenstam made between naturalism and "shoemaker realism" in his essay "Renaissance" ("Renässans"—October, 1889), as well as the distinction made the following year by Heidenstam and Levertin between "little naturalism" and "great naturalism" in *Pepita's Wedding.*[5]
he would be able to put forth his program. But he was once again antici-

Consequently, we can understand Strindberg's annoyance when Heidenstam caused a sensation with "Renaissance," whereas his own essay, published in a Danish journal, was unknown in Sweden. In letters to Ola Hansson in October and November, 1889, he says that Heidenstam had "caught hold of the tail of our *Die Aristokratie des Geistes*" and "prophesies in retrospect."[6] Heidenstam is called a "kleptomaniac . . . who has stolen the cake we baked and is hailed as 'the Renaissance man,' despite my having written 'The Joy of Life' ('Livsglädjen'), *Married I, The People of Hemsö,* and 'Modern Drama.' "[7] He took consolation in the fact that *In the Outer Skerries* would be ready by that spring and in it he would be able to put forth his program. But he was once again anticipated—by Heidenstam's and Levertin's *Pepita's Wedding.*

In a letter of reply to Heidenstam,[8] who in a gesture of courtesy had informed him in advance of the anti-naturalistic viewpoints that would appear in "Renaissance," Strindberg assumed a conciliatory if superior tone. But although he wanted to avoid a complete break if at all possible, he took pains to defend both Zola and naturalism. Earlier, he had sympathized with French reaction against Zola, but these sympathies had clearly abated. "Naturalism as world view can certainly never become outmoded, and when young Frenchmen disavow Zola and call themselves Indépendants, etc., is it only to avoid the role of pupil. They demand the right to go their own way, to be themselves, but they still carry on the movement without restraint." This last suggests that Heidenstam is an ungrateful pupil who denies his master, and Strindberg sharpens this impression by asking: "Is it more enviable to be Wirsén's pupil than Zola's?" —Wirsén being the reactionary permanent secretary of the Swedish Academy, a man despised by both the naturalists and the anti-naturalists.

Although the differences between Heidenstam and Strindberg were settled at a meeting in Stockholm after the publication of "Renaissance," the reconciliation was only temporary. Several months later, in April, 1890, Heidenstam collaborated with Oscar Levertin on their epochal anti-naturalistic critical broadside: *Pepita's Wedding*. As was the case with "Renaissance," Heidenstam tried to explain his motivations to Strindberg before the controversial book appeared in print. He said he was compelled to argue "against the movement [naturalism] of which you were the leader," because it had fulfilled its destiny and should give way to a new movement. But Heidenstam insisted that it had "never been my intention to try to disavow you." He said he longed for Strindberg's great poetic ability to "send a thunderbolt again, but in a manner not commonplace."

Strindberg did not reply to this letter; instead, during a meeting in the middle of August, 1890, he tried to persuade Heidenstam to stop publication of *Pepita's Wedding*.[9] Although Heidenstam refused, Strindberg received the impression that the pamphlet would not attack him and immediately after publication seemed rather indifferent: "I see where Levertin and Heidenstam are closing in on G[ustaf] af G[eijerstam] and Zola!" he told Ola Hansson: "The subject doesn't concern me and I never bother with nonsense."[10]

Several months later, however, he complained bitterly that young people had let themselves be misled by the new calls to action. "If you knew what damage Heidenstam has done! That public enemy!"[11] A few indirect gibes aimed at Heidenstam and Levertin appear in *In the Outer Skerries*. For example, Strindberg notes that Borg's father had said that what the younger generation of writers was turning out was completely worthless; it was just "the distilled thoughts of the older generation that they adopt as their own and try to peddle to the world in a grand manner. . . . All youthful attacks on the established order were hysterical expres-

sions of the inability of the weak to bear pressure."[12] When Strindberg
submitted the novel to K. O. Bonnier in early June, 1890, he said it was
"the promised new whopper of a book in the new Renaissance style," and
indicated that it was a continuation of the trend that had begun with his
"The Battle of the Brains," rather than "with Heidenstam's works of
prophecy, which are apocryphal."

Obviously, Strindberg's intention was to strike a blow in alliance
with Ola Hansson for naturalism on a grand scale based on Nietzscheanism, but a chasm that had developed between the two men began to widen.
This became apparent in 1891, when Hansson published *Materialism in
Belles-Lettres (Materialism i skönlitteraturen)*. Hansson disassociated himself from naturalism's materialistic world view and, while praising Strindberg, regretted that he was trapped in a materialistic attitude toward his
own work—thinking belles-lettres a useless game and believing his true
calling to be that of journalist and scientist.

In a letter sent from Sweden to Ola Hansson in Germany on
October 23, 1891, Strindberg finds this anti-materialism strange, but in any
case he is indifferent to all explanations of the world and maintains his old
conviction that "the universe is a colossal Bosh." Inasmuch as the theosophists, "who are rife here at home," preach spiritual and material unity,
it seems to him that materialism and spiritualism coincide: "Why then
the different names for the same thing?" The statement foreshadows the
monism Strindberg would soon adopt. But his aversion to taking a definite
side in the literary battle indicates that he was perplexed about the route
he should take. "I do not know what I am or snould be called. I shall
just allow my energies to spend themselves, and keep pace with my own
genius. It will be fascinating to see where your new views lead you, and
where we are going in general."

The Pre-Inferno-Crisis Dramas

The same perplexity marks Strindberg's work during the early
1890's. Right after finishing *In the Outer Skerries*, he began *The Keys of
Heaven (Himmelrikets nycklar)*, a drama in verse and prose in the fairy-
tale style of *Lucky Per's Travels*. Evidently Heidenstam's exhortation to
write something "in a manner not commonplace" had its effect.

The play, which Strindberg intended to be a survey of his personal destiny and spiritual development during the 1880's, is an incomplete work. A smith, whose three small children have died of plague (Strindberg had recently lost his three children when Siri was awarded custody in the divorce), is visited by Saint Peter who has carelessly lost the key to the gates of Heaven and requests the smith to make a new one. When the smith asks for directions to the gates in order to make an impression of the lock, Saint Peter remarks only that the path to Heaven is a narrow one. Accompanied by a doctor, the smith goes off on a vain search for the gates. Finally, the doctor advises him to build a heaven of his own on earth. One has the impression that the solution was tacked on in order to give the play a happy ending, because the smith, like Lucky Per, is a fault-finder who finds hell instead of heaven everywhere he goes.

The poetic merit of the play is confined to the beautiful opening scene in which the smith stands before the empty beds of his children and remembers how sweet life was when they were alive. In a letter to Mörner on October 28, 1891, Strindberg wrote, "My children are currently my *idée fixe* and for them I am writing my fairy-tale play to send to [the director of the Royal Opera] Nordqvist."[13] But the eloquent opening scene was not followed up. Instead, we are confronted by a procession of characters from story and legend: Don Quixote, Tom Thumb, Cinderella, the Swedish "Old Man of Ho Mountain," and others. Even when it is possible to understand the satirical allusions, they seem rather pointless. A typical Strindberg spokesman is Don Quixote, now taunted just as much for his skepticism as he once was for his idealism—an obvious reference to Strindberg's own situation, for Young Sweden, which had once found him too romantic, now found his naturalism too outmoded. Another allusion to the contemporary literary scene is contained in Sancho Panza's conceited expectation that Quixote may one day have to saddle his servant's horse. The original manuscript contains a speech in which Don Quixote says that Sancho stole oats from him and foolishly believes that he can trick his master. This is Strindberg rebuking his inferiors for the presumptuousness of *Pepita's Wedding*.

At the same time, we see the reflection of Strindberg's tormented reaction to his isolation. The giant "Old Man of Ho Mountain" kills "the lowly" (here dwarfs and midgets) because they try to undermine his lofty position, but afterwards he finds it dreary "to sit here and be big, / since no one wants to stay with the giant." And when the smith is urged by Saint Peter to crawl to the Cross, the smith says that "no one suffers more than he who believes in nothing, yet he is furthest from the Cross."[14] This is only one of several passages which foreshadow the *To Damascus* trilogy.

In the spring and summer of 1892 Strindberg wrote a group of six long one-act plays, in the style of the Théâtre Libre, for a proposed experimental theatre (which never materialized) in the town of Djursholm, just north of Stockholm. These plays are varied in quality.

Debit and Credit (Debit och Kredit) glorifies a superman of a more vulgar stamp than Strindberg's previous ones. Axel, an explorer, returns home from an African safari to find a group of relatives and acquaintances waiting to collect what he owes them. The situation is reminiscent of Strindberg's own return in 1889 after six years of exile, when he found people waiting to share in the world renown he had earned. Axel settles with his creditors on his own terms, rather ruthlessly, and then skips out, leaving a former associate awed at his daring: "Imagine such a man—being able to unravel his financial embarrassments like that!"[15]

The First Warning (Första varningen), originally titled *The First Tooth (Första tanden)*, is based on an episode in *A Madman's Defense* in which the narrator is delighted when his wife breaks a front tooth since this will make her less attractive to men. The theme is that a couple's jealousy and anxiety about losing each other are indispensable stimulants for love in a marriage. The same theme was executed more successfully in *Playing With Fire (Leka med elden)*. Knut, a painter, stifles a growing infatuation between his wife and his friend and houseguest Axel with a clever piece of strategy: he declares calmly and even jovially that he is prepared to give her up if she will marry his rival. Axel, who discovers quickly that "there's something rotting here under the floor boards!" has some of Strindberg's characteristics and the same marital background. Having just undergone a divorce, he has no intention of allowing himself to be reharnessed. When Kerstin, the young wife, declares to Axel that she and her husband have "never had any serious arguments," it startles him:

> AXEL: Now you're being too candid, Mrs. Lenz!
> KERSTIN: Why, what did I say?
> AXEL: You have revealed that you have never loved your husband![16]

For Strindberg, jealousy, quarreling, and frenetic passion were inseparable from love.

After the divorce, Strindberg was not in the mood for writing comedy; his three other plays before the Inferno Crisis are tragic and point directly to his own situation. Two of them, *Facing Death (Inför döden)* and *Mother Love (Moderskärlek)*, are based on the same idea: the father unselfishly loves his children, and the mother alienates them from him and slanders him. From Strindberg's letters we learn of his fear that his children's upbringing was being neglected and that their mother was trying to "uproot" their memory of him.

Facing Death has a raw dramatic power reminiscent of Tolstoy. The model for the central character was a Lear-like figure Strindberg saw in the Swiss pension where he wrote the first *Married* collection. In the play a father, in order to provide money for his three ungrateful daughters, burns down his villa so that they can collect the fire insurance. Although the mother is dead and not actually part of the action, we learn that she made the daughters detest their father by maligning him to them. In *Mother Love,* on the other hand, the father is the offstage character. Because of the mother's vulgar egoism, he is prevented from taking an interest in his daughter and assisting her in her theatrical career.

After having indirectly touched upon his personal life in these two plays, Strindberg transported his entire divorce proceedings to the stage in *The Bond.* He accomplished this with such masterliness that outside Sweden, where people are less concerned by the unreasonableness of his accusations against his wife, *The Bond* is often regarded as the best of his naturalistic dramas. It has also been a model for plays based on judicial proceedings—Galsworthy's *Justice,* for example. By presenting the story as an apparently random series of transactions in a court session during which a divorce proceeding between a baron and baroness is only one of several cases brought up, Strindberg was to a certain extent putting into effect his old thesis that court records might be the most appropriate form for naturalistic literature, and that an author ought to confine his role to that of a reporter.

Strindberg was embittered by the district court decision giving Siri custody of the children. He believed not only that she had acted treacherously, but that she had actually perjured herself. These accusations are inevitably mirrored in the play, where the wife is made to appear to be at blame, and the husband, a noble martyr. But the fictional outcome is different from real life. In the play, the judge rules that the child be taken from both parents and entrusted to an uneducated peasant couple. Although the Baron is horrified, this was the very verdict Strindberg urged in his own case, since he thought it preferable to having the children remain with their mother.

The misogyny in *The Bond* is not as frenetic and unrelieved as in the marital dramas of the 1880's. Both parents are haunted by the knowledge that the blows they inflict on one another ultimately strike their child, who is "the memory of our most beautiful moments, the bond that unites our souls, the place where we shall always meet, whether we want to or not."[17] Even after the judge grants the separation, they cannot be parted completely. And in the final scene the Baron asks his wife if she really knows with whom they both struggled. "You call him God, but I call him nature! And that tyrant incited us to hate each other, just as he incites people to love. And now we're doomed to slash each other so long as there's a spark of life in us."[18] The Baroness says she wants to hide from the world to "scream myself tired against God who put this devilish love in the world to torment mankind."[19]

Strindberg identified with the Baron's atheistic position. Nature is the force that governs the couple's will and compels them to persecute each other as irresistibly as other people are driven to love each other. But this omnipotent nature is distinguished only in name from the "Powers" that compel people to torture each other mercilessly and unceasingly. Something of the atmosphere of *The Dance of Death* (*Dödsdansen*) already hovers over *The Bond*.

The Departure for Germany

By 1892, when Strindberg wrote his six one-act plays, the "renaissance" prophesied by Heidenstam had begun in Swedish literature. A flock of poetic, non-realistic works were already available in bookstores: Selma Lagerlöf's *Gösta Berling's Saga* (1891), Gustaf Fröding's *Guitar and Concertina* (*Guitarr och dragharmonika*—1891), Oscar Levertin's *Legends and Songs* (*Legender och visor*—1891), Per Hallström's *Lyrics and Fantasies* (*Lyrik och fantasier*)—1891), and Heidenstam's *Hans Alienus* (1892). Under the circumstances it was hopeless to win a hearing for naturalistic dramas that followed the recipes of the 1880's. None of Strindberg's latest plays were performed, and when they were published, they attracted little attention. He had lost his position in the vanguard about which he had been so anxious. He clung stubbornly to a dramatic formula whose possibilities he had exhausted and to an aesthetic program in which he only half-believed. His imagination, moreover, was completely dominated by his marriage problems. He could write about nothing else, because everything seemed meaningless to him. At the same time, he was aware that these problems were making him sterile: "When shall I write well again? My desire to produce has been diminishing since I lost my children and home and live in *misère!*"[20]

It was at this time that he began toying with the idea of writing in German. Of course, some of his works had long appeared in German translation, and he had contributed to German and Austrian newspapers, but only recently had German critics begun to take notice of him. Naturalism, which appeared late in Germany, finally arrived with Hauptmann and Arno Holz, and *The Father* was first presented at the Freie Bühne on October 12, 1890. Strindberg admitted to Heidenstam as early as the fall of 1889 that conditions in Sweden tended to favor a return to idealism, but were "hopeless abroad, since we Scandinavian naturalists are greeted as renaissance [i.e., avant-garde] writers in Germany." Furthermore, Ola Hansson, who had moved permanently to Germany in 1889, had been conducting an enthusiastic publicity campaign for Strindberg in newspaper articles and never tired of pointing out to Strindberg that Germany was El Dorado for Swedish writers.

For a long time Strindberg was incredulous. "Isn't Germany a kind of inferior Sweden?" he asked Ola Hansson in a letter on November 20, 1890.[21] "They have a Sudermann who is infected with hotel-porter liberalism, a Hauptmann who interprets the abc's of Darwinism, but they spurn Ibsen (and Strindberg). I looked over several magazines and reviews. Why, they're written by store clerks!" Ola Hansson alone could not convince him of Germany's advantages and of the sympathy he would encounter there.

Meanwhile, however, Strindberg found the Sweden of the 1890's increasingly intolerable because "reaction has taken over everywhere, so that once again we have romanticism, estheticism, idealism—everything we once purged ourselves of."[22] His desperate financial difficulties and his isolation following the divorce also hastened his decision to leave, if only to "preserve my psychic life, for I could never acquire any prominence in Germany."[23] Finally, in September, 1892, he left for Berlin. Actually, it was Strindberg's good fortune that he never achieved prominence as a

German literary figure. He thereby avoided the tragic fate of Ola Hansson, who gradually lost contact with the Swedish language, temperament, and public and, after a short period of fame in Germany, was forgotten both there and at home.

Strindberg soon turned all his attention to research in natural science, and although he was destined never to win the international renown he hoped for in this area, it led him into his Inferno Crisis which, in spite of all the suffering it caused him, brought about a rebirth of his poetic powers. By the time he returned to Sweden in 1896, he seemed to be taking some of the same paths taken by the "renaissance" writers of the 1890's, but he was following a different drummer: for him it was like a return to the romanticism of his youth. With some justification he called the play *Gustav Vasa* (1899) a sequel to *Master Olof*. Moreover, he retained his old aversion to "the Byronic snob school." When he continued his attacks against the literary leaders of the 1890's in the first decade of the twentieth century (e.g., in *Talks to the Swedish Nation*—1910), they were delayed retaliations for the injustices he felt he had suffered because of "the Pepita outrage," which had caused his writing to stagnate and forced him into exile in Germany.

Notes to Chapter Thirteen

1. In *Edda,* 1936, p. 373, Harald Elovson assumed that Strindberg was inspired here by Valdemar Vedel's attack (in answer to Erik Skram) against naturalism's demand for objectivity, published in *Ny Jord* in the fall of 1888. Since Heidenstam maintained numerous times in his letters to Strindberg that his attacks against dogmatic naturalism in "Renaissance" were aimed primarily at Erik Skram, Elovson's assumption seems reasonable.

2. *SS:*XVII, p. 289.

3. *Ibid.,* p. 287.

4. *Brev,* VII, p. 391.

5. *Cf.* Elovson, p. 338. He believes that Heidenstam's and Levertin's programmatic writings derived inspiration from this Strindberg essay. *Cf.,* too, Hugo Kamras's *Den unge Heidenstam* (1942), pp. 386-87.

6. *Brev,* VII, p. 382.

7. *Ibid.,* p. 391.

8. Concerning the dating of this letter, *see* Örjan Lindberger in *Svensk litteraturtidskrift* (1940), p. 136 n. [and *Brev,* p. 377 n.—Translator]

9. With the help of the feminist writer Ellen Key.

10. *Brev,* VIII, p. 38.

11. *Ibid.,* p. 106.

12. *SS:*XXIV, pp. 48-49. *Cf.* Olle Holmberg, *Gud som haver* (1939), pp. 167-68.

13. *Brev,* VIII, p. 364. As we have seen, the same sense of loss was later handled more factually in "The Silver Marsh."

14. *SS:*XXV, p. 206.

15. *Ibid.,* p. 262.

16. *Ibid.,* pp. 430-31.

17. *Ibid.,* pp. 323-24.

18. *Ibid.,* p. 340.

19. *Ibid.,* pp. 341-42.

20. *Brev,* VIII, p. 157.

21. *Ibid.,* p. 128.

22. *Brev,* IX, p. 54.

23. *Ibid.,* p. 65.

PART TWO

After The Conversion

Chapter Fourteen

THE INFERNO:
PRELUDE (1892-94) AND CRISIS (1894-96)[1]

The spiritual conversions[2] among writers and intellectuals at the turn of the century were motivated by a general reversing of intellectual currents. Materialism provoked a counterthrust of idealism; interest in natural science was replaced by an enthusiasm for hypnotism and the power of suggestion, then occultism and magic. The decadents encouraged refined forms of superstition. There were Black Masses, experiments with witchcraft, and exorcisms; and spiritualism and theosophy were at flood tide.

Similar symptoms had appeared at the end of the Enlightenment, and it was believed that the same causes lay behind the newest trends. Among the converts who supported this view was Huysmans, who declared in *Là-Bas* that these phenomena recur every century after positivism and materialism reach their peaks, and that an era similar to that of Cagliostro, Saint-Germain, and the Rosicrucians a century earlier was being repeated once again. In Scandinavia, the Catholic decadent Johannes Jørgensen made similar observations. More often than not, these psychic crises culminated in monastery sojourns and conversions to Catholicism.

Even before leaving Sweden for Berlin in 1892, Strindberg had been fascinated by hypnotism and the power of suggestion and had expressed sympathy with the decadent movement and with Catholicism. During his Inferno period in Paris, many of his friends had converted to Catholicism and at the very end of the Crisis, in the spring of 1897, he too was inclined to believe that his path would lead eventually to a monastery. It was then that he read Jørgensen's description of the monastery of Beuron in *Rejsebogen*. The following fall he read Huysmans's account of his conversion, *En Route* (1895), and on September 18, 1897, observed in his "Occult Diary" ("Ockulta dagbok"),[3] the notebook he kept during and

291

after the Inferno: "It is striking how his development progresses like mine. From magic and Satanism to Catholicism."

Strindberg, however, never entered a monastery, and his enthusiasm for Catholicism was transitory. As a result, his prospective brethren in the faith regarded him as a convert who stopped half-way; Jørgensen emphasized this superciliously by contrasting Strindberg with Huysmans. On the other hand, Strindberg's colleagues from the 1880's thought he was a miserable renegade. Oscar Levertin, in a review of *Legends* *(Legender*—1898), the sequel to *Inferno,* used a Norse mythological image to describe Strindberg: Loki, the ruthless mischief-maker, with whom Strindberg as a blaspheming fault finder had identified himself in the poem "Loki's Blasphemies" in 1883. Levertin complained that "Loki has come home an Indian fakir."

An examination of Strindberg's personality and environment during this period reveals that the Inferno Crisis developed in a peculiar manner. In later years, when his contemporaries were unable to recognize its importance, he became embittered, for he had dreamed of doing penance for the suffering that he had caused and of being reconciled with his fellow human beings. Instead, he developed an icy contempt for all mankind. The tender compassion for the guilt-burdened and misfortune-struck family of man in *A Dream Play* (1901) was thus followed by the caustic misanthropy of *Black Banners* (1904) and the Chamber Plays (1907).

Strindberg had gone to Berlin in September, 1892, with the hope of building a new future for himself as a writer in the German language, but the attempt was doomed. He was too proud and inflexible to follow the prevailing literary fashions and found himself unproductive in a foreign milieu. He joined the company of young writers and artists at a lively tavern he nicknamed Zum Schwarzen Ferkel, on the corner of Unter den Linden and Neue Wilhelmstrasse; there, according to Strindberg, one felt ready to "purge oneself of the naturalistic leaven": "Everyone was eager to be the first to hit upon a new formula for the art and literature of the forthcoming era."[4] But he was unable to come up with any new ideas and received none from his comrades.

Strindberg's second marriage in May, 1893, to a young Austrian journalist, Frida Uhl, ought to have facilitated his acclimatization, but her well-meaning attempts to advance his international reputation embarrassed him and contributed to the fact that this time his marital journey from Paradise to Gehenna was accomplished in record time: the couple's last meeting was in November, 1894.

After struggling in vain to write—it appears that he was working on a sequel to *In the Outer Skerries*—Strindberg began to devote more and more time to the amateur experiments in natural science he had started during his last years in Sweden, and these, too, drew him toward occultism. The title page of *Antibarbus* (1893/94, 1906), the collection of writings on these experiments, has a statement of the author's intention to prove Darwin's and Ernst Haeckel's monistic theory of "the completeness and oneness of nature" by investigating the characteristics of the elements. But several pages later Strindberg maintained that he was an alchemist and cited Albertus Magnus, Paracelsus, and their German followers. Gradually, he became convinced that alchemy was flourishing anew in Paris and entered into correspondence with French alchemists. In the fall of 1894 he realized his long-cherished plans to return to Paris. Frida accompanied him but left him for good soon afterward.

Landquist[5] has pointed out the significance that Strindberg's utter poverty had on his religious crisis. Without the assistance of the Hanssons, who raised money on his behalf, he could never have left Sweden; and in Germany, Austria, and France he had no income of his own other than the small sums he received from royalties for his plays performed abroad, for newspaper essays and for an occasional translation. While in Austria he was forced to accept food from his wife's relatives; in Paris his only means of sustenance were charitable contributions he got from the Swedish publisher and theosophist Torsten Hedlund (1855-1935), whom he had never met personally and with whom he eventually disagreed and broke off all correspondence. He was also forced to accept charity from such humiliating sources as appeals made by Scandinavian friends in Paris newspapers. The Norwegian writer Knut Hamsun's letters give a vivid picture of how difficult it was to talk to Strindberg and get him to accept the contributions, because he constantly suspected people were plotting against him. Passages in *Inferno* reveal his condition: when passing a boulevard café he sees a stranger who perhaps donated money for his benefit and whose eyes seem to accuse him of being "a beggar who had no right to go to cafés. A beggar! That's the right word. It kept ringing in my ears and brought a burning flush to my cheeks—the flush of shame, humiliation, and rage!"[6]

Poverty and the fear that people might try to limit his freedom of action isolated Strindberg from the Scandinavian circles within which he had first found his friends. Gradually, because of his persecution mania, he alienated the few people who still sought to maintain contact with him. When he heard strange noises in the adjoining rooms at his hotel, he relapsed into his old delusion from the *Married* campaign—that he was being persecuted by a league of Scandinavian women[7]—and at the same time he suspected that his former friends at the Ferkel tavern in Berlin were using telepathy to try to destroy him with electrical currents. In his solitude he felt unprotected against all these attacks: *"Vae soli!* Woe to the solitary one, a sparrow on a roof! Never had the wretchedness of my existence been worse, and I cried like an abandoned child who was afraid of the dark."[8]

Unproductivity, poverty, and loneliness were not new to Strindberg. Except for brief periods, they had tormented him since his divorce from Siri in 1891, but they still alternated, as always, with dreams of grandeur. Sometimes he thought he was on the threshold of world renown as a dramatist; other times he fancied that his method of producing iodine had not only rocked the foundations of the scientific world, but had also prompted dazzling offers from iodine manufacturers.

More fateful, however, for his spiritual equilibrium were the successes he imagined he would have as an alchemist—the chemical production of gold would of course upset the economy of the entire world, and all the international princes of finance would either have to pool their resources in order to buy his formula or have him put out of the way. His associations with Parisian occultists convinced him that he possessed magical powers and was capable of destroying his enemies, but unfortunately, his evil thoughts could also harm those closest to him. Even though he was often literally without bread to eat or a roof over his head and was forced to accept help wherever it was offered, he was confident that he was capable of changing the course of the world. It was no wonder that the Powers had to use all their cunning to wrest the palm of victory from his hand, and that the Eternal One answered his challenge with a clap of thunder. He interpreted all of fate's blows as punishment for his pride;

time after time he preached the necessity of humility, but he could not stifle his arrogant rebellious spirit. The picture of Strindberg as a rather threadbare Titan is a fitting one, but even more appropriate is the image Strindberg himself chose—Jacob wrestling with God.

In the beginning of *Inferno* (describing his first days in Paris), Strindberg states that over a period of years he had "noticed how the unseen Powers left the world to its fate and showed no interest in it" and had become an atheist. This concept of Powers leaving the world to its fate was Strindberg's conclusion toward the end of the Inferno Crisis, but he was not an atheist when he arrived in Paris. Because both *Inferno* and *Legends* were intended as religiously edifying documents, Strindberg tended to exaggerate his earlier spiritual blindness and failure to understand the implications of the Powers when they first began to haunt him with their portents.[9]

While staying with Frida Uhl's relatives in Austria during the summer of 1894 Strindberg found himself moving toward a religious outlook. He wrote to Leopold Littmansson, his long-time friend from the Red Room days, that he felt "the Lord's hand" upon him, but that although he wanted to believe that a divinity was tormenting him only to redeem him in his dying hour, he could not do so. He was still dominated by the Nietzschean hatred of Christianity that he had expressed in *In the Outer Skerries*. It was at this time that a longing emerged that he was never to lose, but never to satisfy: to retreat from the struggle and filth of earthly life into a non-denominational cloister.

The physical and mental sufferings Strindberg endured in Paris led him at first to imagine that his enemies were responsible; they were persecuting him. Although he could never free himself completely from this delusion, he soon began to formulate the idea that supernatural forces were intruding into his life, "the Powers," as he later came to call them in accordance with French occultist terminology. He first conceived of them as completely malign and invidious and not until he studied Swedenborg in Lund in 1896-97 did he transform them into "chastising spirits" whose purpose it was to show him the right path by punishment and trials. (Somewhat earlier he had interpreted Swedenborg's descriptions of Hell as really referring to earthly life, in which we are purified for a higher existence.[10])

In conjunction with this new belief in the Powers, Strindberg undertook a profound self-examination, particularly of his past, and en-

gaged in a struggle that is expressed most movingly in the second part of
Legends—the essay fragment "Jacob Wrestles" ("Jakob brottas"). After
always having been an accuser, he now assumed the role of penitent and
resolved to walk morally purified out of the Crisis.

Strindberg's progress toward spiritual conversion was thus a
gradual one, and he himself was unable to discern how his Crisis would be
resolved. At the conclusion of "Jacob Wrestles" he still awaits—and at
the same time fears—the great miracle that will make him a believer. At
the end of his journey to Canossa he was still questioning and searching
for faith: he returned to Paris from Sweden in the fall of 1897 in order to
convert to Catholicism, but discovered that this was not the answer. As he
ended his stay there, he wrote to Axel Herrlin (March 10, 1898): "My
Crisis, almost seven months long, has not really brought me closer to wisdom, except on several points. Thus, I know what is expected of me ethically, but the expectations seem gradually to increase." He was unable to:

> proceed beyond a moderately warm relationship with the Hereafter
> [*Jenseits*], which should not be approached too intimately, for one is
> punished in that direction with religious fanaticism and led astray. . . .
> My former fatalism has thus been translated into providentialism, and I
> realize completely that I have nothing and can do nothing by myself. But
> I shall never arrive at total humility, for my conscience would not permit
> such self-destruction.

During his later years, when he leaned toward syncretism, Strindberg used to characterize his religion as nondenominational Christianity.
He attempted in some of his *Blue Book* (1908-12) observations to simplify
his religious theories for popular consumption and to harmonize certain
aspects of them with the dogmas of the Swedish Lutheran State Church.

At the end of the Inferno Crisis, however, the religion he professed had more affinity with the Old Testament than with the New. It was
a religion with its own dogmas and with an ethic that is often more Bud-
dhist than Christian. He realized that he had failed in his attempt to draw
near to Christ in "Jacob Wrestles." In a letter to Herrlin on January 31,
1898, he said that for him "the intimacy of *The Imitation of Christ*"—for
a time in Paris he was deeply affected by Kempis's work—"was followed
by damnation and a relapse into hatred." He often found himself returning to an idea expressed by Dr. Anders Eliasson—the doctor in Ystad,
Sweden, to whom he returned for medical advice and attention during the
Inferno—"that religion is occultism and [should be] forbidden, for as

soon as one begins to inquire into the secrets of faith—and of course one has the right to know what to believe—one is afflicted with anguish and damnation and approaches madness."

Even if this statement does not express entirely what Strindberg meant, it is obvious that he did not feel that he had a personal relationship with God. For him, the Eternal One was an imperious master who made harsh demands and chastised man if he did not yield to Him. Christ Himself could be as formidable as an angry Thor: Strindberg is reminded (in the essay "In the Cemetery"—"På kyrkogården"—1896) of a Roman legend in which Christ had "an incomparably handsome outward appearance, but in a moment of wrath His ugliness was frightful, bestial."[11] At the same time, however, Strindberg believed that God preferred a haughty disposition to a completely submissive one: "If I were master, I would hate the rebellious man, but I could not deny him greater respect than the obedient one."[12] In *Inferno*, Strindberg confesses to have "sinned out of arrogance, *hubris,* the one vice the gods do not forgive."[13] But he is also aware that he could not live if his self-esteem were shattered. Among the notes for the play *Gustav Vasa* (1899) is a characteristic observation: "If we were created by God, in God's image, then surely pride is a legacy reminding us of our high origin. And so, it cannot very well be a crime."

"Never quarrel with God!" says the Mother to the Officer in *A Dream Play.* This was also Strindberg's firm resolve, but time after time he caught himself breaking it. Both during and after the Inferno Crisis he was unable to achieve "total humility"; he could not destroy his ego in order to be one with God. Although he had a profound longing to be conquered and to atone, a longing that often emerged in a moving way, he always retained a measure of Promethean defiance.

His consciousness of guilt was genuine; he regretted his past, especially his actions involving religion and morality. During the first years after the Crisis, he attempted to make amends for the injustices he had committed and to reestablish broken friendships, but new conflicts would erupt to frustrate his efforts, and almost immediately he would exchange his penitent's mantle for the cloak of the accuser. Then, because he considered himself summoned to proclaim divine judgment, he was even more merciless than before.

His penitence was also complicated by his belief—inspired by Swedenborg—that vices were punishments imposed upon men for more serious sins. He felt that he was doomed to be ungrateful, "which I detest most of all vices." Every effort to improve himself only engendered new frailties: his celibacy produced unhealthy dreams, his attempt to think well of his fellow man caused him to be deceived, and when through self-denial he achieved inner calm, he became self-satisfied: "I have done penance, I have made amends, but no sooner do I begin resoling my soul than I must add another patch. If I put on new heels, the uppers split."[14]

But if this new religious outlook made life painful for him, it also gave him the anchorage he felt he lacked before. In *The Son of a Servant,* he had said that "he remained like the mistletoe that cannot grow unless carried upward by a tree; he was a climbing plant who had to seek support"[15]; and his letters indicate that he constantly sought advice—and distrusted all advisers. Now, the Powers, with the Eternal One as overlord, became a superior court for him and when other "signs" deceived him, he would "throw open the Bible at random" and interpret the found passage as an answer to his question.

Even during the preliminary stage of the Crisis, Strindberg's letters reveal that he had "relapsed into superstition," and he says the same thing in *Inferno.* For the rest of his life he would continue to wander in the world of revelations and miracles. The most casual everyday occurrence was a message from a higher world, a warning or an exhortation. Everything that happened seemed to have been "staged" for his benefit—and naturally also for the benefit of his fellow men if they were perceptive enough to notice it. This feeling that he was communicating with the transcendental not only sustained him when his depression was most severe, it renewed his faith in life and gave new dimensions to his art.

Believing as he now did in a Providence that intervened everywhere, and in Powers, omens, and revelations, Strindberg was no longer scornful toward "idealists." In fact, he became an idealist himself and admitted, as he wrote later in the novel *Black Banners* (1904/07), that Plato was right "when he considered our ideas about objects to be the true, genuine things, and the objects themselves only schematic shadows, subjective conceptions of the originals."[16] Furthermore, he resorted to the extreme idealism of his old teacher Schopenhauer and declared that matter was devoid of reality.[17] The world exists only in our imagination and is

therefore an illusion, a dream—"Reality Is Only an Illusion"
("Verkligheten är bara illusioner") is the title of an essay in *A Blue Book:*

> It is incomprehensible that we human beings can believe that matter or
> reality is the only actuality. We are constantly thwarted in our grasping
> for reality—it slips through our fingers, disintegrates, disappears—and
> despite this we still grasp for it. . . .
>   Reality is only an illusion; illusions are reality.[18]

Like Schopenhauer, Strindberg found it comforting to believe that this
"world of illusions" was only a brief, passing dream from which death one
day would liberate us. "Do you know what makes life endurable for me?"
he asks in *Legends:*

> I sometimes imagine that it is only a half-reality, a bad dream inflicted
> upon us as punishment. In the moment of death you wake up to the
> reality, that is, you become aware that the other was only a dream, and
> all the evil you have done was merely a dream.[19]

What is suggested here as a comforting fantasy gradually became
the essential truth for Strindberg. For the author of *A Dream Play* and the
Chamber Plays, dream and reality converge. Following Schopenhauer's
example, Strindberg used Indian mythology to express the idea: earthly
existence is the original sin; resignation and compassion are the highest,
indeed, the only virtues.

Man is doomed to suffer on earth not only for his own sins but for
those of others—this departure from the orthodox doctrine of atonement
came from Strindberg's refusal to believe that Christ suffered for mankind, "for if He had, our sufferings would have been abated. But they
have not been; they are just as intensive."[20] Instead, Strindberg proclaimed that each of us can obliterate another's guilt by voluntary suffering, an idea he said[21] he derived from "the theosophists."

This infusion of neo-Platonic mysticism, mediated by Schopenhauer and theosophy, was a moderating influence on the harsh doctrine of
divine retribution in Strindberg's Inferno theology. Pessimistic idealism
erected a bridge to eternity by conceiving of this world as a transitory
dream.[22] In *Legends,* Strindberg says that for several years he had been taking notes on all his dreams and had arrived at the conviction that they possessed a kind of reality, as do fancies and imaginings, and that we are all
spiritual somnambulists. "And the poet's fantasies, which spiritually impoverished souls despise so, are realities."[23] Following the Inferno Crisis,

Strindberg's writings again became richly imaginative after many years of barrenness because he was certain that reality was nothing more than dreams and fictions and that poetry, to quote from *A Dream Play,* was "more than reality," more real than the dream—"waking dreams."

Contemporary critics speculated a great deal about what Strindberg had lost because of the Inferno Crisis. It was true that he would never regain the simple, sparkling joy of storytelling that characterized *The Red Room,* the first volume of *Married,* and *The People of Hemsö.* His palette had lost its enchanting water-color hues and had become darker. When he tried to use his earlier color scale—as in the *Fairhaven* (1898, 1902/03) stories—the effect was a shade too bright. But certain stylistic changes had been evident in his work even before the Crisis. For the most part, the warm appeal of the skerries landscape in *The People of Hemsö* (1887) is absent in *In the Outer Skerries* (1890), and the fifth "somnambulist night," published separately in 1890, five years after the earliest "nights," showed that Strindberg had lost contact with the Stockholm of his youth. Gone, too, was the playful irony.

Nevertheless, it is easier to see what he gained than what he lost because of the Crisis. For example, the last works before his trip abroad in 1892 were dominated entirely by the theme of marital misfortune. After the Inferno this theme was put in different perspective and became a symbol for the imperfection of earthly life and the compulsion human beings have to torment one another throughout their short existences. And although he might allow characters from his earlier works to reappear— such as the characters of *The Red Room* (1879) who appear again in *The Gothic Rooms* (1904) and *Black Banners* (1904/1907)—they were never treated in the same way. The figures have a mystical aura about them and the events have deeper implications. In the poems in *Word-Play and Minor Art* (1902-04/1905), nature scenes have secret meanings. Inanimate things —a deserted room, its furniture, and objects—become living beings in *Black Banners, Easter* (1900/1901), and the novel *Alone (Ensam—*1903), where the settings are as intimately bound up with the lives of the people inhabiting them as is the strongly symbolic interior in *The Dance of Death* (1900/1901).

In all this one can trace the after-effects of the Inferno Crisis. Strindberg might no longer be inclined as he was during the Crisis itself to detect an omen in every bottle cork or scrap of paper in the street, but he had developed a special sensitivity for trivia, and his imagination elaborated on them further. The short story "A Half-Sheet of Paper" ("Ett halvt ark papper") in the collection *Fairy-Tales (Sagor*—1903) tells how the story of a marriage cut short by tragedy can be read in the names and numbers written on a yellowing piece of paper near the telephone; and fascinating things emerge from the rubbish pile of half-burned household furniture in the play *The Burned House* (1907).

In a letter to Geijerstam about *Crime and Crime (Brott och brott)*, Strindberg said that the real "hero, the plot-manipulator in the play, is the Unseen One"; the same could be said of most of his plays after the Inferno, the Eternal One and the Powers are not listed in the cast of characters, but they govern the course of the action. Even when the heroes rebel and believe themselves free, a higher hand holds the strings. (This is the basic theme of the essay "The Mysticism of World History"—"Världshistoriens mystik"—1903, which Strindberg wrote as an explanation of his later historical plays.)

It was obvious that Strindberg was no longer content simply to imitate reality, for his world now lay outside its boundaries, even though it might appear as if he were continuing to follow the naturalistic approach. He preferred to deal with reality at lower levels of consciousness—dreams, daydreams, and ambiguous moods. Even when he tried to depict commonplace reality, he sketched it in jagged contours and violent colors. *Black Banners* and the Chamber Plays are peopled with characters who lack skin and flesh and consist only of entrails and nerves; characters whose faces are distorted into grimaces, and whose words explode. This is how Strindberg became a pioneer of literary "expressionism," never suspecting—as far as we know—that the term existed. "Expressionism" may often seem to be in glaring contrast to the tender "dream" atmospheres, but both moods proceed from Strindberg's conception of the world as "an illusive image."

The element in Strindberg's style least affected by the Inferno was his art of coming straight to the point, of expressing his intention without circumlocutions or ornamentation; here, he was still the unexcelled master. But his register had expanded. He could now stylize his dialogue, either making it short and laconic, or letting it swell out in long, eloquent passages. What probably seems newest is his ability to give dialogue a singing tone that glides effortlessly into free verse.

For the younger generation of Swedish writers, Strindberg's work after the Inferno was more important than his earlier work, and it was at this time that he became a model abroad for modernistic trends, although this was not a role he aspired to: he wanted to be recognized as a religious reviver and renewer. He was aware that through his relentless diatribes against his critics and enemies he was also alienating people who otherwise shared his opinions, but this only drove him to preach his ideas with greater fervor. He had never cultivated the ability to cater to people's feelings and was no more able to be an opportunist now than he had been before.

Notes to Chapter Fourteen

1. Strindberg suffered five psychotic breakdowns during his Inferno
    Crisis: the first in late summer of 1894, the second at the end of
    1894 and the beginning of 1895, the third at the end of 1895
    and the beginning of 1896, the fourth in the summer of 1896, and
    the fifth in November, 1896. *See* "A Biographical Sketch," p. ix.—
    Translator

2. The use of the term "conversion" to describe this particular phase in
    Strindberg's life is a matter of some controversy among critics.
    Generally it refers to Strindberg's change in outlook from atheism
    back to belief in a hereafter *(Jenseits)*.—Translator

3. Strindberg was long uncertain about publishing this highly personal
    document. Selections from it did not appear in print until 1963.—
    Translator

4. *Samlade otryckta skrifter* (1919), II, p. 88.

5. *Aftenbladet,* May 16, 1936.

6. *SS:*XXVIII, p. 19.

7. *Ibid.,* p. 40.

8. *Ibid.,* p. 90.

9   Elsewhere *(Strindberg och makterna,* 1936), I have attempted to
    trace in detail the different phases of his thinking concerning the
    Powers.

10. Strindberg came to this conclusion by comparing the oppressive land-
    scape of an Alpine valley in Austria with Swedenborg's descrip-
    tions of Hell. Thus, Strindberg's concept that the earth is Hell did
    not originate with Swedenborg, as is often claimed. Strindberg
    wrote to Hedlund on October 31, 1896: "The world view I
    arrived at is closest to that of Pythagoras and adopted by Origen:
    We are in an Inferno for sins committed in a previous existence.
    Swedenborg's descriptions of the Inferno are—*without his intend-
    ing it*—obviously and precisely earthly life. Of this I am con-
    vinced."

    On the other hand, both the term and the idea are found in
    Strindberg's long-time favorite—Schopenhauer, who with similar
    references to Pythagoras and Origen advises man to consider this
    world as a place of penance, an institution for punishment, "a
    penal colony," in which one serves time for crimes committed in
    an earlier existence *(Parerga und Paralipomena,* 1851, II, par.

157). Again, in a letter in 1895, Strindberg, without reference to Swedenborg, mentioned life as a time of punishment and the earth as "a penal colony in which one serves time for crimes committed in an earlier existence." And in *The Son of a Servant* *(SS:*XVIII, p. 39), speaking of his first period at school, he says: "Life was a penal institution for crimes committed before one was born." *See also* Eklund, *Strindbergsstudie,* p. 291, where the above quoted passage from Schopenhauer is examined in detail.

When Strindberg presented the idea of the earth as a penal colony for the first time, in the essay "In the Cemetery" published in the journal *Vintergatan* in 1896, he also made a reference to pessimism (*SS:*XXVII, p. 668).

11. *SS:*XXVII, p. 667.
12. *SS:*XXVIII, p. 366.
13. *Ibid.,* p. 80.
14. *Ibid.,* p. 194.
15. *SS:*XVIII, p. 47.
16. *SS:*XLI, p. 185.
17. In an essay "A View Toward Space" ("En blick mot rymden"— translated from the April, 1896, issue of *L'Initiation)* he quotes from Schopenhauer's *Die Welt als Wille und Vorstellung* (1819) to support his view that the world is only a figment of the imagination. *Cf.* H. Taub, who in *Strindbergs Traumspiel* (1918) quite rightly emphasized the importance of this quotation.
18. *SS:*XLVIII, pp. 883-85.
19. *SS:*XXVIII, p. 316.
20. *Ibid.,* p. 393.
21. *SS:*XLVII, p. 703.
22. Eklund (*Strindbergsstudie,* pp. 287-303) has given a number of examples of Strindberg's dependence on Schopenhauer, whose significance for Strindberg's conception of metaphysics he considers greater than that of "any single author." He also points out that they were similar in character and had similar outlooks on life.
23. *SS:*XXVIII, p. 280.

Chapter Fifteen

THE CONFESSIONAL WRITINGS AND THE DRAMAS OF PENITENCE

When Strindberg returned to Sweden for a time in 1896 during the Inferno Crisis, he wrote to Hedlund in August that he felt a compulsion to "write a book about it all in order to liberate myself." Two weeks later he said he intended to write a "poem in prose" in a "grand, exalted tone" with the title *Inferno*. It was to treat the "same theme as *In the Outer Skerries*"—how an individual is crushed by isolation, but saves himself through "work without honor or gold, duty, family, and thus woman—the mother and the child! Resignation comes through the discovery that Providence gives a purpose to each and every person."[1]

Despite his mention of a "poem in prose," when he wrote *Inferno* the following spring in the southern Swedish university town of Lund, he took pains to emphasize that it was "not a novel with pretentions to style and literary structure."[2] And the sequel to *Inferno, Legends,* written the following fall, is less a novel than a series of rambling reflections about his stay in Lund. He began a "third part of *Inferno*," but the work stagnated and was published in fragmentary form under the title "Jacob Wrestles" as a separate section of *Legends.* In a postscript to "Jacob Wrestles," Strindberg explained that he made "an attempt to depict imaginatively the author's religious struggle," but had failed. Strindberg also "cut short" this effort because he had an overwhelming desire to write a purely fictional work. On January 19, 1898, he noted in his diary: "Caught the theatre craze again and planned *Robert le Diable.*"[3] The projected play became Part I of *To Damascus.* After its completion he wrote to Axel Herrlin that he was abandoning nearly all of his "scientific" research into alchemy, occultism, divination, and the secrets of the unseen world; the only exception would be speculative chemistry. "It appears I have regained the grace of being able to write for the theatre and have just finished

an important play. I am thankful that I was able to do it and so admit
that this is a gift of which one can be deprived if it is misused." After a
hiatus of seven years he once again committed himself totally to belles-
lettres, and during the next four years created the finest body of drama in
Swedish literature.

That Strindberg began his return to belles-lettres by dramatizing
his own Crisis was not due to a shortage of other, more objective subject
matter; the same letter to Herrlin mentions a plan to write a drama based
on materials from medieval Sweden. But his spiritual conversion and its
miracles so preoccupied his mind that as a theme it dominated not only
the *Damascus* cycle, but also *Advent, Crime and Crime,* and the first few
of his later historical plays. Not until the summer of 1899, when he returned to Stockholm from Lund, was it possible for Strindberg to write
works in which penitence was no longer the prevailing subject matter; but
even then, it continued to reappear in his writing right up through the
epilogue of his last play, *The Great Highway* (1909).

Inferno and Legends

Strindberg did not believe that a Swedish publisher would accept
Inferno and therefore wrote it in French "so that it will be read—if only in
manuscript."[4] Not only in the book, but in his letters as well, he maintained that *Inferno* was not fiction but "an expanded and rearranged version" of the diary he had kept since 1896. (Some of the excerpts he
presents in the book as actual diary entries are expanded and reinterpreted
versions of short memoranda from the "Occult Diary.")

Inferno was written in May and June, 1897, six months after his
arrival in Lund, a time during which feelings of persecution had abated
and the revelations he had experienced seemed less upsetting. He could
now see a pattern in the events that had occurred and could describe sys-
tematically his realization that supernatural Powers and not human evil
had stalked him. But even while writing the book, he was still uncertain
whether the force manipulating his destiny was an omnipotent Providence
or its rebellious and malevolent satraps. *Inferno* contains suggestions of
the themes that would occupy him in his religious writings—the journey
through Golgotha's twelve stations of the Cross[5] and the image of Jacob
wrestling with God[6]—but they are not yet spelled out clearly. At the end

of the book he says that he has written to a Belgian monastery to plead for refuge, but even if his request were accepted, he does not know what would happen to him. The famous passage in the concluding section of the book—that perhaps the entire Crisis was a jest of the gods, who laugh derisively as we weep—depicts the essential bitterness of the work. The new convert does not yet know whether he has fallen into the hands of God or the devil; he knows only that he has been punished and scourged and must seek reconciliation with a higher world. He knows that he is in an Inferno where everything "is only a masquerade; is pretense and illusion." Only death can grant him full understanding.

Strindberg could never rid himself of the anguish he felt over the enigma of life, no matter how often he vowed that he believed in the Eternal One and was convinced he was being treated justly. His anguish would appear in *A Dream Play* as well as in *The Great Highway*. Time and again he forced himself to be submissive, only to be haunted by the fear that he had surrendered himself to tormentors. In *Inferno* he describes how he hears a wedding march in the distance and thinks it a good omen because he was "enough of a child at heart and sufficiently unhappy to be able to turn the most commonplace and natural occurrences into poetry."[7] This childish trust, however, was coupled with an equally childish distrust, and although misfortunes sometimes compelled him to turn the commonplace into poetry, more frequently he was induced to transform a festive occasion into a nightmare.

Legends, in spite of magnificent passages, is inferior to *Inferno.* It treats the less remarkable miracles—those that Strindberg experienced during the Lund phase of the Crisis, especially the ones concerning his friends. Johan Mortensen is probably correct in saying that these people out of exaggerated kindness invented supernatural tales for Strindberg's benefit. Strindberg was acting in good faith when he said that his entire circle of friends in Lund was in the midst of a penitential journey to Canossa.

"Jacob Wrestles," the last one-third of *Legends,* was written in March, 1898, in Paris, where Strindberg had returned and was experiencing new psychic phenomena. Isolated, he was haunted by persecution fears, but he tried to free himself from them with the thought that he was not being persecuted by ordinary mortals but by Christ, and that Providence was "personally" out "to get him," as he said in a letter to Herrlin.

During this stay in Paris, he spent most of his time in the religious center of the Latin Quarter, attending church services, examining crucifixes and rosaries, and reading Thomas à Kempis and Chateaubriand's *Génie du christianisme*. In Delacroix's mural *Jacob Wrestling with the Angel,* he saw a personification of his own turbulent struggle between self-assertion and self-effacement. But despite the fact that the painting dealt with the subject in an orthodox manner, Strindberg came away with impious, defiant thoughts. What he remembered most of all was the image of "the wrestler, holding himself erect even though his hips were paralyzed."[8]

The most beautiful passage in "Jacob Wrestles" depicts the encounter with the Stranger, here the figure of Christ who, cloaked in an opal-white mantle and surrounded by a glory, reveals Himself to the author as he walks in the Luxembourg Gardens. In anguish Strindberg questions Him, but must provide his own answers. Without actually speaking, the Stranger seems to say: "Why do you ask Me, since you know the answer yourself?" The scene develops into a dialogue with himself in which Strindberg lets his entire life pass in review—accusing, defending, and refuting his defenses anew. Never before did Strindberg seem closer to a solution of his life's problem, and he had never been more successful in attuning poetic form to spiritual content. The poet begs for absolute answers, but the Stranger in the pilgrim's mantle replies only with a smile that frustrates the eager questioning. Finally, He vanishes, leaving the poet alone once more with his brooding.

In the postscript, Strindberg states that "every attempt to approach religion through reasoning leads to absurdities," and that one achieves understanding only by believing without reservation. But even as he felt that he had failed in "Jacob Wrestles" to express the essence of his religious struggle, it is obvious that he was compelled to try again in dramatic dialogue. In "Jacob Wrestles" he had compared himself to Saul who became Paul, and it is this same transformation that he tried to depict in the *To Damascus* cycle.

The *To Damascus* Cycle

In its final version *To Damascus* is a trilogy: the first two parts written in 1898 and the third in 1901. From Strindberg's sketches we know that he intended to have them followed by a fourth part, but this was never written. On the other hand, notations in his diary support Landquist's hypothesis that Strindberg originally did not plan a continuation of the first play, which was begun in January, 1898, under the title *Robert le Diable*⁹ and completed on the eighth of March.

The three separate but closely linked plays of *To Damascus* describe three journeys undertaken by "the Stranger" through despair and hope, dark regions and light, in search of conversion, penitence, and faith. Many of the places visited resemble those in which Strindberg himself wandered before and during his Inferno years: the seashore at Helgoland on the North Sea where he and Frida Uhl spent their honeymoon, the Hôpital de St. Louis (an insane asylum in the play) in Paris where he received treatment for the painful hand infections that resulted from his chemical experiments, and the home of Frida Uhl's grandparents in Austria where he spent time visiting his baby daughter. The characters, too, are part of the author's past: the Stranger of course is Strindberg; the Lady, whom the Stranger eventually marries, is a composite of Siri von Essen and Frida Uhl; the Mother is a portrait of Frida's mother; and the Doctor (also the Lady's first husband) is another composite—Dr. Eliasson and Baron Wrangel, Siri's first husband.

Parts I and II of the trilogy are the most successful artistically. To some extent, Part II is a repetition of the first play, but the two sections differ considerably in treatment. The focus in the first part is on the religious experiences, and the play is pervaded by a tender, poetic dream atmosphere that foreshadows *A Dream Play*. Part II, on the other hand, depicts Strindberg's second marriage and some of his experiences as an alchemist; its harshness suggests what was to come in *The Dance of Death*. But both parts show us Strindberg moving tentatively toward a commitment to Catholicism and a monastic life.

Although Part I deals with themes and ideas similar to those in *Inferno* and "Jacob Wrestles," the period of the author's life dealt with in the play is earlier: the prelude to the Crisis, during which the Stranger moves only a short way on the road to Damascus. In the opening scene the Lady urges the Stranger to accompany her into the church to hear the beautiful music of the vespers, but he refuses because he feels that he is a lost soul who can never enter there. When at the end of Part I she urges him again to go in, he replies: "All right! I guess I can walk through—but I cannot stay!" She suggests that he may hear "new songs." He answers with a skeptical "perhaps" and follows her through the church portal. That Strindberg was as ambivalent as his hero is seen in a letter to Geijerstam in which he discusses whether the Stranger and the Lady should be divorced in Part II: "Shall I have them divorced? Yes! Because their relationship is repugnant. However, as instruments of torture for each other they can still continue to be drawn together." And so, throughout Part II they continue to "plague one another until they reach the Cross," as the Dominican friar says.[10]

Part I is a more compelling version of Strindberg's "unredeemed condition" before his conversion than the confessional writings. In the opening scene the Stranger asks the Lady: "Do you think that some people are already damned here on earth?" Everything has conspired against him from birth: "For you see, I was brought up in hate. Hate!"[11] He was "born out of wedlock while bankruptcy proceedings were going on." There is a legend that he is a changeling, a child of the trolls, and although he had everything he wished for, it was all worthless. "No one in my town was more hated than I, no one more detested. Coming or going, I was alone. If I went into a public place, people moved five yards away from me."[12] Behind the mask of the Stranger, Strindberg is able to express more easily than under his own name in the confessional writings how he suffered from the feeling that he was an outcast, that he was feared and detested as the author of *The New Kingdom*, *Married* and *A Madman's Defense*.

The Stranger's solitude terrifies him more than death:

> because in solitude there is someone waiting for you. I don't know whether it's someone else I sense or myself, but in solitude you're not alone. The air becomes denser and gives rise to beings that are invisible, but alive. You can feel them.[13]

He once hoped for atonement, but the hope was betrayed; he tried to find peace through the rituals of holy water and the ringing of bells, but in vain. His only comfort is that he has the power to end life "when it becomes too wearying." The Lady reproaches him for "playing with death," but the Stranger answers: "As I've played with life. After all, I'm a writer. Despite being born melancholy, I've never been able to take anything really seriously—not even my own greatest sorrows. And there are moments when I doubt that life is more real than my writings."[14] These lines offer a clearer portrait, rendered with more naked honesty, than do the confessional writings, and they contain the gist of the remainder of the play, of the entire cycle; indeed, to a certain extent they could serve as an introduction to all of Strindberg's work after *Inferno*.[15]

In the opening scene we learn that the Stranger has begun to sense a meaning in existence; heretofore he had seen only things and events; now he sees ideas and patterns: "Life, which was total nonsense before, now has meaning. I sense purpose where before I saw only chance."[16] But he still feels damned: "Fate spins its conspiracy; once again I can hear the gavel fall and the chairs being pushed back from the table.---The sentence has been pronounced. But it must have been pronounced before I was born, because I began paying the penalty in my childhood." He cannot remember one moment of happiness in his life, and there is nothing that offers him hope: "There's something false in even the sunshine and calm air. I feel that happiness can never be part of my destiny."[17]

The Mother—the Stranger's mother-in-law—exhorts him to beg for forgiveness and try to atone. She wants him to kneel before Christ, but he refuses: "No not before Him! Not Him! And if I'm forced to do it, I'll take it back—afterwards."[18] The Beggar says that the Stranger "believes only the worst, and so gets only the worst. For once, try to believe in the best. Try!"[19] In the final scene the Lady urges him to go into the post office and pick up the letter he has long avoided asking for: "Go in believing it's good news!" He makes the effort and discovers the letter contains money he had urgently needed. The Stranger now confesses that he misjudged the Unseen One's intentions: "I didn't want to be made a fool of by life—and so I was."[20] The autobiographical reference is clear: Strindberg was aware that his pessimism and misanthropy stood in the way of his salvation. Nevertheless, he always regarded his displeasure with earthly existence as a sign of his nobility; it was proof that he was aware of the perfect original in heaven.

The Stranger warrants such close study because he is in fact the entire drama; the other characters are only sketched in and exist primarily to deliver rejoinders to him. To a significantly greater degree than the following sections, Part I of *To Damascus* is a monodrama and thus is closely related to *The Great Highway*. The conflict is not between the Stranger and the other characters, but between the Stranger and the Unseen One who, though not present in the cast of characters, is responsible for the hero's misfortunes and ultimately wins the battle.

One must admire Strindberg's success in making the Stranger an imposing figure even though he is awed and intimidated by quite ordinary phenomena. He is scared out of his wits in the night scene in his mother-in-law's kitchen although he knows that the things frightening him are harmless: "Yes, it's the moonlight! And that's a stuffed bird. And those are cleaning rags! Everything is so simple and natural, but that's exactly what makes me uneasy."[21]

Strindberg makes no effort to conceal the revealing fact that the Stranger's hostility to the order of things is provoked in part by financial reverses. While on his honeymoon, the Stranger receives a registered letter he hopes contains a royalty check. When he finds that it is just a notice that no money is forthcoming, he angrily tears open his coat and with a threatening look toward the sky shouts: "Come on! Strike me with your lightning if you dare! Frighten me with your storm if you can!" But no bolt of lightning stills the blasphemer who hurls abuse at the Powers, those "little bourgeois gods who parry sword thrusts with pinpricks behind your back."[22] He tells the Mother that although an unpaid bill can make him tremble, "if I were to climb Mount Sinai and face the Eternal One, I would not so much as cover my face!"[23] But the blasphemer is not very consistent or steadfast: it takes only the letter containing money to convince him that he has misjudged the Unseen One.

The Stranger has the same contradictory mixture of candidness and fear of revealing too much as the Captain in *The Father*. Letters to Herrlin indicate that after the publication of *Inferno* Strindberg feared that he would be judged mentally ill and confined, an anxiety that had followed him throughout the entire Inferno Crisis. A doctor's certificate sent to him through Herrlin described Strindberg as someone "extremely feverish, who is able to diagnose himself at any time." The Stranger, too, is feverish for a time in the convent-asylum. When he later asks the Abbess if he had said anything revealing during his delirium, she replies: "The usual feverish dreams all sick people have."[24] But her attempt to reassure him only aggravates his anxiety about the true nature of his condition.[25] He asks if the grotesque and ghostly people he sees in the aslyum are "real," and the Abbess replies that they have a terrifying reality: "If they appear strange to you, it may be because you still have a fever, or— something else."

The Doctor is more frank: when the Stranger asks him if a person can walk about as usual and yet be delirious, he replies that only if the person is insane. When the Stranger wants to know if the institution to which he has been admitted is a hospital or a cloister, the Doctor answers: "No, it's a madhouse."[26] At the same time, he refuses to say whether he considers the Stranger mentally ill. Obviously, Strindberg himself was uncertain of the correct answer. To the Doctor's question of whether he usually had auditory hallucinations, the Stranger replies: "No, not hallucinations, but there are recurrent small incidents, real ones, that seem to be persecuting me."[27]

During Strindberg's second period in Paris, when he wrote Part I of To Damascus, reality had assumed the characteristics of a vision. He talks of seeing curious figures at a sidewalk café, figures who seem to have sprung up from the sewers, and he is struck by the idea that "these are not 'real' people, they are half-visions."[28] The Stranger has the same concern when he touches the Beggar in order to determine if the man is "real"; and in the asylum scene, figures appear who seem to be the Lady, the Doctor, the Stranger's parents, and so forth, yet are not.

In a letter to Geijerstam about the play, Strindberg wrote: "Yes, it is doubtless fiction, but with a terrifying half-reality behind it."[29] The Stranger's world is indeed only partially real. People who have never set eyes on each other converse as if they were acquainted all their lives; they influence each other's actions from afar and read each other's thoughts before they are shaped into words. In the opening scene the Stranger knows instinctively that the Lady will come, and she has sensed that he called to her. On their honeymoon trip the Lady asks of their hotel room: "Is it number eight?" and the Stranger answers: "Then you, too, have been here before?" People become each other's doubles. The Beggar, like the Stranger, has a scar on his forehead, a reminder of a wound received from a close relative. In the scene at the Doctor's the Stranger meets a madman with the same nickname he had in school—Caesar. The scene with the Ystad doctor described in Inferno is a complete nightmare in To Damascus I.[30]

In order to create the impression of "half-reality" and recurrence in Part I, Strindberg used a structural device to which he would later return, although never with such effective results. He made the asylum scene the pivotal point and has the second half of the play repeat in reverse order all the scenes in the first half. This intensifies the dream-like impression: in the first half of the play we feel that the characters are sinking more and more into a trance; in the second half they are roused to a consciousness that becomes clearer and clearer. He used a similar technique in *A Dream Play* and in the "Author's Note" referred to *To Damascus* as "his former dream play." But although the dream atmosphere in *A Dream Play* is to a large extent produced the same way as in the earlier play— by having reality seen in the light of a dream and having the characters "split, double, multiply, evaporate, condense, scatter, converge"—in *To Damascus,* Strindberg did not try "to imitate the disconnected but apparently logical form of the dream."

In spite of the repetition of scenes and transformations of actual experiences into illusions, *To Damascus* gives a harrowing impression of reality. Never had Strindberg succeeded so completely in rendering the essence of the demonic in his own nature, a characteristic that filled him with both awe and horror. In the kitchen scene, as the Mother sits looking out the window, she asks as if to herself: "You beautiful morning star, why have you fallen so far from heaven?" The Stranger answers: "Have you noticed that just before the sun comes up, a shudder goes through us. Are we the children of darkness that we tremble before the light?"[31]

Strindberg also produced a moving expression of the two states of feeling between which he was torn—the dream of grandeur and the sense of inferiority. When the Stranger stands before the sea, he bursts out in a poetic monologue that is more intense than anything in *In the Outer Skerries.* He feels his sense of self expanding and becoming infinite:

> I am everywhere: in the sea which is my blood, in the mountain plateaus which are my skeleton, in the trees, in the flowers. My head reaches up to the heavens, and I can look out over the universe which is me, and I feel all the power of the Creator in me. for I am He. I should like to grasp it all in my hand and mold it into something more perfect, more lasting, more beautiful.[32]

For Strindberg this was blasphemy, and the Stranger pays the penalty for his arrogance. Nevertheless, there is something of Strindberg's innermost self in the outburst, just as there is in the moving passage in which the Stranger talks about his inability to endure loneliness: "I wish I were someone's dog, so I could follow along and never be lonely. A little food once in a while, a kick now and then, and for every pat, two slaps."[33]

Part I of *To Damascus* is one of Strindberg's greatest works; the work to which one always returns when trying to fathom the riddle of his

personality. The same cannot be said for the other parts, for although
Strindberg was always eager to begin sequels to works of which he was
proud, his enthusiasm quickly waned. Only with forced determination was
he able to complete the second part of *To Damascus:* "It was planned in
hate and deals with hateful people. In spite of a sturdy armature and
diverse compositional tricks, it displeases me and makes me sick."[34] He
admitted that he repeatedly bogged down in the writing and thought about
burning the manuscript.

In Part I, the Lady is to a certain extent the Stranger's Beatrice
who finally leads the recalcitrant into church. It is therefore surprising
that concerning Part II Strindberg could write to Geijerstam that he
found the couple's relationship repugnant and wanted to separate them.
The reason for the antagonism was that the references to his wife and her
relatives in Part I had opened old wounds. In Part II, the quiet Lady who
crocheted becomes a shrew who steals and opens her husband's letters,
plants a purse to entice him to theft, and ridicules his experiments in natural science. Even when the Stranger is on the point of entering the monastery he has a bitter word for his wife: "Think how beautifully she can
speak—and yet is so evil! Look at those eyes; they can't cry, but they can
coax and sting and lie! . . . Come, priest, before I change my mind!"[35]

There are, of course, beautiful scenes in the play, the best being
the banquet at the beginning of the third act, in which the Stranger, having
made gold, is feted for his achievement by a gathering of gentlemen in
evening dress decorated with orders. After a short time the gentlemen
evaporate, and the banquet hall becomes a disreputable tavern filled with
felons and loose women drinking out of stone mugs at the bar. This is the
first in the series of "phantom suppers" that Strindberg would later
portray with such masterliness.

The first sketches for Part III reveal Strindberg's old craving for
exposé: the Stranger gains admittance to a monastery to uncover "all the
vice and failings" there. But since he did not write the play until 1901,
three years after the first parts, his view toward the monastic life had
changed. In the final act of the published version, the Stranger enters a
nondenominational refuge, a place not unlike the monastery in the
Ardennes that Strindberg dreamed of establishing during his stay in
Austria or the monastery on Siklaön described in the novel *Black Banners.*

Strindberg was undoubtedly persuaded to complete the last part of the trilogy in the beginning of 1901 by the success that his future wife, Harriet Bosse, had achieved in the role of the Lady in Part I in the fall of 1900. Even before their engagement in March, 1901, she served as model for the Lady in several scenes, but these scenes were replaced by later versions in a different style. As a matter of fact, the play underwent changes and additions right up to its publication in 1904.

Part III has a grandeur in design and isolated scenes that are striking, but it lacks dramatic unity and tension. The optimistic glorification of humanity and the stress on the need for resignation are in sharp contrast to the often savage misogyny. Perhaps because Strindberg worked on it over a long period of time, it became a kind of diary in dialogue form, a running commentary on his life to which he constantly added new entries.

The Cloister
("The Quarantine Master's Second Tale")

In August, 1898, after completing the second part of *To Damascus,* Strindberg entered the Belgian monastery Maredsous, but felt ill at ease and, after a twenty-four-hour visit as a guest, left. It was primarily to describe his "personal impressions from Maredsous in reshaped form" that be began to write the novel *The Cloister (Klostret)* in October of that same year. The first section of the novel is a description of his years in Germany and Austria when his monastery plans first awakened. (Since the real name of the artists' tavern that Strindberg nicknamed Zum Schwarzen Ferkel was The Cloister, he thought that the entire novel could bear this name.)

In essence, however, the final version of *The Cloister* tells the story of Strindberg's second marriage, "reshaped" only slightly and first published as a novella in 1902 under the title "The Quarantine Master's Second Tale" ("Karantänmästarns andra berättelse") in the story collection *Fairhaven and Foulstrand.* The original opening section set in Berlin was omitted, and place names and characters' nationalities were altered. Strindberg also made a number of other deletions in a vain attempt to prevent the reader from associating the hero with the author.[36] Among these were the most moving passages in the book, passages in which Strindberg identified himself with Ishmael, son of the servant woman

Hagar, who, with his mother, was driven out into the desert and became a cruel man and a mocker; the author describes how throughout his life all his achievements were negated. A similar theme dominates the published novella: the hero is a stepchild of existence who cannot find his bearings anywhere and is stripped of his illusions. He feels that a higher Power is responsible for his misfortunes and is attempting to purify him for a coming life. This influence of a higher Power makes the author's hatred of the wife and her relatives appear less irrational than it does in Part II of *To Damascus.*

Although the work cannot compare to *A Madman's Defense* as literature, it is an invaluable autobiographical document since it describes Strindberg's attitude toward his second marriage four years after the divorce. Between the experiences described in *The Cloister* and the actual writing of the work lay the entire Inferno Crisis.

Advent

The two dramas Strindberg wrote during the winter of 1898-99, *Advent* and *Crime and Crime,* are totally different from each other. *Advent*—a combination horror story and children's fairy tale—is a primitive work with an elemental imaginative power that foreshadows *A Dream Play* and *The Ghost Sonata (Spöksonaten). Crime and Crime,* which was obviously written with a French audience in mind, is an elegantly composed piece, devoid of fantastic or ghostly themes. It scarcely lives up to its subtitle of comedy, but among the plays written after the Inferno Crisis it is one of those most frequently performed. Both dramas were published together under the collective title *Before A Higher Court (Vid högre rätt),* and both deal with the administration of higher justice. But whereas *Advent* deals with flagrant crimes that are punished in a palpable way, the crimes in *Crime and Crime* occur only in the mind and consist of evil wishes.

In *Advent,* Strindberg contrasts divine justice with the corruption that attends the application of human justice. A judge and his wife are guilty of a lifetime of perfidy, including the unjust treatment of their son-in-law, Adolf, whom they have separated from his wife and children. In the end, the evil pair is chastised by the Other One, servant of the All-Good One.

The play, begun in November, 1898, and completed in the middle of December, originally bore the title *The Mausoleum (Mausolén)*. The first act does, in fact, take place near a mausoleum, modeled on the structure that Frida Uhl's grandparents had built for themselves. Strindberg speaks sympathetically of the monument in *The Cloister,* but in the play it is a kind of Ibsenesque symbol representing the viciousness and sanctimoniousness of the Judge and his Wife. It stands on a gallows hill, and at one point a terrible ghostly procession issues from it—all those who have been victims of the Judge's deceptions, misappropriations, and unjust decisions. In the final act, the Judge's Wife hears workers singing as they tear it down.

When trying to decide on a title, Strindberg referred to *The Mausoleum* as a children's play and clearly intended it for children's theatre performances at Christmas time. He had reread Dickens's Christmas stories and Hans Christian Andersen's fairy tales, which he found opened up "perspectives inward and upward to *Jenseits.*" The influences from the fairy tales are most noticeable in the somewhat puerile children's scenes. For example, a new playmate for the Judge's grandchildren turns out to be the Christ Child—a sweet, precocious boy. And a final scene cut from the published play is written in the style of a Christmas story, with Adolf telling his children that the family is too poor to be able to afford Christmas presents that year. One can more readily understand the sentiments of these sections when one reads Strindberg's description in a letter to Geijerstam of how he celebrated Christmas alone in his room in Paris with only a can of milk in front of him: "contemplating gratefully all the beautiful Christmas Eves Providence has given me. But the best ones were with my children around our own Christmas tree."

The play concentrates on denouncing the crimes of the Judge and his Wife. In sketching this couple, Strindberg used a number of models in addition to Frida Uhl's grandparents, and when he finished, he had produced his first great specimens of grotesque characterization. The depravity of the Judge and his Wife is almost exceeded by their ability to brag about it. They rejoice over their past crimes and gloat about ones they contemplate. Corpulent and smug, they have a confidence possessed only by people who are completely devoid of conscience. With their fantastic malevolence and their sniggering, malicious gaiety, these characters are brilliantly drawn. The Other One, their chastiser, is a fairy-tale demon: a lean and seedy-looking teacher with a red muffler wound around his neck, carrying in his hand the instrument of chastisement—a cane.

Writing to Geijerstam in January, 1899, Strindberg called the play a Swedenborgian drama and emphasized that he borrowed from Swedenborg the idea that the Evil One "is only an *esprit correcteur,* not evil itself; the dualism of good and evil is thereby cancelled." It was also from Swedenborg that he took the theory that crime was its own punishment and that the Evil Ones suffered by tormenting each other. This is reflected in the Other One's speech to the Judge: "You see, the All-Good One cannot do evil; therefore he leaves it to wretches like me! But to ensure more certain results, you two will have to torment each other and yourselves."[37]

In the fourth act, the Judge and his Wife are placed in "the Waiting Room," a counterpart to Swedenborg's vestibule where the dead come before they are aware they have departed the earth. But Strindberg was not yet completely satisfied with the Swedenborgian formula of allowing the crime to be its own punishment (as he would be in *Crime and Crime*), and so the Judge learns that "there's no complaining here—here the screws are put on without legal formalities." When he hears something he takes to be someone beating clothes, he is told that a person who forgot the significance of the day (Christmas Eve) is receiving "extra caning provisions beyond the law." As the Judge and his Wife enter, a strange ball is in progress with cripples, beggars, and felons waltzing to inaudible music performed by weird musicians; everything is supervised by a seventy-year-old fop with a waxed mustache, a monocle, and a wig. The most distinguished figure present is a small, hunchbacked Prince in a soiled velvet jacket with a lace collar, who later turns out to be the deceased brother of the Judge's Wife. In this grotesque situation Strindberg took pains to avoid any suggestion of comedy. In the stage directions for the Waiting Room scene he notes: "The entire following scene is to be played with an unswervingly melancholy seriousness, without a trace of irony, satire, or humor."[38]

Although Strindberg came to the conclusion during his Inferno that hell was in reality earthly life, he continued to believe that there existed a place of punishment after death. On March 10, 1898, a year before he wrote *Advent,* he wrote to Herrlin: "Is there a hell other than this one? Or is it just an invention with which to frighten children?" Perhaps it was primarily the idea of frightening children that first prompted him to depict the Waiting Room, a chamber of horrors with hair-pulling, beatings, and spitting. During the course of the writing, however, the scene obviously became increasingly real to him, enabling him to produce a graphic and expressive portrait of the lives of the damned. The Witches' Sabbath interludes give *Advent* its strength, whereas the idyllic scenes seem flimsy and mawkish.

Crime and Crime

In *Crime and Crime,* written early in 1899, Strindberg dealt in earnest with problems he barely touched upon in *Advent:* "evil intention, the liabilities of evil thoughts, and the power of the individual to punish himself."[39] A list of contemplated "Occultist dramas—Nemesis dramas" contains the following: "The evil intention is punished as the evil deed. ... Wishes the life out of his own child. The child dies; he is suspected and indicted." This is the basic plot of *Crime and Crime.* Maurice, a playwright, is at long last the toast of Paris when his latest work proves a success. He is drawn into an affair with a beautiful sculptress, Henriette, but has responsibilities that make things awkward: a mistress, Jeanne, and their small daughter, Marion. Several witnesses overhear him say that it would be better if the child did not exist. Shortly thereafter, Marion dies and Maurice is suspected of killing her. Although he is declared innocent after it is discovered that the child died of natural causes, he feels that he is to blame because of his evil wishes. The *raissoneur* of the play, an old Abbé, agrees: "And guiltless you were not, for we are answerable for our thoughts, words and desires. You committed murder in your mind when your evil will wished the life out of your child."[40]

According to a letter to Geijerstam, Strindberg intended the unusual title to be regarded as an ellipsis of the phrase: "There is, of course, crime and crime." He expressed himself somewhat more explicitly in a letter to Littmansson when he suggested that the title of the French translation might be: "Guilty *and* Not Guilty."

In *Inferno* Strindberg accuses himself of an attempt at "bewitchment" when, during his stay in Paris, he performed magical actions upon a portrait of his daughter Kerstin. He longed to be able to return to her and Frida, and believed that through this experiment he would be able to produce a slight illness in Kerstin and be called back to Austria. Later, when he briefly fell in love with a young English sculptress—as Maurice does with Henriette—he reproached himself for almost deserting his responsibilities to his wife and child. Maurice's great triumph with his play reflects the Paris première of *The Father,* and his hesitation to accept a banquet in his honor also had a counterpart in real life. Strindberg wove these personal experiences together with others.

Particularly important, and mentioned by him in *Inferno* and in letters, was the rumor that one of his friends from the tavern group in Berlin was indicted for the murder of his mistress and their children. The inspiration for the beautiful Montparnasse cemetery scene in which Jeanne, Maurice's mistress, is chilled by foreboding at the sight of a woman in black kneeling at a grave, was an actual encounter Strindberg had in the same place with a female stranger dressed in mourning.[41] Originally, Strindberg thought about having the play end with another scene in the cemetery.

An Ibsenic approach to plot construction—which Strindberg much admired at this time—is especially evident in the first two acts. Causal relationships link scene to scene, speech to speech. For example the conversation between Maurice and Henriette during their first meeting at the café contains subtle suggestions of the unhappiness they will experience. Each confesses to the other that during dreams he committed cruel deeds. "If we had to answer for our thoughts, who would stand a chance?" says Maurice. Then, in Act II, in the intoxicating atmosphere of Maurice's triumph at the theatre, the two lovers, almost against their wills, wish the life out of Maurice's child who stands in the way of their complete possession of each other. Just as in Ibsen's work, the past has forced its way between them and has become a Nemesis that demands a blood sacrifice.[42] Marion's death chains the two lovers together, but prevents them from achieving mutual happiness. Henriette complains to Maurice: "We should fly. You offered me wings—but your feet are made of lead."[43]

In an early draft of the play, Strindberg has Maurice undergo an Inferno-like ordeal after his daughter's death. Spied on by detectives, he denies his identity and roams about in cafés and parks. Everyone shuns and despises him, children slap him in the face, and newspaper pages containing the notice of Marion's death fly after him, carried by the wind. For the final version of the play, Strindberg retained only the detectives, whose sole purpose now seems to be to uncover evidence that a psychic murder had been committed. Maurice's period of punishment is shortened to two days, during which he and Henriette torment each other with groundless suspicions.

When it turns out, as Maurice's friend Adolf explains it, that Marion died of "a recognized disease" with a strange name that he cannot remember, there is a change in mood. Maurice, who shortly before wanted to abandon the world and disappear behind the holy walls of a monastery, now wonders whether he should still go to the theatre that evening to accept the homage of the public at a special performance of his play. The Abbé declares: "Since Providence has granted you absolution, I have nothing to add." Maurice chooses a compromise: "This evening I shall meet you at the church to settle accounts with myself about all this—but tomorrow I shall go to the theatre."

"The conclusion of my play is probably banal," Strindberg wrote to Littmansson (who apparently wanted it to end on an even happier note than it does), "the Abbé smiles and jokes, [the proprietress of the café] Madame Catherine guffaws. *Est-ce assez?*" In his eagerness to write a playable comedy, Strindberg allowed Maurice to forget Marion's death and his infidelity rather hastily, but he was careful to emphasize the connection between *Crime and Crime* and *Advent*. "The last act is Swedenborgian—with Hell *déja* on earth—and the real hero, the plot-manipulator of the play, is the Unseen One." The description of the ending is correct, even if it may seem as though the unseen plot-manipulator is sacrificing a woman's happiness and a child's life only to teach a playwright a moral lesson. There are others in the play who become devout through a tormenting sense of guilt over secret crimes—Henriette and even the kind-hearted Adolf. In the last act, Adolf is asked what religion is and replies: "Frankly, I don't know! And I don't believe anyone can tell you. Sometimes, it seems to me to be a punishment, because no one becomes religious unless he has a bad conscience."[44]

As Herrlin pointed out, one inspiration for the play was Beethoven's Sonata in D Minor, the same sonata that inspired one of the Chamber Plays, *The Ghost Sonata*. Strindberg loved it because certain bars in the finale aroused pangs of conscience in him. In connection with the French translation of his play, he wrote to Littmansson on June 21, 1899:

> Please mention Beethoven's D-minor Sonata parenthetically. The finale and
> particularly bars 96 to 107 should be given special attention. These strains
> always bore their way into my conscience like a bit. It has to sound as
> if the musician were practicing these bars, that is, repeating, repeating,
> with pauses in between. And then, again and again.

In *To Damascus*, Strindberg used Mendelssohn's Funeral March to establish a recurrent accompaniment to the action: here he tried to construct
the entire play on the form of a Beethoven sonata, the same technique
later employed for the Chamber Plays.

Even the "concept of chamber music transferred to drama"
(which Strindberg advanced as his ideal in the Chamber Plays, but which
was actually realized only in *Storm—Oväder*) is foreshadowed in *Crime
and Crime*. After the grotesque excesses of *Advent*, where the whistling of
the Other One's cane runs throughout the play, *Crime and Crime* is more
restrained. Compact in composition and with a consistency of style almost
unparalleled in his work, *Crime and Crime* is richly modulated, even if it
lacks *Advent's* strong effects.

The religious outlook is as naive as in *Advent*, but precisely because the characters in *Crime and Crime* are not monsters but ordinary
people of flesh and blood, the modern reader may find the religious harp-
ing in *Crime and Crime* more annoying than in *Advent*. What undermines the effectiveness of Strindberg's religious preaching during the
period immediately following *Inferno* is not so much his unmitigated
superstition as his pedantry: it is no coincidence that the Other One in
Advent is a seedy-looking schoolmaster. There is no parallel figure in
Crime and Crime; instead, virtually all the characters deliver long moral
sermons. Of his later dramas, only in *Easter* would Strindberg emphasize
moral problems so strongly, but the emphasis is less disturbing there because it is more appropriate to the characters involved and the redemptive
ending seems less cheaply purchased.

Notes to Chapter Fifteen

1. Letter to Hedlund, August 23, 1896; reproduced in Landquist's notes for *Inferno* (*SS:*XXVIII, p. 409).
2. *SS:*XXVIII, p. 131.
3. *See* note 9 below.
4. Letter to Hedlund, September 12, 1896 (*SS:*XXVIII, p. 409).
5. *SS:*XXVIII, p. 124.
6. *Ibid.,* p. 155.
7. *Ibid..* p. 174.
8. *Ibid.,* p. 329.
9. This tentative title was connected with Strindberg's fear, during a visit to his mother-in-law in Austria, that the local inhabitants suspected him of being the legendary Robert le Diable and would stone him (*SS:*XXVIII, p. 151). In the play (*SS:*XXIX, p. 103), the Mother says to the Stranger that she believes him to be "the child of the Devil," and he replies: "That seems to be the general opinion about me here." Herrlin (*Skånsk kalender,* 1936, p. 101) is probably correct that Strindberg got the idea for the name from Meyerbeer's opera. There is also a reference in "Jacob Wrestles" (*SS:*XVIII, p. 337) to Robert le Diable who kept company with swine. Although Robert le Diable has no significance in the final version of the *To Damascus* cycle, the projected title shows Strindberg wanted to stress the demonic in his hero.
10. *SS:*XXIX, p. 144.
11. *Ibid.,* p. 13.
12. *Ibid.,* p. 14.
13. *Ibid.,* pp. 9-10.
14. *Ibid.,* p. 9.
15. That Strindberg was aware of the significance of this self-characterization is best exemplified by its repetition—an unusual practice for him—in a slightly altered form, in the opening monologue of Part III of *To Damascus.*
16. *SS:*XXIX, p. 10.
17. *Ibid.,* p. 53.
18. *Ibid.,* p. 109.
19. *Ibid.,* p. 116.
20. *Ibid.,* pp. 134-35.
21. *Ibid.,* p. 106.

22. *Ibid.*, p 58.
23. *Ibid.*, p. 103.
24. *Ibid.*, p. 90.
25. On a postcard to Herrlin on November 4, 1897, after the publication of *Inferno*, Strindberg wrote: "Don't be afraid to let me know if people say I'm crazy. I am prepared for anything! Even the worst!"
26. *SS:*XXIX, p. 130.
27. *Ibid.*, p. 38.
28. *SS:*XXVIII, p. 396.
29. *SS:*XXIX, p. 367. The scenes in the asylum correspond to Strindberg's experiences in the Hôpital de St. Louis in Paris where he was admitted at Christmastime, 1895, on the authority of the Swedish Minister. In a letter to Frida he described the horror of these experiences, and in *Inferno* the description is even more vivid (see Frida Strindberg, *Strindberg ochs hans andra hustru*, 1933-34, II, p. 400 and *SS:*XXVIII, pp. 13-15). These earlier accounts, however, do not convey the impression of half-reality contained in the play. Several of Strindberg's hallucinatory experiences in Paris cafés were inserted directly into Part II of *To Damascus*.
30. Sometimes the inspiration for a grotesque dream sequence was an insignificant observation, as was the case with the funeral scene where the pallbearers wear brown suits and carry a banner with a carpenter's emblem on it. Strindberg noted in his diary on October 15, 1897, that he heard a clicking inside the left side of his coat that sounded like a deathwatch beetle, which superstition says is a portent of death. The same experience is mentioned in "Jacob Wrestles," where Strindberg adds that this beetle is also called "the carpenter." In the play, the First Pallbearer says the deceased was a carpenter and makes a ticking sound like a clock. When the Stranger asks: "A real carpenter or the kind that sits in walls and clicks?" the Pallbearer replies: "Both varieties, but mainly the kind that sits in walls and clicks. What are they called again?" And the Stranger remarks to himself: "The rogue! Now he wants to trick me into saying deathwatch" (*SS:*XXIX, p. 24-25).
31. *SS:*XXIX, p. 111.
32. *Ibid.*, p. 54.
33. *Ibid.*, p. 16.
34. Letter to Emil Kléen, July 1898.

35. *SS:*XXIX, p. 235. The play was written shortly before "The Quarantine Master's Second Tale," a novella about his second marriage and its torments.

36. The complete version of the novella was published in Sweden in 1966 (*Klostret*, ed. C. G. Bjurström).—Translator

37. *SS:*XXX, p. 47.

38. *Ibid.*, p. 71.

39. Letter to Geijerstam, January 4, 1899 (*SS:*XXX, p. 226).

40. *SS:*XXX, p. 220.

41. The encounter was described earlier in "In the Cemetery" *(SS:* XXVII, pp. 659-71).

42. The similarity to the doomed love between Rosmer and Rebecca in *Rosmersholm* is clear; twelve years earlier Strindberg had interpreted Ibsen's play as an example of "psychic murder." See p. 205.

43. *SS:*XXX, p. 158.

44. *Ibid.*, p. 208.

Chapter Sixteen

THE LATER HISTORY PLAYS

Sources and Historical Viewpoint

Strindberg was abroad during the upsurge of nationalism and patriotism that swept Sweden in the 1890's. When the news reached him in Paris that Heidenstam was at work on his monumental *The Charles Men* (*Karolinerna*—1897, 1898), dealing romantically with the tragic destiny of Sweden's last great warrior king, the controversial Charles XII, Strindberg wrote to Birger Mörner on March 21, 1896: "It is ironic that Heidenstam, the cosmopolite, is writing a nationalistic novel and sinking to the level of national minstrel."[1] But it is even more ironic that perhaps Strindberg's greatest achievement after the Inferno is the series of royal portraits[2] in his powerful history plays, since it was he who had savagely attacked Erik Geijer's thesis that the history of the Swedish people was the history of its kings.[3]

The literary historian Johan Mortensen maintained that he was the first to suggest to Strindberg that he choose subjects from Swedish history after *Master Olof* was successfully revived in Stockholm in the fall of 1897. Although unresponsive to the suggestion at first, Strindberg went to Mortensen's home several days later to borrow some books. Apparently, after returning to belles-lettres, he once again found historical writing appealing. On March 10, 1898, shortly after the completion of Part I of *To Damascus,* he wrote to Herrlin from Paris: "Now an item: I must go back up to Lund again quite soon to do research . . . for a play about the Middle Ages in Sweden; it will be written in the fall." We also learn from his diary that after his return to Lund he acquired a copy of Starbäck and Bäckström's *Stories From Swedish History* (*Berättelser ur svenska historien*—1885). But just as he was about to begin work on a play about Magnus Eriksson, he discovered that the pages dealing with this king were

327

missing from his copy, and he interpreted it as "a premonition not to write." Not until the following year, in January, 1899, did he start writing *Magnus the Good (Magnus den Gode)*, as *The Saga of the Folkungs (Folkungasagan)* was then called, but he stopped after a few days and instead wrote *Crime and Crime*. In March, he took up work on the drama again and completed it on April 20, 1899. Immediately thereafter he began *Gustav Vasa*, and finished it on June 12, 1899. One week later he left Lund permanently and went to the Stockholm area, where he continued his historical dramas with *Erik XIV* and *Gustav Adolf*.

Judging from the pace of his activity, it appears that at this time Strindberg's attitude was not as casual as it was during his later years, when he described the writing of historical drama as like writing "a little high school composition on a particular topic."[4] Mortensen—whose extensive knowledge of history no doubt made him valuable to Strindberg— said that once Strindberg decided to write history plays, he talked about virtually nothing else. He borrowed Mortensen's copies of books by the respected historian and Swedish Academy member Anders Fryxell, and the "Great [Clas] Odhner" whose history of Sweden and studies on the origin and development of Swedish cities were favorites with Strindberg. In addition to the Starbäck-Bäckström book, Strindberg himself had long owned A. A. Afzelius's *The Saga Annals of the Swedish People (Svenska folkets sagohävder*—1881), a book he called one of "the cornerstones of ancient Swedish history." From Afzelius, Strindberg borrowed stories of folk superstitions, bits of the Edda songs, and folk ballads and sagas to use in *The Saga of the Folkungs* and *Gustav Vasa*.

With sure artistic instinct, he adopted an imaginative rather than scrupulously accurate approach to historical writing. His two favorite sources were the popular Afzelius and Starbäck-Bäckström, who had intended their works to be regarded primarily as light diversions. Strindberg preferred them to the "official" histories because their shortcomings both as history and art (which he recognized) gave him more opportunity to exercise his imagination. He considered contemporary historical research to be mere dabbling in politics, a confusion of causes and effects, and a deliberate suppression of the truth. He felt, for example, that Anders Fryxell had hesitated to reveal his real views once he was elected to the Swedish Academy, and so had taken a conservative, pro-monarchist position when he expressed doubt that Queen Christina (who never married) had two children by the nobleman Magnus Gabriel De la Gardie. In contrast, the courageous Afzelius had ruined his chances for election to the Academy by daring to suggest that De la Gardie might actually have been Christina's half-brother, born of a youthful affair between King Gustav Adolf and Ebba Brahe De la Gardie.[5]

Although Strindberg found Starbäck and Bäckström useful, he was aware that they had "scraped together an extraordinary amount of material which was so poorly organized and written that one must use a rock drill to get at the nuggets."[6] How Strindberg mined these various sources is indicated by his blue-pencil markings. His criterion for selecting material was its dramatic effectiveness. He paid little attention to primary sources (they were "censored and falsified") or to accuracy in chronological sequence: *The Saga of the Folkungs* opens with a scene in which Erik Magnusson drives Knut Porse out of a barber shop, although Porse had been dead for nine years when Erik was born. Here, as in *Gustav Vasa*, historical events from different periods are arbitrarily combined. But Strindberg always emphasized the distinction between "historical time" and "dramatic time" and hoped that spectators would have "sufficient imagination to be able to watch a play without keeping one eye on the clock or the calendar."[7]

By ignoring historical chronology, Strindberg was able to create the violent peripety in *The Saga of the Folkungs*. Although the misfortunes suffered by King Magnus Eriksson actually occurred over a period of fifteen years, in the play they follow each other in rapid succession, like bolts of lightning from the same thundercloud. The action in *Gustav Vasa* is concentrated in the same way, and individual events as well are telescoped. In history, the king put down a number of peasant revolts between 1525 and 1543 in his successful effort to unite the nation. In the play, the climax of one of these revolts takes place in the home of Måns Nilsson in Aspeboda, where Vasa settles his difficulties with the assembled rebellious leaders of the Dalesmen (men of the Dalecarlia province) by having his subordinates call them out, one at a time, to be executed. Actually, the leaders were captured and liquidated at different times in different places. But few scenes in modern historical drama are as vibrant with tension.

The magnificent final act of *Gustav Vasa* would never have been possible if Strindberg had been faithful to scholarly sources. In the play, the king fears that he is in danger of attack from two directions: rebels from the southern province of Småland led by Nils Dacke and a group of Dalesmen from the north. According to documents in the Royal Registry, the king was by no means surprised that the Dalesmen were marching on Stockholm; on the contrary, he himself had assembled the force of four hundred men and circulated a rumor that it was ten times larger. The Dalesmen were to declare themselves merely the advance party for the entire peasantry of their province and trick Nils Dacke and his followers into believing that the main body of their force was followed behind. The ruse succeeded and Dacke was shortly defeated. Instead of the accurate account, Strindberg chose to follow Afzelius's distorted version of the incident, which has the king fearing that the Dalesmen are marching on the capital city in order to overthrow him. Not until their representatives inform him that they have come to help him does there occur, as Afzelius expressed it, "a change in the king's disposition, and he thanked the good people of Dalecarlia for their loyalty." In the play, the king's anxiety over the impending attack is a form of chastisement the historical Vasa never had to endure.

Another distortion of history occurs in the final act of *Erik XIV*, when Erik's wedding reception turns into a grotesque orgy[8] in the style of the alchemist's banquet in Part II of *To Damascus*. The king—heir and successor to Gustav Vasa but about to be deposed by his brothers—has just married Karin Månsdotter, who is not only a commoner, but the mother of his illegitimate children. The wedding guests are for the most part rabble, and the atmosphere is tawdry and vulgar. The king has the same feeling of displeasure that afflicted Strindberg on similar occasions: "Everything in my life has been dirty and warped. And even this sacred day—when I bring the bride of my youth to the altar of the Lord—this, too, has to be a day of shame! And the children—God's blessings—have to be hidden lest they should expose our shame to the world, which knows about it anyway!"[9] Actually, the wedding of Erik and his mistress was a particularly elaborate affair. Very little was done to conceal the existence of their children; as a matter of fact, they were stationed under the bridal canopy in order to have their legitimacy affirmed. And Karin's relatives, who in the drama demonstrate plebian table manners, shocked many people by behaving as if they were members of the nobility. Sketches for the play show that Strindberg was not ignorant of the historical facts; he altered them to stage a humiliation for the king.

"The anachronisms that occur in . . . [*Gustav Vasa*] are necessary
sacrifices to dramatic technique," Strindberg stated in a note to the reader
in the first edition of the play. When, in spite of this declaration, critics
said that he was ignorant of history, he engaged in extensive research for
his next drama. The huge volume of sketches he assembled for *Gustav
Adolf* is filled with bits of information, anecdotes, and quotations from
every imaginable source: war plans, treaties, letters, and speeches, though
mostly derived from unreliable, third-hand sources. Because of this struggle with material he could not master, it took longer to write *Gustav Adolf*
than the total time that had been required for the three preceding histories. Containing as it does approximately sixty characters and a superfluity
of subplots that obscure the main action, it is no wonder that the play is
disproportionately long. In addition, the playwright's talent for misreading
facts led him into making most peculiar mistakes involving Gustav Adolf's
personal characteristics and political activities.

To Strindberg's contemporaries, the drama seemed a hasty piece
of work in comparison with his earlier ones. Harald Hjärne, discussing
Strindberg's historical plays in the newspaper *Svenska Dagbladet* in 1900,
thought that the earlier dramas—especially *The Saga of the Folkungs*—
showed evidence of "very devoted care," but that *Gustav Adolf* was "a
monstrous block which a thoroughly annoyed Cyclops threw aside without having roughhewn it along more than just a few edges."

Having received so little gratitude for his scholarly labors, Strindberg returned to his old sources for his next plays with casual references to
other works of dubious historical value, such as Crusenstolpe's *Morianen
för Gustav III*. He never doubted that he was proceeding correctly when
he based his plays, as Shakespeare did, on old legends and chronicles
instead of on historical research. The dramatist and novelist must find
more sources than historical evidence: "He who believes otherwise can of
course try to write a history play according to the Scriptures or the Swedish
diplomatics. Then we shall see whether he can succeed in arousing
interest."[10] Unfortunately, he was never able to convince the pedants, who
continued to amuse themselves by searching for historical inaccuracies.

Strindberg's view of history was always influenced by his religious outlook and changed along with it. His first historical dramas after

the Inferno continue the penitential mood of *To Damascus, Advent,* and *Crime and Crime.* Significantly, an early, tentative title for *The Saga of the Folkungs* was *The Penance of the Folkungs (Folkungabot).* The Folkung dynasty, which ruled Sweden from the middle of the thirteenth century to the second half of the fourteenth, did much to civilize and unify the nation and secure for it a measure of international prestige. But the Folkungs were ambitious rulers whose ruthlessness—extending even to fratricide and incest—became legendary. When war, plague, and internal disorder finally combined to undermine and destroy the power of the dynasty, Magnus Eriksson was king, and Strindberg invests the figure with symbolic importance: the guiltless Magnus Eriksson has to expiate the crimes of the Folkungs. The sketches for *Gustav Vasa* indicate a penitential drama on the same pattern. The action was to begin on the king's birthday (Strindberg had recently celebrated his fiftieth birthday) when in the midst of triumph, his misfortunes crash down upon him. In the fourth act of *Gustav Vasa* there is a re-creation of Magnus Eriksson's journey to Golgotha in *The Saga of the Folkungs.* Disguised and unrecognized, Gustav Vasa wanders about in Stockholm, beset by beggars who humiliate him, and the play culminates in a duel between the king and the Eternal One. When Vasa finally yields to the higher power, he is able to vanquish his enemies: "Oh God, Thou hast punished me and I thank Thee!"

The sketches for the dramas immediately following, probably drafted in Lund, also show the influence of the penitential theme. *Erik XIV* was to have been a "Swedenborgian drama," in which the monarch, after having been a heathen, becomes an occultist and alchemist and subsequently sees demons and visions of hell: i.e., another version of the Inferno Crisis.

A play planned (but never written) about Charles IX was to have depicted, according to sketches, the king's "repudiation and destruction by the Powers." Instead, Strindberg chose to have Charles's son, Gustav Adolf—the great warrior king of the Thirty Years War, who died a hero at the battle of Lützen in 1632—expiate his father's crimes, just as Magnus Eriksson did. The title character of *Gustav Adolf* is not at first aware of blood guilt. He is a carefree *viveur* who rashly throws himself into the great religiously inspired conflict. As a typically Strindbergian hero, he gradually perceives that he is a blind instrument of a Providence "whose design we can never fathom." In the scene on the misty battlefield near Lützen, even the ordinary events of war take on apocalyptic dimensions. Through a blanket of fog the king sees three burning wind-mills, the wings of which resemble crosses: "What's that? The three crosses! Is it Golgotha?"[11] He experiences the same vision the Stranger did in Part I of *To Damascus:* "Three crosses! What new Golgotha awaits us now?"

Even *Charles XII,* the first historical drama Strindberg wrote after his third marriage, is haunted by the Inferno. According to a sketch, the hero was supposed to practice magic and live in dread of invisible enemies, frequently practicing sorcery by sticking "his sword in the ceiling above his bed." In *Open Letters to the Intimate Theatre (Öppna brev till Intima teatern)* Strindberg says: "He falls in the struggle against the Powers, having already been made wretched by the revelation of his inner conflicts and doubts."[12]

The later historical dramas have then a common theme: every suffering is a divine punishment for past sins. When Strindberg could not find historical evidence to support his hypotheses, he often invented guilt for his heroes to expiate. Gustav Vasa and Erik XIV are punished for their own sins, but Magnus Eriksson and Gustav Adolf, like Eleonora in *Easter,* must expiate the sins of their predecessors. The Sergeant Major in *Gustav Adolf* explains Strindberg's unusual doctrine of atonement: "The gentle son of cruel Charles IX is atoning for the sins of his father. It's what the quartermaster calls *satisfactio vicaria personalis* or personal vicarious atonement."[13] Strindberg disapproved when the actor playing King Magnus in the original production of *The Saga of the Folkungs* was made up to resemble Christ and carried the Cross on his back as Christ did at Golgotha. It was the author's intention for the king to represent not the Son of God, but an ordinary human being who has, however reluc-tantly, to suffer for others.

Strindberg's religious orientation after the Inferno was often responsible for disturbing anachronisms. The Gustav Vasa of history, for example, did not have the sensitive conscience of a Strindbergian hero; he was bold and ruthless and scarcely inclined to place his hands on the Cross, patiently to await God's punishment and the blow of the poleaxe. And it comes as a surprise in the latter part of *Gustav Adolf* to find the king—one of the great champions of Protestantism in the Thirty Years War—confessing to an aesthetic fondness for Catholicism. It is even more surprising that the basic argument, of a play dealing with what was perhaps the greatest religious conflict in history, is that salvation is open to anyone and everyone, regardless of his denomination.

But despite the anachronisms, the unifying element in this cycle of plays, the element that gives it its greatness, is the theme of atonement. The history of Sweden is made to reflect the different stages of Strindberg's Inferno Crisis. In *The Saga of the Folkungs,* the prevailing force is "the dark, avenging Powers who envy people their good fortune."[14] and in *Gustav Vasa,* it is the Eternal One, who punishes but also rewards. In *Gustav Adolf,* the syncretistic concept that conflicting religious viewpoints should be reconciled (a concept that became Strindberg's final profession of faith) is expressed in the scene in Act Three, where Mohammedans, Jews, Catholics, and Protestants hold separate divine services, but each read prayers that contain the same words, directed to the same God.

Strindberg's statement quoted earlier, that in *Crime and Crime* "the real hero, the plot-manipulator in the play is the Unseen One," also applies to the later historical dramas. At the end of *Charles XII,* the king is killed in battle after having led the nation into a harrowing period of destructive imperialistic war. When Feif, the king's secretary, wonders from which direction the fatal bullet came, Swedenborg points to heaven: "From up there! . . . And if it didn't it should have come from there."[15]

The philosophy of history underlying these events is explained in detail by Strindberg in his essay "The Mysticism of World History" (1903). He describes how at certain times in history parallel events took place in different places and attempts to show that these events did not occur by chance or by the action of ordinary laws of nature. They were brought about by a "conscious will" operating according to prescribed, but to us inscrutable, principles. Everything seems "like a colossal chess game" played "by a solitary player who moves both the black and white pieces."[16] This player is none other than "the Unseen Lawgiver who freely changes laws according to changed situations: the Creator, the Solver, and the Preserver, He may then be called—whatever you like."

For Strindberg, "the grand design of history is Providence's own composition, and Shakespeare is a providentialist just as the classical tragedians were: he did not ignore historical accuracy, he permitted divine justice to be administered even to the point of pettiness."[17] Strindberg followed the same principle in the later history plays. In *The Saga of the Folkungs,* Providence sends a plague to exact penance from Magnus Eriksson for the crimes of his ancestors, and in *Gustav Vasa* the same power uses the Nils Dacke controversy, the Dalecarlian rebellion, and the Lübeckian conspiracy to punish the king's arrogance. When Vasa is humbled, the rebellion against him dies down. The Master Olof of history was one of the first to discover a tragic pattern in the story of the Folkung dynasty, and Strindberg was following in his footsteps when he interpreted their misfortunes as examples of the iniquities of the fathers being visited upon the children to the third and fourth generations.

The Influence of Shakespeare

Strindberg had mixed feelings about Shakespeare; in a diary entry on April 25, 1889 (he had just completed *The Saga of the Folkungs*) he noted that he had always found Shakespeare "repulsive." But while he was in Lund (1898-99) preparing to write his history plays, he studied Shakespeare's histories and tragedies, trying to determine exactly how Shakespeare constructed a play:

> It was then that I noticed that Shakespeare is simultaneously formless and severely, pedantically formalistic. All the plays are cut to the same pattern —five acts, each with four or five tableaus—yet it is not clear how he did it. A play begins, then streaks to the end. The technique does not show through; there are no calculated effects. Great battles take place after well-prepared deployments, and then comes the peaceful ending with drums and trumpets. Someone has said that it seems like nature itself, and I agree wholeheartedly.[18]

Strindberg tried to duplicate the freedom of composition Shakespeare achieved, but the quotation shows that he was also aware that the conventions of the contemporary theatre demanded deliberate compositional effects in drama; he mentions that a "scene" in the French sense was "the fruit of well-thought-out strategy and artful tactics." He also emphasized his preference for parallelisms (subplots paralleling the main action—"my forte!"), which is noticeable in the first dramas after the Inferno Crisis. In making the transition to historical drama, he followed Shakespeare's example by composing in a more carefree manner, but without giving up his tightly controlled tempo or permitting himself

Shakespeare's epic breadth. Whereas earlier he had allowed a play to be dominated by a commanding central character or to be focused on a single line of action, he now tried to create—in common with what Shakespeare achieved in *Hamlet*—"a symphony, polyphonically developed with beautifully interlaced independent motifs."[19]

Strindberg's model "polyphonically" composed drama is *Gustav Vasa*. The brilliant stroke of having the central character appear for the first time in the play in Act Three—after having dominated the two preceding acts like an unseen power—was inspired by *Tartuffe*, about which Strindberg had written admiringly more than a decade earlier.[20] (Johan Mortensen relates that he had reminded Strindberg of Molière's device during their conversations on drama.)

Perhaps the most important influence, though, was *Henry IV, Part I*, which Strindberg had already used as a model for *Master Olof*. Just as Shakespeare contrasts the serious-minded Henry IV and his entourage with the world of Prince Hal, Falstaff, and their happy drinking companions in the Boar's Head Tavern, so Strindberg places the state problems of Vasa and Master Olof in juxtaposition to the dissolute life led by Crown Prince Erik and his plebian companion-adviser, Göran Persson. The Hanseatic League councilor's son, Jacob Israel, with his keen insights into the intrigues of state, contrasts with Erik and his unrestrained tavern manner the way Hotspur contrasts with Hal. The cynicism and gallows-humor fancies of Göran Persson make him a counterpart to Falstaff, despite other personality differences. In Act Two, Strindberg turns away, as Shakespeare often did, from the central action—the relationship between Gustav Vasa and his rebellious subjects—in order to present subordinate characters and parallel actions.

It should be emphasized, however, that the originality of *Gustav Vasa* is not diminished because of the debt Strindberg owed to Shakespearean chronicle drama; none of the characters or scenes in the play is borrowed directly from Shakespeare. What Strindberg took from Shakespeare was the design: the idea of giving a drama some of the richness of life by interlacing different actions and alternating the focus of attention on different worlds and social classes. Just as in Shakespeare's histories, *Gustav Vasa* confronts us with an entire age, and the play is a masterpiece of Swedish historical drama.

The Saga of the Folkungs also has a Shakespearean "polyphonic" composition. The momentous activities of the central action are flanked by colorful scenes involving ordinary people, and throughout the play three couples of different ages and dispositions, but all involved in intrigues to usurp King Magnus's power, are contrasted with one another: the king's mother, Dowager Duchess Ingeborg and her lover Knut Porse, Queen Blanche and her lover Bengt Algotson (the king's best friend), and Erik (Magnus's son and co-ruler) and his consort Beatrice. Ingeborg and Porse are a study of love in which the cup of joy has been emptied and only the dregs remain, Blanche and Algotson represent an intoxicating and sinful love, and Erik and Beatrice are an example of idyllic young love. These youngsters, barely past childhood, are reminiscent of such Shakespearean couples as Florizel and Perdita or Ferdinand and Miranda. Like many of Shakespeare's plays, *Folkungs* opens with a scene showing the ruler at the height of his power: the triumphant Magnus is seated on his throne under a canopy with the queen at his side, accepting tribute from his various provinces. The play follows his fortunes to the moment his enemies are at the gates of the city. But here, as is so often the case in Shakespeare, the dismal atmosphere of impending defeat takes on a lyrical note as a result of the tender scene depicting the death of Erik and Beatrice.

In the subsequent histories, beginning with *Erik XIV*, Strindberg began to be careless about composition and often permitted events to unfold without an apparent scheme. But even in *Erik XIV* and *Queen Christina (Kristina)*, Shakespeare's influence helped induce Strindberg to break with the severely symmetrical structure that characterized earlier Swedish historical drama, as is evident when one compares these last two plays with *Master Olof*.

In his *Open Letters to the Intimate Theatre*, Strindberg writes that "Shakespeare's technique in the play [*Julius*] *Caesar* of depicting historical personages, especially prominent ones, intimately, 'at home,' " was decisive for *Master Olof* "and, with certain reservations, even for those [plays] after 1899."[21] One has difficulty seeing where the reservations apply. The realism of commonplace detail that George Brandes taught Strindberg to look for in Shakespeare is actually more apparent in the historical dramas after 1899 than in the earlier ones. Nearly all the later plays have scenes treating the lives of ordinary people in a manner

similar to Shakespeare's. Moreover, the central characters become involved in family disputes that seem more modern than historical, even
when it is not certain that Strindberg used his own home life as source
material. How directly he drew on contemporary conditions is demonstrated in the various preliminary sketches, where he often identified the
people he contemplated using as models for the historical figures. Few of
these portraits are taken directly from life, however, for as always, Strindberg merged different models.

Again like Shakespeare, Strindberg made references to contemporary manners and mores. The carouses of Prince Erik and Göran Persson at the Blå Duvan Tavern, like the revels of Falstaff and his companions, more accurately reflect the spirit of the author's own time than that
of the historic period he was describing. The same is true of the recurrent
domestic squabbles in Strindberg's last few historical dramas, but he was
apparently no more concerned about the introduction of anachronisms
than Shakespeare was.

At the time he began writing *Gustav Adolf* he lived opposite the
barracks of the Svea Guards (The Yellow Brigade), a group founded in
Gustav Adolf's time.[22] Strindberg studied the drill maneuvers in the barracks yard with great interest and used them in the third act of his play
with little consideration for historical accuracy. In the scene outside
Leipzig, a non-commissioned officer is drilling enlisted men in close-order
marching, military honors, and the recognition of different trumpet signals. Recruits practice shouting "God save the king and the fatherland!"
as a corporal representing the king passes. In the final scene in the castle
church at Wittenberg after Gustav Adolf's death in battle, inscriptions are
read aloud from ribbons on wreaths sent by Germany's Protestant electors
and foreign ambassadors. Even craftsmen and poor old ladies anachro-
nistically send flowers to express their gratitude to Gustav Adolf as the
restorer of freedom of conscience.

Strindberg, fearing criticism, was somewhat more circumspect in
later dramas, but this did not prevent him in *Earl Birger of Bjälbo*
(*Bjälbojarlen*—1909) from introducing another anachronism: the contemporary Swedish convention of celebrating important birthdays. Woe-
begone old Earl Birger complains of his children's hypocritical love: "On
my last birthday they brought me flowers and made me drunk with their
lies!"[23]

Harriet Bosse told the author of this book that at the time Strindberg was writing Act Two of *Charles XII*, which takes place in the king's audience room, he was not sure of the proper protocol at a royal audience. Inquiries were made of August Palme, a leading actor who had recently received a medal—*Literis et artibus*—from King Oscar II. Palme's information about how one conducts oneself at a royal audience was so thorough that Strindberg used it for a special little scene in which the king's secretary gives instructions to those seeking an audience:

> May I just tell you one thing, gentlemen?—One does not inform the king about anything—one only answers his questions more or less completely, depending on how much His Majesty is interested in the answer. . . . As far as etiquette goes, you sit when you are commanded to, either by word or gesture.[24]

Among the lessons he had learned from Shakespeare, Strindberg included "not to avoid the right word."[25] Kings, queens, ministers, and councilors often use the same plain vocabulary as characters from the lower classes. Strindberg's dialogue, which in the earlier plays still retained a mildly archaic quality, was now thoroughly realistic, even in such expressionistically stylized works as *Charles XII*. Undoubtedly it was primarily this bold Shakespearean realism that made these plays repertory pieces abroad and earned Strindberg a position as reviver of historical drama—a literary form long regarded as extinct.

The Characters of the Monarchs

In his commentaries on the later historical dramas in *Open Letters*,[26] Strindberg dwelt primarily on his portraits of the individual monarchs, which he tried to justify historically. His goal in *The Saga of the Folkungs*, for example, was "to epitomize in one person the bloody saga of the Folkungs." Both in this play and in *Gustav Vasa*, the "polyphonic" nature of the composition divided the focus of attention between the central character and certain minor figures. But after *Gustav Adolf*, Strindberg's interest began to be confined to the character of the monarch, and in several of the dramas the subordinate characters are little more than supernumeraries. He was conscious of this change and suggested that his German translator Emil Schering describe *Charles XII* in the German version as "strictly a character drama."

Strindberg's depiction of the different monarchs varied, of course, according to his personal attitude toward them and to a certain extent according to his reaction to the conventional historical interpretations. For example, in his portrait of *Gustav III* in the last of the first cycle of post-Inferno historical dramas, Strindberg deviated less from the traditional Swedish view than in any of the others, partly because he regarded the character as "a difficult-to-manage paradox" and partly because he was deliberately attempting to produce a magnificent figure. The play, with its highly theatrical intrigues and counter-intrigues, resembles many other Scribean-style historical comedies.

Only two of Strindberg's royal portraits are actually transformed to the point where the figures are unrecognizable: Gustav Adolf and Christina. In *Gustav Adolf*, he wanted to revitalize the image of "a Lutheran saint who has become almost a schoolroom decoration" and draw him as "the blond man with the lighthearted disposition, very much the statesman and a bit the musketeer, the man with the dream of a universal monarchy, our Henri Quatre who loved beautiful women as much as a good battle."[27] But Strindberg was not capable of depicting carefree, fortunate Sunday children; nor did he really esteem them. Gustav Adolf's supposed "divine lightheartedness" is shown mainly by his indicating with chalk on a map what he contemplates conquering and concluding international treaties with no intention of keeping them. Only at the end of the play when he begins to brood over why he foolishly threw himself into "this incomprehensible war," does the character assume a commanding stature.

Strindberg's interpretation of Gustav Adolf's daughter Christina is a virtuoso performance in the depiction of vicious femininity, as well as a portrait of modern woman at the turn of the twentieth century. Outside Sweden, especially in Germany, where there is less concern about the historical inaccuracy of the characterization, *Queen Christina* is one of Strindberg's most admired and most often produced plays. But, to Strindberg's indignation, it was condemned in his native land at its publication in 1903 as an utter abortion and met with the same reception in Swedish theatres. Christina is distinguished from Strindberg's earlier feminine portraits by a touch of artistic bohemianism (one of the women from the Berlin tavern Zum Schwarzen Ferkel is mentioned among the models in a sketch). This trait is also pointed out by the queen's chief councilor, Axel

Oxenstierna: "You're so much like an artist—just as careless, just as care-free."[28] From closer to home—Strindberg was now married to the actress Harriet Bosse—he derived the notion of making Christina an actress on a throne, a pampered public favorite who, despite her twenty-seven years, retains her ingénue mannerisms and always speaks of herself as "little Kerstin." She becomes childishly offended when she notices the hatred she has provoked. Magnus Gabriel De la Gardie, the queen's sometime favorite, ruthlessly tells her the truth: "Little Kerstin has been dead a long time, but you keep digging her up."[29]

The masterpiece in Strindberg's royal gallery is, of course, Gustav Vasa. This is the only Swedish monarch he admired without reserva-tion. The king's authority and power is evident even in the few scenes in which he appears in the prose version of *Master Olof,* and during the revisions of the play he grew to such superhuman proportions that Strind-berg had to exclude him from the final poetic version to keep the central character from being overshadowed.

The figure of the young Gustav Eriksson (Vasa was the clan name by which he was known after he became king) appears in two later Strind-berg plays, *The Last of the Knights* (*Siste riddaren*—1908) and *The Regent* (*Riksföreståndaren*—1908/09). In the second act of *The Regent,* the reckless young man makes his entrance by emerging from the water near Stockholm's Blockhus Point. He then dives back into the water and swims away as the blockhouse is conquered by the Danes. His councilor from the Hanseatic League city of Lübeck, Herman Israel, complains that he is a rough-mannered fellow, but nevertheless admires young Eriksson's dedication to his vision of a united Sweden—he will proceed even "on rotten ships and with counterfeit money, straight to his goal as straight as an arrow."

The title figure in *Gustav Vasa* has something of the same vigor-ous force. The leader of the Dalesmen, Engelbrekt, looks at the king's fist in the final scene and says: "It's hard, all right, but clean!" Vasa's wrath is quickly aroused and it can be fearful: "If he gets angry up in the attic, people feel it in the cellar, just as when the thunder rumbles."[30] Devious and suspicious, he tries to use his friends to spy on one another: and he bows to no one: Master Olof reproaches him for "being deficient in piety."

Although he worries about what is best for the kingdom, he does not forget to look out for his own interests. Presumptuous and arrogant, he prevails over everyone through the force of his personality. Crown Prince Erik believes his father is the god Odin himself when the king appears in his huge felt hat and blue cape, and Councilor Israel's son Jacob thinks there is a resemblance between Vasa and Michelangelo's Isaiah in the Sistine Chapel.

Vasa arouses this mixture of admiration and fear in supporters and opponents alike because they regard him as the ambassador of a higher power. The insurgent Måns Nilsson calls the king's life a miracle story; Jacob Israel believes he is guided by the hand of the Lord; and Master Olof, who in the end is made mentor to the king, declares him to be " the miracle man of the Lord, to whom it was given to unite Swedish men and lands into one,"[31] and Vasa shares this belief. He knows that he must sacrifice everything for his mission: "I never make a decision or pronounce a sentence without having asked the Eternal One, the Almighty, for counsel. But once I've fasted, prayed, contemplated, and received the answer from above, I strike joyously, even if I have to chop off the roots of my heart."[32] Although Strindberg deleted most of the direct references to penitence that are in the sketches from the final version of the play, the basic religious theme is still dominant. In his *Open Letters* commentary, Strindberg emphasized his hero's similarity to Job and maintained that the trials to which the character is subjected in the play are the most effective way possible to "portray the great man Gustav Vasa in all his human weaknesses."[33]

Strindberg wisely left it to posterity to decide whether he had, according to certain academicians, "degraded our greatest historical figure."[34] Unlike his studies of other monarchs, his portrait of Gustav Vasa has already won public acceptance and is well on the way to eclipsing history's image. We would not want to dispense with the character's "human weaknesses"—these are the very things that make him so alive. We do not even object to the anachronisms and inconsistencies: we find it entirely proper that he permits himself to be called "a hell of a fellow" by Engelbrekt, but flares up at the liberty taken by the rebel Nils Dacke: "He calls me Eriksson!" And when he asks Master Olof: "Were you the one who said the gods are playing with us?" it should be recalled that the same sentiment is expressed at the conclusion of *Inferno*.

Gustav Vasa is made to undergo his creator's Inferno trials, but in other respects the character is a completely independent figure. Although the characters of Erik XIV and Charles XII also contain autobiographical touches, they represent an attempt to stamp a new impression on two royal portraits much cherished in Swedish literary tradition. The Erik of history was a strange and tragic figure. He was handsome, well educated, and a lover of the arts, but also suspicious, vain, and quick-tempered. He suffered from epilepsy, and when he succeeded his father Gustav Vasa to the throne in 1560, proved to be unstable. He also antagonized public opinion by his choice of confidant—the brilliant and controversial "evil genius" Göran Persson—and aroused the displeasure of the nobility by marrying his mistress, a commoner (Elizabeth of England had turned down his proposal of marriage), and provoked their hatred when he permitted the brutal massacre of his enemies, the noble Sture clan. Erik was finally overthrown by his two half-brothers and died after several years of imprisonment.[35]

Strindberg's interpretation of Erik is considerably different from earlier versions: he is not the royal dilettante with easel and lute of Johan Börjesson's play of the same name (1846), an image that survives to a certain degree in the poetry of Count Carl Snoilsky (1841-1903) and Gustav Fröding (1860-1911). He does not have the sensitivity of his fictional predecessors, and his cruelties are not explained away by a periodic dementia: neither in the drama nor in his statements about it has Strindberg presented Erik as insane in the true sense.[36]

In his commentary on the play, Strindberg declares that his intention was to render "a characterization of a characterless human being."[37] "Characterless," of course, is the term Strindberg used to describe himself in *The Son of a Servant:* a personality compounded of a multiplicity of reflexes and a complex of instincts.

In *Gustav Vasa,* Erik tries to explain the conflicts in his temperament as the result of his being the child of an ill-matched pair and of having had to endure lovelessness ever since childhood. He remembers his father's hatred of his mother: "One day I saw him raise his cane against her—against my mother; and he struck her!—On that day I ceased to be young—and I'll never forgive him—never!"[38] People complain over his heartlessness, but he declares that whatever heart he had was buried with his mother—"I wasn't given any other." "The lovelessness in which I was born and brought up has become a fire in my soul, and it is consuming me. My blood was poisoned by birth and I don't believe there's an antidote."[39] After his mother's death he had a stepmother.

Like Strindberg, he behaves obstinately to his father and rejects all his stepmother's approaches, but after meeting Karin Månsdotter—in an encounter described with visionary radiance—he reconciles himself with his parents and speaks with adolescent pride of his infatuation. In spite of his tavern vocabulary and erratic behavior, he is a more appealing figure here, as a prince, than he is later as a monarch. Karin says shortly after meeting him that she cannot forget his melancholy eyes and long face: "He's very much like a doll I once had that I called my Blinded Bloodless One."[40]

In *Erik XIV*, the lyric tenderness Erik displayed as a prince has vanished, but he is more than ever a man of extremes. His moods change quickly from exhilaration to fury, from burning zeal to passive torpor. He has a seething suspiciousness that ferrets out people's thoughts before they have finished thinking them and a morbid desire to sully everything, taking perverse pleasure in believing himself contemned and hated by everyone. After swelling with pride at the thought of bringing England's Elizabeth to Sweden as his bride, he spits out vulgar invective when he receives the news that she has rejected him. He calls her "sweet whore" and tries to persuade one of his courtiers to murder the Earl of Leicester. The same convulsive reversal of moods takes place at the time of the massacre of the Sture clan, but although Strindberg holds Erik less responsible for the murders than history does, Erik's reactions create a grotesque dramatic effect by giving the impression that the act was done without clear purpose, through a kind of moral insanity.

In the last act, the wedding of Erik and Karin gets its uncanny atmosphere from Erik's change from intoxicated mirth to frenzy. His realization that everything in his life has been "dirty and warped" provokes a wild desire in him to besmirch the wedding reception as well. This Erik is driven by the same demons as Strindberg—suspiciousness and the feeling of being a stepchild—but the portrait is not simply an interesting autobiographical document; it is a brilliant freehand drawing of an unbalanced autocrat's hysterical and capricious proclivities, and it has inner truth.

Charles XII's place in history remains a controversial one. A courageous, ambitious, but reckless soldier (his enemies called him the Madman of the North), he had the misfortune to preside over Sweden's descent from a great power to a devastated minor state. Historians still argue over how much he was to blame for this change. He scored some impressive military victories against Denmark and Poland, but earned the dubious distinction of being the first modern head of state to make an attempt to conquer Russia by marching straight to Moscow. To some Swedes, Charles XII was a genius; to others, such as Strindberg, a good deal less.

As a matter of fact, Strindberg's hatred of the king and the cult built around him became almost an *idée fixe*. In *A Blue Book* he states that anyone reluctant to join in celebrating the anniversary of Charles XII's death in battle (November 30, 1718) risked being "killed outright, just as if he had disturbed public worship."[41] In the Chamber Play *The Burned House*, Strindberg's alter ego, the Stranger, tried to hang himself in a closet when he was ten years old because he was disgusted that he and his schoolmates were sent out with banners and torches to honor "the nation's desolator." But despite such references, including the *Open Letters* statement that the king was "Sweden's corrupter, the great criminal, the bully, the idol of blackguards, the counterfeiter," Strindberg felt a spiritual kinship with him. The short story about the king's death, "At the Wake in Tistedalen," in *Swedish Destinies and Adventures* offers a good illustration of this feeling. In the play, there is a mysterious "Man" who constantly refers to Charles XII as "the villain." But when the king is shot, the Man expresses Strindberg's own conflicting thoughts: "Imagine—I couldn't get really angry at that man! But he was a devil all the same!"[42]

Strindberg was sympathetic toward Charles XII because of certain traits he himself was usually accused of: morbid shyness and a contempt for women. In Act Two, the king has returned from abroad but refuses to set eyes on Stockholm again unless he can make a triumphal entry; he thus remains in a kind of exile in the southern university town of Lund, just as Strindberg stayed in Lund before returning to the capital in 1899. Another autobiographical touch is evident in Act Five, where Charles XII throws a packet of critical anonymous letters into the fire: "I can't fight against lies or the father of lies. . . . I wasn't any angel, but I certainly wasn't that devilishly black, either!"[43] And in Act Four, he admits to his sister Ulrika Eleonora that the only woman he ever loved was

his mother, "because she was my mother and so—not a woman to me!
. . . Oh, you women! I have stood outside windows and looked into
homes; that's why I've seen more than others, because the person inside
sees only his own.—The sweetest, the bitterest!—Love is a hairsbreadth
from hate!"[44] One wonders when Charles XII had opportunities to stand
outside windows and look into homes.

But it is only during unguarded moments that the king reveals his
feelings in this way. In the first act he appears on stage but is mute; in the
second, it is a while before he opens his mouth and even then he is barely
audible. When he finally does begin to speak, the words are abrupt, nervous, and clumsy, delivered in a hushed tone of command. There is a gray
misty light about him; he never discloses the key to his riddle, but, precisely because he never emerges from his shadow, he has a touch of greatness.

It is significant that Strindberg, who often painted his figures
either black or white, was careful to add grays in his portraits of the monarchs. With the exception of Christina, none of the Swedish rulers is arbitrarily censored, and even in Gustav Vasa, whom he loved, he did not
neglect to point out faults. The same tendency is evident in the handling of
the subordinate characters. The Lübeckian councilor Herman Israel in
Gustav Vasa is a mixture of amiable patriarch and conniving diplomat.
In the same play, Göran Persson's disillusionment and cynicism make him
reminiscent of Doctor Borg in *The Red Room,* but in *Erik XIV,* Persson
becomes a dutiful son, a generous and altruistic lover, and a genuine democrat. Even Lady Birgitta—later Saint Birgitta— in *The Saga of the Folkungs,* who in the opening scene is depicted as a ridiculous old witch, subsequently becomes a repentent sinner. But when commenting on the play,
Strindberg's animosity toward this famous medieval "emancipatress" was
stronger, and he concludes his statement: "Using original documents, I
made of this unsympathetic woman the unmanageable fool now found in
the play, although out of respect I permitted her to awaken to a realization of her foolishness and pride."[45]

Birgitta is a mouthpiece for the author, and the same is true to a
greater extent of Master Olof in *Gustav Vasa.* In a conversation between
Master Olof and his son Reginald, the young man declares his bitterness

because the Reformation instituted by his father's generation has created spiritual disorder: "We don't know what to believe." When Master Olof replies: "But we were also . . . deprived of our childhood faith by our prophets," he is reflecting Strindberg's attitude toward the younger generation who accused him of having robbed them of their faith. This Olof is different from the title character of Strindberg's earlier plays; nor does he resemble the bloated canon of the Epilogue. He is still something of a skeptic, but he is also austere and consistent and so a contrast to the impulsive and temperamental Gustav Vasa. By the time Master Olof makes his final appearance in a Strindberg play—in *The Regent*—he has become sternly resolute.

> MÅNS NILSSON: That Master Olof is not an engaging man!
> HERMAN ISRAEL: He's a currycomb!
> ANDERS PERSSON: He demolishes. People like that are needed nowadays.

This is Strindberg's parting word to the hero who once mirrored the tender dreams of his youth.

Strindberg drew a totally different kind of self-portrait in the person of Klas Tott in *Queen Christina*. Tott's ignoble descent from a bastard line of the house of Vasa (he was Erik XIV's great-grandson) enabled Strindberg to give him the same mixture of emotional refinement and brutality that he felt he had received from his socially mismated parents. Moreover, his treatment of Klas Tott's love for Christina is so closely modeled upon Strindberg's last marriage (he was fifty-two and Harriet Bosse, twenty-three) that instead of creating the impression of a twenty-three-year-old man in love with a queen four years his senior, Strindberg makes Tott seem like a typical aging lover, clinging tightly and convulsively to the only precious thing life still has to offer. He is under the illusion that the queen is a being from another world who does not realize it herself: "When the gods sent you, their daughter, down here, they erased your memory."[46] (At this time, Strindberg was developing the character of Indra's Daughter in *A Dream Play* who during her wandering on earth forgets her heavenly origin.) Eventually, however, Tott is totally disillusioned and calls Christina "whore," accusing her of having conveyed him "into a whirlpool of strange desires," of having led his thoughts down paths they must not go, and thus compelling him to destroy himself "in order to sever the bond with these baser regions."

Historical Color and Style

No matter how determinedly Strindberg altered people and events in the later historical dramas or how zealously he defended his modernization of the material, he still had a fervent interest—as he did in *Swedish Destinies*—in re-creating the past. His decision, made in Paris early in 1898, to write a play about Sweden in the Middle Ages, came about primarily because his interest in Catholicism had made him enthusiastic about the period, which he believed was being reborn in France: "The beautiful Middle Ages—when people had the capacity to enjoy and to suffer; when strength and love, beauty in color, contour, and harmonies last appeared before they were drowned and butchered by the heathenistic renaissance called Protestantism."[47] (He even regarded the reappearance of leprosy to be a symptom of the rebirth of the Middle Ages.)

The extravagant contrasts of the Middle Ages dominate the fourth act of *The Saga of the Folkungs,* in which Strindberg portrayed a big crowd scene for the first time since the prose version of *Master Olof.* The setting is a city square with the stench of plague in the air. King Magnus carries a large black crucifix on his expiation journey, and from the church come the sounds of the singing of a *Kyrie eleison,* partially obscured by the trumpet blasts of the army and the screams of half-naked flagellants scourging themselves. The Madwoman who had earlier prophesied the terrible road Magnus would have to follow to expiate the sins of the Folkungs, wanders on the roof of the monastery as if in her sleep; when she reaches the turret, she begins to toll the bell. Down in the square the crowd separates and the vermillion-faced Plague Girl appears, clad in black except for a white cap. She carries a broom over one shoulder and with a piece of chalk marks crosses on entrances to houses, on tables, and on people's clothes. Here is the full range of medieval moods: from raw brutality to boundless ecstasy.

Gustav Vasa is so completely dominated by the monarch that we scarcely notice the accurate re-creation of the historical setting of the middle sixteenth century. In the opening scene in Måns Nilsson's cottage, the tolling of a church bell and the ominous rolling of drums provide a grim accompaniment as the insurgent Dalesmen are called to their executions, one at a time. Three bloody coats are then brought in and thrown on the table. The scene is similar to an actual incident in 1528 at Tuna Church in Dalecarlia, when Vasa assembled all the yeomen of the province and had several of their leaders executed. There are other memorable historical images in the play: the scene in the Hanseatic League office where crucifixes and monstrances confiscated from Catholic churches and cloisters are weighed and appraised as payment of the kingdom's debt to the city of Lübeck, the colorful moments in the Blå Duvan Inn, and the brilliant final-act scene on the palace terrace where the king listens anxiously as the sounds of the Dalesmen's birchbark horns and drums come closer and closer.

In *Gustav Adolf,* the entire opening act—as is the case with Schiller's *Wallensteins Lager*—is devoted to the rendering of a picture of Germany during the Thirty Years War in the early 1630's. Like his predecessor, Strindberg depicted life behind the lines and thus created an intense atmosphere of war without bringing large masses of men on stage. Stragglers from the rear guard of the German Imperial Army appear: a Kronoberger (Bavarian cavalryman) with a white death's-head on his helmet, a Croatian laden with plunder, and two Walloons who gaze out toward the sea and the thunderclouds above it. They are watched by two civilians, an impoverished miller and his wife who occupy a cloister ruin that has been transformed into a mill. The struggle to survive during wartime has made the miller a sensitive interpreter of the sounds of battle: "Those are hoofbeats and the clashing of weapons.- - - Evil is at hand, wife! Worse than the year the Croatians murdered people upstream at the river source, when the mill waterfall ran red and the big wheel churned up blood like at autumn slaughter."[48]

A similar description of war-ravaged Sweden in 1715 opens *Charles XII.* A cottage, its windows broken, its roof tiles torn away, and its door removed, is half-buried in a field of shifting sand on the coast of southern Sweden. A man dressed in rags searches the ruins for the remains of the home he left fifteen years earlier when he was called to war. He finds the stove on which his wife cooked oatmeal and, in the sand, the sole of a shoe: "It's my wife's—she had a pretty little foot that walked quietly and gently—right here! . . . I suppose this is the way the whole kingdom looks!- - - A ruin, a scrap heap—and a rotten apple on top."[49]

Strindberg's last masterpiece in the series of historical vignettes he began with the tavern scene in *Master Olof* is the opening of *Gustav III* in Holmberg's bookstore in Stockholm. The time is the late 1780's, shortly before the revolutionary fever of the eighteenth century made Gustav III the target of an assassin at a masked ball. In Holmberg's store gather literary people and politicians to discuss the king's extravagances, freedom of the press, and incipient revolt. When the rumor comes that a riot has started, the store is closed by the commissioner of police. While the others scatter in alarm, and drums are heard in the streets, the revolutionary writer Thomas Thorild (1757-1808) remains behind, unruffled, and delivers a heroic tirade against kings and tyranny.

Thus far, this discussion has been limited to Strindberg's use of historical material in large panoramas, but of course he was also capable of sketching striking cameo scenes. In the portrait of the Swedish bugle boy in *Gustav Adolf,* he created his most powerful image of the ferocity and senselessness of war. The lad has traveled with the army all his life; born in Livonia in Russia with a drum for a crib, he was rocked in a baggage wagon across Poland. He has never seen Sweden, but has heard wonderful campfire stories about the land of his ancestors: "I want to go home, I want to go home," he mumbles on the eve of the battle of Lützen, as he lies dying of fever with the big drum in his arms. This is not the only time in these dramas that Strindberg epitomized the entire course of action in a single symbolic scene.

Contemporary critics were convinced that whenever the sense of historical period in these plays did not ring true it was because Strindberg had neglected to provide sufficient background material. The reverse is probably true. Whenever Strindberg felt unsure of himself, he took great care with details involving historical personages and events. *The Saga of the Folkungs* and *Gustav Vasa* are examples of how he could encumber a play with superfluous historical material. Magnus Eriksson delivers a long account of the history of the Folkung dynasty to Queen Blanche, and the history is continued in *Gustav Vasa* by the king as he explains to his queen how she too belongs to the clan and is even related to Valdemar the Victorious. In these plays, however, Strindberg wisely refrained from speculating about state politics. In *Erik XIV* he ignored this principle, and by the time he wrote *Gustav Adolf,* had succumbed completely to the temptation of inundating the spectator with his observations on world history.

After Strindberg's third marriage, another gratuitous element asserted itself in the historical dramas: the woman question. The real Charles XII was thought by his court to be afraid of women: Strindberg's character, to the contrary, shows himself to be a brilliant woman-tamer. Gustav III is made to relive Strindberg's own domestic martyrdom: his queen, Sofia Magdalena, provoked by the obnoxious man-hater Fru Schröderheim, harasses the king constantly with demands for her independence, and although she despises his effeminacy, becomes angry the moment he shows himself capable of manly action. Mannish women are severely criticized in *The Saga of the Folkungs* and *Gustav Vasa*, and in *Queen Christina* Strindberg devoted an entire play to this kind of female.

Comments on state politics and the satire against women combined to wear away the historical veneer from Strindberg's dialogue. Even in the earliest of the later histories, *The Saga of the Folkungs*, the relationship between the rough-mannered Knut Porse and his mistress, the power-hungry Queen Dowager, Duchess Ingeborg, contains the ambivalent "love-hatred" that appeared in Strindberg's dramas of the 1880's. Ingeborg expresses her contempt for men in approximately the same naturalistic tone as Miss Julie's: "I hate you . . . so much, I'd like to see your eyes on a fishhook and your liver chopped up for cats."[50]

Strindberg attempted in several scenes of the play to suggest archaic speech, though it lacks a specifically medieval quality. The dialogue in the final act has a lyrical ring strikingly similar to that of Maeterlinck, whom Strindberg had already read but did not yet really appreciate. When King Magnus listens to the song of the wind through a chink in the door, he says: "It sounds like when sick people wail or when children cry over lost toys—have you noticed the special way they cry then?- - - And why does the wind lament only in autumn? The same air is present in summer!"[51] And when the two royal lovers Erik and Beatrice— like a fairy prince and princess out of some Maeterlinck medieval drama —lie dying from the plague, their mumblings have a mysterious quality.

When Strindberg sent the manuscript of *The Saga of the Folkungs* to Geijerstam on April 23, 1899, he wrote: "The difficult thing was to bring out the intimate relationships between people in the midst of state affairs. Have I succeeded?" At this time he had already planned *Gustav Vasa*, in which he would solve this problem.

Many speeches in *The Saga of the Folkungs* retain the ballad style of those earliest plays where Strindberg attempted to re-create medie-

val language. For *Gustav Vasa* he returned to the realistic dialogue of
Master Olof, which despite its modern syntax does suggest a past era.
Ordinarily, authors who write about Gustav Vasa regard his letters and
speeches as a gold mine; one can often identify long tirades taken right out
of the Royal Registry. Strindberg was familiar with these sources only at
second hand and scarcely bothered with them. There is not a phrase in
the entire play that is dusty with pedantry. The journals of the historical
Master Olof inspired him only to the extent of making the character's
speeches abrupt and forceful. The diction and certain images in *Gustav
Vasa* suggest Hagberg's unique translations of Shakespearean prose, but
these passages were not necessarily borrowed from Hagberg.[52]

In the later post-Inferno historical dramas, Strindberg yielded to
the temptation to have the characters speak with the author's voice and
intonations, but he avoided this in *Gustav Vasa* even when a character
became the mouthpiece for his ideas, as is the case with Master Olof. Seldom do Strindberg's people characterize themselves so unmistakably
through their speeches. Anyone who reads the play can hear Gustav
Vasa's deep, ringing voice, Erik's thin falsetto, and Göran Persson's cynical grunting. The dry and unmusical Swedish that Strindberg has the
Lübeckians speak gives the impression that it is spoken by foreigners, in
spite of the fact that it contains no grammatical errors. Then, too, the
suggestion of dialect is not over-emphasized in the ingenious and conceited
speech of the Dalesmen. It is not surprising that Strindberg was not
able to repeat this impressive feat: even a more consistent writer would
have had a difficult time doing so.

By the time he wrote *Erik XIV,* Strindberg had abandoned efforts
to suggest archiac speech; the dialogue is bold, candid conversational
speech, unparalleled in Swedish historical drama at that time. During the
opening act, King Erik tosses off so many strong words—particularly
when he thinks about Elizabeth's rejection of his proposal—that Göran
Persson, who is not otherwise squeamish, feels obliged to protest: "My
king and friend, you use that word 'hate' so often that soon you're going
to imagine yourself the enemy of the human race. Put it away!"[53] We do
not see Erik accepting this admonition *ad notam,* however, and his fondness for harsh words seems gradually to infect the other characters in the
play.

In *Queen Christina,* Strindberg is straightforwardly colloquial, as if indifferent to the problems of writing period dialogue. Furthermore, the figures are handled so presumptuously that the play has the flavor of a scandalous historical masquerade: Carl Gustav (later Charles X) is a genial epicure; Magnus Gabriel De la Gardie (nobleman and Christina's first favorite), a professional jester; and Axel Oxenstierna (Sweden's greatest statesman), an indulgent and slow-witted old man. When *Queen Christina* was first produced by August Falck at the Intimate Theatre on March 27, 1908, the criticism was devastating and disturbed Strindberg deeply; in a letter to Falck on March 30, he called the play his "finest work." However, he was of a different opinion earlier, during rehearsals, when he wrote to Falck: "Aim higher than I did! Elevate these historical personages! And try to evoke a bit of grandeur and . . . [historicity]. A bit of formality in the playing, which the costumes require; a bit of elegance (Molière), otherwise we shall descend without fail into travesty."[54]

For *Gustav III,* Strindberg tried to provide dialogue appropriate to the period in the last quarter of the eighteenth century which is called the "Gustavian," the era of the first great flowering of elegance in Swedish arts and letters. He also made it more "historical" by occasionally inserting actual speeches. For example, the revolutionary Thorild reads aloud long passages from his letters and writings, which Strindberg had already used in *The Swedish People.* In developing dialogue for Captain Anckarström, the fanatic officer who assassinated Gustav III at the masked ball in 1792, Strindberg used excerpts from Anckarström's trial proceedings which he found in the *Swedish Biographical Dictionary (Svenskt biografiskt lexikon).* In other words, Strindberg resorted to a rather cheap way of fabricating historical effect, something he did not do in *Gustav Vasa.*

The Last Post-Inferno Historical Dramas

After *Gustav III* (1902), Strindberg stopped writing plays about Swedish history for a time because his most recent works were not accepted by the theatres: the premiere of *Engelbrekt*—a completely uninspired piece written in the summer of 1901—had been a fiasco, six years would elapse before *Queen Christina* was performed, and *Gustav III* was not produced until after his death. Since several other of his plays had also been rejected (among them *A Dream Play*), he turned from Swedish to world history in hopes of having better luck abroad.

The Nightingale of Wittenberg (Näktergalen i Wittenberg), a play about Luther written in 1903, was intended for a German audience and is actually an inferior version of *Master Olof*. It is almost a travesty, consisting of a parade of Reformation figures making famous statements, such as Ulrich von Hutten's remark to Dr. Johannes Faust about being happy to be alive in a time when spirits were awakening, with Faust replying: "Whom have I the honor of . . . ?" and Lucas Cranach's leading question to Hans Sachs: "Well, friend Sachs, you haven't sung in several years, have you?"

A trilogy, written in 1903 but published posthumously—*Moses, Socrates,* and *Christ*—was intended to initiate a cycle of dramas on world history, but to some extent seems to be a joke on the audience. In any case, Strindberg abandoned the plan and recast the trilogy in story form for the collection *Historical Miniatures (Historiska miniatyrer*—1905).

It was quite another story with the three plays Strindberg wrote in the fall of 1908, primarily with the thought of producing something the big theatres would accept. These plays—*The Last of the Knights, The Regent,* and *Earl Birger of Bjälbo*—were greeted with surprisingly indulgent criticism: one reviewer even rated *The Last of the Knights* above *Gustav Vasa.* The probable reason for this approval was that Strindberg had taken more pains with historical accuracy and tried to avoid disturbing anachronisms. But the plays disappeared rather quickly from theatre repertoires and have not since been revived. *The Last of the Knights* and *The Regent* were intended to constitute a trilogy with *Gustav Vasa.* In *The Last of the Knights,* Sten Sture the Younger, a member of the clan displaced by the Vasas, represents the dying idealism of the age of chivalry, whereas the practical politics of the new era is personified by young Gustav Eriksson (Vasa). Strindberg had already brought out this contrast less deliberately in *Master Olof.* In the beautiful final act, Sten Sture is a vitual copy of the banished Magnus in *The Saga of the Folkungs,* and Strindberg was aware of the resemblance.[55]

The Regent, also dealing with Gustav Vasa's earlier years, has lively traces of folk drama, but the characterizations are devoid of subtlety. Of *Earl Birger of Bjälbo* Strindberg said that he brought the chief character alive "by taking blood and nerves out of my own life." This is especially true of the title character, a self-portrait of the aging, life-weary Strindberg (he was almost sixty). An unfriendly fate has denied Earl Birger the crown that he, above anyone else, merited. In order to bring peace to the nation, he had to perjure himself and commit crimes, and for ten years has worn a hairshirt and given up meat and wine. His court astrologer tells him that his crime is expiated and that he may burn his hairshirt. But he is gloomy and distrustful: "I am going to throw off my mask, Willibald. I now know what life and human beings are, and I want to use this dearly bought wisdom. Human beings? Call them scoundrels! Friends? Fellow criminals, that's what friends are! Love? Say hate! They all hate each other! My children hate me, as I hate them."[56] Disgusted with people, the Earl wants to retreat into solitude on Visingö, the large island in Lake Vätter in central Sweden. "I shall walk in the woods, look at the lake, think about what I've lived through, try to become reconciled with the past, and prepare myself for what lies ahead."[57] A few months earlier, on July 10, 1908, Strindberg had moved into the Blue Tower—the house at 85 Drottning Street where he would die four years later. *Earl Birger of Bjälbo* contains the bitter misanthropy of his later years, but also his longing for atonement and his sense that the end was near.

Notes to Chapter Sixteen

1. Mörner, p. 120.
2. The following table indicates the reigns, in chronological order, of the Swedish rulers discussed in detail in this chapter:

PLAY	RULER
Earl Birger of Bjälbo (1908)	Earl Birger, regent (1250-66)
The Saga of the Folkungs (1899)	Magnus Eriksson, king (1319-64)
The Regent (1908) and *Gustav*	Erik XII, co-king (1357-59)
Vasa (1899)	Gustav Vasa, regent (1521-23)
Erik XIV (1899)	king (1523-60)
Gustav Adolf (1900)	Erik XIV, king (1560-68)
Queen Christina (1901)	Gustav II Adolf, king (1611-32)
Charles XII (1901)	Christina, queen (1632-54)
Gustav III (1902)	Charles XII, king (1697-1718)
	Gustav III, king (1771-92)

A table listing the reigns of all the important historical figures in the plays can be found in Walter Johnson's valuable study *Strindberg and the Historical Drama* (1963) pp. 13-14—Translator

3. *See* p. 103.—Translator
4. *SS:*L, p. 109.
5. *SS:*XLVII, p. 545.
6. *SS:*L, p. 296.
7. *Ibid.,* p. 255.
8. It is difficult to understand why this brilliant scene has not become as renowned as Professor Stenkåhl's "phantom supper" in the novel *Black Banners.*
9. *SS:*XXXI, p. 379.
10. *SS:*L, p. 258.
11. *SS:*XXXII, p. 272.
12. *SS:*L, p. 251.
13. *SS:*XXXII, p. 39.
14. *SS:*XXXI, p. 58.
15. *SS:*XXXV, p. 223.
16. *SS:*LIV, p. 353.
17. *SS:*L, p. 114.
18. *Ibid.,* p. 52.
19. *Ibid.,* p. 69.

20. *See* p. 215.
21. *SS:*L, p. 123.
22. He had just moved to 31 Banér Street (named for Johan Banér, one of Gustav Adolf's close associates) and wrote with delight in his diary on October 13, 1899, that he was living "directly opposite Gustav Adolf's Church."
23. *SS:*XLIX, p. 278.
24. *SS:*XXXV, p. 136.
25. *SS:*L, p. 240.
26. *Ibid.*, pp. 237-53.
27. *Ibid.*, p. 249.
28. *SS:*XXXIX, p. 228.
29. *Ibid.*, p. 220.
30. *SS:*XXXI, p. 183.
31. *Ibid.*, p. 261.
32. *Ibid.*, p. 210.
33. *SS:*L, p. 247.
34. *Ibid.*, p. 248.
35. A theory has persisted since the king's death that he was murdered. When his body was disinterred recently, it was discovered to be full of arsenic.—Translator
36. In Strindberg's analysis of *Hamlet* he states that Hamlet, like Erik XIV, was "insane or simulating [insanity]" (*SS:*L, p. 75).
37. *SS:*L, p. 248.
38. *SS:*XXXI, p. 172.
39. *Ibid.*, pp. 172-73.
40. *Ibid.*, p. 230.
41. *SS:*XLVII, p. 614.
42. *SS:*XXXV, p. 223.
43. *Ibid.*, p. 217.
44. *Ibid.*, p. 200.
45. *SS:*L, p. 243.
46. *SS:*XXXIX, p. 217.
47. *SS:*XXVIII, p. 347.
48. *SS:*XXXII, p. 9.
49. Also present in this scene, and in the entire play, are Maeterlinck's fatalism and mysticism, his dream-like atmosphere and gloom.
50. *SS:*XXXI, p. 55.
51. *Ibid.*, p. 118.
52. *See* Joan Bulman, *Strindberg and Shakespeare* (1933), p. 217.

53. *SS:XXXI*, p. 305.
54. August Falck, *Fem år med Strindberg* (1935), p. 138.
55. *SS:L*, p. 256.
56. *SS:XLIX*, p. 278.
57. *Ibid.*, p. 347.

Chapter Seventeen

MODERN PLAYS AND DRAMATIZED FOLK TALES

Strindberg was occupied with *Erik XIV* and *Gustav Adolf* during the year immediately following his departure from Lund in midsummer, 1899. His working pace was slower than before, and although the cycle of historical dramas would be continued in the following years, it was punctuated by long interruptions. It is apparent from his correspondence and diary that he longed to experiment with other literary forms. Moreover, he veered constantly between optimism and pessimism, and these moods are reflected in his work during the first years of the new century.

In certain respects the time he spent in Lund—lasting, except for the period August, 1897, to March, 1898, from December, 1896, to June, 1899—was unique in Strindberg's life. It is true that in *Inferno* and *Legends* he had felt obliged to complain about the exquisite cunning with which the Powers had chosen the small university town for his prison, forcing him to associate with students—"bachelors who are addicted to a dissolute tavern life." But he was probably more honest several years later when he called Lund "this mysterious little town, which one can never figure out; secretive, inscrutable; friendly, but not with open arms; as serious and industrious as a cloister which one has not entered voluntarily, yet which one leaves with regret; a place from which one believes one can flee, but to which one returns again."[1] This was the very atmosphere Strindberg needed after the troubled Inferno years. Furthermore, he established friendships there that lasted for the rest of his life. Strindberg loved the company of academicians—a fact attested to by the dominant role played by the academic profession in his gallery of characters. In Lund he made friends with a number of university people trained in medicine and psychology, and they respected and understood him. They also tolerated with good-humored equanimity his casting them in the role of penitential sinners in *Legends*.

It was his longing for the skerries that induced him to return north. He left Lund on June 20, 1899, stayed for two days with friends on Lillön in Lake Mälar and on Midsummer Eve arrived at Furusund in the skerries: "the most beautiful place I know in Sweden." When he returned from there to Stockholm after a number of weeks, he noted in his diary (August 8, 1899): "Received a tremendously strong impression of something new [and] shining that has brightened up Stockholm, and all the old, dark houses from the 1870's and 1880's look dirty." Once again, his native city and its archipelago became the focal point of his writing, in which they had not had a place since the 1880's.

In the beginning, the new spirit he felt in Stockholm induced in him an almost cloying optimism most clearly reflected in the drama *Midsummer,* but disappointment soon cropped up. He had begun his Furusund visit with the great reconciliation with his family that he had hopefully anticipated on several occasions in his works. It was quickly followed by new conflicts, however, and at his departure from Furusund he noted in his diary: "This *séjour* seems like a beautiful Midsummer Night's dream to me, now that I look back on it. But the details were dreadful." The renewals of old friendships were only temporary and followed by new breaks. When he got a close look at the theatre situation, he was distressed and thought again of starting his own theatre if he were "forced to because of the obstacles."

He no longer tried to blame his interpersonal difficulties on others. He admitted in a letter to his painter friend Richard Bergh on February 18, 1901: "By isolating myself from life's banalities, I grow so sensitive that soon I shall not even be able to endure people's glances." On February 16, he had written Bergh that he was thinking of going into an Italian monastery:

> Even if I did not enter for life, I long to be there and away from here. I believe my presence here at home has only an irritating, disturbing effect on the peaceful work of others. - - - Now that I have redeemed the promise of my youth and fulfilled my obligations to my country, I think it might be proper to disappear, almost believing I have a duty to public modesty to conceal my bulky, untidy person. And allow my works—alone! —to speak for themselves!

It was at this time that Strindberg resumed the *To Damascus* cycle and in Part III had his hero end up in a monastery dedicated to "Humanity! and Resignation!"

During the time Strindberg was "preparing for the departure," as he described it to Bergh, he realized that he was hopelessly in love once again. Harriet Bosse, who had been a success as the Lady in Part I of *To Damascus* and was now rehearsing the role of Eleonora in *Easter*, haunted his dreams and filled his waking thoughts. "Felt as if life was about to smile again," he observed in his diary after one of her visits in the middle of February, 1901. He sensed he had entered a new phase: "Longing for purity, beauty, and harmony." But at the same time he feared new disappointments: "If the High Powers are joking with me, I am ready to bear that, too!"

The courtship was conducted in the solemn imagery of the *Damascus* dramas. When Strindberg asked Harriet if she thought "The Stranger" should follow through with his plans to enter a monastery, the young actress said she would like to reconcile him with the world and show him how good and happy it could be. They became engaged, but then there were discussions about a home and children, and Harriet began to have doubts. Before long, arguments ensued, and Strindberg was once again in torment. He remembered his earlier matrimonial unhappinesses and determined to proceed cautiously. This is most evident in the beautiful, tenderly phrased letters he wrote to Harriet, totally different from his usual brusque and matter-of-fact style of correspondence, and the same determination can be seen in his love poems and in the play *Swanwhite* (*Svanevit*—1901). The years, however, had made him touchier and more difficult to live with than ever.[2] They were married in May, 1901, but the poetic dream world Strindberg created around himself and his loved one collapsed after several months: they were divorced in October, 1904, after having been separated for a year. During their marriage, he was bitter toward Harriet only during the stormy periods, and even then we can see in his letters, diary entries, and poetry that he truly regretted their conflicts. After the divorce, he began to court Harriet again, and he was once more the troubadour celebrating his lady in poems and letters. But whenever they saw each other for any length of time the old wounds were torn open again.

He was always grateful for the rejuvenation the new love had brought him and regarded the suffering as the cost he had to pay for the precious moments: "Do you think happiness exists unalloyed, or that it has a price?" he asked in a letter in 1904. "It is paid for with suffering and hardship, yet it can be so intense that one can live on the memory of it for many years. The memory of *one* Sunday morning still keeps me alive."[3] Even after Harriet had married again, Strindberg was convinced that their relationship lay outside time and space and that they continued to communicate with one another telepathically long after they had stopped corresponding.

During the first years after his return to Stockholm, Strindberg was occupied exclusively with drama, and it occurred to him that perhaps his life had been a series of trials sent by the Powers to temper him for his calling. On January 25, 1901, he wrote in his diary:

> Is it possible that all the dreadful things I experienced were staged for my benefit so that I might become a dramatist and depict all states of mind and all situations? I was a dramatist at twenty. But if my life had passed quietly and calmly, I would have had nothing to depict.

At this time he was indeed involved with depicting "all states of mind and all situations." In addition to his history plays—which were rather different from their predecessors—he experimented with other genre: serious comedy, naturalistic domestic drama, peasant drama, dramatized folk or fairy tales, and finally the extraordinary *A Dream Play*. It may not seem possible to discern the connecting links between such diverse works as *Midsummer, Easter, The Dance of Death,* and *The Crown Bride (Kronbruden)* which were produced in rapid succession during the last half of 1900 (judging from diary entries, Strindberg wrote *Easter* and *The Dance of Death* simultaneously), but when we survey all the drama of the period, a line of development becomes apparent.

The idea of penitence was still a dominant theme in the plays written in 1900. It is found in *Gustav Adolf, Easter,* and *The Crown Bride,* and glimpses of it are also evident in *Midsummer* and *The Dance of Death.* But in the dramas from 1901 on—the year Strindberg fell in love and married—it disappears. Instead, love is the principal theme; in *Swanwhite* it is pictured as a warm and happy experience, whereas in the dramas following, it becomes imbued with increasing sadness and bitterness. In works such as *Charles XII, A Dream Play,* and the fragment *The Dutchman (Holländarn),* love is portrayed as both the sweetest and bitterest thing life has to offer, the point of view uppermost in Strindberg's mind as he developed his image of the hard and thorny path humanity had to follow.

After the years in Paris and Lund, the first period in Stockholm was a sudden return to reality. The bright and sunny outside world dazzled Strindberg, who had not written a work with a contemporary Swedish setting since the beginning of the 1890's. In *Midsummer* he tried to express his delight in his native city is it appeared to him after his long absence. But he had not allowed his impressions to mature and realized that the play's failure was deserved. As a result, in *Easter* he returned to his Lund memories and in *The Dance of Death* resumed his 1880's naturalism, with an exaggeration in the delineation of characters and situations that foreshadowed the Chamber Plays.

The evolution of *The Crown Bride* from original concept to published play reflects a basic transformation that took place in Strindberg's style. The piece was first conceived as a "Grand Swedish Dalecarlia play" with the typical red cottages, white birches, and green spruces of that northern province. In the sketches it became a modern, realistic peasant drama, and finally turned into a dramatized folk tale based on ballads and legends and—for practical purposes—removed to the reign of Charles XV (1859-72). This change in stylistic approach from realistic to unrealistic continued with *Swanwhite* and reached its first peak in *A Dream Play* where Strindberg found it necessary to invent a new form to depict the external reality blooming around him in Stockholm and the archipelago: the inner reality of the world of dreams. The second peak was the Chamber Plays.

Midsummer

Ten years earlier in 1889, when Strindberg returned to Stockholm after his first long stay abroad, he had described in the fifth "somnambulist night" how dark and alien the city seemed to have become for him. Now he was delighted with the bright new innovations introduced after the industrial exposition of 1897. The light and sinuous art nouveau architecture—with its turrets and playful, arabesque-like ornamentation—had succeeded the traditional styles. And the same festive quality began to appear in interiors: airy curtains, bright wallpaper designs, and whimsically carved birch and oak furniture. Until his death Strindberg remained an admirer of the Swedish version of the *Jugendstil*.

The new trend in taste was in harmony with the cultural national-ism that began to color everyday life in Sweden. There were special folk festivals in Skansen, Stockholm's newly opened park and ethnographical museum, and a surge of popular interest in folk dances, peasant furniture, domestic handicrafts, and especially the picturesque folk qualities of the provinces of Dalecarlia and Värmland. School children were enthusiastic about the outdoors and went skiing, rode bicycles, and played tennis. Sports-minded young people became an ingredient in all of Strindberg's works, even the gloomy *Dance of Death*. There were lively debates about the reformation of the national defense forces along democratic lines, and people demanded universal suffrage and improved social conditions. The curve of the business cycle was upward, and public opinion favored trade unions and their demonstrations. There was general support for the tem-perance movement, and the growing respect for the democratic tendencies of the different new religious sects and missions that sprang up led to talk of replacing the established State Lutheran Church with a truly popular and nationalistic state church. Even the boisterous emergence of the Sal-vation Army was in harmony with the contemporary demand for festivals and parades.

Strindberg sensed the trend toward national democracy while he was in Lund. His characterization of Gustav Vasa, the peasant king, was an expression of this—in the final scene of the play the king shakes hands with the simple Dalesman, Engelbrekt. But Strindberg's past bitterness toward Heidenstam and Levertin made it impossible for him to appreciate fully the lyrical nationalism in the literature of the 1890's, which meant not only the work of the authors of the "Pepita" outrage, but also that of Selma Lagerlöf, Gustav Fröding, and Per Hallström. Every time they are mentioned in his writings, it is with a certain condescension, and in *The Gothic Rooms* a discussion of European literature in the 1890's omits any reference to its Swedish representatives. On the other hand, he showed full understanding of how the *fin de siècle* was reflected in the graphic arts in Sweden, especially in the painters Anders Zorn, Bruno Liljefors, and above all Carl Larsson. He also loved the folk-ballad echoes evident in the music of such Swedish composers as Tor Aulin and Wilhelm Peterson-Ber-ger: in Lund he started collecting Swedish folk ballads and melodies, and their influence is especially apparent in *The Crown Bride* and *Swanwhite*.

The new milieu tempted Strindberg to abandon historical drama. On August 5, 1899, he wrote to Geijerstam that "[I have] a fully planned Swedish dramatic fairy tale in verse, which has intoxicated me, and I am burning to write it." (This might have been *The Crown Bride*.) But it was in the realistic contemporary play *Midsummer* that Strindberg gave full expression to his naive rapture for what he called "new Sweden."

Midsummer was begun in March, 1900, and completed at the end of July. Its earliest title was *In the Leaf Market (I lövmarknaden)*, referring to the traditional market set up on the day before Midsummer Eve where birch branches and leaves were sold to decorate homes and streets in honor of the holiday. The play was then retitled *Midsummer Journey (Midsommarresan)*, the same title Strindberg first gave to his poem in hexameters, "Journey to Town." The inspiration for both the play and the poem was the midsummer visit in 1899 to friends on Lillön. It was shortly after this visit that Strindberg once again set eyes on his native city. One of the scenes in the play has small children dancing midsummer dances around a gravestone in Klara churchyard—his first playground. And the drama ends with the annual Midsummer Eve festivities at Skansen. *Midsummer's* merits are in its portrayal of Stockholm, although Strindberg's old memories gave the atmosphere a strange mixture of the 1870's and the turn of the century. Gradually, the play develops into a comparison between Stockholm past and present.

Originally, Strindberg had thought of calling the piece a "religious comedy," and it does deal with penitence although in a new and somewhat surprising form. A fussy, unsociable, and conceited young man, Ivar Lundberg, returns to Stockholm after a ten-year absence. His sense of alienation from the sports-loving and optimistic young people he encounters is obviously a reflection of Strindberg's own feeling at his return.

During the course of the play, Lundberg is exposed to all the new and beautiful things Stockholm has to offer, and after enduring a series of humiliating misadventures he is cured of his pride, petulance, and fondness for fault-finding. His egocentricity and lack of consideration for others is typical of Strindberg himself; when he is urged to drink his mother's wretched coffee just to make her happy, he says: "But it would be an agony for me. How could she be made happy by my agony?" An old schoolmate, now a respected police officer, lectures him about his failure to keep abreast of the times: "You're like a perpetual undergraduate from the middle of the last century. You see, all the goals we drank to and sang and made speeches about when we were younger are now being realized, and people have begun to treat each other more humanely."[4] Lundberg's misadventures, which end when he is converted by a woman from the Salvation Army, are only one element of the overabundant action described in traditional folk comedy style. The play might well have been called *Country Folk on a Stockholm Spree.*

"Everything has changed while we were away, sir!" says the helmsman of the skerries boat to Lundberg. The drama glorifies the new era— a time, supposedly, when class distinctions have been erased, education made universal, and people are concerned about owning their own homes and about medical attention, care of the aged, and child welfare. In the end, Lundberg joins the celebration of the "new" Swedish *joie de vivre* at the folk-art festivities at Skansen where folk songs expressing the new nationalistic spirit are sung: "Manliness, Courage, and Men of Daring" ("Mandom, mod, och morske män) and "the new song of the people," "There's a Land I Know Far Up North" ("Jag vet ett land längt upp i höga nord"). Strindberg was secretly more touched by what he called "jingoism" than he cared to admit—he was even interested in the efforts to find a new national anthem. The manuscript for *Gustav Adolf* is adorned with a crayon drawing of the Swedish flag colored in the newly adopted bright shades of yellow and blue.

But clashing with the happy pictureque mood of *Midsummer* is the somber view of life shared by a number of the characters. A porter observes that everything repeats itself, and the steamboat waitress expresses what would become the central theme of *A Dream Play:* "Det är synd om alla människor," a statement that has an interesting ambiguity in Swedish, for it can be translated either as "man is to be pitied," "it's a shame about human beings," or "It's too bad about people." The Count, who is ashamed because his father was a murderer, comes to realize that through his suffering he has expiated his father's crime. The theory that by suffering for others we can expiate their guilt would shortly become the principal theme in *Easter,* where the bright summer clouds of *Midsummer* gather ominously and darkly but eventually let the sun shine through.

Easter

Easter should be included among the dramas of penitence since
their principal theme—"punishment first, atonement afterwards"—is formulated simply by Eleonora: "Today the birch rod, tomorrow, Easter
eggs!" The drama was written in Stockholm several months after the
completion of *Midsummer,* but the setting is Lund where an incident that
took place in a flower shop gave Strindberg the idea of how to create sus-
pense for the plot.[5] There are strong suggestions in the play of the religious and collegiate atmosphere that Strindberg felt pervaded the town:
the important events of the year were church confirmations, university-
qualifying examinations and doctoral dissertation defenses, and entertainment consisted mainly of concerts in the cathedral.

Guilt, suffering, and penitence hang heavily over the Heyst home,
and the family's eventual redemption is symbolically associated with the
season of atonement and reconciliation: Act One takes place on Maundy
Thursday, Act Two on Good Friday, and Act Three on Easter Eve. The
father, who never appears in the play, is serving a prison sentence for embezzlement, but his wife stubbornly insists that her husband is innocent.
Elis, the son, knows his father was guilty and is bitter because he is forced
to share the family shame and suffering. In contrast, the daughter, the
mystical Eleonora, who has just returned home from an institution and
seems strangely ill, desperately tries to accept her father's guilt as though
it were her own. Guilt and atonement are balanced in terms of debt and
payment, and throughout the play the family awaits the arrival of a fearful
creditor—Lindkist—who has the power to strip them of all they possess.

As a model for the central character of Eleonora, Strindberg used
his unmarried sister Elizabeth who was confined in the Eppsala Mental
Hospital during the time he was in Lund. When she died in 1904, he sent
her picture to Harriet Bosse: "She was like my twin, and when she died,
we were grateful for her sake. I only want to show you 'the Easter girl,'
who suffered for others, and because she took on their evils as her own,
was unable to be really good."[6] When Strindberg wrote that his sister
"suffered for others," he was referring—as we can see in *Easter*— to the
suffering caused by his father's bankruptcy which the entire family regarded as a disgrace. It is also clear from the letter that Strindberg felt that

he was spiritually allied with his sister, as if her affliction had something in common with his own Inferno Crisis which he never considered mental illness: his nerves had become hypersensitive, and he had developed the ability to see across great distances. He was always anxious to impress upon the different actresses who played Eleonora that they must avoid "the conventional interpretation of a mentally ill person."

On several occasions Strindberg emphasized his heroine's kinship with Balzac's Séraphita. Séraphita, too, is thought to be deranged, but is actually a member of a higher species, a visitor from another world who only partially shares earthly pleasures and sufferings. In a letter written but never sent to Harriet Bosse, Strindberg said of the "Easter girl":

> Family tribulations have reduced Eleonora to the mental state—called illness by some—wherein she makes contact (telepathic), sometimes with her relatives, sometimes with all of humanity, and finally with higher creation, so that she suffers along with every living thing and is a materialization of "Christ in Man." Therefore she is kin to Balzac's Séraphita, Swedenborg's niece.[7]

The statement could almost serve as a description of Indra's Daughter in *A Dream Play*, and the kinship is further suggested in notes for a contemplated sequel to *Easter* in which Eleonora would endure "the suffering of all humanity and the torment of existence."

When the delicate and ethereal Eleonora comes home, Benjamin, the young man boarding with the Heyst family, is surprised because he has never heard of her. "People don't talk about the dead," she replies. She feels she no longer has an individual existence:

> For me there is neither time nor space; I am everywhere and of all times! I am in my father's prison and in my brother's schoolroom. I am in my mother's kitchen and in my sister's store, far away in America. When business is good for my sister, I feel her happiness, and when it's bad I suffer. But I suffer most when she does something bad.[8]

She identifies with others and thereby adopts their suffering, interpreting their sins as her own: "Yes, I've embezzled trust funds—It doesn't matter very much though, because ill-gotten gains never prosper. But to blame my old father and put him in prison, you see, that can never be forgiven."[9] In the middle of a speech she breaks off: "Oh, now my father is in great trouble! They're being cruel to him.[10] . . . He and I are one and the same person."

She is knowing and precocious, having grown up remote from the games and occupations of children: "I was born old—I knew everything when I was born, and when I learned anything, it was just like remembering."[1] Her mental state is similar to Strindberg's during the Lund years when the terrible scourges of the Crisis had subsided, but his hypersensitivity continued and he brooded about religion, only half-believing that he belonged to the world of the living. Eleonora's strange observations about nature also appeared in notes for "The Book of Miracles" ("Mirakelboken"), a sequel to *Legends* he planned in Lund but never wrote. According to Eleonora, the only place nightingales sing is in the Garden of the Deaf and Dumb, because people with normal hearing do not hear what the nightingales say. The flowers have a silent language in which every scent expresses "a whole multitude of thoughts." Eleonora's sensitivity also extends to inanimate objects. For example, she can feel the difference between the good clock that beats like a heart, speeding up during hours of misfortune and slowing down when times are brighter, and the wicked clock that cannot tolerate music and must be carried out into the kitchen. The effect created by these childish superstitions woven into the character of a half-grown girl who cherishes a fantasy life isolated from human beings is beautiful and poetic. Strindberg never found a more expressive instrument for his occultism.

Coming from Eleonora's lips the rigid dogmas of the Inferno theology sound like tidings of reconciliation. When she preaches that crime itself is a punishment one is commanded to endure and that every punishment is a mercy, it does not sound cruel, but thoughtful and understanding. On her way home from the institution where she was confined, Eleonora took a daffodil from a closed flower shop, but left money behind for the florist. Although she fears the money will not be discovered and she will be accused of having stolen the flower, she forbids Benjamin to telephone the florist to report the circumstances. Her fear is a kind of punishment: "No, I did wrong, and I must be punished with this anxiety."[2] When the newspaper subsequently publishes a story about a burglary at the florist shop and Eleonora feels threatened with either prison or the asylum, she bows her head resignedly· "Then I must suffer that, too." She longs for the dreaded creditor to come and take all their possesssions:

> All the old furniture Father brought home—I've known them since I was little! Yes, we should never own anything that binds us to the earth.

We must take the stony paths that bruise our feet, for that route leads
upward and is hard.[13]

Through Eleonora's suffering and resignation the family achieves
redemption. Mrs. Heyst realizes that she was foolish when she believed
her husband was innocent despite his confession and the clear evidence
against him, and she now knows that it was pride that brought about his
misfortune. When Elis questions why the innocent have to suffer with the
guilty, she cuts him off with the eloquent: "Be still!" To her, Eleonora is
wise "because she knows how to bear life's burdens better than I do, than
we do."[14]

In *Open Letters* Strindberg points out that there are several references in the play to Algren, Benjamin's Latin teacher, who was intended
at first to represent Providence. The creditor Lindkvist replaced Algren in
this role, undoubtedly because Strindberg wanted a more literal representation of *satisfactio vicaria*, which he interpreted as one person paying the
debts of another. In the first act Elis asks his fiancée: "Can you understand this—that the Redeemer suffered for our sins, and yet we have to go
on paying? No one is paying for me!" But when Kristina asks in return:
"If someone were paying for you, would you understand then?" Elis replies:"Yes, then I'd understand."[15]

In the last act a miracle takes place—old Lindkvist remembering
that Mr. Heyst once befriended him, declines to press his claims for money
from the Heyst family, but not before he has frightened Elis and humbled
his pride. As a redeemer, Lindkvist is an unlikely figure in his guise as
"the giant from Skinflint Mountain," with his fur-collared overcoat, car-
nelian rings, and cane. During the two preceding acts, his ominous presence has an extraordinary effect, although we see only his shadow outlined
on the curtains and hear his laughter, the tapping of his cane, and the
squeaking of his leather galoshes. When he appears, the spell is broken.
Although, according to the stage directions, "he is an elderly, serious man
with a frightening appearance"—bushy eyebrows, black whiskers, and
black horn-rimmed glasses—the spectator is hardly likely to consider him
an ogre. When the play was revived by the Intimate Theatre in 1908,
Strindberg urged that "the old man should be good-natured and good-
hearted and only *pretend* to be irascible! Grunting and growling! but
good!"[16]

Elis's ultimate confession of humility is genuine, even though induced by Lindkvist's threats: Strindberg himself had been prodded onto the penitential road and burned with the desire to drag fellow sinners to the Cross. In the final scene, Inferno theology is portioned out in larger doses than the spectator can digest, but it cannot destroy the beauty of the play. Strindberg subtly cast a visionary aura over the commonplace. The supernatural is not seen, but it is talked about and believed in. It is present in the atmosphere, in the somber Easter mood, and above all in the figure of Eleonora.

The moods of the three days of the Passion represented by the three acts of the play are established by the different movements of Haydn's *Seven Last Words of Christ* that introduce each act. The use of these simple and moving melodies was a prelude to Strindberg's experiments in the coordination of musical and dramatic form that culminated in the Chamber Plays. An undertone of rhythm and music permeates the dialogue in *Easter,* although the play has neither the more obvious lyricism of *Swanwhite* nor the songs and ballads that are scattered throughout *The Crown Bride.* And, interestingly enough, although nature plays a role in all three of these plays, its presence is most strongly felt in *Easter,* in spite of the fact that the spectator can see no more landscape than the backdrop of trees in bloom that is visible through the windows of the meagerly furnished glass veranda.

A mood of happiness, albeit melancholy, glows in the first act, but dies out in the second. Good Friday, the day of suffering, has frozen over all the promises of spring. But Eleonora, who lives more in the future than in the present, feels that the weather is breaking: "You can feel the snow melting, even in here—and tomorrow the violets will be out against the south wall! The clouds have lifted—I can sense it when I breathe. Oh, I can always tell when the skies are clear!"[17]

The next morning her expectations seem to have been frustrated. The blue hepaticas she bought at the market are half-frozen. But when Benjamin asks where the sun she promised is, she answers with implicit faith: "Behind the mist. There are no clouds today—only mist from the sea. It smells of salt."[18]

At the end of the play the sun shines warmly into the room, and Eleonora shouts jubilantly: "We'll be able to go to the country, Benjamin! In two months! Oh, if only they would pass quickly!" She tears sheet after sheet from the calendar and throws them into the streaming sunlight: "See how the days go by! April, May, June! And the sun is shining on them all! See? Now you must thank God for helping us get to the country!" Benjamin asks shyly if he may say it quietly, to himself, and Eleonora replies: "Yes, you can say it quietly! For now the clouds are gone, and we can be heard up there."[9]

This ingenuous hymn of thanksgiving to a protective, paternal Power who minute by minute regulates the changes of nature and man's destiny is captivating because it stands out in relief against a background of suffering. "Happiness makes everything else trivial."

The Dance of Death

The same summer that Strindberg completed the brightly optimistic *Midsummer* he found himself once again embroiled with the relatives with whom he had recently been reconciled. The bitter memories that were reawakened, especially those involving his first divorce and the loss of his children, are reflected in *The Dance of Death*, which was written the same time as *Easter*.

In *Easter* a mood of peace and reconciliation marks the final family scenes, but in the two parts of *The Dance of Death* Strindberg returns to the living hell of marital conflict. An artillery captain and his wife have spent the nearly twenty-five years of their married life tormenting each other mercilessly. When Alice plays the piano to accompany Edgar's grotesque sword dance, she secretly hopes that he will fall dead of apoplexy, that his performance will be an actual "dance of death." Ironically, when the Captain dies at the end of Part II, she realizes that she will miss him because her compulsion to torment him made her feel alive.

The third major character is Alice's cousin Kurt, a quarantine master separated from his family by divorce. As was the case with Strindberg, the court awarded custody of Kurt's children to the mother. In Part I Kurt discovers that the Captain conspired against him in his divorce and is still acting in collusion with his divorced wife. In Part II, the Captain continues to interfere in Kurt's private affairs, draining his life, vampire-fashion, of every element of joy and hope.

The fundamental difference between this play and the marital dramas of the 1880's is that in *The Dance of Death* Strindberg takes an impartial attitude toward both parties. When the Captain asks Kurt's opinion about who is in the right, Kurt replies: "Neither! But I pity you both deeply, perhaps you a bit more."[20] In other respects, Part I of the drama is similar to the earlier plays: the main characters are reduced to three, and the setting is a prison-like tower room where for a quarter of a century the walls have reverberated with the cruel and stinging remarks that now fall so heavily and wearily.

Originally, Strindberg planned to use the title *Danse Macabre* and have Saint-Saëns's music accompany the horrifying scene in Act I where the Captain collapses during his Hungarian sword dance and falls senseless to the floor. But since Ibsen had used *Danse Macabre* in *John Gabriel Borkman* to underscore the atmosphere of terror, Strindberg had Alice play the *Entry of the Boyars* march instead. In Part II, Alice explains that the Captain's fall virtually killed him and that he has been living the half-life of a parasite ever since. According to sketches for the play, this parasite image was to be the central one in Part I, and in a letter to Schering, Strindberg mentioned *The Vampire (Vampiren)* as a possible title. But the theme was not really used until the artistically weaker second part.

Strindberg apparently considered several occupations before making his hero a retired captain of artillery, a familiar figure in Sweden at the time. The Captain had never been promoted to the rank of major and regarded himself as a great man who had never achieved proper recognition. He brags about his rifle textbook which is still "number one, although they've tried to throw it out for an inferior one---which is used now, it's true, but is completely worthless." He is an expert on everything from establishing quarantine stations to cooking hazel hens. In Part II he tries to place his talents at the service of his ungrateful country by running for public office.

But the Captain's blustering tone of command, his raucous guffaws and noisy energy are all contrived, and his jovial exhilaration, which he hopes will be taken for a sense of humor, is as false as his effusive benevolence. He has, to use some of Strindberg's favorite expressions, " 'lied together' a character for himself." At the end of Part I, Kurt says to the Captain, "I've noticed that you've actually fabricated your life and surroundings in your imagination," and the Captain replies that he would not have been able to live otherwise. "But there comes a moment," he admits, "when the ability to fabricate, as you call it, fails. Then reality stands revealed in all its nakedness!"[21]

His mask has become his other self, and although the apoplectic fit he suffers deprives him for a time of his ability to play a role, he is able to recover it again. Sometimes he falls into a trance while sitting in his chair, appearing not to see or hear anything. But just as a distant trumpet call can break the trance, make him reach mechanically for his sword and uniform tunic and dash out to inspect the posts, so can he rouse himself out of a state of whining impotence, resume his cynical, bullying tone, and think up new means of tormenting those around him. "That's his vampire nature, all right," says Alice, "to interfere in the fates of others, to suck interest from their lives, to order and arrange things for them, since his own life is of absolutely no interest to him."[22] As a dying person with the need to cling tightly to the lives of others, he is more interested in intimidating people than in actually hurting them. Returning from a visit to town, he tells Kurt and Alice of a number of malicious deeds he committed against them. Moments later, however, when his mood changes to an anxious fear of dying, he confesses that he made up the story.

Strindberg created a masterpiece in the Captain: he had a genius for exposing the truth behind a character's assumed mask. In real life he seemed constantly to run into people who tried to disguise themselves in this way; sketches for the play mention a half-dozen models for the Captain. He took elements from several of them and fused them into a characterization which, despite its fantastic and grotesque dimensions, has the stamp of life upon it.

Alice is to some extent drawn in darker colors than the Captain. Her only passion is her hate for her husband and her only desire is to see him dead. The result is a great portrait: a graying coquette who cannot forget her few moments in the limelight as an actress and cannot forgive her husband for snatching her away from an artistic career whose only remnants are some dried-out laurel wreaths hanging on the wall. She too wears a mask, picturing herself as "an actress with a free and easy manner," and tries her best to give her untidy home a bohemian flavor.

The Captain and Alice are so spiteful and malicious because their more sympathetic features have been eroded away by the terrible marriage within which they feel indissolubly bound to each other: "Twice we broke off our engagement," says Alice, "and since then not a day has gone by in which we haven't tried to separate. But we are welded together and can't get free! We did separate once in our own home—for five years! Now only death can separate us. We know that, and so we wait for the deliverer!"[23]

Actually, each begrudges the other the joy of freedom. When the Captain says that he applied for a divorce during his visit to town, Alice flies into a rage and tells Kurt that the Captain is apprehensive about dying largely because he fears she will remarry. Alice describes their feelings for each other as "the most unreasoning hatred—without cause, without purpose, but also without end."[24] She says she will "laugh out loud" the day her husband dies. The Captain, who once tried to shove Alice into the sea, cannot give Kurt a clear motive for his action: "I don't know! As I watched her on the pier it just seemed perfectly natural that she should go in."[25] Both Alice and the Captain are driven by what Kurt in Swedenborgian terminology calls "love-hatred," which comes "from the bottom of Hell."

The most bizarre elements in the play are the frustrations and repetitions, the recurrent realization that actions seem to have no consequences and everything remains the same. The Captain has apoplectic fits but, until the last one, recovers from each attack more malicious than ever; his devilish intrigues against Kurt and Alice are empty threats; and Alice's charge of embezzlement against the Captain is based on error. In the last scene of Part I, we are right back where we were at the beginning: as if nothing has happened, the Captain and Alice resume the gallows-humor discussion of their approaching silver wedding anniversary that Kurt has interrupted in the opening scene. The Captain reminds Alice of the silver wedding of a fellow officer, when the bride had to wear the ring on her right hand because the bridegroom, in a tender moment, had chopped off her left ring finger with a billhook. "So, silver wedding it is," says the Captain, finishing with the phrase that is his motto: "Cross it out and go on!---So, let us go on!"[26]

"I wonder if everyone's life is like this?" the Captain asks Alice earlier in the play, and she replies: "Perhaps, although they don't talk about it, as we do!"[27] Phrased slightly differently, Alice is expressing one of Strindberg's firmest convictions: that the frenzied battle the Captain and his wife wage against each other is not only a portrait of marriage, but of life itself. On a sheet of sketches for various plays during this period is the following notation: *"Prisoners* (a Dream Play). People torment each other exactly as prisoners or madmen do." Strindberg would develop this idea in *A Dream Play,* but to a certain extent it is anticipated in *The Dance of Death.* The humid tower room on the little island—where a guard marches back and forth unceasingly outside the glass doors and all connection with the outside world is severed—becomes a symbol for humanity's prison.

However melancholy their situation may be, Alice and the Captain see a possibility for eventual relief. The two galley slaves welded together have retained some consciousness of their dignity as human beings and consequently hope for a better existence than the one they are experiencing. "Perhaps when death comes, life begins," the Captain says in answer to Alice's question about whether they have not tormented each other enough.[28] Strindberg had already expressed this theme in *Inferno* and it would become a prominent one in *A Dream Play.*

Part II of *The Dance of Death* appears to be an unnecessary addition to Part I, but Strindberg's original plan had called for depicting the Captain's vampire life and ultimate death. In Part II of the play written at the end of 1900, the Captain is spiritually dead, able to survive only as a parasite, and has been transformed into a ruthless speculator who liquidates his bad investments in the nick of time while allowing Kurt to lose his money. Alice has become harder and more inhuman than before. An early sketch indicates that Strindberg intended to develop a new theme: two feuding families can be brought together by their children. In the final version of Part II the Captain's daughter Judith does want to marry Kurt's son Allan, but her father has him sent away. Strindberg did not succeed in developing this theme until *The Crown Bride.* As Judith is portrayed in Part II of *The Dance of Death*—a vampire in her teens—one can only conclude that the same, hopeless, vicious circle of "love-hatred" will be repeated from generation to generation.

The Crown Bride

In *The Crown Bride* and *Swanwhite,* Strindberg experimented with a genre that has a long tradition in Scandinavian drama—the dramatized folk tale or ballad, represented in Denmark by Henrik Hertz (1798-1870), in Norway by Ibsen's early works, and in Sweden by Frans Hedberg (1828-1908), Maeterlinck is sometimes cited as an important influence on the two plays, but the evidence to support this thesis is contradictory and inconclusive.

On the one hand, in *Open Letters* Strindberg says unequivocally that he wrote *Swanwhite* under Maeterlinck's influence, and in a letter never sent to Harriet Bosse he said that *The Crown Bride* was "an attempt . . . to penetrate Maeterlinck's wonderful world of beauty, forgetting analyses, questions, and viewpoints, searching only for the beauty in color and mood."[29] An entry in Strindberg's diary on February 4, 1901, indicates that he had recently read Maeterlinck's folk-tale-like *La Princesse Maleine,* and another entry a month earlier, on January 5, 1901, mentions that *The Crown Bride* had been completed.

On the other hand, Strindberg had long been occupied with plans to write "a Great Swedish Dalecarlian play" and as early as August 8, 1900, had written to ask Carl Larsson to design settings for the play. As for *Swanwhite,* he declared that long before Maeterlinck came to his attention he had thought about "skimming through our most beautiful chivalric ballads . . . [with a view toward] adapting them for the stage."[30] The most likely conclusion is that Maeterlinck's influence played no role at all in the creation of *The Crown Bride* and did not affect *Swanwhite* until work on the play was in progress.[31]

In the letter to Carl Larsson, written at the same time that Strindberg was busy with *Midsummer,* he said he could picture the planned drama as "bright and beautiful" and believed the settings should have the same flavor as the picturesque domestic scenes that Larsson painted of his home in Sundborn. But when Strindberg set to work, the great nationalistic optimism which he felt while writing *Midsummer* had evaporated, and *The Crown Bride* has virtually nothing in common with Larsson's water colors.

The play's title refers to the still prevalent custom of a bride wearing a small crown on her wedding day. Two young lovers, Kersti and Mats, have a child out of wedlock and keep it hidden. At first they are satisfied to pledge their love in a touching little mock wedding ceremony alone in the forest, but later Kersti wants to be married in a church. However, Mats's family has always wanted him to marry a crown bride

(i.e., a maiden). Kersti angrily demands, "What is a crown bride? Someone who wears a crown!" and Mats answers, "With honor!" But Kersti
is determined to have her wedding: she suffocates the baby and obtains a
wedding crown from the Midwife in exchange for the body. On the
wedding day, her crown falls into the waterfall of Mats's mill. When the
guests search for it, they find the baby's body instead. The tragedy reopens
an old feud between Kersti's and Mats's families and not until the end
of the play when Kersti drowns after having repented her sin, are the
families reconciled.

John Landquist's assumption[32] that the inspiration for the drama
is the antiphonal song sung at the opening by Mats and Kersti is supported by the sketches in which the song is mentioned as the point of
departure. Strindberg found it in *Swedish Herdsmen's Songs and Horn
Melodies (Svenska vallvisor och hornlåtar*—1846) collected by Richard
Dybeck, who provided an accompanying narrative framework describing
how a young shepherd and shepherdess have a child and hold their own
wedding ceremony in the forest. The affair is discovered and ultimately
they are married by a minister.

In his sketches for the play, Strindberg planned a conclusion that
would have the young people's union dissolved by divorce. Since the beautiful song was inappropriate in the modern turn-of-the-century Dalecarlian
farm milieu he first contemplated—with its mowing machines, railroads,
and adult education courses—he placed the action in the time of his own
childhood, during the reign of Charles XV (1859-72).

The theme of the child who is hidden away had a personal significance for Strindberg, as earlier scholars have pointed out.[33] Several weeks
after his marriage to Siri von Essen, their newborn child was left with a
midwife and died at the age of two days. In the play this theme is combined with another motif common to folk tales about peasants: enmity
between the families of two lovers. Often this kind of love is at first depicted as sweet and happy—as in the work of Bjørnson and Gottfried
Keller (1819-90)[34]—but in *The Crown Bride* the sweetness has disappeared when the play begins.

Kersti, sullen and resolute in contrast with the gentle Mats, is
already hostile toward her child since it stands in the way of a proper
marriage. When she kills the baby and gives its body to the witch-like
Midwife (the most interesting character in the play), she does not indulge

in sentimental reflections but is pursued by pangs of conscience and by anxiety over the punishments of the law and of Hell. Her fears take shape as terrifying nature spirits: the kelpie (represented in human form in Swedish folk-lore), a Christ-like child dressed in white, and others. The moment she is alone, inanimate objects begin to move by themselves: a spinning wheel whirs, a loom operates, and a stove takes a turn around the room as if bent on persecuting her. This same scourging technique was used in *Advent,* but the "sorcery" in the *The Crown Bride* seems better explained as the fantasies of a mind frightened by popular superstitions. Here, too, for the most part, Strindberg leaned on Dybeck's notes for support.

The most powerful effects in the play are achieved through Strindberg's study of the psychology of the characters. For example, there is the scene in which Kersti asks Mats to pray for her because she cannot do it herself. When the little bell in the rural church rings for Vespers, Mats can hear it, but she cannot, and her anguish increases: she can hear "the rushing of water in the woods, the flailing of grain in the barn, the ringing of wheel rims; but not the bell!" And Mats reflects: "This is evil! I remember—at the funeral of the former bailiff all the bells rang, we saw them moving, but no one heard anything! It's evil!"[35]

Kersti's fear that her sin will be discovered gives her away. She tries to avoid people, becomes brusque when she meets them, and detects accusations in the most innocent remarks. But although almost everyone eventually suspects what has happened, only Mats's wicked sister Brita— a folk-tale figure hovering between the fantastic and the real—wants the crime exposed. When the body of the child is fished out of the mill waterfall, scarcely anyone is surprised but the innocent Mats.

The first three acts of the play, with their constricted atmosphere of anguish and continually rising tension, are dramatically effective, but are surpassed in poetic beauty by Kersti's touching journey to martydom in the final acts. Among Strindberg's penitential figures, she is one of the most human and most moving. Condemned to death, Kersti is placed in the stocks outside the whitewashed rural church. By this time, she has been chastened by the loneliness of her imprisonment; she is not daunted by the shame her own family feels or the hatred from Mats's relatives. Although she shudders involuntarily at the sight of Blackman, the solemnly dressed executioner, carrying his terrible black box and axe, she is not afraid to die and is actually disappointed when her death penalty is commuted to life imprisonment by royal order.

When Kersti drowns in the final scene during the bloody battle on the ice between the two warring families—which starts as she is about to keep her vow to serve a year in the church—her death is interpreted as a conciliatory sacrifice because it stops the fighting and brings the families together: "And behold, it was good that someone died for the people!" Strindberg's theory of atonement seems somewhat more convincing here than usual.

In his letter to Carl Larsson, who had close ties with the province of Dalecarlia, Strindberg asked if it would be proper to allow the peasants in the area around Lake Siljan in that province to speak "everyday Swedish" instead of the local dialect: "I mean ordinary written language with a moderate accent. Because . . . [the dialect used] in *Gustav Vasa* is tiresome and ugly." In a note in the manuscript relating to production of the play, he expressly forbade the use of authentic Dalecarlian dialect, suggesting instead "a moderate singing accent." However, the dialogue in *The Crown Bride* is anything but "everyday Swedish": it is extremely stylized and intended to harmonize with the ballads, songs, proverbs, and Bible quotations inserted throughout the play. Occasionally, it glides almost unnoticeably into a rhythmic prose close to verse, and its spareness is extraordinarily appropriate for the dour and laconic people of the play.

Strindberg felt most akin to the minor key in the Swedish temperament, and the most memorable aspects of *The Crown Bride* are its pine-forest atmosphere, folk-ballad melancholy, and the mixture of anguish-filled superstition and gentle piety. The characters are never seen in bright daylight; they are delineated as passing shadows. Instead of knowing them, we have an inkling of their natures. The forest and its treacherous powers spin a web about them. Along with *Gustav Vasa*, this peasant drama is perhaps Strindberg's most national work.

Swanwhite

It is significant that the only play Strindberg wrote that contains a conventionally romantic love story, *Swanwhite,* was conceived and partially written before his marriage to Harriet Bosse when they had had as yet but a few chance encounters and had exchanged letters solely in connection with her appearance in his plays: he had not yet dared to confess his love for her. Perhaps this is why *Swanwhite* is so bright and ends on an optimistic note. "The nearer, the more remote" is a line in Part III of *To Damascus*.

It was at this time, in January, 1901, that Strindberg first became familiar with Maeterlinck's *Le Trésor des humbles* (1896), which in a letter to Schering in April, he called "the greatest book I have ever read." He told Richard Bergh that Maeterlinck was inspired by the same Parisian occultism that influenced his own Inferno outlook. Maeterlinck believed, just as Strindberg did, in the existence of dark, malevolent powers who played games with human beings and in a divine guidance whose intentions no one knew or could know. But it was Maeterlinck's pronounced spiritualism that particularly fascinated Strindberg: supposedly, souls would soon be able to communicate directly with each other without the intermediary of the senses; already there were invisible links of silences, not words, that united soul with soul. Strindberg translated these and other thoughts about "the soul's awakening," "inner beauty," and "invisible goodness" from a chapter in Maeterlinck's book and dedicated the manuscript to Harriet.

Strindberg was always more responsive to philosophy than to literary trends and this explains his attraction to Maeterlinck's exotic but extremely tenuous ideas. He admired the spiritualistic elements in Maeterlinck's dramas: "His people exist on a plane that is from the one we live on; he is in contact with a higher world."[36]

As has been mentioned, Strindberg said that even before he was enthusiastic about Maeterlinck he had had plans for a drama based entirely on folk ballads and fairy tales, and this is supported by the first outline for *Swanwhite* which, under the title *Flores and Blanzeflor*, consists primarily of quotations from folk ballads, some of which were used in the completed play. It was in the interim between this outline and the writing of the drama that he read Maeterlinck's first play, *La Princesse Maleine* (1889), a kind of dramatized folk ballad. Here, Strindberg found another example of the stepmother theme which he claimed to have "discovered" in no fewer than twenty-six Swedish fairy tales. Strindberg's heroine's name, Svanevit (Swanwhite), was obviously taken from the fairy tale written by Gunnar Olof Hyltén-Cavallius and Georg Stephens about the virgins Svanvita and Rävrumpa, in which the stepmother tries to marry off her ugly daughter to the king and destroy her stepdaughter Svanvita, with whom the king is in love.

In the play, the Stepmother becomes angry when the Prince falls in love with Swanwhite instead of with her own daughter and has him locked up in the Blue Tower, where his hair turns gray overnight. Swanwhite and the Prince are reunited but soon begin to argue over trifles; disillusionment sets in, and she leaves him. Strindberg added a theme from the folk ballad "The Royal Children" ("Kungabarnen"), about a prince who drowns one night when he tries to swim to his loved one. For a time, when Strindberg thought his association with Harriet was ended, he contemplated the same fate for the Prince in *Swanwhite*. In the completed drama the Prince does drown attempting to swim back to Swanwhite but is awakened from the dead through the power of love and reunited with his beloved.

That *Swanwhite* does not have much in common with Maeterlinck's dramas, despite the similarity in themes, is due to its bright mood and the recurrent folk ballad phrases that clash with the stylized, suggestive dialogue Strindberg tried to achieve. Clearly with Princesse Maleine in mind, Strindberg gives Swanwhite a childishness that is seen in her playing with a doll, a rattle, and a toy horse.

By the second act, however, she is mature enough to be involved in a marital quarrel which is not yet caustic since it is couched in a fairy-tale-like discussion of flowers. But the lovers become disenchanted with each other. She notices for the first time that her beloved has gray hair. According to the Prince, it turned gray "out of sorrow over the loss of my Swanwhite, who is no more." This last idea was borrowed from a folk ballad about Duke Fröjdenborg, but Strindberg could not resist the impulse to have the Prince's hair turn dark again at the end of the play, whereas the Stepmother and the Maids who had "laughed at the young suitor with his gray hair" become gray instead. Although the Stepmother is later forgiven and regains her original beauty, Strindberg's manipulations with hair coloration obviously constitute a veiled threat against those who found the graying author's engagement to a woman thirty years his junior ludicrous.

Strindberg included other personal allusions to his courtship of Harriet which are rather inappropriate within the medieval context, such as the Prince using a clock to take Swanwhite's pulse or the couple exchanging thoughts from a distance through a helmet that was a christening gift to the Prince from his godmother—obviously a medieval counterpart of the telephone.

What prevents the play from becoming puerile is its spiritualized eroticism. Swanwhite and the Prince are happiest when they regard each other from a distance. The moment they are close enough for a kiss, they lose the blessed feeling of a union of souls. They imagine they have lost each other and long to meet in another world, "in the land of dreams."

Before the première of *Swanwhite* in October, 1908, at the Intimate Theatre, Strindberg interpreted the play in a letter to the actress Anna Flygare:

> Eros is not the central theme: the symbolism relates to *Caritas,* the great Love, which suffers everything, survives everything, which forgives, hopes, and believes, no matter how much it is betrayed! This is better illustrated by the Stepmother's change of character—but best by the final scene: Love is stronger than death. Emphasize the essence of love in spirit and intention rather than in external beauty and allurement.[37]

By the time these words were written Strindberg had lost Harriet forever, and they reveal his feelings. But even years earlier during the writing of *Swanwhite,* he had written in his diary on February 17, 1901, that the gospel for that Sunday, according to the calendar, dealt with "love = *Caritas,* not Eros-Amor." It is this suggestion of a love of a higher variety than the earthly, a love that suffers and survives everything, that gives *Swanwhite* its undeniable charm and makes it unique among Strindberg's works.

Notes to Chapter Seventeen

1. *SS:*LIV, p. 336.
2. His spiritualism also complicated their relationship. In one of his last letters to Harriet, on April 8, 1908, he said: "You remember our first days, when the evil radiation from alien souls disturbed us, ruined things for us, merely by thinking about us!" (*Brev till Harriet Bosse,* 1932, p. 286).
3. *Brev till Harriet Bosse,* p. 97.
4. *SS:*XXXIII, p. 243.
5. *SS:*LIII, p. 468.
6. *Brev till Harriet Bosse,* pp. 131-32.
7. Published in *Teaterdraken* (1937).
8. *SS:*XXXIII, pp. 61-62.
9. *Ibid.,* p. 59.
10. *Ibid.,* p. 63.
11. *Ibid.,* p. 69.
12. *Ibid.,* p. 92.
13. *Ibid.,* p. 95.
14. *Ibid.,* p. 105.
15. *Ibid.,* p. 52.
16. Falck, p. 162.
17. *SS:*XXXIII, p. 97.
18. *Ibid.,* p. 99.
19. *Ibid.,* p. 127.
20. *SS:*XXXIV, p. 113.
21. *Ibid.,* pp. 108-9.
22. *Ibid.,* pp. 82-83.
23. *Ibid.,* p. 43.
24. *Ibid.,* p. 45.
25. *Ibid.,* p. 112.
26. *Ibid.,* pp. 121-22.
27. *Ibid.,* p. 56.
28. *Ibid.,* p. 121.
29. February 8, 1901. *Teaterdraken* (1937).
30. *SS:*L, p. 300.
31. It may seem presumptuous to doubt Strindberg's assertion that he was a disciple of Maeterlinck at the time, but concerning writers whom he admired, he was all too generous when it came to

acknowledging their influence. *See* Jolivet, pp. 293 ff., who generally believes Strindberg overestimated his dependence on Maeterlinck.

32. *SS*:XXXVI, p. 345.
33. *See* Hedén, *Strindberg,* p. 318.
34. Particularly in Keller's beautiful short story *Romeo und Julia auf
      dem Dorfe* (1856).
35. *SS*:XXXVI, p. 61.
36. *SS*:L, p. 294.
37. May 5, 1908. Falck, p. 222.

Chapter Eighteen

A DREAM PLAY

There was no work that Strindberg was prouder of than *A Dream Play*. In a letter to K. O. Bonnier on August 31, 1906, he ranked it highest among his writings, and in a letter to Schering written the night of the play's première, April 17, 1907, he called it "my most beloved drama, the child of my greatest torment."

A Dream Play is the most personal of Strindberg's works written after the Inferno Crisis and provides the deepest insight into his world view. From an artistic standpoint, it is one of his most daring creations, marking the point of departure for his Chamber Plays, and its influence is frequently discernible in modern drama.

Like *To Damascus, A Dream Play* concerns a pilgrimage: Indra, the Hindu god of skies and storms, sends his daughter to earth to see if the complaints and lamentations of mankind are justified. The Daughter meets many people on her travels and finds that the human condition always implies disillusion and suffering. She concludes that "Man is to be pitied" and returns to the heavens. During her earthly wandering she becomes closely involved with three men: the Officer she discovers imprisoned in a castle, who has spent a considerable part of his life waiting in vain outside the stage door of an opera house for his beloved Victoria, a singer; the Lawyer, to whom she is married briefly and unhappily, and whose hideous face mirrors the crimes and sufferings of his clients; and the Poet, who descends from his lofty spheres to wallow in mud, thus hardening himself against the stings of gadflies, and who searches for truth but is always dissatisfied since the moment his songs are acclaimed he no longer believes them worthwhile.

The action unfolds in an unrealistic manner. Time is distorted: in one scene the Officer enters and exits several times, each time growing visibly older. Inanimate objects seem to have mysterious lives of their own: from the gilded roof of a "growing castle" a flower buds and blooms; and a cupboard door with a clover-leaf opening becomes a stage door that conceals a secret, but before the door can be opened and the secret discovered, the door turns into the front of a deed cabinet, then the entrance to the vestry of a church, and finally the stage door again, but always retaining the clover-leaf opening.

In its finished form *A Dream Play* gives the impressions of a loose improvisation without any inner coherence other than that of the dream. The early sketches demonstrate, however, that the play required what was for Strindberg an unusually long period of preparation; originally it was not conceived as a "dream play" and did not have Indra's Daughter as the heroine.

The most important sketch bears the title *The Stage Alley Drama (Korridordramat)* and reveals the genesis of the most powerful scene in *A Dream Play*—the scene outside the stage door of the opera house where the Officer is waiting for Victoria. In this version he is a composer who has waited seven years to have a successful opera and seven years for a wife. Now he waits for his fiancée, the opera singer Carita, who has achieved success in his opera. After their joint triumph, they are to get married and travel south. It is spring when he arrives for the first time to wait for her, and he is carrying a bouquet of roses.

More obvious here than in the completed play are references to Strindberg's personal life. While waiting for Harriet Bosse outside the theatre during rehearsals of *Easter,* Strindberg felt himself transported to the past when he had waited in the same alley and under the same conditions for Siri von Essen.

In the sketch, the composer waits in vain: summer comes and goes, the roses wither, and he learns that his fiancée has gone abroad alone. Strindberg's first great disappointment in his third marriage came when Harriet went abroad by herself and left him behind. They had made plans for a honeymoon trip abroad, but Strindberg felt that he had received a warning from the Powers not to leave Sweden. In the sketch the faithful lover continues to return with his flower bouquet until, broken with age, he sinks down dead: "The Doorkeeper's daughter strews roses on him, for she has loved him. He blesses her who abandoned him."

As in *A Dream Play,* the hero in *The Stage Alley Drama* is flanked by two individuals who also have to live through a lifetime of disappointments: the Billposter and the Doorkeeper, a woman who for twenty-seven years has been crocheting stars to be made into a great bed-spread. A section of dialogue excluded from the final version of the play tells us that when she was young, she was a dancer engaged to a tenor but he abandoned her, and after that she could no longer dance: "Love takes happiness with it when it goes and leaves sorrow behind." Now she has only one goal: to prevent her daughter from choosing a career in the theatre. But at the end of the sketch, the girl becomes a ballet dancer, and her mother must resign herself to the situation.

The Stage Alley Drama (which in a somewhat different form bears the title Waiting [Väntan] and suggests that it would have been completed in the style of a Hans Christian Andersen fairy tale) contains one of the basic themes of A Dream Play: that life never fulfills man's expectations. Either people achieve what they hope for and inevitably are bitterly disillusioned or they are cruelly frustrated in everything they attempt.

In the completed drama, the theme is expressed most clearly in the fate of the poor Billposter, who at the age of fifty obtains his life's modest goal—a fishing net and green fishing box: "The net was all right, I guess," he says after returning from fishing, "but not exactly what I expected." The Officer replies: " 'Not exactly what I expected!'---That's very well put! Nothing ever turns out as I expected it to—because the thought is greater than the deed and goes beyond the material object."[1]

Strindberg's work on The Stage Alley Drama was interrupted when he and Harriet were reunited in Hornbæk on the Danish coast north of Copenhagen, after a separation of two weeks. According to a diary entry, he went back to work on the sketch on August 22, 1901, the same day that the severest crisis in his marriage began. After a quarrel Harriet wrote him a letter saying that she was leaving him forever. Not until after "exactly forty days of suffering, among the most difficult I have under-gone,"[2] were they reconciled. At this time the sketch was titled The Grow-ing Castle (Det växande slottet); work on the play was finished at the end of 1901. It is no wonder he called it "the child of my greatest torment."

The poem "Chrysáëtos"[3] (1902) presents a picture of the despair Strindberg felt after the break with his wife. And his diary entries, which during this time grew from short comments into page-long observations, show how he conceived of the world as a bewildering, uninhabitable dream state. On September 6, 1901, he wrote in his diary:

> This love story that I thought so great and extraordinarily beautiful, dissolved into a mockery and convinced me completely that life is illusion, and that the most beautiful stories, which dissolve like bubbles of dirty wash water, were created to instill in us a contempt for life. We do not belong here and we are too good for this wretched existence. . . . People are not born evil; life makes them evil. Therefore, life cannot be a time of enlightenment or punishment (which reforms), but only of evil.

The same despair is repeated in *A Dream Play* and is most beautifully expressed in the Lamentation of the Winds:

> Earth is not clean,
> life is not just,
> men are not evil,
> nor are they good. . . .
>
> They were given feet,
> but no wings.
> Dust-covered they become.
> Is the fault theirs
> or Thine?[4]

Throughout the fall of 1901 Strindberg's feelings toward Harriet changed from day to day. Sometimes he complained that his spirit was "fettered in the baser regions frequented by my wife" (September 6). But when he reread his diary and letters to her: "All the great and beautiful things came back; I blessed her memory and thanked her for having spread light and joy in my life" (August 25). He complained that when she left their apartment, it became dark, "literally, not figuratively." "But her bright little spirit could not prevail over my darkness, and when I noticed this, I begged her to save me. But it was too late" (September 28). Indra's Daughter, who had descended from above to liberate the prisoner in the castle, is sullied by earthly life and torn asunder by marriage: "My thoughts can no longer fly. There is clay on their wings---dirt on their feet. . . . Alas, I am earthbound!"[5]

From the beginning of his relationship with Harriet, Strindberg imagined he was wandering in a world of dreams. One week after their engagement he wrote to an old Lund friend Nils Andersson (March 13, 1901): "I don't know what kind of Dreamer's Land I am living in, but I cannot descend to reality again without dread." And after a quarrel with

Harriet he wrote to Carl Larsson (November 2, 1901) : "Life is becoming increasingly dream-like and inexplicable to me—possibly death is really the awakening."

In the Author's Note to *A Dream Play,* Strindberg described the nature of dreams so strikingly that since then it has often been cited in scientific studies of dreams. It is not easy, however, to harmonize the claims of the Author's Note with the facts of the play. He begins by asserting that he tried to imitate a dream's "disconnected but apparently logical form," as he had done in his former dream play *To Damascus,* but the similarity between the two plays extends only to the sequential order of scenes and to elements of the stage setting. (The reference in the Author's Note to *To Damascus* was actually added later to the manuscript.) For example, whereas all the scenes in the first half of *To Damascus* recur in reverse order in the second half, this sequential device was employed only in part in *A Dream Play:* after the prologue in the sky between Indra and his daughter, the play begins and ends outside the Growing Castle, and the scene outside the stage door follows the first Growing Castle scene and precedes the last.

For *To Damascus,* a permanent inner proscenium arch was used, and properties such as furniture were painted on the backdrops—all to facilitate rapid scene changes in darkness with the curtain open. For *A Dream Play,* Strindberg was even more concerned about the action, moving quickly from one setting to another. The stage directions call for permanent side wings which are to serve as "stylized decorations, simultaneously rooms, architecture and landscapes," and during the play a number of free-standing objects and minor characters in one scene remain on stage to represent other things or characters in the following scenes. The gate into the theatre, for example, becomes the railing gate in the Lawyer's office, and then the chancel rail in the church. The theatre's billboard becomes a bulletin board in the Lawyer's office and in the church serves as an announcement board showing the order of the hymns to be sung. In the same way, the male choristers from *Die Meistersinger* and the female dancers from *Aïda* in the opera scene remain to represent people seeking help in the Lawyer's office and are then ushers and carriers of laurel wreaths in the church.

Clearly, Strindberg knew that an audience could accept the fact that in a dream visual images retain certain basic features as they change from one form into another. All of this is ingeniously thought out, but has always proved more effective in the reading than on the stage. Strindberg himself thought the setting for the original production in 1907 was "too tangible for the Dream Image."[6]

In the Author's Note Strindberg says that although anything can happen in a dream—personalities can split and events occur without causal connections—it all seems logical because a single consciousness guides everything: that of the dreamer. "For him there are no secrets, no inconsistencies, no scruples, no laws. He neither condemns nor acquits, but only narrates." To conclude from this, however, that the play depicts the dreams of one individual, and that one character can be singled out as the dreamer would be a mistake. Although Indra's Daughter is present in every scene, she does not belong to the earthly world. On several occasions during her visit she fancies that she has dreamed everything she experienced, but this is part of the general impression of the dream-like quality of life that Strindberg was trying to create.

We are all sleepwalkers; one person's dream coincides, in part, with another's,[7] and everything is twisted together into the single tangle of dreams that is the inextricable nightmare of earthly life. Like the characters in the play, we too stumble about, transforming our life into a dream in order to escape the cruelties of reality. Ironically, however, as Strindberg explains in the Author's Note, "sleep, the liberator," can often cause us so much pain that waking up "reconciles the sufferer with reality which, no matter how painful it may be, is still a pleasure, compared with the tormenting dream." The implication is that death is the final awakening, liberating us from the anguish of both nightmares: the world of dreams and that of reality. "Surely suffering is redemption and death deliverance?" asks the Poet in the final scene.

Strindberg used many of his own experiences to produce the simultaneous effect of dream and reality that the play evokes. But although he had recorded his dreams very carefully since the beginning of the Inferno Crisis, only several scenes are actually based on real dreams. The source for the scene showing the conferral of doctoral degrees in the church was probably a dream (recorded in his diary in July, 1896) in which he pictured himself being awarded an honorary doctorate. He certainly hoped for such an award and was constantly encouraged by rumors and newspaper stories. And the most typically dream-like scene in the play —the one in which the Officer is humiliatingly treated as a schoolboy by the Schoolmaster—was only too vivid to Strindberg. One of his most agonizing nightmares as an adult was to find himself once again in Klara school, threatened with Latin lessons and the cane.[8]

Most of the play, as Strindberg states in the Author's Note, is "a mixture of memories, experiences, complete inventions, absurdities, and improvisations." The scene between the Officer and his parents is from Strindberg's own childhood. The inspiration for the strange door with the clover-leaf opening was a door in the old Royal Dramatic Theatre, and Harriet Bosse told me that when Strindberg waited for her, he constantly wondered where the door led. For the scenes on the Riviera, Strindberg used notes he had gathered during his travels in 1884.[9] The character of the Billposter is patterned after the fishermen whose unusual scoop-net fishing is a traditional activity in Norrström, the waterway in front of the Royal Palace in Stockholm (references to these fishermen can be found in Strindberg's diary). And a manuscript notation indicates that the model for the Officer was a friend from the Red Room period, Jean Lundin, a carefree lieutenant who was always in financial straits.

Some of his raw material had been collected for use elsewhere; indeed, a number of the same characters and situations appear in other works in different forms. One of Strindberg's friends in Lund, whom he later used as the model for the hero of the novel *The Scapegoat* (*Syndabocken*—1906-07), had a law office, and Strindberg was concerned that this friend, because of his work, "lives only in human misery" and would grow old before his time.[10] In the play, the Lawyer's face "mirrors all the crime and vice with which his profession forced him to come into contact."[11]

Two of the most striking scenes are set on contrasting resort islands: Foulstrand, with its blighted landscape and rich people howling with pain as they submit to the torturous physical therapy necessitated by their sinful living; and Fairhaven, more inviting than Foulstrand at a distance because it has pleasant greenery, lovely villas, white boats, and a dance hall, but actually offering no greater chance of happiness than its opposite across the narrow strait. Both scenes were based on memories from Strindberg's first summers on Furusund. In his diary in the summer of 1899 he compared Köpmanholm and Furusund to Ebal, the Mount of Curses, and Gerizim, the Mount of Blessing (Deuteronomy 11:29); in the stage directions of *A Dream Play* there is a description of the islands that is later repeated almost verbatim in his introduction to the story collection *Fairhaven and Foulstrand.* Characters and situations only fleetingly suggested in the play reappear in these stories and later works.

Many scenes in *A Dream Play* contain visual impressions that Strindberg gathered from the windows of his apartment at 40 Karla Way, where he lived from 1901 to 1908. To the far left, beyond the tree tops, he could see "the growing castle," which provided the first title for the final version of the play. It was a cavalry barracks built during his Inferno period and still stands today, a building with a black roof topped by a gold crown. He wrote a beautiful poem about this "magic castle" in *Word-Play and Minor Art,* and in the long prose narrative *Alone* (1903) he described how he watched it every day—when it was illuminated by the morning sun or when the lights were turned on in the evening—and how he wished he might retreat into it to find peace.[12]

Even the visions seen by the Poet and Indra's Daughter in the Fingal's Cave scene were inspired by things Strindberg saw from his apartment. As he wrote in *Alone,* it pleased him to stand on his balcony and be able to see "heaths, sea, and bluish woods in the distance out toward the seacoast."[13] In the play, the Poet thinks he sees a boat in distress, but when he looks more carefully, the ship turns out to be a two-story house and a telephone pole. When the Poet has a strange vision of a snow-covered parade ground over which a little church casts its long shadow, the image calls to mind Ladugård's Field[14] and Gustav Adolf's Church.

From evidence in Strindberg's diary entries and sketches, we could track down the source for virtually every detail in *A Dream Play.* The intriguing fact is that Strindberg succeeded in producing one of his most consummate works from extremely disparate material collected on loose scraps of paper. He did it by molding this material into "the disconnected but apparently logical form of the dream." The sequence of events is rarely continuous; usually a single absurd idea is sufficient to transport us into new surroundings. After being liberated from the Growing Castle, the Officer goes to the opera, bouquet in hand, to wait for Victoria. He wonders what lies behind the mysterious clover-leaf door and sends for a locksmith to have it opened. The Glazier arrives with his diamond cutter instead, but before he can proceed, the Policeman forbids him to open the door. The Officer rushes from the opera to the Lawyer's office for legal assistance in the matter but by the time he receives an audience, he has forgotten his errand: "I only want to ask if Miss Victoria has gone." After being reassured by the Lawyer, the Officer pokes around for a moment at the clover-leaf door, now the front of a cabinet for storing documents, then abruptly goes to change clothes for the doctorate ceremony.

In *To Damascus,* everything seemed mysterious and inexplicable to the Stranger. But in *A Dream Play* the characters use the half-logic of dreams and regard most things as self-explanatory. As Strindberg himself indicated in the Author's Note, his dreamers are not guided by ethical principles or social amenities; they behave in a capricious and unaccountable manner and candidly reveal all their hopes and fears. They help each other, comfort each other, support, hate, and torment each other, according to the whim of the moment. They turn suddenly hostile but are quickly pacified; they complain but their grumbling fades away, as does their laughter. The dream spins its web over everything and puts a damper on every extreme: to the sinister it gives a nuance of grotesque unreality and to the cheerful, a melancholy note of transience.

When Strindberg portrayed Fairhaven and Foulstrand as the Mount of Blessing and the Mount of Curses in his story collection a year later, he was too heavy-handed. In *A Dream Play* the colors are more brilliant and the scenes more fantastic and we are not burdened with the Sunday School preaching found in the later work. In the strange atmosphere of the resort on Foulstrand as depicted in the play, people, actions, and objects are both metaphorical and real. The frightful Quarantine Master wears a blackamoor mask, but he is going to a masquerade and so has made himself "a bit blacker" than he really is. The oven with blue sulphurous flames into which he puts the young lovers belongs to the regular quarantine station equipment, the mud that besmirches everything beautiful is part of the established bathing regimen, and the dreadful torture instruments are medical-mechanical gymnastic equipment. The Quarantine Master takes malicious pleasure in showing off his wealthy patients: "Look at that man on the rack! He's eaten too much *pâté de foie gras* with truffles, and drunk so much Burgundy that his feet have curled into knots! . . . And that one lying on the guillotine has drunk so much brandy that his spine has to be put through a wringer!" The Officer responds rather indifferently: "And that can't be very pleasant."[15] The grotesque exaggeration lends an aura of unreality to this house of correction which the rich have chosen for themselves.

The Fairhaven of *A Dream Play* does not have the sentimentally pretty appearance it has in the story collection. When the scene changes in the play from Foulstrand to Fairhaven, the summer landscape that looked so attractive at a distance is covered with snow, the trees have lost their leaves, and although everyone is dancing and seems gay, all are unhappy. Never has Strindberg's optimism been so mournful and his pessimism so sanguine as in *A Dream Play*. The shifting dream contours wipe out the dividing line between laughter and tears.

"The characters split, double, multiply, evaporate, condense, scatter, converge," says Strindberg in the Author's Note. The Officer, whose childhood martyrdom is Strindberg's own, has a double in the Lawyer who is criticized for looking at the world wrong-side up: "People said I was a malcontent, that I look at the world through the devil's eye, and so forth."[16] And this personification of the Strindberg of the 1880's— the social reformer rewarded with ingratitude—is complemented in turn by the Poet who presents Strindberg's Inferno outlook.

One could also say that these three characters, who have no definite relation to one another, represent different sides of Strindberg's temperament. The Officer is something of a carefree loafer, an aspect of the young Strindberg which was still present in his old age and especially apparent in letters and personal associations. As the play's most typical dreamer, he is only intermittently conscious of the absurdity of his experiences.

In the first act, he finds it not at all surprising that his deceased parents are present and conversing with him until he catches sight of the cupboard with the strange clover-leaf door: "Think of that cupboard still being there after twenty years.---We've moved so many times, and my mother died ten years ago!" When his Mother replies: "Well, what of it? You always have to question everything, and so you spoil the best things in life for yourself!"[17] he calms down.

He is an inveterate optimist in his belief that Victoria will come to the champagne supper he has planned. When finally, as a white-haired and tattered old man he toddles into the alley near the stage door and asks the Ballet Girl whether Victoria has left yet, he learns: "No, she hasn't left! She never leaves!" He replies trustfully: "That's because she loves me."[18]

In the Foulstrand scene, he sees a pair of lovers sailing toward the island and shouts joyfully: "It's Victoria!" When the Quarantine Master retorts dryly: "Well, what of it!" the Officer briefly explains what he meant, trying not to admit his mistake: "That's his Victoria. I have my own, and no one will ever see her!"[19]

When the church bells ring for the conferring of the doctoral degrees, the Lawyer asks the Officer if he would like to receive a doctor's laurel wreath: "Why not? At least it would be a diversion."[20] But the doctoral wreath somehow returns him to a classroom where he is treated as a schoolboy and has to recite the same lessons he recited throughout his childhood.[21] In this amusing scene, we see the aging Officer, uneasy and troubled, sitting among the small boys and trying vainly to answer the terrifying Schoolmaster's question: "What is two times two?" He has a vague awareness that he is an adult and a graduate with a degree, but when the Schoolmaster tells him that he must remain until he is mature, he is once again powerless and remains subdued until the Schoolmaster asks whether anyone will buy drinks before they all go swimming. The Officer protests: "This is a *posterus prius*—a turned-around world. Usually the swim comes first and then the drink." "Don't be so conceited, Doctor," the Schoolmaster says quietly, but the Officer flares up: "Captain, if you please! I am an officer, and I don't understand why I should have to sit among a lot of schoolboys and be scolded."[22]

The Lawyer—with his furrowed face and his cracked and bleeding hands—has more of his creator's outward appearance, touchiness, and opinionatedness than the other two figures. Also evident is Strindberg's persecution mania. For example, in the church scene, the Lawyer is refused a degree because he pleaded humanity's cause, took an interest in the poor, and put in a good word for the guilty. His reward is a crown of thorns instead of a laurel wreath. Fortunately, Strindberg stopped short of total deification of the figure by underscoring his harshness and impetuousness.

The kinds of cases the Lawyer finds most distasteful are divorces, because no one really knows why the couples quarreled: "Oh, once it had something to do with a salad, another time with a word. Most of the time it's about nothing at all. But the pain, the suffering! These are the things I have to bear."[23]

When Indra's Daughter offers the Lawyer her hand in marriage, they both determine to "avoid the rocks, now that we know them so well:" "We ought to be able to smile at trifles!"[24] But in spite of all their resolutions, the small vexations of everyday life make their marriage unbearable. The Daughter is impulsive and inconsiderate, and the Lawyer is set in his ways. Everything becomes a torment; for the Lawyer, it is careless housecleaning and the morning newspaper that was burned before he had a chance to read it. For the Daughter, it is Kristin, the maid, who is closing out every breath of fresh air by pasting over all openings to the outside world. He likes cabbage soup, but she hates it, and so "pleasure for one is torment for the other!" Domestic life is a nightmare.

The third of Strindberg's alter egos in *A Dream Play,* the Poet, is depicted with irony at his entrance: he walks in looking up at the sky and carrying a bucket of mud. Originally, Strindberg had someone else in mind to serve as a model for the figure before he identified himself with it. As the Poet converses with the Daughter in Fingal's Cave, he becomes dreamy and poetic: the happy moments of marriage pass in review. He writes poems that she speaks aloud from memory, but she objects to his gloomy view of existence. They are beyond time and space in a world where winds and waves sing an eternal lament over the agony of being born.

Taken together, the three major male characters sum up the mixture of incurable illusions and pessimism that is the play. All three have some of Strindberg's features, yet they are also sharply defined as individuals, and no one of them can be taken as the author's spokesman; this is the function of Indra's Daughter.

The stately prologue to *A Dream Play,* in which Indra sends his daughter down to earth, was not part of the original completed manuscript; it was added in 1906. The earlier version of the play begins with the scene outside the Growing Castle where a mystical young woman appears as the Glazier's daughter. She believes there is a prisoner inside who is waiting for her to liberate him. In the next scene the Officer calls her Agnes and pays tribute to her as "the beautiful, which is the harmony of the universe. There are lines in your form which I have found only in the orbits of the solar system, in the beautiful melody of strings, in the

vibrations of light.---You are a child of heaven."[25] He does not yet know
her real identity, but his mother whispers to him that she is said to be
Indra's Daughter, "who begged to come down to earth to learn how things
really are for human beings."[26] In the stage-door alley scene the Daughter
takes the Doorkeeper's place: "Because I want to know about people and
life, to find out if it really is as hard as they say."[27] She borrows the Doorkeeper's shawl, which has soaked up thirty years of suffering, and in the
Lawyer's office she tries to gather up in the shawl all the confidences he
has received concerning crimes, vices, unjust imprisonments, slander, and
libels.

With Indra's Daughter thus introduced as just one of the many
dream figures, although more innocent than they about the world's pleasures and pains, it does not seem strange for her to marry the Lawyer and
have a child by him in order to experience "the sweetest thing, but also the
bitterest—love!" And it is no surprise that she does not live up to his
expectations as a proper housewife. She hates and loves just as mortals do
and is tormented by the imperfection of earthly life. Later in the play she
feels dirtied by the mire and longs to burn her earthly possessions and
return to her heavenly origin. Yet even as she is about to depart, she half-
regrets leaving her human harbor and her fellow-sufferers:

> To want to go, and want to stay—
> And so the heart is split in two,
> Feelings torn apart by the galloping steeds
> Of conflict, indecision and discord—[28]

On one occasion the Poet compares her to "Harun the Just," who
went among the people in disguise "to see how justice was operating."[29]
But he remembers, too, that in spite of the fact that Indra once sent down
his Son, the human condition was not improved by more than an insignificant degree. And so, although Indra's Daughter—half-mortal, half-Christ
figure—has witnessed all the miseries of mankind, it is doubtful that
earthly existence will become more pleasant after she has borne their
complaints to the Throne, since existence is itself a Fall, made more bitter
by man's want of compassion toward his fellow man.

Like Eleonora in *Easter,* Indra's Daughter has shared more intensively than ordinary mortals in humanity's martyrdom: "I have suffered
all your sufferings a hundred-fold, because my sensations were keener."[30]
For her, too, all earthly experiences seem like a dream. She is the ideal

feminine divinity, ethereally beautiful and filled with maternal compassion. Her proper place is at the Poet's side, and at her departure she praises him as the dreamer who knows best how to live:

> Floating on wings above the earth,
> You sometimes dive to touch the soil
> But just to graze it, not to be trapped!

Her power is slight, however, and when she is asked the ultimate questions, she remains mute. Nevertheless, she gives man the confidence that he has not lost contact entirely with a higher world.

There are a host of images that offer clues to the meaning of *A Dream Play.* Mentioned earlier, for example, was the notation of the first outline for the play: *"Prisoners* (a Dream Play). People torment each other exactly as prisoners do or madmen." This concept dominated Strindberg during the crisis in his third marriage. Other important images are the Growing Castle (which has a beautiful exterior but a cold prison-like interior) and the recurrent desire to escape from dirt and filth. When the Glazier is asked why flowers grow out of dirt, he says: "They're not happy in the dirt, so they hurry upward into the light—in order to blossom and die!" The image is less grim in the scene between the Daughter and the Officer in the Castle. When he asks her why he has to tend the horses, take care of the stables, and cart out the droppings, she replies: "So that you'll long to get away from it!"[31]

Strindberg himself indicated that not until he had completed the drama did he realize its meaning. On November 18, 1901, as he worked on the ending of the play, he wrote in his diary that he was studying "the doctrines of the Indian religion." From Arvid Ahnfelt's *The History of World Literature (Verldslitteraturens historia)* he had borrowed the myth of how the divine primal force, Brahma, allowed himself to be seduced by Maja, the procreative spirit, thereby giving rise to our world. "The world thus exists," the diary entry continues, "only because of a sin, if indeed it does exist—for it is only a dream image (Therefore my *Dream Play* [is] an image of life), an illusive image. . . . This seems to be the solution to the riddle of the world!" He explored Buddhism "the entire day," and found "the explanation for my *Dream Play* and the significance of Indra's Daughter. The Secret of the [clover-leaf] Door = Nothing."

In the play, Indra's Daughter explains the myth about Brahma's indiscretion to the Poet, but shortly before this, the strange door with the clover-leaf aperture is opened and the secret behind it is disclosed: "Nothing! That's the solution of the riddle of the universe," shouts the Dean of the theological faculty. "Out of nothing God created heaven and earth in the beginning." His medical colleague adds: "Bosh!"[32] the same word that Doctor Borg uses at the end of the first version of *The Red Room* when he is asked what life is. Indra's Daughter tells the Dean that he spoke the truth without realizing its significance. Strindberg emphasized in the same diary entry quoted above that the world is "Bosh or relative nothingness."

When the Growing Castle goes up in flames in the final scene, the background is illuminated, revealing "a wall of human faces, questioning, mourning, despairing." But at the same time, the flower bud on the roof bursts into a giant chrysanthemum, perhaps implying a new era emerging from the old. In the poem "Journey to Town," Strindberg mentions *Ragnarök*, "the last conflagration" that will cleanse the earth in order to create a better existence: "Then the golden age of dreamers will be at hand."

Strindberg's attitude toward sex and sexuality, as toward most things in life, was highly ambivalent. On the one hand, he could write: "Life disgusts me and it always has," as he did in his diary on September 6, 1901, during the crisis in his marriage to Harriet Bosse. To support his argument he cited Schopenhauer, Hartmann, and Hegel, and noted that "the organ of love is identical with one of the organs of elimination! Now, isn't that characteristic?!" On the other hand, in the first volume of *Married* he had fought more openly and more daringly than any of his contemporaries for the recognition of sexual desire and relations as proper and natural parts of life. He would return to the same theme in 1908 in the third volume of *A Blue Book,* where an essay on the beauty and symbolism of the human body includes a beautiful description of the physiology of love-making.

Strindberg's ambivalence was perhaps most clearly illustrated in the story "Evolution" in *Swedish Destinies,* in which Botvid and Giacomo represent the different sides of the author's nature. In Strindberg, the monk's and the satyr's viewpoints found a common focus.[33] It was thus quite appropriate for him to explain the fall from heaven in terms of Brahma's love affair and to conclude that it was through love that sin and death entered life. Man is torn between "the penitent's agonies and the sensualist's delights."

The disgust with life that erupted in *A Dream Play* colored all of Strindberg's later writings. Especially in such works as *Black Banners* and *The Great Highway*, misanthropy and a striving for atonement are placed in almost untenable juxtaposition. They become more comprehensible, however, when seen in the light of *A Dream Play's* conception of life and humanity.

In *A Dream Play*, the misanthropy is not yet intensified into the black pessimism of the later works. Life is imperfect, filled with baffling illusions, and the human body is really a prison that confines and torments us. When Indra's Daughter is asked what she has suffered most from on earth, she answers: "From—being alive. From feeling my vision dimmed because I have eyes, my hearing dulled because of ears, and my thoughts, my airy, luminous thoughts, imprisoned within a labyrinth of fat."[34] If man's sense organs are so burdensome to a higher spirit, what of his other physical functions:

> The soul expected a different attire
> Than this of blood and filth!

This lament is from the petition that the Poet presents to the rulers of the universe from humanity.[35] Additional encumbrances are the problems involved in being part of human society. "These are my children," Indra's Daughter says near the end of the play. "Individually, they are good, but the moment they come together they fight and turn into devils."[36] Social reform will not help, for "all reformers end up in prison or the madhouse."[37] Indra's Son was crucified by the "righteous ones" because He wanted to liberate men, who are compelled to ask endlessly and with ever-increasing anguish why they were sent into this existence and what their final lot will be.

In the Author's Note, Strindberg says that since the dream is more often painful than pleasureful, "a tone of melancholy and of compassion for all living things, runs through the swaying narrative." It is this warm sympathy that gives *A Dream Play* its unique position among Strindberg's works.

In a letter to Harriet Bosse, Strindberg described how airy, grand, and beautiful he could envision a play during "the surging joy of conception." But when he tried to "put it down on paper, it [became] something different or nothing at all. It's almost a sin to write. To write something down is to debase it! To make prose out of poetry! In brief, to reduce it to the commonplace."[38] Despite extensive revision, *A Dream Play* was to some extent written "in the surging joy of conception." The original plans were not followed, and the themes are hinted at rather than spelled out. When a portion of these plans was later carried out in *Fairhaven and Foulstrand,* it lost much of its poetry. In the play, the characters are only sketched in and the philosophical viewpoint is not developed as a series of definite theses. Perhaps it is this lightness of touch that gives *A Dream Play* its brilliance.

After the Inferno Crisis, Strindberg tried to suggest in his writings that "anything can happen; everything is possible and probable," as he wrote in the Author's Note. But he had a difficult time realizing his intention successfully. In plays like *Advent* and *The Crown Bride* supernatural forces intervene like bits of stage magic. In other works, characters simply talk about their occult experiences and make pedantic observations. Repeatedly, dissonances arise between the naturalistic and occultist elements, sometimes breaking a work into two disparate halves, as in *Black Banners.*

A Dream Play is devoid of this kind of tension between different materials and different styles. Everything is simultaneously real and unreal; it is reality transformed by the dream. Strindberg accomplished this transformation largely through exaggeration carried to an extreme. Kristin, the Lawyer's maid, pastes windows closed until people suffocate; when the Lawyer turns a door handle the squeaking makes Indra's Daughter feel as though her husband were twisting her heartstrings; the rich people in the physical therapy gymnasium in Foulstrand roar with pain as they are stretched on racks; and the newlyweds, who are deliriously happy, wish to die: "In the midst of happiness grows a seed of unhappiness. Happiness consumes itself like a flame. - - - It cannot burn forever; it must die out. And this premonition of the end destroys bliss at its peak."[39] One might call this technique surrealistic; Indra's Daughter describes poetry as "not reality, but more than reality - - - not dreams, but waking dreams."

To give unity to the composition of the play, Strindberg shaped it "polyphonically," to borrow the word he used in his studies of Shakespeare in *Open Letters*. No individual situation or character is permitted to dominate the drama, and a continuity of action is created by an ingenious device—one character picking up the train of thought of another. At times, however, the absence of a strong focal point makes the play seem too complicated. Strindberg was tempted, especially toward the end when his inspiration ebbed, to include any chance impression that popped into his mind. In the Fingal's Cave scene, for example, one has difficulty finding a justification, either as art or idea, for the Poet describing his vision of soldiers marching in the shadow of a church tower on a snow-covered parade ground.[40] This is one of the instances in *A Dream Play* in which the reader is lured into fruitless attempts at interpretation. But in spite of its surfeit of riches, the drama is made coherent by the variations in the basic unifying theme of mankind's suffering, each variation leading to new, always unanswered questions.

A subordinate theme of class distinctions and conflicts was only fleetingly suggested in the original manuscript, principally through the three servant girls who stand on an empty box outside the Fairhaven casino, enviously watching the dance in which they are forbidden to participate. It was during one of his final revisions that Strindberg inserted the bitter scene on the Riviera, in which two coal heavers who worry about getting enough to eat get angry when they hear that rich people must go for a walk in order to work up an appetite.

We might have expected that Strindberg would have used a stylized dialogue in *A Dream Play*, not only because he was trying to create a dual illusion of dream and reality, but also because this had been his approach in the two immediately preceding plays, *The Crown Bride* and *Swanwhite*. We might also have expected that in order for the dialogue in the main body of the play to harmonize with the wonderful lyricism in the prologue, epilogue, and the songs of the winds and waves, it would have to have a rhythmic quality, similar to large sections of the dialogue in Part III of *To Damascus* and the dramatic fragment *The Dutchman*. In the 1921 production of *A Dream Play* at Stockholm's Royal Dramatic Theatre, Max Reinhardt apparently believed that the profundity of the play demanded a solemn presentation and had the lines literally chanted

by the actors. The pretentious effects which were produced only underscored the distinctive nature of the dialogue: it is conversational speech.
The key phrase—"Man is to be pitied"—has a colloquial ring in Swedish,
but some translators have felt the necessity to make it sound more imposing.

After the Inferno, Strindberg's diction contained so many nuances
that he was able to give a grandeur to his style without having to make
the vocabulary or syntax more literary. Often he accomplished this merely
through a variation in intonation, either supported by a nimble inversion
or an isolated Biblical word that suddenly illuminated the text.

But the dialogue in *A Dream Play* never becomes so ordinary
that it dispels the dream-like atmosphere. For example, the tension between
the Lawyer and Indra's Daughter after their marriage is so similar to the
countless other realistic Strindbergian portraits of married life that we
expect the inevitable quarrel and mutual invective to erupt at any moment.
Instead, the pasting over of windows and the screeching door handle
cause the scene to dissolve into a nightmare. And in the Foulstrand scene
the Quarantine Master's gallows humor creates a totally different effect
from the fairy-tale image of Hell in *Advent's* Waiting Room scene.

In the solemn, almost reverent scene between the Poet and Indra's
Daughter, Strindberg was able to introduce a half-comic situation without
creating a ludicrous effect. After much lamenting over the wretchedness
of life and the liberation offered by death, the Poet sees the tragic vision
of a ship in distress, and at the same time the water in the cave begins
to rise, threatening to drag him under. "Don't you want to be set free?"
Indra's Daughter asks when she notices his alarm, and the Poet replies:
"Yes, of course, of course I do, but not now - - - and not by water!"[41]
Strindberg manages to make the irrational will to live, which compels
man to desire a prolongation of his earthly suffering, seem both humorous
and pathetic.

A Dream Play is not, as many have surmised, a naked drama of
ideas; nor is it an incoherent muddle; and it is least of all a manipulated
theatrical experiment. As a work of art, it is more representative of Strindberg's view of reality after the Inferno than his more realistic works. The
author of *The Red Room* could no longer see people and objects in firm
contours and sharp outlines. Moreover, he had lost some of his curiosity
about reality and his appetite for realism. A short essay titled "Stockholm

at Seven in the Morning" ("Stockholm sju på morgonen"—1905) concludes with a mention of the "growing castle" with the sun shining on
every window and a white object visible beneath the roof balcony: "I
have never resolved what that white-painted thing is, nor do I care to
know, for it is much more fun this way."[42] Memories and notions replaced
the here and now. He saw the world through a dreamy veil that made it
more frightening, but because the veil made things less real, the world
was less cruel.

He began work on the play by recalling his entire inner treasure
of memories and fantasies, somewhat as he had begun the captivating
short autobiographical novel *Alone* (1903). Only during the course of
the writing did he realize that he was working with dreams, not reality.
Toward the end of his work, he concluded that earthly existence is a meaningless dream, a heavy coma, from which we would awaken only through
death. He became preoccupied with thoughts about the Fall and man's
guilt, but could not resolve the questions they raised in his mind. *A Dream
Play* may appear a capricious drama, devoid of a firm foundation, but it is
artistically consistent and the most spontaneous poetic work Strindberg
produced after the Inferno.[43] "Tell me your sorrows!" the Poet urges
Indra's Daughter near the end of the play, and she replies: "Poet, could
you tell your own so that every word was true?" In *A Dream Play*, Strindberg told his own greatest sorrow "so that every word was true."

In the unfinished drama *The Dutchman*,[44] which Strindberg
wrote in the summer of 1902, a half-year after *A Dream Play*, his growing
bitterness over the failure of his third marriage is the dominant theme,
although it is not as strong as it would be in the third song of the verse
cycle of the same name, based on the play, in *Word-Play and Minor Art*.

The image in the title of the play fragment is mentioned in the
Fingal's Cave scene in *A Dream Play*, where Indra's Daughter and the
Poet think they see the ghost ship *The Flying Dutchman* outside a reef.
"Why is he punished so cruelly, and why doesn't he come ashore?" asks
Indra's Daughter. "Because he had seven unfaithful wives," answers the
Poet.[45] In the original manuscript of *A Dream Play*, the Poet's reply to
Indra's Daughter's next question of how the Dutchman might be freed of
the curse was: "When he encounters a faithful woman." In the fragment,

the Dutchman has had six unfaithful wives, and his mother prophesies
that one day he will find a faithful woman and "achieve atonement
through a loving wife."

The portion of the play that was completed—two acts and part
of a third—shows that the seventh marriage is no happier than the six
previous ones. At the opening of the play the Dutchman has returned to
land after sailing for seven years; the action takes place in a city square
and inside "the new red house," obviously the same house on Karla Way
in which Strindberg lived during his third marriage.

The fragment's merit lies in its beautiful lyricism. Transitions
between prose and verse are often imperceptible, and the lovely songs of
the Dutchman were later inserted virtually unchanged into *Word-Play
and Minor Art*. This same mixture of prose and free verse can be found at
the conclusion of *A Dream Play,* and certain of the scenes in the fragment
also have a pronounced dream character. The Dutchman fancies he walks
in a dream through a sleeping city: "You see, when you've lived as long as
I have, dreams and experiences merge."[46]

The Dutchman foreshadows the Chamber Plays, partly through
the shattering of the dream atmosphere by bitter and cutting invective,
and partly by the image of a house as a living being that determines the
fates of the occupants and whose fate is determined in turn by them. In his
first monologue the Dutchman says:

> So many human destinies have accumulated in these houses, piling up on
> each other. Each family treads over the heads of others; they marry, have
> children, fight, suffer, without knowing each other, separated only by a
> layer of timbers and a little sawdust. Sometimes a sound penetrates the
> double flooring: a child's scream, a chord of music from some instrument,
> the banging of a door . . . and then the silence closes in again and the
> stranger's destiny is complete.[47]

The figure of the Dutchman has some of the features of the Customs Agent in *Men of the Skerries,* the Stranger in *To Damascus* (especially in Part III), and the Prince in *Swanwhite*. In his tranquil observations on old age and in his outbursts of misogyny he foreshadows the
hero in the Chamber Play *Storm*. When his beloved Lilith reproaches him
for living entirely in memory instead of in the present, he says:

> The moment that just passed is already memory;
> only what was, *is!* . . .
> what is this minute that is passing;

> what is this *now* you talk about?
> Something not yet finished: Illusion![48]

His new love also fills him with misgivings. Anticipation and presentiment are actually more important in his life than fulfillment: "I don't drink wine; the colors alone intoxicate me."

In the unfinished third act, he is a newlywed, but does not feel completely happy:

> You fill my life and yet it is empty!
> You are enough for me and yet something
>   is missing,
> I know not what.
> You come so close I cannot see you;
> as when you are in my arms---[49]

It takes only one careless word to tear apart this fragile web of eroticism, and when it is spoken and the Dutchman's beloved leaves forever the marriage she thinks is a spiritual prison, the Dutchman also feels liberated. Now, for the first time, he can breathe freely:

> She who brought me happiness almost suffocated me. . . . She obscured the light in here; she took up all the space, forcing me out. . . . Now I feel I can paint her portrait, which I could not do when she was present. . . . Not as she is, but as I see her in my mind's eye. As such, however, neither color nor line can render her, for I remember only her soul . . . which I love.[50]

Strindberg would take up this theme again in the beautiful autobiographically inspired story about Erik XIV, "The Tragedy at Örby House" ("Sorgespelet på Örbyhus") in *Sagas of the Rulers* (*Hövdingaminnen*).

Like *To Damascus* and *The Great Highway*, the fragment *The Dutchman* is virtually a monodrama in which only the central character is realized. Neither his servant Ukko nor Lilith is a psychologically consistent character, and his mother, to whom he confesses his erotic misadventures in the first act, is scarcely more than a listener. It was thus rather easy for Strindberg to transform this lovely fragment into a series of lyrical monologues in *Word-Play*. Nevertheless, much was lost in these reworkings, for in them his bitterness over his lost love spilled over into venomous accusations that never emerge in the play.

Notes to Chapter Eighteen

1. *SS*:XXXVI, p. 239.
2. *SS*:XLVI, p. 405.
3. *See* p. 417.—Translator
4. *SS*:XXXVI, pp. 298-99.
5. *Ibid.*, p. 302.
6. *SS*:L, p. 288.
7. Kipling's short story "The Brushwood Boy" (*The Day's Work,* 1898) made a deep impression on Strindberg for the very reason that it portrayed two people who have a common dream in which they encounter each other. Strindberg wrote to Geijerstam (February 24, 1899): "I was frightened when I read ['The Brushwood Boy'] because the author believes in it and so tricks the reader into believing."
8. *SS*:XVIII, p. 38.
9. *SS*:XVI, pp. 251 ff.
10. Expressed in a letter to Nils Andersson a year before the writing of *A Dream Play.*
11. *SS*:XXXVI, p. 244.
12. *SS*:XXXVIII, pp. 148-49.
13. *Ibid.*, p. 139.
14. *See* p. 76.—Translator
15. *SS*:XXXVI, p. 266.
16. *Ibid.*, p. 249.
17. *Ibid.*, p. 227.
18. *Ibid.*, pp. 241-42.
19. *Ibid.*, p. 272.
20. *Ibid.*, p. 247.
21. *Cf.* Strindberg's description in *The Son of a Servant* of how as a teacher in the lowest class in an elementary school he imagined he was reexperiencing his days in the Klara school (*SS*:XVIII, pp. 249-50).
22. *SS*:XXXVI, p. 282.
23. *Ibid.*, pp. 245-46.
24. *Ibid.*, p. 260.
25. *Ibid.*, p. 223.
26. *Ibid.*, p. 226.
27. *Ibid.*, p. 236.
28. *Ibid.*, pp. 329-30.

29. *Ibid.*, p. 271.
30. *Ibid.*, p. 325.
31. *Ibid.*, p. 224.
32. *Ibid.*, p. 317.
33. The same mixed feelings are evident in the marital plays from the 1880's and in his autobiographical writings, especially in *A Madman's Defense*. The passion of *Swanwhite* follows close upon the agony of *The Dance of Death*.
34. *SS:*XXXVI, p. 326.
35. *Ibid.*, p. 304.
36. *Ibid.*, p. 322.
37. *Ibid.*, p. 294.
38. April 1, 1906. *Brev till Harriet Bosse*, p. 229.
39. *SS:*XXXVI, p. 284.
40. *Ibid.*, p. 309.
41. *Ibid.*, p. 306.
42. *SS:*LIV, p. 452.
43. In a very thorough investigation ("Bidrag til tolkningen af 'Ett Drömspel,'" *Orbis litterarum*, 1943) Ejnar Thomsen has shown the inner contradictions in the play. Eklund has strongly emphasized the influence of Schopenhauer (*Strindbergsstudie*, pp. 293 ff.).
44. *SOS:*I, pp. 201-310.
45. *SS:*XXXVI, pp. 306-7.
46. *SOS:*I, p. 235.
47. *Ibid.*, p. 205.
48. *Ibid.*, p. 243.
49. *Ibid.*, p. 250.
50. *Ibid.*, p. 253.

Chapter Nineteen

PROSE AND LYRICS

Fairhaven and Foulstrand

After his disappointment over the failure of his realistic play *Midsummer,* Strindberg resorted to the dream form whenever he dealt with his impressions of Stockholm and the skerries. But he had many sketches of such impressions, especially from Furusund, and when in 1902 he found the theatres unwilling to perform his plays, he resolved to publish a collection of realistic stories under the title *Fairhaven and Foulstrand.* He indicated in his diary on May 11, 1902, that he was working on the collection and a week later wrote to Geijerstam that he had "seventy pages of the Narratives finished" but sounded pessimistic about being able to continue. By May 13, 1902, he wrote to Schering: "Now I sit idle, believing I am written out—as in 1892."

It had obviously been his intention to fill an entire volume with stories set in Furusund, but a portion of the material had gone into *A Dream Play* and undoubtedly he sensed that a realistic depiction of the skerries did not suit him as well now as it had earlier. As a result, two stories not connected with Furusund were added to the book, both narrated by the skerries figure the Quarantine Master. One of these stories, "The Quarantine Master's Second Tale," was the aforementioned unfinished novel, *The Cloister* (begun in 1898), about Strindberg's second marriage, and the other, "The Quarantine Master's First Tale" ("Karantänmästarns första berättelse"), a newly written short story based in part on an incident which took place in the southern province of Skåne (and is mentioned in *A Dream Play*), but dealing primarily with Strindberg's third marriage.

By the fall he had written his verse confession "Trinity Eve" ("Trefaldighetsnatten"); apparently it was now easier for him to write poetry than prose, and on September 8, a month before publication of the stories, he suggested to Geijerstam that a small group of poems (which included "Trinity Eve") be added to the volume "to act as a rear guard to protect the Quarantine Master's somewhat dangerous tales." Ironically, this "rear guard," called *Word-Play and Minor Art,* turned out to be the best thing in the book, making the prose pieces seem like filler.

The only pieces written specifically for the story collection were the Introduction, the story "A Nursery Tale" ("En barnsaga"), and two anecdotes—"The Lowliest and the Foremost" ("De yttersta och de främsta") and "Bypassed" ("Den kvarlåtne"). The common theme in these stories is the contrast between the smiling Furusund (Fairhaven) and the melancholy island lying opposite, Köpmanholm (Foulstrand). During his first summers on Furusund, in 1899 and 1900, Strindberg observed in his diary that this contrast reminded him of Gerizim, the Mount of Blessing, and Ebal, the Mount of Curses, and he made a number of notes about the islands, obviously with the intention of dealing with them in dramatic form. In *A Dream Play,* Fairhaven's joyous summer paradise conceals as much unhappiness as exists among the cold rocks of Foulstrand, and the same is true in the stories. Torkel, the young man in "A Nursery Tale," longs to leave Foulstrand's shores and go to Fairhaven with its beautiful villas, curtains wafted by summer breezes, flagpoles, and rose gardens. But when he gets a position as a uniformed servant at the hotel on Fairhaven, he learns that people there were not fundamentally better than on the other side: "They just wore finer clothes, concealing the dirtiness underneath, and they actually came here to get clean."[1] And in "The Lowliest and the Foremost," an artist who provokes a scandal in the resort lodge at Fairhaven by dancing with a scullery maid, sails over to Foulstrand, never more to set foot on Fairhaven: " 'It's beautiful, all right,' he thought, 'but only on the surface! And I wonder in which place a person has most to be ashamed of! Ebal isn't Gerizim, but the question is where the Mount of Blessing is really located—perhaps in the middle of the sound!' "[2]

Strindberg suggests that Fairhaven's happy holiday environment owed a debt to the harsh climate of Foulstrand. In the Introduction he says that the island of Fairhaven would not be so beautiful "if Foulstrand, lying directly opposite, did not serve as a breakwater, protecting against heavy seas and intercepting the raw northeastern winds."[3] This probably accounts for the absence of sympathetic warmth in Strindberg's descriptions of Fairhaven—with its small white, blue, or rose-red candystand villas, fruit trees and flowerbeds, piers and bathhouses, its pennant-bedecked sailboats, and ladies dressed in white on the piers. Or perhaps it just seems this way because today we find these motley seaside resort surroundings uninteresting—the inn terrace, music pavilion, skittles alley, and summer theatre—and tend to prefer the reed-edged coves and open bays of Hemsö or perhaps even the cold hills, red cottages, and pigsties of Foulstrand. Not until he turned to verse did Strindberg bring Fairhaven to life. In "Trinity Eve" he excluded Foulstrand entirely and was thus able, with the help of his wonderful hexameters, to portray Fairhaven's splendor with a clear conscience.

The longest Furusund story in the collection, "A Nursery Tale," is obviously a fragment of an intended novel. The first part is the best, portraying Torkel Öman's alcoholic father, a ship's pilot who lost his job when he ran a Finnish schooner aground. Now a rebel, he lives a lawless life poaching fish and plundering wrecks, until one day he is pursued by a revenue cutter and sails off to an unknown fate. The story is reminiscent of Strindberg's narratives in *Men of the Skerries,* and it is possible that the idea originated at the time the earlier book was written.

The real hero of the story is Torkel. The sketches show that Strindberg had originally planned to depict his future as a lighthouse keeper: apparently he was to experience reverses which turn him into a cynic, misanthrope, and enemy of society. The final version of the story, however, ends with Torkel as a young boy being accepted as a seaman aboard a cutter belonging to an old naval officer. He is on his first voyage, peering with curiosity into the distance toward Stockholm, "the big city into which all the ships sailed, and which he had never seen!"[4]

As long as Strindberg is describing the fantasies of this isolated young boy, the portrayal is splendid. What we find is a spiritual brother of the romantic Råno organist. (In one sketch, Strindberg actually indicated that Torkel was born on Årdala, where the real-life model for the organist had had his home.) In a crevice between two flat rocks Torkel finds a treasure that sets his imagination in motion: wonderful corks with bits of silver and gold on them lying in the midst of purple loosestrife and violet asters. And when he goes into the woods, he fancies that he is still on the sea:

> It was dark within and smelled damp. Mushrooms grew there and looked like jellyfish and sea urchins; he half-expected the stomachs of the fungi to heave in and out to enable them to float up between the mast-like spruce trees. The winds murmured in the trees as in rigging, and the flexible yards swayed in the green top rigging—he was still on the sea with all its memories and illusions.[5]

After the father's disappearance, the story takes on an unctuous tone. According to the sketches, Torkel was to develop into a "Pietist," and even in the final version a number of uplifting observations are made. Sometimes, these are pure Sunday school stories, such as when Ruten, a horse who is Foulstrand's only sober being, converts Vicksberg, a drunken pilot, to sobriety by frightening him. As the pilot lies dead drunk on the beach, the horse takes hold of the man's pea jacket between his teeth and dips him three times in the sea.

The other two Furusund stories are only anecdotes, variations on the theme of the contrast between Fairhaven and Foulstrand. As with "A Nursery Tale," their real merit lies in the passages in which they show us the raw material for the wonderful skerries idylls in *Word-Play and Minor Art.*

Word-Play and Minor Art

Many of the poems included in *Fairhaven and Foulstrand* and later added to for the separately published edition of *Word-Play and Minor Art* in 1905[6] grew spontaneously out of Strindberg's dramas. *The Crown Bride* and *Swanwhite,* because they were inspired by folk ballads, have dialogue passages with a lyrical quality close to poetry, but they also have many insignificant fillers that resemble popular songs. In *A Dream Play,* however, his free verse has assumed some of the characteristics that would give it distinction in *Word-Play,* especially in the Lamentation of the Winds and the Song of the Waves with their tendency towards alliteration and onomatopoeia:

> Det är vi, vi, vindarne   It is we, we, the winds
> som vina och vinsla   who whine and whistle
> ve! ve! ve!   woe! woe! woe!

or:

Det är vi, vi, vågorna	It is we, we, the waves
som vagga vindarne	that rock the winds
till vila!	to rest!
Gröna vaggor, vi vågor.	Green cradles, we waves.
Våta äro vi, och salta.	Wet are we, and salt.

In *Word-Play* these are two verse cycles based directly on earlier drama fragments: "The Dutchman" and "Trinity Eve." The sketch and outline for the origin of "Trinity Eve," *Walpurgis Night on Fairhaven (Valborgsafton på Fagervik)*, was reconstructed by Gunnar Ollén from Strindberg's manuscript.[7]

The alteration between prose and verse in the drama *The Dutchman* is a technique to which Strindberg would return in several of his later plays: the last Chamber Play, *The Black Glove (Svarta handsken)*, is subtitled a "lyrical fantasy"; the Arabian fairy tale *Abu Casem's Slippers (Abu Casems tofflor)* is to a large extent written in "uncounted iambs"; and in the lyrical monologues in *The Great Highway*, Strindberg's verse achieved a beauty unmatched by any of the poems in *Word-Play*.

Some poems in *Word-Play* have similar themes to the stories in *Fairhaven and Foulstrand,* and others have their origin in the prose observations of *Alone.* Because of its intimate connection with his drama and prose fiction, Strindberg's later verse has a quality different from what is generally meant by lyricism. With the exception of a few simple short songs in folk-ballad style, his lyrics are intended to be spoken, rather than sung, and for the most part are presented either in the form of a narrative, a dialogue, or a series of dramatic monologues, as is the case with the intimate personal confessions in "Trinity Eve."

In order to understand some of the lyrics completely, it is necessary to read the commentaries that Strindberg provided for them. This is true, for example, of a number of the separate poems included within "Trinity Eve" or of "The Wolves Howl" ("Vargarne tjuta"), which would be almost incomprehensible without the reference in *Alone* that depicts the psychological process that preceded the writing of the poem:

> In my solitude, isolated events seem connected, and much of what happens seems to be staged expressly for me. Thus, one evening I witnessed a fire in the city and at the same time heard the howling of wolves from Skansen [Park]. These two ends of different threads entwined in my imagination, became part of a single context, and were woven on an appropriate warp into a poem.[8]

The connection Strindberg sensed between the fire and the wolves' howling is the animals' wild, malicious delight in humanity's misfortune:

> A howling arose from the wolves' pits
> as if they had been stabbed with knives—
> hateful, vengeful sounds; in the laughter from
> the foxes' den was the hunger for arson,
> the joy of the kill, a happy, uncanny satisfaction.[9]

Only dogs are unhappy and whine like lost souls:

> They have compassion, only they—the dogs,
> for their human friends—such sympathy![10]

Another event that seems "staged" for the poet's benefit is found
in "Summer Shower" ("Åskregn"). The poet and his wife sit at a table in
the sunshine and talk "in embarrassing dashes,/and perhaps mostly question marks." But the sky darkens and suddenly there is a clap of thunder
and a shower covers the windowpanes "with exclamation points":

> So the heavens respond with a crash
> to the children's foolish questions.[11]

The Eternal One silences presumptuous inquiries.

Sometimes there are no clues to interpretation in the poem itself,
as, for example, in the third section of "Street Scenes" ("Gatubilder"):

> Dark is the house and dark outside—
> but it is darkest in the cellar—
> underground, no light, no air—
> the entrance serves as window and door—
> and down deep in the darkness
> flying sparks reveal a buzzing generator;
> black and frightful in the void
> it grinds out light for all nearby.[12]

In a letter to Harriet Bosse dated Easter Sunday, 1901, Strindberg wondered whether his suffering, like Eleonora's in *Easter,* could not be transformed into happiness for others: "I think of that frightful black electric
machine down in the cellar on Grev Magni Street. It sits there darkly in
the darkness, grinding out light for the entire block."[13] Not a word in the
poem suggests this personal application, and there is certainly nothing
particularly unusual about a machine to produce light being located in a
dark cellar. But the contrast stimulated Strindberg, and his imagination

must have pictured the generator suffering because it was doomed to remain in darkness, scaring everyone with its din.

Similar personal elements appear in Strindberg's most famous poems, such as "Chrysáëtos" in "Trinity Eve." As Ollén has demonstrated, it is based on the same marital crisis that inspired *A Dream Play*. It begins with a haunting introduction in which Strindberg describes all the portents in his neighborhood that ominously suggest the same thing—death and burial:

> What are they waiting for,
> those tiresome crows,
> down on the autumnal moor? . . .
>
> Is it carrion and bait
> on the butcher's cart?
> Or is there an animal
> lying in a litter, dying? . . .
>
> What are they doing,
> those stooped men,
> at the entrance to my home? . . .
>
> [scattering] spruce branches[14] in the snow.[15]

Whenever misfortunes occurred, Strindberg would examine his diary to trace the events that foreshadowed them. In a way, *Word-Play* is a supplemental diary in which he used verse to capture and preserve impressions from his morning promenades ("Street Scenes"), from the lonely evenings in the apartment ("Long Somber Evenings"—"Långa tunga kvällar"), or from his wife's piano playing in the summer villa on Furusund ("At the Last Headland"—"Vid sista udden"). Sometimes views from his window call up the past ("At Day's End"—"Vid dagens slut"):

> Beyond those blue woods
> near the sea,
> is my youth, long gone
> out there in the bracing bays—
> Where are the hearths I dreamed about,
> and the friends who have departed?
> Buried.
> Life took the best!
>
> I don't want to look out there,
> not in that direction!
> So I sink back in my chaise,
> where I can see only clouds—

> And the setting sun in the clouds
> is like the glow of a fire in coals!
> Then—in here!
> Here, too, day's end is awaited![16]

These mood poems have the virtues of improvisation—charm and spontaneity—but also the shortcomings. All too often a rhyme goes wrong or a thought is not expressed completely.

The most beautiful of these daydreams is "Cloud Pictures" ("Molnbilder"), in which the poet—once again from his window—follows the visions that clouds conjure up for him. Now they form castles and palace ruins, cathedrals and town hall gables, now desert landscapes with oases, camels, and pyramids. The next moment they call to mind the skerries and Kymmendö:

> Verdant shores, shady alders,
> swaying reeds in quiet bays,
> here I feel I belong,
> here are my lands, my leas!
>
> Oh, verdant isle I call my own,
> flower basket on the waves of the sea![17]

The poet is overcome by homesickness and wants to leave the earth and follow the clouds on their journey, but then a black cloud dissolves in rain over the dirty field:

> Alas! They are clouds, they are vapors only![18]

The same mixture of reality and dream can be found in the poems written in hexameters. Nothing could be more resolutely realistic than the opening lines of "Trinity Eve," which depict a spring evening in the resort inn at Fairhaven. The inn's storm windows are being taken down in preparation for the coming season. Three men are drinking at a table: the Customs Collector, the Master Pilot, and the Postmaster; shortly thereafter, they are joined by several more men: the Will Executor (the first summer guest of the year), the Curate, the Poet, and the Accountant, each of whom has stories in verse to tell, or poems to recite. The Customs Collector speaks first, and his joy at the arrival of spring changes very quickly into a detailed order for supper:

> It's spring again! Break open the windows like the billow broke the ice!
> Let out the winter air, let the tile stove cool in shame in its corner.
> Youth and spring await us at the door with anemones and sallow;

dear Mrs. Lundström, put the brandy on ice and get a supper ready,
supper for seven with crayfish and beer and fresh new radishes;
don't forget the Burträsk cheese and the crispest Bergman hard rye;
then fill the tankards with foaming Saint Erik's pilsner;
That's how a meal's arranged in the good old Swedish way—I have
   spoken![19]

The Executor's sensual description of summer's culinary pleasures
sometimes turns into prim domestic advice, not very different from the
kind with which readers were regaled in eighteenth-century landscape
poetry:

cucumbers are my fruit, the fruit of my life, I have to admit;
I grow prime ones myself and put them in jars,
jars made of blue-green glass from a quarter-gallon size to a half,
bought from the Kosta factory, located near Munk Bridge, I think.[20]

But at the same time, a suggestion of melancholy intrudes in this
section, for with summer come the resort tourists, putting an end to God's
peace in nature and renewing the "law of conflict":

everything young and beautiful is brief
like summer in the North.

The Curate transforms reality into dream in his description of a
hay barn concealed in a clearing in the woods and bordered by junipers,
ferns, and close-cropped grass. As he speaks about it, the barn begins to
resemble a temple consecrated to a nature god, "exuding the fragrance of
sweet vernal grass and clover."[21] And when, using Linnaeus's botanical
terminology, he describes the "annual miracle" taking place in the steaming rye as flowers are fertilized, the hexameter loses every trace of a heavy
accent and becomes as flexible and melodic as a lyrical meter.

If dream and reality fuse in these passages, they are wrenched
apart in other "Trinity Eve" poems—"Chrysáëtos" and "I Dreamed" ("Jag
drömde"), which although clothed in the forms of a dream are anguished
and brimming over with reality's bitter disappointments.

"Journey to Town" is a straightforward narrative poem, but contains the same contrasts as "Trinity Eve." An organist from Årby who is
on his way to Stockholm stands on the foredeck of the Lake Mälar boat
"amidst goods and drunken peasants."[22] As he sweats and suffers, the
boat's engines smell of tallow and from the dining salon below rises a
tantalizing aroma of "steaming beefsteak and soy sauce."[23] But beyond
the ship is the serene world of nature celebrating its midsummer holiday:

A warm summer calm hovers in the air and in the trees, over water,
    and land;
Sunday's peace covets the earth and silence reigns,
and from the bell tower's humble home the Sabbath rest is rung out.
The mill wheel is stopped and the stream runs dry in its channel;
Draught animals rest in their cribs and stalls, free of the harness.[24]

The image brings to mind the summer peace of *The People of Hemsö,* and passages in the opening stanza are similar to the novel's sprightly descriptions of bird life in the outer skerries and the hay mowing:

Out on a Mälar bay as bright and smooth as a mirror
the gulls are awake and screech themselves hoarse from hunger;
And then from the land, from the whitewashed stones of the alder beaches,
comes the cheering verse of the snipe, whistling and trilling;
the fieldfare clicks his castanet from sky-high alders on the shore;
deep in the elders, rustling like a spring brook over well-washed stones,
can be heard the willow warbler's ingenious song; but the singer does
    not show himself.[25]

Strindberg had conceived the theme for "Journey to Town" before he wrote *The People of Hemsö* and had even decided at that time to develop it as in idyll in hexameters.[26] In the summer of 1886 he promised his publisher that he would shortly send "a Swedish idyll in verse called 'The Birthday' dealing with the Organist's new piano and the circumstances connected with it, landscapes, a peasant church, etc." Had the poem been completed then, it probably would have had largely the same sequence of events as the final version, including the Organist's dreams of glory: with stiff fingers he plays the same Bach toccata on his piano that he played as a young and promising performer in an organ concert at Stockholm's Klara Church during his time at the Academy.[27] But the basic mood would have been very different if the poem had been written earlier. Even the opening section of "Journey to Town" suggests that the idyllic cheer depicted is only a quiet interlude, and the suggestion becomes explicit when in his playing of Beethoven's Apassionata Sonata the Organist expresses his feeling that

Life has made everything bitter; cynical
    mocking life,
making foolish all our earnestness, and
    deriding sacred emotions,
demanding sacrifice and duty, then
    laughing at the sacrifice;

People are compelled to "slash and hurt" their dearest possessions. Their intentions are good, but life's are evil, and so "you hear the prisoners screaming from their earthly prison."[28] The melancholy tone is identical to that of *A Dream Play* and prevails throughout *Word-Play*. The great hymn in "The Dutchman" to the beauty of woman's body ends with bitter words about her hair:

> Alas, I, too, have rested in the
>   shadow of tresses
> At a mother's breast and at a wife's
>   bosom . . .
>
> once, they were black as cypress;
> like a scourge of lean snakes
> they lashed across my eyes;
> and entwined themselves into a hair
>   shirt
> I was forced to wear, even as it
>   chilled me!
> Oh, benign scourge—[29]

The beautiful monologue "I Dreamed" included in "Trinity Eve" portrays the same transition from joyous dream to nightmare as does the Lawyer's marriage to Indra's Daughter, except that the contrasts are stronger. Here, the Accountant says that he dreamed he was a cripple, unworthy to be loved by a woman. But love renewed and transformed him, and he celebrated "a marriage in which two souls were wed." But a single careless word turned the marriage into a Gehenna:

> We battled finally and we cried
> so bitterly at our humiliation—
> reconciled and caressed, swore oaths of love,
> and then we quarreled again and battled—
> So I shouted loudly: "Is there no end,
> is there no end to this hell?"
> There was no end; and every night my dream returned,
> the dream that is like my second life![30]

In the later enlarged edition of *Word-Play*, published separately from *Fairhaven and Foulstrand* in 1905, self-accusations give way to accusations; Strindberg persuaded the publisher to remove the third Dutchman song from the already printed book. But the final poem in the revised edition was still the sad little song for a lost love that is as moving as a drowning man's call for help:

Villemo, Villemo
why did you go, did you go?

Strindberg was just as hostile toward the "finger-counting" of verse feet as when he published *Poems* in 1883. And during his later years he was very anxious to point out the revolution he had initiated with the loose *knittelvers*[31] of *Somnambulist Nights*. But if critics no longer found his verse as bold as it had been, it was not only because they had become accustomed to innovations of this sort during the twenty years that had passed, but because Strindberg himself had become less daring in his use of both metrics and vocabulary. It is significant that the original subtitle for "Journey to Town," describing it as being written "in free hexameters," was omitted at publication. And when in a 1903 review the classicist Johannes Paulsson sharply critcized Strindberg's failure to adhere to form in the hexameters, Strindberg meekly made basic revisions for the 1905 edition so that the metric accents could be "counted on the fingers by those skilled in counting."

An essay in *Talks to the Swedish Nation* demonstrates that Strindberg found the same shortcomings in Heidenstam's lyrics that the critics in 1883 had found in his own *Poems*.[32] This might have been just a polemical tactic against an old enemy, but it could also have been a manifestation of a change in taste. In any case, Strindberg's descriptive account of what constituted good lyricism corresponds approximately to what he believed he achieved in *Word-Play*. He regarded the lyrical, nationalistic "Pepita poetry"[33] of the 1890's as "pure prose" and characterized it as "shoemaker realism," using the very term Heidenstam and Levertin had used in *Pepita's Wedding* to attack the realism of the 1880's.[34]

In *Word-Play*, Strindberg cultivated to excess such devices as alliteration, assonance, internal rhyme, and echo sounds. Not content to have the winds sing in *A Dream Play*, he amused himself in *Word-Play* (in "The Weathercock Sings"—"Flöjeln sjunger") by allowing a rusty weathercock to speak nonsense words as a way of reproducing the appropriate squeaking, scraping sounds. Of course, in this poem and in the similar "Song of the Nightingale" ("Näktergalens säng"), Strindberg defied contemporary critcism just as much as he did in the cycle "Exile" in *Poems*, but his purpose was different. In *Poems* he aimed primarily at experimenting with metrical effects and with words that jarred the contexts in which they were introduced. Now, he took pains with sound imitation and word music, attempting from time to time to construct his poems according to musical forms—sonatas, fugues, and so forth.

Ollén has emphasized[35] that *Word-Play* was not influenced to any large extent by the Swedish lyric poets of the 1890's, but one must take exception in the case of Ola Hansson. One wonders, too, whether Erik Karlfeldt (1864-1931) did not have a certain impact on Strindberg, for the same subject matter that dominated Karlfeldt's lyrics dominated Strindberg's—nature and eroticism. Karlfeldt was also interested in folk wisdom and folk mysticism, and he, too, admired the seventeenth-century masters and amused himself with rhyme play, echo effects, and onomatopoeia. In fact, Karlfeldt achieved the blending of verse and music for which Strindberg strove.

As far as I can recall, however, neither in his letters nor his notebooks did "the idea-builder from central Sweden" who signed his name to *Word-Play* indicate that he took notice of the popular fictional poet-peasant hero of two volumes of Karlfeldt's verse: *Fridolin's Songs (Fridolins visor* —1898) and *Fridolin's Pleasure Garden (Fridolins lustgård*—1901). But one can hardly imagine that Strindberg was totally unfamiliar with the most esteemed lyric poet in the country during these years; a poet, moreover, who had the additional advantage in Strindberg's eyes of being outside the "Pepita" coterie he detested.

The similarities between the two writers are not great, but we are reminded of Karlfeldt when we read the opening stanzas of "Chrysáëtos," with their swinging trisyllabic rhymes and somber rocking rhythms:

Vad skrika de gula ugglorna	What do the yellow owls screech
på tobaksladornas tak,	on the roofs of the tobacco barns,
när rostiga flöjeln med bugglorna	when the rusty, battered weathercock
knappt håller i vinden sig rak?	can scarce keep its perch in the wind?
Vad sjunger den rostiga flöjeln	What does the rusty weathercock sing
vid nattvindens sorgemusik?	in the night wind's mournful dirge?[36]

Another figure from the 1890's whose influence should be mentioned in connection with *Word-Play* is the satirical writer, magazine editor *(Strix),* and caricaturist Albert Engström (1869-1940). Strindberg is generally given credit for writing the first hexameters of literary merit in Sweden since the days of Esias Tegnér (1782-1846) and Johan Runeberg (1804-77), and he himself probably felt the claim was justified. In the list of his literary qualifications that he drew up in 1909 as a preface to the fourth part of *The Son of a Servant,* Strindberg says the following about *Word-Play:* "The hexameter in the style of Stiernhielm[37] is revived again in Swedish nature depiction."

But Engström had anticipated Strindberg with a short description of spring and the powerful hexameter poem "The Christmas Day Early Service" ("Julotta") which depicts Christmas morning in the cottage of a tenant farmer through the eyes of moose hunters. The poem was included in the 1901 Christmas issue of *Strix.* Engström's influence seems apparent in the first hexameters Strindberg wrote the following spring for the drama fragment *Walpurgis Night on Fairhaven* (later continued as "Trinity Eve") and "Journey to Town," although Strindberg had made plans to write Swedish idylls in hexameters back in the 1880's. And just as Engström did, Strindberg set his descriptions of Swedish nature and landscapes in holiday atmosphere: Walpurgis Night, Trinity Eve, and Midsummer Eve.

The influence of classicism may be more obvious in Albert Engström's hexameters than in Strindberg's, but in "Trinity Eve" Strindberg paid direct tribute to Stiernhielm as his master and identified himself with neoclassicism. In a letter to Schering on September 19, 1902, Strindberg said that twenty-five years earlier he had dreamed of being able to write a counterpart of Johann Voss's "Luise" (1795)—the idyllic poem generally regarded as the finest work of this German poet and translator —and had now finally accomplished his dream with "Journey to Town."[38] Several scholars have pointed out Stiernhielm's influence on Strindberg, particularly Stiernhielm's poem "Recollections of Wedding Inconveniences" ("Bröllopsbesvärs ihugkommelse") which Strindberg had praised in *The Swedish People* for its scences of lusty humor and realism that could hold their own with "the most savage of contemporary French naturalists."[39] Although there are no conspicuous traces of Voss's influence in "Journey to Town," it was surely passed on to Strindberg through the works of Frans Franzén 1772-1847) and Tegnér who, together with Johan Wallin (1779-1839), were included among the classical Swedish lyricists in Strindberg's father's library.[40]

In spite of his worship of Charles XII, Tegnér was always one of Strindberg's favorites. In *The Swedish People* there is mention of joy Tegnér spread "in palace and cottage" by means of *Frithiof's Saga* (1825), a romantic narrative cycle, and *The Children of the Lord's Supper*

(Nattvardsbarnen—1820), a religious idyll. Strindberg further asserted that posterity "never denied [Tegnér] the honor of being Sweden's greatest poet."[41] In *Talks to the Swedish Nation,* Strindberg said that after Stiernhielm's day the art of poetry in Sweden did not reach a similar high point "until Tegnér dealt with Swedish themes in the most beautiful Swedish ever written."[42] Furthermore, the enchanting opening note of "Journey to Town"

> Midsommarafton går in, då en enda Midsummer Eve sets in, as a single,
>   och bleknande stjärna . . .   fading star . . .

is reminiscent of a line in Tegnér's "The Crown Bride":

> Midsommaraftonen låg som ett   Midsummer Eve lay like a
>   grönskande flor over Värend.   greening veil over Värend.

And in Strindberg's description of the church in the third "song" or section of "Journey to Town," one seems to sense Tegnérian moods and images:

> The Lord's day is ordained and the Lord's house is open;
> the largest house in town, the loveliest in the parish—
> white as the wing of a dove and high-arched like the canopy of heaven,
> the ceiling is high, as though built for giants, for gods.
> A forest of columns supports the lofty arches, and deep beneath
> the dragons and trolls they tread upon, like the roots of the tree
> of the world, treads the ancient serpent, the great
> canker, the disintegrator Nidhögg.[43]

The passage is more than a bit reminiscent of the whitewashed church with its leafy entrance and the silver-plated dove under the pulpit in Tegnér's *The Children of the Lord's Supper.* And Strindberg could have found an accessible inspiration for the image of "the ancient serpent, the great canker, the disintegrator Nidhögg" in the section "Atonement" ("Försoningen") in Tegnér's *Frithiof's Saga,* where a *Ragnarök* is presented as the necessary preamble for a happier age, in the same way as Strindberg's Organist interprets the myth.

The Stiernhielmian and Tegnérian elements are so discreetly placed in "Journey to Town" that there is no suggestion of a pastiche. The narrator's voice is unmistakably Strindberg's—in the depiction of bird life in the Lake Mälar landscape, the images of the bells of Riddarholm Church being answered by Tyska Church to the east, and Munk Bridge brightened at midsummer by the leaf market's diverse stands.[44] Nevertheless, the strains from Swedish classical poetry enrich "Journey to Town" with another dimension.

Alone

Strindberg's unique and enchanting little book *Alone* is intimately associated with his lyrics; indeed, in places, its tranquil, fluid, melodic prose flows effortlessly into verse passages. It was published in the fall of 1903, when Harriet and their infant daughter left Strindberg for the last time, and it has been assumed that the work portrays his solitude after the end of his third marriage. But the book was begun in March and completed in June, 1903, when he had not yet irrevocably lost his wife and child, although new marital disputes had once again brought up the question of divorce. He says in the book that married life, which is supposed to be a form of education, is actually a "coeducational school for vices"; that it is torture for someone with a sense of beauty to have to see ugliness every day, and that one becomes a hypocrite and a coward by becoming accustomed to repressing one's opinions.

The prospect of a lonely old age—plus the memory of earlier years in Stockholm and the periods of loneliness during his third marriage —induced Strindberg to take stock of his resources for enduring the burden of solitude. The result was *Alone,* a quiet inventory, partly imaginary, partly real, of memories, hopes, impressions, and moods. He tried to sound an optimistic keynote: to live alone is only to "spin a cocoon of the silk of one's own soul. . . . Meanwhile, you survive on your experiences and telepathically live the lives of others."[45] At the end of the book he exults in being able to "enjoy the happiness of others without a trace of chagrin, regret, or contrived misgivings."[46] He takes pleasure in being his own master, in being relieved of all painful personal contacts, in being able to watch life pass by like a shadow play until the final moment when he is spirited away completely into the Sleeping Beauty Castle of fantasy.

At the same time, Strindberg is conscious of how difficult it is for him to endure isolation. He has a desperate need to be with people. He sits in a streetcar just to share the same space with others, to read the faces of his fellow passengers and listen to their conversation, as if he were listening to people talk at a social gathering: "When it got crowded, I found it pleasant to feel my elbow making contact with another human creature."[47]

In his apartment he is kept company by the sounds coming from his neighbors in the house, but when summer comes and nearly everyone in Stockholm moves out to the country, the house is empty: "I collapse as if my contact with humanity were broken; all the trivial sounds from the different apartments stimulated me, and I miss them; even the dog who woke me to nightly meditations or stirred me to a healthy rage has left a void behind."[48] He is relieved in August when the street lamps are lit, the neighbors move back, and the dog begins "to bark again, night and day."[49]

Often solitude seems like a restraint, or a form of ostracism, and he winces when a beggar tells him that evil people are punished by solitude. He tries to persuade himself that it is better for him to be alone than in the company of other people. "I believe it is my fate to be alone, and it is to my advantage." But he adds hesitatingly: "I want to believe this, for otherwise it would all be too unbearable."[50]

He no longer wants direct contact with nature; only people interest him. He knows that spring has returned by the sea and that wood anemones and blue anemones are growing under the spruces, but he gets more enjoyment out of imagining them than actually seeing them, "for I have long ago outgrown the nature that is manifested as minerals, plants, and animals. What interests me is the nature and fate of man."[51] But he has been afraid of people ever since he was born, and even when he goes to see a friend, he generally feels like a beggar and is ashamed; when he reaches the bellpull, he turns around and leaves.

Gunnar Ollén has pointed out[52] that *Alone* is similar in design to Rousseau's *Rêveries du promeneur solitaire,* with its descriptions of the author's wanderings, his dreams, and his references to the reading of classical literature. Strindberg, however, believed the book to have been inspired by Balzac.[53] It seems also to have some kinship with the street scenes in Hjalmar Söderberg's *Martin Birck's Youth (Martin Bircks ungdom*—1901), one of the few works of the younger generation that Strindberg had read and appreciated. But it is scarcely necessary to seek literary models for a work that bears its creator's mark so strongly and is occasionally a direct elaboration of his diary observations.

In *Rêveries,* Rousseau believes that he has forsworn human company and desires to devote himself entirely to the pleasure of conversing with his own soul. The only thing that still charms him on this strange planet is nature. At the same time, he knows that his happiness is an inner state and does not need nature as a background: "This kind of reverie can be enjoyed anywhere one can remain undisturbed, and I have often thought that in the Bastille, and even in a dungeon, with nothing at all to catch my eye, I should be able to dream delightfully."

Strindberg was equally shy of people, but his need of company was greater. Even as he isolates himself, his thoughts are constantly focused on the unknown destinies being played out around him. On his morning promenades he usually takes the same route so as to encounter the same people day after day, year after year, and to try, without ever coming into contact with them, to discover what their feelings are toward him. An unguarded gesture or a covert facial expression tells him their entire life stories. In his apartment he listens with strained attentiveness to all the sounds from the other apartments, making predictions and drawing conclusions. Solitude for Strindberg was thus like working on an endless piece of fiction, without plan or purpose, and as much without regard for an audience as was possible in an author who was always exposing his innermost being to public view.

A year after the publication of *Alone,* Strindberg instructed Bonniers that after his death the book was to be reissued as the last in the series of his autobiographical writings, following *Inferno* and *Legends.* But unlike them, it is not a conventional, chronologically organized autobiography. What it depicts are inner moods rather than outer events, and the basic tone is different. Life once again had an ordinary everyday rhythm, but it also had solemn and mysterious elements. In the stream of commonplace experiences, Strindberg attached importance to certain minor events that seemed to be "staged" for his benefit and so have special significance. He made the same kinds of notations in his sketches, outlines, and diary entries, and they, too, often are like detached, formless daydreams.

Strindberg says in *Alone* that when he picks up scraps of paper from the street he pays heed only to those that are "expressions of my innermost unborn thoughts." The same is true when he gathers impressions of people, scenes, sights, and sounds on his promenades, in his apartment, or from his balcony; he singles out the ones which evoke an inner response. A sickly child cries somewhere; the telephone wire sings sadly in the wall; two passersby down on the street utter mysterious words; or the sound of a melody being played on a piano comes up through the double flooring.

He looks through his telescope toward Värta Beach in the northeast where a brightly dressed ten-year-old girl steps ashore from a skiff and cuts spruce branches with an axe. She is frightened by the sudden appearance of a cow but gathers up courage, raises her axe, and advances on the animal who, uncertain and "indignant that its friendliness was unappreciated," turns tail into the woods. "Imagine!" says the author, "sitting in one's own quiet home and being drawn into such far-off dramas!"[54]

New impressions stir up memories: the old houses and tobacco barns he remembers from the 1850's, the parish office where he had his first marriage banns registered, the linden trees on Nortulls Street, and the small back streets he took to avoid Drottning Street when going to school. "There were trees and flowering plants; cows grazed and chickens cackled; at that time it was country!—My thoughts drifted back to the dreadfulness of childhood, when the unknown destiny that lay before me was frightening, and everything oppressed and crushed me!"[55]

His memories torment him: he recalls that in his writings he had profaned the Mysteries just as Alcibiades had done and had toppled the idols' images. "I know now that I was right, but when I took malicious pleasure in the conflagration I had lit—that was wrong. If only I had had a spark of compassion for the feelings that I wounded!"[56] But memories are also the basic ingredients of his writings; in one passage he says that he can assemble them "like fragments from a load of bricks," and that from one memory he can distill the most disparate elements into a single imaginative construction. A glance through a window into an old house reveals "a writing table covered with practical and dull accessories,"[57] an ugly aspidistra, and an open damper on a four-cornered tile stove that sets his imagination in motion. He conjures up a vision of "a somewhat affluent petty bourgeois home" and of people who torture and torment each other: "Upon arriving home, I wrote down the drama. And it came from an open damper!"[58] Another time, when he felt drained as a writer, an ugly color lithograph gave him the inspiration for a crucial scene in a play.

Alone also introduces us to the "impersonal associates" that had become Strindberg's only real contacts with the outside world—books. Over a period of ten years the fifty volumes of Balzac's works had made the Frenchman a personal friend who taught him about nondenominational Christianity and reconciled him to suffering. He is disturbed that Balzac has been called a compassionless materialist and is hailed by "that physiologist Zola" as a teacher; Strindberg has eyes only for Balzac's mysticism. "The same situation exists regarding my other literary friend, Goethe, who in recent times has been exploited for all sorts of purposes, mostly for the idiotic revival of heathenism." Goethe rejected pantheism in the end and turned, according to Strindberg, to mysticism and Swedenborg: "The Faust of Part I, whose wrestling with God made him appear a victorious Saul, becomes the fallen Paul of Part II. This is my Goethe!"[59]

Nevertheless, Strindberg does not transform Goethe into an image of himself during the storms of the Inferno period. He finds pleasure in reading him because it is as if Goethe "could not take life completely seriously; either it lacked firm reality, or did not merit our grief and our tears." And Strindberg stresses "the intrepidity with which [Goethe] approaches the divine Powers, with whom he felt related."[60]

That this was an ideal toward which Strindberg himself was striving is evident in his description of the devotional books he selected to read: one is a Catholic book, but he does not feel like a Catholic "for I cannot bind myself to a confession"; another is a seventeenth-century Lutheran book that he uses to scourge himself, but he is critical of its severity and its proclamation of suffering as a gift of grace. He is most comfortable with a book from the Enlightenment. Its author is anonymous, but "he is what I call a reasonable man, who has both eyes open and assigns right and wrong as they should be assigned."[61] Now and then, on important occasions, Strindberg has recourse to the Bible, but he no longer cares to read David's and Jeremiah's curses against their enemies. He prefers those parts of the Old Testament where one does not encounter "the pitiless, vindictive God." And:

> . . . finally, there are times when the only help is Buddhism. As one so seldom gets what one wishes for, what good does it do to wish? Wish for nothing, ask nothing of people and life, and you will always believe you received more than you could have asked for.[62]

It is obvious that Strindberg's religious outlook had assumed a calmer form, but his anxiety had not completely subsided. He says that sometimes he asks himself: "Do you believe in this?" but quickly suppresses the question because he does not think faith is an intellectual activity but "a spiritual condition" that is "beneficial" for him. At other times, he revolts "against unreasonable expectations, too rigid demands," and "inhuman punishments," and abandons his devotional books, but is soon compelled to return to them, "admonished by a shouting voice from the far distant past: 'Remember that thou hast been a slave in Egypt and the Lord thy God hath liberated thee from thence!' "[63] He is only too aware of the difficulty of achieving the fearless relationship with the divine Powers that he found so attractive in Goethe.

Devoted admirers of the young Strindberg often regard his work after the Inferno Crisis with a certain amount of mistrust. They find his confession pieces excessively unctuous and the fantasy in his plays and fiction excessively contrived. In *Alone,* there are no excesses. And although it was primarily intended to be a description of the solitary life he led in crowded Stockholm, it became a self-inventory, but a more profound and thoroughgoing one than the term might suggest.

Fairy Tales

The tales Strindberg submitted to his publisher several months after *Alone* indicated a turning point in his writing. In a letter to Schering in December, 1902, he promised a collection of fairy tales—in "Andersen's poetic style"—tales that he said he had told to his own children. Some of them do seem to have been written only as children's stories, but others are expressions of his growing bitterness toward his wife and also reveal a desire to return to social satire, a tendency not noticeable in *Alone.* As a result, it is a motley collection. "Saint Gotthard's Saga," as John Landquist pointed out, was based on an 1886 sketch and is another variation on one of the *Utopias* themes: the need for fraternization between people of different backgrounds.

The influence of Andersen's fairy tales is most apparent in "The Big Gravel Screen" (Stora grusharpan"). Strindberg later suggested his indebtedness to Andersen in an article he wrote for the Andersen Jubilee (April 2, 1905). He described the impression made on him by Andersen's "The Great Sea Serpent" ("Den stora sjöormen") in which fish puzzle over an intruder in their world: a telegraph cable, apparently a new kind of fish that lacked head or tail. In Strindberg's story the foreign object is a mine inspector's old piano that falls into three fathoms of water as it is being carried ashore. As in Andersen, fish speculate about the purpose of the strange object and finally conclude that it is a device for screening gravel. But when Strindberg has nearby resort guests react in surprise to the inexplicable music rising from the bottom of the sea, he places greater demands on the credulousness of the reader than Andersen usually does.

"The Trials of the Pilot" ("Lotsens vedermödor") is also in the form of a child's fairy tale, although more in the style of Ernst Hoffman. A pilot who with difficulty boards a ship in heavy seas discovers that the vessel is not only crewless but enchanted. The description of the ship was inspired—as Strindberg himself indicated[64]—by Coleridge's "The Ancient Mariner."

One of the most beautiful tales is "When the Tree Swallow Was in the Buckthorn" ("När träsvalan kom i getapeln"), a moving story of how a criminal serving a life sentence at Långholm prison is reconciled with his lot when a little girl charitably offers him a glass of wine as he works on a road.

In other tales Strindberg began to bridge the distance between fairy tales and realism by yielding to his old habit of describing people who were usually identifiable, as he does in the stories in which certain opera artists are punished severely for the arrogance and ingratitude they display toward people who helped them toward success. Even suggestions of the discord in his last marriage began to appear, but were introduced subtly and cautiously, because the tales were completed on Blidö where he was staying with his wife and child, and the idea of divorce had been postponed. In "At Midsummer" ("I midsommartider"), for example, an "unfortunate little wife" and her child withstand all kinds of trials while "in a foreign land" the child's father "tended his sorrow, which was twice as great as the mother's,"[65] and in "The Deep Sleeper" ("Sjusovaren") there is a lonely man, an orchestra leader, who piously worships his deceased wife's memory: "Poor little thing, she didn't belong here—she just made a guest appearance and departed."[66]

The marital theme is handled with acidity in the story "The Pintorpa Wife's Christmas Eve" (Pintorpafruns julafton"), and Strindberg withdrew the story from the collection before publication.[67] The title is derived from a famous old Swedish legend about the Pintorpa (now the town of Eriksberg) matron Beata Gyllenstierna who tormented her husband to death and for this wicked deed was sent to Hell—a story found, among other places, in Afzelius's *The Saga Annals of the Swedish People.*

Strindberg's story is of a good-hearted chamberlain who marries a wife who makes life so sour for him that he gradually realizes "that he was married not to a human being, but to a devil."[68] The couple's mutual hate finally makes their home an unbearable place to live: "There was so much hate that the brass and gilt turned black, the furniture dried out and opened at the joints, and the paneling burst. There was so much hate that the tile stove smoked up the apartment, plants died, and food curdled."[69] Thus far, the tale seems like a grotesque late-born *Married* story. The sketches seem to indicate that the present somewhat arbitrary happy ending came about when the story was later transformed into a Christmas tale. On Christmas Eve, the wicked wife falls victim to a curious set of mishaps. She gets stuck for three hours in an elevator, her telephone ceases to operate, the water stops running, and the electric lights go out. But when she repents her sins, everything changes as if by a stroke of magic. She hears a brisk rushing sound at the water tap, the apartment is flooded with light, the table is set for Christmas dinner, and her husband returns: "A warm hand moved lightly along her cold cheek, and she heard a familiar voice whisper like a summer breeze through the flowers on a forest slope: 'Beloved!' "[70]

Once he had returned to realistic description, Strindberg felt a need to express his displeasure with society, as in "The Golden Helmets in Ålleberg" ("Gullhjälmarne i Ålleberg"). Based on an old folk legend, the story concerns a soldier, Kask, who wanders down into the mountain in Skansen Park and encounters the golden helmets: Sweden's kings from the past. The economist among them, Charles XI (1655-97), learns to his dismay that half of Sweden's land has been pawned abroad for 300 million kroner, that municipal debts amount to almost 200 million, and that the annual wage for a bishop is 30,000 kroner:[71] "Just think of it," says soldier Kask, "they've boozed away old Sweden and trampled on it abroad! - - - It's positively awful; if it's true!"[72] The same legend had been used at the conclusion of an early draft of *Midsummer*, but there, all the great Charleses and Gustavs had been assembled in order to inspect the glory of the new age. In the interim, Strindberg had read a volume of Sweden's official statistics and was convinced that the country was on the brink of ruin. He used the same statistics to elaborate on and support his thesis in *The Gothic Rooms*. In *Midsummer* the Skansen ethnographical museum is glorified as an abridged representation of "our great beautiful land"; in *Fairy Tales* it is called "a mountain upon which has been collected all the memories of the fatherland, as when someone has a premonition of the end, makes a will, and gathers together souvenirs of the past."[73]

"The Pintorpa Wife's Christmas Eve" and "The Golden Helmets in Ålleberg" signify that the day of the idyll and melancholy dream was over in Strindberg's writing. Harder times were setting in.

Notes to Chapter Nineteen

1. *SS:*XXXVII, pp. 47-48.
2. *Ibid.,* p. 220.
3. *Ibid.,* p. 8.
4. *Ibid.,* p. 57.
5. *Ibid.,* pp. 20-21.
6. The poems have been dealt with by Gunnar Ollén in his definitive study *Strindberg's Twentieth Century Lyrics (Strindbergs 1900-talslyrik*—1941).
7. Ollén, pp. 321-37.
8. *SS:*XXXVIII, p. 192.
9. *Ibid.,* p. 194.
10. *Ibid.,* p. 195.
11. *SS:*XXXVII, pp. 236-37.
12. *Ibid.,* p. 233.
13. *Brev till Harriet Bosse,* p. 37.
14. These are signs of mourning in Sweden.—Translator
15. *SS:*XXXVII, pp. 276, 278.
16. *Ibid.,* pp. 234-35.
17. *Ibid.,* p. 243.
18. *Ibid.,* p. 244.
19. *Ibid.,* p. 263.
20. *Ibid.,* p. 274.
21. *Ibid.,* p. 293.
22. *Ibid.,* p. 251.
23. *Ibid.,* p. 252.
24. *Ibid.,* p. 255.
25. *Ibid.,* p. 245.
26. *See* my essay "The History of Strindberg's *The People of Hemsö*" ("Förhistorien till Strindbergs *Hemsöborna,*" *Svensk litteraturtidskrift,* 1938) and Gunnar Ollén, p. 137.
27. This is the same theme, of course, that Strindberg dealt with in "The Romantic Organist on Rånö" (*see* p. 248), whose central character was based on the same real-life models as the Årby organist in "Journey to Town."
28. *SS:*XXXVII, p. 260.
29. *Ibid.,* pp. 311-12.
30. *Ibid.,* pp. 288-89.

31. *See* p. 130.
32. Gunnar Ollén has shown (p. 86 n. 1) that Strindberg even used the same venomous remarks against Heidenstam's verse that were once directed against his own.
33. *See* p. 238.
34. Strindberg also objected to verse that was too readable and free: "Verse, even if it is rhymed, must also have an inner euphony, either through assonance or alliteration, consonant rhyme or internal vowel rhyme" (*SS:*LIII, p. 76). He was irritated by P. D. A. Atterbom's (1790-1855) "The Choir of the Winds" ("Upp genom luften") : "The winds compose an essay instead of singing" (*Ibid.*, p. 104).
35. Ollén, p. 108.
36. *SS:*XXXVII, p. 277.
37. Georg Stiernhielm (1598-1672) is considered to have been the best Swedish poet of his day.—Translator
38. *See* Ollén, p. 57.
39. *SS:*VIII, p. 117.
40. *SS:*XVIII, p. 99.
41. *SS:*VIII, p. 434.
42. *SS:*LIII, p. 117.
43. In ancient Norse mythology, Nidhögg was a serpent that fed on corpses.—Translator
44. *See* p. 420.—Translator
45. *SS:*XXXVIII, p. 145.
46. *Ibid.*, p. 216.
47. *Ibid.*, p. 152.
48. *Ibid.*, p. 177.
49. *Ibid.*, p. 191.
50. *Ibid.*, p. 153.
51. *Ibid.*, p. 162.
52. Ollén, p. 184.
53. See *Brev till Harriet Bosse*, p. 239.
54. *SS:*XXXVIII, pp. 176, 177.
55. *Ibid.*, p. 150.
56. *Ibid.*, pp. 151-52.
57. *Ibid.*, p. 163.
58. *Ibid.*, p. 164.
59. *Ibid.*, p. 198.

60. *Ibid.*, p. 199.
61. *Ibid.*, p. 157.
62. *Ibid.*, p. 160.
63. *Ibid.*
64. *Ibid.*, p. 37.
65. *Ibid.*, p. 9.
66. *Ibid.*, p. 32.
67. The story did not appear in print until 1908 in a Christmas magazine. It was reprinted in Strindberg's collected works (*SS:*LIV, pp. 124-36).
68. *SS:*LIV, p. 131.
69. *Ibid.*, p. 132.
70. *Ibid.*, p. 136.
71. In 1969 the exchange rate was slightly more than five Swedish kroner to one American dollar.—Translator
72. *SS:*XXXVIII, p. 110.
73. *Ibid.*

Chapter Twenty

THE TWENTIETH CENTURY NOVELS
AND HISTORICAL SHORT STORIES

The Gothic Rooms

In a letter to his publisher on January 6, 1904, Strindberg called *The Gothic Rooms* "a continuation of *The Red Room*." Many of his writings at the turn of the century were extensions of past activities: his old love for the skerries produced *Fairhaven and Foulstrand,* and a renewal of his interest in Swedish history resulted in the later history plays; now the social criticism of the Red Room days beckoned to him.

The new novel begins with a superb description of a gathering of artists at a dinner in Bern's Restaurant's Gothic Rooms, part of which was the redecorated Red Room. Some of the former members of the coterie are present, and Doctor Borg's nephew, Kurt Borg, an architect, paces off the area where the old retreat had been. But neither the author nor his characters succeed in recovering the old carefree bohemian tone. The most striking description in the scene is the picture of the mentally ill painter Ernst Josephson (1851-1906), disguised under the fictional name Syrach, who sits at a marble table in the salon below the Gothic Rooms, wearing a red fez and staring vacantly, lost in his dreams. When Strindberg returns to the Gothic Rooms in the final chapter to portray the Borg clan's New Year's celebration, we discover that this meeting place, too, is out of fashion, "and when someone tried to talk about the Red Room, it sounded like ancient history."[1]

It was difficult for Strindberg to return to social satire; he had lived too long outside the world of politics to be able to generate an authentic sense of outrage. We can see from the sketches that he examined government statistics and studies of the national economy and carefully compiled long lists of material and speeches that were later inserted at

439

random in the novel. His basic hypothesis seems to have been that Sweden
had been ruined through debts and depopulated through emigration: one
sketch for the novel bears the title *Wasteland (Ödeland)*.

But the handling of statistics was never one of Strindberg's strong
points. He concluded that the one million employable Swedish men had to
maintain two-and-one-half million unproductive women and children, in
addition to 133,000 military personnel and 170,000 civil servants, of which
28,000 were clergymen. Contemporary critics immediately pointed out
that the figures for civil servants and clergymen also included their wives,
children, and servants. Equally peculiar were his calculations regarding
the Swedish national debt: bank savings could not be regarded as assets,
since the funds provided by savers were "lent out to an equal number of
borrowers."

He demonstrates the wretchedness of the agricultural situation by
pointing out that it was necessary to import fertilizers from abroad and
that the importation of oil cake proves that "we cannot even feed our
livestock." Because the forests are depleted, and as much iron is imported
as exported, Sweden exists on loans and will soon be unable to pay the
interest on its debts: "Imagine if everything in Sweden were to be confiscated, like the possessions of a reckless debtor."[2]

Social satire is not presented, as it was in *The Red Room,*
through vividly depicted situations from different areas of national life. It
is now offered in seemingly endless debates on politics, economics, sex,
and other weighty subjects, generally among members of the Borg family
and others, such as between Ester Borg, who is a doctor, and her lover,
Count Max. Almost all the debaters scatter statistics about with abandon,
but the character who shouts them most vehemently is old Doctor Borg,
no longer the blunt scapegrace of *The Red Room,* but a peevish Faultfinder
who is unimpressed with the new ideas and inventions of the twentieth
century; they are only "trivial applications of older ideas, variations on
other people's themes." His slogan is "Demolish, that's all, demolish! You
can't grow anything under snow. Nothing can be built until the old house
is demolished." Just as Doctor Borg still uses his favorite expression
"Bosh!" to describe the corruption he sees, so does Strindberg still offer
a "boulevard system"[3] as a solution to all problems.

Although Strindberg had not been overly scrupulous about his
choice of subject matter and methods in *The Red Room* and *The New*

Kingdom, the younger generation had found these books exhilarating because he had given voice to its resentment toward what was outmoded in Swedish society. He had uttered the indignant words that many people would have preferred left unsaid. But *The Gothic Rooms* was just a rehash of what anyone could read for himself in the newspapers or records of Parliament and is tamer than his other books, even in literary style. Strindberg still used the technique of veiled allusions and disguised names when dealing with identifiable people and events, but this furtiveness now seemed oddly old-fashioned.

The word "decadence" is recurrent in *The Gothic Rooms,* probably inspired by the series of novels *La Décadence latine* by the occulist Joséphin (Sâr) Péladan. Péladan proclaimed the deterioration and downfall of the Latin race, and Strindberg follows in his footsteps when he predicts the approaching destruction of Sweden and the Swedish people. But these gloomy visions of the future are not very convincing; in places, even Strindberg seems skeptical. The symptoms of decadence upon which Strindberg dwells in *The Gothic Rooms* were applicable not only to the Swedes, but to the entire human race. For Strindberg, the basic issue was not the decadence of the day, it was the overwhelming loathing he felt for existence itself, and it is significant that his distaste should be expressed primarily in terms of relations between the sexes.

When Strindberg and Harriet were separated in the fall of 1903, his attitude toward married life was marked by the same frenzy he had felt in the late 1880's. Unpleasant memories were dredged up from all three marriages. In the novel, Doctor Borg has been married only twice, once to a Norwegian woman (Harriet Bosse, of course, was Norwegian), but a string of relatives suffer the same marital torment. "All these Borg men, whom Strindberg depicts as typical husbands, have incredibly poor taste in the choice of wives," wrote Oscar Levertin in his review of the novel. "They are divorced, remarry, and seem to end up with the same woman again, the same horrid bluestocking and selfish emancipation fool." Levertin's point is well taken: it is difficult to distinguish among the different marriages and wives in the novel.

Strindberg reiterates his old viewpoints and arguments with stubborn consistency. When one reads his characterization of the turn-of-the-century suffragette—who has her hair closely bobbed, wears mannish clothing, and sips port wine in secret—one's thoughts go back immediately to the *Married* campaign. And Strindberg pursues the same old enemies: "the hysterical nincompoop" Nora of *A Doll's House* and Svava from Bjørnson's play *The Gauntlet,* with her exaggerated ideals of masculine purity. It pleased him enormously that the feminist leader Ellen Key had abandoned her emancipatory ideas, but he still used her as a target; from the sketches we see that it was his original intention to include in *The Gothic Rooms* the description of the Christmas Eve visit in her home, used later in *Black Banners.*

Other old themes appear in almost unaltered form: Doctor Borg gives the same definition of woman's purpose that was the motivation for the original title of Strindberg's first drama on the woman question, *Marauders-Comrades:* "When everything is ready, they come to collect; when the battlefield is sown with the dead and the wounded, the female bone gatherers arrive."[4] Another version of the lamp-throwing episode in *The Father* appears as an anecdote about an American justice of the peace who was supposed to have shouted, "What a monstrous woman!" on learning that a man threw a burning lamp in his wife's face. And Strindberg adds: "Yes, the man who loved that woman must have had a vision of Hell to make him forget himself to such an extent."[5]

In *The Gothic Rooms,* woman is pictured as the radical evil in existence, a filthy vermin, like a dog.[6] But there is something new in Strindberg's misogyny. No longer, as in *Married,* does he plead the cause of sexual love in opposition to Ibsen's and Bjørnson's idealism. Instead, he shows an aversion to eroticism that is unparalleled in his earlier writings.

> Do you know, Ester, I was never an idealist [says Count Max], but surely reality is a caricature of our ideas about things. . . . There are times when I think the deranged Stagnelius was right when he complained about our human souls having to creep into animal bodies. We behave like animals; we kiss with the same mouth we eat with, and make love with our eliminatory organs![7]

Count Max and his fiancée, the ugly Ester, who appears briefly as an unhappy figure in the Fairhaven scene of *A Dream Play* and in a sketch for an unwritten novel, are the only sympathetic couple in *The Gothic Rooms.* They move on a higher plane than the others and tell each other about the "miracles that take place every day, but which pass unnoticed by insensitive observers."[8] They hope to keep their love pure by living together without getting married, but soon discover that this arrangement produces the same mutual hostilities as marriage. "I think our bodies hate each other," says Max, "and that's often the case in marriage."[9] As a result, they separate for long periods. Max tells Ester, "I understand you best in silence and from a distance; then you're closest to me and there are no misunderstandings."[10] This hypersensitive aristocrat prefers human contact to be between souls rather than bodies, and probably expresses Strindberg's own loathing of humanity in his remark: "Do you know, once in swimming class I looked at all the ruddy, yellowish-white human bodies and was struck by the similarity to—not apes, but young swine. They, too, are rosy-red and hairless."[11] But even more repulsive, according to Max, are people's thoughts and desires: "What a horrid masquerade life is! I can never be with people, for I can hear their thoughts, read their faces."[12] (This theme of thought-reading would reappear in *Black Banners* and *A Blue Book*.)

Strindberg devoted little space to descriptions of literary life in this black portrait. The eighth chapter of the novel is called "The 1890's" but treats the period only in terms of a general European reaction against the positivism of the 1880's and as a time of the reawakening of religious mysticism. The sketches show that Strindberg had considered attacking the "Pepita School" in this chapter but decided instead to bypass entirely the Swedish literature of the 1890's.

Another opportunity for literary satire not completely exploited in the novel was the funeral of Viktor Rydberg (1828-95) which, according to sketches, was supposed to be the most important scene in the novel. Strindberg was disturbed that Rydberg, whom he mentioned during the Inferno Crisis as one who had misled him in his youth, was honored at his death.[13] The scene was replaced in the completed novel by a conversation between Doctor Borg and Count Max in Operakällaren Restaurant the day before Rydberg's funeral, but the purport has changed. Borg interprets the impressive arrangements made for the funeral as a sign that the age of humbug had found a new saint. Max is, however, more sympathetic toward Rydberg and feels Borg's opinion is antiquated. After Borg leaves, Max says to Ester: "The good doctor has an 1880's view of things, but he forgets that we are in the 1890's. He doesn't understand this new era that is dawning; he doesn't understand us young people."[14]

Here, as in the chapter on the 1890's, Strindberg seems uncertain about what position to take. He does not want to repudiate his work from the 1880's, but wants even less to appear to be retaining his viewpoints from that time. He solves the problem by calling the nineties "neurasthenic," and toward the end of the novel de-emphasizes the character of Doctor Borg who, with his biting, vulgar cynicism, seemed to be the author's spokesman in the beginning. To Count Max, Borg is a "faultfinder who serves his profession like a man," but is "a bit simple": "He believes in wireless telegraphy, but denies the soul's ability to communicate across distances."[15]

The least successful sections in *The Gothic Rooms* are those in which Strindberg tried to return to the realism of *The Red Room* and the *Married* stories. He had the same stylistic means at his disposal, but lacked the spontaneity, sense of humor, and zest for battle of the earlier period. For once, Strindberg seemed to have trouble finding targets for his satire, and worked himself up over situations toward which he was actually indifferent.

The only genuine and moving section in the novel is based on memories of his first divorce proceedings, when Strindberg felt most rejected. Because he now found himself in much the same situation, the memories took on renewed immediacy. Gustav Borg, who loses his position as editor and is threatened with divorce, flees to the skerries and seeks refuge with his son. But he is greeted with shocking inhospitality, and the night before he is to face the vestry board he is close to committing suicide. Borg's feeling of homelessness is reflected in a striking way in a description of the desolate skerries landscape. In the same episode the uneasiness pervading an interior scene is depicted in a grotesque style that Strindberg would develop further in *Black Banners*.

Criticism of *The Gothic Rooms* included unfavorable comparisons with *The Red Room* and struck Strindberg deeply: he mentioned "the Gothic storm" in a letter to Nils Andersson and protested that he wrote the work "at a higher behest." The same orders from above, according to Strindberg, compelled him to follow this novel with *Black Banners*, a settling of accounts with his literary adversaries.

Black Banners

Black Banners is the result of a fusion of a novel and a collection of religious observations that Strindberg called "cloister writings" which he had originally intended publishing separately. The novel is a satire whose central theme is that the world of letters, especially journalism, exploits people ruthlessly and uses lies to ensure a literary work's success. The chief villain is Zachris (who appeared as "little Sakris"[16] in *The Gothic Rooms*), in reality Strindberg's former close friend and business associate, Gustaf af Geijerstam. Zachris is a parasite who lives off other people by stealing their literary ideas and even their women. One of the people he wrongs is Falkenström (i.e., Strindberg). Zachris helps Falkenström sell his writings, the same way Geijerstam did for Strindberg after the Inferno Crisis, but he cheats him in the process. Zachris hounds Falkenström throughout the novel, sucking him dry of ideas, and he contributes to the destruction of one of his three unhappy marriages. Zachris and his wife Jenny hate each other with a fervor characteristic of the Strindbergian marital hell. When Jenny becomes ill and dies, Zachris is exultant and exploits her death to make himself a martyr and a prominent figure in literary circles. (Geijerstam's wife died several years before *Black Banners* was written, and her death was reflected in some of his writings.) Jenny is as ruthless as Zachris, but just as he is forgiven for many things "because he lived in Jenny's hell," so Jenny is not judged too harshly because she was subject to the evil influence of feminism, notably through the "emancipatress" Hanna Paj, whose real-life model was the feminist leader Ellen Key.

Falkenström's marital difficulties force him to retreat into a non-denominational cloister on Siklaön, an island near Stockholm, where Count Max, one of the several characters from *The Gothic Rooms* who reappear in *Black Banners*, is staying. Strindberg used the "cloister writings" in the chapters about Siklaön. The inspiration for these observations in the form of Platonic dialogues originated before Strindberg thought of writing the novel and are to a certain degree a continuation of the conversations between Max and Ester in *The Gothic Rooms*. They were first called *Gothic Fugues (Götiska fugor)*[17] and were still planned as a separate book with the title *Fugues and Preludes (Fugor och preludier)* as late as December, 1904, when Strindberg was working on *Black Banners.* Not until the first half of the novel was completed did he decide to include them as anecdotes, debates, and parables presented by the residents of the cloister.

Even before the Inferno Crisis, Strindberg had had plans to establish a "cloister for higher spirits" in a castle in the Ardennes. He frequently returned to the idea and once intended to incorporate it into the novel *The Cloister,* in a section that was never written. He wrote to Littmansson on September 25, 1902, that he continued to dream about such a cloister and had found a suitable site for it near Stockholm across from Blockhus Point on a hill that offered a view of the city and the island of Vaxholm.

These "cloister writings," which foreshadow *A Blue Book,*[18] are inserted rather arbitrarily into the novel. For example, the first reflections are spoken by a young Count Max even though the comments made about past events would be more appropriate coming from the fifty-year-old man. Not only is the unity of the story line broken by the cloister chapters, but the beauty of the observations is spoiled by being grafted onto the plot of the novel. Furthermore, one wonders why high-minded spirits who live aloof from the mundane world spend so much time in petty discussion about a vulgar "pathological liar"[19] such as Zachris.

Although they contain a number of eccentric speculations on natural science and some bitter statements on the woman question, the "cloister writings" also include some of Strindberg's most profound psychological and religious reflections, based to a large extent on entries in his diary. Miracles and portents were no longer his main interest, although he reports several of them; he was primarily occupied with the spiritual reality of ordinary occurrences: "Everyday life is filled with mysticism," says Falkenström, "but you observe so poorly. You must be a naturalist in order to be a mystic."[20] Under the somewhat misleading promise of a statement "about matter as living essence,"[21] there is a description of how a room can appear different when viewed during different moods. If one returns home from a journey, the room seems changed, even though nothing has been moved: "You are confronted with something cold and empty that does not correspond to what you imagined while away, and you feel alien from the surroundings."[22] If one spends the evening at a party, returning to the room again can be "downright fright-

ening. The unslept-in bed with its winding sheets stands there like an
accusation. You feel as if a crime had been committed, perhaps a crime
against the laws of nature."[23] If one has been away for a long time on
distasteful business, one is gripped with horror on returning:

> You are confronted by an unknown presence that has taken possession of
> the room, forcing you out; someone is sitting on your sofa, someone you
> cannot see, and this someone is a threatening shadow of yourself, a part
> of your better self that will contemptuously and reproachfully drive out
> its degrading twin brother. But you may also meet most alien essences,
> corrupt products of your person, which in the abandoned room have
> assumed life-like form, and it is not good to meet them, for they are the
> children of deserts, burned houses, ruins, silences, and empty rooms.[24]

As would be the case later in the Chamber Plays, a room to Strindberg
was a place palpitating with life, changing its character according to the
feelings of its occupants. Even the furniture has moods; it shines as
brightly as a smile:

> as long as love and order prevail. . . . But if hate and strife come into
> the house, the dining-room lamp will smoke, the flames in the fireplace
> will burn so unevenly that you cannot close the damper, the brass will
> darken, the piano get out of tune, and the dining-room clock strike at
> the wrong times.[25]

The passage concludes with a description of how different plants react to
happenings in the home.

Other "cloister writings" deal with the relationship between
memory and imagination, and Strindberg tries to show in a series of
examples "how you can completely obliterate a painful impression from
your memory so that it no longer exists."[26]

Strindberg warned his German translator Schering on January
27, 1905, that although "the book has great merit . . . this may diminish if
it is turned into a lampoon." The reference, of course, alludes to the main
action of the novel, whose outlines and sketches bear the titles *Decadents
(Dekadenter)*, *Wretched People (Förfallna människor)*, and *Phantoms
(Spöken)*. The first title is connected with *The Gothic Rooms*, which was
a series of variations on the theme of "contemporary decadent men." The
novel was later called *The Black Flags (Svarta flaggorna)*, presumably
after a notorious band of pirates who roamed the Bay of Tonkin when

Strindberg was young; *Flags* was changed to *Banners* in the final manuscript. In a separately published preface written in February, 1908, for the second edition, Strindberg speaks of his "penetrating, true picture of the life and manners of a corrupt age and the wretched people who carry its banners." From then on, he called all his adversaries "black banners," especially the remnants of the Young Sweden group.

Strindberg had long thought of sentencing Gustaf af Geijerstam to a literary execution. He still remembered that during the 1880's Geijerstam had not supported him when conservative forces attacked Strindberg's works as immoral.[27] In letters to Bengt Lidforss and Karl Warburg in February, 1894, he described Geijerstam in the same way as he did later in *The Gothic Rooms:*[28] "born bare-headed, with eyeglasses, paunch, and pension," and equipped with a mania for "taking care of . . . [people] in a way that is objectionable and always to his advantage." He added that up to then he had been considerate toward Geijerstam, but would one day get revenge: "I shall certainly return [to Sweden] again, and if no one wants to give me justice, I shall have to administer it myself."

From 1897 to 1902, however, Geijerstam (as literary director of the Gernandt publishing house) saw to it that Strindberg's works were printed at a time when it was risky for a publisher to be associated with the author of *Inferno.* When Strindberg returned to Stockholm, they patched up their broken friendship, and for a few years Geijerstam was his closest intimate, but the intimacy provided new material to feed Strindberg's suspiciousness. He thought Geijerstam was pocketing a portion of his royalties, just as earlier he had thought Geijerstam guilty of stealing his ideas. Veiled accusations of this kind appear as early as Part II of *The Dance of Death,* and Geijerstam was mentioned in sketches for the play as one of the models for the Captain.

After breaking all ties with Geijerstam (except for their business relationship) in a solemn, formal letter, Strindberg was haunted by the fear of being persecuted by him. At the same time, he felt it a religious duty to expose him. A month after the break he recorded in his diary (January 24, 1901) that he thought he saw Geijerstam at a dress rehearsal of *The Saga of the Folkungs* and added: "Perhaps Providence prescribes warfare to enable people to defend their personalities against attacks by others, and perhaps compliancy is laziness and cowardice." When the business association ended with the bankruptcy of Gernandt's in 1903, Strindberg followed through with his literary execution in *Black Banners,* although the novel was not published until the spring of 1907, because his friends tried to dissuade him and publishers rejected it.

Strindberg took the form for his attack from Ernst Hoffmann's "Klein Zaches, genannt Zinnober" (1819) in which a literary parasite is portrayed in a fantastic fairy-tale manner. The ugly dwarf Klein Zaches accepts the applause for a beautiful violin solo played by someone else and reaps the tribute paid to a poem he did not write. Hoffmann's influence is indicated in a passage in *Black Banners:* Falkenström refuses to write about Zachris since Hoffmann did it "so well in his Zacherle or Cinnober [sic]."[29] And in the sketches for *Black Banners,* the character is alternately called Zachris and Cinnober.[30] But although Strindberg calls Zachris a sorcerer, *Black Banners,* unlike Hoffmann's tale, has a realistic plot.

Strindberg's original intention was to let Zachris appear good-natured and thus be doubly dangerous. But his desire to crucify Geijerstam was so strong that he gave Zachris no real motivation to be good-natured: all Zachris's plans are wrecked by his clumsy maneuvers; he is repudiated as head of the literary opposition party, rejected by his friends, and betrayed by his wife. In his review of *Black Banners,* Tor Hedberg wrote that Strindberg "either intentionally or accidentally" achieved "cruel and merciless, that is to say, great satire," and that Zachris must be regarded as:

> the archetype of the literary vampire. The vampire who sucks the lifeblood of those closest to him—his friends, his loved ones—in order to create literature. . . . In this portrayal . . . [Strindberg] is often blinded by personal rancor, but at times he hates the character so intensely that the satire in all its appallingness achieves great dimensions. It must also be pointed out that consciously or unconsciously he even pierces deeply into his own heart, a boundless self-hater in spite of his boundless self-love.

Hedberg's last point is interesting, but Strindberg probably suggested similarities between his own life and Zachris's more because of his general contempt for anyone engaged in the profession of writing than out of self-hatred. Similar to the feelings of the narrator in *A Madman's Defense,* Zachris longs for his wife to become pregnant and grow old and ugly so that he may eventually gain the upper hand. He transforms all his marital misfortunes into literature. When his wife betrays him with a friend, he wants to free himself of the "poison" by "putting everything down on paper and then either burning the manuscript after it has been read by his closest friends, or if he needed money, publishing it in Germany."[31] Strindberg, as we know, chose the second alternative, whereas Geijerstam gave a prettified picture of his marriage in *The Book About Little Brother* (*Boken om lillebror*—1900).

Zachris must always have his wife close at hand—as Strindberg required during the writing of *A Madman's Defense*—in order to write his story: "As long as she was present in the house he could regain all the power he had deposited in her, without which he could not destroy her."[32] Even during her final illness he is totally preoccupied with how to exploit it in literary form. From time to time he leaves the sick room and rushes to his desk to record the " 'choice remarks' so picturesquely expressed" that he heard her speak. "As she lay dying, she served as model, dictating notes."[33] An indication that Strindberg knew he too suffered from an incurable desire to transform everything into literature is apparent when he has Falkenström devise "the last chapter of his novel, unwittingly using Zachris for a model."[34]

Zachris's approach to his book about his marriage illustrates *Black Banner's* basic theme: that literary life poisons all human values. Like *The Gothic Rooms,* the novel opens with a dinner; a group of literary people are gathered for a grotesque "phantom supper" at the home of Professor Stenkåhl (another vindictive portrait of an old friend, the literary historian and critic, Professor Karl Warburg) where the atmosphere is heavy with evil. The guests envy each other and have in common only their mutual hatred. They steal each other's friends and overwhelm each other with hypocritical compliments. The newspaper on which Zachris is an underling survives on bribes, adulterates all values, and tears down everything great in order to evaluate the shabby and the foolish. The "emancipatress" Hanna Paj ("who is infatuated with young women") goes around ruining marriages on the pretext of trying to put everything right. In the middle of this web of lies and hypocrisy, Zachris is the spider. Everything that is said he records for later use; he writes scathing criticism of his colleagues while continuously beating a drum for himself. He will use any opportunity to get publicity, even his wife's death. At her funeral he feels like the leader of a literary school addressing his followers and talks grandly "about his literary merits, the great revolution, and about those who lead and those who follow."[35]

One may wonder why Strindberg did not attack the Ninety-ists, the most fashionable literary coterie in Sweden at the turn of the century, instead of the out-dated survivors of Young Sweden. According to sketches for the novel, this had been his original intention: they contain notes about "the Pepita attack," "Hilma Lageröl" (Selma Lagerlöf), and Heidenstam,[36] who was to have been presented as a clown dressed up as Charles XII.

But this approach would have made it impossible to sustain the fiction of Geijerstam as the leading exponent of Strindberg's chief target: the 1880's viewpoint. He had repudiated its anti-metaphysical positivism during the Inferno Crisis and reiterated his opposition in *The Gothic Rooms*. Positivism is also condemned in the last chapter of *Black Banners* in a letter the dying Smartman sends to his son. When Strindberg's plays were not performed in the theatres and *The Gothic Rooms* was annihilated by the critics, he believed that the intrigues of the remaining members of Young Sweden were responsible and that Geijerstam was the chief instigator. Strindberg was unforgetting in his hatred, and we can see from notes for an intended preface that he wanted to exact vengeance for reviews and magazine articles that were nearly twenty years old.

The bitterness against Young Sweden notwithstanding, one must acknowledge that the satire in *Black Banners* is directed at a larger issue than a literary movement. It is aimed against the writer's life in general, a life that pollutes society. The final judgment is pronounced by Zachris's wife Jenny on her deathbed:

> You know, I sometimes wonder if your books don't do more harm than good. You authors stand outside life and society; you're like birds who live above in the atmosphere, gazing down on the world and people. Can you see things truthfully? . . . Your work is a game and your life a party. . . . I curse the moment I landed in your gypsy world with its criminal morality.[37]

This anathema against the useless game of belles-lettres is an almost perfect echo of the opinion Strindberg first presented in *The Red Room* and in many subsequent works in the 1880's. Actually, it is *Black Banners* and not *The Gothic Rooms* that has a kinship with the early novel; it has the same basic theme: literature, the press, and indeed all of society are debased by high finance and degrading press-agentry. The satire, is, however, more ruthless, the touch heavier, and although the author tries to play his former role of wounded idealist, he is not as persuasive. His whip lashes out right and left and often strikes innocent bystanders, but it is guided by the same fiery indignation and sometimes also has the same verve.

In the beginning of *Black Banners,* Dickens, Balzac, and Zola are called "the giants of literature," and there are traces of the influence of all three in the novel. The mystical *Séraphita* and *Louis Lambert* were the first of Balzac's works to enchant Strindberg, and he felt his "cloister writings" showed him to be the Frenchman's pupil. In *Alone* he said that Balzac told the history of his time in his novels; and when in *Black Banners* he satirized literature and journalism, he was dealing with the same themes as Balzac's *Illusions perdues.* The basic idea in *Black Banners* is the same as that in Balzac's novel: Intrigue, humbug, and publicity are the only means by which a literary work can be made successful, and newspapers live on and exist in corruption. And in both Balzac and Strindberg, the power of money dominates everything.

But although Balzac's satire was merciless, it was not as sweeping as Strindberg's. Balzac is most severe when dealing with a character whose ambitions are like his own and who travels the same devious paths he himself had to take to achieve success. During the criticism over *Lucien de Rubempré* Balzac showed that for all his self-centeredness he could be objective about his own faults. If Strindberg had possessed the same capacity for self-criticism and generosity, he would not have tried to make Falkenström the hero and pathetic Zachris the villain. Nevertheless, Strindberg did achieve something akin to Balzac's great vigor in style. Like Balzac, he exaggerated the emotions of his characters to the point of manias, and intrigues are no longer means, but ends; people conspire against and persecute one another out of pure malice.

Strindberg's descriptive technique, however, has more in common with Dickens than with Balzac; as a matter of fact, one of his sketches bears the subtitle "The Dickens Novel" ("Dickensromanen"). Lindblad[38] has said that Dickens's evident influence in *The Red Room* reappears in *Black Banners,* and he shows the parallel between the "phantom supper" at Professor Stenkåhl's and a description of a supper in *Little Dorrit;* other parallels could be pointed out in *Martin Chuzzlewit* or *Our Mutual Friend.* Dickens took delight in depicting great banquets in which food is devoured with wild appetite by hungry guests. In *Martin Chuzzlewit* turkeys and chickens seem to fly down people's throats, and whole cucumbers disappear as if they had been pickled cherries. And after consuming the heavier courses, the undernourished guests stare greedily at the pastries. The same frenzy exists at Professor Stenkåhl's in *Black Banners,* although the participants are more quickly satiated. When the asparagus is served, the gentlemen raise their mustaches and show their teeth like angry dogs with bones in their mouths, but by the time the eighth dish is brought in, a calm has settled over the gathering: "There were only idiotic faces staring disconsolately at wine glasses, and the more they drank the more idiotic they became."[39]

Strindberg differs from Dickens, however, in his intensified naturalism. As the soup is being consumed, a slurping is heard, and "sixteen craniums were bent forward, . . . some white and bare like bathers' backsides."[40] At the end of the dinner the entire dining room smells of perspiration "and under the ladies' arms dampness stains began to show, forming sea charts and maps." Finally, everyone rises "after two hours of torture," leaving behind "round-bottomed impressions in the cane chairs" and napkins:

> twisted up like entrails. . . . In other respects the table was simultaneously a glass shop, for it was set with eight glasses; a porcelain store; [and] a garbage dump, with orange peels, cheese rinds and bread crusts, fruit cores, cigarettes . . . matches, ashes. The finger bowls had been spat in and were reminiscent of washbasins. A garbage dump and washbasin![41]

Lindblad believes that this unappetizing inventory shows the influence of Zola. But is not this tendency to regard everything human as ugly merely another expression of Strindberg's basic misanthropy? In *The Red Room* Struve advises Arvid Falk to think of existence as a garbage dump and people as "the garbage—egg shells, carrot tops, cabbage leaves, rags"; and the coarse description of the reception at Norrbacka after the funeral of Struve's child anticipates to some degree the supper at Professor Stenkåhl's. Strindberg's disgust with man's physical functions had intensified with the years, and it turns the repugnant details of the meal into a grotesque "phantom supper" without the introduction of supernatural elements.

The characterization, too, is in the caricatural style of Dickens, but the ugly, animalistic features are underscored with an extraordinary intensity. Professor Stenkåhl interrupts everyone with his bellowing voice, and as he gestures widely, he knocks down "a whatnot with false antiques."[42] When he yawns, "an immense gap" opens "with gift fruits of cadmium and gold fillings, like a bedroom alcove with paintings on the walls." But this is no good-natured Rabelaisian giant. He is an executioner who has invited his guests to their own destruction. Mercilessly, he incites them against each other and even uses his small stepdaughter to hurt and humiliate them. As she asks embarrassing questions, he sits back and pretends innocence, "this man-eater, who was probably too cowardly to do the biting himself."[43]

It was evident in *The Red Room* that Strindberg's technique of indicating his character's personalities by outward appearances, recurrent mannerisms, and the environments in which they live was borrowed from Dickens and various American humorists. But there, the exaggeration often gave the reader an unclear image. In *Black Banners* the same impetuous caricatural approach is used, but the characters are more vivid. Zachris "seemed to have been born with eyeglasses, for no one had ever had a good look at his eyes, probably because these unnaturally large objects, like two fertilized duck eggs, were always bloodshot from whiskey and yellow from tobacco and frenzy." He hypnotizes people with his eyeglasses and puts them at ease with his provincial dialect, "which was a jumble from Dalecarlia, Jönköping, and Skänninge."[44]

Whenever the character appears, Strindberg reminds us of these outward characteristics. Zachris weeps whiskey tears, smiles humorously with one side of his mustache, and always chews on a fifteen öre (three-cent) cigar that seems to be too big for him. He laughs with his stomach and soft palate, and when he snores, it sounds like sleeping swine. Like Dickens's characters, Zachris uses certain stock phrases, but the benignity they appear to express is false and misleading. Whenever he exclaims "dear friend," one knows he is planning something treacherous.

Again as in Dickens, the insidiousness of Zachris's personality is reflected in his home where "all the furnishings seemed assembled through theft" and everything is sham: "An osprey is referred to as a sea eagle, two bookshelves are called a library, and a plaster bust of a grinning Voltaire is called a work of art." But the *pièce de résistance* is a large washbasin that Zachris alleges was used by visiting foreign authors: "and when he accompanied the statement with a gesture toward the stove cornice, one could almost see Zola and Bjørnson using the brown-painted washbasin."[45]

The entire family is infected by the same mendaciousness—right down to the servant girl, "a 'faithful retainer' (who stole) now in her third year of service." Jenny tries to pass herself off as an artist because she went to a Paris studio several times and managed, with the cooperation of a male friend, to have a painting accepted in an exhibition. Zachris, "in his role of self-embellisher," heralded the births of his two sons as if princes and universal geniuses had arrived: "When one saw this little author in this environment, . . . his repellent, insignificant figure diminished even more."[46]

In his book on Geijerstam,[47] Melker Johnsson emphasizes how untrue and distorted a picture Strindberg gave of the original, but at the same time he exaggerates when he says that as a portrait of the literary vampire, Zachris is "one of the great figures in world literature." Strindberg's fervent hatred for the model gave the portrait its power, but also its absurdity; for even as he was careful to include factual details from his association with Geijerstam, he magnified their significance out of proportion—Zachris's actual offenses seem unimportant in relation to the indignation they provoke.

On the whole, the figures in *Black Banners* are not independent characters like, for example, the characters in *The People of Hemsö,* but caricatures. Often the grotesquely comic effects produced are due entirely to the distortions, and unless the reader is somewhat familiar with the original, he may not appreciate the caricature completely. For example, the "emancipatress" Hanna Paj, with her port-wine red nose and her interminable verbiage, is one of the most striking minor characters, and the most amusing episode in the book is the scene in which she takes in Zachris's wife Jenny, his two ill-bred sons, and their dog on Christmas Eve. Although Hanna had encouraged Jenny to leave her husband, she had not foreseen the uncomfortable consequences of the Zachris family descending upon her; for one thing, "dogs were her *bête noire.*" It does not take long for the domestic chaos and Jenny's presumptuous demands to undermine Hanna's modern, tolerant, humanitarian attitudes, and she asks the family to leave.

The chapter first appeared in the Christmas issue of Albert

Engström's humor magazine *Strix,* two years before *Black Banners* was published, but since the heroine was called Hanna Lindgren at that time, it seems that most of the readers did not realize Strindberg was ridiculing Ellen Key and were only mildly entertained by the description.[48]

Interestingly enough, although the same caricatural technique was employed in *The Red Room* and *The New Kingdom,* these earlier works probably gain by the fact that we no longer recognize the people represented. Perhaps part of the explanation is that at that time Strindberg still possessed, as he says in his autobiography, "the ability to conjure up characters and scenes from his imagination." He had also placed "false masks" on the characters so as "not to expose private persons." Obviously, he regarded such humanitarianism as inappropriate when he wrote *Black Banners,* for he handled the private lives of the people alluded to with far less consideration.

Falkenström is in the cloister when he hears of Jenny's death and becomes angry as he thinks of the suffering caused by Zachris's selfish and rapacious nature. His cloister brothers try to quiet him, but he replies: "Yes, I'll keep quiet about the dead woman, but I'm going to talk about Zachris."[49] Strindberg had a similar intention to be discreet in his treatment of Jenny and her relationship with her husband, but he could not hold to it, and the section in *Black Banners* that brings the most discredit to its author is his description of Zachris's marriage; even at publication Strindberg could bring himself to cut only the most revolting passages.[50]

As a character, Jenny is more sympathetically drawn than her husband. It is true that she states the usual grievances of the Strindbergian woman: her husband devastated her youth, ruined her career as an artist, and gave her children she did not want. "Think of it—carrying that ox's brat!" says Jenny to her former boyfriend Kilo in Zachris's presence. "I have a good mind to drown it, for it'll surely come into the world with eyeglasses, a paunch, and a fifteen-öre [cigar] in the corner of its mouth."[51] Yet Strindberg suggests that Jenny once possessed a certain French elegance and feminine charm that were worn away by the degrading life that she shared with Zachris. During her final illness, by which time she has been transformed into a fat, blowzy matron, she develops some of the psychic powers that Strindberg esteemed so highly. She reads her husband's thoughts before he has spoken them and has ecstasies during which she feels herself possessed by strange beings. She longs to cross over to the other side and is anxious to "root out" her husband from both her body and soul so that he will not accompany her there. She tells him:

> You don't know what the other side is like, so you'll stay on this shore, where you thrive. I know there is another side, for I have seen it; I saw my mother and my sisters there. They were simple but respectable people who lived in duty and privation and were patient in their hope, never expecting to find bliss down here.[52]

Although an immoderate amount of space is devoted to Jenny's expressions of loathing for the mate whose person is "nauseating" to her, Strindberg managed to endow her with something of the visionary aura often present in his characters after the Inferno Crisis.

No assessment of *Black Banners* can ignore the self-portrait Strindberg drew in the character of Falkenström. In *The Gothic Rooms,* the presence of Strindberg's *persona* from *The Red Room*—Arvid Falk— is felt briefly: he is the subject of observations by Count Max regarding a bust of Falk in an exhibition. Count Max says Falk combined the strongest self-esteem with "the most candid self-contempt." But Falk is not satirized in *The Gothic Rooms;* on the contrary, he is seen in a sympathetic and, to a certain extent, heroic light.

Falkenström in *Black Banners* is presented as "spirited, carefree, independent, and unconcerned about honor and social standing,"[53] but the description fits him rather badly. At Professor Stenkåhl's dinner party at the beginning of the book, he appears as a hollow-eyed and burned-out roué. His cynical comments have a chilling instead of amusing effect on the other guests, and even the brutal Doctor Borg seems more jovial.

Throughout the novel there is a frigid zone around Falkenström. He carries on an indiscreet flirtation with Jenny without becoming physically aroused and makes cynical disclosures about his sexual experiences. Even as he complains that outsiders have torn his marriage apart, he tries to win everyone's support against his divorced wife. Strindberg went back to the harrowing years after his first divorce for material for Falkenström, but he also afflicted the character with the infirmities of old age that he himself was suffering as he wrote the novel.

It is impossible for Falkenström to forget the wrongs done to him by Zachris, and the moment someone mentions his name, Falkenström flares up and is incapable of talking about anything else: "Unless I hate evil, I cannot love goodness." His description of Zachris as a vampire is the harshest denunciation in the novel.

For twenty years Zachris has hounded Falkenström with his company; he has stolen friends, publishers, and theatre directors from him, eaten him out of house and home, lured his wife away, and opposed and spoiled all his plans. Toward the end of the novel, Falkenström says: "It now occurs to me that this sterile soul wanted to drain my manly strength, and each time I broke off contact with him he ran dry." When Falkenström is urged to forgive Zachris, he replies: "To forgive is to take back, and therefore I can never forgive him."[54]

Like Strindberg, Falkenström cannot remain in a cloister and once outside its walls relapses "into his wild ways, forgetting all the spiritual exercises."[55] There is clearly a certain amount of self-criticism in Strindberg's description of this cloister novice; Falkenström says he is reacting "against the baseness" in himself when he punishes others.[56] Ultimately, self-esteem prevails over self-contempt, and Falkenström triumphs. The reader is expected to regard him as a great and renowned author who was unjustly betrayed and overshadowed by Zachris.

Strindberg's style, which was fettered and monotonous in *The Gothic Rooms,* is bold and varied in *Black Banners,* particularly in his masterly use of dialogue to characterize. He returned to the expressive device of *verbum dicendi* used in *The Red Room,* where he had his characters "fire pointed bullets" or "hurl shells" at each other in their speech; now they go a bit further and "roar" or "brawl" their remarks, when they are not simply spitting "gobs" at each other. His dialogue becomes increasingly cutting and his characters more hostile. In the scene outside Professor Stenkåhl's door in the opening of the novel, Falkenström asks whether there will be any "baiting" that evening, and the bookseller Kilo answers: "It wouldn't be a phantom supper without baiting." Similar "baiting" continues throughout the book.

Although *The Red Room* lacked Dickens's humor, it had sparkling wit, tender nuances, and here and there a touch of youthful lyricism. In *Black Banners* harsh colors clash with each other, and an atmosphere of ordinary, everyday life is apt to change suddenly into a wild witches' Sabbath. This is true at Professor Stenkåhl's phantom supper and in many of the best sections in the book. But Strindberg was not able to exploit this style completely until the Chamber Plays, in which he used fantastic elements to create a suggestive nightmare mood not apparent in *Black Banners*.

The element that gives power to *Black Banners*, despite the novel's shortcomings, is the intense misanthropy, sometimes reminiscent of Swift. Strindberg's loathing of the animal in man emerges not only in the descriptive passages, but in the preaching of Falkenström and his cloister brothers. Hanna Paj, who claims no depth of feeling other than humanitarianism, is induced by Falkenström to throw off her mask and reveal her animal instincts; and on her deathbed Jenny complains to Zachris: "I went astray in your zoo, for animal is what you are."[57]

It would be easy to conclude that the theme of misanthropic bestiality became almost an automatic reference for Strindberg because it appears so often in his later writings, but it would be more accurate to describe it as an obsession from which he could not free himself. In a diary entry, obviously never intended for publication, he wrote that life was so ugly that if a writer were to describe everything he saw and heard, no one could bear reading it. "Education and social training seem to be only masks for the bestial, and virtues only pretense. The highest to which we can attain is the concealment of the wretchedness.---Life is so loathsome that only a swine can thrive in it. And whoever is able to regard the ugliness of life as beautiful is a swine."

> [Falkenström] always dreamed about beautiful poems, but experienced only life's ugly side. On a number of occasions he tried to transform reality's abominations into something beautiful, but was then despised by his colleagues and called a gilder. He admitted to himself that to represent the wretchedness in cheerful colors was roguery.[58]

We have certainly not noticed any earlier tendency in Strindberg to gild existence. But *Black Banners* is the first work in which he allowed absolute pessimism to prevail, and his later writings are constant variations on man's bestiality. *Black Banners* is a preparatory study for *The Ghost Sonata*.

Historical Short Stories

Inasmuch as *Black Banners* was rejected by both Swedish and German publishers (it did not appear in Sweden until the limited edition of 1907), Strindberg had to produce a work quickly that would bring in some income. In one month in the spring of 1905 he compiled *Historical*

Miniatures, an ambitious attempt to cover the period from Moses to Napoleon. There was, of course, no time for historical research; apparently all he did was skim through a popular text on world history and select personalities and anecdotes at random.

For the first part, Strindberg used his unpublished dramatic cycle on world history,[59] which was reproduced virtually unchanged except for an occasional narrative transition inserted between sections of dialogue. The second part contains several good stories, especially "Laocoön" in which he depicts the contrast between ,a decaying Catholicism and a heathenish Renaissance, the same theme he had dealt with in "Evolution" in *Swedish Destinies.* The portraits of Peter the Great and the aging Voltaire have some power but lack subtlety. Strindberg is often content just to relate a bit of the history of the characters without constructing real plots. In the first story he introduces the Jew Eleazar; it was clearly his intention to have this Ahasuerus figure reappear as the connecting link in the entire story series which was to conclude with the Hague Peace Conference of 1899, but he was to fulfill his idea only partially.

Strindberg hoped that the story collection would have a cumulative effect on the reader. "Each piece is quite foolish by itself, but the collection should succeed," he wrote to the publisher. The public, however, was indifferent to *Historical Miniatures,* and it occasioned Oscar Levertin's harshest review of a Strindberg work.

Strindberg's short stories from Swedish history in *New Swedish Destinies (Ny svenska öden),* written immediately after *Historical Miniatures,* encountered just as sour a reception, primarily because they prompted comparisons with his historical stories from the 1880's. In contrast with the earlier *Destinies, New Swedish Destinies* deals with major figures of history rather than ordinary people; Strindberg had thought of calling the collection *Sagas of the Rulers*[60] or *Sagas of the Kings (Konungasagor).*

Except for a few well-written passages, he did not go to a great deal of trouble describing milieu. The stories consist largely of conversations between a monarch and his intimates or adversaries. Sometimes entire dialogue exchanges are taken from the post-Inferno historical dramas, such as in "The Öland King and the Little Queen" ("Ölandskungen och den lilla drottningen") where Queen Christina's reputation is blackened even more than in the play. She is so unattractive and even repellent in her masculine clothes that her adviser Count Oxenstierna cannot stay in the same room with her: "The rough masculine voice, the flat chest, and the large coquettish eyes created a hideous monster that frightened normal men."[61] Her morals are illustrated by the fact—duly supported by a reference to the *Swedish Biographical Dictionary*—that after her break with Magnus Gabriel De la Gardie she had four lovers at one time. The other female figures in the stories are equally unpleasant, particularly Queen Joanna I of Naples (1326-82) whom Strindberg called his "most beautiful and truest female portrait in the naive innocence."[62] She "meekly and childishly" tells Karl Ulfsson how she murdered her first husband and makes such advances that the knight burst out: "But you're married, woman!"[63]

The kings are let off more lightly, especially if, like Johan III and Sigismund, they show a taste for Strindberg's Catholically oriented syncretism or, like Erik XIV, experience occult sensations. Urban Hjärne, physician to Charles XI (1655-97), regrets the rationalism that he displayed while serving on a witchcraft commission and comes to believe in the power of witches to destroy by their evil will. Moreover, he is "deeply interested in all abnormal manifestations of the secret emotional life."[64]

Strindberg selected bits of information at random from his old sources and inserted them wherever he felt they would be most effective. For a scene set during the time Gustav Vasa was breaking the hold of the Vatican over the Swedish Church and confiscating church property, Strindberg used actual records of a meeting between Vasa and the clergy at Vadstena cloister. The king shows that the cloister establishment is "illegal and based upon a roguish trick,"[65] and in the process cites the exact dates when certain papal bulls were issued. Characters speak with absolute certainty about controversial questions and are assiduous "who's who" specialists when it comes to family relationships. Gustav Adolf's military commanders bombard each other with theological and historical polemics in order to prove that the Thirty Years War was a piratical expedition and not a religious struggle.

It is evident from Strindberg's letters that while he was writing he became thoroughly tired of "the coal mines of Swedish history." Several times he thought of breaking off work but continued under the pressure of financial considerations. Perhaps because he was somewhat inspired at the beginning, the best story in the collection is the first one, "The Saga of

Stig Storverk's Son" ("Sagan om Stig Storverks son"), based on an old
Scandinavian legend retold in Starbäck and Bäckström's *Stories From
Swedish History.*

The fate of Storverk's son Starkodd reminded Strindberg of his
own. Each gift Starkodd receives from Odin is accompanied by a curse
from Thor. It is prophesied that he will live three lives, but he is doomed
to commit a terrible deed in each one. He receives the gift of song, but
cannot remember what he composed and so "could never feel his greatness or be someone on his own." Strindberg endows Starkodd with the
additional fate of winning and losing women, although this has no counterpart in the legend.[66] All of Starkodd's inner contradictions are Strindberg's: stern defiance and feminine tenderness, egotism and a sense of
inferiority, the desire for revenge and the pangs of remorse. More candidly
than in any other work, Strindberg admitted his faults.

In "The Beginning of Ån Bogsveig's Saga," Strindberg had depicted himself in the person of the youngest son, despised by all, unaware
of the magnitude of his powers, and incapable of controlling them. "Stig
Storverk's Son" is a continuation of that fragment. Starkodd becomes the
"greatest Nordic warrior"[67] and poet, but no one will acknowledge his
greatness. People remember only the terrible deeds, and he himself has
forgotten his triumphs. When he learns after the Battle of Bråvalla
(c. 750) that he was wounded and carried home by seven kings, he replies:
"Seven? Surely I dreamed it and so have you."[68]

He marries the Valkyrie Veborg, but this cripples his power. After
they have a child, he has to sit by the cradle and wind wool into balls.[69]
Alf, his young squire, points out to him the ignominious slavery in which
he lives, whereupon he "curses all women, flying into a berserker[70] rage,"
as is noted in a sketch. Alf proves to be a faithless friend who robs him of
his ability to remember and takes credit for his feats and ballads: "A thief
of souls, an assassin of men, a secret assassin is what he was."[71]

In the sketches, Geijerstam is indicated as the model for this
faithless friend who claims to be the author of Starkodd's poem about the
Battle of Bråvalla. After killing a king, Starkodd offers to atone by immo-
lating himself on the king's funeral pyre. While standing on the pyre, he
regains his gift of song, and as those present hear him sing they realize
that Alf acquired his reputation falsely. When Alf speaks disparagingly of
the dead Starkodd, he is thrown onto the burning pyre.

In this story, Strindberg probably came as close to self-accusation as it was possible for him to do. Starkodd, who "sniffs like a wolf" at the midwinter sacrificial feast, assassinates his foster brother and murders his wife, but although he is tormented by pangs of remorse after each terrible deed, he is compelled to commit new ones because he knows that only by drinking human heart blood can he regain his manly power. Even in details one notices how Strindberg modeled the figure after his own image. When it becomes necessary to route the enemy forces, Starkodd is frightened and ventures to join in only after Alf rides ahead of him at full gallop. "I think *I* serve *you!*" is Starkodd's first reflection afterwards.[72]

But these personal insertions do not spoil the historical flavor. Without resorting to as many archaisms as in "Ån Bogsveig's Saga," Strindberg managed to create an equally strong impression of Viking savagery. The story, which was written while Strindberg was hesitating to submit *Black Banners,* is among the finest works of his last years. It is a pity he was never able to follow through on a planned dramatization, for he seldom had at his disposal material so extraordinarily suited to his talents or a hero so appropriate as a mirror of his own personality.

Another story in the collection, also interesting from the autobiographical standpoint, is "The Tragedy at Örby House," which is set in the palace in which Erik XIV was imprisoned at the time of his death.[73] A prematurely aged Erik XIV repents the evil he has done and realizes that there are many innocent people in this world who suffer. For his own part, he is resigned to the imprisonment that followed his deposal and does not even long for a visit from his wife and children. When they come to visit they seem larger than life, and he feels they are suffocating him:

> You see, I am a painter, and I want to see paintings I painted myself. But it is necessary to be distant from things in order to see them beautifully. When in the distance I see Karin in a boat on the sea, preferably in moonlight, then all is well. Furthermore, I don't have to see them; they are always with me in here, and in the way I want them, too. See these three empty chairs at the table? There, my mother sits; this is Sigrid's place, that is Gustav's . . . . Things will do as they are. Solitude has made me irritable, so I cannot endure reality.[74]

At the time Strindberg wrote these lines he had spent a summer alone on Furusund and pretended to himself that Harriet and their daughter were there with him. He considered this summer his happiest and described it in detail in the short novel *The Roof-Topping-Off Ceremony (Taklagsöl).*

The Roof-Topping-Off Ceremony

During the spring of 1906, Strindberg wrote his last two prose narratives, *The Roof-Topping-Off Ceremony* and *The Scapegoat.* They were first published as serials in periodicals and then issued together in one volume in 1907 (*The Scapegoat,* the more artistically successful of the two works, was originally planned as a part of *The Roof-Topping-Off Ceremony*).

The inspiration for *The Roof-Topping-Off Ceremony* came to Strindberg in 1905 when he was alone on Furusund and hoped that his wife and child would join him. His letters dealt with the provisions he was making for their comfort: he picked up pieces of glass from the grass so his little girl would not hurt herself, had the swing painted, raised the flag, and so forth. When they did not come, he comforted himself with the thought that they were with him in spirit: "I have lived with you here; everything was done for your sake—perhaps I shall write a beautiful book about this *séjour.*"[75]

But the book was not written until the following spring and dealt largely with the wrongs Strindberg suffered during his third marriage. Nevertheless, the description of the Furusund summer is the best thing in the novel next to the unusual and enchanting plot framework: a curator who has undergone an operation lies dying. Under the influence of morphine he becomes loquacious, and old memories crop up in his mind. The story is a monologue interrupted only by short conversations between the curator and his nurse or pieces of information concerning changes in his condition. The memories of the wonderful summer occur near the end. The old man recalls the arrangements he made to receive his anxiously expected guests and the experiences he shared "with my dear shadows, a shadow life in a phantom house."[76] It is clear to him that the summer when his wife and child were with him only in his imagination was his happiest, "with everything pleasant, and nothing disturbing."

A basic idea throughout the story is that the curator's enemy, "the green eye," will now have the opportunity to slake his revenge. The person alluded to, according to letters to Schering, is Siri von Essen's first husband, Baron Wrangel, who lived nearly opposite Strindberg's house and whose green lampshade Strindberg could see from his bedroom until a newly built house obscured his view.

The topping-off ceremony for this new house was the inspiration for the title of the novel. At the end of the story, the curator's enemy sends word by telephone that "he who has suffered has no enemies." The old man can see a nearby topping-off ceremony from his bed and hears the workmen cheering. Past hatred is extinguished, and the curator's anguished features resolve into the peaceful smile of the sleep of death: "And so he lay there smiling as if he were seeing only beautiful things: green meadows, children and flowers, blue water, and flags in the sunshine."[77]

By having the curator's personality and attitudes change according to his physical condition—vehement during fever crises and pain, subsiding into sweet memories under the influence of morphine—Strindberg was able to motivate the rapid changes in the plot: the hopping about from one conversational subject to another and the alternating of temperamental outbursts with moments of nostalgia and tender forgiveness. In a striking way, the flow of the narrative reveals the disparate elements in Strindberg's own personality:

> Sometimes new personalities seemed to develop within him; either "reaction residue" from his ancestors or the influence of all the people he was thinking about. He could thus be wicked and venomous one moment, and haughty and supercilious the next. And so there emerged in turn a wise old man, a child, and a rudimentary woman.[78]

The difference between *The Roof-Topping-Off Ceremony* and earlier works is that here the different "personalities" do not exist as separate entities, they mix and merge with each other in sudden and unexpected ways. The book is more illustrative of the lightning changes in Strindberg's temperament than *Alone,* and the line between dream and painful reality is even more blurred than in *A Dream Play.* There is a tense, shrill quality present that is motivated by having the curator remember the Graphophone he gave his child; the wax recordings were introduced by a rough Prussian voice shouting titles: "Falkensteinmarsch, Nachtigallrekord." When the curator becomes delirious with fever, he begins to speak in the same way, "striking up again, like a Graphophone without a ratchet."

Strindberg was aware that *The Roof-Topping-Off Ceremony* was his most experimental work in the narrative genre. In a letter to Schering he called it one of the best things he had written. He also said that he originally planned it as a play, and that it could be considered a Chamber Play. Indeed, with a framework in which the real and the dream-like blend together and personalities are unraveled and transformed, it does foreshadow the Chamber Plays.

The Scapegoat

Immediately after completing *The Roof-Topping-Off Ceremony,* Strindberg thought of expanding it into a novel in the style of Balzac. In a letter to Harriet Bosse on April 15, 1906, he said: "Balzac's type of novel interests me most just now. Like *Alone,* there you can explain yourself, be expansive, interpret people, examine them within—basically."[79] The result of his plans was his last novel, *The Scapegoat,* portions of which were actually written with the intention of including them in *The Roof-Topping-Off Ceremony.* It even has some of the same characters: the restaurant keeper who fails in his attempt to establish a restaurant and his protégé, the considerate lawyer. But Strindberg seemed to have become quickly aware that the idea could be used in a separate story. After sending *The Scapegoat* to the publisher, he described it in a letter to Schering: "It is Balzac's method: insignificant people, great points of view."[80]

It is strange that Strindberg first thought of including *The Scapegoat* within the unrealistic structure of *The Roof-Topping-Off Ceremony,* for it is a straightforwardly realistic novel of small-town life. Perhaps it was Balzac's example that persuaded him to define a small town as a home for "elderly pensioners, widows, and sick people,"[81] a place where streets appear empty most of the time, and people spy on each other through mirrors mounted outside their windows when they are not dozing on benches on the big esplanade. The first title for the novel was *Small-Town Life (Småstadsliv),* and although the book does not contain detailed description, a small-town atmosphere prevails throughout. Comparisons may be drawn with the impressions of Lund in *Easter,* and as a matter of fact, the central characters are fashioned after models from Lund.

Of the two central characters, restaurant keeper Askanius resembles Balzac's petty tradespeople most closely; they, too, generally have delusions of grandeur and are eventually ruined. The large restaurant founded by Askanius to put the City Restaurant out of business has fewer customers every day, and so he begins "a terrible battle with himself and against his destiny." He takes his meals near the windows facing the square to give the impression that the place is busy, invites acquaintances to free suppers, keeps all the electric lights on, and even buys an orchestrion. But business not does improve, his wife dies, and he becomes a dotty old man whom relatives want to put under the care of a guardian. A syndicate supported by one of his enemies plans a competitive enterprise—a "Grand Hotel"—to deprive him of his liquor license. But to all advice that he go out of business, he always answers proudly: "I'll never close." The restaurant is finally closed, however, by the public prosecutor, and on the same day that the new Grand Hotel is to open, Askanius is found dead, sitting like a marble statue in the dining room of his empty restaurant, a bottle of maraschino liqueur and a silver bowl in front of him, while his orchestrion, which has broken down, spews forth infernal sounds: "the most horrible fanfares, mixed with chorales, waltzes, overtures, and parade marches."[82]

This restaurant keeper with Napoleonic dreams, who battles vainly against the Powers, is contrasted with the lawyer Libotz, who yields humbly to every blow.[83] In the beginning of the novel we learn that Libotz "was doomed to suffer for himself and for others, and people felt a kind of compulsive duty to contribute to the fulfillment of his fate by tormenting him."[84] The old doctrine of *satisfactio vicaria* proclaimed in earlier works such as *Easter* appears again, but now Strindberg was more closely identified with the sufferer.[85]

Ironically, Libotz's unique position is also his protection. "It was as if he were marked by destiny, and no one dared to touch him; it was as if people were afraid of coming under his spell, of having their destinies connected with his."[86] At the end of the novel, Libotz hears people calling him "The Scapegoat." He then recalls "the atonement ceremony in the Old Testament in which a goat laden with everyone's sins was driven out into the desert as a consecration to Asasel; that is, to the Evil One, who thereby got his own back again."[87] But although Strindberg's sympathies were undoubtedly with this figure who is marked by fate and burdened by the sins of others, he resisted the temptation to create a martyr with a persecution complex. On the contrary, Libotz is the most kindhearted and unassuming of people, although everything he does places him in a suspicious light; in the end, the town makes him an outcast.

At his first appearance in the narrative, Libotz has already learned resignation. Because "he looks like a poor musician" and a foreigner when he arrives in town, he is thought poorly of and is shoved and trampled in the crush in front of Askanius's smörgåsbord table, but he has only kind words for those who despise him. As a result, he is regarded as a sycophant. And since he never tries to shift blame on anyone else, people drag him into suspicious situations in which he always seems to be the villain. But precisely because they believe that he would not shrink from using any means necessary to gain his ends, people frequently turn to him for legal assistance:

> Because of his undeserved bad reputation he made a handsome living. He realized this and could read in his clients' eyes how they felt they were, so to speak, in collusion with the blackguard that they had created and grafted onto him. Finally, he got into the habit of regarding his other self as a separate person against whose existence he fought.[88]

The description of Libotz's wretched dealings with his clients and intimates is rendered with a fresh narrative zest that is unexpected in Strindberg at this time, and in episodes such as Libotz's brief engagement, there are flashes of the bantering spirit of the *Married* stories. The lawyer grows attached to one of Askanius's waitresses, "better known for her dependability than her beauty." After a period of acquaintance they become engaged and, according to custom, exchange rings.

In contrast with the couples in most of Strindberg's love stories, both parties have the best intentions, but there can never be any real meeting of minds; the girl is uneducated and Libotz is too shy and self-deprecating. During a Sunday outing, their inability to communicate with each other makes them both miserable. Libotz tries to sustain the conversation by rattling on about his goals in life, and they discuss a little politics, but even attempts at small talk are doomed. When Libotz grows desperate and says, "It's funny how all shoemakers are named Andersson," Karin replies, "But my father was a shoemaker and his name was Lundberg." They wander aimlessly through the woods, throw "stones in the water for the tenth time, and . . . [look] up into the pines as if they felt like hanging themselves in the branches." After they have eaten, Libotz, who is used to napping in the middle of the day, becomes helplessly sleepy and dozes off. The foxy public prosecutor Tjärne pops up like a good fairy coming to the rescue and converses with the girl. He organizes a game of skittles and eventually the three of them have supper together at the City Hotel, but poor Libotz is excluded from the conversation more and more and finally he leaves them. The following day he returns her ring with a letter in which he assumes all responsibility for breaking the engagement, explaining that someone with gloomy temperament cannot bring joy to another person's life. And so he is forever relegated to the life of a bachelor and the company of his false friends.

Things go from bad to worse for Libotz; his clerk, who stole from him, brings action against him for false accusations. In the first proceedings Libotz is ordered to pay damages of 3,000 kroner to the thief. The circuit court acquits him, but the entire town is moved to sympathy for the thievish clerk who is assisted in establishing his own law firm in order to drive Libotz out of business. Although this effort is unsuccessful, Libotz is evicted from his lodgings, and no one in town will rent him a room.

The acquittal decision restores Libotz's faith that humane treatment still has a place in the order of things, but he must regularly pass by the shop window where his caricature hangs in every weekly issue of the newspaper and turn a deaf ear to the jeering words expressed behind his back. He must live his life "as if enclosed in an impenetrable diving suit, avoiding both the important and the unimportant people." When he finally leaves town with a bank draft in his pocket, he feels like a criminal who has been discharged. On the other side of the mountain he is a stranger, "but people only had to look at him to turn somber and quiet, and no one dared to address him, let alone affront him. He bore the scar, but its protective shield enveloped him."[89]

Before he left the town, his only comfort in distress was to wander out to the mountain, his Mount Tabor, and speak to his God. "It was a strange sight to see this town dweller in his top hat up on the desolate mountain." There he bared "his head and mumbled words, sometimes defiant and complaining, sometimes submissive." Then he would wander back again "after he lifted his hat and bowed to the Invisible One." His meditations bring him to the conclusion that " 'one person has to suffer for another,' he sighed, 'some more, others less.' "[90] As he is about to leave for good, he ascends the mountain once again and looks out over the town, and although he feels it is a prison he has left, he is still able to think about the good things he enjoyed there.

At his departure he encounters the pharmacist's assistant who tells him what people have said and thought about him. Libotz remarks that there is a great difference in people's destinies, "but for what reason 'one could not explain,' and that was probably the way it should be."[91]

Through this long-suffering little lawyer, Strindberg gave profound expression to the spirit of resignation in the face of "the riddle of the world" that he himself had such difficulty in achieving.

Notes to Chapter Twenty

1. *SS:*XL, p. 277.
2. *Ibid.,* p. 45.
3. *See* p. 33.
4. *SS:*XL, p. 236.
5. *Ibid.,* p. 189.
6. Strindberg's dislike of dogs was as enduring as his misogyny (*see* p. 194). At one point in *The Gothic Rooms,* Doctor Borg voices his disapproval of societies for the protection of dumb animals: "Women have joined forces with animals; an animal may bite me, but if I defend myself with a kick, I get thrown in jail. Is this the end of the world, or what?"—Translator
7. *SS:*XL, p. 195. Strindberg reread Erik Johan Stagnelius (1793-1823) in the fall of 1899. [A respected romantic poet, Stagnelius was tortured by frustrated eroticism.—Translator] In a letter to Nils Andersson (September 9, 1899) Strindberg stated that in common with Stagnelius he believed that he was "an ion sent down from a superior atmosphere to be tormented here."
8. *SS:*XL, p. 243.
9. *Ibid.,* p. 212.
10. *Ibid.,* p. 244.
11. *Ibid.,* p. 195.
12. *Ibid.,* p. 294.
13. Strindberg was particularly upset that Rydberg was honored as a follower of the spiritualist theologian Waldemar Rudin and that Rydberg had even been forgiven for his defense of Oscar Björck's "lewd paintings in Operakällaren" Restaurant.
14. *SS:*XL, p. 247. Regarding this passage, *see* Olle Holmberg, "Viktor Rydberg och August Strindberg" (*Samlaren,* 1935, pp. 50-51). It might be mentioned in passing that Holmberg's assumption that Strindberg felt he was the model for the figure of the dogmatic schoolmaster Lars in Rydberg's historical novel *The Armorer* (*Vapensmeden*—1891) is supported by a statement about *The Armorer* in the sketches for *The Gothic Rooms.*
15. *SS:*XL, p. 248.
16. In *The Gothic Rooms,* "Sakris" is ridiculed by Borg as "born with a paunch, eyeglasses, tonsure and pension, the patron of literature, the friend of the ladies" (*SS:*XL, p. 88). The mentioning, however,

of the mentally ill Fröding as someone who blasphemously defied the Lord in "Hinnoms dal" and was therefore punished
(*Ibid.*, p. 290) must be regarded not as a personal attack, but as
part of Strindberg's religious propaganda.

17.   Strindberg gave the name "fugues" to those conversations in *The
Gothic Rooms* in which arguments and counterarguments are not
divided between different speakers. One of these fugues, which
was omitted from *The Gothic Rooms* at the publisher's request,
reappears in the second chapter of *Black Banners* (*see* Landquist's
notes, *SS:*XLI, p. 292).

18.   As a matter of fact, after the novel was published Strindberg considered reprinting them in *A Blue Book* (*see* August Falck, pp.
220-21).

19.   *SS:*XLI, p. 99.

20.   *Ibid.*, p. 200.

21.   *Ibid.*, pp. 186-95.

22.   *Ibid.*, p. 186.

23.   *Ibid.*

24.   *Ibid.*, p. 188.

25.   *Ibid.*, p. 189.

26.   *Ibid.*, p. 128.

27.   For discussions of the relationship between Strindberg and Geijerstam and their final break, *see* Landquist in the newspaper *Dagens
Nyheter*, March 25, 1917; Melker Johnsson, *En åttitalist* (1934),
pp. 301 ff.; Eklund, *Strindbergsstudie, passim* [and Walter A.
Berendsohn, *Strindbergsproblem* (1946), pp. 20-23.—Translator]

28.   *Brev*, X, pp. 5, 22. *Cf.* note 16 above.

29.   *SS:*XLI, p. 271. In a section crossed out in the manuscript of *The
Gothic Rooms* "Little Sakris" (Geijerstam) is referred to as "the
[parasitic] ichneumon fly."

30.   For a further discussion of the resemblances between the two works
see P. J. Vilhelm Ljungdorff, E[rnst] T[heodor] A[madeus] Hoffmann (1924), p. 418.

31.   *SS:*XLI, pp. 213-14.

32.   *Ibid.*, p. 214.

33.   *Ibid.*, p. 259.

34.   *Ibid.*, p. 54. In another episode in the novel, Strindberg quite consciously transferred one of his own experiences to Zachris. To his
horror, Zachris's son by his first marriage turns up and wins a
position on the same newspaper as his father, despite Zachris's

energetic attempts to shake him off. The real-life basis for this episode can be found in Strindberg's diary, in which he describes how he was scared out of his wits by the news of an impending visit from his son Hans, which later proved to be a false alarm (December 3, 1900). He used the same episode in *Alone* and describes his intentions to keep his unwelcome son at a distance, prevent the boy from preying on his relatives, and reject the demands for economic assistance that were certain to be made, for his "obligations to him ceased when he reached the age of fifteen." Strindberg alleges that although the experience was a bitter memory, he did not reproach himself: "for I had not abandoned him!" (*SS:*XXXVIII, p. 187).

In *Black Banners* the anguished expectation of the visit is fulfilled. On Christmas Eve, Zachris is called on by his son, who had been in America. He tries to get rid of him with the same argument that Strindberg thought of using on his own son: "You have no claims after the age of fifteen, and you're eighteen now!" (*SS:*XLI, p. 157). When the son asks whether his father intends throwing him out the way he did his mother, the young man is put off with a bit of charity and retorts: "A fiver, on Christmas Eve! Damn it to hell!" (*Ibid.*) After being kicked out, he shows his face at the window and sticks out his tongue.

It is obvious that Strindberg wanted Zachris to suffer the anguish he did. But again, it is difficult to assume self-hatred. On the contrary, Zachris's moral paltriness is contrasted with Falkenström's gnawing sense of loss over the children he lost through divorce.

35. *SS:*XLI, p. 276.
36. *See also* pp. 327 and 277-80.
37. *SS:*XLI, p. 248.
38. Lindblad, *Strindberg som berättare*, pp. 99-100.
39. *SS:*XLI, p. 13.
40. *Ibid.*, p. 8.
41. *Ibid.*, p. 19.
42. *Ibid.*, p. 26.
43. *Ibid.*, p. 17.
44. *Ibid.*, p. 54.
45. *Ibid.*, pp. 42-43!
46. *Ibid.*
47. *En åttitalist: Gustaf af Geijerstam 1858-1890* (1934), pp. 302 ff.

48. According to an oral statement by Albert Engström.

49. *SS:*XLI, p. 270.

50. A frequently made assertion—by, among others, Albert Engström
     (*Strindberg och jag,* p. 36)—that there was a manuscript older
     than the one in the Royal Library is probably without foundation.
     The Royal Library manuscript bears all the traces of being the
     original; the cloister conversations are in the form of inserts out-
     side the original pagination. It is true that Strindberg indicated
     in his diary that he was cutting *Black Banners* for publication, but
     this seems to have consisted of just striking out several details.

51. *SS:*XLI, p. 46.

52. *Ibid.,* pp. 247-48.

53. *Ibid.,* p. 50.

54. *Ibid.,* pp. 270-71.

55. *Ibid.,* p. 272.

56. *Ibid.,* p. 196.

57. *Ibid.,* p. 248.

58. *Ibid.,* pp. 72-73.

59. *See* p. 354.

60. It was reprinted under this title in Volume XLIII of the *Samlade
     Skrifter.*

61. *SS:*XLIII, p. 358.

62. In a letter to Schering.

63. *SS:*XLIII, p. 199.

64. *Ibid.,* p. 362.

65. *Ibid.,* p. 268.

66. Strindberg also worked on a dramatization of the story; the prologue
     was published in the Christmas periodical *Julkvällen* in 1906, and
     the opening scenes for the first act are in *Samlade otryckta skrifter,*
     I, pp. 282 ff. The publisher, Carlheim-Gyllensköld, dates the frag-
     ment from 1903, but letters indicate that it was written in the
     spring of 1906.

67. *SS:*XLIII, p. 34.

68. *Ibid.,* p. 43.

69. Strindberg originally provided the story with a scholarly commentary
     in which he justified the introduction of the Omphale theme by
     means of the saga's affinity to the Hercules legend.

70. *See* p. 21.

71. *SS:*XLIII, p. 50.

72. *Ibid.,* p. 37.

73. *See* p. 408.

74. *SS:* XLIII, p. 282.

75. July 23, 1905. *Brev till Harriet Bosse,* p. 147.

76. *SS:*XLIV, p. 63.

77. *Ibid.,* p. 81.

78. *Ibid.,* p. 79.

79. *Brev till Harriet Bosse,* p. 239.

80. April 7, 1907.

81. *SS:*XLIV, p. 85.

82. *Ibid.,* p. 199.

83. The following was written about the restaurant keeper in the first version: "Spiteful gods practiced bending a human being to the ground." The lawyer here did not yet play the role intended by the title *The Scapegoat.*

84. *SS:*XLIV, pp. 93-94.

85. Nils Erdmann has pointed out that Strindberg was reminded of his own early experience (*see SS:*XVIII, p. 67) while writing the description of Libotz's suffering as a schoolboy, and biographical details support this supposition. The idea of being a scapegoat for the sins of other people reappears in *The Great Highway.*

86. *SS:*XLIV, p. 100.

87. *Ibid.,* p. 200.

88. *Ibid.,* p. 172.

89. *Ibid.,* p. 201.

90. *Ibid.,* pp. 105-6.

91. *Ibid.,* p. 203.

Chapter Twenty-one

THE CHAMBER PLAYS

When after a long interval Strindberg resumed his dramatic writing early in 1907, his never-abandoned plans to found an "experimental theatre" were at the point of fulfillment. The previous autumn he had become acquainted with the young director August Falck, and together they planned the establishment of the Intimate Theatre.[1] It was in anticipation of the opening of this theatre that Strindberg, during the first half of 1907, wrote the four Chamber Plays which more than any other of his works have secured his reputation as a theatrical revolutionary.

Strindberg's term "Chamber Play" was adopted from Reinhardt's Kammerspiel-Haus; German articles about this theatre, with passages marked, can be found in Strindberg's library. His basic idea was to create an intimate theatre whose repertoire would consist of plays in a subtle, naturalistic style. This is evident in a letter to the author Adolf Paul written on January 6, 1907:

> If you write anything new, let me hear about it; but try for the intimate in form, the little motif, exhaustively treated, few characters, great points of view; freely imaginative, but based on observation, experience, well-studied, simple, but not too simple; no great apparatus, no superfluous minor characters, no rule-bound five-act plays or "old machines," no drawn-out whole evening affairs. *Miss Julie* (with no intermission curtain) withstood the test of fire[2] and proved to be the form desired by the impatient people of today. Thorough, but short.[3]

But as he began writing his Chamber Plays, it became clear that subtle naturalism alone was not adequate to express what he had to say. *Storm,* the first of the plays (written in January, 1907), satisfies the requirements set down in the letter to Paul, but it also fits the definition of the Chamber Play he published a year later: "the idea of chamber music transferred to drama."[4] After completing *The Burned House* and *The Ghost Sonata* (both in March, 1907), he indicated the new direction in which he was working when he wrote that *Storm* was "complete (lower) reality, or an

excellent Philistine play that should succeed."[5] Time had made obsolete
the ideas contained in his preface to *Miss Julie,* which was written when
naturalism was the fashion, "reflecting the contemporary materialistic striving toward faithfulness to reality."[6] The turn of the century had brought
a reawakening of imagination and the triumph of the spiritual over the
material.

But perhaps the strongest influence affecting Strindberg's change
in stylistic method was his occupation with preparations and revisions for
two very different works: *A Dream Play,* which was to be premièred in the
spring of 1907, and *Black Banners,* which had been accepted for publication the same year. And so it was the interaction of dream atmosphere and
brutal naturalism that helped to give the Chamber Plays their special
quality. Whereas *A Dream Play* thrusts the spectator directly into the
world of the dream, the Chamber Plays open with realistically drawn
scenes.

In *The Burned House* we are taken to a burned-out dwelling on
Norrtulls Street, made somber because of its nearness to a cemetery. All
the tenants are associated in some way with death and funerals. Diagonally
across the street is The Coffin Nail, a tavern where hearse drivers stop and
where once criminals were given a last glass before they were taken to the
gallows hill. Like the castle in *A Dream Play,* the littered site of the burned
house is a symbol of man's existence. Each of the worn-out items on the
scrap heap has a story to tell. On top of the broken parlor clock is a small
globe of the world: "You tiny Earth: densest and heaviest of planets.
That's why we find it so burdensome on you, so hard to breathe, so hard
to carry things. The Cross is your symbol, but it could have been a cap and
bells or a strait jacket—a world of illusion and madmen."[7] The same
mood dominates the prologue to *A Dream Play,* which was written at the
same time.

The opening scene of *The Ghost Sonata* presents a typical Stockholm street scene in the fashionable Östermalm district. It is Sunday; the
bass notes of an organ from a nearby church mingle with the clanging of
steamboat bells. Bedclothes are hanging out on the service balcony of a
modern house in the background, and the Superintendent's Wife is polishing the brass on the gateposts and watering the laurel trees on either side
of the entrance. In front of the house, the Student, unshaven and pale
from keeping late hours, pictures the luxury and beauty that must exist

within: "Imagine having an apartment there, four flights up, with a lovely young wife, two beautiful little children, and an income of twenty thousand kroner a year in dividends."[8] But behind the beautiful façade is unspeakable human misery.

Strindberg tried to bring out the same contrast in *The Pelican (Pelikanen)*. At the première at the Intimate Theatre he was pleased that the bourgeois living room represented by the setting seemed comfortable and elegant "in l'art nouveau style, with furniture to match":

> It was both correct and attractive, but there was something more in the room; there was an atmosphere, a white scent of sickroom and nursery with something green on a bureau as if placed there by an invisible hand. "I want to live in that room," I remarked, although one could sense the tragedy whose last act would be played there; the most horrible theme in ancient tragedy; innocently suffering children and the false mother Medea.[9]

The passage reveals Strindberg's intentions: the bright, peaceful interior that acquires a touch of melancholy only through its "white" sickroom scent is calculated to make the action doubly moving. Max Reinhardt's chamber-of-horrors setting for his extraordinary production of *The Pelican* in 1920 was definitely a departure from the stage directions.

For Strindberg, a feeling of comfort and well-being was a false dream-like illusion which is destroyed when people are forced to see existence in its true light. On March 29, 1907, he wrote to Schering about *The Ghost Sonata*: "It is *schauderhaft* as life is when the scales fall from the eyes and one sees *das Ding an sich*." He describes how most people live in imagined happiness and only gradually have their eyes opened to reality: "This is the way the Weaveress of the World weaves the fates of men; there are that many secrets in *every* home."

In *The Pelican*, which for a time Strindberg thought of calling *Somnambulist (Sömngångare)*, the central characters imagine they are walking in their sleep and shudder at the prospect of being awakened. The Son says that he has read about great criminals who believed they had acted rightly "even up to the moment they are discovered and woke up! If that isn't dreaming, it's at least sleeping!"[10] And in *The Burned House* the Stranger explains that he rarely takes life seriously now: "I am like a sleepwalker on a ledge—I know I'm asleep, but I'm awake—and I'm only waiting to be awakened."[11]

To illustrate this awakening Strindberg placed in a central position in each play a hero who sees life "without a film over his eyes." Either he strips the masks from his fellow beings as mercilessly as the Stranger does in *The Burned House,* or he exposes them with compassion, as the Student does in *The Ghost Sonata* and the Son does in *The Pelican.*

Strindberg thus strayed rather far from his intention of creating intimate dramas with simple motifs. Despite the limitations implied in its chamber music title, *The Ghost Sonata* exceeds the possibilities of stage presentation in its attempt to depict simultaneously how people can show one personality to the world and live another within themselves. Strindberg probably did not consider this a problem: the feeling that he could see directly through people was a daily experience for him, as is evident in *A Blue Book.* But in his definition of a Chamber Play he was careful to emphasize that an author should not feel bound to a fixed form, since the theme conditions the form: "And so, there should be freedom of treatment restricted only by the unity of the idea and the feeling for style."[12]

Storm

In spite of its title, *Storm,* written in January, 1907, is the most tranquil of Strindberg's Chamber Plays. It deals with "old age and its quiet repose." But there is thunder in the air, and behind the placid dialogue we sense the tragedy of a broken marriage. When the Gentleman and his wife Gerda meet in Scene Two after a separation of five years, they become hostile, and the familiar elements of a Strindbergian marital conflict are in evidence. But the story line is not autobiographical. With his marriage shattered, Strindberg's imagination was engrossed with terrifying expectations of what the future held in store for Harriet and their child.

In the play, Gerda's new husband, an adventurer who runs dance clubs, manhandles her and runs off with a young girl, taking with him Gerda's and the Gentleman's child. A mood of anxiety hangs over Scene Three, when it is still not known whether the child will be recovered, and the Gentleman complains bitterly over the tyranny he suffered at the hands of his wife, their child, and the servants: treacherous slander and warmed-over food. It is difficult to recognize here the tranquil old man whose boundless kindness was mentioned earlier in the play. At the end, relief comes with the comforting news that the child is safe. Moreover, the threatening storm that gives the play its title has passed by—its only trace some heat lightning and a few warm raindrops. "Lightning passed over us, directly overhead, but didn't strike us! False alarm!"[13]

The merit of the play is not in the plot but in the portrayal of the aging Gentleman's loneliness. The beautiful letters Strindberg wrote in the summer of 1906 to Harriet[14] constitute a commentary on the Gentleman's mood. In one letter Strindberg called *Storm* "a painful poem with which I tried to write you and Lillan[15] out of my heart. I tried to remove ahead of time the pain I anticipated."[16]

After fruitless efforts to rent a summer place, Strindberg remained in his old apartment with its memories of his marriage. One family after another moved out to the country, and the silence became an increasingly heavier burden; he even missed a screaming child in a neighborhood apartment. The solitary mealtimes tormented him, but he was still more uncomfortable when he had to go out among people. Occasionally, his brother Axel came to play the piano for him; these were the only visits he could tolerate. In the middle of July he mentioned that the gas lamps on the street were turned on—a sign that the tormenting half-daylight of the Scandinavian summer nights was approaching its end. In the beginning of August there was thunder, lightning, and rain: "One can breathe."

The play gives a similar picture of the empty, desolate feeling that permeates Stockholm in the summer. A sketch for *Storm* bears the title *The First Street Lamp (Första lyktan),* and in the opening scene of the final version the Gentleman says to his brother, the Consul: "These light nights make me nervous. They're undoubtedly beautiful in the country, but in town they seem unnatural, almost sinister. Not until the first street lamp is lit do I become calm. Then I can take my evening walk."[17] At the end of the play the first street lamp is lit outside his window: "The first street lamp! Now it's autumn! That's our season, my friends! It begins to get dark, but wisdom comes and shines its dark lantern to guide our way."[18]

Storm describes the kind of reality to which Strindberg was becoming accustomed; a reality composed of memories of the past and a feeling of resignation toward what was to come. "There is no present," says the Gentleman, "what is happening now is empty nothingness. Look ahead or look back—preferably ahead, for there hope lies!"[19] He sinks into his hermit's life seeing only his brother, but avoids engaging him in too intimate conversation so as not to call up disturbing memories. "I've learned to keep quiet in this house," says the young Maid in the play. Even the truly kindhearted Confectioner from the ground floor apartment, with whom the Gentleman chats from time to time, finds it best to see and hear as little as possible. "We old people love the twilight. It hides so many faults—our own and other people's."[20]

As in *Alone,* the aged recluse keeps abreast of the destinies of all the people around him through telepathy. The house and its tenants tell him their stories without his having to ask: "They're brought here in wedding carriages and taken away in funeral carriages, and that mailbox on the corner has held many secrets."[21] He is thankful for his ability to "keep neutral with people" and so keep them at a distance.

At the same time he is tormented by the isolation that makes him hypersensitive. He attempts to persuade the Maid and later the Confectioner to play chess with him, and tries in vain to strike up a conversation with the Iceman. "They all go home, to listen to the sound of their own voices and find company." And when he is alone in the room, he exclaims in disillusionment: "The peace of old age—ha!" He wanders about, strikes a few chords on the piano, tries to read a newspaper, lights matches, and puts them out. His brother says "he's had enough of solitude," but the troubled emotions stirred up by seeing his wife and child again cure him of his longing for company: "Close the windows and pull down the shades, so our memories can go to sleep in peace! The peace of old age! In autumn I shall leave this silent house."[22]

If one were to look for parallels to *Storm,* one would probably turn to Maeterlinck's one-act plays set in contemporary milieus, and *Intérieur,* the most exquisite of these, has in fact a setting similar to that of the first and second scenes of *Storm:* the front façade of a house in half-twilight. Through a window we can see into an illuminated room that has a mood that plays a part in the drama, and the occupants of the room make facial and bodily movements that constitute a kind of accompaniment to the dialogue outside. Maeterlinck had also pointed out in *Le Trésor des humbles* that a depiction of the moods of an old man was an appropriate subject for tragedy.

There is no trace of occultism in *Storm,* but there is the suggestion that memories could become frightened phantoms: "They don't haunt me. They're poems I make out of real events. But if the dead reappeared, *they* would be ghosts!"[23] At the end, when Gerda and the child go off to live in the country, the Gentleman makes several comments about people who cannot face up to the existence of such things as justice and Nemesis: "And you're supposed to treat *their* filth kindly!" This is a foreshadowing of *The Burned House,* where memories take on a phantom-like reality and humanity is deprived of all pleasant illusions.

The Burned House

The setting for *The Burned House* is the house on Norrtulls Street where Strindberg lived when he experienced "the events that stand out most strongly in *The Son of a Servant,* my mother's death, my father's remarriage, and my university-qualifying examination."[24] Falck recalls that he and Strindberg were on a morning walk when the latter spotted the ruins of his old home, ravaged by fire during the night:

> A large quantity of household goods was assembled in the courtyard. We stopped. Strindberg put his hand on my arm and pointed past the yard. In an instant he had seized upon the theatrical effect of an apple tree, iced over, that had bloomed under the heat of the fire and stood there like a revelation in the midst of the soot and the homelessness.[25]

In the play, a Stranger on his way to visit his parents' grave stops before an old, half-burned hovel, behind which is a fruit orchard that has bloomed in the heat of a fire the night before. As he pokes about in the litter, it comes alive. Old pieces of wall, fragments of wallpaper, and furniture coalesce into visions of interiors from the past which torment him, and he feels himself falling "down through time, sixty years, down into my childhood."

Strindberg regarded his childhood and the time in which he grew up in a darker light as he became older, as if the injustices he suffered then had been doubly painful. He also came to feel that as a child he had been filled with more disgust for life than was expressed in *The Son of a Servant,* as can be seen in the novel fragment *Armageddon* and in a statement made in an interview in 1909 about the most vivid recollection of his childhood. He remembered that injustices had wounded him so deeply that he wanted to take his own life "at the age of seven or eight (I do not remember precisely)," and he cried much over "the pain of existing, perhaps surmising my dreadful destiny."[26]

In *The Burned House,* we learn that the Stranger had attempted
to hang himself at the age of twelve, and was removed to a mortuary since
he was thought to be dead. Speaking of the event to his brother, the
Stranger says:

> Whether I *was* dead, I don't know—but when I woke up I had forgotten
> most of my previous life and so began a new one, but in such a way that
> you people considered me strange. . . . When I regained consciousness, I
> seemed to be another person. I took life with cynical calmness. Surely,
> this is the way it ought to be! . . . From that time on, I considered myself
> as someone else; I observed and studied this other self and his fate, and
> this made me insensitive to my own suffering. But in death I had acquired
> new faculties—I could see through people, read their thoughts, and hear
> their intentions. When I was in a group, they appeared naked to me.[27]

The Stranger spent thirty years in America and "saw life from all
quarters and points, from above and below, but always as if it were staged
especially for me." But although he says that he has thereby become reconciled with some of his past and has forgiven "the so-called faults of
others and myself," he constantly reiterates the injustices he suffered as a
child, for which Nemesis always demanded punishment. Even objects in
nature that provoked him had to pay the penalty. His brother once stole
some apples and blamed him. The Stranger "got angry with the tree and
cursed it.—Two years later that big branch died and was sawed off. It
brought to mind the fig tree Our Savior once cursed, but I didn't draw any
presumptuous conclusions."[28]

In the above-mentioned interview Strindberg told the story as a
true experience from his childhood, and again mentioned the fig tree
cursed by Christ.[29] He also said that after his mother's death he felt as if
he "ceased to be related to his father and brothers and sisters" and felt
"alienated from the whole human race."[30] The same alienation is felt by
his spokesman in *The Burned House.* Years earlier the Stranger learned
that his family consisted of scoundrels and smugglers who had been pillo-
ried. His brother reproaches him for enjoying the idea of his family
exposed to scandal, but he retorts: "My family? I've never felt related to
you, never had any feelings for my fellow human beings or for myself. I
just think it's interesting to observe them."[31]

During the time he spends at the site of the fire, he succeeds in
ripping the masks off all the people around him, shattering their illusions
about their departed ones, and showing them that everything they value is

false and corrupt. "If we wanted to be just, we could put a rope around the neck of the whole human family, but we don't want to! It's an abominable family: ugly, sweaty, stinking; dirty linen, filthy stockings with holes in them; sores, bunions, ugh! No, an apple tree in bloom is far more beautiful."[32] To the Stranger, this view of humanity implies something better, a prospect of a higher existence: "You have to be a pig to feel at home in the muck here."

The Stranger says that he can see the secret bond that weaves together everything and everyone. When one is young, one sees the loom set up, and later on in life one can discern the woof. "In old age, when the eye can really see, you discover that all the curlicues form a pattern—a monogram, an ornament, hieroglyphics—which only now can be deciphered: this is life! The World Weaveress wove it."[33] Originally, Strindberg had considered calling the play *The World Weaveress (Världsväverskan)*.

August Falck describes the difficulty Strindberg had getting a firm hold on the play because he obviously tried to squeeze too many elements into it.[34] The basic idea, however, is brilliant in its simplicity. A Stranger on his way to the cemetery passes by his childhood and finds it in ruins. He reconstructs in his memory what had once constituted his entire world: "There's the site. Imagine such a little spot holding so many destinies! There's the dining room with the paintings on the walls: palms, cypresses, and temples under a rose-red sky. That's the way I used to think the world was once you got away from home!"[35] His brother warns him not to dig about in the ruins, but he replies: "Why not? When something's burned, you can read the ashes, as we used to read coals when we were children." And he reassures his apprehensive brother: "There's no purpose to my chatter; memories just pop up."

Undoubtedly, this was also Strindberg's first impulse: simply to revive half-forgotten melancholy childhood memories. But every memory becomes an accusation, and the Stranger's questioning of his relatives and childhood friends takes on the aspects of a detective's inquiry. In the rather awkwardly handled subplot a plainclothes policeman investigates the possibility of arson, but the conclusion is that the fire was accidentally caused. "The debt is canceled!" decrees the Stranger. "The case is closed; it cannot be solved. The litigants retire."[36] The wreath he had intended to place on his parents' grave he now places on the ruins of the family home: "And now: out into the wide world again, wanderer!"

The Ghost Sonata

Strindberg's most enigmatic work, *The Ghost*[37] *Sonata,* is easier
to understand when one realizes that it was written at the same time as
The Burned House and has the same basic theme.[38] The difference between
the two plays is that in *The Burned House* only the Stranger was born
"without a veil over his eyes" and is able to see life and people as they
really are. In *The Ghost Sonata* almost all of the characters in the play
eventually acquire this faculty. The phantom supper, which gave the play
its first title, concludes with everyone unmasking everyone else. In *The
Burned House,* the Stranger describes how although he once admired his
family, especially his parents, he was compelled to unmask them once he
learned the truth: "I had to repaint their portraits, strip them naked, pull
them down, and get them out of my mind. It was horrible! Later, they
began to haunt me. The pieces of shattered images reassembled themselves,
but didn't fit together properly. They became a waxworks of monsters."[39]

We meet a similar "waxworks of monsters" in *The Ghost Sonata.*
But whereas in *The Burned House* the Stranger exults in his ability to see
through people, in *The Ghost Sonata* the gift is regarded as a tragic one.
Strindberg himself is the central character, the Student, who "is said to
have come into the world in the midst of bankruptcy proceedings," and
who cannot resist telling his beloved what he thinks of her, even when the
results may be disastrous.

Scenes and characters in the play are a mixture of the real and the
unreal. The first scene takes place in a city square, and in the background
is the façade of the house that the Student believes contains happy people.
He meets a dream-life figure, the Milk maid, who is invisible to the Student's supposed benefactor, the vampire-like old man Hummel. The second scene, inside the house, reveals how false an impression the façade
gave. Gathered for a "phantom supper" is a bizarre collection of people, the
strangest of whom is the "Mummy," a woman who is kept in a closet
and talks like a parrot. Among the revelations made during the supper is
that the Mummy was once Hummel's lover and is the mother of Hummel's
daughter, the beautiful, ethereal Young Lady.

The lyrical third and last scene takes place in the Hyacinth Room
of the house between the Young Lady and the Student, who loves her. He
woos her with a discourse on the mysterious symbolism of flowers, but her

death frustrates his efforts to possess her. For a time he thought he had entered paradise, and now his dream is destroyed. Earlier, he had seen a harp he wanted to play but could not because the instrument had lost its sound. Now, when the Young Lady dies, the strings begin to murmur, the room is filled with white light, and the Student is able to sing the praises of the liberator Death.

In a letter to Schering, Strindberg said that he "suffered as if in Kama-Loka (Scheol) during the writing" and wrote with the feeling "that these are my last sonatas."[40] *The Ghost Sonata* is a stronger and more harrowing expression of self-penetration and confession than many other of Strindberg's works because it portrays so clearly the anguish his pessimism caused him:

> Why should the most beautiful flowers be so poisonous, the *most* poisonous. This curse hangs over all creation, all life . . . Jesus Christ descended into Hell when He made His pilgrimage to earth—to this madhouse, this prison, this morgue we call earth. And the madmen killed Him when He tried to set them free, but the robber they released. The robber always gets the sympathy! Woe! Woe to us all. Saviour of the world, save us! We are perishing![41]

The core of this pessimism is black misanthropy. In *A Blue Book,* Strindberg contrasts human beings with "superterrestrially" beautiful nature. He admits that sometimes he has felt at ease in the company of others, but only for "two minutes at a time." Often at a party he would discover suddenly that the entire gathering appeared naked to him. He could see "the dirty linen through their clothes, their infirmities, and their unwashed feet, but worst of all . . . hear the thoughts behind their words."[42] His diary notations confirm that he frequently had such sensations at social occasions. An earlier attempt to portray these feelings in fiction was in Professor Stenkåhl's phantom supper in *Black Banners,* but there Strindberg was satisfied to compare the diners to loathsome wild animals, without overstepping the bounds of naturalistic technique. In *The Ghost Sonata,* he shows people as they are inside and lets them speak their innermost thoughts.

The transformations in *The Ghost Sonata* are for the most part from the real to the grotesque. In the first scene, Hummel tells the Student that a statue visible in a window of the house is the Colonel's wife as a young woman, and now the model sits "like a mummy" admiring it. In the second scene, she is actually called the Mummy.

Hummel, who unmasks all the guests and reveals their secrets, is himself unmasked and turns into a creature with a parrot-like voice. What begins as an ordinary tea supper, develops into a gathering of phantoms who stir occasionally or abruptly acquire the ability to speak, but only to express a longing for final annihilation: "God, if we were allowed to die! If *only* we could die!"

The Student recalls a parallel to this phantom supper and describes a social gathering at which his father raised his glass to give a toast: "Then something loosed the trigger, and in a long speech he stripped the whole company naked, one after the other, telling them of their treachery."[43] The guests rushed for the doors, his parents began to fight with each other, and his father was taken to a madhouse. (In *A Blue Book,* Strindberg tells the same story about a friend.[44])

As if to defend the grotesqueness of the situation, Strindberg said in a letter to Schering that every family had secrets to hide, although people were too proud to admit it and generally concealed their corruption. But he knew he was no longer depicting "complete (lower) reality," as in *Storm,* but a kind of higher reality where things were seen in their proper light. Seldom had Strindberg's prose taken on such a powerful lyrical ring as in the dialogue between the Student and the Young Lady in the final scene. It is the same atmosphere as in the scenes between Indra's Daughter and the Poet in *A Dream Play.* That play's theme of life's illusory appearance and death's liberating mission is the same one that the Student preaches in the conclusion of *The Ghost Sonata* when he sings the strange, sad verses about corruption in the Song of the Sun, while in the background Arnold Boecklin's painting "The Isle of the Dead" rises like a vision.

But before this, in the earlier conversation between the Student and the Young Lady concerning the spiritual life of flowers and the longing of earth to become heaven, they talk of life's sternest tests: of counting the wash, fixing the stove damper cord that was broken by the maid, drying glasses, and rinsing the water decanter. But despite all "the dirt of life," the Student is determined to get married. "Don't talk like that!--- You can never have me!" the Young Lady answers, but will not explain why. She accuses the fat Cook who appears in the doorway with a Japanese bottle in her hand of devouring her, of "devouring all of us." When the Student is overcome by a compulsion to expose the truth about everything, he seizes upon the following accusation:

> Why wouldn't you be my bride? Because at the very source of your life you are sick.---Now I can feel that vampire in the kitchen beginning to suck my blood. I believe she is one of those Lamias who suck the blood of children. It's always in the kitchen that the seed leaves of children are nipped, if it hasn't already happened in the bedroom.[45]

The sketches show that Strindberg originally thought of having the Young Lady suffer from cancer; the idea of having her drained, vampire-like by the Cook, first arose during his work on the play. At the time he was finishing the writing, household problems were creating a hell for him, and in both his diary and *A Blue Book* he describes the strange martyrdom he underwent:

> My servant left. The whole house was topsy-turvy. I had to change servants six times in forty days, one worse than the other. Finally I had to take care of myself, set the table and light the fire. I ate black swill out of a container; in short, I had to suffer everything bitter that life has to offer, without understanding the reason.[46]

When Strindberg sent the manuscript to his German translator, he was worried that Schering would exclude the scene in which the Cook is accused of substituting water that is colored with soya sauce for more nourishing gravies and soups. Apparently, Strindberg felt that he, too, was being cheated in the same way, for he wrote to Schering: "N.B.! Don't forget the soya bottle, the coloring of which has made me suffer now for thirteen days; was eating colored water."[47] The bottle is an undeniably comic element, but to Strindberg it signified something of the deepest seriousness. The disgust he felt for life during his later years was closely associated with his worries over food and household problems. His sufferings are compared to the ordeals of Job and Hezekial, and he could not resist finding a place for them in the picture of human wretchedness he was attempting to portray in *The Ghost Sonata* and later in *The Pelican*.

There is probably no work that is as revealing of the ways in which its creator experienced life as *The Ghost Sonata:* the almost imperceptible transitions from reality to dream, and the abrupt alternations between the sublime and the grotesque, the significant and the trivial. It also contains some of the figures who appear most frequently in his gallery of characters.

The fictional ancestor of the credulous young student who is gradually forced to see life in its true light is Arvid Falk: at a crucial moment we hear him express the familiar Strindbergian suspicion that something is rotting between the floorboards. In old man Hummel we have the male vampire who "steals people." He is revealed as a former valet who was a "sponger" in the pantry and who compelled the family he worked for to eat his warmed-over leavings and take their bouillon diluted with water. His female counterpart is the Cook, with her bottle of colored water. Then, there is the recently deceased Consul whose vanity is such that he rises from the dead and goes out into the street in his winding-sheet in order to see whether the flag has been lowered to half-mast in his honor: "He'll probably count all the wreaths and check the visiting cards.---Pity the person whose name is missing!"[48] The Colonel, who uses a false title and a false noble name and wears a wig and false teeth, is also a former valet and "sponger." And the Young Lady is another example of a creature who has "lost the desire to live, without knowing why.---She withered in this air, so heavy with crime, deception, and falsehood."[49] We met this entire cast of characters earlier in Strindberg's writings, and yet they seem new and surprising.

Much in the play—certainly more than we know—was derived from a reality that was familiar and commonplace to Strindberg: "a mosaic from the lives of others and from my own," as he wrote to Schering.[50] But we seem lost in a tangle of unexplained mysteries, as if we were among creatures who do not belong on our earth. *The Ghost Sonata* appears to be a fantasy of terror in which people scream out brutal truths. Strindberg, however, had a different view and told Schering that in the play "one lives in a world of suggestion, where people talk in half-tones, mutedly, because they are ashamed to be human beings."[51] It is difficult to find muted tones in *The Ghost Sonata,* but in spite of the misanthropy, a note of compassion emerges for the inhabitants of "this world of illusion, guilt, suffering, and death; this world of eternal change, disappointment, and pain."[52]

The Pelican

In April, 1907, Strindberg tried to write a play, *Toteninsel (Isle of the Dead),* inspired by the same Boecklin painting used at the conclusion of *The Ghost Sonata.* The sketchy fragment that remains[53] depicts how a dead teacher arrives in the spirit world but continues to believe that he is on earth and is tormented by his unpaid bills, his uncorrected exercise books, and his wife's bad cooking. Then Strindberg lost interest, "as if I lost interest in life and have a foreboding of the end,"[54] and chose instead to portray the family the deceased teacher left behind. This was the genesis of *The Pelican,* which, because of its explosive force and vivid characterization became the most frequently performed of the Chamber Plays.

On many points *The Pelican* is reminiscent of the dramas of the naturalistic period: the cast is small and the action is drastically simplified and performed in a single setting. Strindberg indicated in the manuscript that it could be performed as a long one-act play. The cast includes only five characters—mother, son, daughter, daughter's husband, and cook— and the setting is a living room. The theme as well—"the false mother"— is reminiscent of a pair of one-act plays from the beginning of the 1890's: *Facing Death* and *Mother Love.* The title, *The Pelican,* refers to the fact that the inhuman Mother who tormented her husband to death and allows her children to freeze and go hungry, believes she is self-sacrificing and compares herself to the pelican who gives its blood to its children.

Although there are no supernatural details in the play, *The Pelican* has a stronger nightmare mood than any of the earlier plays. The wind howls like a lost soul in the room, and papers fly off the table. Everything stirs up the Mother's conscience. The red chaise lounge in which her husband died seems to her to be a bloody slaughtering-block. A rocking chair, set in motion by the wind, frightens her: "That chair drives me crazy! Whenever he rocked in it, the sound was like two chopping knives hacking away—chopping at my heart."[55] And when her son drunkenly bellows in the next room, she thinks she hears her dead husband in the garden crying out the sense of loss he feels for his wife and children: "It's him! In the tobacco garden! Isn't he dead? What shall I do? Where shall I go?"[56]

The Mother is one of those people Strindberg describes in *A Blue Book* as "so lethargic that they never wake up, and so unintelligent that they cannot realize how evil they are."[57] She has become as fat as a toad by drinking all the gravy and nutritive juices from the family's meat dishes and the cream from the milk, but she is convinced that she is young and enchanting. "Poor Mama," says the Daughter, "you're still walking in your sleep, as we all did. Won't you ever wake up? Don't you see how people laugh at you?[58] For a moment the Mother comes to her senses in the face of the Son's violent reproaches: "Yes, I'm waking up, as if out of a long, long sleep! It's terrible! Why didn't someone wake me up before?"[59] But she soon returns to her self-delusion.

The conclusion of *The Pelican* is one of the most psychologically baffling passages in all of Strindberg's works. A letter left behind by the father reveals the full extent of the Mother's vampire crimes. The half-intoxicated Son finds no way out but to set fire to the house, and the Mother throws herself off the balcony. Brother and sister die in each other's arms in the flames, but during their death struggle they experience beautiful hallucinations in which they ecstatically relive their childhood memories and finish by missing "poor Mama, who was evil, so evil."

The play's naturalistic style makes the references to food and eating more disturbing than similar references in *The Ghost Sonata* which seemed appropriate among the other grotesque elements. The children quiver with righteous indignation when they remember how their mother robbed them of nourishment, and their greatest triumph is when they serve her the porridge and skim milk she used to prepare for them and the dog. The play has numerous absurd situations and speeches, but it also has a wild, theatrical verve, reminiscent of *The Dance of Death*.

The Black Glove

The hero of *Storm* says that he is through with the world and people and has "already begun to pack for the journey." *The Burned House* also has a settling of accounts, *The Ghost Sonata* culminates in a vision of "The Isle of the Dead," and the fire in *The Pelican* is a kind of *Ragnarök* (for a time Strindberg considered the title *Purgatory—Skärseld*). A similar mood of finality is expressed in a more placid way in the Chamber Play *The Black Glove*, written a year after the others.

The main plot of *The Black Glove*, originally intended as a Christmas play for the Intimate Theatre,[60] was derived from the story "The Pintorpa Wife's Christmas Eve"[61] that Strindberg published the same year in a Christmas magazine. But in order to make it more suitable for children, Strindberg centered most of the action on a Christmas Brownie and a Christmas Angel. As in the story, the Wife is frightened into repentance for being mean to her husband. The most interesting character, however, is one who did not appear in the story: the Wife's father, an eighty-year-old taxidermist who is totally occupied with trying to find a solution to the riddle of the world. The old man has some of Strindberg's characteristics, and his vigorous, defiant verse speeches contrast with the cloying style of the play.

Like Strindberg in his final years, the Taxidermist is resentful toward life. The old man has worked for sixty years on a theory for the riddle, and when his theory is easily demolished by the Brownie, he wants to die. The Brownie advises him to reconcile himself with existence, but he refuses:

> Reconciled?---To be bound once again to the stake?
> No, never be reconciled! Otherwise you can never leave—
> "Join the crowd and have one for the road!"
> "Oh, stay a little longer!"---And so you remain—
> No, board your mount, break off the battle
> and wrench yourself free! You'll have no longing to go back![62]

But the Brownie brings out a bridal crown and a white veil to remind the old man of the life he abandoned to pursue the coldness of thought; music plays, and the Taxidermist is plunged into bittersweet memories:

> Ah! What fragances! Is the clover in bloom?
> In rosy May, when the apple trees blossomed,
> the lilacs rocked their spires to the West Wind
> and newly-ploughed garden land, just recently white
> with snow, stretched its black garb
> over seeds that lay buried and ready to grow.[63]

In his imagination he sees a white farmhouse with green shutters and, in a room deep within, "the most beautiful thing in life"—a young mother dressing her child:

> Music! Those melodies from younger
>   days,
> half-forgotten, emerge again—
> The little stream gliding by under alders,
> a boat, midsummer garlands, strawberry baskets,
> and fresh pike, sparkling beside you.[64]

(The same nostalgic visions would loom before the Hunter in *The Great Highway*.)

Strindberg and Problems of Staging

Strindberg's involvement with the Intimate Theatre gave him an interest in stage production that he pursued with an unselfishness that was not typical of him. He was interested in everything, from the acting to insignificant details of costuming and stage properties. Since personal contacts made him uncomfortable, he generally transmitted his character analyses and instructions in writing to the actors. He also wrote a series of essays for the ensemble of the Intimate Theatre; they were published during 1908 and 1909 and later collected in one volume under the title *Open Letters to the Intimate Theatre.* Most of the essays deal with Shakespeare's plays, and one is about Goethe's *Faust,* but there are also several on his own plays, and in virtually all of them, regardless of the subject, he touches upon his own attitude toward drama and his conception of how it ought to be presented.

Strindberg built upon his experiences as a novice actor. In the autobiography there is a memorable account of how as a supernumerary at the Royal Dramatic Theatre he watched a rehearsal of Bjørnson's *Maria Stuart* from backstage. Although the actors were in street dress—the men in hats and overcoats and the ladies in coats and muffs—as they stood about the nail-scarred stage floor in front of gray linen backdrops, when the play began with the Puritans calling down woe upon the corruption of the court, "the effect was moving, and he felt how it took hold of him."[65] He learned a valuable lesson: that the theatre could do without scenery and costumes, that it lived through "the spoken word." "One can play a scene in darkness and enjoy it, as long as it is spoken well."[66] His preference for simplicity in staging was not new: in the 1880's he had said that a table and two chairs were the only set pieces required to produce his naturalistic dramas. And in a letter to August Falck in March, 1908, he described his "ideal" as: "A table and two chairs!"[67]

How then did Strindberg help provoke a revolution in modern European stage design? It was because he wrote his most original dramas during a time when he had no direct contact with the theatre or theatre people—the period in Lund and the first years after his return to Stockholm. Unhampered by all practical considerations, he created the fantastic images that modern directors have tried to come to grips with as best they could. For the dramas he wrote in Lund he had in mind the kind of setting he was used to seeing in his youth, which had slight pretensions to creating an illusion. One can take *Advent* as an example, with its rattling handcuffs, a twig dancing in the air, and a *"changement à vue"* that Strindberg thought of accomplishing by means of trap doors and collapsible settings. After his return to Stockholm he became superficially acquainted with the stage machinery of the new century and put it to a hard test.

But despite the increased demands that Strindberg's later dramas placed on theatrical facilities, he retained his Spartan preferences. This is evident in the stage directions for *A Dream Play* in which scene changes are to be made by changing the backdrops, while the wings that remain in place throughout the play are to be "stylized wall paintings, at once architecture and landscape." To achieve such an effect was not easy, and Strindberg discovered during production that "the entire performance became 'a phenomenon of materialization' instead of the intended opposite (dematerialization)."[68]

Strindberg wrote his Chamber Plays before the opening of the tiny Intimate Theatre, and therefore made no provisions at all for its limited stage space. It turned out that the "construction activities" necessary on stage during performances caused long intermissions and ruined the intended effect. His awareness of contemporary German attempts to present Shakespeare's plays without scene changes led him to demand a stage virtually devoid of scenery:

> The spoken word is of course the main thing and if Shakespeare's highly sophisticated contemporaries could do without scenery, then we too should be able to imagine partitions, walls, and trees. . . . And if actors can pretend to be kings and queens, then we should certainly be able to pretend that what we have before us is a forest or a room in a castle. Everything is pretense on the stage.[69]

"Pretense" is the watchword of Strindberg's stage directions. Otherwise one reverts to "realism and naturalism which are things of the past."[70] For a projected production of *A Dream Play* at the Intimate Theatre, he considered as sufficient one backcloth which would remain in place throughout the performance. A few simple stage properties placed on a railing could suggest the locality: several shells, the sea; a couple of cypresses, Italy; a board with psalm numbers, a church; and so forth. But later he feared that even these symbols might lead to a "stumbling into reality again and into the baroque."[71]

The Great Highway, his last play, was written for an extremely simplified and stylized staging system using symbolic stage properties: for example, a signpost wih two arms, one pointing upward and the other down, represents the Alps, and two windmills, the plain. At this point he was so obsessed by his idea that everything on the stage was "pretense" that in the introduction to *Abu Casem's Slippers* he wrote: "Abu Casem sits in his shop and pretends to smoke."

It should be emphasized, however, that Strindberg's striving for simplified settings was not prompted merely by consideration for the Intimate Theatre's modest resources. It was in keeping with his earlier tastes and his newly adopted spirituality: "The image in the poet's imagination is profaned when it is committed to paper, and in a way the written drama is profaned through performance."[72] The magnificent descriptive passages about nature in *The Great Highway* perhaps would not have been written if Strindberg had not wanted to compensate for the austerity of the stage pictures. He pointed out that because Shakespeare did not have scenery at his disposal he was compelled to paint "portraits of nature and other valuable pictures in words."[73]

Strindberg and Dramatic Form

On a page of manuscript written around the turn of the century, Strindberg proposed a universally applicable formula for dramatic composition:

> An effective drama
> ought to operate through suggestion,
> contain a secret which the spectator learns either in the beginning or
>   toward the end,*
> an outburst of feeling, wrath, indignation,
> a turning point *(revirement),* a reversal.
> a surprise, well-prepared,
> a discovery,
> a punishment (Nemesis), a humiliation,
> a deliberate conclusion, either with or without atonement.
> A *quidproquo,* a parallelism.

> *If the spectator knows the secret and the characters do not, then he can enjoy their game of blindman's bluff. If the spectator does not know the secret, his curiosity is provoked and he is kept interested.

Of these ingredients, the "outburst" and the "humiliation" are probably the ones found most often in Strindberg's drama. And he clearly showed his preference for "parallelisms," that is, the repetition of similar situations with altered significance: "This is my forte!" he wrote in *Open Letters*.[74] The other devices occur more infrequently, for although Strindberg regarded his dramas as products of a refined technique and used such terminology as "counterpoint" and "putting themes into the form of fugues," he was by no means unaware that he achieved his greatest triumphs when he wrote without an excessive dedication to logical coherence.

It is indicative that both in *Easter* and *The Burned House* he refused to eliminate undeveloped themes that were called to his attention by his German translator. "The incomplete (abortive) intentions must stand as they are, because they give a natural fidelity to the depiction of life, since life is full of stranded plans, passing fancies, and projects which serve to fill out conversation yet still constitute sources of energy."[75] This is in complete agreement with what he wrote to the same correspondent on May 13, 1902, after completing *A Dream Play:* "A work of art should be a little untidy, as imperfect as a work of nature in which not a single crystal is free of fault, not a single plant is without a miscarried leaf." He admired Shakespeare's "slovenly" composition and felt that Schiller could proceed no further than a draft of *Demetrius* because he had lost the joy of creation by dissipating it on detail work. "He used it up ahead of time. It happened to me once," Strindberg explained.[76] The role of chance in artistic creation interested him greatly; and during the Inferno Crisis he wrote an essay about it. It was because of his reliance on the gusts of inspiration that Strindberg came to have such a liberating influence on modern drama, which was in the process of petrifying into rigid forms.

Notes to Chapter Twenty-one

1. The Intimate Theatre was in operation from November, 1907, to December, 1910. For more information regarding the theatre, *see* Falck's *Fem år med Strindberg.*
2. The test of fire to which the letter refers was August Falck's Swedish première of *Miss Julie* at Lund in September, 1906.
3. Adolf Paul, *Min Strindbergsbok* (1930), p. 178.
4. *SS:*L, p. 11.
5. Letter to Schering, March 29, 1907.
6. *SS:*L, p. 284.
7. *SS:*XLV, p. 114.
8. *Ibid.,* p. 157.
9. *SS:*L, p. 291.
10. *SS:*XLV, p. 246.
11. *Ibid.,* p. 138.
12. *SS:*L, p. 12.
13. *SS:*XLV, p. 47.
14. She stayed for a time in Denmark and in the mountain resort of Åre in western Sweden.
15. Literally, the Little One, Strindberg's pet name for his daughter Anne-Marie.—Translator
16. *Brev till Harriet Bosse,* p. 282.
17. *SS:*XLV, pp. 10-11.
18. *Ibid.,* p. 74.
19. *Ibid.,* p. 39.
20. *Ibid.,* p. 18.
21. *Ibid.,* p. 12.
22. *Ibid.,* p. 74.
23. *Ibid.,* p. 39.
24. Letter to Bonniers, January 28, 1909.
25. Falck, p. 84. Falck states that it was 14 Norrtulls Street that burned down, but this Strindberg house had been razed to make way for the Public Orphanage in the 1880's. Falck's statement that the site was "behind the Hamburger Brewery" indicates that the building referred to was probably number 12, where the Strindberg family lived on several occasions. In the later descriptions of his childhood, Strindberg himself confused the two houses.
26. *SS:*LIV, p. 465.

27. *SS:*XLV, pp. 105-6.
28. *Ibid.,* p. 99.
29. *SS:*LIV, pp. 466-67.
30. *Ibid.,* p. 467.
31. *SS:*XLV, p. 107.
32. *Ibid.,* p. 118.
33. *Ibid.,* p. 97.
34. Falck, pp. 90-91.
35. *SS:*XLV, pp. 94-95.
36. *Ibid.,* p. 145.
37. Although the word *phantom* is perhaps more appropriately sugges-
    tive than *ghost,* I have retained the title by which the play is best
    known.—Translator
38. Strindberg noted in his diary on March 6, 1907, that he was writing
    The Burned House, and on March 8 that he had finished his third
    Chamber Play, *The Phantom Supper (Spöksupén).* August Falck
    also states that Strindberg wrote *The Burned House* at the same
    time as he planned and executed *The Ghost Sonata* (Falck, p. 91).
39. *SS:*XLV, p. 102.
40. The drama in manuscript bears the subtitle *Kama-Loka,* a term used
    by theosophists (*Scheol* is another) to signify Hades. Strindberg's
    interpretation was that it referred to our own earthly inferno.
41. *SS:*XLV, pp. 209-10.
42. *SS:*XLVI, p. 62.
43. *SS:*XLV, p. 208.
44. *SS:*XLVI, pp. 62-63.
45. *SS:*XLV, p. 209.
46. *SS:*XLVI, p. 405.
47. April 7, 1907.
48. *SS:*XLV, p. 166.
49. *Ibid.,* p. 191.
50. Old man Hummel, according to August Falck, was modeled after a
    well-known Stockholm wholesaler whose habit of ostentatiously
    distributing charities annoyed Strindberg during his morning
    promenades.
51. April 26, 1907.
52. *SS:*XLV, p. 211.
53. *SOS:*I, pp. 293-310 [*See* Richard B. Vowles's article and translation,
    "Strindberg's *The Isle of the Dead,*" *Modern Drama,* V (Decem-
    ber, 1962), pp. 366-78.—Translator]

54. Letter to Schering, April 26, 1907.
55. *SS:*XLV, p. 268.
56. *Ibid.,* p. 271.
57. *SS:*XLVI, p. 61.
58. *SS:*XLV, p. 274.
59. *Ibid.,* p. 269.
60. Several months earlier Strindberg had written the trifling Arabian nights play *Abu Casem's Slippers* for the same purpose.
61. *See* p. 432.
62. *SS:*XLV, p. 320.
63. *Ibid.,* p. 322.
64. *Ibid.*
65. *SS:*XVIII, pp. 333 ff.
66. *SS:*L, p. 17.
67. Falck, p. 192.
68. *SS:*L, p. 289.
69. *Ibid.,* p. 70.
70. Falck, p. 208.
71. *Ibid.,* p. 275.
72. *SS:*L, p. 220.
73. *Ibid.,* p. 196.
74. *Ibid.,* p. 53.
75. Letter to Schering, April 24, 1907. Cf. *SS:*L, p. 171.
76. Letter to Schering, January 18, 1902.

Chapter Twenty-two

THE FINAL YEARS

The publication of *Black Banners* in 1907, three years after it was written, was a turning point in Strindberg's life. He had just achieved success at The Swedish Theatre (Svenska teatern) with *A Dream Play* and was waiting impatiently for the Intimate Theatre to open with the Chamber Plays. His reputation abroad was growing, and in Sweden his later works were attracting more and more attention. Even his anger toward Geijerstam had abated, since the two men had had no contact with one another for several years. (On October 28, 1906, Strindberg noted in his diary that he was reading Geijerstam's *The Forest and the Sea* [*Skogen och sjön*] and almost felt reconciled with him.)

While going through the proofs for *Black Banners* in April, 1907, Strindberg felt uneasy about the book and wondered "whether it was an outrage and ought to be suppressed." He resorted to his habit of opening the Bible at random for advice "and happened upon the Book of Jonah in which the prophet is compelled to prophesy even though he tries to hide [to escape the Lord's command]. This comforted me.—But it is a horrible book."[1] While reading the final proof he noted in his diary: "Now it remains to drain the final cup,"[2] a feeling that recalls his state of mind prior to the publication of *The New Kingdom*. In the conclusion of the first part of *A Blue Book*, Strindberg tries to indicate that after the publication of Black Banners things went better for him than they had before, "and I gained new and better friends than those I lost."[3] But in a letter to Schering several weeks after the novel was published he said: "With *Black Banners* I stand alone on a rock in the sea, with a starry sky above me and only my conscience for company. I no longer have friends, or wife, and even my last child has been stolen from me."[4]

When Harriet Bosse remarried in the summer of 1908 Strindberg believed the event was part of the persecution campaign waged against him by Young Sweden, since he had attacked them in *Black Banners*. He even thought that friends and relatives were conspiring to rob him of his wife and child. As a result, his contacts with the outside world became more limited. When in July, 1908, he left 40 Karla Way and moved into the house on Drottning Street that he christened The Blue Tower, he began a secluded life interrupted only by infrequent visits; it was in this house that he died on May 14, 1912.

Most of the descriptions we have of Strindberg from these years are the same: a recluse, shy of people, who cautiously barricaded himself behind a safety lock and door chain and admitted only those who identified themselves with special knocks or whom he recognized through the opening in his mail slot. People who crossed his path during his morning promenades were lucky if they did not attract his attention. Fanny Falkner, the young actress who was the object of his last, fleeting dream of love, relates that he said he deliberately stepped on the heels of a stranger to punish her for having stared at him. In *A Blue Book* he says that being famous makes life unbearable for a sensitive person. "Finally, it becomes impossible for him to go out because people's glances touch him, go through his skin, and poke at his heart."[5]

Outwardly, Strindberg's life was uneventful, but he never lost his curiosity about the world. From his Blue Tower he issued ukases and bulls of excommunication concerning everything that came within his range of observation. Since his pronouncements were generally sternly condemnatory, he appeared to many of his contemporaries to be a reactionary crank, but this was not the case. He had lost the ability to deal ironically with hypocrisy; gone was the spirit of mischief that had earlier helped him cope with reverses. Misanthropy had burrowed so deeply into his nature that he was no longer cynically amused by people's pettiness and shabbiness. There are flashes of bitter humor in his works as late as *The Scapegoat* (1906), but not afterward.

Beneath his loathing for existence we detect more clearly than ever before his dissatisfaction with himself. As a rule every self-accusation was followed by an expression of self-defense, because he was desperately afraid that his contemporaries would take advantage of the weak spots he had exposed. But on the whole, he viewed himself more critically, and characteristics that he had once regarded as virtues he now thought of as failings. The stern mask of the elderly Strindberg concealed a greater insecurity than he had felt in his younger days. He was capable of being more hardhearted than before, especially when he thought he was acting upon a higher exhortation, but most of the time he was gentler. His judgments might be more brusque, but when he gave himself time to think through a problem, the results could be more penetrating and level-headed.[6]

On one point, however, Strindberg remained uncompromising: his hostility toward "the black banners," the survivors of the Young Sweden group. The nearly unanimous public disapproval of *Black Banners* had convinced him that he was carrying on a holy crusade against the agents of evil. Both in his final contributions to belles-lettres and in *A Blue Book* he continued his battle against Geijerstam, even after the latter's death in 1909. Anyone who might be suspected of belonging to Geijerstam's coterie or who objected to Strindberg's actions became a target for his hatred. Even his attack on the literature of the 1890's in *Talks to the Swedish Nation* was primarily a continuation of the campaign against Young Sweden.

A Blue Book

The work Strindberg placed highest among the products of his last years was the four-volume *A Blue Book,* a collection of short random essays, many less than a page in length. He began accumulating material during the last half of 1906 and continued to do so for the remainder of his life. The first part came out in 1907, and the fourth and final part was published posthumously as *An Extra Blue Book (En extra blå bok)* in the fall of 1912.

Strindberg said that the idea for *A Blue Book* came from a plan Goethe once had to write a *"breviarium universale,* or edifying guide for confessors of all religions." Originally, Strindberg's book was to contain a religious adage for every day in the year, with accompanying comments. But a draft for the work with the title "Breviarium, A Word of Wisdom for Every Day in the Year by Johannes Damascenus"[7] consists only partially of adages, mostly derived from the Bible. During the writing, the plan was altered to include "purely wordly wisdom about people," but the items in the original manuscript of the first volume of *A Blue Book* are still designated for different days of the year. They are in the form of conversations between Johannes Damascenus—a pseudonym Strindberg borrowed from a medieval theologian—and his teacher who is well versed in Swedenborg, to whom the work is dedicated. (One of Strindberg's models was obviously Swedenborg's *Diarium Spirituale:* in a letter to Schering on November 7, 1906, he referred to *A Blue Book* as *Diarium.*)

The first part of *A Blue Book* appeared in September, 1907, only a few months after *Black Banners* was published and during the time that the controversy over the novel was still occupying the press. Strindberg therefore called it *"A Blue Book* Delivered to the Authorities and Constituting a Commentary on *Black Banners."* Although the same complete title was used for the later volumes, the polemic against "the black banners," which plays a prominent role in the first volume, diminishes in importance in the succeeding ones. In the later volumes he also stopped using the dialogue form and discontinued the attempt to keep terminology consistent, such as using The Abode of Anguish (Kvalhem) for the earth, Tophet[6] for Stockholm, Dung Droppings (Bönorna) or Philistines for contemporary atheists, the Dung Master for the Devil, and so forth. Furthermore, the barbarous expressions borrowed from the German race theorist Jörgen Lanz-Liebenfels—"ape-lings," "baboons," "ape-marshalls," etc. —appear less and less frequently in the later parts.

Strindberg probably patterned *A Blue Book* on the cloister chapters in *Black Banners:* the opening observations in *A Blue Book* are mostly religious in nature. Soon, however, he joined battle with contemporary science, which in his opinion was the foremost obstacle to the religious renaissance he tried to further. *A Blue Book,* therefore, became a rather haphazard kind of encyclopedia in which all branches of science were subjected to harsh criticism and all current problems aired. Polemical attacks against "decadent science" are interspersed among short edifying observations and essays in which Strindberg relates episodes from his life or engages in rather bloody settlings of accounts with relatives and friends, both alive and dead. It need scarcely be added that prominence is given to intimate pictures of his married life and bitter comments on the woman question.

Both in letters to Schering and in the preface to *The Author,* the fourth part of *The Son of a Servant,* Strindberg called *A Blue Book* "my life's synthesis." The description may seem strange since it is applied to a work without a discernible structure—a series of rambling meditations jotted down as they occurred to him. But for this very reason they are exceptionally vivid, and a close study of *A Blue Book* provides an insight into Strindberg's temperament and outlook that few of his later works can offer. To be sure, there is an abundance of absurd scientific hypotheses in the book, as well as outrageous personal attacks on easily recognizable contemporaries. Nevertheless, one cannot help being impressed by Strindberg's sharp psychological insights, not only concerning other people but especially himself. The wisdom and resignation of old age are also evident in *A Blue Book*. And although Strindberg took few pains with form, several of the essays are exquisite short prose poems.

In the complex apparent tangle of subjects that runs through the book, the easiest thread to follow is Strindberg's negative attitude toward science. Ever since his youth he had distrusted all knowledge and research that bore the stamp of authority and official acceptance, and his distrust was aggravated when his own contributions to natural science during the 1890's were ridiculed. In one of the essays from *A Blue Book* he concludes that X-rays and radium are hoaxes: "Radium does not exist! And yet it wins the Nobel Prize, costs 50,000 marks per gram and 400 kroner per gram in duty."[9]

For him, modern science was a natural enemy of religion. At the beginning of the Inferno Crisis he had responded affirmatively to the French battle cry about "the bankruptcy of science," and an essay with this title appears in *A Blue Book;* in it Strindberg says that the history of science demonstrates "the ineffectuality of human knowledge. . . . Christ never talked about science [or scholarship] other than when He spoke of the follies of the Pharisees and the interpreters of the Scriptures. If He had considered astronomy and physics important, He would certainly have interpreted their secrets, but He avoided doing so."[10]

Even before the Inferno Crisis Strindberg opposed the scientific belief in the laws of nature. In a letter to his botanist friend in Lund, Bengt Lidforss, on March 15, 1891, he said, "I have always associated laws with lawgivers, and I do not believe in laws in nature except in a limited sense."[11] At that time, Strindberg's reluctance to acknowledge the existence of a lawgiver caused him to believe in a "great chaos." Now, in *A Blue Book*, he attacks "the laws" for precisely the opposite reason. They are attempts to avoid the acceptance of a God or at best make Him subject to laws governing all phenomena. "When people see the same set of circumstances occurring regularly under prescribed conditions, they think they have discovered 'a law,' whereas I think I have discerned an instance of Divine judgement, implying the existence of a tribunal whose decisions we can see, but whose composition and location we can only surmise."[12]

Strindberg also finds scientific "laws" in the humanities. He is disturbed that philology had entered into the service of "the Dung Master" and tried "to demonstrate the non-existence of God by means of immanent self-enacted phonetic laws."[13] But it was primarily the natural sciences and especially biology that aroused his ire: "Lowest on the scale of development at present are the zoologists, since they deal with unsubstantiated facts, false inferences, inadequate materials, and an absolutely incomprehensible logic."[14]

Strindberg had old positions to defend here; he had ridiculed Darwinism as early as *Somnambulist Nights*—a feat about which he never ceased to boast. And it was against the theory of evolution that he now directed his sharpest attacks. He finds gaps in the description of the continuity of evolution in Ernst Haeckel's *Natural History of Creation (Natürliche Schöpfungsgeschichte)* and calls it "unnatural, irrational, and unscientific rubbish." Nothing seems as degrading to Strindberg as the belief that men are descendants of apes. He finds it more plausible that apes originated "from wretched human beings, escaped convicts, Robinson Crusoe's shipwrecked and cast ashore on islands in the sea."[15]

As Strindberg saw it, Darwinism had developed into a theology whose first article of faith read: "The different forms of plants and animals were not created." He reproaches the biologists for having neglected the fact that the word "create" implies "shaped by hand."[16] For support, Strindberg cites Darwin who acknowledged his belief in a Creator and whose theory of the origin of life was in accord with the Book of Genesis. "This is different from the ape-ling theory advanced by his successors, which states that [life] . . . came into being spontaneously."[17]

The concept that the species were "shaped by hand" originated with Strindberg. During the Inferno Crisis he loved to wander in the Jardin des Plantes where he discovered the Creator: "that great Artist who develops as He creates, makes rough drafts and casts them aside, takes up abortive ideas anew, perfects and multiplies primitive forms. Most certainly, everything is shaped by His hand."[18] This is the same story of creation that he contrasts with Haeckel's in *A Blue Book*. God has proceeded in the manner of a spontaneously creative artist:

> Out of formless material He begins testing and discarding simple sketches (the extinct species); invents new and better ones, amusing Himself (not us) with improvisations, forestalling and repeating; getting an entirely new idea, unrestrainedly and omnipotently; deriving a new form from a lower one that existed earlier in the cosmic context.[19]

In the essay "The Beauty and Symbolism of the Human Body" ("Manniskokroppens skönhet och symbolik") he discusses the muscles and finds that they constitute "an eternally constant proof that they did not create themselves or arise, but that they were shaped by hand, the products of a Mechanic, a Surgical Instrument-Maker, a Truss-Maker, and a mighty Artist."[20] Throughout *A Blue Book* is the recurrent assertion that all the famous mountain formations—Fingal's Cave, Tempel Mountain in Spitsbergen, the Rocky Mountains, and even the Halle and Hunne Mountains[21]—were fashioned "by living hands."[22] And in an essay dealing with mysterious numerical repetitions and correspondence in nature, he notes that the base of the Cheops pyramid is 365 sacred cubits, reflecting the 365 days of the year. Everywhere he detects traces of the Master Builder "who shaped the world in numbers and measurements."[23]

Inasmuch as Strindberg held this concept of God as a creative and continually evolving artist following His whims, he finds all talk of adherence to the laws of nature to be blasphemous. He condemns anything and everything in which a living nature does not have a role to play. The laws of logic are completely worthless and have interest only as an intellectual game. And mathematics, which deals with "false definitions, unproven axioms," and irrational numbers "must of course culminate in madness."[24]

It is hardly worthwhile to analyze all Strindberg's anathemas against the different sciences. His skepticism toward them is basic and universal and begins with a rejection of the proposition that two times two is four. He is convinced that all modern scientists, like the majority of the ancients who are still accorded recognition, belong to "a learned Camorra." To combat the "Camorra," he cites as references either an obsolete and forgotten old study or a new work regarded as of dubious value by orthodox scholars. Sometimes he makes exceptions among members of the "guild," such as in the case of the universally respected Linnaeus, his

long-time favorite, who fulfills his requirement that the scientist see the
Creator's hand in everything in nature. In an analysis of Linnaeus's system-
atization of the sexes, he finds that the great botanist was closer to
"Swedenborg than people believe."[25]

Strindberg is usually satisfied to quote the Bible or Swedenborg
as his authority.[26] The theory of the Fall is valuable, says Strindberg, because it helps to explain the struggle that prevails in nature. And botany,
which deteriorated into a worthless science after it abandoned horticul-
ture, could be rehabilitated if, under the guidance of Swedenborg's theory
of correspondence, it drew its conclusions about the inner natures of
flowers on the basis of their outer forms. The old term *signatura rerum*
occurs often in Strindberg's botanical speculations. Flowers are perhaps
"corpses that arose from corruption and are living a nirvana existence, a
painless, unconscious dream life."[27]

If Strindberg's conception of nature has something of a romantic,
medieval flavor, it is because after the Inferno Crisis he was an enthusiastic admirer of the Middle Ages— a time of blossoming for science, religion, and art. According to him, one of the most serious wrongs committed
by historians was to have failed to recognize this and to have glorified
the Renaissance, whose "neo-heathenism" Strindberg found comparable
to that of the turn of the century. He felt that in Sweden this modern paganism was foreshadowed by Viktor Rydberg's criticism of the Bible in
The Teachings of the Bible about Christ (Bibelns lära om Kristus—1862)
and his glorification of a moribund antiquity in the novel *The Last Athenian* (1859). He also believed that a libertine and permissive morality was
as dominant in the Renaissance as in his own day.

Since all science was worthless, Strindberg asks why the state
should maintain "these armies of guessers and diviners."[28] Peasants can
predict more accurately than weather bureaus, and it is an illusion that
reaping and threshing machines are worksavers. People sleep away the
time they earlier used threshing with a flail and this is a loss of energy and
therefore of capital. "This is Rousseau!---Yes, it's Rousseau!"[29] In thus
calling science to account, Strindberg is led back again to Rousseau:

> Life has become so troublesome, and half the day is wasted on trivia:
> unnecessary visits, telephone calls, letters about nothing at all, reading
> newspapers, and above all, preparations to use the toilet, which used to
> involve an attractive looking cloak and a rope and have now "advanced"

to a cumbersome harness of buttons, loops, hooks, laces, straps, strings, pins, buckles, and clasps. This is civilization in miniature—with all its time-consuming nuisances, of which the greatest portion is useless nonsense. The man who lives in the country and cultivates the soil has no need of art, science, or literature. Churches can be found everywhere, but only in the cities are there museums, theatres, bookstores, and bars. Whether or not they are necessary is another question. This is Rousseau![30]

The fundamental principles of the religion for whose benefit Strindberg wishes to sacrifice all science and culture are set forth in a cate-chistic form and are almost unchanged from the Inferno period. But the main thing for Strindberg is no longer *what* one believes, but *that* one believes. He has no patience with those who deny God. "All atheists are rogues, and all rogues are atheists." *A Blue Book* begins with a statement of Euclid's twelfth axiom and the speculation: "If this is a self-evident proposition, which neither can nor needs to be proved, then how much clearer is not the axiom about the existence of God!" To dispute it is a sign of mental aberration, and to say that one does not believe in a deity is to admit to being "a godless dog, a perverse ape-ling, an unprincipled swindler and thief from whom people flee and whom detectives ought to watch."[31] Similar statements appear time and again, often illustrated by stories of how badly things go for the godless and what tribulations Strindberg himself had to endure during his atheistic period.

When it comes to expressing a preference for a particular sect, however, Strindberg is very open-minded and eclectic. He finds no real difference between Protestantism and Catholicism; the most practical course of action is to retain one's childhood faith. He has scant interest in dogmatic disputes and is in agreement with Luther who supposedly ad-vised a skeptical disciple to "go out and get respectably drunk instead of quarreling over the doctrine of justification by faith."[32]

Strindberg was an uncompromising enemy of Biblical criticism: it constantly missed the mark and in any case was completely nullified by Swedenborg's allegorical interpretation. For the most part, Strindberg condemns all scientific investigation of religion. "All prying into religion is only an indication of denial and doubt, masquerading as 'love of truth.'"[33] The first requisite for believing is to accept everything without reservation. If one wishes to convert to Christianity, "then one must ac-cept it all: the impure, the long and the short, the dogmas and miracles.

The way to consume it is uncritically, naively, in big gulps. Then it goes down like castor oil in hot coffee.—Open your mouth and close your eyes! That's the only way."[34] Laymen do not have to behave as if they were clergymen, but on the other hand, religion must "not only be a Sunday coat. Instead, it should serve as a silent accompaniment to the somber melody of everyday life."[35] "A jaunty Christianity for everyday use, and a more austere one for holidays."[36]

But Strindberg is not always this cocksure in *A Blue Book*. His approach to religion, largely unchanged since the Inferno, had been complicated by new elements and an intensification of the theodicean issue: How can one reconcile a belief in an all-good and all-wise Creator, as Strindberg unconditionally demands, with a creation as imperfect as our earth? Even if one accepts as fact that man and his culture have poisoned existence, is it still possible to believe that we were sent into the best of all worlds? Strindberg's theory that the great Artist needs to experiment with His creative projects in order to achieve progress was not really sufficient to explain the world's wretchedness, which he now saw in an even darker light than he did during the Inferno. And so he persisted in the idea that earthly life is a hell through which we have to pass.

In *A Blue Book* the disciple asks whether this was also Swedenborg's opinion, but the teacher gives an evasive answer: "I don't know; it's possible that what he had in mind was not a place, but a state of mind. However, when his descriptions of the other side coincide perfectly with those of this side, . . . then a hell certainly exists, whether it is here or there."[37]

Another problem for Strindberg was the concept of the redemption of man through Christ:

> [This] has been difficult for me to explain, and I have tried to interpret it to my own satisfaction many times, but without success. If God sacrificed His son for mankind's atonement, then reconciliation and paradisical tranquility ought to exist on earth, but such is not the case.[38]

The two millennia that elapsed since Christ descended to earth have not appreciably improved the situation here, but Strindberg hopes that the third millennium will end "with a complete reconciliation between humanity and God."

Strindberg has no answer to give to the question of why we are compelled to live on this earth. "As a Christian I have of course learned that mankind suffered a Fall and was damned; indeed, life seems to me to be not so much a school as an inferno and a prison, for nothing endures to hold on to. The loveliest things seem to have been created only to become ugly, and the good, evil."[39] The meaning of existence is therefore a mystery, and it is sinful to try to penetrate it. "The arrogance in wishing to comprehend God and His plans and wishing to understand one's fate, is like wishing to steer a frigate with an oar. Every Greek tragedy ends with an exhortation to beware of presumptuousness, hubris."[40]

But although man can never receive answers to the most difficult questions, not even concerning his own fate, Strindberg was convinced that Providence guides our every step. Citing Swedenborg for support, he asserts that any person who learns to detest evil will be given guardian angels to assist and advise along the new path. They make their presence known through various warning signals, such as the sound of crickets chirping in one's ear or the sensation of pinchings in one's foot—pinchings in the left foot signifying yes, in the right foot, no. But the primary signals are knocking sounds in walls. Strindberg maintains that he had been receiving such signs ever since 1896, but did not always obey them "because I was perplexed about whether it was a trial I should withstand or a warning I should heed."[41] In his diary and letters we can see that he was still somewhat uncertain about how to interpret the various omens.

But he is confident that such phenomena are heavenly intimations, even when he has to admit that ordinary mortals were responsible for the knocking sounds, for these cases, too, were due to "an urging, because although the person doing the knocking might be driving a nail in the wall for a practical reason, he received an exhortation to do it at that precise moment." One evening he himself received an "exhortation" to move a painting, and although he was reluctant to disturb his neighbors, he overcame his hesitation. "Afterwards it occurred to me that . . . perhaps I had played the role of a warner in some dangerous situation about which I knew nothing and learned nothing!"[42]

When even things he could explain naturally assumed aspects of the miraculous, one can imagine how he would interpret the inexplicable. Incidents of bad luck become a series of miraculous events with a definite purpose:

> Yes, it has to be this way. How does it happen that I fail in every enterprise, encounter only enemies on the streets, am cheated in every store,

purchase the worst food in the market, read only malice in the newspaper, have good letters withheld from me although they were definitely mailed? . . . It cannot be an accident, but what is it then?---It is something else, but we shall never learn the answer, since we know so little about the most ordinary of everyday events.[43]

It is not enough to be on guard against evil actions: evil thoughts are even more dangerous, although it takes a long time to discover that "thoughts are the soul's action." Not until Strindberg began guarding his thoughts did he understand "why so often in life I thought I was unjustly accused of and punished for crimes I had not committed. I admit now that I committed them in my thoughts." He wonders how his fellow men could have known this and concludes that there is "an immanent justice" that punishes sins of intention, " and when people guess things about each other on the basis of suspicions, ugly facial expressions, or feeling, they are guessing correctly! These are unpleasant things to have to say, but they are undeniably true."[44]

In other words, a double-entry ledger of our transgressions is kept, and the life we lead is double as well. As we wander through this vale of tears, we pursue what Strindberg in theosophical terminology calls an unconscious life on the astral plane, and more and more this other life became the essential one for him: "We do not live in reality, but in our ideas of reality."[45] And therefore we have the gift of being able to blind ourselves temporarily to life's wretchedness. "Perhaps it is our duty to conceal and blind ourselves to certain things, just as we conceal our natural functions." Our life in this existence, seven times blacker than Zola pictured it, more often than not is a tolerable state of somnambulism. But sometimes we awaken and see reality and people in their true light.

It was during the 1880's that Strindberg became familiar with the psychological discoveries that were the basis for his experiments with occultism, hypnotism, and the power of suggestion. In several places in *A Blue Book* he says that materialism actually paved the way for religion:

Everything serves a purpose, and delusion often furthers truth. At the end of the last century the materialists began to pry into the unseen world. One fine day they discovered man's ability to perceive the remote while under a hypnotic trance, to see the invisible and penetrate the future. They thereby fulfilled the important function—at quite a cost—of demonstrating the truths of the arts of prophesy and divination and the possibility of miracles.[46]

It is obvious from this statement that Strindberg's faith in these phenomena was now unlimited. In the 1880's, of course, he thought that the power of suggestion could be defined as the influence one person can exercise over another, even under ordinary, everyday conditions. Now, he had no difficulty believing in the existence of vampires and witches. A witch was quite simply "a woman (mostly women!) who has by chance discovered the ability of the soul to leave the body or exert influence over someone from a distance, mostly over the baser instincts."[47] Mind reading "is practiced daily and constantly in married life"[48] and is similar to the ability to monitor a person's train of thought by observing his facial expressions, the tones of his voice, his gestures, and so forth. A "seventh sense" is operating here—an "exteriorized sensitivity."

Thanks to this ability, Strindberg can sense at a distance either when enemies are threatening him or when people are speaking well of him. On the street he can distinguish between friend and enemy, and he can experience illnesses and operations undergone by others as if they were actually happening to him. "This makes life painful, but rich and interesting."[49]

Human beings radiate and receive psychic power, and they can transfer it to inanimate objects.

> If a tribe of primitive people begin to worship a meteorite, and if this rock is continually worshiped by a nation for centuries, then the rock accumulates psychic power or becomes a holy object that can transmit power to those who possess the receiving apparatus—Faith. Consequently, it can accomplish miracles that are incomprehensible to nonbelievers.[50]

Statements like this seem to indicate that Strindberg approved of the most primitive kind of animism, but other statements involving his intensive probing into the unconscious show that occasionally he anticipated what modern psychology has made common knowledge. This is true, for example, of the chapter "The Imaginary Invalid" ("Inbillade sjuke")[51] in which he describes what has subsequently been called "escaping into illness," although he exaggerated and went so far as to express doubt that tuberculosis actually existed.

The pious and occasionally sanctimonious tones of the religious observations in *A Blue Book* seem irreconcilable with the merciless vengeance Strindberg was exacting—often in almost the same breath—upon ancient enemies, especially Geijerstam, but even upon others whose only crime, as in the case of Carl Larsson, was to have disapproved of *Black Banners*. In several essays he tries to justify his attacks by quoting the same exhortation from the Law of Moses: "Thou shalt not hate thy brother in thine heart,"[52] but rather punish him so that his guilt is not passed on to you. Strindberg interprets this to mean, among other things, that "you should not keep false friends by remaining silent, for this corrupts both you and them. Instead, you must first speak out and then break off with them." For him, to speak out meant to write: "If they too could write, then of course they would!"[53]

Strindberg also maintains that he was not false and disloyal when he revealed unpleasant things about his friends. His pen had "written away" their unpleasantness, and they had changed themselves. He loves their better selves and hates their worse selves.[54] "If I awaken a dulled, self-deceived person with a description of his twisted character, then I have done this person an incalculable service." It pains him to have to do this, just as it pains a father to have to punish his child, and as God is said to be pained to have to do us evil. But he cannot regret what he did.

Strindberg has to admit, however, that the intention of his attacks was not always reform. But even in these instances, he denies that he was vengeful:

> Christianity forbids one to seek revenge, but this is such an ambiguous concept. For if I react against a person's evil, he calls it revenge; if I punish a scoundrel, he calls it revenge; if I tell how a scoundrel wronged me, especially if I put it in writing and have it published, everyone—society, the state, the nation—screams: "He seeks revenge!" The only alternative is to keep quiet and suffer! But this is intolerable; there are times when one must cry out.[55]

In a section that contains an obvious allusion to his relationship with Geijerstam, he says that one who had called himself his friend treated him badly:

> Since I had kept quiet long enough, I had to complain; so I related his evil deeds. Then came the outcry (against me, of course): "Look at the way he uses his friends!" But he was the one who used me, and I only related what he did. Now, I ask you, aren't people ridiculous?[56]

In this passage as well as others, Strindberg makes no distinction between private criticisms and published accusations. If his friends "had not written, they would have talked, and the same effect would have been produced, outwardly as well as inwardly!" In a very significant reflection entitled "Betrayal" ("Förräderi") he admits that he often regretted betraying confidences in anger ("justified reaction against evil"), but he thinks he had the right to do so in his writings:

> As a writer . . . I have often trespassed on inviolable ground, but have regarded it as a burdensome duty. In doing so, I have naively relied on the honor of those who have the peculiar mission of allowing their casual opinions about a book to be published. If they betray a confidence, the fault is not mine. I entrusted it to the silent printed word on a piece of white paper. It was a confidential statement; the one who betrayed it was the betrayer. Books are made to be read silently, to be whispered in the ear; but a newspaper's voice is always audible, it shouts out secrets, and so it must assume the blame.[57]

This paradoxical attempt to blame his indiscretions on the reviewers who denounced them seems to indicate that Strindberg was coming to realize in his final years that he was morbidly suspicious and suffering from persecution mania. In an essay on what Swedenborg called "being punished through imaginings," Strindberg identifies this experience with the things doctors "vulgarly call obsessions" and admits that in his own life "punishment through imaginings" played the dominant role. "The most difficult thing is suspiciousness, since I feel compelled to suspect the innocent; it is uncontrollable, and my thoughts alternate between trust and mistrust."

At the same time, he insists that someone who suffers from persecution mania is actually persecuted. "The sufferer reviews in his mind the entire list of people he injured. And if the injured are really numerous and their hatred justified, then one can readily see that the sufferer is persecuted by their hatred, of which his aroused conscience now becomes the recipient."[58] Strindberg maintains here and in other passages that he has now come to a realization of his own guilt and is managing to overcome his suspiciousness by being unjust to himself or responding to treachery with resignation, but his arguments are not convincing, for if anyone spoke well of his enemies, it was "just like speaking ill of me!"[59]

Among the confidences Strindberg entrusted "to the silent printed word on a piece of white paper" in *A Blue Book* are a large number dealing with his third marriage. Since Harriet Bosse remarried while *A Blue Book* was being written, the observations are often marked by irrational bitterness, as are the more general statements on the woman question which are not conspicuously different from his earlier ones. He detected the interference of women everywhere. Especially interesting are references to *King Lear* in two different essays. In one, Lear's wife, not present, of course, in Shakespeare's play, is declared responsible for the harshness of the two older daughters. In the other essay, Strindberg pictures a hypothetical argument between Cordelia and her father in which she speaks in defense of her sisters and tries to exculpate them, "in a word, [she] ranges herself on the side of villainy." "Cordelia loves her father more than anything else on earth, but as a daughter, as a woman, she hates him!"[60] Shakespeare's conception of woman turns out to be surprisingly similar to Strindberg's:

> For good or evil, with her roots in dung and her flower in the light, the loveliest grafted onto the ugliest, the masterpiece of creation, but spoiled through misguidance, hating when she loves and loving when she hates— this is the way Shakespeare portrayed woman, the sphinx whose riddle cannot be solved, because it is either unsolvable or does not exist![61]

But even when Strindberg is speaking about personal matters in *A Blue Book,* he can write beautifully about love and marriage. "Marriage is more than a bond sealed in blood and vows; it is a holy act. It is so pure and so fragile that one unguarded word—yes, even a jest—can kill it forever."[62] Cohabitation is, consequently, an impossibility for Strindberg:

> There is a woman whose presence I cannot bear, but at a distance she is precious to me. We correspond, always respectfully and amiably. When we have longed for each other for a time, we must be together, but immediately we get into arguments, become mean and unsympathetic, and separate in anger. We are fond of each other on a higher plane, but cannot stay in the same room together. We dream of a reunion, dematerialized, on a verdant isle, where only we two are present or at most, with our child. I remember one half-hour when we three actually walked hand in hand along the shore of a verdant isle, and I had the impression it was heaven. Then, the dinner bell rang and we were once again on earth, and directly thereafter in hell.[63]

After the divorce became final in 1904 his bitterness was more evident, but even then he was able to write poignant observations about the cleansing and sanctifying power of his great sorrow. He has the hope that someone who is forsaken may ultimately win back the loved ones he lost through divorce if he treats his sorrow respectfully, like a cherished guest:

> The ancients represented Eros with a mournful expression. A great love resembles sorrow, and is manifested in the same way. There is first a nourishing of something that has to die, and a nourishing of something that wants to live; a rebirth after death. And love's highest moment resembles death's: the closed eyes, the deathly pallor, the suspension of consciousness.[64]

The third volume of *A Blue Book,* the last to be published in his lifetime, contains several essays that sum up Strindberg's life and works. The essay "The Wretch" ("Hundsfotten") depicts his life as a series of sufferings and injustices from birth to old age. "Wretched all his life! And yet people demanded that he write beautifully about them! Sometimes he did, but the thoughts expressed were his own ideas of beauty in a dream world that did not exist."[65] In another essay, "Different Preachers" ("Olika predikare"), he tries to explain why he, whose *Dream Play* described innocent humanity corrupted by life, spoke so harshly in his later works: "All human beings are harsh to one another in their words and judgments. But who has a greater right to be harsh than he who has atoned for his own harshness through suffering and now labors against evil?" He says that Christ called humans the "generation of vipers"[66] and notes that Swedenborg has scarcely one good word for them, finding them all "fundamentally corrupt."[67]

The last essay in Volume III describes a higher form of existence after death. As was the case with his unfinished Chamber Play *Toteninsel,* Strindberg was influenced by Boecklin and calls this first phase after death "The Isle of the Dead," but depicts it in a free interpretation of Swedenborg. Men and women live "in clean, beautiful cottages" with roofs open to the sky so that the stars can shine in upon them at night. The cottages are located on islands that float in a substance that could be either air or water. People's bodies are composed "of a finer material and of foodstuffs so subtle" that no digestive processes are necessary. "Liberated from their human animal bodies and from evil and mendacity, they are all fair and pure. They are partly transparent, so that they cannot dissemble and lie."[68] Teachers instruct them in the meaning of their past earthly life. "The entire strange fabric of life is unraveled, and they can see the threads in their destiny: Why they were compelled to commit the very deeds they most disapproved of; why other people were allowed to torment them unjustly." In this way, a light is diffused over "the dreadful past. . . . Everything— including the most appalling things—acquires an aura of reconciliation and in this way, and only in this way, are these horrible memories blotted out, memories from which they never believed they could be free."[69]

Those who have reached "The Isle of the Dead" praise God, for they have been able to atone for their pasts, whereas "before, they had only wished to forget everything they experienced."[70] At the end of every day they long for the next, so that they may learn more of their destiny.

Strindberg emphasizes that one cannot become reconciled with one's "dreadful past" by drinking Lethe's waters; one must have the past illuminated in a clear light. His feeling that he was the object of constant injustices and that he had committed injustices to others in turn, is of course one of the central themes in all his later work, especially in *A Blue Book*. Despite the certainty with which he defends himself in one situation or another, we sense that he was more tormented by pangs of conscience than he was willing to admit even to himself, and that he could not forget or forgive any injustice, although it might have occurred in his earliest childhood. And so in his letters and his writings, he never ceased to declare that he would die unreconciled with life.

Talks to the Swedish Nation

Whereas the weighty volumes of *A Blue Book* attracted scant attention, Strindberg once more, against all expectations, set Sweden ablaze with the essay collection *Talks to the Swedish Nation*. It went through eight editions, and "The Strindberg Controversy" provoked by the tract raged long after the author's death. *Talks,* along with the pamphlets that followed—*The People's State (Folkstaten), Religious Renaissance (Religiös renässans)*, and *The Czar's Courier, or The Saw Filer's Secrets (Tsarens kurir eller sågfilarens hemligheter)*—attacked the upper classes and the monarchy and made Strindberg the literary champion of the working class, although he declined to become a part of any party program and made it clear that he stood to the left of everyone.

There was hardly anything in *A Blue Book* to suggest that Strind-

berg would finish his career as a tribune of the people. He did believe, of
course, that everything in society was perverse, but although he acknowledged that Rousseau, Max Nordau, and Tolstoy were correct in their criticism, he felt they had drawn false conclusions. The socialism they advocated had restored the guilds, restricted the right to pursue a trade through
the persecution of non-strikers, and reintroduced the Inquisition through
the ostracism of heretics: "Non-socialists were denied water service and
light, and bread and milk for their children during the general strike."[71]

He believed that the Parliamentary Reform of 1866, which extended the franchise to hitherto unprivileged classes, had only led to a
tyranny of the majority, and he distrusted the recently established universal
suffrage for men that was certain to produce a conservative majority.[72] He
believed with Swedenborg that public affairs were unimportant, and emphasized, furthermore, that Christianity was "more radical than radical-
ism."[73] It did not seem likely that the author of *A Blue Book* would two
years later write a pamphlet demanding a radical democratic reform of the
constitution.

In 1910, 1911, and the beginning of 1912, the new radical Stockholm newspaper *Aftontidningen* provided Strindberg with a forum for
polemical essays and thus enticed him out onto the battlefield. He started
off with an article, "Pharaoh Worship" ("Faraodyrkan"), about the cult
that had grown up around Sweden's romantic, imperialistic Charles XII
and boldly resumed his old campaign against "Sweden's Destroyer," while
at the same time taking side swipes at Charles's modern panegyrist, Heidenstam. As time went on, the number of Strindberg's targets grew. He
attacked Viktor Rydberg and modern critics of the Bible in the essay series
Religious Renaissance, in which he also zealously propagandized for the
same syncretism he had advocated in the play *Gustav Adolf.*

A by-product of his preoccupation with the history of the Caro-
line period was an attempt to demonstrate that the geographical discoveries of the great arctic explorer Sven Hedin (1865-1952) were actually
made much earlier by other explorers. One searches in vain for new ideas
in this profusion of journalistic pieces. Old weapons from the Strindbergian
arsenal are reintroduced, and arguments and paradoxes have a familiar
ring. But because he had regained his old verve as a polemicist, his attacks
on the Ninety-ists aroused a great commotion.

Ever since the appearance of "Renaissance" (1889) and *Pepita's*

Wedding (1890),[74] Strindberg had felt bitter toward the Ninety-ists, especially Heidenstam, but had not attacked them publicly. In the chapter concerning the 1890's in *The Gothic Rooms,* he had been content to mention foreign ideas and writers he thought were significant and to bypass developments in Sweden. In *Black Banners,* tempted by his hatred of Geijerstam, he had turned his fire toward the surviving representatives of Young Sweden, although he recognized that it was not Young Sweden but the romanticism of the 1890's that had overshadowed his work.

In the survey of his writings that prefaced *The Author* (1909), the fourth part of his autobiography, he placed special emphasis on the romantic elements in his earlier 1880's works, referring to the "reaction against atheism and the theory of evolution" in *Somnambulist Nights* and characterizing *The People of Hemsö* and *Men of the Skerries* as "liberation from social problems; pure portrayal of nature and the life of the people; *L'art pour l'art* as early as 1889, in other words, prior to the *Pepita* outrage and the return of the Byronic Snob School." One thing he neglected to point out was that his historical plays had been an important contribution to the national poetic renaissance of the 1890's, and he neglects the same point in *Talks to the Swedish Nation.* He declares that he was unjustly treated and feels compelled to defend his position in Swedish literature, but does so by stubbornly asserting his own pre-eminence and stating that the renaissance of the 1890's was unnecessary.[75]

On the whole, Strindberg's approach in *Talks to the Swedish Nation* is the same as the one with which he greeted the publication of "Renaissance" and *Pepita's Wedding.* He attacks Heidenstam's lyricism, defends Zola's naturalism, and condemns French symbolism.[76] But the heat of battle had driven him to take a literary position that could justly be called old-fashioned and contrary to the non-realistic modernism of *A Dream Play* and the Chamber Plays. He was undoubtedly aware of this; in the article "Stylistic Taste (in Painting)" ("Stilkänsla [inom målarkonsten]") he praised the painter Bruno Liljefors:

> Liljefors's sea eagles are not painted realistically and the ocean waves are almost decorations, *because* the painter *this* time wanted to paint something more than a predatory murder, or a mealtime at sea. This is a tragedy portrayed with a sureness of artistic taste.[77]

Painting was another area in which Strindberg could take pride in having pointed the way. Time and again in the 1870's and 1880's he had ques-

tioned why Swedish artists should spend their apprenticeship in Paris. He
had urged that they return home to recapture the essence of Swedish nature.
But even after the turn of the century he refused to acknowledge that what
he had advocated for the graphic arts had already taken place in Swedish
literature, asserting in *Talks* that he found the new patriotic intonations
"cracked, thin and above all false."[78]

One assumption of Strindberg's campaign was correct: that because
of the critical enthusiasm for the literary achievements of the 1890's and
the first years of the new century, his own contributions had been forgotten,
particularly his work after *Inferno*. But his aesthetic criticism of "The
Gigerl [Fop] School of Literature" cannot withstand close inspection, and
he went too far when he tried to demonstrate that he had anticipated
everything viable in the movement inaugurated by Heidenstam and Levertin. Nevertheless, he had touched upon a sore point, and his words aroused
strong approbation and opposition. From all accounts, Strindberg was
exhilarated at being the focal point of battle once again. His letters do
not complain about the counterblows he received, and his retorts bear
witness to his unquenchable warrior temperament.

The approaching World War cast an increasingly darker shadow
over Sweden during Strindberg's final years, but he was firmly convinced
that all the warnings and preparations for war were invented by the upper
classes as means of battling "the enemy within." His last pamphlet, a
collection of eight short essays published as *The Czar's Courier, or The
Saw Filer's Secrets,* was written following a narrow brush with death during an attack of pneumonia at Christmastime in 1911 and seems strangely
out of touch with world affairs.

Shortly before he was confined to his bed for the last time, he
wrote his final article "Dangerous Gifts" ("Farliga gåvor"), which was
published in the newspaper *Socialdemokraten* on March 23, 1912.[79] It
contains an urgent warning to the government not to accept the gift of a
new type of warship—the F-boat. The funds for the warship had been
raised by patriotic public subscription after the government had canceled
orders for the ship as an economy measure. Strindberg asserts that the
money was collected through lies and extortion, largely by playing on the
traditional Swedish fear of Russian expansionist policies. Furthermore,
the money is not in cash, but in IOU's, which are not binding: "Thus we
have a new trick or swindle characteristic of the political morality of the

upper classes."[80] The donors are counting on the government's paying for the ships, "since in all probability the dried-up promissory notes will not be honored." Moreover, the annual cost for maintaining such a ship would be 490,000 kroner. "I wonder," concludes Strindberg, "if any other nation, or entire people, has ever allowed itself to be deluded by such transparent treachery." The contentious Strindberg of old—of *The Red Room, The New Kingdom,* and *This and That*—was resurrected for the last time.

The Great Highway

The Great Highway (1909) is the last of Strindberg's plays and his farewell to art. The novel fragment *Armageddon* (written at the end of June, 1907, and published in a Christmas magazine in 1908),[81] in which Strindberg started a retrospective survey of his life, may be regarded as a kind of preparatory study for the play. The title is the name of "a secret, invisible society"—i.e., the Young Sweden coterie. Here, they are called "black sorcerers," a phrase Strindberg borrowed from a theosophical pamphlet by Georg Ljungström that came into his hands just at the time *Black Banners* was to appear. Ljungström's pamphlet describes in Swedenborgian style an extraordinary society that the great practitioners of black magic have established for themselves under the South Pole. The law of the society is that anyone who does a good deed is banished to earth, but retains a vivid memory of the hell he experienced. Strindberg thought he recognized his own "situation, when I was at the point of breaking with the black sorcerers (Banners)."[82]

In the novel, the black sorcerers, who believe themselves descended from a wart hog, are united in the Armageddon society. The hero, who bears the strange name Joy-Kiss (Fröjdkyss), is cast down to them from heaven, strangely enough because up there he was not regarded as sufficiently outspoken. Joy-Kiss is then reborn on earth, and Strindberg writes another black portrait of his own childhood. The fragment ends at this point, but a prophecy gives us the main outline of what was to happen. The hero would flounder about in delusions and vices, but also reveal to mankind the futility of life and teach them that they were prisoners. On reaching manhood, he would discover that he served the black sorcerers and could not free himself from them, for they hold him prisoner and torment him. When he finally attacks them, both the white and the black sorcerers would assail him. Not until death would he be able to bring "all the seeds of his humanity to the purest, highest, and most complete fruition."

One notices in this pale Swedenborgian pastiche the device of having the central character, like Indra's Daughter, descend to earth; Strindberg would repeat it in *The Great Highway*, in which the Hunter wanders down from the Alps to the dwelling places of men. The taste for Biblical place names is also common to the fragment and the play. Another detail that appears in both works is the fateful refusal on the part of the hero to believe in the theory of evolution. In *Black Banners* Strindberg had already mentioned the heresies concerning this issue that he had presented in *Somnambulist Nights,* the volume he believed to be the cause of his break with the Young Sweden group.

The Great Highway, submitted for publication on August 25, 1909, got its name from the road in north Stockholm that runs from Norrtulls Street out to the New Cemetery. The subtitle of the play is "A Drama of a Journey with Seven Stations" ("Ett vandringsdrama med sju stationer"), and the first sketch bears the title *On the Journey (På vandring).* Strindberg's intention to portray a journey to death is clearer in the sketch than in the completed drama. The route he had planned to have his hero take passes the Blue Tower—his final home at 85 Drottning Street—and further north, his burned-out childhood home. Both places figure in the sketch, but do not appear in the play. An unfinished second part was to have the hero continue his journey past the grave to the Isle of the Dead and the shore beyond. Only later did Strindberg follow the pattern of *A Dream Play* and frame the drama with the two scenes that contain the most beautiful lyricism: the Hunter's descent from the alpine regions down to life's dusty highway and his decision at the end to return to the eternal snows.

The subtitle for *The Great Highway* is reminiscent of the *To Damascus* cycle, and, as was the case in the earlier drama, Strindberg is candidly autobiographical. It is a monodrama, completely dominated by the character of the Hunter, whose thoughts are often broken off in the middle of sentences and completed by other characters who are only unsubstantial shadows, now his doubles, now his opposites. The play is devoid of all dramatic conflict; Strindberg indicated to his publisher that the play was a closet drama.

It is also devoid of the religious concept that gave *To Damascus* its stature. The Hunter had once been an evangelist, but found it futile and ceased preaching in order to avoid being called hypocrite. What disturbed him most was that when he publicly confessed his own sins, people thought of themselves as guiltless, but after he had suffered ten years of atonement and proclaimed their sins as well, they became indignant.

Strindberg, of course, was still obsessed with his need to defend *Black Banners*. It is no accident that when the Hunter confronts the urns containing the ashes of his enemies, he reviles the "idolator" (Geijerstam) whose "dreary wife and detestable children"[83] one was forced to worship.

Strindberg found it easier to be penitent when speaking through one of the Hunter's doubles than through the Hunter himself. The dying Japanese man the Hunter meets confesses that fifteen years earlier he had been awakened:

> It was as if everything I had experienced and done was written in a book, and now the book was opened. Day and night, night and day, I read all the false entries, all the irregularities. And I have struggled, but in vain. Death alone can liberate me, for the greatest evil is in my flesh. My soul I have purified through suffering.[84]

The dying man also expresses Strindberg's belief that nothing is as degrading as:

> the basic fact of life—
> the humiliation of wandering about
> as just a skeleton clothed in flesh.

The Hunter complains that it is more bitter than death to have "to take the great joke seriously / and treat as holy what was so coarse." Once he had raised "bright flags to the mast" but now has found that beauty cannot be realized on earth. To this the Japanese replies:

> I know it---but it's a memory,
> a hope, a beacon to navigate by—
> and therefore: make the signals ready!
> Let the flags unfurl!
> They fly high, but are easy to see
> and they point the way—upward—toward
> the sun![85]

Throughout this dialogue that Strindberg carries on with himself, rancor and desire for self-vindication battle with remorse and yearning for atonement. "I was the defender of the only True One against the idolators," the Hunter declares to the Woman. "You always wanted someone to worship—yourselves, your relatives, your friends, but you never wanted to render simple justice."[86] He admits, however, that he is confused: "Therefore, I am not the person I am." In "this hellish forge[87] known as society" he has become like the others, a highwayman, a robber in the woods.

This strangely painful and ambivalent play contains a number of passages that are only barely understandable. It also has a great deal of pointless and heavy-footed literary satire aimed at the same target as the attack on the Ninety-ists in *Talks to the Swedish Nation:* Heidenstam, here represented as the fatuous Blacksmith in Assessville who won a prize for his memorial address on "the destroyer of the nation," a reference, of course, to Heidenstam's study of Charles XII, *The Charles Men.* But Strindberg no longer had the playfully ironic imagination that created *Lucky Per's Travels* and was aware of it:

> Poor human being!
> Your half-mask is torn,
> and when you show your teeth,
> one cannot tell whether it's to bite or smile.[88]

In spite of everything, he feels he cannot stay away from the thick of the battle. When the Hermit gives the Hunter good advice on how to deal with people, the Hunter replies:

> I'm more than aware of that. If only I could
> remain a spectator and sit in the audience.
> But I want to be up on the stage, act, and take part;
> and as soon as I play a part, I'm lost,
> forgetting who I am.[89]

He knows, too, that for him married life means only conflict. When the Hunter reaches the final station on his journey and meets his daughter at the Forester's home, he is happy, both for her sake and his, that she does not recognize him. He gratefully acknowledges that such a thing as happiness exists in life, but knows, too, that it is:

> brief as lightning,
> as sunshine or convolvulus—
> *one* blossom and *one* day,
> and then it's over.[90]

It is therefore best to live in memories:

> I know your tunes and your hand,
> but have no desire to meet you—
> At the right distance the fire warms
> but get too close and it burns![91]

And so, the solitude of nature—the solitude he constantly longs to escape from but toward which he is driven back again—becomes the Hunter's lot. Nowhere did Strindberg give as magnificent a lyric expression of his feeling for nature as in the soaring free verse of the opening monologue of *The Great Highway:*

> Here I can breathe, and the seed leaves of my heart—
> the tender lungs—can swell out;
> no dust, no smoke, no air breathed by others
> to poison my blood.
> White, pure snow—
> vapor made sublime! Water diamonds,
> you lily flowers, stone-hardened by frost;
> stained through the black sieve of clouds like flour from heaven.
> You blessed silence, draw your silken quilt
> over the head of the tired wanderer
> who seeks sleep, whispering his prayer!

Absent from the Hunter's epitaph, which he hopes the Hermit will write in the snow, is the self-pleading that occurs so often within the play. The result is a simple statement of the tragedy of Strindberg's life:

> Here rests Ishmael, the son of Hagar,
> who was once called Israel,
> because he fought a fight with God,
> and never stopped struggling until he was down,
> overcome by His almighty goodness.

The epitaph gives the impression that *The Great Highway* was intended to be what in fact it became—Strindberg's farewell to poetic art. He continued, however, to be occupied not only with ideas for plays, but with other literary plans as well. During the final months of his life, he was working on a play about the French Revolution with Robespierre as the central character: *The Bloody Bread (Det blodiga brödet)*. But the sketches give no clear indication of how it was to be worked out.

Notes to Chapter Twenty-two

1. *SS:*XLVI, pp. 407-8.
2. May 16, 1907.
3. *SS:*XLVI, p. 415. His previous reverses, he insists, were the result of having served "the black ones, and that was no blessing!" *(Ibid.).*
4. June 10, 1907.
5. *SS:*XLVIII, p. 834.
6. A beautiful and well-documented picture of Strindberg during his final years is given by Walter Berendsohn in *Strindbergs sista levnadsår* (1948).
7. In *SOS:*II, pp. 267 ff.
8. Another name for Hell. See 2 Kings 23:10; Isaiah 30:33; and Jer. 7:31-33.—Translator
9. *SS:*XLVIII, p. 1044.
10. *SS:*XLVII, pp. 662, 664.
11. *Brev,* VIII, p. 215.
12. *SS:*XLVI, p. 389.
13. *Ibid.,* p. 327.
14. *SS:*XLVIII, p. 1059.
15. *SS:*XLVI, p. 302.
16. *SS:*XLVIII, p. 1059.
17. *Ibid.*
18. *SS:*XXVIII, p. 93.
19. *SS:*XLVII, p. 458.
20. *SS:*XLVIII, p. 810.
21. The site of a Swedish royal hunting preserve.—Translator
22. *SS:*XLVI, pp. 335 *et passim.*
23. *Ibid.,* p. 403.
24. *SS:*XLVIII, p. 1112.
25. *SS:*XLVI, p. 314.
26. The Bible's zoology had apparently been unjustly derided by the freethinker zoologists who refused to believe, as the Bible states, that the hare chews its cud. (*SS:*XLVII, p. 724).
27. *SS:*XLVI, p. 313.
28. *SS:*XLVII, p. 805.
29. *Ibid.,* p. 664.
30. *Ibid.,* p. 656.

31. *SS:*XLVI, p. 215.
32. *Ibid.*, p. 59.
33. *SS:*XLVII, p. 631.
34. *SS:*XLVI, p. 102.
35. *Ibid.*, p. 79.
36. *Ibid.*, p. 100.
37. *Ibid.*, pp. 26-27.
38. *Ibid.*, p. 159.
39. *Ibid.*, p. 60.
40. *Ibid.*, p. 65.
41. *SS:*XLVIII, p. 894.
42. *Ibid.*
43. *SS:*XLVI, p. 18.
44. *Ibid.*, p. 84.
45. *Ibid.*, p. 169.
46. *Ibid.*, pp. 106-7.
47. *SS:*XLVII, p. 611.
48. *SS:*XLVI, p. 84.
49. *Ibid.*, p. 185.
50. *Ibid.*, p. 31.
51. *SS:*XLVIII, pp. 876-80.
52. Leviticus 19:17.
53. *SS:*XLVIII, p. 1024.
54. *Ibid.*, pp. 873-74.
55. *SS:*XLVII, p. 708.
56. *SS:*XLVIII, p. 1018.
57. *Ibid.*, pp. 941-42.
58. *SS:*XLVI, pp. 147-48.
59. *SS:*XLVIII, p. 1011.
60. *Ibid.*, p. 873.
61. *SS:*XLVII, pp. 758-59.
62. *Ibid.*, p. 734.
63. *SS:*XLVI, p. 175.
64. *SS:*XLVII, p. 776.
65. *SS:*XLVIII, p. 1026.
66. Matthew 3:7 attributes this phrase to John the Baptist.—Translator
67. *SS:*XLVIII, pp. 1022-23.
68. *Ibid.*, pp. 1034-35.
69. *Ibid.*, p. 1035.
70. *Ibid.*, p. 1036.

71. *SS:*XLVII, p. 618.
72. *Ibid.,* pp. 668-71.
73. *Ibid.,* p. 617.
74. *See* p. 248 and 278.
75. Strindberg denies that Swedish poetry was "in such danger around 1890 that it had to be regenerated" (*SS:*LIII, p. 97), and asserts that his works were ignored in "Renaissance." He proceeds to formulate a very pedantic criticism of Heidenstam's lyrics—partly inspired by Nils Linder's attack on Heidenstam's style (*Svenska språket i modern diktkonst. En studie,* Stockholm, 1902)—and in general devaluates the entire literary contribution of the *fin-de-siècle* generation.
76. In attacking Heidenstam's lyricism, he contrasts it not only with the work of the great Esias Tegnér (1782-1846), but also with Count Snoilsky (1841-1903) and the minor poet Herman Sätherberg (1812-97). And in reference to the admiration for provincialism and folk art on the part of the Ninety-ists, Strindberg reminds "all provincial dialecticians and pseudo-peasants' sons" that a more genuine pioneer in this area was Fredrik August Dahlgren (1816-95), whose nationalistic opera *Värmlänningarne* (1846) was one of the most popular stage pieces in the history of the Swedish theatre. He also aims jibes at the Ninety-ists Per Hallström and Selma Lagerlöf.
77. *SS:*LIII, p. 124.
78. *Ibid.,* p. 86.
79. *Ibid.,* pp. 546-48.
80. *Ibid.,* p. 547.
81. It was reprinted in *SS:*LIV, pp. 145-63. *Cf.* Berendsohn, *Strindbergs-problem,* pp. 98-106.
82. *SS:*XLVI, p. 414.
83. *SS:*LI, p. 77.
84. *Ibid.,* p. 69.
85. *Ibid.,* pp. 82-83.
86. *Ibid.,* p. 91.
87. *See* note 6, Chapter I.—Translator
88. *SS:*LI, p. 19.
89. *Ibid.,* p. 12.
90. *Ibid.,* p. 85.
91. *Ibid.,* p. 99.

Chapter Twenty-three

CONCLUSION

When Strindberg was on the verge of suicide during his marital crisis in September, 1901, he wrote in his diary:

> My past? Can a writer's life be analyzed? Does one have the right to repent a past from which one has learned?—and which has been staged by someone else? One has lived as one was able to—and not as one wished. The fact that I am being dragged through filth is itself a punishment. Most of the evil I committed was due to imprudence and impetuous moods—as is true of other people. And have I not been punished enough?

These are the questions that are reiterated in an even more anguished, personal tone in the famous final verses of *The Great Highway*.

Strindberg felt that his inability to resist acting on impulse was an obstacle preventing him from "being the person he wanted to be." "I believe you're stronger than I am," says Master Olof to Kristina in the prose version of the play. "You're the master of your will, but I'm not master of mine." Strindberg was thinking primarily of his compulsion for revealing the truth, as in the bizarre and moving scene in *The Ghost Sonata* in which the Student, intoxicated by love, is seized by an irresistible craving to tell the Young Lady everything he is thinking about her, although he knows it will cost her her life. Vainly, she tries to stop him: "It's in asylums that people say everything they think." But he goes on, relentlessly: "I must, otherwise I'll die!" He was born with a poison that prevents him from closing his eyes to life, "for I cannot see what is ugly as beautiful nor call evil good. I cannot!"

"It's in asylums that people say everything they think." This could have been a sentence from one of the reviews of his most disturbing works—*A Madman's Defense* or *Black Banners*. Even today some people try to defend Strindberg by asserting that these works were produced during periods of temporary insanity. But then why did Strindberg publish them several years after they were written? Furthermore, he never expressed regret over having written them, nor did he ever ask to be judged morally irresponsible.

The numerous foreign psychopathologist-biographers[1] who studied Strindberg are probably correct in saying that his two most severe psychotic episodes—during the *Married* campaign and during the Inferno Crisis—were of a schizophrenic nature.[2] But since the researchers did not have access to primary source materials in Swedish, they present a distorted picture of his condition during the somewhat calmer periods in between. In Torsten Eklund's exhaustive analysis,[3] Strindberg is described as neurotic or hysterical. As someone trying to make a living as a writer, he had a natural desire to be noticed, and although the sensational aspects of his works helped to advance his international reputation, one is tempted to agree with Eklund's assertion that he was not simply an opportunist, for he often acted against his own best interests, which is typical of hysterical people.[4] Eklund also points out how Strindberg balanced between fantasy and reality and had a preference for the somnambulistic state—other symptoms of hysteria—and that after the Inferno Crisis his attitude toward life was built on the idea that reality was a dream.[5]

But it is difficult to demarcate the symptoms of hysteria from the signs of radical literary innovation. Strindberg's statements on *The Father* and *A Dream Play*[6] show that he himself was uncertain about where to draw the line. Ever since his youth he had been haunted by the fear of going insane and being confined. But his mania for self-confession drove him to defy all risks, and his preference for bold expression led him to exaggerate his illness, a tendency typical of the hysterical temperament. There is no reason, of course, to accept all his assertions at face value, but on the other hand one ought not to distrust them on principle.

Strindberg's constant attempts to defend and excuse himself often obscure the candidness and psychological brilliance with which he revealed the truth of his emotional life. A critic or biographer risks, as is the case with most of the painters and sculptors who tried to capture the essence of his character, rendering more of the outer pose than of the inner life. Not even the statements that he made about himself create a satisfactory portrait, because they were either expressions of moods that dominated him only briefly, or visions of a state of being that glittered in his imagination like an unattainable ideal.

Ernst Kretschmer, who considers Strindberg a schizoid recluse,[7] supports his hypothesis with the passage from *Alone* about enclosing one-self in a cocoon spun from the silk of one's own soul. But Strindberg was not really a recluse. Although he yearned for solitude, he could not bear long isolation: after two weeks or so he usually complained that he could no longer listen to the sound of his own voice. His most profound psychic crisis occurred when he wandered aimlessly and alone in Paris, and it was not resolved until he was again among friends in Lund. Not even the hermit of the Blue Tower broke off contact entirely with the outside world.

The reason that the company of others became periodically un-bearable for him was that he was simultaneously cruel and abnormally sensitive; it was extraordinary how easily he could hurt others or how they could hurt him. This was, of course, especially true of the most intimate form of human contact—marriage. In one of his first letters to Siri von Essen he wrote: "I don't believe anyone could become bored with me, for I am very changeable, but sooner or later everyone is unhappy with me, that I can promise."[8] In his most beautiful ballad in *Word-Play and Minor Art* he described with classical simplicity what a tragic gift his love was:

Semele, Semele,	Semele, Semele,
vem narrade dig, du kära,	who tricked you, you dear one,
att älskarens anlet se?	into beholding your lover's counte-
Ej kommer man makter nära,	nance?
om icke för att dem be.	One doesn't approach the Powers,
Semele, Semele,	unless it is to beseech them.
din älskare komi i glansen	Semele, Semele,
bland väsande blixtar ställd,	your lover came in splendor
din brudkrans blev offerkransen;	in the midst of lightning flashes,
nu brinner du opp i hans eld.	your bridal bouquet became a sacrifi-
	cial wreath;
	and now you are consumed in his fire.

But this poem presents only one side of Strindberg's eroticism. Though he considered himself a Zeus whose lightning bolts destroyed those who got close to him, he suffered from a feeling of inferiority toward woman,[9] and it emerges in many of his works. In *A Blue Book* he made an ironically revealing survey of himself as a lover and as a married man:

> When I approach a woman as a lover, I look up to her. I see something of the mother in her, and this I respect. I assume a subordinate position, become childish and puerile and actually am subordinate, like most men. I do not know how well meaning I am. But I have a clumsy hand, do foolish things with good intentions, hurt others with my gift of love, receive rebukes, and become a bit ridiculous. Her beauty inspires me, and

> I have a propensity for beautifying, for seeing more than is there; I put her on a pedestal. She becomes, so to speak, older than I, although she is younger; and when she treats me as if I were a boy, I no longer feel my age, but she loses an advantage. When I serve my mistress then, I constantly let her know that her power over me is something she received from me, and that if she misuses her power, the lion will awaken, roaring. Strangely enough, this does not frighten her; instead, she just says: "You're so small when you're like that."[10]

This worship of woman that was so quickly transformed into hatred was an aspect of all of Strindberg's marriages. During the first one, he was tossed between ecstasy and fury. His second marriage taught him that love "has all the symptoms of insanity: hallucinations or seeing beauty where none exists, a melancholy as profound as possible, alternating with a boisterous hilarity." At that time he was convinced that marriage was a purgatory through which man must pass during his earthly Inferno wandering.[11] The third marriage was less stormy because Strindberg had acquired a new attitude toward love: as a union of souls which physical love only profanes. In Part III of *To Damascus* the Tempter says that he does not understand "what this powerful love—which is the wedding of souls—has to do with procreation."[12] And on New Year's Day, 1905, several months after his divorce from Harriet Bosse, he wrote to her:

> It was possible to break our visible bond, but not the invisible one! I think the situation is beautiful as it is, and from a distance I picture you as having come from on high. I don't think we are true mortal spirits; we come from a place somewhat higher and have been cast deep down here. This is why there is a tension within our bodies, and why we are ill at ease.

What was applicable to marriage was also applicable to friendship: the more intimate the association, the more violent the break. The motto with which Strindberg prefaced *Inferno*—to burn what he worshiped and worship what he burned[13]—was one he practiced his entire life.

For the wounds caused by his contacts with people, Strindberg sought a balm in nature. For him, the Alps and the Stockholm archipelago were the quintessence of all beauty. During the Inferno Crisis he imagined that human beings originated in a higher land, similar to Switzerland, but they could remember it only dimly. And, of course, it is up in the snow of the Alps that the Hunter in *The Great Highway* hopes he will be buried.

The skerries, too, had an ethereal quality for him: they resembled "the clouds in the ether, upon which the gods live, and the blessed ones, liberated, wander in purity near the aquamarine water."[14] In his last effort at a novel, *Armageddon,* he planned to depict higher existence as a combination of the Alps and the skerries. The home of the blessed ones was to be located in a dell in an alpine chain, and from the highest pinnacle one would be able to see the ocean on all sides:

> Innumerable islands, large and small, hovered freely over the sea; all were covered with plants, bushes, and trees down to the water's edge, where charming coves covered with golden sand invited swimming. On each island were pretty cottages and villas, and above them perched a temple-like fortress. These freely moving islets and islands caused the appearance of the landscape to change ceaselessly, and the same contour could never be repeated. And there were all types of landscapes.[15]

Strindberg could not conceive of an Eden without gleaming Alpine tops, skerries islands with villas and swimming coves, and endless change. But he quickly tired of the solitude of nature after any extended length of time. Natural phenomena would begin to frighten him and he felt that he was an unwelcome guest. In his early poem "Haze" ("Solrök" —1881)[16] there is a description of oyster catchers and seagulls screaming anxiously at his approach and even a gray viper quickly wriggling away: "Everything flees the feared one who fled people." Suddenly, he finds footprints in the sand. "He cursed and wanted to flee, but then he realized that he had cursed himself. Now he understood why the seagulls fled and the viper and the others, and he trod again in his footprints, for of course he could not flee himself." In reality, he was as homeless in the world of nature as in the world of men, in solitude as in company. He had begun by conceiving of himself as the stepchild of the family; gradually he became the stepchild of life. The Flying Dutchman and Ahasuerus, the Wandering Jew, were his natural symbols.

His stormy and changeable temperament found an immediate release in writing, which even as an old man he regarded as "a pure salvation as long as the work is in progress." To write was to surrender himself and everything and everyone around him to public inspection. In a letter to Schering on October 25, 1902, he quotes Goethe's *Dichtung und Wahr-*

heit to the effect that he transformed into poetry and pictures everything that delighted or tormented him or caught his attention, and that everything he published was a fragment of one huge continuous confession. In a passage in *A Blue Book* Strindberg uses Shakespeare as a similar example: "There is scarcely anything ugly or squalid that he did not experience; not a passion that he did not suffer; hate and love, revenge and lust, murder and fire—he seemed to have participated in them all as a writer. And a true writer will, should, or must sacrifice his person for his art."[17]

Because Strindberg restricted his subject matter to himself and his environment, his gallery of characters and range of themes are limited. This narrowness dictated constant repetitions, new variants of the same type, new modulations on the same theme. Whether his characters are historical figures or men and women from the dream world, they are involved in the same reckless marital quarrels or return to the same arguments on questions close to Stindberg's heart. But this very fact—that the works are confessions that he lived and suffered through—gives them a feverish intensity that makes them compelling, because we sense his need both to mask and expose. They remind us of Strindberg's strange oil painting of a landscape in which the outline of a cliff that wrestles with a stormy sea is revealed as a profile of the artist himself when the canvas is turned upside down.[18]

The clash between romanticism and naturalism that Strindberg knew was reflected in his earlier writings, had a counterpart in his later works in the battle between naturalism and symbolism. Before the Inferno Crisis, his instinctive urge to move against the current caused him to profess himself a late-born romantic. He adopted naturalism with great reservation, and he had been ready by the end of the 1880's—before anyone else in Sweden—to abandon it.

After the Inferno Crisis, when symbolism was the leading literary style, Strindberg's same ineradicable contrariness made him support naturalism. Of course, he did not become an orthodox naturalist, but he emphasized more strongly than before his admiration for Zola, "the father of symbolism, which has taken an antagonistic position toward its teacher."[19] In a letter to Gauguin in February, 1895, Strindberg repudiated the term symbolism as "an unfortunate name for something as old as *alle-*

gory."[20] His judgment of "the French symbolistic trend in lyricism" was even less sympathetic in *Talks to the Swedish Nation:* it was obscene and absurd and "regarded by wiser Frenchmen as *blague,* or a way to *epater les bourgeois* [dupe *(sic)* the Philistines]."[21] Naturally, he expressed even more contempt for the Swedish offspring of this trend. At the same time, he was careful to point out that he had anticipated the lyricism of the Ninety-ists in his 1880's reaction to naturalism.

During "The Strindberg Controversy" of his final years, he was reminded many times that his critical position was untenable, and the impetuous way with which he stood his ground was not really indicative of his actual preferences. He was not at all as hostile to French symbolism as he pretended to be: he had read Baudelaire and Villiers de l'Isle-Adam with admiration, assimilated from Huysmans's later works the demands of the symbolists, and included Maeterlinck and Péladan among his household gods. During the Inferno Crisis, the years in Lund, and the first period after his return to Stockholm, his writing showed a rather strong affinity for symbolism. But even then, he emphasized his desire to serve as a bridge between occultism and naturalism, to become "the Zola of occultism." Thereafter, he often called himself a "neo-naturalist," apparently meaning that he wanted to retain naturalism's conquest of reality without yielding to its overestimation of science. No more "science in art!" he said in a letter to Schering on May 13, 1902.

His later work cannot be confined within the limits of either one of these styles, nor can it be regarded as a result of a fusion of the two. It cuts its own path and foreshadows literary currents with which his name is often associated but which did not assert themselves until after his death. With certain justification he has been called an expressionist, and one might also call a portion of his work surrealistic.

Strindberg was aware that his writing magnified and distorted the reality that was his point of departure. In a passage in *A Blue Book* he says that over the course of the years he had sketched several thousand characters, but cannot remember a single portrait that was not a caricature. "Probably I am an impressionist who looks at movement, gesture, and expression, and not at physical objects."[22] He also believed that only a visionary was able to conceive of and render reality in this way. After re-reading *David Copperfield,* he wrote of Dickens: "Using only small, crooked black type, he evokes the same illusion the theatre does with its

huge apparatus. Or to be more precise, reading him provides one with hallucinations of actual events."[23] As early as 1884 he had told Jonas Lie that
he was not a realist: "I write best when I hallucinate."[24]

Strindberg's reluctance to align himself with any contemporary
school of writing meant that his work was not given the recognition it
merited. In the 1880's he found himself slighted in favor of more doctri-
naire naturalists, and during the new century his work after *Inferno* was
considered inferior. This was Oscar Levertin's basic opinion, despite his
obvious efforts to be just. But Heidenstam took the opposite view in his
otherwise harsh reply to Strindberg's attack on him in *Talks to the Swedish
Nation*. He maintained that Strindberg's originality, like Tolstoy's, had
grown with the years:

> The People of Hemsö is a narrative that satisfied contemporary taste, but
> what about the uniqueness of the beautiful little play Easter? Master Olof
> is constructed like other plays, but To Damascus stands alone: a constel-
> lation sparkles over the curious events, a constellation that shines right
> through the proscenium arch. Likewise, the fragmented forms of the other
> dream plays and the Chamber Plays are different from everything else.

Heidenstam overlooked the fact that *Master Olof* and *The People of
Hemsö* were just as uncommon in their day, and that in many ways
Strindberg's efforts in the 1880's prepared the way for the poetic renaissance of the 1890's. But he was correct in that Strindberg had found a new
style of expression at an age when most writers can only continue to tread
well-worn paths.

Today it is no longer fruitful to speculate about whether his later
production is superior to his earlier, just as it is impossible to decide
whether he was greatest as a dramatist or as a prose stylist. Drama was
the child of his sorrow. Even when he had established himself firmly with
The Red Room, he was unable to get *Master Olof* produced. And so, during the entire decade of the 1880's, he called his skerries narratives light
entertainment that he was forced to turn out so that he could afford to
write plays. By the 1900's, his work as a novelist was totally overshadowed
by his dramatic writing which had won him a world reputation. However,
it was characteristic of him that he now often placed the art of fiction
above that of drama. In a letter to Harriet Bosse on April 15, 1906, he
asserted: "The novel attracts me most, I detest the theatre. Posing! Super-
ficiality, calculation."[25] But when he was asked in an interview in 1909 why

he chose the dramatic form for his debut, he replied: "I found it easiest to write dramas; characters and actions took form and wove themselves together."[26]

His restless spirit lived continually at high tension and saw everything in terms of conflict. It is no exaggeration to say that he literally thought in dialogue form. This is evident in his novels, his lyrics, his *Blue Book* observations, and his letters. Even his diary entries, which were not intended for publication, are often in the form of questions and answers, self-accusations and refutations. It was as if Strindberg were carrying on a constant conversation with an invisible reader who was leaning over his shoulder. But although dialogue was Strindberg's natural medium, and he had little difficulty shaping it to suit his needs, he was as inconsistent here as in his characterization. His figures speak the same language no matter what their age or social position, whether they belong to contemporary reality, to history, or to the worlds of fairy tales and dreams. Nevertheless, his dialogue has great range—from lyrical pathos to colloquial bickering—and what one may find abrupt and disturbing when reading his plays often disappears when one sees them performed on stage, for halftones and subtleties emerge that had escaped one's attention earlier.

But much of his literary talent found no outlet in the drama. In most of his plays he is portentously solemn; and if humor occasionally appears, it never dominates the action. Then, too, most of the dramas are either period pieces or set in a stylized contemporary milieu; actual locales were ordinarily transformed, fantastically or grotesquely. Only in narrative literature could Strindberg find a place for his satire: sometimes pungent, sometimes exhilarating. His fiction gives us a picture of Swedish society that is often highly subjective, but it renders the life and landscapes of the time as had never before been done in Swedish literature. Above all, his fiction reveals Strindberg in his greatness and his weakness, with his lightning changes in mood, his buoyancy, his virulence, and· his absurdities.

Few literary figures are more difficult to assess than Johan August Strindberg. As Count Arvid Horn says of the king in Strindberg's *Charles XII*: "He doesn't conform to ordinary scales of measurement.---I have seen him as great as a Theseus and as petty as a page!" And in the same play Swedenborg answers the question of the king's significance in terms that are also applicable to Strindberg: "Great, not great! Can we measure a man with such small words?"

Notes to Chapter Twenty-three

1. The two most important contributions in this area were probably made by Karl Jaspers in *Strindberg und van Gogh* (Bremen, 1949), and Alfred Storch in *August Strindberg im Lichte seiner Selbstbiographie* (Munich, 1921).—Translator
2. This has been disputed by Gunnar Brandell in his definitive study *Strindbergs infernokris* (Stockholm, 1950). *See also* Sven Hedenberg, *Strindberg i skärselden* (Gothenburg, 1961), pp. 74-75 *et passim.*—Translator
3. In the chapter "Själssjukdom och kriser," *Strindbergsstudie.*
4. *Ibid.,* p. 176.
5. *Ibid.,* p. 178.
6. *See* pp. 205-12 and pp. 387-408.
7. Kretschmer also uses the term *sensitive Beziehungswahn* as a diagnosis of Strindberg's condition (see *Kroppsbyggnaden och karaktären,* Stockholm, 1939).—Translator
8. *Brev, I,* pp. 221-22.
9. For the psychological causes of this, *see* the chapter "Kvinnan och äktenskapet," in Eklund's *Strindbergsstudie,* pp. 109 ff.
10. *SS:XLVIII,* pp. 866-67.
11. *SS:XXXVII,* pp. 187-88.
12. *SS:XXIX,* p. 340.
13. St. Remy, while baptizing Clovis the Frank at Rheims, said, "Courbe la tête, fier Sicambre!/Adore ce que tu as brûlé/Brûle ce que tu as adoré!"—Translator
14. *Brev till Harriet Bosse,* p. 74.
15. *SS:LIV,* p. 147.
16. *SS:XIII,* pp. 93-105.
17. Cited by Linder, pp. 19-20.
18. *See* frontispiece, Mörner.—Translator
19. *SS:XLVI,* p. 167.
20. *SS:LIV,* p. 327.
21. *SS:LIII,* p. 94.
22. *SS:XLVIII,* p. 818.
23. *SS:L,* pp. 130-31.
24. *Brev, IV,* p. 180.
25. *Brev till Harriet Bosse,* p. 238.
26. *SS:LIV,* p. 467.

BIBLIOGRAPHY

Bibliographies

BRYER, JACKSON R. "Strindberg 1951-62: A Bibliography," *Modern Drama*, V (December, 1962), pp. 269-75.

GUSTAFSON, ALRIK. "A Bibliographical Guide," in *A History of Swedish Literature*. Minneapolis: Published for the American-Scandinavian Foundation by the University of Minnesota Press, 1961, pp. 602-609, 651-54.

RAPP, ESTHER H. "Strindberg's Reception in England and America," *Scandinavian Studies*, XXIII (February, 1951), pp. 1-22; XXIII (May, 1951), pp. 49-59; XXIII (August, 1951), pp. 109-37.

(*See also* "American Scandinavian Bibliography," published annually in *Scandinavian Studies*.)

Biographical and Critical Studies in English, French, and German

BENTLEY, ERIC. *The Playwright as Thinker*. New York: Harcourt, Brace and World, 1946; Meridian Books, 1955.

BRUSTEIN, ROBERT. *The Theatre of Revolt*. Boston: Little, Brown, 1964.

BULMAN, JOAN. *Strindberg and Shakespeare*. London: Jonathan Cape, 1933.

DAHLSTRÖM, CARL ENOCH WILLIAM LEONARD. *Strindberg's Dramatic Expressionism*. Second edition with the author's essay "Origins of Strindberg's Expressionism." New York: Benjamin Blom, 1965.

SMEDMARK, CARL REINHOLD (Ed.). *Essays on Strindberg*. Stockholm: Beckmans Bokförlag, 1966.

GRAVIER, MAURICE. *Strindberg et le théâtre moderne*, Vol. I: *L'Allemagne*. Lyon: Bibliothèque de la Société des études germaniques, 1949.

GUSTAFSON, ALRIK. "Strindberg and the Realistic Breakthrough," in *A History of Swedish Literature*. Minneapolis: Published for the American-Scandinavian Foundation by the University of Minnesota Press, 1961, pp. 243-87.

JASPERS, KARL. *Strindberg und van Gogh.* Bremen, Germany; Johns Storm, 1926, 1949.

JOHNSON, WALTER. *Strindberg and the Historical Drama.* Seattle: University of Washington Press, 1963.

JOLIVET, ALFRED. *Le Théâtre de Strindberg.* Paris: Boivin, 1931.

KRUTCH, JOSEPH WOOD. *"Modernism" in Modern Drama.* Ithaca, New York: Cornell University Press, 1953.

LAGERKVIST, PÄR. "Modern Theatre: Points of View and Attack," in *Modern Theatre: Seven Plays and an Essay,* translated with an Introduction by Thomas R. Buckman. Lincoln: University of Nebraska Press, 1966, pp. 3-38.

LAMM, MARTIN, "August Strindberg," in *Modern Drama,* translated by Karin Elliott. Oxford: Basil Blackwell, 1952, pp. 135-51.

LUCAS, F. L. *Ibsen and Strindberg.* London: Joseph Cassell, 1962.

McGILL, V. J. *August Strindberg, the Bedeviled Viking.* London: Noel Douglas, 1930.

MADSEN, BØRGE. *Strindberg's Naturalistic Theatre: Its Relation to French Naturalism.* Copenhagen: Munksgaard, 1962; Seattle: University of Washington Press, 1962.

MORTENSEN, BRITA M. E. and DOWNS, BRIAN W. *Strindberg: An Introduction to his Life and Work.* Cambridge, 1949, 1965.

SPRIGGE, ELIZABETH. *The Strange Life of August Strindberg.* New York: Macmillan, 1949.

STRINDBERG, FRU FRIDA (Uhl). *Marriage with Genius.* London: Jonathan Cape, 1940.

VALENCY, MAURICE. *The Flower and the Castle.* New York: Macmillan, 1963; Universal Library, 1966.

WILLIAMS, RAYMOND. "August Strindberg," in *Drama From Ibsen to Eliot.* London: Chatto & Windus, 1952; Oxford University Press, 1953, pp. 98-125.

Biographical and Critical Studies in Swedish

BERENDSOHN, WALTER A. *Strindbergsproblem.* Stockholm: Kooperativa förbundets bokförlag, 1946.

BRANDELL, GUNNAR. *Strindbergs Infernokris.* Stockholm: Albert Bonniers Förlag, 1950.

EKLUND, TORSTEN. *Tjänstekvinnans son, En psykologisk Strindbergs-studie.* Stockholm: Albert Bonniers Förlag, 1948.

FALCK AUGUST. *Fem år med Strindberg.* Stockholm: Wahlström & Widstrand, 1935.

HEDÉN, ERIK. *Strindberg: en ledtråd vid studiet av hans verk.* Stockholm: Tidens Förlag, 1926.

LAMM, MARTIN. *Strindberg och makterna.* Stockholm: Svenska kyrkans diakonistyrelses bokförlag, 1936.

—————. *Strindbergs dramer.* Two vols. Stockholm: Albert Bonniers Förlag, 1924-26.

OLLÉN, GUNNAR. *Strindbergs dramatik.* Stockholm: Radiotjänst, 1949, 1961.

—————. *Strindbergs 1900-talslyrik,* Stockholm: Seelig, 1941.

RINMAN, SVEN. "Strindberg," *Ny illustrerad svensk litteraturhistoria.* Stockholm: Albert Bonniers Förlag, 1948, pp. 383-97.

SMEDMARK, CARL REINHOLD. *Mäster Olof och Röda rummet.* Stockholm: Almqvist & Wiksell, 1952.

Strindberg's Works in English Translation

Plays in Collections

The Chamber Plays [*Storm Weather, The Burned House, The Ghost Sonata, The Pelican*], translated by Evert Sprinchorn and Seabury Quinn, Jr., with an Introduction by Evert Sprinchorn. New York: E. P. Dutton, 1962.

A Dream Play and The Ghost Sonata, translated by Carl Richard Mueller with an Introduction by Robert W. Corrigan. San Francisco: Chandler, 1965.

Eight Expressionist Plays by August Strindberg [*Lucky Per's Journey, The Keys to Heaven, To Damascus, I, II, III, A Dream Play, The Ghost Sonata, The Great Highway*], translated by Arvid Paulson with an introduction by John Gassner. New York: Bantam Books, 1965.

The Father and A Dream Play, translated and edited by Valborg Anderson. New York: Appleton-Century-Crofts, 1964.

Five Plays of Strindberg [*Creditors, Crime and Crime, The Dance of Death, Swanwhite, The Great Highway*], translated by Elizabeth Sprigge. Garden City: Doubleday Anchor, 1960.

Miss Julie and Other Plays by August Strindberg [*Miss Julie, Creditors, The Ghost Sonata, The Stronger*], English adaptations by Max Faber. London: William Heinemann, 1960.

The Plays of Strindberg, Volume I [*The Father, Miss Julie, Creditors, The Stronger, Playing With Fire, Erik the Fourteenth, Storm, The Ghost Sonata*], translated with Foreword and Introductions by Michael Meyer. New York: Random House, 1964.

Selected History Plays, translated with Introductions by Walter Johnson. Seattle: University of Washington Press.
   Queen Christina, Charles XII, Gustaf III (1955).
   The Last of the Knights, The Regent, Earl Birger of Bjälbo (1956).
   Gustav Adolf (1957).
   The Vasa Trilogy: Master Olof, Gustav Vasa, and *Erik XIV* (1959, 1966).
   The Saga of the Folkungs and Engelbrekt (1959).

Seven Plays by August Strindberg [*The Father, Miss Julie, Comrades, The Stronger, The Bond, Crime and Crime, Easter*], translated by Arvid Paulson with an Introduction by John Gassner. New York: Bantam Books, 1960.

Six Plays of Strindberg [*The Father, Miss Julie, The Stronger, Easter, A Dream Play, The Ghost Sonata*], translated by Elizabeth Sprigge. Garden City: Doubleday Anchor, 1955.

Strindberg: Selected Plays and Prose [*The Father, Miss Julie, A Dream Play*, Selections from *Inferno*], translated by N. Erichsen, Evert Sprinchorn, and Robert Brustein, with an Introduction by Robert Brustein. New York: Holt, Rinehart and Winston, 1964.

Three Plays by August Strindberg [*The Father, Miss Julie, Easter*], translated by Peter Watts. London: Penguin Books, 1958.

To Damascus. A Trilogy, English version by Graham Rawson with an Introduction by Gunnar Ollén. New York: Grove Press, 1960.

World Historical Plays [*The Nightingale of Wittenberg (Martin Luther), Through Deserts to Ancestral Lands (Moses), Hellas (Socrates), The Lamb and the Beast (Christ)*, translated by Arvid Paulson, with an Introduction by Gunnar Ollen. New York: Published for the American-Scandinavian Foundation by Twayne Publishers, Inc., 1970.

Fiction and Nonfiction

From An Occult Diary, translated by Mary Sandbach; edited with an Introduction and Notes by Torsten Eklund. New York: Hill and Wang, 1965.

Inferno, translated by Mary Sandbach, with an Introduction by F. L. Lucas. London: Hutchinson, 1962.

Letters of Strindberg to Harriet Bosse, translated and edited with an Introduction by Arvid Paulson. New York: Thomas Nelson, 1959.

A Madman's Defense, translated with an Introduction and Notes by Evert Sprinchorn. New York: Doubleday Anchor, 1967.

Open Letters to the Intimate Theater, translated with an Introduction by Walter Johnson. Seattle: University of Washington Press, 1967.

The People of Hemsö, translated by Elspeth Harley Schubert. Stockholm and London: Bonniers, 1959. (Also translated by Arvid Paulson as *The Natives of Hemsö*, with an Introduction by Richard B. Vowles. New York: Paul S. Eriksson, 1965).

The Red Room, translated by Elizabeth Sprigge. New York: E. P. Dutton, 1967.

The Scapegoat, translated by Arvid Paulson, with an Introduction by Richard B. Vowles. New York: Paul S. Eriksson, 1967.

The Son of a Servant; The Story of the Evolution of a Human Being (1849-1867), translated with an Introduction and Notes by Evert Sprinchorn. New York: Doubleday Anchor, 1966.

Strindberg's Works in Swedish

August Strindbergs brev. Edited by Torsten Eklund. Eleven vols. to date. Stockholm: Albert Bonniers Förlag, 1948-1969.

August Strindbergs dramer. Edited with Introductions and Commentaries by Carl Reinhold Smedmark. Three vols. to date. Stockholm: Albert Bonniers Förlag, 1962-1964.

Före Röda rummet. Edited by Torsten Eklund. Stockholm: Albert Bonniers Förlag, 1946.

Samlade otryckta skrifter. Two vols. Stockholm: Albert Bonniers Förlag, 1918-1919.

Samlade skrifter. Edited with Notes by John Landquist. 55 vols. Stockholm: Albert Bonniers Förlag, 1912-1919.

Strindbergs brev till Harriet Bosse. Stockholm: Bokförlaget Natur och kultur, 1932.

Ur Ockulta dagboken. Edited by Torsten Eklund. Stockholm: Albert Bonniers Förlag, 1963.

INDEX

Alphabetization follows customary American style except in the case of titles in Swedish, which are alphabetized according to the Swedish style (vowels with diacritical marks follow the letter *z;* articles are included in alphabetization).

"Tvekamp" (Strindberg). See "Duel, A"
Ude og Hjemme, journal, 165
Uhl, Frida
  as character source, 309
  divorce, xvi
  honeymoon, 309
  marriage, xv, 292-293
  separation, 293
Ulf, Härved (Strindberg pseudonym), 13
Uli, der Knecht, Gotthelf work, 236, 255 (n. 6)
"Ungdom och ideal" (Strindberg). See *Poems*
University of Uppsala, 9-10
"Uppsyningsman" (Strindberg). See "Customs Agent, The"
Ur dagens krönika, newspaper, 102
Utopias i verkligheten (Strindberg). See *Utopias in Reality*
Utopias in Reality (Utopias i verkligheten), Strindberg story collection, 132, 146, 163-175, 267
"Utveckling" (Strindberg). See "Evolution"
Valborgsafton pa Fagervik (Strindberg). See *Walpurgis Night on Fairhaven*
Vallès, Jules, 180
"Vargarne tjuta" (Strindberg). See "Wolves Howl, The"
"Victim, The" ("Offret"), Strindberg *Town and Gown* story, 49-51
"Vid dagens slut" (Strindberg). See "At Day's End"
Vid högre rätt (Strindberg). See *Before A Higher Court*
"Vid höstlåttern" (Hedberg). See "At Mowing Time"
"Vid likvaken i Tistedalen" (Strindberg). See "At the Wake in Tistedalen"
"View Toward Space, A" ("En blick mot rymden"), Strindberg essay, 304 (n. 17)
Villgrund, Henry, observations on Strindberg's theatrical experiences, 89 (n. 12)
"Virtue's Rewards" ("Dygdens lön"), Strindberg *Married* story, 12 (n. 9), 143, 146-147, 191

Vivisections (Vivisektioner), Strindberg essays, 177 (n. 19), 201-204, 237
Väntan (Strindberg). See *Waiting*
"Världshistoriens mystik" (Strindberg). See "Mysticism of World History, The"
Waiting (Väntan), Strindberg play, 389
Wall, Rudolf, editor *Dagens Nyheter,* 42
Wallenberg, A. O., banker, 134 (n. 36)
Walpurgis Night on Fairhaven (Valborgsafton på Fagervik), Strindberg sketch, 415
Warburg, Karl, critic, 71, 109, 152, 450
"Weathercock Sings, The" ("Flöjeln sjunger"), Strindberg poem, 422
Wedding at Ulvåsa (Bröllopet på Ulvåsa), Hedberg play, 11
Werin, Algot, analysis of *The Red Room* characters, 90 (n. 35)
"What Is the Battle About? and What Has Happened?" ("Vad gäller striden? och Vad har hänt?"). See "Literary Reactionism in Sweden"
What Is to Be Done? Tchernishevski novel, 167-168
Wieselgren, Oscar, 105
Wirsén, Carl David af, xx, 122, 253
"Witch, A" ("En häxa"), Strindberg *Swedish Destinies* story, 111
"Wolves Howl, The" ("Vargarne tjuta"), Strindberg poem, 415
Word-Play and Minor Art (Ordalek och småkonst), Strindberg lyric poetry, 126, 300, 394, 406, 407, 412, 414-426
Working People (Arbeidsfolk), Kielland novel, 63
"Wound-Fever" ("Sårfeber"). See *Poems*
Wrangel, Baron Carl Gustaf, xi, 309, 464
Young Sweden, 51, 95, 102-103, 109, 156, 277, 448, 451, 501, 503, 520, 522
"Youth and Ideals" ("Ungdom och ideal"). See *Poems*
Zola, Émile, 69, 95, 102, 110, 118, 119, 131, 137 (n. 78), 145, 147, 171, 182, 212, 214, 243, 253, 278